Lecture Notes in Computer Science 16496

The series Lecture Notes in Computer Science (LNCS), including its subseries Lecture Notes in Artificial Intelligence (LNAI) and Lecture Notes in Bioinformatics (LNBI), has established itself as a medium for the publication of new developments in computer science and information technology research, teaching, and education.

LNCS enjoys close cooperation with the computer science R & D community, the series counts many renowned academics among its volume editors and paper authors, and collaborates with prestigious societies. Its mission is to serve this international community by providing an invaluable service, mainly focused on the publication of conference and workshop proceedings and postproceedings. LNCS commenced publication in 1973.

Feng-Hao Liu
Editor

Topics in Cryptology – CT-RSAC 2026

Cryptographers' Track at the RSAC 2026 Conference San Francisco, CA, USA, March 23–26, 2026 Proceedings

Editor
Feng-Hao Liu
Washington State University
Pullman, WA, USA

ISSN 0302-9743 ISSN 1611-3349 (electronic)
Lecture Notes in Computer Science
ISBN 978-3-032-22930-4 ISBN 978-3-032-22931-1 (eBook)
https://doi.org/10.1007/978-3-032-22931-1

This Springer imprint is published by the registered company Springer Nature Switzerland AG
The registered company address is: Gewerbestrasse 11, 6330 Cham, Switzerland

Preface

The RSAC Conference has been the premier trade show for the security industry since 1991, bringing together more than 40,000 attendees annually from industry, government, and academia. The Cryptographers' Track (CT-RSAC) serves as RSAC's dedicated venue for scientific research in cryptography. Historically, the main conference was known as the RSA Conference, and its cryptography track as CT-RSA. Beginning in 2025, the names were updated to RSAC Conference and CT-RSAC, respectively.

This volume represents the proceedings of the 2026 edition of the Cryptographers' Track at the RSAC Conference, which took place in San Francisco, California, USA, during March 23–March 26, 2026. We received 39 submissions. Two submissions were deemed out of scope and desk rejected by the program committee chair. The remaining 37 full papers were each assigned at least three reviewers. The reviewing process was double-blind and carried out using the HotCRP conference management system. We followed the IACR policy for conflicts of interest.

The review process concluded with the acceptance of 12 papers, including three papers accepted with conditions. These 12 papers comprised the final scientific program. The acceptance rate was $12/37 \approx 32.4\%$. CT-RSAC would not have been possible without the valuable contributions of many volunteers. My sincere thanks go out to all program committee members, as well as additional reviewers, for their consistently thoughtful, constructive reviews, and for actively participating in the paper selection discussions.

Special thanks are due to:

- the committee members who shepherded conditionally accepted papers;
- Mike Rosulek (CT-RSA 2023 program chair) and Arpita Patra (CT-RSA 2025 program chair) for graciously sharing institutional knowledge about the role of program chair;
- the RSA Conference team, in particular Samantha Mello, Christie Ross, and Britta J. Glade, for their support with scheduling and procedural matters;
- Guangbei Yi for helping with the system and maintaining the webpage.

February 2026 Feng-Hao Liu

Organization

Program Committee Chair

Feng-Hao Liu	Washington State University, USA

Program Committee

Adam O'Neill	University of Massachusetts Amherst, USA
Amin Sakzad	Monash University, Australia
Anca Nitulescu	Input Output, Paris, France
Antonio Flórez-Gutiérrez	NTT Social Informatics Laboratories, Japan
Arnab Roy	University of Innsbruck, Austria
Bart Mennink	Maastricht University, The Netherlands
Bart Preneel	KU Leuven, Belgium
Benjamin Fuller	University of Connecticut, USA
Chester Rebeiro	Indian Institute of Technology Madras, India
Claudio Orlandi	Aarhus University, Denmark
Fuyuki Kitagawa	NTT Social Informatics Laboratories, Japan
Jiayu Xu	Oregon State University, USA
Khoa Nguyen	University of Wollongong, Australia
Maxime Bombar	Université de Bordeaux, France
Nicky Mouha	National Institute of Standards and Technology (NIST), USA
Nigel P. Smart	KU Leuven and Zama, Belgium
Paola de Perthuis	Centrum Wiskunde en Informatica (CWI), The Netherlands
Qiqi Lai	Shaanxi Normal University, China
Rupeng Yang	University of Wollongong, Australia
Seung Geol Choi	United States Naval Academy, USA
Sylvain Guilley	Secure-IC, France
Tetsu Iwata	Nagoya University, Japan
Valerio Cini	Bocconi University, Italy
Victor Mateu	Technology Innovation Institute (TII), United Arab Emirates
Yiannis Tselekounis	Royal Holloway, University of London, UK
Yu Shen	Ruhr-Universität Bochum, Germany
Zhedong Wang	Shanghai Jiao Tong University, China

Additional Reviewers

Akira Nakashima
Atsushi Takayasu
Charles Liu
Chris van Noorden
Daniel Augot
Diego F. Aranha
Joachim Vandersmissen
Jules Maire
Maiwenn Racouchot
Masayuki Tezuka
Minzhang Li
Tianyu Zhao
Yijian Zhang
Yu-Te Ku
Yusuke Sakai
Zuoxia Yu
Guangbei Yi

Contents

Homomorphic and Searchable Encryption

Fully Homomorphic Encryption on the Ring of Gaussian Periods

Yimeng He[1], San Ling[1], Yimin Shi[1(✉)], Benjamin Hong Meng Tan[2], Huaxiong Wang[1], and Allen Siwei Yang[1,2]

[1] School of Physical & Mathematical Sciences, Nanyang Technological University, Singapore, Singapore
{yimeng002,yimin005,yang0788}@e.ntu.edu.sg, {lingsan,hxwang}@ntu.edu.sg
[2] Institute for Infocomm Research, Agency for Science, Technology and Research (A*STAR), Singapore, Singapore
benjamin_tan@a-star.edu.sg

Abstract. In Geelen and Vercauteren (Eurocrypt 2025), a Generalized BFV (GBFV) fully homomorphic encryption scheme was proposed. Here, a plaintext space of form $\mathbb{Z}[x]/(\Phi(x), t(x))$ was utilized to reduce the number of Single Instruction Multiple Data (SIMD) slots within the initial BFV plaintext space. This lowered its dimension and thus enabled lower latencies as well as greater flexibility in parameter selection. However, to obtain slots of degree 1, the methods of Geelen and Vercauteren limit the choice of plaintext modulus to that of large primes, which can be unnecessary for various use cases.

To resolve this, we propose a generalized method to perform FHE based on a subring of the plaintext polynomial ring. We utilize the decomposition ring $\mathcal{O}_{\mathbf{K}}$, with which when taking quotient with a rational prime p, already factors into residual fields of dimension 1. From here, we develop methods to perform FHE on subrings of the decomposition ring $\mathcal{O}_{\mathbf{K}}$, which we refer to as the decomposition subring $\mathcal{O}_{\mathbf{M}}$. We introduce novel methods to enable both encoding and decoding maps within the decomposition subring $\mathcal{O}_{\mathbf{M}} \subset \mathcal{O}_{\mathbf{K}}$. By utilizing $\mathcal{O}_{\mathbf{M}}$, we further lower the dimension of the underlying ring, improving upon efficiency while retaining sufficient security. In experiments, we provide a proof-of-concept implementation, demonstrating up to a 5.06× improvement in the latency of operations for selected parameters. This approach offers enhanced flexibility in the selection of parameters for FHE with the subring dimension being any suitable divisor of r. This direction also represents the first generalization of the subring approach for FHE.

Keywords: Fully Homomorphic Encryption · Decomposition Rings

1 Introduction

Fully Homomorphic Encryption (FHE) constitutes a type of encryption that enables arbitrary computations on encrypted data [8]. Its robustness in preserving privacy lends itself to an extensive range of applications both inside

F. -H. Liu (Ed.): CT-RSAC 2026, LNCS 16496, pp. 3–31, 2026.
https://doi.org/10.1007/978-3-032-22931-1_1

and outside cryptography. A substantial portion of FHE-related research has been devoted to enhancing efficiency. This ranges from works that focus on accelerating the bootstrapping procedure [17,28] to works that target more fundamental components such as homomorphic matrix multiplication operations [4]. Homomorphic encryption (HE) schemes typically consist of two types. The first includes schemes that support Single Instruction Multiple Data (SIMD) [25] operations on the encryption of multiple elements. Examples of this include BGV [8], BFV [7,15] and CKKS [10]. The second prioritizes lower latencies with smaller parameters. Representatives for this type include FHEW [14] and TFHE [11,12]. The focus of this work is on the first category of FHE schemes.

1.1 Contributions

Most relevant to our work is that of GBFV [16]. Here, they attempted to reduce the number of slots in the plaintext space to lower its dimension. This was applied to the BFV cryptosystem [7,15]. To do so, they extended the work of [9] from a linear polynomial plaintext modulus to that of a binomial modulus and eventually to a general non-linear polynomial plaintext modulus. The work of [16] computes a specific quotient of the cyclotomic ring which then enables (SIMD) operations over a subset of the slots. Specifically, they obtained the quotient of the cyclotomic ring, by this polynomial modulus, and set this to be the plaintext space. This was shown to correspond to a subset of the slots in the initial BFV plaintext space under certain conditions. This enabled lower latencies as well as improved flexibility in the parameter selection. Specifically, new, lower latency parameters could be obtained where typical BFV parameters would first be selected followed by selecting a subset of the slots.

In most use cases, which require slots of degree 1, a large prime modulus plaintext space corresponding to a large number of slots of degree 1 would first have to be selected. From there, a specified quotient of the plaintext ring would be applied to reduce the dimension and obtain the desired number of slots as the subset. However, this limits the choice of plaintext modulus to that of large primes, which can be unnecessary for various use cases.

Motivated by the work of [16], we attempt to reduce both the degree of each slot as well as the slot count to expand the options available for parameter selection. We find that the decomposition ring [2] exhibits some special properties that support our idea. To obtain slots of degree 1, the work of [2] had attempted to first select parameters whose slots had degree larger than 1. From here, by moving down to the decomposition ring, this would then decrease the degree of each slot to 1 as desired. However, in the context of the decomposition ring, the ideas of [16] do not necessarily apply as the ring utilized in [2] will not be a polynomial quotient ring. Drawing upon the works of [2,16], we therefore instead propose a form of FHE on the ring of Gaussian periods. Here, we propose methods to go further down the decomposition ring $\mathcal{O}_{\mathbf{K}}$, yielding subrings of smaller dimension. These subrings are referred to as decomposition subrings $\mathcal{O}_{\mathrm{M}}$ and their structure is discussed in Sect. 2.2. However, the methods of [2] are not applicable in this context, as the CRT basis elements τ_i are no longer idempotents. To overcome this, we introduce novel methods for encoding and decoding. Here, we obtain an element F_i in the decomposition subring $\mathcal{O}_{\mathbf{M}}$ such that every factor of a given prime p is contained in (F_i) except for a specified prime ideal. We demonstrate that this construction of $F_i \in \mathcal{O}_{\mathbf{M}}$ enables us to find the desired encoding and decoding maps to work over the decomposition subring $\mathcal{O}_{\mathbf{M}}$. Our work could therefore be viewed as the first instance of a generalized subring FHE. This is detailed in Sect. 3.

Following this, the novel encoding and decoding maps introduced are utilized as the building blocks for the operations of an FHE scheme. A comparison between the operations performed over the decomposition subring $\mathcal{O}_{\mathbf{M}}$ and the decomposition ring $\mathcal{O}_{\mathbf{K}}$ is conducted. Let r denote the dimension of the decomposition ring $\mathcal{O}_{\mathbf{K}}$ and $n < r$ denote the dimension of the decomposition subring $\mathcal{O}_{\mathbf{M}}$. It is observed that the time complexity of the operations is decreased from, for encryption and decryption, $O(r \log r)$ to $O(n \log n)$, for addition, $O(r)$ to $O(n)$ and for multiplication, $O(l_w \cdot r \log r)$ to $O(l_w \cdot n \log n)$ in Sect. 4. Concretely, this implies that greater efficiency is obtained for the operations performed, lowering latency. We further verify this by providing a proof-of-concept implementation in Sect. 5. Here, the implementation demonstrates up to a 5.06× improvement in the latency of operations for selected parameters. We emphasize that this latency improvement demonstrates that previously available parameters can now be instead utilized in a lower latency setting, while still retaining acceptable security levels. We further note that while the FHE scheme proposed is a BFV-variant, our techniques are not restricted to the BFV cryptosystem. The methods introduced could also be applied to BGV-styled cryptosystems, directly following from the work of [3].

Finally, the utilization of low-dimension decomposition subrings for FHE provides flexibility in the choice of parameters. Compared to [16], the choice of our prime number p could be small while matching the number of slots in the parameters of [16]. This optimizes for use-cases where a large dimension and a large plaintext integer modulus are not required. Our scheme therefore unlocks new sets of parameters that can be utilized for FHE, offering greater flexibility in the choice of parameters in practice. This technique could additionally be applied to optimize key FHE operations, such as blind rotations and bootstrapping [21]. For instance, for 2048 many slots at 128-bit security, the smallest plaintext integer modulus of the recommended parameters from [16] is a 16-bit prime 65537. On the other hand, with our techniques we achieve approximately this number of slots and security level with a plaintext integer modulus of 113. This is discussed in Table 6 of Sect. 5. This fine-grained selection of the plaintext modulus consequently also applies when compared with the typical power-of-two cyclotomic ring utilized in BFV. Unlike the case involving the power-of-two cyclotomic rings, the smaller plaintext modulus from our techniques would be better suited for applications such as circuit-oriented equality comparisons [24, 26].

1.2 Related Work

Alongside the aforementioned works, there have been several others that focus on obtaining subring structures or on applications of the subring plaintext spaces. [18] explored the use of the conjugate-invariant subring, which was specific to the CKKS cryptosystem [10]. [3] extended the work of [2], providing both refinements to the original BFV-based cryptosystem [7,15] and an added BGV-based variant. [29] further explored conditions in which subfields of the cyclotomic field could be utilized for cryptosystems. Recently, [21] utilized the subring technique of [2] to efficiently perform slot-wise blind rotation in the context of bootstrapping.

2 Preliminaries

2.1 Notation

For a positive integer number m, $\Phi_m(x)$ refers to the m-th cyclotomic polynomial. Denote $\mathbb{Z}$ as the integer ring and $\mathbb{Z}_p := \mathbb{Z}/p\mathbb{Z}$. Denote $\mathcal{R}$ to be the polynomial ring $\mathbb{Z}[x]/f(x)$ where $f(x)$ is irreducible and $\mathcal{R}_q := \mathcal{R}/q\mathcal{R}$. By default, bold uppercase letters such as $\mathbf{A}$ will be interpreted as matrices. The symbol $||\cdot||_\infty$ refers to the L_∞ norm and $||\cdot||_2$ refers to the L_2 norm. Denote $\mathbb{Q}$ as the field of rational numbers and $\mathbf{K}$, $\mathbf{L}$, $\mathbf{M}$ etc. as its extension fields. The relative trace map $\mathbf{Tr}^{\mathbf{L}}_{\mathbf{K}}(\cdot)$ for any two number fields $\mathbf{K} \subset \mathbf{L}$ is defined to be the sum $\sum_{i=1}^{n} \sigma_i(\cdot)$, where each σ_i is one of the $n = [\mathbf{L} : \mathbf{K}]$ embeddings of $\mathbf{L}$ in $\mathbb{C}$ which fixes $\mathbf{K}$ pointwise. This takes as input an element of $\mathbf{L}$. Exact division of ideals is denoted by $||$ and is defined as $P^k \mid\mid u \iff (P^{k+1}, u) = P^k$, for ideals P, u and some integer $k \geq 0$.

2.2 Gaussian Periods

Gaussian periods serve as the building blocks of and characterize a large class of number fields which possess a normal integral basis. Consequently, fields of Gaussian periods are well-suited for instantiating cryptographic protocols founded on the Ring-LWE assumption, offering a viable alternative to the traditional reliance on cyclotomic fields. Specifically, the Ring-LWE assumption on the decomposition subring $\mathcal{O}_{\mathbf{M}}$ is utilized to instantiate our FHE scheme, as opposed to being over $\mathbb{Z}[\zeta_m]$. Here, we describe how the decomposition subrings as well as their respective period-basis are obtained. More generally, we first define the decomposition field and its corresponding decomposition subfields. From the decomposition subfield, we then obtain the corresponding decomposition subring $\mathcal{O}_{\mathbf{M}}$ and period-basis.

Let $q > 2$ be an odd prime, $g > 0$ be a multiplicative generator of $\mathbb{Z}_q^\times$. Select positive integers $n, f > 0$ such that $q = nf + 1$. Let ζ_q denote a primitive q^{th} root of unity.

Definition 1 (Gaussian Periods). *The Gaussian periods of degree n and length f are algebraic integers $\eta_0, \ldots, \eta_{n-1}$ satisfying:*

$$\forall 0 \leq i < n : \eta_i := \sum_{k=0}^{f-1} \zeta_q^{g^{i+nk}}$$

For ease of notation, we denote $\eta_i := \eta_{i \bmod n}$ for $i \in \mathbb{Z}$.

2.2.1 Decomposition Rings

We first define the decomposition ring. Suppose $m > 0$ and let $\mathbf{L} = \mathbb{Q}(\zeta_m)$, $\mathcal{O}_\mathbf{L} = \mathbb{Z}[\zeta_m]$. Choose a prime $p \nmid m$, then p is unramified and the ideal $p\mathcal{O}_\mathbf{L}$ factorizes as:

$$p\mathcal{O}_\mathbf{L} = \prod_{i=1}^{r} \mathfrak{P}_i$$

In the factorization above, each prime ideal $\mathfrak{P}_i$ has inertial degree $d = \mathsf{ord}_m^\times(p)$, the multiplicative order of $p \in \mathbb{Z}_m^\times$. The number of prime ideals $r = \frac{\varphi(m)}{d}$ where $\varphi(\cdot)$ denotes the Euler totient function.

The *Decomposition Group* $\mathbf{H} = \langle \phi_p \rangle \subset \mathsf{Gal}\left(\mathbb{Q}(\zeta_m) \,/\, \mathbb{Q}\right)$ of p is the subgroup generated by the Frobenius map $\phi_p : \zeta_m \mapsto \zeta_m^p$. The subgroup $\mathbf{H}$ is the (unique) subgroup of order d in $\mathbb{Z}_q^\times$. Let $\mathbf{K} = \mathbf{L}^{\langle \phi_p \rangle}$ and $\mathcal{O}_\mathbf{K}$ be its ring of integers. A standard result in algebraic number theory tells us that the prime ideal $p\mathcal{O}_\mathbf{K}$ "splits completely" in $\mathcal{O}_\mathbf{K}$:

$$p\mathcal{O}_\mathbf{K} = \prod_{i=1}^{r} \mathfrak{p}_i$$

i.e. each $\mathfrak{p}_i$ is a prime ideal in $\mathcal{O}_\mathbf{K}$ with inertial degree 1. Equivalently,

$$\mathcal{O}_\mathbf{K}/p\mathcal{O}_\mathbf{K} \cong \prod_{i=1}^{r} \mathcal{O}_\mathbf{K}/\mathfrak{p}_i \cong \prod^{r} \mathbb{F}_p$$

where $\mathbb{F}_p$ is the finite field of cardinality p.

The ring $\mathcal{O}_\mathbf{K}$ is therefore referred to as the *Decomposition ring*. The splitting structure described above represents the single instruction, multiple data (SIMD) slot packing [25], with each $\mathcal{O}_\mathbf{K}/\mathfrak{p}_i$ representing a slot. In [2,3], the left and right ends of the isomorphism above have the basis elements η_i and ξ_i respectively. The conversion between the two bases is performed via multiplication by matrix $\Omega_Z^{(p)}$. Further information on the conversion can be found in [2,3]. It is noted that the decomposition ring $\mathcal{O}_\mathbf{K}$ is not the only subring of $\mathbb{Z}[\zeta_m]$ in which the prime p splits completely, but is however the largest. This is detailed in Theorem 2.

Theorem 2 ([20]). *Under the notation above, let $\mathbf{M} \subset \mathbf{L}$ be any subfield of $\mathbf{L}$, with ring of integers $\mathcal{O}_\mathbf{M}$. The prime p splits completely in $\mathcal{O}_\mathbf{M}$ iff $\mathbf{M} \subset \mathbf{K}$ is a subfield of the Decomposition field $\mathbf{K}$.*

2.2.2 Decomposition Subrings

Following the notation of Theorem 2, we obtain the decomposition subring $\mathcal{O}_{\mathbf{M}}$ by first selecting a subfield $\mathbf{M} \subset \mathbf{K}$ and obtaining the corresponding ring of integers. Specifically, this is performed below in terms of the Gaussian periods, obtaining the decomposition subring $\mathcal{O}_{\mathbf{M}} = \mathbb{Z}[\eta_0, \ldots, \eta_{n-1}]$. The splitting behavior of the decomposition subring $\mathcal{O}_{\mathbf{M}}$ is also described below. Set $m = q$ to be an odd prime, then $\varphi(q) = q - 1$, $q - 1 = rd$, where $d = ord_q^{\times}(p)$. Let $k \mid r$ be any divisor of r and define $n = \frac{r}{k}$, $f = dk$. Since $q - 1 = nf$, the Gaussian periods of degree n and length f, $\eta_0, \ldots, \eta_{n-1}$ (cf. Definition 1), forms a subfield $\mathbb{Q}(\eta_0) \subset \mathbb{Q}(\zeta_q)$ whose Galois group $\mathsf{Gal}\left(\mathbb{Q}(\zeta_q) \,/\, \mathbb{Q}(\eta_0)\right) \rhd \mathbf{H}$ has order $f = dk$. By the Galois correspondence, $\mathbb{Q}(\eta_0) \subset \mathbf{K}$ is a subfield and by Theorem 2 the prime p also splits completely in $\mathbb{Z}[\eta_0, \ldots, \eta_{n-1}]$. This is described in Proposition 3.

Proposition 3. *Let $q > 2$ be an odd prime. Choose $n, f > 0$ such that $q = nf + 1$. Let $\eta_0, \ldots, \eta_{n-1}$ be the Gaussian periods of degree n and length f. Suppose p is a prime whose multiplicative order* $\bmod q$ *divides f, then the ideal $p\mathbb{Z}[\eta_0, \ldots, \eta_{n-1}]$ splits completely in $\mathbb{Z}[\eta_0, \ldots, \eta_{n-1}]$.*

Basis Elements. For a given decomposition subring $\mathcal{O}_{\mathbf{M}}$, the associated Gaussian period forms a basis of $\mathcal{O}_{\mathbf{M}}$. This is referred to as the period-basis. By considering both the decomposition rings and their subrings as subfields of a cyclotomic field, this is shown in Proposition 4. Let $\mathbb{Q}(\zeta_q)$ be the cyclotomic field of prime conductor $q > 2$. The Galois group $\mathbf{G} := \mathsf{Gal}\left(\mathbb{Q}(\zeta_q) \,/\, \mathbb{Q}\right) \cong \mathbb{Z}_q^{\times}$ is cyclic of order $q-1$. Let g be a generator of $\mathbb{Z}_q^{\times}$. The automorphism $\sigma : \mathbb{Q}(\zeta_q) \to \mathbb{Q}(\zeta_q)$ sending $\zeta_q \mapsto \zeta_q^g$ is a generator of the Galois group $\mathbf{G}$. The relation between the Gaussian periods in Definition 1 and the cyclotomic field $\mathbb{Q}(\zeta_q)$ is captured in the following proposition.

Proposition 4. *Let $\mathbf{H}$ be the (unique) subgroup of order f in $\mathbf{G}$. Then $\mathbf{H} = \langle \sigma^n \rangle$, and the following is true:*

1. *$\forall i \in \mathbb{Z} : \sigma^n(\eta_i) = \eta_i$.*
2. *$\forall i \in \mathbb{Z} : \mathbb{Q}(\eta_i) = \mathbb{Q}(\eta_0)$. $\mathbb{Q}(\eta_0)$ is the fixed field corresponding to $\mathbf{H}$.*
3. *$\forall i \in \mathbb{Z} : \eta_i = \mathbf{Tr}_{\mathbb{Q}(\eta_0)}^{\mathbb{Q}(\zeta_q)}(\zeta_q^i)$. The minimal polynomial of η_0 is $p_{\eta_0}(x) = \prod_{i=0}^{n-1}(x - \eta_i) \in \mathbb{Z}[x]$.*
4. *The vector $(\eta_0, \ldots, \eta_{n-1})$ forms a normal, integral basis of $\mathbb{Q}(\eta_0)$. In particular, $\mathbb{Z}[\eta_0, \ldots, \eta_{n-1}]$ is the ring of integers of $\mathbb{Q}(\eta_0)$.*

Proof. The proof is included in the Appendix.

In summary we have,

$$\underset{\text{Decomposition Subring}}{\mathcal{O}_{\mathbf{M}}} \subset \underset{\text{Decomposition Ring}}{\mathcal{O}_{\mathbf{K}}} \subset \underset{\text{Ring of Integers}}{\mathcal{O}_{\mathbf{L}}}$$

with $\mathcal{O}_{\mathbf{L}} = \mathbb{Z}[\zeta_m]$ corresponding to the typical BGV/BFV plaintext space. An overview of the notation introduced is also provided in Table 1.

Table 1. A summary of the main notation utilized.

Symbol	Definition
r	Number of slots/η_i period-basis elements under Decomposition Ring $\mathcal{O}_{\mathbf{K}}$.
n	Number of slots/η_i period-basis elements under Decomposition Ring $\mathcal{O}_{\mathbf{M}}$.
q	Gaussian period root of unity parameter, set to be equal to cyclotomic m and is an odd prime.
p	Plaintext prime modulus whose multiplicative order mod q divides f.
f	Length parameter of Gaussian periods.

2.3 Fully Homomorphic Encryption

Modern realizations of practical FHE are built upon lattice assumptions, particularly the decisional variants of the learning with errors (LWE) [23] and ring learning with errors (RLWE) [19] problems. The RLWE problem is based on the LWE problem. Both of them are commonly used to construct homomorphic encryption schemes. In this work, we employ the ring-variant problem.

Definition 5 (Ring-LWE Distribution). *For any secret* $\mathbf{s} \in \mathcal{R}_Q$, *error distribution* Φ *over* $\mathcal{R}_Q$, *the Ring-LWE distribution* $A_{\mathbf{s},\Phi}$ *over* $\mathcal{R}_Q^2$ *is defined by sampling* $\mathbf{a} \leftarrow \mathcal{U}(\mathcal{R}_Q)$, $\mathbf{e} \leftarrow \Phi$ *independently and output* $(\mathbf{a}, \mathbf{b} = \mathbf{a} \cdot \mathbf{s} + \mathbf{e} \bmod q)$.

Definition 6 (Ring-LWE Problem, average-case decision). *Let* Υ *be a family of error distributions over* $\mathcal{R}_Q$. *Ring-LWE*$_{Q,\Upsilon}$ *asks to distinguish, with non-negligible advantage, between independent samples* $A_{\mathbf{s},\Phi}$, *where* $\mathbf{s}, \Phi \leftarrow \mathcal{R}_Q, \Upsilon$ *are randomly chosen; and the same number of uniform, independent samples from* $\mathcal{U}(\mathcal{R}_Q^2)$.

In practice each component of $\mathbf{s}$, over some fixed basis, is uniformly and independently sampled from a small set $\mathcal{S}$. When the secret $\mathbf{s}$ is sampled this way, we refer to the Ring-LWE problem as the small-secret Ring-LWE.

A homomorphic encryption (HE) scheme is a collection of algorithms - (Setup, KeyGen, Enc, Dec, EvalKeyGen, Evaluate). Setup gives the parameter set for following procedures. KeyGen generates a secret key sk. Enc encrypts a plaintext element from the plaintext space to a ciphertext from the ciphertext space using the public key. Dec decrypts a ciphertext ct to a plaintext using the secret key. EvalKeyGen generates an evaluation key evk. Evaluate allows the evaluation of ciphertexts $\mathsf{ct}_1, \ldots, \mathsf{ct}_n$ on a function f and outputs a new ciphertext encrypting $f(\mathsf{ct}_1, \ldots, \mathsf{ct}_n)$ using the evaluation key evk.

2.3.1 BFV Cryptosystem

The BFV cryptosystem is an FHE scheme where the message and the noise are separated by storing the message in the higher bits and the noise in the lower bits (LSB). We present the BFV scheme here as a variant is utilized in Sect. 2.4. The BFV encryption scheme is as follows:

- $\mathsf{BFV.Setup}(1^\lambda)$: Given the security parameter λ, set ring $\mathcal{R}$, plaintext and ciphertext moduli t and q, the secret key distribution ψ and the error distribution χ, output the parameter set $\mathsf{pp} := (t, q, \psi, \chi)$.
- $\mathsf{BFV.KeyGen}(\mathsf{pp})$: Given the parameter set pp, sample secret key $\mathsf{sk} \leftarrow \psi$.
- $\mathsf{BFV.Enc}(m, \mathsf{sk})$: Given message $m \in \mathcal{R}_t$, sample $a \stackrel{\$}{\leftarrow} \mathcal{R}_q$ and $e \leftarrow \chi$. Define the scaling factor Δ to be $\lfloor \frac{q}{t} \rceil$. Encrypt it using secret key sk and output $\mathsf{ct} := (\mathsf{ct}_0, \mathsf{ct}_1)$ where $\mathsf{ct}_0 := a$, $\mathsf{ct}_1 := \mathsf{ct}_0 \cdot \mathsf{sk} + \Delta \cdot m + e$.
- $\mathsf{BFV.Dec}(\mathsf{ct}, \mathsf{sk})$: Given the ciphertext $\mathsf{ct} = (\mathsf{ct}_0, \mathsf{ct}_1)$ and secret key sk, recover the message $m := \lfloor \frac{\mathsf{ct}_1 - \mathsf{ct}_0 \cdot \mathsf{sk}}{\Delta} \rceil$.
- $\mathsf{BFV.EvalKeyGen}(\mathsf{sk})$: Given the secret key sk, output the evaluation key $\mathsf{evk} := \mathsf{BFV.Enc}(\mathsf{sk}^2, \mathsf{sk})$.
- $\mathsf{BFV.Evaluate}(f, \mathsf{ct}^{(1)}, \ldots, \mathsf{ct}^{(n)}, \mathsf{evk})$: Given a sequence of ciphertexts $\mathsf{ct}_1, \ldots, \mathsf{ct}_n$, a function f and evaluation key evk, output a ciphertext $\mathsf{ct}_{\mathsf{eval}}$ which satisfies $\mathsf{Dec}(\mathsf{ct}_{\mathsf{eval}}, \mathsf{sk}) = f(\mathsf{ct}^{(1)}, \ldots, \mathsf{ct}^{(n)})$.

2.4 Subring Homomorphic Encryption

In BFV-based FHE schemes, the plaintext is set to be a vector of slots. Each slot represents an element of the Galois field $\mathrm{GF}(p^d)$ of degree d [25]. Addition and multiplication in plaintext space corresponds to slot-wise addition and multiplication over the Galois field $\mathrm{GF}(p^d)$. In [2], it was noted that in practice, a plaintext slot space of form $\mathbb{Z}_{p^l}$ is often preferred. Subring homomorphic encryption was therefore presented in [2]. The idea was to first go down from $\mathbb{Z}[\zeta_q]$ to $\mathcal{O}_K$ as discussed in Sect. 2.2.1, take the quotient of the ring under modulo p and then perform Hensel lifting over to $q' = p^l$. This decreased the slot degree from d to 1. In addition, a BFV-based homomorphic scheme [25] over the decomposition ring $\mathcal{O}_K$ was realized. The encoding and decoding algorithms, along with the complete scheme, are summarized in the following sections.

2.4.1 Encoding/Decoding

The encoding and decoding techniques of [2] involve transformations between the η-vectors and ξ-vectors. The η-vectors form the basis of the decomposition ring $\mathcal{O}_K$ and the ξ-vectors form the basis for the other end of the isomorphism (slot space) of the decomposition ring described in Sect. 2.2.1. The conversions are analogous to conversions between the power(ful) and Chinese Remainder Theorem(CRT) bases respectively. As before, let q be a prime index of the cyclotomic ring R. Let $p \neq q$ be a prime and $d = ord_q^\times(p)$ and the number of slots $r = \frac{q-1}{d}$. Let the integer modulus $q' = p^m$ and $t = p^l$, for $l < m$. Let $\vec{a} \in \mathbb{Z}^r$ denote an η-vector and let its encoding be denoted as $a = \vec{\eta}^T \cdot \vec{a} \in \mathcal{O}_\mathbf{K}$.

We present the transformations, between the η basis and the ξ basis, in Algorithm 1 and Algorithm 2. These perform the transformations between the ring $\mathcal{O}_\mathbf{K}/p^m\mathcal{O}_\mathbf{K}$ and the slots $\prod_{i=1}^{r} \mathbb{Z}_{p^m}$, mapping the ring elements to their slots and vice versa. We refer the reader to Sect. 3 of [2] for the definitions of the matrices $\Omega_Z^{(q')}$ and $\bar{\Omega}_Z^{(q')}$ as these are not utilized for the rest of the paper.

Algorithm 1. `eta_to_xi`

Input: η-vector $\vec{a}$, prime power q'.
Output: ξ-vector $\vec{b}$.
1: Set $a(X) = a_0 + a_{r-1}X + \cdots + a_1 X^{r-1}$.
2: Set $c(X) = \eta_0 + \eta_1 X + \cdot + \eta_{r-1}X^{r-1}$ where $(\eta_i)_{i=0}^{r-1}$ is the first row of $\Omega_Z^{(q')}$.
3: Compute $b(X) = a(X)c(X) \bmod (q', X^{r-1})$.
4: **Return** $\vec{b} = (b_0, \ldots, b_{r-1})$.

Algorithm 2. `xi_to_eta`

Input: ξ-vector $\vec{b}$, prime power q'.
Output: η-vector $\vec{a}$.
1: Set $b(X) = b_0 + b_{r-1}X + \cdots + b_1 X^{r-1}$.
2: Set $c(X) = \bar{\eta}_0 + \bar{\eta}_1 X + \cdots + \bar{\eta}_{r-1}X^{r-1}$ where $(\bar{\eta}_i)_{i=0}^{r-1}$ is the first row of $\bar{\Omega}_Z^{(q')}$.
3: Compute $a(X) = b(X)c(X) \bmod (q', X^{r-1})$.
4: Compute $t = b_0 + \cdots + b_{r-1} \bmod q'$.
5: **Return** $\vec{a} = (q^{-1}(a_i - dt) \bmod q')_{i=0}^{r-1}$.

To multiply two vectors encoded by η-vectors $\vec{a}$ and $\vec{b}$ modulo $q' = p^m$, we first convert the η-vectors to ξ-vectors modulo q', that is, they become elements of the slot space. From here, we multiply the resulting ξ-vectors component-wise and convert the result back to an η-vector modulo q'. The procedure is detailed in Algorithm 3. This is utilized in their proposed scheme to perform multiplication between elements of the ring $\mathcal{O}_{\mathbf{K}}/p^m\mathcal{O}_{\mathbf{K}}$, forming the building block of the scheme. That is, for two elements of the ring $\mathcal{O}_{\mathbf{K}}/p^m\mathcal{O}_{\mathbf{K}}$, their η-vectors are obtained and converted to the slot space, with the component-wise multiplication then applied and finally converted back.

Algorithm 3. `mult_eta`

Input: η-vectors $\vec{a}, \vec{b}$, prime power q'.
Output: Multiplication product η-vector $\vec{c}$.
1: Set $\vec{\alpha} = \text{eta\_to\_xi}(\vec{a}, q')$.
2: Set $\vec{\beta} = \text{eta\_to\_xi}(\vec{b}, q')$.
3: **for** i in range $0 \leq i \leq r-1$ **do**
4: Compute $\gamma_i = \alpha_i \beta_i \bmod q'$.
5: **end for**
6: **Return** $\vec{c} = \text{xi\_to\_eta}(\vec{\gamma}, q')$.

2.4.2 Scheme

The subring homomorphic encryption scheme is based on the decomposition ring $\mathcal{O}_{\mathbf{K}}$ and the BFV scheme [7,15]. We describe the symmetric key variant below.

- SubringHE.SecretKeyGen(): Sample secret key from the key distribution $\vec{s} \leftarrow \chi_{key}$. Return $\mathsf{sk} = \vec{s} \in \mathbb{Z}^r$.
- SubringHE.Enc($\mathsf{sk} = \vec{s} \in \mathbb{Z}^r$, $\vec{m} \in \mathbb{Z}_t^r$): Sample $\vec{a} \xleftarrow{\$} \mathbb{Z}_{q'}^r$, $\vec{e} \leftarrow \chi_{err}$, $\vec{n} =$ `xi_to_eta` $(\vec{m}, t)$. Calculate $\vec{b} :=$ `mult_eta`$(\vec{a}, \vec{s}, q') + \Delta \cdot \vec{n} + \vec{e} \bmod q'$. Return $\mathsf{ct} = (\vec{a}, \vec{b})$.
- SubringHE.Dec($\mathsf{sk} = \vec{s} \in \mathbb{Z}^r$, $\mathsf{ct} = (\vec{a}, \vec{b})$): Calculate $\vec{n} = \lfloor \frac{1}{\Delta}(\vec{b} -$ `mult_eta`$(\vec{a}, \vec{s}, q') \bmod q') \rceil$. Define message vector as $\vec{m} =$ `eta_to_xi`$(\vec{n}, t)$. Return $\vec{m}$.
- SubringHE.Add($\mathsf{ct}_1 = (\vec{a}_1, \vec{b}_1)$, $\mathsf{ct}_2 = (\vec{a}_2, \vec{b}_2)$): Given two pairs of ciphertexts, calculate $\vec{a} := (\vec{a}_1 + \vec{a}_2) \bmod q'$, $\vec{b} := (\vec{b}_1 + \vec{b}_2) \bmod q'$. Return $\mathsf{ct}_{\mathsf{add}} = (\vec{a}, \vec{b})$.
- SubringHE.EvalKeyGen($\vec{s}$): Given secret key vector $\vec{s}$, calculate $\vec{\gamma} =$ `mult_eta` $(\vec{s}, \vec{s}, q')$. For k from 0 to $l_w - 1$, sample $\vec{\alpha}_k \xleftarrow{\$} \mathbb{Z}_{q'}^r$, $\vec{x}_k \leftarrow \chi_{err}$ and calculate $\vec{\beta}_k =$ `mult_eta`$(\vec{\alpha}_k, \vec{s}, q') + w^k \vec{\gamma} + \vec{x}_k \bmod q'$. Return an evaluation key $\mathsf{evk} = ((\vec{\alpha}_k, \vec{\beta}_k))_{k=0}^{l_w-1}$.
- SubringHE.Mult($\mathsf{ct}_1 = (\vec{a}_1, \vec{b}_1)$, $\mathsf{ct}_2 = (\vec{a}_2, \vec{b}_2)$, $\mathsf{evk} = ((\vec{\alpha}_k, \vec{\beta}_k))_k$): Given two pairs of ciphertexts and evaluation key ek, calculate $\vec{e} = \lfloor \frac{1}{\Delta} \cdot$ `mult_eta`$(\vec{b}_1, \vec{b}_2, \frac{q'^2}{t}) \rceil$, $\vec{c} = \lfloor \frac{1}{\Delta} \cdot$ `mult_eta`$(\vec{a}_1, \vec{b}_2, \frac{q'^2}{t}) +$ `mult_eta`$(\vec{a}_2, \vec{b}_1, \frac{q'^2}{t}) \rceil$, $\vec{d} = \lfloor$`mult_eta`$(\vec{a}_1, \vec{a}_2, \frac{q'^2}{t}) \rceil$. Define $(\vec{d}_0, \cdots, \vec{d}_{l_w-1}) =$ `WD`$(\vec{d})$, which satisfies $l_w = \lfloor \log_w(q') \rceil + 1, \vec{d} = \sum_{k=0}^{l_w-1} w^k \ \vec{d}_k$, $\vec{d}_k \in \mathbb{Z}_w^r$. Calculate $\vec{a} = \vec{c} + \sum_{k=0}^{l_w-1}$ `mult_eta`$(\vec{d}_k, \vec{\alpha}_k, q') \bmod q'$, $\vec{b} = \vec{e} + \sum_{k=0}^{l_w-1}$ `mult_eta`$(\vec{d}_k, \vec{\beta}_k, q') \bmod q'$. Return $\mathsf{ct}_{\mathsf{mult}} = (\vec{a}, \vec{b})$.

3 Decomposition Subring

To perform FHE more efficiently, we utilize the decomposition subring $\mathcal{O}_{\mathbf{M}}$ introduced in Sect. 2.2.2, to perform FHE over a ring of smaller dimension n. This is as opposed to performing FHE over the decomposition ring $\mathcal{O}_{\mathbf{K}}$ with dimension $r > n$. To enable this, encoding and decoding maps specific to the structure of $\mathcal{O}_{\mathbf{M}}$ are introduced in this section. From here, the encoding and decoding maps are later utilized for the operations within FHE. By decreasing the dimension, significant gains in efficiency are observed. This is later discussed in Sect. 4.

In the context of [2], encoding and decoding serve as fundamental operations in their scheme as described in Sect. 2.4.2. Crucially, they are utilized to define Algorithm 3 which is then heavily used in the subsequent homomorphic operations, forming the building block of their scheme. In general, to perform encoding and decoding, the fundamental idea involves a conversion between two bases. One is of the decomposition (sub)ring and the other, the slots form. This is analogous to the power(ful) and CRT bases in FHE.

Let $q > 2$ be an odd prime, $\Phi_q(x)$ be the qth cyclotomic polynomial, $\mathbb{Q}(\zeta_q) \cong \mathbb{Q}[x]/(\Phi_q(x))$ the qth cyclotomic field with the ring of integers $\mathbb{Z}[\zeta_q] \cong \mathbb{Z}[x]/(\Phi_q(x))$ and p be another prime distinct from q. Note that from this section onward, m is utilized to denote the power of the plaintext prime modulus and not the cyclotomic parameter. The famous Kummer-Dedekind theorem tells us exactly how the prime ideal $p\mathbb{Z}[\zeta_q]$ factorizes:

$$\mathbb{Z}[\zeta_q]/p\mathbb{Z}[\zeta_q] \cong \mathbb{Z}[x]/(p, \Phi_q(x)) \cong \prod_{i=1}^{r} \mathbb{Z}[x]/(p, f_i(x))$$

where $f_1(x) \dots f_r(x) \equiv \Phi_q(x) \pmod p$ are the irreducible divisors of $\Phi_q(x)$ over $\mathbb{F}_p[x]$. $\forall i$: $\deg(f_i) := f = \mathsf{ord}_q^{\times}(p)$ and $r = \frac{\phi(q)}{f} = \frac{q-1}{f}$.

Prior Approach. In [2], the authors consider the decomposition ring $\mathbf{K} = \mathbb{Q}(\eta_0)$, $\mathcal{O}_{\mathbf{K}} = \mathbb{Z}[\eta_0, \dots, \eta_{r-1}]$ where $\forall i$: $\eta_i := \sum_{t=0}^{f-1} \zeta_q^{g^{i+rt}}$, g is a multiplicative generator of $\mathbb{Z}_q^{\times}$, r, f are as in the previous paragraph. As discussed in Sect. 2.2.1, the prime ideal factorization of $p\mathcal{O}_{\mathbf{K}}$ is given by:

$$p\mathcal{O}_{\mathbf{K}} = \prod_{i=1}^{r} \mathfrak{P}_i, \quad \mathcal{O}_{\mathbf{K}}/p\mathcal{O}_{\mathbf{K}} \cong \prod_{i=1}^{r} \mathcal{O}_{\mathbf{K}}/\mathfrak{P}_i \cong \prod_{i=1}^{r} \mathbb{Z}_p$$

where each $\mathfrak{P}_i$ is a prime ideal factor of $p\mathcal{O}_{\mathbf{K}}$. In addition, $\forall m \geq 1$:

$$\mathcal{O}_{\mathbf{K}}/p^m\mathcal{O}_{\mathbf{K}} \cong \prod_{i=1}^{r} \mathcal{O}_{\mathbf{K}}/\mathfrak{P}_i^m \cong \prod_{i=1}^{r} \mathbb{Z}_{p^m}$$

The LHS of the equation above corresponds to the plaintext/ciphertext space of the BFV scheme. It has a basis $(\eta_0, \dots, \eta_{r-1})$ and multiplication follows the ring arithmetic of $\mathcal{O}_{\mathbf{K}} = \mathbb{Z}[\eta_0, \dots, \eta_{r-1}]$. The RHS corresponds to the slot space of the BFV scheme. It possesses "standard basis" $(\varepsilon_0, \dots, \varepsilon_{r-1})$ and follows the point-wise multiplication rule. We note that the authors of [2] refer to the basis on the RHS as the ξ basis. They define the ξ basis in terms of the canonical embedding but we find their formalism slightly extraneous. We deviate from their notation and emphasize that the isomorphism above is simply an application of the Chinese Remainder Theorem.

An explicit conversion between the slot space and the plaintext/ciphertext space can be found in Sect. 3.4 of [2]. Their general strategy can be summarized as follows:

- From the factorization $\Phi_q(x) \equiv f_1(x) \dots f_r(x) \pmod p$, calculate a CRT basis

$$\tau_i := \left(\prod_{j \neq i} f_j(x)^{-1} \bmod (p, f_i(x)) \right) \prod_{j \neq i} f_j(x) \bmod p$$

  Identify τ_i with an element of $\mathbb{Z}[\zeta_q]$. It turns out that $\tau_i \in \mathcal{O}_{\mathbf{K}}$ and τ_i is an idempotent element with respect to the ideal $\mathfrak{P}_i$.
- Hensel lift the idempotents to $\bar{\tau}_i \in \mathcal{O}_{\mathbf{K}}$ such that $\bar{\tau}_i$ is an idempotent element with respect to the ideal $\mathfrak{P}_i^m$
- For each i, calculate an $a_i \in \mathbb{Z}_{p^m}$ satisfying $a_i \cdot \bar{\tau}_i \equiv \eta_0 \cdot \bar{\tau}_i \pmod{p^m}$ over $\mathcal{O}_{\mathbf{K}}$

- Finally, to translate the basis component vector $\mathbf{v}$ of the LHS to the slot component vector $\mathbf{w}$, compute $\mathbf{w} = \mathbf{A}\mathbf{v}$ where $\mathbf{A} \in \mathbb{Z}_{p^m}^{r \times r}$ is a circulant matrix, with first row $(a_j)_{j=1}^r$.

Our Approach. The approach in [2] depends essentially on $q - 1 = rf$, where $f = \mathsf{ord}_q^\times(p)$, $r = \frac{q-1}{f}$. In our case in which we wish to decrease r and work in a subring of $\mathcal{O}_\mathbf{K}$, which we refer to as the decomposition subring $\mathcal{O}_\mathbf{M}$. This method breaks down because the τ_i terms are no longer idempotents in our setting. Therefore, we propose a new method that handles both the decomposition ring and decomposition subring cases. Furthermore, this approach is simpler than the previous one. To overcome the difficulty of finding the idempotents, we attempt to find a member, F_i, of the decomposition subring $\mathcal{O}_\mathbf{M}$, such that a principal ideal (F_i) contains every factor of a prime p except a specific prime ideal $\mathbf{P}_i$. In a sense F_i represents the complement of $\mathbf{P}_i$. This F_i is then used to compute the decoding map as first discussed in Sect. 3.1. From here the encoding map is computed from the decoding map. The details are discussed in Sect. 3.2.

3.1 Decoding Map

Given the period-basis elements $\eta_0, \ldots, \eta_{n-1}$ of the decomposition subring $\mathcal{O}_\mathbf{M}$, we consider the prime ideal factorization of $\mathcal{O}_\mathbf{M}$ and show that, up to permutation, any prime ideal $\mathbf{P}_i = (p, f_i(\zeta_q))$ from $p\mathbb{Z}[\zeta_q] = \prod_{i=1}^r (p, f_i(\zeta_q))$ can be used to calculate decoding kernel $(a_i)_{i=0}^{n-1}$. This is detailed in Algorithm 4. Here the decoding kernel corresponds to the first row of a circulant matrix $\mathbf{A}$. This decoding kernel is subsequently employed to compute the decoding map, mapping elements from $\mathcal{O}_\mathbf{M}/p^m\mathcal{O}_\mathbf{M} \to \prod_{i=1}^n \mathbb{Z}_{p^m}$. This is performed via taking the product of a polynomial containing the coefficients to be decoded and a polynomial containing decoding kernel as its coefficients. The details are presented in Algorithm 5.

To give a technical overview, a factor $\mathfrak{P}_i$ of $p\mathcal{O}_\mathbf{M} = p\mathbb{Z}[\eta_0, \ldots, \eta_{n-1}] = \prod_{i=0}^{n-1} \mathfrak{P}_i$ is first selected. Any factor can be chosen, and without loss of generality, denote this factor as $\mathfrak{P}_i$. From here, we consider $\mathfrak{P}_i\mathbb{Z}[\zeta_q] = \prod_k \mathbf{P}_{i_k}$ and select one of the $\mathbf{P}_{i_k}$. Again, any factor can be chosen and without loss of generality, denote this factor as $\mathbf{P}_i$. A special polynomial $F_i(x)$ is constructed such that for any element u, $\mathfrak{P}_i$ exactly divides u if and only if $\mathbf{P}_i$ exactly divides u. This is as per Proposition 7. Furthermore this is if and only if p exactly divides $uF_i(x)^2$. This polynomial enables us to find the a_i such that $\eta_i \equiv a_i (\bmod \mathfrak{P}_i^m)$, by the proof of correctness for Algorithm 4.

Let $q - 1 = nf$, now f can be a multiple of $\mathsf{ord}_q^\times(p)$. Again designate $\mathbf{M} = \mathbb{Q}(\eta_0)$, $\mathcal{O}_\mathbf{M} = \mathbb{Z}[\eta_0, \ldots, \eta_{n-1}]$ where $\forall i : \ \eta_i := \sum_{t=0}^{f-1} \zeta_q^{g^{i+tn}}$, again g is a fixed multiplicative generator of $\mathbb{Z}_q^\times$. Let $m \geq 1$, the ideal $p^m\mathcal{O}_\mathbf{M}$ factorizes as:

$$p^m\mathcal{O}_\mathbf{M} = \prod_{i=1}^n \mathfrak{P}_i^m, \quad \forall i : \ \mathcal{O}_\mathbf{M}/\mathfrak{P}_i^m \cong \mathbb{Z}_{p^m}$$

Each $\mathfrak{P}_i$ is a prime ideal divisor of $p\mathcal{O}_{\mathbf{M}}$. Fix any prime ideal divisor, say $\mathfrak{P}_0$. For each $0 \le i < n$ our goal is to calculate the unique $a_i \in \mathbb{Z}_{p^m}$ satisfying

$$\eta_i \equiv a_i \pmod{\mathfrak{P}_0^m}$$

Because the Galois group $\mathsf{Gal}\left(\mathbb{Q}(\eta_0)\,/\,\mathbb{Q}\right) \cong C_n$ is cyclic of order n, the Chinese Remainder isomorphism can be captured by a circulant matrix $\mathbf{A}$ with a first row of form $(a_i)_{i=0}^{n-1}$.

To compute a_i, recall that over the cyclotomic ring $\mathbb{Z}[\zeta_q]$, $p\mathbb{Z}[\zeta_q] = \prod_{i=1}^{r}(p, f_i(\zeta_q))$ where $\Phi_q(x) \equiv \prod_{i=1}^{r} f_i(x) \pmod{p}$ and $r = \mathsf{ord}_q^{\times}(p)$.

Proposition 7. *Fix an index i, and let $\mathbf{P}_i = (p, f_i(\zeta_q))$ be a prime ideal divisor of $p\mathbb{Z}[\zeta_q]$. Define $F_i(x) := \Phi_q(x) \cdot f_i(x)^{-1} \bmod p$. The element $F_i(\zeta_q) \in \mathbb{Z}[\zeta_q]$ separates the prime ideal $\mathbf{P}_i$ in the following sense:*

For any element $u \in \mathbb{Z}[\zeta_q]$, $\mathbf{P}_i^k \parallel u$ if and only if $p^k \parallel u \cdot F_i(\zeta_q)^{k+1}$ over $\mathbb{Z}[\zeta_q]$. i.e. $\mathbf{P}_i^k$ exactly divides u if and only if p^k exactly divides $u \cdot F_i(\zeta_q)^{k+1}$ over $\mathbb{Z}[\zeta_q]$.

Proof. The proof is provided in the Appendix.

As $\mathcal{O}_{\mathbf{M}} \subset \mathbb{Z}[\zeta_q]$, for any fixed index i, the lifted ideal $\mathfrak{P}_i\mathbb{Z}[\zeta_q]$ factorizes as $\mathfrak{P}_i\mathbb{Z}[\zeta_q] = \prod_l (p, f_{i_l}(\zeta_q))$ for some distinct indices i_l over $\mathbb{Z}[\zeta_q]$. We can use the valuation index of any prime ideal $(p, f_{i_l}(\zeta_q))$ to calculate the valuation index over $\mathfrak{P}_i$. In other words, for any $u \in \mathbb{Z}[\eta_0, \ldots, \eta_{n-1}]$

$$\mathfrak{P}_i^k \parallel u \text{ over } \mathcal{O}_{\mathbf{M}} \iff (p, f_{i_l}(\zeta_q))^k \parallel u \text{ over } \mathbb{Z}[\zeta_q] \qquad (1)$$

Up to permutation, any prime ideal $\mathfrak{P}_i$ can serve as an "anchor" as $\mathcal{O}_{\mathbf{M}}/\mathfrak{P}_i^m$ are all isomorphic to $\mathbb{Z}_{p^m}$. The discussion above implies that we may essentially use any prime ideal $(p, f_i(\zeta_q))$ to calculate $(a_i)_{i=0}^{n-1}$. Specifically, denote a chosen $f_i(X)$ as an irreducible factor $f(x)$ of $\Phi_q(x)$ mod p. Similarly, denote the corresponding $\mathfrak{P}_i$ as $\mathfrak{P}$. Also, denote the coefficient of x^i in a given the polynomial $H(x)$ as $H[i]$. Moreover, all indices i are implicitly taken to be i mod n. Algorithm 4 is then used to compute the decoding kernel. This then enables the use of the decoding map, detailed in Algorithm 5. This produces the map of the left-to-right direction of the Chinese Remainder isomorphism discussed above.

Algorithm 4 takes as its input a prime p where p^m forms the modulus to be utilized. It then takes in prime q corresponding to the cyclotomic polynomial $\Phi_q(x)$ as discussed above as well as the period basis. The irreducible factor $f(x)$ is selected and the relevant polynomials are computed as previously discussed. From here, as $\eta_i \in \mathbb{Z}[\zeta_q]$ we then express it as the polynomial $\eta_i(x)$. The polynomial $A_i(x)$ is then computed as per Proposition 7. Furthermore, according to Proposition 7 and the proof below, the polynomial $A_i(x)$ should be an a_i multiple of $\phi(x)$ mod p^m. This implies that the degree j coefficient of $A_i(x)$ is also an a_i multiple of the degree j coefficient of $\phi(x)$ for all $0 \le j \le \deg(\phi(x))$. We therefore choose any "good" index idx such that the degree idx coefficient of $\phi(x)$ is coprime to p, which then uniquely determines the constant multiple a_i using the modular division in Step 8 of Algorithm 4. Additionally, an example demonstrating how Algorithm 4 works is provided in the Appendix.

Algorithm 4. DecodeKerGen

Input: Prime q, period-basis $\eta_0, \ldots, \eta_{n-1}$, modulus p^m.

Output: Decoding kernel $(a_i)_{i=0}^{n-1} \in \mathbb{Z}_{p^m}^n$, where $\eta_i \equiv a_i \pmod{\mathfrak{P}^m}$ for some prime ideal $\mathfrak{P}|p$.

1: Obtain an irreducible factor $f(x)$ of $\Phi_q(x) \bmod p$.
2: Compute $F(x) = \Phi_q(x)f(x)^{-1} \bmod p$.
3: Compute $\phi(x) = F(x)^m \bmod (p^m, \Phi_q(x))$. ▷ Taken to power of m to fulfill the requirement/congruence on page 12.
4: Obtain an index idx where $gcd(\phi[\mathsf{idx}], p) = 1$. ▷ To allow for computation of the inverse in Step 8.
5: **for** each basis element η_i **do**
6: Represent η_i as a polynomial $\eta_i(x) = \sum_{t=0}^{f-1} x^{g^{i+nt} \bmod q} \in \mathbb{Z}[x]$. ▷ Replacing ζ_q with a variable x.
7: Compute $A_i(x) = \eta_i(x)\phi(x) \bmod (p^m, \Phi_q(x))$.
8: Compute $a_i = A_i[\mathsf{idx}] \cdot \phi[\mathsf{idx}]^{-1} \bmod p^m$.
9: **end for**
10: **Return** $(a_i)_{i=0}^{n-1} \in \mathbb{Z}_{p^m}^n$

Correctness of Algorithm 4: Let $f(x)$ be the mod p irreducible polynomial chosen by the Algorithm 4, and let $\mathfrak{P}$ be the unique prime ideal in $\mathcal{O}_{\mathrm{M}} = \mathbb{Z}[\eta_0, \ldots, \eta_{n-1}]$ such that $\mathfrak{P} \mid (p, f(\zeta_q))$ over $\mathbb{Z}[\zeta_q]$. The correctness is obtained from the correctness of Steps 7 and 8 of the algorithm.

For the correctness of Step 7,

$$\begin{aligned}
&\eta_i \equiv a_i \pmod{\mathfrak{P}^m} \iff \mathfrak{P}^m \mid (\eta_i - a_i)\\
&\iff (p, f(\zeta_q))^m \mid (\eta_i - a_i) \text{ over } \mathbb{Z}[\zeta_q] \text{ by Equation (1)}\\
&\iff p^m \mid (\eta_i - a_i)F(\zeta_q)^m \text{ by Proposition 7}\\
&\iff (\eta_i(x) - a_i)F(x)^m \equiv 0 \bmod (p^m, \Phi_q(x)) \text{ lifting cyclotomic integers to } \mathbb{Z}[x]\\
&\iff \eta_i(x)F(x)^m \bmod (p^m, \Phi_q(x)) \text{ is an } a_i \text{ multiple of } F(x)^m \bmod (p^m, \Phi_q(x))
\end{aligned}$$

The ratio mod p^m of an appropriate pair of coefficients will yield the constant $a_i \in \mathbb{Z}_{p^m}$.

For the correctness of Step 8, denote the result of Step 7 after modular reduction to be of the form

$$A_i(x) = \sum_{j=0}^{q-2} r_j x^j = a_i \sum_{j=0}^{q-2} t_j x^j \bmod (p^m, \Phi_q(x)).$$

Here, we denote $\phi(x) = \sum_{j=0}^{q-2} t_j x^j$ and denote by r_j the coefficients of the reduced $A_i(x)$. Again, note that this form is due to the result of Step 7 being an a_i multiple of $\phi(x) = F(x)^m \bmod (p^m, \Phi_q(x))$. Choose index idx such that $gcd(\phi[\mathsf{idx}], p) = 1$. By equating the coefficients of the reduced equation, we obtain $a_i \cdot t_{\mathsf{idx}} x^{\mathsf{idx}} = r_{\mathsf{idx}} x^{\mathsf{idx}}$. As $\phi[\mathsf{idx}]$ is invertible under modulo p by the choice of idx, we can obtain $a_i = r_{\mathsf{idx}} \cdot t_{\mathsf{idx}}^{-1}$. □

Algorithm 5. Decode

Input: Encoded polynomial $c(X) = \sum_{i=0}^{n-1} c_i X^i \in \mathbb{Z}_{p^m}[X]$, decoding kernel $(a_i)_{i=0}^{n-1} \in \mathbb{Z}_{p^m}^n$, modulus p^m.
Output: Polynomial $c'(X)$ containing the slot entries in its coefficients.
1: Initialize decoding polynomial $t(X) = \sum_{i=0}^{n-1} t_i X^i$.
2: **for** i in range $0 \leq i \leq n-1$ **do**
3: Set $t_i \leftarrow a_{-i \pmod n}$
4: **end for**
5: Compute $c'(X) = t(X) \cdot c(X) \bmod (X^n - 1, p^m)$.
6: **Return** $c'(X)$

The resulting decoding map is described in Algorithm 5. Here, it utilizes the decoding kernel computed using Algorithm 4, first converting it into a polynomial $t(X)$. This is then multiplied with an encoded polynomial, resulting in the desired decoded polynomial $c'(X)$. This contains the slot-wise entries as its coefficients. The correctness of Algorithm 5 follows directly from the discussion of Sect. 3.1, the correctness of Algorithm 4 and the standard properties of circulant matrices. It is routine to see that the computation in Algorithm 5 corresponds to multiplication by the circulant matrix $\mathbf{A}$. The time complexity of Algorithm 5 is $O(n \log n)$. This arises from the multiplication of the two polynomials in Step 5 of the algorithm, which is performed using the Fast Fourier Transformation(FFT).

3.2 Encoding Map

The encoding map, which performs the map from $\prod_{i=1}^{n} \mathbb{Z}_{p^m} \to \mathcal{O}_{\mathrm{M}}/p^m\mathcal{O}_{\mathrm{M}}$, is subsequently derived from the decoding map. Here, we first observe that for a circulant matrix $\mathbf{A}$ corresponding to the decoding map, the circulant matrix $\mathbf{B}$ corresponding to the encoding map can be derived. From there, Algorithm 6 is utilized to compute the first row of the matrix $\mathbf{B}$, referred to as the encoding kernel $(b_j)_{j=0}^{n-1} \in \mathbb{Z}_{p^m}^n$. The encoding kernel is then utilized in Algorithm 7, which details the encoding procedure.

For consistency, we use the same notation and variables as Sect. 3.1. To recap, let $\mathbf{v} \in \mathbb{Z}_{p^m}^n$ be a component vector of $\mathcal{O}_{\mathrm{M}}/p^m\mathcal{O}_{\mathrm{M}}$ with the basis $(\eta_0, \ldots, \eta_{n-1})$. The corresponding component vector $\mathbf{w} \in \mathbb{Z}_{p^m}^n$ in the slot space $\prod_{i=1}^{n} \mathbb{Z}_{p^m}$ with "standard basis" $(\varepsilon_0, \ldots, \varepsilon_{n-1})$ is determined by the Chinese Remainder isomorphism

$$\varphi : \mathcal{O}_{\mathrm{M}}/p^m\mathcal{O}_{\mathrm{M}} \to \prod_{i=1}^{n} \mathbb{Z}_{p^m}$$
$$\eta_i \mapsto \sum_{j=0}^{n-1} (\eta_i \bmod \mathfrak{P}_j^m)\varepsilon_j = \sum_{j=0}^{n-1} \sigma^j(\eta_{i-j} \bmod \mathfrak{P}_0^m)\varepsilon_j = \sum_{j=0}^{n-1} a_{i-j}\varepsilon_j$$

Or equivalently $\mathbf{w} = \mathbf{A}\mathbf{v}$, $\quad \mathbf{A}_{i,j} = a_{j-i}$ where $\mathfrak{P}$ is the unspecified prime ideal and $(a_i)_{i=0}^{n-1}$ the output of Algorithm 4. The generator of the Galois group is $\langle\sigma\rangle = \mathsf{Gal}(\mathbb{Q}(\eta_0)\,/\,\mathbb{Q})$ with $\sigma(\eta_i) = \eta_{i+1}$.

According to Equations (8) and (20) of [13],

$$\sum_{i=0}^{n-1} \eta_i = -1 \tag{*}$$

$$\sum_{i=0}^{n-1} \eta_i \eta_{i+k} = q \cdot d_k - f \text{ where} \tag{**}$$

$$d_k = \delta_{0,k} \text{ if } f \text{ is even, } d_k = \delta_{e/2,k} \text{ if } f \text{ is odd}$$

The inverse isomophism φ^{-1} can be easily obtained from these 2 facts.

Proposition 8. *The inverse of the matrix* $\mathbf{A} \in \mathbb{Z}_{p^m}^{n \times n}$ *given above is a circulant matrix* $\mathbf{B} \in \mathbb{Z}_{p^m}^{n \times n}$*, whose first row is given by* $(b_j)_{j=0}^{n-1}$ *such that for any* $0 \leq j \leq n-1$*:*

- *If* f *is even,* $b_j = q^{-1} \cdot (a_{-j} - f) \bmod p^m$
- *If* f *is odd,* $b_j = q^{-1} \cdot (a_{e/2-j} - f) \bmod p^m$

Proof. The proof is provided in the Appendix.

To summarize the computation for the encoding map described above, we present Algorithm 6. This computes the first row of the circulant matrix **B**, which we refer to as the encoding kernel $(b_j)_{j=0}^{n-1} \in \mathbb{Z}_{p^m}^n$. Here, the identities obtained from Proposition 8 are utilized to compute the respective coefficients of the encoding kernel. The correctness of Algorithm 6 follows directly from Proposition 8.

Algorithm 6. `EncodeKerGen`

Input: Decoding kernel $(a_i)_{i=0}^{n-1} \in \mathbb{Z}_{p^m}^n$,, modulus p^m, prime q.
Output: Encoding kernel $(b_j)_{j=0}^{n-1} \in \mathbb{Z}_{p^m}^n$.
1: Compute $f = \frac{q-1}{e}$.
2: Compute inverse $q^{-1} \bmod p^m$.
3: **if** f is even **then**
4:     **for** j in range $0 \leq j \leq n-1$ **do**
5:         $b_j \leftarrow (a_{-j \bmod n} - f) \cdot q^{-1} \bmod p^m$
6:     **end for**
7: **else**
8:     **for** j in range $0 \leq j \leq n-1$ **do**
9:         $b_j \leftarrow (a_{\frac{e}{2}-j} - f) \cdot q^{-1} \bmod p^m$
10:     **end for**
11: **end if**
12: **Return** $(b_j)_{j=0}^{n-1} \in \mathbb{Z}_{p^m}^n$

The encoding map is described in Algorithm 7. Here, it utilizes the encoding kernel computed using Algorithm 6. The encoding kernel is first converted into a

Algorithm 7. `Encode`

Input: Polynomial $c(X) = \sum_{j=0}^{n-1} c_j X^j \in \mathbb{Z}_{p^m}[X]$ with slot entries in coefficients, encoding kernel $(b_j)_{j=0}^{n-1} \in \mathbb{Z}_{p^m}^n$, modulus p^m.
Output: Polynomial $c'(X)$ containing c_js in slots.
1: Initialize encoding polynomial $t(X) = \sum_{j=0}^{n-1} t_j X^j$.
2: **for** j in range $0 \leq j \leq n-1$ **do**
3: Set $t_j \leftarrow b_{-j \pmod n}$
4: **end for**
5: Compute $c'(X) = t(X) \cdot c(X) \bmod (X^n - 1, p^m)$
6: **Return** $c'(X)$

polynomial $t(X)$. This is then multiplied with a polynomial containing the slot entries in the coefficients, resulting in the desired encoded polynomial $c'(X)$. The correctness of Algorithm 7 follows directly from the discussion above in Sect. 3.2, the correctness of Algorithm 6 and the standard properties of circulant matrices. Similar to Algorithm 5, the computation in Algorithm 7 corresponds to multiplication by the circulant matrix $\mathbf{B}$. The time complexity of Algorithm 7 is $O(n \log n)$. This arises from the multiplication of the polynomials in Step 5 of the algorithm, which is performed using FFT.

4 Homomorphic Operations

Here, the encoding and decoding techniques of Sect. 3 are applied to develop a homomorphic scheme. For the purpose of comparing the effects of using the decomposition subring $\mathcal{O}_{\mathbf{M}}$ against using the decomposition ring $\mathcal{O}_{\mathbf{K}}$, this scheme will be similar to the one in Sect. 2.4.2. The `Encode` and `Decode` functions enable the use of the decomposition subring, which has a lower dimension compared to the decomposition ring. We show that this therefore provides greater efficiency.

Algorithm 8. `GaussMult`

Input: Polynomials $c_1(X) = \sum_{j=0}^{n-1} c_{1,j} X^j \in \mathbb{Z}_{p^m}[X]$, $c_2(X) = \sum_{j=0}^{n-1} c_{2,j} X^j \in \mathbb{Z}_{p^m}[X]$ where the coefficients are the components in the period-basis, encoding kernel $(b_j)_{j=0}^{n-1} \in \mathbb{Z}_{p^m}^n$, decoding kernel $(a_i)_{i=0}^{n-1} \in \mathbb{Z}_{p^m}^n$, modulus p^m.
Output: Encoded polynomial $t(X)$ containing in its slots the slot-wise product of $c_1(X), c_2(X)$.
1: Set $c_1'(X) \leftarrow$ `Decode`$(c_1(X), (a_i)_{i=0}^{n-1}, p^m)$
2: Set $c_2'(X) \leftarrow$ `Decode`$(c_2(X), (a_i)_{i=0}^{n-1}, p^m)$
3: Initialize polynomial $t'(X) = \sum_{j=0}^{n-1} t_j' X^j$.
4: **for** j in range $0 \leq j \leq n-1$ **do**
5: Set $t_j' \leftarrow c_1'(X)[j] \cdot c_2'(X)[j] \bmod p^m$
6: **end for**
7: Set $t(X) \leftarrow$ `Encode`$(t'(X), (b_j)_{j=0}^{n-1}, p^m)$
8: **Return** $t(X)$

To construct the scheme, first recall that the function described in Sect. 2.4.1 as Algorithm 3 forms the main building block of the homomorphic scheme described in Sect. 2.4.2. It is heavily utilized, being a component of almost all the FHE operations in Sect. 2.4.2. Here, we provide a variant of Algorithm 3, labeled Algorithm 8, based on the encoding and decoding maps described in Sect. 3. From there, we utilize it in the scheme described in Sect. 2.4.2 and analyze the effects on the complexity of the FHE operations. It is shown that the operations of the proposed scheme exhibit a lower complexity due to the lower dimension of the decomposition subring. Following this, the security analysis of the scheme is performed. It is shown that the proposed scheme is secure assuming the hardness of the small-secret Ring-LWE$_{Q,\Phi}$. Finally, the correctness of the scheme is shown. Here, error bounds are described for each operation.

Algorithm 8 describes the slot-wise multiplication procedure. It functions similar to Algorithm 3, with the main difference being the calls to our encoding and decoding functions. Specifically, Algorithm 5 is utilized in the first two steps while Algorithm 7 is utilized in the last step. Correctness follows directly from Sect. 2.4.1 and the correctness of Algorithms 5 and 7. Crucially, we note that the modulus p^m utilized changes depending on which operation Algorithm 8 is utilized for in Sect. 2.4.2. As Algorithms 5 and 7 are both performed with time complexity $O(n \log n)$, Algorithm 8 has time complexity $O(n \log n)$.

Complexity Analysis. From here, we directly replace Algorithm 3 with Algorithm 8 and apply it to the FHE scheme presented in Sect. 2.4.2. Similarly Algorithms 1, 2 are replaced with Algorithms 5 and 7, our `Decode` and `Encode` algorithms, respectively. Following the notation introduced at the beginning of Sect. 3, we denote n as the dimension of our decomposition subring $\mathcal{O}_{\mathbf{M}}$ and we let r be the dimension of the decomposition ring $\mathcal{O}_{\mathbf{K}}$ utilized in [2].

For encryption, as shown in Sect. 2.4.2, a single call to the `Encode` and `GaussMult` functions is invoked. This dominates the complexity of encryption as both functions are of $O(n \log n)$ complexity, from the discussion above as well as in Sect. 3.2. Encryption therefore requires $O(n \log n)$ time complexity in our context and $O(r \log r)$ in theirs. Similarly, decryption invokes a single call to the `Decode` and `GaussMult` functions which both require $O(n \log n)$ complexity due to the discussion above as well as Sect. 3.1. Therefore decryption requires $O(n \log n)$ time complexity in our context and $O(r \log r)$ in theirs. For addition as described in Sect. 2.4.2, it is trivial to see that ours requires $O(n)$ time complexity while theirs requires $O(r)$. For multiplication, the procedure is dominated by the sum of l_w calls to `GaussMult`, where l_w is the parameter selected for decomposition. Its complexity is therefore $O(l_w \cdot n \log n)$ time complexity in our context and $O(l_w \cdot r \log r)$ in theirs. The complexity analysis is summarized in Table 2. By choosing the parameters such that $n < r$, our framework therefore outperforms theirs in terms of complexity.

4.1 Analysis of the Scheme

Security Analysis. The security of our scheme is based on a variant of the decisional version of the Ring-LWE assumption, defined on an arbitrary number

Table 2. Comparison of efficiency between the use of Algorithm 3 of [2] against the use of our Algorithm 8 in the homomorphic scheme described in Sect. 2.4.2.

Multiplication Algorithm	Encryption	Decryption	Addition	Multiplication
Algorithm 3	$O(r \log r)$	$O(r \log r)$	$O(r)$	$O(l_w \cdot r \log r)$
Algorithm 8	$O(n \log n)$	$O(n \log n)$	$O(n)$	$O(l_w \cdot n \log n)$

field. Compared to the standard assumption, this assumes that the underlying ring can be an arbitrary ring of integers and that the coefficients of the secret key are binary. This is described in Theorem 9 below.

Theorem 9 (Security). *Assume the hardness of the small-secret Ring-DLWE$_{Q,\Phi}$ [6,22] where Q is the ciphertext modulus and Φ a distribution on $\mathbf{K}_{\mathbb{R}}$ specified in the BFV scheme. The scheme is* IND-CPA *secure.*

Proof. The proof is provided in the Appendix.

Correctness. Here, we provide the noise analysis for the decryption as well as the addition and multiplication operations for our scheme. A bound[1] for the multiplication depth supported by the scheme is also provided. The results are presented in Theorem 11.

Let $\mathbf{K} = \mathbb{Q}[\eta_0]$, $Q > 0$ be the ciphertext modulus, $0 < t < Q$ be the plaintext modulus and $\Delta := \lfloor \frac{Q}{t} \rceil$ be the scaling factor. Define $\|a\|_{\eta,\infty} := \max_{0 \leq i < n} |a_i|$, where a_i are the components of a in the period basis and let δ be the multiplication expansion factor defined as the smallest $\delta > 0$ such that $\forall x, y \in \mathbf{K}_{\mathbb{R}}$: $\|xy\|_{\eta,\infty} \leq \delta \|x\|_{\eta,\infty} \|y\|_{\eta,\infty}$. Let $w > 0 \in \mathbb{Z}$ be the relinearization modulus, and $l = \lfloor \log_w Q \rfloor + 1$ be the relinearization depth.

For decryption correctness, let $\mathsf{ct} = (\mathsf{ct}_0, \mathsf{ct}_1)$ be a ciphertext satisfying $\mathsf{ct}_1 - s \cdot \mathsf{ct}_0 \equiv \Delta m + e \bmod Q$ for some message $m = \sum m_i \eta_i$, $\|m\|_{\eta,\infty} \leq \frac{t}{2}$ and error $e \in \mathbf{K}_{\mathbb{R}}$. Then decrypting ct correctly recovers m if $\|e\|_{\eta,\infty} < \frac{Q}{2t} - \frac{Q - \Delta t}{2}$.

For addition, suppose $\mathsf{ct}^{(1)}$ has an inherent noise $e_{\mathsf{inh}}^{(1)}$ corresponding to $m_1 \in \mathbb{R}_t$, $\mathsf{ct}^{(2)}$ has an inherent noise $e_{\mathsf{inh}}^{(2)}$ corresponding to $m_1 \in \mathbb{R}_t$. Then the ciphertext resulting from homomorphic addition $\mathsf{ct}^{(1+2)}$ has an inherent noise $e_{\mathsf{inh}}^{(1+2)}$ satisfying $\|e_{\mathsf{inh}}^{(1+2)}\|_{\eta,\infty} \leq |Q - \Delta t| + \|e_{\mathsf{inh}}^{(1)}\|_{\eta,\infty} + \|e_{\mathsf{inh}}^{(2)}\|_{\eta,\infty}$.

For multiplication, assume each evaluation key has the same noise bound $\|e_{\mathsf{ev}}\|_{\eta,\infty}$.

Lemma 10. *For each $A \in \mathcal{R} = \mathbb{Z}[\eta_0]$, write the w-decomposition of A as $A = \sum_{i=0}^{l-1} A^{(i)w^i}$, $A^{(i)} \in \mathcal{R}$, $\|A^{(i)}\|_{\eta,\infty} < w$. To obtain the decomposition we decompose each coefficient into w-ary representation and then collect the terms with the same arity into each $A^{(i)}$. For any "relinearization"* $\mathsf{ct}^{\mathsf{rel}} = (\mathsf{ct}_0^{\mathsf{rel}}, \mathsf{ct}_1^{\mathsf{rel}})$ *defined by:*

$$\mathsf{ct}_0^{\mathsf{rel}} := \sum_{i=0}^{l-1} A^{(i)} \cdot \mathsf{ev}_0^{(i)} \bmod Q, \quad \mathsf{ct}_1^{\mathsf{rel}} := \sum_{i=0}^{l-1} A^{(i)} \cdot \mathsf{ev}_1^{(i)} \bmod Q$$

[1] Further derivations of these bounds will be included in the full version of the paper.

There exists $e_{\mathsf{inh}}^{(\mathsf{rel})}$ *such that* $\mathsf{ct}_1^{\mathsf{rel}} - s \cdot \mathsf{ct}_0^{\mathsf{rel}} \equiv A \cdot s^2 + e_{\mathsf{inh}}^{(\mathsf{rel})} \pmod Q$ *with an inherent noise bound* $\|e_{\mathsf{inh}}^{(\mathsf{rel})}\|_{\eta,\infty} \leq w\delta \sum_{i=0}^{l-1} \|e_{\mathsf{ev}}^{(i)}\|_{\eta,\infty}$.

Let $\mathsf{ct}^{\mathsf{rel}}$ be the relinearization ciphertext defined in Lemma 10. Let the ciphertext $\mathsf{ct}^{(1\times 2)} = (\mathsf{ct}_0^{(1\times 2)}, \mathsf{ct}_1^{(1\times 2)}) \in \mathcal{R}_Q^2$ be the result of homomorphic multiplication defined by:

$$d_0 := \lfloor \frac{t}{Q} \mathsf{ct}_0^{(1)} \mathsf{ct}_0^{(2)} \rceil \bmod Q$$

$$d_1 := \lfloor \frac{t}{Q} (\mathsf{ct}_0^{(1)} \mathsf{ct}_1^{(2)} + \mathsf{ct}_1^{(1)} \mathsf{ct}_0^{(2)}) \rceil \bmod Q$$

$$d_2 := \lfloor \frac{t}{Q} \mathsf{ct}_1^{(1)} \mathsf{ct}_1^{(2)} \rceil \bmod Q$$

$$\mathsf{ct}^{\mathsf{rel}} = (\mathsf{ct}_0^{\mathsf{rel}}, \mathsf{ct}_1^{\mathsf{rel}}) := \left(\sum_i {d_0}^{(i)} \cdot \mathsf{ev}_0^{(i)} \bmod Q, \sum_i {d_0}^{(i)} \cdot \mathsf{ev}_1^{(i)} \bmod Q \right)$$

$$\mathsf{ct}^{(1\times 2)} = (\mathsf{ct}_0^{(1\times 2)}, \mathsf{ct}_1^{(1\times 2)}) := (d_1 + \mathsf{ct}_0^{\mathsf{rel}} \bmod Q, d_2 + \mathsf{ct}_1^{\mathsf{rel}} \bmod Q)$$

Then $\mathsf{ct}^{(1\times 2)}$ has an inherent noise $e_{\mathsf{inh}}^{(1\times 2)}$ satisfying $\mathsf{ct}_1^{(1\times 2)} - s \cdot \mathsf{ct}_0^{(1\times 2)} \equiv \Delta(m_1 m_2 \bmod t) + e_{\mathsf{inh}}^{(1\times 2)} \pmod Q$, upper bounded by:

$$\|e_{\mathsf{inh}}^{(1\times 2)}\|_{\eta,\infty} \leq \left\{ \frac{\delta t}{2}(\delta + t)(Q - \Delta t) + \frac{\delta^2 t}{2}(\|e_{\mathsf{inh}}^{(1)}\|_{\eta,\infty} + \|e_{\mathsf{inh}}^{(2)}\|_{\eta,\infty}) + \frac{2\delta t}{Q}\|e_{\mathsf{inh}}^{(1)}\|_{\eta,\infty}\|e_{\mathsf{inh}}^{(2)}\|_{\eta,\infty} + w\delta l \|e_{\mathsf{ev}}\|_{\eta,\infty} \right\} (1 + o(1))$$

For the multiplication depth, under the additional assumptions that $Q = \Delta t$ and that each multiplicand has roughly the same inherent noise magnitude: $\|e_{\mathsf{inh}}^{(1)}\|_{\eta,\infty} \approx \|e_{\mathsf{inh}}^{(1)}\|_{\eta,\infty}$, the BFV scheme supports repeated homomorphic multiplication with the multiplication depth being

$$L \lesssim \frac{\log \frac{Q}{2t} - \log \|e_{\mathsf{inh}}^{\mathsf{init}}\|_{\eta,\infty} - \log w\delta l}{\log 2t + 2 \log \delta}$$

where $\|e_{\mathsf{inh}}^{\mathsf{init}}\|_{\eta,\infty}$ is the magnitude of the inherent noise in a fresh ciphertext.

Theorem 11. *Let* $\mathsf{ct} = (\mathsf{ct}_0, \mathsf{ct}_1)$ *be a ciphertext of the FHE scheme discussed. Let the error term of* ct *satisfy* $\|e\|_{\eta,\infty} < \frac{Q}{2t} - \frac{Q - \Delta t}{2}$. *The decryption of* ct *then yields the correct output. Furthermore, assuming the bound on multiplicative depth provided above holds, our scheme correctly evaluates any circuit of multiplication depth* L. *The correctness of the FHE scheme discussed therefore follows.*

5 Experiments

We provide a proof-of-concept implementation of the BFV-based FHE scheme on the ring of Gaussian periods as discussed in Sect. 4. This was implemented and

Table 3. Parameters for our FHE framework described in Sect. 4.

Parameter Set	Cyclotomic q	Ring Dimension n	Plaintext Modulus	Ciphertext Modulus	Error Var.	Security (bits)
1-A	45319	6474	11^2	$(11^2)^8$	4	444.2
1-B		2158				127.6
2-A	41761	5220	17	17^8		-
2-B		1044				103.4
3-A	44983	6426	113	113^8		447.6
3-B		2142				128.4
4-A	41761	5220	17	17^{16}	8	292.4
4-B		1740				88.7
5-A	28057	9352	167	167^{16}		290.2
5-B		4676				133.1
6-A	41203	4578	29	29^{16}		206.7
6-B		2289				98

benchmarked using SageMath [27] on an Intel(R) Core(TM) i7-7700HQ CPU @ (2.80GHz, 2.80GHz).

Experiments were conducted with the six sets of parameters listed in Table 3. For each parameter set, the cyclotomic q value is first chosen. Following this, for a given prime, the corresponding decomposition ring dimension(A) and the smallest decomposition subring dimension(B) we can decrease it to, are listed. The ring dimension is decreased as much possible while still retaining at least 80-bit security. Parameter sets 1, 3 and 5 correspond to approximately 128-bit security. The security estimates were obtained from the Lattice-Estimator [1]. The binary secret key was sampled from a uniform distribution. The error terms were sampled from a discrete Gaussian distribution, with the variance listed in Table 3. Parameter sets 1 to 3 correspond to having a smaller ciphertext modulus while the parameter sets 4 to 6 correspond to a larger ciphertext modulus. The benchmark timings of the experiments are listed in Table 4 for each operation.

As observed in Tables 4, 5, significant latency improvements are obtained. Specifically, for the parameter set 2, we obtain up to a 5.06× speed-up with our techniques. Based on the data in Table 5, it is also observed that the proportion of the latency improvement for each operation is roughly similar to the proportion of the decrease in the ring dimension n. It is noted that, compared to the other parameters, the parameter set 5 exhibits a marginally greater degree of improvement in Table 5. This may be attributed to the SageMath libraries employed within the implementation for our scheme. It is also noted that the size of the parameters utilized was restricted by the capabilities of our hardware. If larger parameters were employed, it is likely that the latency would be further improved through greater reductions in the dimension. Tables 4 and 5 also represent a form of comparison between the techniques of [2,3] (A parameter sets) with our work (B parameter sets). Note that the works of [2,3] utilize similar techniques to form their plaintext spaces. However, a direct comparison with their proposed parameters is not provided here, as applying our techniques to

Table 4. Timings for our FHE framework described in Sect. 4.

Parameter Set	Encryption(ms)	Decryption(ms)	Addition(ms)	Multiplication(ms)
1-A	106.65	126.83	5.83	1829.98
1-B	38.58	42.19	2.05	683.28
2-A	108.43	100.41	4.44	1982.82
2-B	21.42	21.13	0.91	414.07
3-A	161.85	149.97	5.59	4449.5
3-B	52.35	54.5	2.09	1665.39
4-A	110.07	102.46	4.58	2203.22
4-B	36.95	45.94	1.91	629.92
5-A	289.81	272.52	9.12	8767.55
5-B	125.70	126.40	4.49	4157.89
6-A	94.73	105.63	4.33	2198.2
6-B	47.83	49.21	2.21	1109.54

their proposed parameter sets would result in there being less than sufficient security due to the decrease in the dimension.

Table 5. Relation between change in dimension and change in timings for our FHE framework described in Sect. 4.

Parameter Set	Change in Dimension	Change in Encryption	Change in Decryption	Change in Addition	Change in Multiplication
1-A $\leftrightarrow$ 1-B	$\times 3$	$\times 2.76$	$\times 3.01$	$\times 2.84$	$\times 2.68$
2-A $\leftrightarrow$ 2-B	$\times 5$	$\times 5.06$	$\times 4.75$	$\times 4.88$	$\times 4.79$
3-A $\leftrightarrow$ 3-B	$\times 3$	$\times 3.09$	$\times 2.75$	$\times 2.67$	$\times 2.67$
4-A $\leftrightarrow$ 4-B	$\times 3$	$\times 2.98$	$\times 2.23$	$\times 2.40$	$\times 3.50$
5-A $\leftrightarrow$ 5-B	$\times 2$	$\times 2.31$	$\times 2.16$	$\times 2.03$	$\times 2.11$
6-A $\leftrightarrow$ 6-B	$\times 2$	$\times 1.98$	$\times 2.15$	$\times 1.96$	$\times 1.98$

A comparison between our work and that of [16] is performed in Table 6. Amongst the recommended parameters of [16], the parameters with the smallest plaintext modulus are selected. We compare them with our parameters while approximately equating for the number of slots and security. As observed in Table 6, for a similar number of slots and security, our methods can attain plaintext modulus values that are significantly smaller than theirs. This demonstrates an accessibility to new parameters not previously available with the techniques of [16], which instead restricts their plaintext modulus to large primes.

It is noted that for our proof-of-concept parameters, the number of multiplication levels available is lower than that of [16], as observed in Table 6. This

Table 6. A comparison between our parameters and the proposed parameters of [16] with their smallest plaintext modulus $2^{16} + 1 = 65537$.

Parameter Set	2-B	[16]	3-B	[16]	5-B	[16]
Plaintext Modulus	17	$2^{16} + 1$	113	$2^{16} + 1$	167	$2^{16} + 1$
Number of slots	1044	1024	2142	2048	4676	4096
Security	103.4	128	128.4	128	133.1	128
Multiplication levels	< 4	~ 25	< 4	~ 25	< 6	~ 25

is likely due to the implementation-level differences between the schemes of the two works. However, it is crucial to note that the primary contribution of our work is the construction of a new plaintext space which allows for parameter selection through a reduction of both the slot degree and the number of slots, and not the scheme itself. We leave it to future works to adapt and optimize our techniques within the typical BFV framework, which would provide a more exact comparison to the work of [16].

Table 7. A comparison of communication cost between our parameters and the proposed parameters of [16] with their smallest plaintext modulus $2^{16} + 1 = 65537$.

Parameter Set	2-B	3-B	5-B	[16]
Ciphertext size (MB)	0.01	0.03	0.14	1.72
Public key size (MB)	0.01	0.03	0.14	1.72
Evaluation key size (MB)	0.18	1.02	10.36	37.84
Total size (MB)	0.20	1.08	10.64	41.28

Additionally, although our parameters support fewer levels, our scheme exhibits a significantly improved communication cost. This is detailed in Table 7 which compares the communication cost of our scheme to the estimated communication cost of [16]. Specifically, for both the size of the ciphertexts and public keys in our proposed parameters, an improvement of up to $172\times$ is obtained over the work of [16]. For the size of the evaluation key, an improvement of up to $210.2\times$ is observed. Overall, this translates into an improvement of up to $206.4\times$ in communication cost. Again, optimizing and implementing our plaintext space within the standard BFV framework is beyond the scope of this work and is left to future research, where a more precise comparison with [16] may be conducted, for factors such as the communication cost.

6 Conclusion

To conclude, we introduced FHE on the ring of Gaussian periods. By proceeding further down the decomposition ring and utilizing the decomposition subring, the dimension is lowered from r to n, therefore lowering the latency. To achieve this, we introduced novel methods for both encoding and decoding. These methods were then applied to the operations within FHE, decreasing the time complexity from, for encryption and decryption, $O(r \log r)$ to $O(n \log n)$, for addition, $O(r)$ to $O(n)$ and for multiplication, $O(l_w \cdot r \log r)$ to $O(l_w \cdot n \log n)$. This was further validated in a proof-of-concept implementation, achieving up to a $5.06\times$ latency improvement for selected parameters. To summarize, we introduced a novel method which is optimized for lower-dimension use-cases and offers an increased flexibility in the selection of parameters. Future studies could explore the application of these techniques within the context of bootstrapping. Our techniques may also be applied to the work of [21], allowing for greater flexibility in their bootstrapping procedure. Furthermore, additional algebraic constructions could be explored. For instance, we could take the minimal polynomial $p_{\eta_0}(x) \in \mathbb{Z}[x]$ of η_0 and work over the order $\mathbb{Z}[x]/(p_{\eta_0}(x)) \subsetneq \mathbb{Z}[\eta_0, \ldots, \eta_{n-1}]$. Under Order-LWE assumption [5], this order would support FHE instantiations based on polynomial arithmetic. This direction of research would be non-trivial as the Gaussian periods $\eta_1, \ldots, \eta_{n-1}$ do not generally lie inside $\mathbb{Z}[x]/(p_{\eta_0}(x))$. We leave a more detailed comparison between the ring of integers and its suborder to future work.

Acknowledgments. This research is supported by the National Research Foundation, Singapore and Infocomm Media Development Authority under its Trust Tech Funding Initiative, Trust Tech Funding Initiative (DTC-IGC-01) and Singapore Ministry of Education Academic Research Fund Tier 2 Grant MOE-T2EP20223-0016. Any opinions, findings and conclusions or recommendations expressed in this material are those of the author(s) and do not reflect the views of National Research Foundation, Singapore and Infocomm Media Development Authority. Allen Siwei Yang is supported by the Institute for Infocomm Research of Agency for Science, Technology and Research (A*STAR). The authors would like to thank Dr Khoa Nguyen for his insightful discussions on these topics. We also thank the anonymous CT-RSA reviewers for their helpful comments.

7 Appendix

Proof of Proposition 4.

Proof. Items 1 to 3 are immediate consequences of Galois theory and cyclotomic fields. For Item 4, first observe that all the summands within η_i, $0 \leq i < n$ form a partition of all the primitive q^{th} roots of unity $\{\zeta_q^j : 0 \leq j < q\}$. Since the latter set is linearly independent over $\mathbb{Q}$, $\{\eta_i, 0 \leq i < n\}$ are also linearly independent over $\mathbb{Q}$. It is a basis of $\mathbb{Q}(\eta_0)$ because of dimensionality.

Suppose $a \in \mathbb{Q}(\eta_0)$ is integral. Viewing $\mathbb{Q}(\eta_0) \subset \mathbb{Q}(\zeta_q)$ as a subfield and recalling that $\{\zeta_q^j : 0 \leq j < q\}$ is a normal, integral basis of $\mathbb{Q}(\zeta_q)$, we may write $a = \sum_{j=0}^{q-1} a_j \zeta_q^j$ where all $a_j \in \mathbb{Z}$. By applying the automorphisms σ^{nk}, $1 \leq k < f$ to a and comparing the coefficients with a, we see that all ζ_q^j that appear as summands in the same Gaussian period share the same coefficient. Consequently, a can be written as integer combinations of the periods. $\square$

Proof of Proposition 7.

Proof. Since $F_i(x) = \prod_{j \neq i} f_j(x) \bmod p$, the ideal $(p, F_i(x)) = (p, \prod_{j \neq i} f_j(x))$ holds over $\mathbb{Z}[x]$. Next we claim that $(p, \prod_{j \neq i} f_j(x)) = \prod_{j \neq i}(p, f_j(x))$ over $\mathbb{Z}[x]$.

On one hand, $\prod_{j \neq i}(p, f_j(x)) \subseteq (p, \prod_{j \neq i} f_j(x))$ because each ideal generator of the LHS belongs to the RHS. On the other hand, $p \in \prod_{j \neq i}(p, f_j(x))$ since the $f_j(x)$ are pairwise relatively prime mod p. Therefore equality holds.

Hence $\gcd(p, F_i(\zeta_q)) = \prod_{j \neq i} \mathbf{P}_j$, $\mathbf{P}_j := (p, f_j(\zeta_q))$ over $\mathbb{Z}[\zeta_q]$. In other words, $F_i(\zeta_q)$ is divisible by all the prime ideal factors of $p\mathbb{Z}[\zeta_q]$ except $\mathbf{P}_i$. Note that when considering just division when restricted to the case of k,

$$\mathbf{P}_i^k \mid u \iff \mathbf{P}_i^k \cdot F_i(\zeta_q)^k \mid u \cdot F_i(\zeta_q)^k \iff p^k \mid u \cdot F_i(\zeta_q)^k$$

can be obtained. For exact division in the case of $k+1$ as per the theorem, since $\mathbb{Z}[\zeta_q]$ is a Dedekind domain and integral ideals have a unique factorization,

$$\begin{aligned}
\mathbf{P}_i^k \parallel u &\iff (\mathbf{P}_i^{k+1}, u) = \mathbf{P}_i^k \\
&\iff (\mathbf{P}_i^{k+1} \cdot F_i(\zeta_q)^{k+1}, u \cdot F_i(\zeta_q)^{k+1}) = \mathbf{P}_i^k \cdot F_i(\zeta_q)^{k+1} = (p)^k \cdot F_i(\zeta_q) \\
&\iff p^k \parallel u \cdot F_i(\zeta_q)^{k+1}.
\end{aligned}$$

For the forward direction of the last step, $p^k \mid u \cdot F_i(\zeta_q)^{k+1}$ follows directly from the previous step. To show exact division, suppose not, that is, suppose $p^{k+1} \mid u \cdot F_i(\zeta_q)^{k+1}$. This implies $\mathbf{P}_i^{k+1} \cdot F_i(\zeta_q)^{k+1} \mid u \cdot F_i(\zeta_q)^{k+1}$ which implies $\mathbf{P}_i^{k+1} \mid u$, leading to a contradiction.

□

An example for Algorithm 4. As an example of how Algorithm 4 works, consider the thirteenth cyclotomic field with cyclotomic polynomial $\Phi_{13}(x) = x^{12} + x^{11} + \cdots + x^2 + x + 1$. Now let $p = 3$. It is not difficult to compute:

$$\Phi_{13}(x) \equiv (x^3 + 2x + 2)(x^3 + x^2 + 2)(x^3 + x^2 + x + 2)(x^3 + 2x^2 + 2x + 2) \bmod 3.$$

By the CRT we have:

$$\mathbb{Z}[x]/(3, \Phi_{13}(x)) \cong \prod_{i=1}^{4} \mathbb{F}_{27}.$$

In the BFV terminology the RHS contains 4 slots, each with degree 3 over $\mathbb{F}_3$. By looking at a subring $\mathcal{O}_\mathrm{M} \subset \mathbb{Z}[x]/(\Phi_{13}(x))$ and using structure theorems from algebraic number theory, it is possible to obtain a simpler CRT factorization:

$$\mathcal{O}_\mathrm{M}/3\mathcal{O}_\mathrm{M} \cong \prod_{i=1}^{2} \mathbb{F}_3.$$

Both the degree of each slot and the number of slots have shrunk in the subring.

A priori, $\mathcal{O}_\mathrm{M}$ contains an integral normal basis $\{\eta_0, \eta_1\}$, and each element of $\mathcal{O}_\mathrm{M}/3\mathcal{O}_\mathrm{M}$ can be represented by $a\eta_0 + b\eta_1$, $a, b \in \mathbb{Z}_3$. It is not immediately clear though, for example, which element in $\mathbb{F}_3 \times \mathbb{F}_3$ corresponds to η_0 mod 3 in the CRT factorization.

The idea is therefore to leverage our knowledge of the explicit factorization $\Phi_{13}(x)$ mod 3. This is what is utilized by Proposition 7 and Algorithm 4. In this particular example, the procedure becomes the following:

1. Use the unique prime ideal $\mathbf{P} \subset \mathcal{O}_{\mathbf{M}}$ lying under $(3, \zeta_{13}^3 + 2\zeta_{13} + 2)$ as an anchor.
2. Compute the polynomial $F(x) = \Phi_{13}(x)/(x^3 + 2x + 2) \bmod 3 = x^9 + x^8 + 2x^7 + x^5 + 2x^3 + 2x^2 + 2$.
3. Use the definition of η_0 to represent it as a polynomial $\eta_0(x) = x + x^4 + x^3 + x^{12} + x^9 + x^{10}$.
4. Compute $\eta_0(x)F(x) \bmod \Phi_{13}(x) \bmod 3 = 2x^9 + 2x^8 + x^7 + 2x^5 + x^3 + x^2 + 1$, and notice that this is $2\,F(x) \bmod 3$. Therefore, $\eta_0 \equiv 2 \bmod \mathbf{P}$.
5. Similarly, we obtain $\eta_1 \equiv 0 \bmod \mathbf{P} \iff \eta_0 \equiv 0 \bmod \sigma^{-1}(\mathbf{P})$, where σ is a generator of the Galois group. Specifically, $\sigma(\zeta_{13}) \to \zeta_{13}^2$.
6. We conclude that up to permutation, η_0 mod 3 corresponds to $(2, 0) \in \mathbb{F}_3 \times \mathbb{F}_3$ under the CRT map above.

Proof of Proposition 8.

Proof. In the case where f is even,

$$\begin{aligned}
\mathbf{BA}_{i,j} &= \sum_k \mathbf{B}_{i,k}\mathbf{A}_{k,j} \bmod p^m = \sum_k b_{k-i}a_{j-k} \bmod p^m \\
&= q^{-1}\sum_k (a_{i-k} - f)a_{j-k} \bmod p^m \\
&= q^{-1}\left(\sum_k \eta_{i-k}\eta_{j-k} - f\sum_k \eta_{j-k}\right) \bmod \mathfrak{P}^m \text{ as } \eta_i \equiv a_i \bmod \mathfrak{P}^m. \\
&= q^{-1}(q\delta_{i,j} - f + f) \text{ by (*) and (**) } = \delta_{i,j}.
\end{aligned}$$

In the case where f is odd,

$$\begin{aligned}
\mathbf{BA}_{i,j} &= \sum_k \mathbf{B}_{i,k}\mathbf{A}_{k,j} \bmod p^m = \sum_k b_{k-i}a_{j-k} \bmod p^m \\
&= q^{-1}\sum_k (a_{\frac{e}{2}+i-k} - f)a_{j-k} \bmod p^m \\
&= q^{-1}\left(\sum_k \eta_{\frac{e}{2}+i-k}\eta_{j-k} - f\sum_k \eta_{j-k}\right) \bmod \mathfrak{P}^m \text{ as } \eta_i \equiv a_i \bmod \mathfrak{P}^m. \\
&= q^{-1}(q\delta_{i,j} - f + f) \text{ by (*) and (**) } = \delta_{i,j}.
\end{aligned}$$

$\square$

Proof of Theorem 9.

Proof. The proof is the same as the standard BFV scheme instantiated over power-of-two cyclotomic fields. Below we sketch the basic idea:

1. The public key $(\mathsf{pk}_0, \mathsf{pk}_1)$ is pseudorandom. $\mathsf{pk}_0 = a \xleftarrow{\$} \mathcal{R}_Q$, $\mathsf{pk}_1 = as + e$ and $s \xleftarrow{\$} \mathcal{S}$, $e \xleftarrow{\$} \Phi$. $(\mathsf{pk}_0, \mathsf{pk}_1)$ therefore comes from the small secret Ring-LWE$_{Q,\Phi}$ sample and hence is indistinguishable from being random by the small-secret Ring-DLWE assumption.
2. Assume $(\mathsf{pk}_0, \mathsf{pk}_1)$ is truly random, then $(\mathsf{ct}_0, \mathsf{ct}_1)$ is pseudorandom. Note that $\mathsf{ct} = (\mathsf{ct}_0, \mathsf{ct}_1) = (\mathsf{pk}_0 \cdot u + e_1 \bmod Q, \mathsf{pk}_1 \cdot u + \Delta m + e_2 \bmod Q)$ where u, e_1, e_2 are independent and u has the same distribution as s, $e_1, e_2 \xleftarrow{\$} \Phi$ are from the error distribution.
   Under the small secret Ring-DLWE assumption, $(\mathsf{pk}_0 \cdot u + e_1, \mathsf{pk}_1 \cdot u + e_2)$ is pseudorandom. It therefore completely masks the scaled message Δm, so ct is pseudorandom. □

References

1. Albrecht, M.R., Player, R., Scott, S.: On the concrete hardness of learning with errors. J. Math. Crypt. **9**(3), 169–203 (2015)
2. Arita, S., Handa, S.: Subring homomorphic encryption. In: Kim, H., Kim, D.-C. (eds.) ICISC 2017. LNCS, vol. 10779, pp. 112–136. Springer, Cham (2018). https://doi.org/10.1007/978-3-319-78556-1_7
3. Arita, S., Handa, S.: Fully homomorphic encryption scheme based on decomposition ring. IEICE Trans. Fundam. Electron. Commun. Comput. Sci. **103**(1), 195–211 (2020)
4. Bae, Y., Cheon, J.H., Hanrot, G., Park, J.H., Stehlé, D.: Plaintext-ciphertext matrix multiplication and FHE bootstrapping: fast and fused. In: Reyzin, L., Stebila, D. (eds.) CRYPTO 2024, Part III. LNCS, vol. 14922, pp. 387–421. Springer, Cham (Aug (2024)
5. Bolboceanu, M., Brakerski, Z., Perlman, R., Sharma, D.: Order-LWE and the hardness of ring-LWE with entropic secrets. In: Galbraith, S.D., Moriai, S. (eds.) ASIACRYPT 2019. LNCS, vol. 11922, pp. 91–120. Springer, Cham (2019). https://doi.org/10.1007/978-3-030-34621-8_4
6. Boudgoust, K., Jeudy, C., Roux-Langlois, A., Wen, W.: On the hardness of module-LWE with binary secret. In: Paterson, K.G. (ed.) CT-RSA 2021. LNCS, vol. 12704, pp. 503–526. Springer, Cham (May (2021)
7. Brakerski, Z.: Fully homomorphic encryption without modulus switching from classical GapSVP. In: Safavi-Naini, R., Canetti, R. (eds.) CRYPTO 2012. LNCS, vol. 7417, pp. 868–886. Springer, Heidelberg (2012). https://doi.org/10.1007/978-3-642-32009-5_50
8. Brakerski, Z., Gentry, C., Vaikuntanathan, V.: (Leveled) fully homomorphic encryption without bootstrapping. In: Goldwasser, S. (ed.) ITCS 2012, pp. 309–325. ACM (Jan 2012)
9. Chen, H., Laine, K., Player, R., Xia, Y.: High-precision arithmetic in homomorphic encryption. In: Smart, N.P. (ed.) CT-RSA 2018. LNCS, vol. 10808, pp. 116–136. Springer, Cham (Apr (2018)

10. Cheon, J.H., Kim, A., Kim, M., Song, Y.: Homomorphic encryption for arithmetic of approximate numbers. In: Takagi, T., Peyrin, T. (eds.) ASIACRYPT 2017. LNCS, vol. 10624, pp. 409–437. Springer, Cham (2017). https://doi.org/10.1007/978-3-319-70694-8_15
11. Chillotti, I., Gama, N., Georgieva, M., Izabachène, M.: Faster fully homomorphic encryption: bootstrapping in less than 0.1 seconds. In: Cheon, J.H., Takagi, T. (eds.) ASIACRYPT 2016. LNCS, vol. 10031, pp. 3–33. Springer, Heidelberg (2016). https://doi.org/10.1007/978-3-662-53887-6_1
12. Chillotti, I., Gama, N., Georgieva, M., Izabachène, M.: Faster packed homomorphic operations and efficient circuit bootstrapping for TFHE. In: Takagi, T., Peyrin, T. (eds.) ASIACRYPT 2017. LNCS, vol. 10624, pp. 377–408. Springer, Cham (2017). https://doi.org/10.1007/978-3-319-70694-8_14
13. Dickson, L.E.: Cyclotomy, higher congruences, and waring's problem. Am. J. Math. **57**(2), 391–424 (1935)
14. Ducas, L., Micciancio, D.: FHEW: bootstrapping homomorphic encryption in less than a second. In: Oswald, E., Fischlin, M. (eds.) EUROCRYPT 2015. LNCS, vol. 9056, pp. 617–640. Springer, Heidelberg (2015). https://doi.org/10.1007/978-3-662-46800-5_24
15. Fan, J., Vercauteren, F.: Somewhat practical fully homomorphic encryption. Cryptology ePrint Archive, Report 2012/144 (2012). https://eprint.iacr.org/2012/144
16. Geelen, R., Vercauteren, F.: Fully homomorphic encryption for cyclotomic prime moduli. In: Fehr, S., Fouque, P.A. (eds.) EUROCRYPT 2025, Part III. LNCS, vol. 15603, pp. 366–397. Springer, Cham (May (2025)
17. Ho, M.C., et al.: Invited paper: efficient design of FHEW/TFHE bootstrapping implementation with scalable parameters. In: Proceedings of the 43rd IEEE/ACM International Conference on Computer-Aided Design. Association for Computing Machinery (2025)
18. Kim, D., Song, Y.: Approximate Homomorphic Encryption over the Conjugate-Invariant Ring. In: Lee, K. (ed.) ICISC 2018. LNCS, vol. 11396, pp. 85–102. Springer, Cham (2019). https://doi.org/10.1007/978-3-030-12146-4_6
19. Lyubashevsky, V., Peikert, C., Regev, O.: On ideal lattices and learning with errors over rings. In: Gilbert, H. (ed.) EUROCRYPT 2010. LNCS, vol. 6110, pp. 1–23. Springer, Heidelberg (2010). https://doi.org/10.1007/978-3-642-13190-5_1
20. Marcus, D.A., Sacco, E.: Number Fields, vol. 1995. Springer (1977)
21. Min, S., Song, Y.: Carousel: fully homomorphic encryption from slot blind rotation technique. Cryptology ePrint Archive, Report 2024/2032 (2024). https://eprint.iacr.org/2024/2032
22. Peikert, C., Regev, O., Stephens-Davidowitz, N.: Pseudorandomness of ring-LWE for any ring and modulus. In: Hatami, H., McKenzie, P., King, V. (eds.) 49th ACM STOC, pp. 461–473. ACM Press (2017)
23. Regev, O.: On lattices, learning with errors, random linear codes, and cryptography. In: Gabow, H.N., Fagin, R. (eds.) 37th ACM STOC, pp. 84–93. ACM Press (May 2005)
24. Ren, S.Q., Meng, T.H., Yibin, N., Mi Aung, K.M.: Privacy-preserved multi-party data merging with secure equality evaluation. In: 2016 International Conference on Cloud Computing Research and Innovations (ICCCRI), pp. 34–41 (2016)
25. Smart, N.P., Vercauteren, F.: Fully homomorphic SIMD operations. DCC **71**(1), 57–81 (2014)
26. Tan, B.H.M., Lee, H.T., Wang, H., Ren, S., Aung, K.M.M.: Efficient private comparison queries over encrypted databases using fully homomorphic encryption with finite fields. IEEE Trans. Dependable Secure Comput. **18**(6), 2861–2874 (2021)

27. The Sage Developers: SageMath, the Sage Mathematics Software System (Version 10.5) (2024). https://www.sagemath.org
28. Xia, H., Liu, F.H., Wang, H.: More efficient functional bootstrapping for general functions in polynomial modulus. In: Boyle, E., Mahmoody, M. (eds.) TCC 2024, Part IV. LNCS, vol. 15367, pp. 130–163. Springer, Cham (Dec (2024)
29. Yamada, R., Okumura, S., Miyaji, A.: Consideration on defining field for efficient ring-LWE. In: 2024 19th Asia Joint Conference on Information Security (AsiaJ-CIS), pp. 25–32. IEEE (2024)

ProxCode: Efficient Proximity Searchable Encryption from Error Correcting Codes

Maryam Rezapour(✉) and Benjamin Fuller

University of Connecticut, Storrs, CT 06269, USA
{maryam.rezapour,benjamin.fuller}@uconn.edu

Abstract. This work builds approximate proximity searchable encryption. Secure biometric databases are the primary application. Prior work (Kuzu, Islam, and Kantarcioglu, ICDE 2012) combines locality-sensitive hashes, or LSHs, (Indyk, STOC '98), and secure multimaps. The multimap associates LSH outputs as keywords to biometrics as values.

When the desired result set is of size at most one, we show a new preprocessing technique and system called `ProxCode` that inserts shares of a linear secret sharing into the map instead of the full biometric. Instead of choosing shares independently, shares are correlated so exactly one share is associated with each keyword/LSH output. As a result, one can rely on a map instead of a multimap. Secure maps are easier to construct with lower leakage than multimaps.

This approach reduces the required number of LSHs for a fixed accuracy for many parameters. Our scheme improves most when combining a high accuracy requirement with a biometric with large underlying noise. Our approach builds on any secure map. To benchmark, we implement the scheme using the tree based oblivious map of Wang et al. (CCS, 2014) and evaluate efficiency and accuracy for iris, synthetic, and random data.

Compared to the recent work of Ha et al. (Codaspy 2025), for the largest parameters tested and a comparable true accept rate, our work reduces the number of LSHs by a factor of 4.3. This reduction impacts all efficiency metrics; our rounds are smaller by 2, storage by a factor of 6.5, and parallel time by a factor of 8.

Keywords: Applied Cryptography · Biometrics · Searchable Encryption · Linear Secret Sharing

1 Introduction

This work builds approximate proximity searchable encryption, called APSS [1–6]. Secure biometric databases [7–9] are a major application of APSS. Searchable encryption considers two parties a client, denoted as Client, and a server, denoted as Server. The goal of the searchable encryption is for Client to outsource a database, $\mathcal{DB}$, to Server and be able to query this outsourced database. The system should limit what is learned by a semi-honest Server while still allowing

F. -H. Liu (Ed.): CT-RSAC 2026, LNCS 16496, pp. 32–62, 2026.
https://doi.org/10.1007/978-3-032-22931-1_2

the client to retrieve the relevant results from the database. See prior reviews [10–14] of searchable encryption.

We now set notation of APSS and provide a review of prior work. Let $\mathcal{DB} = x_1, ..., x_M$ be a collection of records. For metric $\mathcal{D}$, a distance parameter t, and query y, the goal of the search is to find the set $\texttt{Res} = \{x_i \in \mathcal{DB} | \mathcal{D}(x_i, y) \leq t\}$. Our system is designed for 1-to-n matching, for query y, one is trying to retrieve the single record $x_i \in \mathcal{DB}$ such that $\mathcal{D}(y, x_i) \leq t$. Most work in APSS uses preprocessing techniques and encrypted multimaps.

Encrypted Multimaps. Multimaps [15], MMs, allow association of keywords with values x_i.[1] An encrypted multimap is the same except there are interactive protocols between the Client and Server. We use the following notation for the encrypted version (with the Client's inputs and outputs on the top row and the Server's inputs and outputs on the bottom row):

$$\begin{pmatrix} K \\ \mathsf{EMM} \end{pmatrix} \leftarrow \mathsf{MM.Setup} \begin{pmatrix} \mathsf{MM} \\ \perp \end{pmatrix}$$

$$\begin{pmatrix} \mathsf{MM}[\texttt{keyword}] \\ \perp \end{pmatrix} \leftarrow \mathsf{MM.Search} \begin{pmatrix} \texttt{keyword}, K \\ \mathsf{EMM} \end{pmatrix}$$

The goal of preprocessing is to create accurate search while minimizing the size of the multimap, which impacts storage, bandwidth, computation, and communication rounds.

Preprocessing Data for APSS. Prior work [1–3] use locality sensitive hashes or LSHs [16] to preprocess. We provide a brief overview of LSHs and then explain how they are used for preprocessing. LSHs map close items to the same value more frequently than they map far items to the same value. For some n number of LSHs, a multimap MM, and LSH family LSH, the Client proceeds as follows, $\mathsf{APSS.Init}(\mathcal{DB} = x_1, ..., x_M)$:

1. Sample n LSHs, $\mathsf{LSH}_1, ..., \mathsf{LSH}_n \leftarrow \mathsf{LSH}$.
2. For $j = 1, ..., n$ & $i = 1, ..., M$: $\mathsf{MM.add}(\texttt{keyword} = (j, \mathsf{LSH}_j(x_i)), \texttt{value} = x_i)$.
3. Store MM on Server by executing

$$\begin{pmatrix} K \\ \mathsf{EMM} \end{pmatrix} \leftarrow \mathsf{MM.Init} \begin{pmatrix} \mathsf{MM} \\ \perp \end{pmatrix}.$$

Then, $\mathsf{APSS.Search}(y)$ is:

1. Client computes $\mathsf{LSH}_1(y), ..., \mathsf{LSH}_n(y)$.

[1] A multimap has two operations: 1) $\mathsf{MM.Init}(\{\texttt{keyword}, \texttt{value}\})$ that takes a set of $\texttt{keyword}, \texttt{value}$ pairs and associates $\texttt{value}$ with $\texttt{keyword}$, and 2) $\mathsf{Resp} \leftarrow \mathsf{MM}[\texttt{keyword}]$ which returns all values associated with $\texttt{value}$.

2. For $i = 1$ to n:

$$\begin{pmatrix} \mathsf{Resp}_i \\ \perp \end{pmatrix} \leftarrow \mathsf{MM.Search}\begin{pmatrix} \mathsf{LSH}_i(y), K \\ \mathsf{EMM} \end{pmatrix}.$$

3. Output all returned records across all queries.

There are two aspects to understand for the above construction for a fixed number of LSH's n: security and accuracy. We discuss these issues below.

Security. The security of the above construction derives from the encrypted multimap. Constructions of (dynamic) multimaps [13,17–24][2] have nonzero leakage including query equality. Patel et al. [24] showed that avoiding query equality leakage for multimaps requires high overhead techniques similar to ORAM.

Accuracy. LSH-based preprocessing solutions have imperfect accuracy. The two accuracy parameters are:

1. $\delta_{\texttt{Close}}$ measures how frequently the close record is not returned, and
2. $\delta_{\texttt{Far}}$ measures what fraction of the database is (incorrectly) returned.

High accuracy systems have three advantages:

1. Returned records are more likely to be relevant. Many leakage attacks [25] are based on identifying the correlation between returned values, so decreasing erroneously returned values improves security.
2. A decrease in the maximum number of values associated with a keyword, a key efficiency metric for secure multimaps. If this is made to a small constant, one can use a map instead.
3. In a three party system where the querier does not know the whole dataset it reduces unintentional exposure of biometrics (discussion in Sect. 1.2).

1.1 Our Contribution

This work contributes 1) a data preprocessing method for accurate proximity search, 2) an implementation of this processing technique using an oblivious tree-based map [34], and 3) an evaluation of accuracy and efficiency on iris and random data. Our approach is to transform the query from a disjunction, where one concatenates the list of all records that match some LSH, to a k-out-of-n query, where one retrieves at most a single record that matches at least k LSHs. We call the system `ProxCode` for efficient proximity search from error correcting codes.[3] The high-level approach proceeds in five steps:

[2] This generation of low leakage maps followed attacks on the prior generation of map constructions [25–33].

[3] In the majority of our discussion, we use the notation of Reed-Solomon codes, as we discuss in the Conclusion, it may be possible to achieve better parameters with custom codes. We use map notation instead of multimap notation. In our system one only associates one value with each keyword.

1. Compute n LSHs and for every record x, compute $\mathsf{LSH}_i(x)$ for $1 \leq i \leq n$.
2. For each x_i, define $P_{x_i} = \{p \mid \text{degree(p)} \leq k \wedge p(0) = x_i\}$,[4]
3. For each pair $1 \leq i < j \leq M$ do the following:
   (a) If p_{x_i} has not been defined, set $p_{x_i} \leftarrow P_{x_i}$ uniformly.
   (b) For each $1 \leq \beta \leq n$ if $\mathsf{LSH}_\beta(x_i) = \mathsf{LSH}_\beta(x_j)$ remove those $p_j \in P_{x_j}$ such that $p_i(\beta) \neq p_j(\beta)$.
   (c) If $P_{x_j} = \emptyset$, go to step 1.
4. Set p_{x_M} as a uniformly random element of P_{x_M}.
5. Associate in the map for all i, j

$$\mathsf{Map}[(j, \mathsf{LSH}_j(x_i))] = p_{x_i}(j).$$

At search time, the client queries the map for all $(j, \mathsf{LSH}_j(x'))$, collects results from the map, and uses polynomial interpolation to reconstruct the relevant record.

Roughly, instead of associating x_i with LSH values, we associate polynomial points. If a querier gets enough points on the same polynomial, they can reconstruct the original value. Each LSH collision between records x_i, x_j of the database, where $i < j$, removes a degree of freedom from the polynomial of x_j, denoted as P_{x_j}; but does not require one to associate multiple values with the same LSH keyword. The procedure succeeds as long as no record x_j has no more than $k-1$ LSH collisions with other x_i (more precisely, more than $k-1$ distinct LSHs have collisions).

Improving n for Fixed Accuracy. Our analysis shows that for the error regimes present in biometrics, we can sample a set of M polynomials using fewer LSHs than the Baseline disjunctive search's requirement described by the recent work of Ha et al. [3].

Mean FHD (Fractional Hamming Distance) is the Hamming distance divided by the length of the vector. FHD for biometrics varies between $10\% - 30\%$ depending on the biometric, collection conditions, and the feature extractor. Ha et al. [3] point out it is necessary to consider distance higher than the mean of biometric error rate to achieve low $\delta_{\texttt{Close}}$. For one accuracy regime, their analysis suggests $n = 80$ LSHs suffices to capture the distribution mean but $n \approx 1000$ LSHs are needed to capture the distribution tail.

Theoretic Improvement. We show theoretical improvement in the number of required LSHs in Table 1 for a dataset of size 10,000. This directly translates to the overall size of the $|\mathsf{Map}|$ that must be stored. Many cryptographic constructions have storage of $\omega(|\mathsf{Map}|)$.

The accuracy level of $\delta_{\texttt{Far}}$ presented in Table 1 has a slightly different meaning for the baseline and `ProxCode`. Roughly for `ProxCode` it is the probability of a

[4] The system works perfectly well if one associates the value i and uses a separate mechanism to retrieve x_i from i. Associating x_i prevents a second lookup with associated leakage [20,35].

query returning a far value. For the baseline, it is the fraction of far records that are returned. Our efficiency improvements are highest for high-accuracy regimes with large underlying biometric noise.

Concrete Improvements. Table 2 shows a concrete comparison between representative parameters for synthetic and random data for Ha et al. and this work. We focus our parameters on achieving TAR of $\approx .90$. On a random dataset of the same size, `ProxCode` reduces the number of required LSHs by a factor of 4.3. For synthetic data, we are able to reduce the number of LSHs by nearly a factor of 2 on a dataset 5 times larger.

Improving the number of LSHs, n, directly results in a smaller map. A smaller map means less storage, fewer rounds for our tree-based OMap construction, and faster parallel search. As we discuss in Sect. 5, Ha et al. use a filtering technique to search fewer items in the map, this technique works in our setting as well but is not reported. As a result, parallel time is the appropriate comparison.

Table 1. Summary of improvement in number of required LSHs across biometric error rates $(1 - \epsilon_t')$ and accuracy of the scheme with respect to false accepts denoted as δ_{Far}, fully described in Appendix A. We note the substantial improvement for the high error rate regime. Dataset of size $M = 10^4$.

Error	Improvement ($\log_{10}(n)$)				
Rate	.10	.15	.20	.25	.30
$\delta_{\mathsf{Far}} = 10^{-3}$	-0.5	-0.2	0.3	2.1	1.3
$\delta_{\mathsf{Far}} = 10^{-4}$	-0.2	0.1	0.7	1.6	2.8
$\delta_{\mathsf{Far}} = 10^{-6}$	0	0.6	1.4	2.4	3.9

Security and Cryptographic overhead. `ProxCode` can be secured using any map. Our implementation and efficiency results consider an oblivious tree-based map [34]. We consider security when instantiated with 1) a map that leaks search [33,36] & access pattern [17,37] and 2) an oblivious map [2,34,38]. When the map reveals query and access pattern, our scheme reveals the query and access pattern for each individual search term which we call subquery and subaccess pattern leakage using the language of Falzon et al. [39]. If one uses a map with access pattern leakage, subquery and subaccess leakage are in 1-1 correspondence. For our real iris data, we observe roughly 3000 repeats on 200 queries when $n = 100$. This is on queries of different irises. One expects much higher subquery equality if multiple readings of the same iris are in the set of queries.

We present a prototype implementation of the above `ProxCode` scheme integrated into an implementation of Wang et al.'s [34] oblivious map (Github). We evaluate accuracy and overhead on

1. The IITD iris data set [40] for realism using a feature extractor designed for an LSH-based fuzzy extractor [41],
2. A synthetic dataset designed to have the same degrees of freedom as the above feature extractor, and
3. Random data.

For the synthetic and random data, the number of errors follows the distribution from real data. Table 2 compares the largest tested parameters between `ProxCode` and Ha et al. [3]. The main comparison point is the number of LSHs. Improving this improves all other values. See further results in Sect. 5.

Table 2. Comparison of largest tested parameters. In Ha et al. [3] there is a filtering phase that finds non-null values and only searches for 72/20 (for synthetic and random respectively) items in the map. As we discuss in Sect. 5, if one implements a similar phase in our scheme we estimate the sequential time to be .26 seconds. The fairest comparison is parallel search time which is agnostic to such an optimization.

System	Data Type	M	LSHs n	|Map|	Setup	Storage	Search Seq.	Search Par.	TAR
[3]	Synthetic	5000	1300	6.5M	12.5 hrs	35.6 GB	8.8	.023	.83
	Random	25000	3500	87.5M	153 hrs	285 GB	7.9	.035	.91
`ProxCode`	Synthetic	25000	800	20M	6.6 hrs	43.5 GB	7.2	.0042	.88
	Random	25000	800	20M	6.8 hrs	43.5 GB	7.5	.0051	.88

1.2 Implications for Client Security

Throughout the body of this work, we define a traditional two-party setting of searchable encryption where there is a data owner that outsources data to a server. Some searchable encryption systems operate in the three party setting where there is a data owner, server, and a client [42–44]. In this setting, the database contents and queries are both private. In this setting, the data owner gives the client a token that allows them to execute their query. Our scheme shows that the client is unlikely to gain enough code symbols to learn anything about any records far from their query. In the body, we measure for real data how many code symbols are gained by a client across multiple queries. We compare this to the number of biometrics that are completely leaked using the baseline setting (Sect. 5.3). In `ProxCode`, learning anything about a non-queried biometric requires a persistent adversary [45] with many queries.

Further Prior Work. Boldyreva and Tang considered the related problem of zero-leakage k-nearest-neighbor search [2]. In (approximate) k-nearest neighbors, the goal is to retrieve the k closest records [2,46,47]. There have been leakage abuse attacks against k-nearest neighbor systems that reveal access pattern [31,48–50].

Organization. Section 2 introduces preliminary notation including the definition of APSS. Section 3 introduces the Baseline construction described in the Introduction and describes the required number of LSHs for fixed accuracy parameters. Section 4 presents ProxCode and proves correctness and security. Section 5 presents our implementation and evaluation. Section 6 concludes and discusses future work.

2 Preliminaries

Throughout this work we use the following notation:

1. Let λ be a security parameter.
2. Let stored records x_i be values over $\{0,1\}^\gamma$.
3. Let $M = |\mathcal{DB}|$, the number of records.
4. We consider prime fields over prime power p, denoted $\mathbb{F}_p$.
5. For a Reed Solomon code, let k be the dimension, $\mathsf{k}_{correct}$ be the required number of correct symbols, and k_{error} be the maximum number of incorrect symbols. See Definition 2.
6. Let n denote the number of LSHs, and,
7. If one uses an extended LSH, let α denote the number of concatenated LSHs.

We use $z = (z_1, ..., z_\ell)$ to denote a vector. We focus on the Hamming distance. For vectors $x, y \in \{0,1\}^\gamma$, let $\mathcal{D}(x,y) = |\{i | x_i \neq y_i\}|$ denote the Hamming distance between x and y. The Hamming distance metric is frequently used in iris recognition [51]. Our techniques apply to any metric with locality sensitive hashes [16]. For a positive integer x, let $[x]$ denote the set $\{1, ..., x\}$. TAR stands for True Accept Rate; FAR stands for False Accept Rate. For a protocol, Prot, between a client Client and a server Server we use notation

$$\begin{pmatrix} o_{\mathsf{Client}} \\ o_{\mathsf{Server}} \end{pmatrix} \leftarrow \mathsf{Prot} \begin{pmatrix} i_{\mathsf{Client}} \\ i_{\mathsf{Server}} \end{pmatrix}$$

with $i_{\mathsf{Client}}, o_{\mathsf{Client}}, i_{\mathsf{Server}}, o_{\mathsf{Server}}$ denoting the client's and the server's inputs and outputs respectively. Protocols are written from the client's perspective.

Definition 1 (Locality-sensitive Hashing (LSH)). *Let $t \in \mathbb{N}$, $c > 1$ and $\epsilon_{\mathtt{t}}, \epsilon_{\mathtt{f}} \in [0,1]$ with $\epsilon_{\mathtt{t}} > \epsilon_{\mathtt{f}}$. $\mathcal{H}$ defines a $(t, ct, \epsilon_{\mathtt{t}}, \epsilon_{\mathtt{f}})$-sensitive hash family if for any $x, y \in \{0,1\}^\gamma$ one has:*

- *If $\mathcal{D}(x,y) \leq t$ then $\Pr_{h \leftarrow \mathcal{H}}[h(x) = h(y)] \geq \epsilon_{\mathtt{t}}$*
- *If $\mathcal{D}(x,y) \geq ct$ then $\Pr_{h \leftarrow \mathcal{H}}[h(x) = h(y)] \leq \epsilon_{\mathtt{f}}$*

where $\mathcal{D}(x,y)$ denotes the Hamming distance between binary vectors x and y.

An extended LSH is formed by concatenating α independently sampled LSHs. This output is an LSH, with parameters $\epsilon_{\mathtt{t}} = \epsilon_{\mathtt{t}}'^{\alpha}$ and $\epsilon_{\mathtt{f}} = \epsilon_{\mathtt{f}}'^{\alpha}$. This is used to compute parameters but can just be considered an LSH with smaller $\epsilon_{\mathtt{t}}, \epsilon_{\mathtt{f}}$.

Definition 2 (Reed-Solomon Codes). *An (n, k) Reed-Solomon code over $\mathbb{F}_p$ is*

$$\mathsf{RS}_{(n,k)} := \{\mathsf{C} | \mathsf{C}_i = P(i) \text{ for some } k-1 \text{ degree polynomial } P\}.$$

Such codes are linear with the Vandermonde matrix representing one encoding matrix. An (n, k) Reed-Solomon code has the following features:

1. *Let $\mathsf{C}_1, ..., \mathsf{C}_n \in \mathsf{RS}_{n,k}$ and let $\mathsf{C}'_1, ..., \mathsf{C}'_n$ be some value. Define*

$$k_{correct} = |\{i | \mathsf{C}_i = \mathsf{C}'_i\}|. \qquad k_{error} = |\{i | \mathsf{C}_i \neq \mathsf{C}'_i \wedge \mathsf{C}'_i \neq \perp\}|.$$

$$e_{erase} = |\{i | \mathsf{C}'_i = \perp\}|.$$

   where $k_{correct} + k_{error} + e_{erase} = n$. There exists an efficient procedure $\mathsf{Decode}(\mathsf{C}'_1, ..., \mathsf{C}'_n) = \mathsf{C}_1, ..., \mathsf{C}_n$ when $2k_{error} + e_{erase} < n - k$. The Berlekamp-Welch algorithm is one such procedure. We assume that $\mathsf{Decode}_{\mathsf{RS}}$ outputs $\perp$ if $e_{erase} > n - k$.
2. *For any $\ell \leq k$, $\mathtt{Agree} = (i_1, y_{i_1}, ..., i_\ell, y_{i_\ell})$ there exists a nonempty set $\mathsf{RS}_{\mathtt{Agree}}$ such that for all $\mathsf{C} \in \mathsf{RS}_{\mathtt{Agree}}$, $\mathsf{C}_{i_j} = y_{i_j}$ for $j = 1, ..., \ell$. (This is because all $k \times k$ minors of the Vandermonde matrix are full rank.)*
3. *One can efficiently sample from $\mathsf{RS}_{\mathtt{Agree}}$ using an algorithm denoted as $\mathsf{Inv}_{\mathsf{RS}}$. $\mathsf{Inv}_{\mathsf{RS}}$ takes the inverse of the square Vandermonde matrix corresponding to $i_1, ..., i_\ell$ multiplied by $y_{i_1}, ..., y_{i_\ell}$ to define the first ℓ components of the polynomial coefficients, the remaining $k - \ell$ coefficients are chosen uniformly.*

Definition 3. *A map $\mathsf{Map} = (\mathit{insert}, \mathit{retrieve})$ is a pair of algorithms where,*

1. *$\mathsf{Map}.\mathit{insert}(L, R)$: Adds (L, R) where L is the key and R is its assigned value.*
2. *$\mathsf{Map}.\mathit{retrieve}(L)$: Given L, it returns the last assigned value R or $\perp$ if no value has been assigned.*

We assume that values L and R are both binary strings of a fixed length. Looking ahead, values R will be from a field $\mathbb{F}_p$ we assume that $|\log p|$ is at most the supported length of the map. In a multimap*, denoted as MM, $\mathsf{MM}.\mathit{retrieve}(L)$ returns all previously assigned values R_i.*

2.1 Approximate Proximity Search

We now turn to defining our cryptographic goal. We begin with the notion of a well-spread database which captures the intuition that its records are far apart.

Definition 4 (Well-spread database). *For parameters $c > 1, t \in \mathbb{Z}^+$. For some value $y \in \{0,1\}^\gamma$ and $\mathcal{DB} \in \{0,1\}^{\gamma \times M}$, define*

$$\mathtt{Close}(y, \mathcal{DB}) = \{x_i \mid x_i \in \mathcal{DB} \,\&\, \mathcal{D}(x_i, y) \leq t\},$$
$$\mathtt{Far}(y, \mathcal{DB}) = \{x_i \mid x_i \in \mathcal{DB} \,\&\, \mathcal{D}(x_i, y) \geq ct\}.$$

A database $\mathcal{DB} \in \{0,1\}^{\gamma \times M}$ is said to be (c, t)-well-spread if

$$\forall y \in \{0,1\}^\gamma, |\mathtt{Far}(y, \mathcal{DB})| \geq |\mathcal{DB}| - 1.$$

This implies that $\forall y \in \{0,1\}^\gamma, |\mathtt{Close}(y, \mathcal{DB})| \leq 1$.

As discussed in the Introduction, Definition 4 is a strong condition useful for analysis. Accuracy measurements in Sect. 5 consider real data.

Definition 5 (Approximate Proximity Search Scheme). *Let* $\mathsf{APSS} = (\mathsf{Init}, \mathsf{Setup}, \mathsf{Search})$. *For* $c > 1, t \in \mathbb{Z}^+$ APSS *is a* $(t, c, q, \delta_{\texttt{Far}}, \delta_{\texttt{Close}})$*-approximate proximity search scheme if for all* (c,t)*-well-spread* $\mathcal{DB} \in \{0,1\}^{\gamma M}, y_1, ..., y_q \in \{0,1\}^{\gamma}$, *define*

$$\begin{pmatrix} \mathsf{sk}, \mathsf{pp} \\ \mathsf{pp} \end{pmatrix} \leftarrow \mathsf{APSS.Init}\begin{pmatrix} 1^\lambda \\ 1^\lambda \end{pmatrix},$$
$$\begin{pmatrix} \perp \\ \mathcal{I}_0 \end{pmatrix} \leftarrow \mathsf{APSS.Setup}\begin{pmatrix} \mathcal{DB}, \mathsf{sk} \\ \mathsf{pp} \end{pmatrix},$$
$$\begin{pmatrix} J_i \\ \mathcal{I}_i \end{pmatrix} \leftarrow \mathsf{APSS.Search}\begin{pmatrix} y_i, \mathsf{sk} \\ \mathcal{I}_{I-1}, \mathsf{pp} \end{pmatrix}.$$

Then, for `Far` & `Close` *defined as in Definition 4, it is true that,* $\forall i, 1 \leq i \leq q$,

$$\Pr\left[\texttt{Far}(y_i, \mathcal{DB}) \cap J_i = \emptyset\right] \geq 1 - \delta_{\texttt{Far}},$$
$$\Pr\left[\texttt{Close}(y_i, \mathcal{DB}) \subseteq J_i\right] \geq 1 - \delta_{\texttt{Close}}.$$

Definition 6 (Adaptive Security for Search Protocol). *Let* $\mathsf{SSE} = (\mathsf{Init}, \mathsf{Setup}, \mathsf{Search})$ *be a triple of algorithms with associated leakage functions* $(\mathcal{L}^{\mathsf{Setup}}, \mathcal{L}^{\mathsf{Search}})$. *Let* λ *be a security parameter.*

For an adversary $\mathcal{A}$ *and simulator* $\mathcal{S}$ *define* $Exp_{\mathsf{SSE},\mathcal{A}}(\cdot)$ *and* $Exp_{\mathcal{S},\mathcal{A}}(\mathcal{L} = (\mathcal{L}^{\mathsf{Setup}}, \mathcal{L}^{\mathsf{Search}}))$ *as in Fig. 1. We say* SSE *is semantically secure in the adaptive setting if for all PPT* $\mathcal{A}$, *there exists a PPT simulator* $\mathcal{S}$ *such that*

$$\left| \begin{array}{r} \Pr[\mathrm{Exp}_{\mathsf{SSE},\mathcal{A}}(\cdot) = 1] - \\ \Pr[\mathrm{Exp}_{\mathcal{S},\mathcal{A}}(\mathcal{L}^{\mathsf{Setup}}, \mathcal{L}^{\mathsf{Search}}) = 1] \end{array} \right| \leq \mathtt{ngl}(\lambda).$$

We use Definition 6 for maps, multimaps, and approximate proximity schemes, which we denote at Map, MM and APSS respectively. We consider the following leakage functions:

1. $\mathcal{L}^{\mathsf{Setup}}_{\mathsf{Size}}$ which leaks the size of the created $\mathcal{DB}$. For the case of a map this leaks the number of (keyword, value) pairs inserted. Size is often padded to a power of 2 [3,52].
2. $\mathcal{L}^{\mathsf{Search}}_{0}$, leaks the occurrence of a query [2,53].
3. $\mathcal{L}^{\mathsf{Search}}_{\mathsf{AccPatt}}$ which leaks identifiers returned with a query [17,37]. These identifiers are consistent across queries.
4. $\mathcal{L}^{\mathsf{Search}}_{\mathsf{QueryEq}}$ which leaks when queries repeat in a sequence [33,36].

Experiment $\text{Exp}_{\text{SSE},\mathcal{A}}(\cdot)$:

1. $\begin{pmatrix} \text{sk} \\ \text{pp} \end{pmatrix} \leftarrow \text{SSE.Init}\begin{pmatrix} 1^\lambda \\ 1^\lambda \end{pmatrix}$.
   Let ts_{Init} be the server's view.
2. $D \leftarrow \mathcal{A}(\text{ts}_{\text{Init}})$.
3. $\begin{pmatrix} \perp \\ \mathcal{I}_0 \end{pmatrix} \leftarrow \text{SSE.Setup}\begin{pmatrix} D, \text{sk} \\ \text{pp} \end{pmatrix}$.
   Let ts_0 be the server's view.
4. For $i = 1$ to q:
   (a) $y_i \leftarrow \mathcal{A}(\text{ts}_{i-1})$.
   (b) $\begin{pmatrix} J_i \\ \mathcal{I}_i \end{pmatrix} \leftarrow \text{SSE.Search}\begin{pmatrix} y_i, \text{sk} \\ \mathcal{I}_{i-1}, \text{pp} \end{pmatrix}$.
   Let ts_i be the server's view.
5. Output $b \leftarrow \mathcal{A}(\text{ts}_q)$.

Experiment $\text{Exp}_{\mathcal{S},\mathcal{A}}(\mathcal{L}^{\text{Setup}}, \mathcal{L}^{\text{Search}})$:

1. $\text{ts}_{\text{Init}} \leftarrow \mathcal{S}(1^\lambda)$.
2. $D \leftarrow \mathcal{A}(\text{ts}_{\text{Init}})$.
3. $\text{ts}_0 \leftarrow \mathcal{S}(\mathcal{L}^{\text{Setup}}(D)))$.
4. For $i = 1$ to q:
   (a) $y_i \leftarrow \mathcal{A}(tk_{i-1})$.
   (b) $\text{ts}_i \leftarrow \mathcal{S}(\mathcal{L}^{\text{Search}}(y_i))$.
5. Output $b \leftarrow \mathcal{A}(\text{ts}_q)$.

Fig. 1. Adaptive Experiments for search protocols and Adversary interacting with the Simulator in the ideal world using $\mathcal{L}$. Both $\mathcal{A}$ and $\mathcal{S}$ keep state between stages but this state is omitted for notational clarity.

During our construction we make n calls to the underlying map, in the case of $\mathcal{L}_0^{\text{Search}}$ this creates a straightforward leakage function as there are n calls to that map. Below we define two modifications of the above leakage functions. These leakage functions when one uses multiple LSHs in conjunction with a map. That is, they apply for the baseline or `ProxCode` system. They are a function of making multiple calls to the underlying map [1 3]. For a query y and an integer n, we consider subqueries of the form $y_1, \ldots, y_n$.

1. $\mathcal{L}^{\text{Search}}_{\text{SubAccPatt}}$ for an integer n, for each returned identifier ι leaks the pair (i, ι) of each subquery y_i that caused the identifier ι to be returned where $1 \leq i \leq n$.
2. $\mathcal{L}^{\text{Search}}_{\text{SubQueryEq}}$ for an integer n, leaks query equality over subqueries.

3 Baseline Construction

The goal of searching for a value y is to retrieve the set `Close` without receiving any indices in `Far`. We informally present the baseline LSH scheme, as described in prior work [1–6], to introduce the relevant accuracy parameters. Let $\text{LSH}_1, \ldots, \text{LSH}_n$ be a sampled set of LSHs and treat a as relevant for a value y if they agree on a single LSH value. The output is the set for $1 \leq j \leq n$:

$$\{x_i | \{(j, \text{LSH}_j(x_i))\} \cap \{(j, \text{LSH}_j(y))\} \neq \emptyset\}.$$

Construction 1 (LSH and Multimap based APSS). *Let t be a distance parameter, $c > 1$ and let $\mathcal{DB} \in \{0,1\}^{\gamma \times M}$. Let LSH be a $(t, ct, \epsilon_{\mathsf{t}}, \epsilon_{\mathsf{f}})$-LSH family.*

$\texttt{Init}\begin{pmatrix}1^\lambda\\1^\lambda\end{pmatrix} = \mathsf{MM.Init}\begin{pmatrix}1^\lambda\\1^\lambda\end{pmatrix}$

$\mathsf{APSS.Setup}_n\begin{pmatrix}\mathcal{DB}=(x_1,...,x_M),\mathsf{sk}\\ \mathsf{pp}\end{pmatrix}$:

1. Sample n LSHs $\mathsf{LSH}_1, ..., \mathsf{LSH}_n \leftarrow \mathsf{LSH}$.
2. Set $\mathcal{DB}_{\mathsf{MM}} = \{(j, \mathsf{LSH}_j(x_i)), x_i\}_{j=1,...,M,i=1,...,n}$.
3. Execute $\begin{pmatrix}\perp\\ \mathcal{I}_0\end{pmatrix} \leftarrow \mathsf{MM.Setup}_n\begin{pmatrix}\mathcal{DB}_{\mathsf{MM}},\mathsf{sk}\\ \mathsf{pp}\end{pmatrix}$.
4. Output $(\mathsf{LSH}_1, ..., \mathsf{LSH}_n)$ to Client.

$\mathsf{APSS.Search}_n\begin{pmatrix}y_i,\mathsf{LSH}_1,...,\mathsf{LSH}_n\\ \mathcal{I}_{(i-1)\cdot n}\end{pmatrix}$:

1. For $j = 1$ to n, compute $\begin{pmatrix}x_j\\ \mathcal{I}_{(i-1)\cdot n+j}\end{pmatrix} \leftarrow \mathsf{MM.Search}_n\begin{pmatrix}(j,\mathsf{LSH}_j(y))\\ \mathcal{I}_{(i-1)\cdot n+(j-1)}\end{pmatrix}$.
2. Output $J_i = \cup_{j=1}^n x_j$.

Algorithm 1: Baseline construction of APSS from LSH and MM.All procedures from perspective of Client with calls to underlying interactive protocols.

Let MM *be a multimap. Define APSS = (APSS.Init, APSS.Setup, APSS.Search) as in Algorithm 1. Then following notation from Definition 5, for all $y_1, ..., y_q$, and all well-spread $\mathcal{DB}$, $\forall i$*

$$\Pr[\texttt{Far}(y_i,\mathcal{DB}) \cap J_i = \emptyset] \geq 1 - \delta_{\texttt{Far}},$$
$$\Pr[\texttt{Close}(y_i,\mathcal{DB}) \subseteq J_i] \geq 1 - \delta_{\texttt{Close}},$$

For

$$\delta_{\texttt{Far}} = 1-(1-\epsilon_{\texttt{f}})^{nM}, \qquad \delta_{\texttt{Close}} = (1-\epsilon_{\texttt{t}})^n.$$

That is, APSS is a $(t, c, \delta_{\texttt{Far}}, \delta_{\texttt{Close}})$-approximate proximity search scheme.

$\delta_{\texttt{Close}}$ exactly corresponds with TAR for a well-spread database. However, $\delta_{\texttt{Far}}$ controls the overall probability of a false accept and is a much stronger condition than controlling the FAR. Below we analyze the FAR of the baseline scheme for random data where each record in the database has exactly $\epsilon_{\texttt{f}}$ probability of matching an LSH and each query that is a noisy version of a stored x_i has probability exactly $\epsilon_{\texttt{t}}$ of colliding LSH with the stored reading of the biometric.

We use report FAR as $\delta_{\mathtt{FAR}}$ for consistency with ProxCode, which is presented shortly. This means we are comparing ProxCode against a baseline scheme with a weaker correctness guarantee.

As described in the Introduction, there are three main issues with Construction 1:

1. The use of a multimap. Constructing oblivious multimaps is a difficult prospect (see discussion in [13,18–21]).
2. The use of a disjunctive query requires $\epsilon_{\mathtt{f}}$ to be very small and n to be very large to support reasonable $\delta_{\mathtt{Close}}, \delta_{\mathtt{Far}}$.
3. In the three party searchable encryption scenario, unintended biometrics are (occasionally) leaked to clients.

3.1 Finding n for Baseline Construction

For fixed $\epsilon_{\mathtt{t}}, \epsilon_{\mathtt{f}}$ it suffices to set

$$\frac{\log(\delta_{\mathtt{Close}})}{\log(1-\epsilon_{\mathtt{t}})} \leq n \leq \frac{\log(\delta_{\mathtt{Far}})}{M\log(1-\epsilon_{\mathtt{f}})}. \tag{1}$$

In particular, in the setting when $\delta_{\mathtt{Close}} \approx \delta_{\mathtt{Far}}$ and for small $\epsilon_{\mathtt{t}}, \epsilon_{\mathtt{f}}$ where $\log(1-x) \approx -x$ for n to exist in Eq. 1 it must be the case that $\epsilon_{\mathtt{t}} \geq M\epsilon_{\mathtt{f}}$.

In the case when the LSH is an extended LSH with underlying error rates of $\epsilon'_{\mathtt{t}}, \epsilon'_{\mathtt{f}}$ with α concatenated copies and $\epsilon'_{\mathtt{t}} > \epsilon'_{\mathtt{f}}$ then setting

$$\alpha \geq \frac{\log(M)}{\log(\epsilon'_{\mathtt{t}}/\epsilon'_{\mathtt{f}})}. \tag{2}$$

suffices for

$$\left(\frac{\epsilon'_{\mathtt{t}}}{\epsilon'_{\mathtt{f}}}\right)^{\alpha} = \frac{\epsilon_{\mathtt{t}}}{\epsilon_{\mathtt{f}}} \geq M.$$

This means that $n \approx M\log(\delta_{\mathtt{Close}})/\log(\delta_{\mathtt{Far}})$.

4 ProxCode

This section formally introduces ProxCode, and gives the proof that it is secure and accurate under the well-spread condition (Definition 4). This condition is not assumed in our evaluation in Sect. 5.

Our construction combines LSHs and secure map. Instead of assigning LSH outputs with records, we assign them with points on a random polynomial whose intercept is the record. Later, multiple shares are collected and decoded. Search only reveals a matching record x_i when there is *enough* LSH matches.

To handle LSH collisions, when $z = \mathsf{LSH}_\beta(x_i) = \mathsf{LSH}_\beta(x_j)$, we constrain the two polynomials to have the same value at position β. That is, that $\mathsf{c}_{i,\beta} = \mathsf{c}_{j,\beta}$. We can do this without impacting either $\mathsf{c}_{i,1}$ or $\mathsf{c}_{k,1}$ as long as this occurs in no more than $k-1$ positions for each codeword. We present this scheme formally in Algorithm 2 and Construction 2.

As mentioned in the Introduction, the goal can be retrieval of the indices, i, or the actual values, x_i (see discussion in Gui et al. [20,35]). Usually in encrypted search, one focuses on building an index data structure with the actual records being obtained through a second oblivious structure. Our system works equally well in both settings, assuming the map can hold entire records (as long as they are distinct) since our encoding technique does not increase the size of values inserted in the map (beyond the additional space to encode them in a field). A separate lookup of the value x_i from i often has leakage, so we associate x_i to prevent the second lookup.

Construction 2 *Let t be a distance and let $c > 1$ be a distance parameter. Let $\mathcal{DB} \in \{0,1\}^{\gamma \times M}$ be a (c,t)-well-spread database. Let $n \in \mathbb{Z}^+$ and $\mu, k \in \mathbb{Z}^+$ such that $\mu \leq k < n$.*

1. *Let LSH be a family of $(t, ct, \epsilon_{\mathtt{t}}, \epsilon_{\mathtt{f}})$-LSHs with domain of $\{0,1\}^r$.*
2. *Let p be a prime power such that $p \geq M$. Let $\mathsf{RS}_{(n+1,k)}$ be a Reed-Solomon code with associated algorithms $\mathsf{Decode}_{\mathsf{RS}}, \mathsf{Inv}_{\mathsf{RS}}$.*
3. *Let $\mathsf{Map} = (\mathsf{Map}.\mathit{insert}, \mathsf{Map}.\mathit{retrieve})$ be a map.*

Define APSS as in Algorithm 2.

We provide some intuition for the scheme before presenting our formal results. There are two main ideas in Construction 2:

Polynomial Evaluations in the Map. First, we replace x_i as the value inserted into the map with a polynomial whose intercept is x_i. That is, $\mathsf{c}_{i,1} = x_i$. The idea behind this change is that if one can reconstruct c_i then one can easily recover the value x_i. We then insert pairs $((j, \mathsf{LSH}_j(x_i)), \mathsf{c}_{i,j})$ into the map.

Align Codewords with LSH Collisions. We add a preprocessing step so that codewords are chosen in a correlated manner. We precompute Eq, the set of all LSH collisions in the database. If two values x_i, x_k share some $\mathsf{LSH}_\beta(x_i) = \mathsf{LSH}_\beta(x_j)$ then we fix $\mathsf{c}_{i,\beta} = \mathsf{c}_{j,\beta}$. We rely on the fact that one can interpolate a degree $k-1$ polynomial for any k points to ensure this is possible. Theorem 1 bounds the probability that such sampling cannot complete over the choice of LSH_is. Importantly, this probability holds for all well-spread $\mathcal{DB}$ and does not depend on the chosen codewords. We check this condition by examining Eq.

Once Setup is complete, there is now a one-to-one correspondence between the LSH outputs and the codeword symbols. Let $x_i \in \mathcal{DB}$, if one searched for the value x_i one would retrieve $\mathsf{c}_{i,2}, ..., \mathsf{c}_{i,n+1}$ which determines $\mathsf{c}_{i,1}$ and allow retrieval. If one searches for a value y then the returned values will be a mix of different codewords and $\perp$ if nothing in the database matched the LSH value. We first consider the correctness of this scheme deferring security until Sect. 4.2.

$\texttt{Init}\begin{pmatrix}1^\lambda\\1^\lambda\end{pmatrix} = \mathsf{Map.Init}\begin{pmatrix}1^\lambda\\1^\lambda\end{pmatrix}$

$\begin{pmatrix}\mathsf{LSH}_1, ..., \mathsf{LSH}_n\\ \mathcal{I}\end{pmatrix} \leftarrow \texttt{Setup}\begin{pmatrix}\mathcal{DB}, \mathsf{sk}\\ \mathsf{pp}\end{pmatrix}$:

1. Sample $\mathsf{LSH}_1, ..., \mathsf{LSH}_n \leftarrow \mathsf{LSH}$. Define $L \in (\{0,1\}^r)^{M\times n}$ where $L_{i,j} = \mathsf{LSH}_j(x_i)$.
2. Define $\texttt{Eq} \in [M]^{M\times n}$ where $\texttt{Eq}_{i,j} = \arg\min_{i'<i}(L_{i',j} = L_{i,j})$ where $\texttt{Eq}_{i,j} = 0$ if no such i' exists.
3. If there exists a row of $\texttt{Eq}$ with more than $k-1$ nonzero coordinates go to Step 1 (up to ℓ times, then output $\perp$).
4. Initialize $\mathbf{C} \in (\mathbb{F}_p \cup \perp)^{M\times(n+1)} = \perp^{M\times(n+1)}$
5. For $i = 1, ..., M$:
   (a) $\mathbf{C}_{i,1} = x_i$.
   (b) For $j = 1, ..., n$, if $\texttt{Eq}_{i,j} \neq 0$, set $\mathbf{C}_{i,j+1} = \mathbf{C}_{\texttt{Eq}_{i,j},j+1}$.
   (c) $\mathbf{C}_i = \mathsf{Inv}_{\mathsf{RS}}(\texttt{NEmpty}(\mathbf{C}_i))$. $\texttt{NEmpty}$ outputs the indices and values of positions that are not $\perp$.
6. $\mathcal{DB} = (j||\mathsf{LSH}_j(x_i), \mathbf{C}_{i,j+1})$ for $i = 1, ..., M, j = 1, ..., n$.
7. $\begin{pmatrix}\perp\\ \mathcal{I}_0\end{pmatrix} \leftarrow \mathsf{Map.Setup}\begin{pmatrix}\mathcal{DB}, \mathsf{sk}\\ \mathsf{pp}\end{pmatrix}$.

$\texttt{Search}\begin{pmatrix}y, \mathsf{LSH}_1, ..., \mathsf{LSH}_n, \mathsf{sk}\\ \mathcal{I}_{(i-1)\cdot n}, \mathsf{pp}\end{pmatrix}$:

1. Compute $L_j = \mathsf{LSH}_j(y)$ for all $j = 1, ..., n$.
2. Initialize $\mathsf{e}_{erase} = n$.
3. For $j = 1, .., n$,
   (a) Client retrieves $\begin{pmatrix}\mathsf{c}_{j+1}\\ \mathcal{I}_{(i-1)\cdot n+j}\end{pmatrix} = \mathsf{Map.Search}\begin{pmatrix}(j, L_j), \mathsf{sk}\\ \mathcal{I}_{(i-1)\cdot n+(j-1)}, \mathsf{pp}\end{pmatrix}$.
   (b) If $\mathsf{c}_{j+1} \neq \perp$, $\mathsf{e}_{erase} := \mathsf{e}_{erase} - 1$.
4. If $\mathsf{e}_{erase} > n-k$ output $\perp$.
5. Compute $\mathsf{c}_1, ..., \mathsf{c}_k \leftarrow \mathsf{Decode}_{\mathsf{RS}}(\perp ||\mathsf{c}_2||...||\mathsf{c}_n)$, output c_1

Algorithm 2: $\texttt{ProxCode}$: APSS from maps and linear codes. Procedures are run by Client unless calling an underlying interactive protocol.

4.1 Correctness

Theorem 1. *Let $c, c_1, c_2 > 0$ be constants. Let LSH be a family of $(t, ct, \epsilon_t, \epsilon_f)$-locality sensitive hashes. Let $\mathcal{DB}$ be a (c,t)-well-spread database where $|\mathcal{DB}| = M$. Let $n \in \mathbb{Z}^+, k \in \mathbb{Z}^+$ be parameters. Suppose the following are true:*

$$\epsilon_t > \frac{2k}{(1-c_2)n}, \tag{3}$$

$$\epsilon_f < \frac{k}{Mn(1+c_1)}, \tag{4}$$

and define

$$\forall i \leq M, \delta_{\mathtt{Far}_i} = exp\left(\frac{-c_1^2}{2+c_1} \cdot \epsilon_{\mathtt{f}} \cdot n \cdot (i-1)\right),$$

$$\delta_{\mathtt{Far}} = \delta_{\mathtt{Far}_M} = exp\left(\frac{-c_1^2}{2+c_1} \cdot \epsilon_{\mathtt{f}} \cdot n \cdot (M-1)\right),$$

$$\delta_{\mathtt{Close}} = exp\left(\frac{-c_2^2 \epsilon_{\mathtt{t}} n}{2}\right) + \delta_{\mathtt{Far}_{M-1}}.$$

Construction 2 instantiated with $\mathsf{RS}_{(n+1,k)}$ *and* n *LSHs from* LSH *is an* $(t, c, \delta_{\mathtt{Far}}, \delta_{\mathtt{Close}}) - \mathsf{APSS}$*. Furthermore,*

$$\Pr[\mathsf{Setup}\ outputs\ \perp] \leq \left(1 - \prod_{i=2}^{M}(1-\delta_{\mathtt{Far},i})\right)^{\ell} \leq \left(1-(1-\delta_{\mathtt{Far}})^{M-1}\right)^{\ell}$$

Theorem 1 is proved through Lemmas 1, 2, and 3 which focus on the number of LSH matches between close records, far records, and the ability of the setup to complete. Roughly, each of these lemmas is proved using a Chernoff bound since LSH outputs are independent (if data is fixed before sampling). The constants c_1, c_2 represent the constant of the Binomial deviating from its expectation. The proofs of the lemmas are deferred to Appendix B.

Lemma 1. *Let all parameters be as in Theorem 1. Define*

$$\mathsf{Match}_{j,x,x^*} = \begin{cases} 1 & LSH_j(x) = LSH_j(x^*) \\ 0 & otherwise \end{cases}.$$

And define $\mathsf{Match}_{x,x^*} = \sum_{j=1}^{n} \mathsf{Match}_{j,x,x^*}$*. If* $\mathcal{D}(x,x^*) \leq t$ *then*

$$\Pr[\mathsf{Match}_{x,x^*} \leq 2k] < exp\left(\frac{-c_2^2}{2} \cdot \epsilon_{\mathtt{t}} \cdot n\right).$$

Lemma 2. *Let all parameters be as in Theorem 1. Define random variable* $\mathsf{Match}_{j,\mathcal{DB},x}$ *as follows for* $j \in \{1, ..., n\}$*:*

$$\mathsf{Match}_{j,\mathcal{DB},x} = |\{x_i \in \mathcal{DB} | \mathsf{LSH}_j(x_i) = \mathsf{LSH}_j(x)\}|.$$

and $\mathsf{Match}_{\mathcal{DB},x} = \sum_{j=1}^{n} \mathsf{Match}_{j,\mathcal{DB},x}$*, denoting the number of* LSH*'s where there exists some collision between the value* x' *and some record in the* $\mathcal{DB}$*. For all* x *such that* $\forall x_i \in \mathcal{DB}$ *it is true that* $\mathcal{D}(x, x_i) \geq ct$ *it is true that*

$$\Pr[\mathsf{Match}_{\mathcal{DB},x} \geq k] \leq exp\left(\frac{-c_1^2}{2+c_1} \cdot \epsilon_{\mathtt{f}} \cdot n \cdot M\right).$$

Lemma 3. *Let all parameters be as in Lemma 2 and Theorem 1 letting*

$$\delta_{\texttt{Far},i} = exp\left(\frac{-c_1^2}{2+c_1} \cdot \epsilon_{\texttt{f}} \cdot n \cdot (i-1)\right).$$

Then the probability that Setup *outputs* $\perp$ *is at most*

$$\Pr[\mathsf{Setup}\ outputs\ \perp] \leq \left(1 - \prod_{i=2}^{M} (1 - \delta_{\texttt{Far},i})\right)^{\ell} \tag{5}$$

Proof (Proof of Theorem 1). There are three parts to proving Theorem 1 that setup completes with high probability, that the close item is included in the result set and that far items are not included in the result set. The probability of setup completing follows directly from Lemma 3.

Close Item in Result Set. Let x be the search term where x is close to at most one item in $\mathcal{DB}$ denoted as x_i with corresponding codeword c_i. That is, $\mathcal{D}(x, x_i) \leq t$. If such a x_i exists, its uniqueness is guaranteed by Definition 4. Let c_i denote the corresponding codeword. Define the following parameters:

$$\delta_{\texttt{Close},1} = exp\left(\frac{-c_2^2}{2} \cdot \epsilon_{\texttt{t}} \cdot n\right), \qquad \delta_{\texttt{Close},2} = \delta_{\texttt{Far},(M-1)}.$$

Let c' denote the recovered symbols (including $\perp$). By Lemma 1 there are at least $2k$ symbols from c_i with probability $1 - \delta_{\texttt{Close},1}$. By Lemma 2 there are at most k_{error} symbols from the other LSH values $M - 1$. By union bound, both of these conditions hold with probability $1 - (\delta_{\texttt{Close},1} + \delta_{\texttt{Close},2})$ Conditioned on both of these events occurring $\mathsf{Decode}_{\mathsf{RS}}$ outputs c_i with probability 1.

Far Items not in Result Set. By Lemma 2 the probability that c' has more than $k - 1$ symbols other than $\perp$ is at most $\delta_{\texttt{Far}}$.
This completes the proof of Theorem 1.

4.2 Security and Leakage

This section shows that when the Map in Construction 2 is an appropriate encrypted map, one achieves a secure APSS. We consider two commonly used leakage patterns in secure maps: 1) the zero-leakage setting where the server learns the size of the dataset M and when a query occurs, such as [2,53] and 2) access and search pattern where the server learns the identifiers associated with each query response and whether the queries have been repeated [17,37]. Of course, if one uses a zero-leakage map [2,34], the resulting APSS is zero-leakage as well (treating n as a public system parameter). Since each query of the APSS translates to n queries to the underlying map, we additionally leak when subqueries repeat and the subquery associated with a returned identifier.

Lemma 4. *Let λ be a security parameter. Let* $\mathsf{Map} = (\mathsf{Map}.\mathit{Setup}, \mathsf{Map}.\mathit{Search})$ *be a map that is secure according to Definition 6 for*

$$\mathcal{L}_{\mathsf{Map}} = \mathcal{L}^{\mathsf{Setup}} = |\mathsf{Map}|, \qquad \mathcal{L}^{\mathsf{Search}} = (\mathcal{L}^{\mathsf{Search}}_{\mathit{AccPatt}}, \mathcal{L}^{\mathsf{Search}}_{\mathit{QueryEq}}).$$

Then the $\mathit{APSS} = (\mathit{APSS.Init}, \mathit{APSS.Setup}, \mathit{APSS.Search})$ *scheme defined in Construction 2 is secure according to Definition 6 for*

$$\mathcal{L}^{\mathsf{Setup}} = n \cdot |\mathsf{Map}|, \qquad \mathcal{L}^{\mathsf{Search}} = (\mathcal{L}^{\mathsf{Search}}_{\mathit{SubAccPatt}}, \mathcal{L}^{\mathsf{Search}}_{\mathit{SubQueryEq}}).$$

$\mathcal{A}_{\mathsf{Map}}.\mathsf{Setup}(1^\lambda)$:

1. Initialize $\mathcal{A}^{\mathsf{APSS}}$ and receive $\mathcal{DB} \in (\{0,1\}^\gamma)^M$.
2. Run steps 1-6 of $\mathsf{APSS.Setup}(\mathcal{DB})$ from algorithm 2 to receive vector LSH and matrices L and C as described in steps 1, 2 and 6 respectively. If Step 4 outputs $\perp$ output $\perp$.
3. Output $\mathcal{DB}_{\mathsf{Map}} = \{(L_{i,j}, \mathsf{C}_{i,j+1})\}_{j=1,\ldots,n}^{i=1,\ldots,M}$.

$\mathcal{A}_{\mathsf{Map}}.\mathsf{Search}(\mathsf{LSH}, L, \mathsf{C})$:

1. Receive $q \in \{0,1\}^\gamma$ from $\mathcal{A}^{\mathsf{APSS}}$.
2. Compute $q_1, \ldots, q_n = \mathsf{LSH}_1(q), \ldots, \mathsf{LSH}_n(q)$.
3. Output $q_1, \ldots, q_n$.
4. Receive tk and send to $\mathcal{A}^{\mathsf{APSS}}$.

Fig. 2. Construction of $\mathcal{A}_{\mathsf{Map}}$ from $\mathcal{A}_{\mathsf{APSS}}$.

Proof. Let $\mathcal{A}_{\mathsf{APSS}}$ denote some PPT adversary for the APSS scheme. Our goal is to construct a $\mathcal{S}_{\mathsf{APSS}}$. As noted in Fig. 2 for any valid $\mathcal{A}_{\mathsf{APSS}}$ adversary there exists some $\mathcal{A}_{\mathsf{Map}}$ that is a valid Map adversary. Let $\mathcal{S}_{\mathsf{Map}}$ be one such simulator for $\mathcal{A}_{\mathsf{Map}}$. Note that setup leakage is the same in both settings. For the search leakage, $(\mathcal{L}^{\mathsf{Search}}_{\mathsf{SubAccPatt}}, \mathcal{L}^{\mathsf{Search}}_{\mathsf{SubQueryEq}})$ this allows $\mathcal{S}_{\mathsf{APSS}}$ to expand the q queries into qn subqueries which is the required leakage for $\mathcal{S}_{\mathsf{Map}}$. Then

$$|\Pr[\mathrm{Exp}_{\mathsf{APSS},\mathcal{A}_{\mathsf{APSS}}}(\cdot)) = 1] - \Pr[\mathrm{Exp}_{\mathcal{S}_{\mathsf{APSS}},\mathcal{A}_{\mathsf{APSS}}}(\mathcal{L}_0^{\mathtt{init}}, \mathcal{L}^{\mathsf{Search}}_{\mathsf{SubQueryEq},\mathsf{SubAccPatt}}]) = 1]| =$$
$$|\Pr[\mathrm{Exp}_{\mathsf{Map},\mathcal{A}_{\mathsf{Map}}}(\cdot)) = 1] - \Pr[\mathrm{Exp}_{\mathcal{S}_{\mathsf{Map}},\mathcal{A}_{\mathsf{Map}}}(\mathcal{L}_0^{\mathtt{init}}, \mathcal{L}^{\mathsf{Search}}_{\mathsf{QueryEq},\mathsf{AccPatt}}) = 1]|$$

This completes the proof of Lemma 4.

4.3 Discussion

Handling Dynamic Data. Assuming a dynamic map, one can naturally handle new data x^* being added to the database by searching for x^* and retrieving codeword symbols that x^*'s codeword should be consistent with. Then one can sample the codeword (under the constraints described above) and add the missing codeword symbols to the corresponding maps. Handling data deletion and updates requires care; map values have information about multiple biometrics. One way to handle deletes is to maintain a counter with each value indicating how many records are using this value, this counter could be decremented with each delete. The leakage and efficiency of the above depends strongly on the underlying map. Further study is required.

5 Implementation and Accuracy

We implemented `ProxCode` using Python 3. Our implementation uses an implementation of the tree-based oblivious map of Wang et al. [34]. The source code can be found in (Github).

5.1 Used Data

We perform tests on iris, synthetic, and random data. Iris datasets are not available for large M.

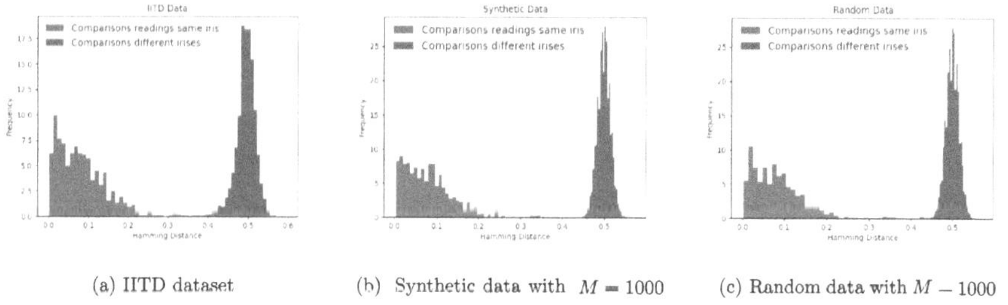

(a) IITD dataset (b) Synthetic data with $M = 1000$ (c) Random data with $M = 1000$

Fig. 3. FHD histogram for real data from IITD dataset, synthetic data, and random data. Comparisons between readings of the same biometric are in blue. Comparisons between readings of different biometrics are in red. The x-axis differs. (Color figure online)

Real Data. The IITD dataset [40] consists of 224 persons and 2240 images. We process these data using a recent feature extractor used for LSH-based fuzzy extractors [41] and segmentation system of Ahmad and Fuller [54]. We use their regime of left irises for training and right irises for testing. After removing unsuitable right irises without two readings, there are $M = 202$ right irises suitable for testing. We choose this feature extractor as it is designed to produce good features for extended LSHs.

Synthetic Data. Since the existing Real datasets such as IITD are small, to test our construction on a larger dataset with a distribution closer to the real world than random, we used synthetic dataset. To generate an initial reading of irises we perform the following:

1. Measure the degrees of freedom and closest fit binomial distribution for the real data in the previous subsection. This is the standard mechanism for estimating the entropy of an iris after applying a feature extractor [51].
2. This yielded a binomial with parameters of $n = 391, p = .4939$.
3. For each starting iris we sampled from a binomial with (n, p) as above.
4. Converted the output to 512 bit features by multiplying by 512/391 and rounding.
5. This specified how many 1s to put in the feature vector.
6. We then randomly placed the chosen number of 1s in the feature vector.

For generating noise between readings of the same iris, we use the probability mass function for number of errors from our real-data and randomly place errors.

Random Data. Random data uses the same error distribution as synthetic data but all feature vectors are uniformly distributed. Histograms for all three datatypes are shown in Fig. 3.

5.2 Time Efficiency

Our savings in n will translate to any encrypted map, see discussion in the Introduction. For our cryptographic implementation, we use a tree-based oblivious map due to Wang et al. [34]. At a high level, the construction is a tree of oblivious arrays where one stores the current logical position of all children for a node in addition to the node value. This storage allows one to use non-recursive ORAM, as long as one always traverses the tree from the root to some predetermined depth. In our setting, we always traverse to a leaf node for each LSH subquery. One can traverse the tree using PathORAM [55] using depth + 1 rounds of communication.

Usually one queries the map on all n LSH values of the search term. Ha et al. [3] build a preprocessing step using private set intersection where one first finds out which terms exist in the map and then uses the map to search only a constant number of non-null terms. They find the cryptographic overhead of this first stage is small compared to overhead of the second stage.

We use κ to denote the required number of parallel accesses to ORAM that doesn't impact accuracy. Let $\max_{\texttt{error}}$ be the maximum number of errors observed in the query set. Then $\kappa = k + 2\max_{\texttt{error}} + 1$. By making κ queries in this way, one always retains enough codeword symbols to reconstruct the value without having to query all n terms. Often $\kappa/n \approx .1$ improving performance by an order of magnitude. Furthermore, κ is usually of the scale that queries could be processed in parallel by a modern server.

We consider two timing experiments below, how long to preprocess in `ProxCode` and timing for `Search` and `Setup` of the full implementation. These evaluations are on a Ryzen Threadripper PRO 7995WX with 384MB L3 cache and 768GB of DDR5 RAM.

Finding Parameters. We manually find the relevant n, k, α for each dataset. We choose a target TAR of .90 for a parameter set to be acceptable. We consider dataset sizes for synthetic and random of $M = \{1000, 2500, 5000, 10000, 25000\}$.

ProxCode preprocessing time We first measure time to run Algorithm 2 ignoring the map, note this algorithm has complexity $\Theta(n \times M)$, assuming constant cost to evaluate each LSH. Results are reported in Table 3. On our largest tested parameter sets finding the relevant polynomials takes at most 5 minutes. Looking ahead, this time is dwarfed by the time to build the relevant oblivious map which on the same data set is nearly 7 hours. For all of our chosen parameters, Setup completes in a single iteration so we don't report the number of iterations.

Table 3. PreProcessing Times (in seconds) for Tested Concrete Parameters.

ℓ	Dataset type	# Queries	n	k	α	Sample LSH	Eq. Matrix
202	IITD	202	100	4	17	.15	.051
1000	Synth	200	500	12	17	3.7	1.4
1000	Rand					3.6	1.5
2500	Synth	200	600	10	20	12.1	5.1
2500	Rand					11.8	5.1
5000	Synth	200	700	13	21	31.0	13.4
5000	Rand					30.9	12.9
10000	Synth	200	800	10	23	70.6	34.2
10000	Rand					71.0	34.2
25000	Synth	200	800	10	25	191	98.4
25000	Rand					190	95.0

Cryptographic Efficiency. In Table 4 we report the time to set up all the oblivious RAM arrays, the number of rounds, the number of ORAM reads, the overall search time, and the parallel search time which is the average (across queries) of the maximum time required for each subquery. The overall search time includes decoding the code and as such is more than n times the parallel search time. Network delay is not modeled. While setup time is in hours for our largest datasets, parallel search still requires $< 10ms$. On a relatively fast network with a 100ms RTT, overall query time would be roughly 2.5s. As we discuss above we can use the same filtering technique of Ha et al. [3] to only search κ times in the map and κ remains small enough that all requests could be reasonably handled by a modern server. We do note that our κ are much smaller than Ha et al. who use $\kappa = 72$ on synthetic data of size 5000 (they use δ for the number of searched items in the map).

5.3 Implications of ProxCode for Client Security

Throughout this work, we defined and considered the two party SSE setting for notational simplicity. Since ProxCode is primarily a preprocessing technique it naturally extends to a three party SSE setting. A three party SSE consider a data owner, server, and a client [56]. In this setting, in addition to limiting leakage to the server, the data owner wishes to limit unintended data learned by a client. The three party setting highlights the importance of an accurate system. To demonstrate the difference between the baseline and ProxCode we demonstrate the difference in information available between map outputs to the client. This information is available even if one uses a fully oblivious map.

Table 4. Cryptographic Efficiency results. Map sizes and number of Reads (number of ORAM accesses per search) are in thousands. Setup Time and Sequential Search Times are in seconds, Parallel Search time in ms. GB is 10^9 bytes.

ℓ	Dataset type	# q	n	k	α	TAR	Map K Size	Par Rnds	Crypto Setup Time	GB	O Reads	Search Time Seq.	Par.	κ
202	IITD	202	100	4	17	.97	20.2	16	13	.04	1.5	.76	1.4	9
1000	Synth	200	500	12	17	.96	500	19	418	1.1	9.5	3.0	2.5	27
1000	Rand					.91			421			3.0	2.4	27
2500	Synth	200	600	10	20	.94	1500	21	1430	3.3	12.6	4.11	2.9	23
2500	Rand					.92			1430			4.11	3.0	23
5000	Synth	200	700	13	21	.90	3500	22	3560	7.6	15.4	5.20	3.4	22
5000	Rand					.89			3500			5.32	3.2	22
10000	Synth	200	800	10	23	.90	8000	23	8600	17.4	18.4	6.82	3.5	17
10000	Rand					.86			8520			6.73	3.5	17
25000	Synth	200	800	10	25	.88	20000	25	23700	43.5	20.0	7.17	4.2	17
25000	Rand					.88			24300			7.53	5.1	19

- **Baseline:** For fixed value $n = 100$ we found the α for Baseline with comparable TAR. This value is $\alpha = 22$, producing a TAR of .923. For these values across the query set, this produced 4 false positives across the 202 queries. Each false positive represents a biometric of a non-relevant person incidentally exposed to the client.
- **ProxCode:** For parameters $\alpha = 17, n = 100, k = 8$ (first row in Table 4), we fixed a single value x_i and issued queries corresponding to the other irises in the dataset. We then measured how many values $\mathbf{C}_{i,j}$ for $2 \leq \mathbf{C}_{i,j} \leq n + 1$ are returned by some other query. That is, we measure how many "shares" of

$\mathbf{C}_i$ are obtained after 201 queries for each of other irises. This produced the average of 1.4 shares across 201 queries, with STD of .66, and the max of 4 shares. No iris has at least k symbols returned after issuing 201 queries.

To summarize, in the Baseline system a client who issues a small number of queries has a small probability of learning some non-relevant iris. In `ProxCode` a client may be able to decode a single iris after 200 queries. Analysis assumes client queries come from irises in the dataset. One expects higher success with specifically crafted queries [27,57].

6 Conclusion

In this work, we consider approximate proximity searchable encryption in both zero and access pattern leakage settings. Our scheme allows use of a map and reduces leakage over the baseline scheme.

This work considers Reed-Solomon codes that correct arbitrary errors. However, observed errors are not arbitrary. Assume that the $\epsilon_{\mathtt{t}}$ is tuned so that $k' > k$ LSH matches occur for a nearby value with good probability. The actual errors are defined by the following process:

1. Sample M codewords $\mathsf{c}_1, ..., \mathsf{c}_M$ (under the collision constraint defined above).
2. Consider codeword c_i corresponding to a search for a value x^* that is close to x_i. Consider a fixed a symbol j. With probability at least $1 - \epsilon'_{\mathtt{t}}$ the symbol $\mathsf{c}_{i,j}$ is correctly transmitted. Otherwise there are two cases:
   (a) With probability at most $(M-1)\epsilon'_{\mathtt{f}}$ is replaced by $\mathsf{c}_{i,k}$ for some $k \neq j$. Each of these replacements occur with probability at most $\epsilon'_{\mathtt{f}}$.
   (b) Otherwise, the symbol is converted to $\perp$.

There are two aspects of the above error model: 1) errors come from symbols of other codewords, and 2) these codewords are not independently sampled.

It is an open problem to design codes that correct more of such errors than is possible in traditional error models. Furthermore, it seems possible to argue some independence and randomness of the errors (Shannon model [58]) using the secret sharing properties of the code. We were not able to prove this or find a counterexample. The sticking point was the coupled sampling of the codewords. We also consider using list decoding for Reed Solomon codes. There are three reasons `ProxCode` could not work:

1. Setup doesn't complete,
2. There are too many errors to successfully decode, and
3. There were too few LSH matches between noisy readings, which creates too many erasures.

In our experience, items 1 and 3 were bigger issues when working with real data. This can be seen by the relatively small values of κ. For example, the largest number of errors in the random 25000 query set was only 4. We didn't find the need to implement more complex correction beyond Berlekamp Welch.

`ProxCode` has a dramatic impact on the efficiency of LSH based proximity searchable encryption. These improvements lead to major improvements in all aspects of system efficiency. We present an open-source prototype implementation with testing for real, synthetic, and random data.

Acknowledgments. The authors are grateful to the reviewers for their important comments in improving this work. The work of B.F. and M.R. is supported by NSF grants #2141033 and #2232813. This research is based upon work supported in part by the Office of the Director of National Intelligence (ODNI), Intelligence Advanced Research Projects Activity (IARPA), via Contract No. 2019-19020700008. This material is based upon work supported by the Defense Advanced Research Projects Agency, DARPA, under Air Force Contract No. FA8702-15-D-0001. Any opinions, findings, conclusions, or recommendations expressed in this material are those of the author(s) and do not necessarily reflect the views of DARPA. The views and conclusions contained herein are those of the authors and should not be interpreted as necessarily representing the official policies, either expressed or implied, of ODNI, IARPA, or the U.S. Government. The U.S. Government is authorized to reproduce and distribute reprints for governmental purposes notwithstanding any copyright annotation therein.

Disclosure of Interests. The authors have no competing interests to declare that are relevant to the content of this article.

A Algorithmic Parameter Analysis for Random Data

This section compares the efficiency of the baseline scheme with `ProxCode`. During this discussion, we assume that all biometrics in the database are far yielding probability $\epsilon_{\mathtt{f}}$ of their LSHs matching, and that all queries are closing yielding probability of $\epsilon_{\mathtt{t}}$ of matching an LSH with the relevant stored record. These assumptions are useful for analysis but not true in practice, see discussion in Sect. 5. Our evaluation focuses on the number of required LSHs. We first compute accuracy parameters for `ProxCode` and then find corresponding parameters for the baseline scheme for the same accuracy.

A.1 Evaluation Methodology

We take the smallest values for α, n, and k that satisfy Eqs. 3 and 4 simultaneously Our parameter finding was done in Python 3.9.

Recall that for a (n, k)-Reed-Solomon Code to decode successfully (Definition 2) it suffices that $\mathsf{k}_{correct} > 2k$ and $\mathsf{k}_{error} \leq k$. Our evaluation uses an augmented LSH so we assume for some $\alpha \in \mathbb{Z}^+$ that $\epsilon_{\mathtt{t}} = \epsilon_{\mathtt{t}}'^{\alpha}$ and $\epsilon_{\mathtt{f}} = \epsilon_{\mathtt{f}}'^{\alpha}$.

We assume the bit selection LSH $\mathsf{LSH}_i(x) = x_i$ which has the property that

$$\Pr[\mathsf{LSH}(x) = \mathsf{LSH}(y)] = \frac{\gamma - \mathcal{D}(x, y)}{\gamma} = 1 - \mathcal{D}(x, y)/\gamma.$$

We test with different parameters $\epsilon'_{\mathtt{t}}, \epsilon'_{\mathtt{f}}$ which represent the noise between different readings of the same biometric and readings of different biometrics respectively. Errors between readings of the same biometric and differences between readings of different biometrics both come from distributions. So for two different values $x_i, x_j \in \mathcal{DB}$, one will frequently observe $\mathcal{D}(x, y) < .5\gamma$. Even if the average FHD between readings of the same biometric is .1 one observes errors of at least .2. See Fig. 3. This is why we test for values of $\epsilon'_{\mathtt{f}} \in \{.5, .6, .7\}$. We consider $\epsilon'_{\mathtt{t}} \in \{.7, .75, .80, .85, .9\}$. Our results exclude values where no solutions could be found with $\log_{10}(n) \leq 20$. We provide a full methodology next.

Detailed Methodology. For input constants c_1, c_2 we search for settings of α, n, k such that

$$(\epsilon'_{\mathtt{t}})^{\alpha} > \frac{2k}{(1-c_2)n}, \tag{6}$$

$$(\epsilon'_{\mathtt{f}})^{\alpha} \leq \frac{k}{Mn(1+c_1)}. \tag{7}$$

Increasing α exponentially decreases both the true accept rate and false accept rate. Thus, we first find the minimum α that produces a solution for n, k. Combining the Eqs. 6 and 7 one has that:

$$M(1+c_1)(\epsilon'_{\mathtt{f}})^{\alpha} \leq \frac{k}{n} < \frac{1}{2}(1-c_2)(\epsilon'_{\mathtt{t}})^{\alpha}.$$

We compute the minimum α such that

$$M \cdot (1+c_1)(\epsilon'_{\mathtt{f}})^{\alpha} \leq \frac{1}{2}(1-c_2)(\epsilon'_{\mathtt{t}})^{\alpha}$$

Using the computed α, we find the first n that satisfies the following inequality:

$$M \cdot (1+c_1)(\epsilon'_{\mathtt{f}})^{\alpha} \cdot n \leq \left(\frac{1}{2}(1-c_2)(\epsilon'_{\mathtt{t}})^{\alpha} + 1\right) \cdot n$$

With α, and n we can easily find the set of possible as solutions to:

$$M \cdot (1+c_1)(\epsilon'_{\mathtt{f}})^{\alpha} \cdot n \leq k < \frac{1}{2}(1-c_2)(\epsilon'_{\mathtt{t}})^{\alpha} \cdot n. \tag{8}$$

As we show next the value of k, is strongly connected to the error probabilities in Lemma 1 and Lemma 2. Thus, we exclude solutions where $k < 20$ or k is not an integer.

Lastly, we check the probability that setup fails according to Lemma 3. We compute

$$\delta_{\mathtt{Far}} \leq exp\left(\frac{-c_1^2}{2+c_1} \cdot \epsilon_{\mathtt{f}}'^{\alpha} \cdot n \cdot M\right) \approx exp\left(\frac{-c_1^2 k}{(2+c_1)(1+c_1)}\right)$$

$$\delta_{\mathtt{Close}} \leq exp\left(\frac{-c_2^2}{2} \cdot \epsilon_{\mathtt{t}}'^{\alpha} \cdot n\right) + \delta_{\mathtt{Far}} \approx exp\left(\frac{-c_2^2 k}{1-c_2}\right) + \delta_{\mathtt{Far}}$$

We estimated the minimum value of ℓ such that Setup has probability of at least .99 of completing within ℓ iterations using Eq. 5.

Computing Parameters for Baseline Scheme. Recall for the baseline scheme described in Construction 1 one has $\delta_{\mathtt{Far}} = (1 - \epsilon_{\mathtt{f}}'^{\alpha})^{nM}$ and $\delta_{\mathtt{Close}} = (1 - \epsilon_{\mathtt{t}}'^{\alpha})^{n}$. We solve the following two equations to compute α and n in the Baseline scheme.

$$\mathtt{FAR} = Mn\epsilon_{\mathtt{f}}'^{\alpha}, \qquad \delta_{\mathtt{Close}} = (1 - \epsilon_{\mathtt{t}}'^{\alpha})^{n}$$

As mentioned above, we require the baseline scheme to have the same FAR as our $\delta_{\mathtt{Far}}$. This is a much weaker condition. For example, for a dataset of size $M = 10^6$ and $\delta_{\mathtt{Far}} = 10^{-4}$ corresponds to a FAR $\approx 10^{-10}$.

A.2 Required Number of LSHs

Our parameter analysis focuses on three different database sizes when $M = 10^6, 10^4$ and $M = 10^3$ representing a country wide specialized database, a large organization, and a medium size organization.

Discussion. The smaller the value of $\delta_{\mathtt{Far}}$ the more ProxCode improves over the baseline scheme. Furthermore, the more noise is present, represented by a decrease in $\epsilon_{\mathtt{t}}$ the more ProxCode improves over the baseline scheme.

For $\epsilon_{\mathtt{t}}' = .9$ the difference in $\log n$ between ProxCode and in baseline scheme is negative (across all three accuracy regimes). As error increases, for example, $\epsilon_{\mathtt{t}}'$ to .7, ProxCode presents major improvement. This improvement is largest in higher accuracy regime with $\delta_{\mathtt{Far}} = 10^{-6}$ and smaller with $\delta_{\mathtt{Far}} = 10^{-3}$. The gap between $\log n$ is similar across sizes of databases M though the absolute size has a strong dependence on M. The summary comparison is presented in Table 1.

For instance, looking at Table 5, setting $c_1 = 3$, and $c_2 = .4$ results in a high accuracy setting yielding:

- $\delta_{\mathtt{Far}} = 10^{-4}$.
- $\delta_{\mathtt{Close}}$ varies in size between the order of 10^{-4} and 10^{-3}.

The improvements are most pronounced when the gap between $\epsilon_{\mathtt{t}}'$ and $\epsilon_{\mathtt{f}}'$ is smallest. As an example, when $\epsilon_{\mathtt{f}}' = .6$ and $\epsilon_{\mathtt{t}}' = .75$ (represented in Table 5), for $M = 10^4$ records in the Baseline scheme we need $n = 10^{12.1}$ (with LSHs of size $\alpha = 91$), ProxCode requires $n = 10^{8.4}$ (with $\alpha = 53$). There are some cases where there is a large difference between underlying LSH error rates ($\epsilon_{\mathtt{t}}' = .9, \epsilon_{\mathtt{f}}' = .5$) where ProxCode performs worse requiring approximately 60% more LSHs. These are "easy cases" when few LSHs are required. However, ProxCode often makes drastic improvements: when $\epsilon_{\mathtt{f}}' = .6$ and $\epsilon_{\mathtt{t}}' = .80$ one moves from almost a 100 million LSHs to a million. Improvements follow the same pattern for the setting of $M = 10^3$ and $M = 10^6$.

Impact of Reducing α. Although our prime interest is to decrease n, we can see that we also have improvement in the value of α. This improvement is in

Table 5. Parameters Comparison between our ProxCode and Baseline scheme where $M \cdot \epsilon_{\mathtt{f}}'^{\alpha}.n = \delta_{\mathtt{Far}}$ and $(1 - \epsilon_{\mathtt{t}}'^{\alpha})^n = \delta_{\mathtt{Close}}$. In ProxCode parameters are computed as in Sect. A. The numbers for α, n, k are the first found solutions. For the baseline scheme we measure FAR while in ProxCode we measure $\delta_{\mathtt{Far}}$ this allows the baseline scheme to have more errors for the same accuracy. Accuracy $\delta_{\mathtt{Far}} \approx 10^{-3}$ from $c_1 = 2$ and $c_2 = .4$. Accuracy $\delta_{\mathtt{Far}} \approx 10^{-4}$ from $c_1 = 3, c_2 = .4$ and accuracy $\delta_{\mathtt{Far}} \approx 10^{-6}$ from $c_1 = 5, c_2 = .4$. Logarithms are base 10.

		$M = 10^6$						$M = 10^4$						$M = 10^3$					
$\delta_{\mathtt{Far}} = 10^{-3}$		Baseline		ProxCode				Baseline		ProxCode				Baseline		ProxCode			
$\epsilon_{\mathtt{f}}'$	$\epsilon_{\mathtt{t}}'$	α	$\log n$	α	$\log n$	k	$\delta_{\mathtt{Close}}$	α	$\log n$	α	$\log n$	k	$\delta_{\mathtt{Close}}$	α	$\log n$	α	$\log n$	k	$\delta_{\mathtt{Close}}$
.7	.85	117	9.1	84	7.8	24	10^{-3}	93	7.4	60	6.1	22	2×10^{-3}	81	6.5	48	5.2	22	2×10^{-3}
.7	.9	91	5.0	65	4.8	24	10^{-3}	72	4.1	46	3.9	20	3×10^{-3}	63	3.7	37	3.5	21	2×10^{-3}
.6	.75	102	13.6	73	11.0	22	10^{-3}	81	10.9	52	8.3	21	2×10^{-3}	71	9.7	42	7.1	23	10^{-3}
.6	.8	79	8.5	57	7.5	26	8×10^{-4}	63	6.9	41	5.9	26	8×10^{-4}	55	6.2	33	5.1	26	8×10^{-4}
.6	.85	66	5.6	47	5.3	25	10^{-3}	53	4.7	34	4.3	27	6×10^{-4}	46	4.2	27	3.8	24	10^{-3}
.6	.9	56	3.4	40	3.7	22	2×10^{-3}	45	2.9	26	3.2	25	10^{-3}	39	2.6	23	2.9	22	2×10^{-3}
.5	.7	67	11.1	48	9.3	20	4×10^{-3}	49	8.4	34	7.1	27	2×10^{-3}	42	7.3	27	6	26	3×10^{-3}
.5	.75	56	7.8	40	6.9	22	2×10^{-3}	41	6.0	20	3.9	36	4×10^{-4}	35	5.2	23	4.8	33	7×10^{-4}
.5	.8	49	5.7	35	5.4	27	5×10^{-4}	38	4.7	25	4.4	37	2×10^{-4}	31	4.0	20	3.9	36	4×10^{-4}
.5	.85	43	3.9	31	4.2	27	5×10^{-4}	32	3.3	22	3.5	35	5×10^{-4}	28	3.1	18	3.3	41	10^{-4}
.5	.9	39	2.7	28	3.2	28	5×10^{-4}	29	2.4	20	2.9	38	2×10^{-4}	25	2.2	16	2.7	36	4×10^{-4}
$\delta_{\mathtt{Far}} = 10^{-4}$		Baseline		ProxCode				Baseline		ProxCode				Baseline		ProxCode			
$\epsilon_{\mathtt{f}}'$	$\epsilon_{\mathtt{t}}'$	α	$\log n$	α	$\log n$	k	$\delta_{\mathtt{Close}}$	α	$\log n$	α	$\log n$	k	$\delta_{\mathtt{Close}}$	α	$\log n$	α	$\log n$	k	$\delta_{\mathtt{Close}}$
.7	.85	129	9.9	85	7.8	21	2×10^{-3}	104	8.1	61	6.1	20	3×10^{-3}	92	7.2	49	5.2	20	4×10^{-3}
.7	.9	100	5.4	66	4.9	21	10^{-3}	81	4.5	47	3.9	20	4×10^{-3}	72	4.1	38	3.5	21	3×10^{-3}
.6	.75	112	14.8	74	11.1	21	2×10^{-3}	91	12.1	53	8.4	20	4×10^{-3}	81	10.9	43	7.2	22	2×10^{-3}
.6	.8	87	9.3	58	7.5	21	8×10^{-4}	71	7.7	42	6.0	26	8×10^{-4}	63	6.9	34	5.2	26	8×10^{-4}
.6	.85	72	5.9	48	5.3	21	6×10^{-4}	58	4.8	34	4.2	20	3×10^{-3}	52	4.5	28	3.9	25	10^{-3}
.6	.9	62	3.7	41	3.7	21	10^{-3}	51	3.3	30	3.3	28	4×10^{-4}	45	2.9	24	3.0	25	10^{-3}
.5	.7	74	12.2	49	9.4	26	3×10^{-3}	61	10.3	36	7.5	27	6×10^{-4}	54	9.2	29	6.4	25	9×10^{-4}
.5	.75	62	8.6	41	7.0	30	10^{-3}	51	7.3	30	5.7	28	4×10^{-4}	45	6.5	24	4.9	25	10^{-3}
.5	.8	53	5.9	35	5.2	25	3×10^{-3}	44	5.2	26	4.5	30	2×10^{-4}	39	4.7	21	4.0	29	4×10^{-4}
.5	.85	47	4.1	31	4.0	25	3×10^{-3}	39	3.7	**23**	**3.6**	**29**	$\mathbf{3 \times 10^{-4}}$	34	3.2	18	3.1	21	3×10^{-3}
.5	.9	43	2.9	28	3.1	26	3×10^{-3}	36	2.8	**21**	**3.0**	**34**	$\mathbf{10^{-4}}$	32	2.6	17	2.8	32	10^{-4}
$\delta_{\mathtt{Far}} = 10^{-6}$		Baseline		ProxCode				Baseline		ProxCode				Baseline		ProxCode			
$\epsilon_{\mathtt{f}}'$	$\epsilon_{\mathtt{t}}'$	α	$\log n$	α	$\log n$	k	$\delta_{\mathtt{Close}}$	α	$\log n$	α	$\log n$	k	$\delta_{\mathtt{Close}}$	α	$\log n$	α	$\log n$	k	$\delta_{\mathtt{Close}}$
.7	.85	142	10.7	87	7.9	21	4×10^{-3}	119	9.2	63	6.2	20	4×10^{-3}	108	8.5	52	5.5	24	10^{-3}
.7	.9	110	5.8	67	4.9	20	3×10^{-3}	92	5.0	49	4.1	22	2×10^{-3}	83	4.6	40	3.7	23	2×10^{-3}
.6	.75	124	16.2	76	11.3	23	2×10^{-3}	104	13.8	55	8.7	21	3×10^{-3}	94	12.6	45	7.5	22	2×10^{-3}
.6	.8	96	10.0	59	7.6	23	10^{-3}	81	8.7	43	6.0	23	10^{-3}	73	7.9	35	5.2	23	10^{-3}
.6	.85	79	6.3	49	5.3	25	10^{-3}	67	5.6	36	4.5	27	5×10^{-4}	60	5.0	29	3.9	24	10^{-3}
.6	.9	68	3.8	42	3.8	24	10^{-3}	58	3.6	31	3.4	28	4×10^{-4}	52	3.3	25	3.0	25	10^{-3}
.5	.7	83	13.6	50	9.5	20	4×10^{-3}	69	11.5	37	7.6	25	10^{-3}	63	10.7	30	6.5	24	10^{-3}
.5	.75	69	9.5	42	7.1	24	10^{-3}	58	8.2	31	5.8	28	4×10^{-4}	52	7.4	25	5.0	25	10^{-3}
.5	.8	59	6.5	36	5.3	22	2×10^{-3}	50	5.7	26	4.3	20	4×10^{-3}	45	5.3	22	4.1	30	2×10^{-4}
.5	.85	53	4.7	30	3.5	23	2×10^{-3}	45	4.3	**24**	**3.7**	**33**	$\mathbf{10^{-4}}$	40	3.8	19	3.2	23	10^{-3}
.5	.9	48	3.2	29	3.2	25	10^{-3}	40	2.8	**21**	**2.8**	**22**	$\mathbf{2 \times 10^{-3}}$	36	2.6	17	2.6	21	2×10^{-3}

all testing parameters. Current oblivious maps [2,3] build trees and obliviously traverse them, the LSH values are used to decide which child to visit. Decreasing α allows one to use a tree with a larger branching factor. This in turn decreases the number of communication rounds. So decreasing α improves efficiency even if n remains the same.

Probability of Setup Completing. Assuming ℓ to be the number of iterations for the Setup to succeed. For the setting of $\delta_{\mathtt{Far}}$, one has

$$\left(1 - \prod_{i=2}^{M} (1 - \delta_{\mathtt{Far},i})\right)^{\ell} \leq \eta$$

where η is the probability of failure. Requires that

$$\ell \geq \frac{\log(\eta)}{\log\left(1 - \prod_{i=2}^{M}(1 - \delta_{\mathtt{Far},i})\right)}.$$

For our choice of parameters $\delta_{\mathtt{Far}}$, and n, we always have $1 - \prod_{i=2}^{M}(1 - \delta_{\mathtt{Far},i}) \approx 0$.

This behavior held true regardless of the size of the dataset, giving evidence that $\ell = 1$ suffices. We note that we performed this computation with floating point arithmetic and its known inaccuracies. For our implementation, Sect. 5, we do observe parameters where setup takes a multiple ≤ 10 iterations to succeed.

B Correctness Proofs

B.1 Proof of Lemma 1

Proof. Let x, x^* be two values where $\mathcal{D}(x, x^*) \leq t$. One has

$$\forall j, \mathsf{Exp}[\mathsf{Match}_{j,x,x^*}] > \frac{2k}{(1-c_2)n}$$

by Eq. 3. By independence of the LSHs, Match_{x,x^*} is bounded below by a $(n, \frac{2k}{(1-c_2)n})$ binomial distribution with $\mathsf{Exp}[\mathsf{Match}_{x,x^*}] = \frac{2k}{(1-c_2)}$. Then by a standard Chernoff bound, it is true that

$$\Pr[\mathsf{Match}_{x,x^*} \leq 2k] = \Pr[\mathsf{Match}_{x,x^*} < (1-c_2)\mathsf{Exp}[\mathsf{Match}_{x,x^*}]] \quad < exp\left(\frac{-c_2^2}{2} \cdot \epsilon_{\mathtt{t}} \cdot n\right).$$

This completes the proof of Lemma 1.

B.2 Proof of Lemma 2

Proof. For each pair x, x' such that $\mathcal{D}(x, x') \geq ct$ it is true that

$$\Pr_{\mathsf{LSH} \leftarrow \mathrm{H}_{\mathtt{lsh}}}[\mathsf{LSH}(x) = \mathsf{LSH}(x')] \leq \epsilon_{\mathtt{f}}.$$

This means that $\mathsf{Match}_{\mathcal{DB},x}$ is bounded above by a $(nM, \epsilon_{\mathtt{f}})$ binomial distribution. By a standard Chernoff bound one has

$$\Pr[\mathsf{Match}_{\mathcal{DB},x} > k] = \Pr\left[\mathsf{Match}_{\mathcal{DB},x} > (1+c_1)\mathsf{Exp}[\mathsf{Match}_{x,\mathcal{DB}}]\right] \leq exp\left(\frac{-c_1^2}{2+c_1} \cdot \epsilon_{\mathtt{f}} \cdot n \cdot M\right)$$

This completes the proof of Lemma 2.

B.3 Proof of Lemma 3

Detailed Methodology

Proof. Let $(x_1, ..., x_M) = \mathcal{DB}$ For all $x_i \in \mathcal{DB}$ define $\mathcal{DB}_{x_i} = x_1, ..., x_{i-1}$. By the (c, t)-well-spread condition of $\mathcal{DB}$ and Lemma 2 it is true that

$$\Pr\left[\mathsf{Match}_{\mathcal{DB}_{x_i}, x_i} \geq k\right] \leq \delta_{\mathtt{Far},i}.$$

Setup succeeds in an iteration if it is true for all $x_i \in \mathcal{DB}$ that $\mathsf{Match}_{\mathcal{DB}_{x_i}, x_i} < k$. Let 1_{x_i} be an indicator random variable where $1_{x_i} = 1$ if $\mathsf{Match}_{\mathcal{DB}_{x_i}, x_i} < k$. Then

$$\Pr\left[\sum_{i=2}^{M} 1_{x_i} = 0\right] \geq \prod_{i=2}^{M}(1 - \Pr[\mathsf{Match}_{\mathcal{DB}_{x_i}, x_i} \geq k]).$$

So the chance that an iteration of setup fails is at most

$$\Pr\left[\sum_{x_i} 1_{x_i} > 0\right] \leq 1 - \prod_{i=2}^{M}(1 - \Pr[\mathsf{Match}_{\mathcal{DB}_{x_i}, x_i} \geq k]).$$

The chance that all ℓ iterations fail is then at most

$$\left(1 - \prod_{i=2}^{M}(1 - \Pr[\mathsf{Match}_{\mathcal{DB}_{x_i}, x_i} \geq k])\right)^{\ell}.$$

This completes the proof of Lemma 3.

References

1. Mehmet Kuzu, Mohammad Saiful Islam, and Murat Kantarcioglu. Efficient similarity search over encrypted data. In *IEEE Data Engineering*, pages 1156–1167. IEEE, 2012
2. Alexandra Boldyreva and Tianxin Tang. Privacy-preserving approximate k-nearest-neighbors search that hides access, query and volume patterns. *PoPETS*, 2021
3. Julie Ha, Chloe Cachet, Luke Demarest, Sohaib Ahmad, and Benjamin Fuller. Private eyes: Zero-leakage iris searchable encryption. In *ACM Codaspy*, 2025. https://eprint.iacr.org/2023/736
4. Zhangjie, F., Xinle, W., Guan, C., Sun, X., Ren, K.: Toward efficient multi-keyword fuzzy search over encrypted outsourced data with accuracy improvement. IEEE TIFS **11**(12), 2706–2716 (2016)
5. Bing Wang, Shucheng Yu, Wenjing Lou, and Y Thomas Hou. Privacy-preserving multi-keyword fuzzy search over encrypted data in the cloud. In *IEEE INFOCOM*, pages 2112–2120. IEEE, 2014
6. Qin Liu, Yu., Peng, J.W., Wang, T., Wang, G.: Secure multi-keyword fuzzy searches with enhanced service quality in cloud computing. IEEE Trans. Netw. Serv. Manage. **18**(2), 2046–2062 (2020)

7. Brislawn, C.M., Bradley, J.N., Onyshczak, R.J., Hopper, T.: The FBI compression standard for digitized fingerprint images. In: Proceedings of SPIE, vol. 2847, pp. 344–355 (1996)
8. Daugman, J.: 600 million citizens of India are now enrolled with biometric ID. SPIE newsroom (2014)
9. Electronic Frontier Foundation. Mandatory national ids and biometric databases (2016)
10. Bösch, C., Hartel, P., Jonker, W., Peter, A.: A survey of provably secure searchable encryption. ACM Comput. Surv. (CSUR) **47**(2), 1–51 (2014)
11. Fuller, B., et al.: SoK: Cryptographically protected database search. In: IEEE S&P, pp. 172–191. IEEE (2017)
12. Kamara, S., Kati, A., Moataz, T., Schneider, T., Treiber, A., Yonli, M.: Sok: Cryptanalysis of encrypted search with leaker - a framework for leakage attack evaluation on real-world data. In: Euro S&P (2022)
13. Ren, K., Wang, C.: Security impact of leakage profiles: threats and countermeasures. In Searchable Encryption: From Concepts to Systems, pp. 77–105. Springer, Cham (2023). https://doi.org/10.1007/978-3-031-21377-9_5
14. Islam, M.S., Kuzu, M., Kantarcioglu, M.: Access pattern disclosure on searchable encryption: ramification, attack and mitigation. In: NDSS, vol. 20, p. 12. Citeseer (2012)
15. Kamara, S., Moataz, T.: Computationally volume-hiding structured encryption. In: Ishai, Y., Rijmen, V. (eds.) EUROCRYPT 2019. LNCS, vol. 11477, pp. 183–213. Springer, Cham (2019). https://doi.org/10.1007/978-3-030-17656-3_7
16. Indyk, P., Motwani, R.: Approximate nearest neighbors: towards removing the curse of dimensionality. In: STOC, pp. 604–613 (1998)
17. Song, D.X., Wagner, D., Perrig, A.: Practical techniques for searches on encrypted data. In: IEEE S&P, pp. 44–55. IEEE (2000)
18. Kamara, S., Moataz, T., Ohrimenko, O.: Structured encryption and leakage suppression. In: Shacham, H., Boldyreva, A. (eds.) CRYPTO 2018. LNCS, vol. 10991, pp. 339–370. Springer, Cham (2018). https://doi.org/10.1007/978-3-319-96884-1_12
19. George, M., Kamara, S., Moataz, T.: Structured encryption and dynamic leakage suppression. In: Canteaut, A., Standaert, F.-X. (eds.) EUROCRYPT 2021. LNCS, vol. 12698, pp. 370–396. Springer, Cham (2021). https://doi.org/10.1007/978-3-030-77883-5_13
20. Gui, Z., Paterson, K.G., Patranabis, S.: Rethinking searchable symmetric encryption. In: IEEE S&P (2023)
21. Ando, M., George, M.: On the cost of suppressing volume for encrypted multi-maps. In: Proceedings on Privacy Enhancing Technologies, vol. 4 (2022)
22. Amjad, G., Patel, S., Persiano, G., Yeo, K., Yung, M.: Dynamic volume-hiding encrypted multi-maps with applications to searchable encryption. PoPETS **1**, 417–436 (2023)
23. Wang, J., Sun, S.-F., Li, T., Qi, S., Chen, X.: Practical volume-hiding encrypted multi-maps with optimal overhead and beyond. In: CCS, pp. 2825–2839, New York, NY, USA. Association for Computing Machinery (2022)
24. Patel, S., Persiano, G., Yeo, K., Yung, M.: Mitigating leakage in secure cloud-hosted data structures: volume-hiding for multi-maps via hashing. In: CCS (2019)
25. Cash, D., Grubbs, P., Perry, J., Ristenpart, T.: Leakage-abuse attacks against searchable encryption. In: CCS, pp. 668–679 (2015)
26. Kellaris, G., Kollios, G., Nissim, K., O'Neill, A.: Generic attacks on secure outsourced databases. In: CCS, pp. 1329–1340 (2016)

27. Zhang, Y., Katz, J., Papamanthou, C.: All your queries are belong to us: the power of file-injection attacks on searchable encryption. In: 25th USENIX Security Symposium, pp. 707–720 (2016)
28. Grubbs, P., Lacharité, M.-S., Minaud, B., Paterson, K.G.: Pump up the volume: practical database reconstruction from volume leakage on range queries. In: CCS, pp. 315–331 (2018)
29. Grubbs, P., Lacharité, M.-S., Minaud, B., Paterson, K.G.: Learning to reconstruct: statistical learning theory and encrypted database attacks. In: 2019 IEEE Symposium on Security and Privacy (SP), pp. 1067–1083 (2019)
30. Gui, Z., Johnson, O., Warinschi, B.: Encrypted databases: new volume attacks against range queries. In: CCS, pp. 361–378 (2019)
31. Kornaropoulos, E.M., Papamanthou, C., Tamassia, R.: The state of the uniform: attacks on encrypted databases beyond the uniform query distribution. In: IEEE S&P, pp. 1223–1240 (2020)
32. Damie, M., Hahn, F., Peter, A.: A highly accurate query-recovery attack against searchable encryption using non-indexed documents. In: USENIX Security, pp. 143–160 (2021)
33. Oya, S., Kerschbaum, F.: Hiding the access pattern is not enough: exploiting search pattern leakage in searchable encryption. In: USENIX Security (2021)
34. Wang, X.S., et al.: Oblivious data structures. In: CCS (2014)
35. Gui, Z., Paterson, K.G., Patranabis, S., Warinschi, B.: SWiSSSE: system-wide security for searchable symmetric encryption. In: Proceedings on Privacy Enhancing Technologies (2024)
36. Liu, C., Zhu, L., Wang, M., Tan, Y.A.: Attacks and new construction: search pattern leakage in searchable encryption. Inf. Sci. **265**, 176–188 (2014)
37. Curtmola, R., Garay, J., Kamara, S., Ostrovsky, R.: Searchable symmetric encryption: improved definitions and efficient constructions. In: CCS, pp. 79–88 (2006)
38. Micciancio, D.: Oblivious data structures: applications to cryptography. In STOC, pp. 456–464, New York, NY, USA. Association for Computing Machinery (1997)
39. Falzon, F., Markatou, E.A., Espiritu, Z., Tamassia, R.: Range search over encrypted multi-attribute data. In: Proceedings of the VLDB Endowment **16**(4), 587–600 (2022)
40. Kumar, A., Passi, A.: Comparison and combination of iris matchers for reliable personal authentication. Pattern Recogn. **43**(3), 1016–1026 (2010)
41. Shukla, A., et al.: Cryptographic strength key derivation from the iris. In: CCS, Fuzzy Extractors are Practical (2025)
42. Fuller, B., et al.: Security and privacy assurance research (SPAR) pilot final report. Technical report, MIT Lincoln Laboratory (2015)
43. Hamlin, A., Shelat, A., Weiss, M., Wichs, D.: Multi-key searchable encryption, revisited. In: Abdalla, M., Dahab, R. (eds.) PKC 2018. LNCS, vol. 10769, pp. 95–124. Springer, Cham (2018). https://doi.org/10.1007/978-3-319-76578-5_4
44. Wang, Y., Papadopoulos, D.: Multi-user collusion-resistant searchable encryption with optimal search time. In: Asia CCS, pp. 252–264 (2021)
45. Grubbs, P., Ristenpart, T., Shmatikov, V.: Why your encrypted database is not secure. In: Proceedings of the 16th Workshop on Hot Topics in Operating Systems, pp. 162–168 (2017)
46. Wang, B., Hou, Y., Li, M.: Practical and secure nearest neighbor search on encrypted large-scale data. In: INFOCOM, pp. 1–9. IEEE (2016)
47. Wang, B., Hou, Y., Li, M.: QuickN: practical and secure nearest neighbor search on encrypted large-scale data. IEEE Trans. Cloud Comput. **10**(3), 2066–2078 (2020)

48. Kornaropoulos, E.M., Papamanthou, C., Tamassia, R.: Data recovery on encrypted databases with k-nearest neighbor query leakage. In: IEEE S&P, pp. 1033–1050. IEEE (2019)
49. Larsen, K.G., Malkin, T., Weinstein, O., Yeo, K.: Lower bounds for oblivious near-neighbor search. In: SODA, pp. 1116–1134. SIAM (2020)
50. Chen, H., Chillotti, I., Dong, Y., Poburinnaya, O., Razenshteyn, I., Riazi, M.S.: SANNS: scaling up secure approximate k-Nearest neighbors search. In: USENIX Security, pp. 2111–2128 (2020)
51. Daugman, J.: How iris recognition works. In: The Essential Guide to Image Processing, pp. 715–739. Elsevier (2009)
52. Grubbs, P., et al.: Pancake: frequency smoothing for encrypted data stores. In: 29th USENIX Security Symposium, pp. 2451–2468 (2020)
53. Boyle, E., Ishai, Y., Pass, R., Wootters, M.: Can we access a database both locally and privately? In: Kalai, Y., Reyzin, L. (eds) TCC (2), pp. 662–693. Springer, Cham (2017). https://doi.org/10.1007/978-3-319-70503-3_22
54. Ahmad, S., Fuller, B.: Unconstrained iris segmentation using convolutional neural networks. In: Carneiro, G., You, S. (eds.) ACCV 2018. LNCS, vol. 11367, pp. 450–466. Springer, Cham (2019). https://doi.org/10.1007/978-3-030-21074-8_36
55. Stefanov, E., et al.: Path ORAM: an extremely simple oblivious ram protocol. J. ACM (JACM) **65**(4), 1–26 (2018)
56. Fisch, B.A., Vo, B., Krell, F., Kumarasubramanian, A., Kolesnikov, V., Malkin, T., Bellovin, S.M.: Malicious-client security in blind seer: a scalable private DBMs. In: IEEE S&P, pp. 395–410. IEEE (2015)
57. Zhang, X., Wang, W., Xu, P., Yang, L.T., Liang, K.: High recovery with fewer injections: practical binary volumetric injection attacks against dynamic searchable encryption. In: USENIX Security, pp. 5953–5970 (2023)
58. Guruswami, V., Rudra, A., Sudan, M.: Essential Coding Theory (2022)

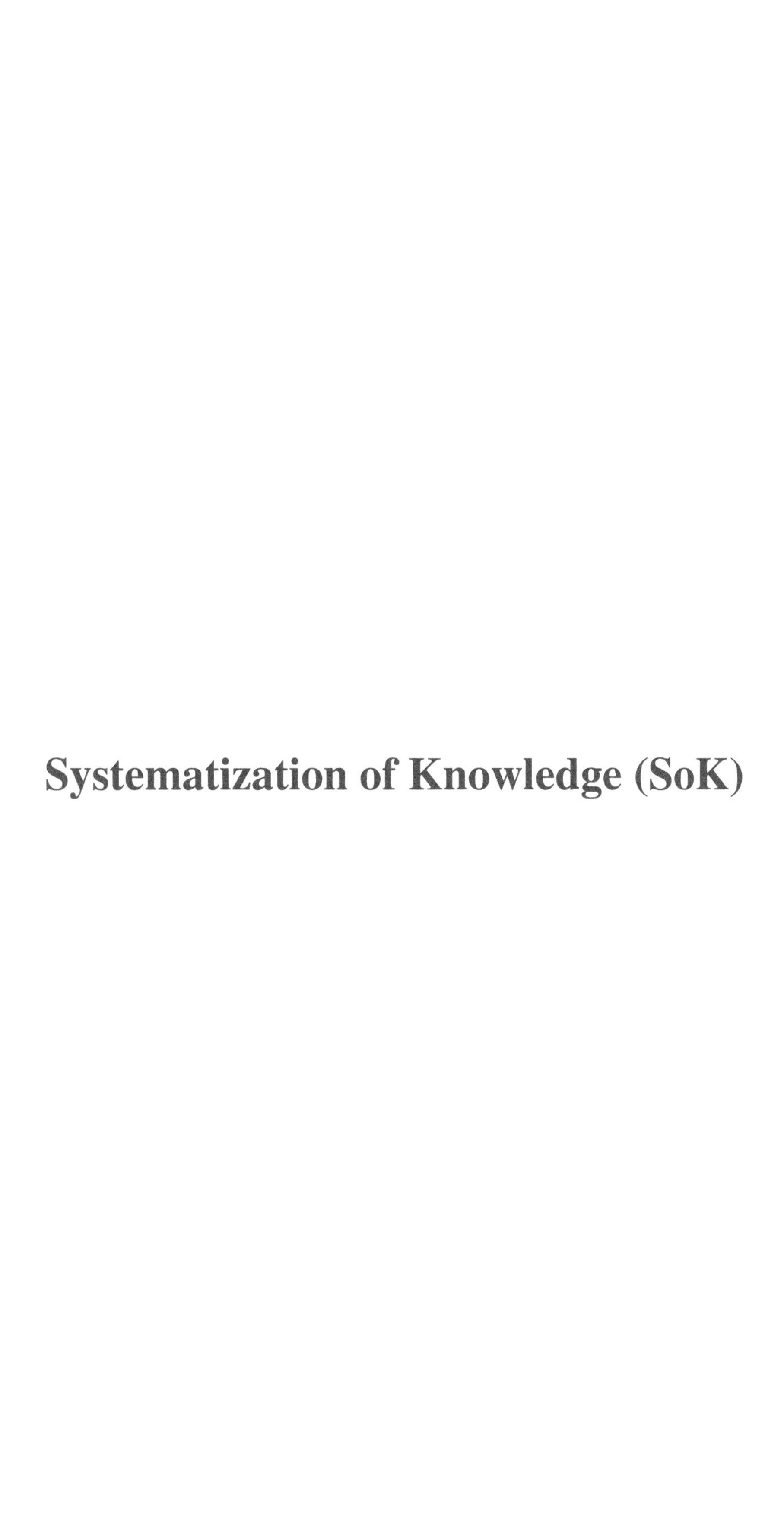

Systematization of Knowledge (SoK)

SoK: On Cryptography for Multi-cloud Storage

Dayane Horkos[1,2(✉)] and Ludovic Perret[2,3(✉)]

[1] Astran, Paris, France
dayane.horkos@astran.ai
[2] EPITA, EPITA Research Lab (LRE), Le Kremlin-Bicêtre, France
ludovic.perret@epita.fr
[3] Sorbonne Université, CNRS, LIP6, 75005 Paris, France

Abstract. This paper is a Systematization of Knowledge (SoK) on cryptography applied in Multi-Cloud Storage (MCS) schemes. Such techniques distribute and fragment data among multiple cloud providers to strengthen confidentiality, integrity, and availability compared to single-cloud deployments. Over the past decade, many cryptographic mechanisms have been proposed to secure outsourced data. However, the lack of unified framework has led to fragmented terminology, inconsistent trust assumptions, and unclear comparisons between existing protocols. In this SoK, we analyze and classify existing MCS approaches along two complementary dimensions: (*i*) their architectural trust models, and (*ii*) the cryptographic primitives they employ to achieve confidentiality, integrity, availability, access control, and auditability. This taxonomy allows us to highlight recurring design patterns, evaluate trade-offs between security and efficiency, and identify redundancies and research gaps. By unifying terminology and mapping the landscape of cryptographic techniques in MCS, this SoK provides both researchers and practitioners a structured foundation to guide future designs and deployments.

Keywords: SoK · Multi-Cloud Storage · Cryptography · Cryptographic Protocols

1 Introduction

With the growing demand for data storage, cloud solutions have become the default choice for individuals and enterprises alike, thanks to their flexibility, scalability, and low cost. However, relying on a single cloud provider raises well-known concerns about data confidentiality, integrity, and availability [29,93]. For example, outages in major providers such as AWS, Microsoft Azure, or Alibaba Cloud [48], and other real world incidents reported in [105], have repeatedly shown that entrusting data to a single entity creates a critical single point of failure and risks of vendor lock-in. As emphasized in [4], clouds should not be treated as secure vaults for cryptographic secrets, since this corresponds to sharing ownership of the underlying assets with the provider.

F. -H. Liu (Ed.): CT-RSAC 2026, LNCS 16496, pp. 65–99, 2026.
https://doi.org/10.1007/978-3-032-22931-1_3

These risks have motivated a shift towards multi-cloud (also called cloud-of-clouds or intercloud [107]), where services are distributed across multiple independent providers. From a research perspective, the concept of utilizing multiple cloud environments has evolved significantly over the past decade. Early visions framed a "cloud of clouds" as a loosely interconnected ecosystem inspired by the Internet; this concept evolved into federated cloud models [27] and intercloud frameworks with standardized protocols and fault-tolerant coordination [109,118]. In practice, systems such as RACS [3] pioneered distributing data across multiple cloud vendors to improve availability, resilience, and reduce vendor lock-in. This paradigm has moved from research to practice, with platforms like Google Anthos, Astran, Vawlt, and MultCloud enabling fragmentation, dispersion, and orchestration across heterogeneous infrastructures.

Today, Multi-Cloud Storage (MCS), broadly refers to splitting and allocating partial data across several providers to balance security, availability, cost, and performance. For instance, Yang et al. [118] model share allocation among providers as a multi-objective optimization problem that trades off trust-based security, access time, and cost. Most secure MCS schemes achieve this by fragmenting, dispersing, and cryptographically protecting data shares prior to storage. Indeed, the only robust way to prevent unauthorized access or misuse is to make such actions cryptographically impossible without possession of specific secrets, and to withhold those secrets from untrusted parties.

Despite rapid deployment of MCS, e.g. [2,17,19,28,46,66,68,75,90,97,108, 116,117], the academic literature remains fragmented. As Alqahtani et al. [7] note, there are still no standard definitions or classifications that capture the features of existing MCS models. This lack of consensus motivates the need for a systematization of knowledge (SoK) that connects architectural trust models with the cryptographic foundations that underpin security guarantees.

1.1 Related Works

Several surveys and reviews have examined cloud and multi-cloud security. Below, we position our SoK within this landscape.

Single-Cloud Security Surveys. Papers such as [47], which reviews threats and cryptographic countermeasures for cloud storage (e.g. encryption, hashing), or [51], which analyzes client-side cryptographic defenses (e.g. encryption, PDP, POR, access control), remain insufficient because they address only single-provider architectures which risk vendor lock-in.

One PrimitiveFocused Review. Since the core challenge is securely splitting data among multiple parties, secret sharing has been extensively studied as a basis for confidentiality, availability, and integrity in cloud storage [35]. Likewise, [11] surveys variants of Shamir's Secret Sharing and their applications to privacy and secure computation. In addition, [41] explores All-Or-Nothing Transforms (AONTs) for distributed storage, and [14] examines erasure coding for fault tolerance. While valuable, such works focus on isolated primitives, whereas MCS schemes integrate and combine multiple cryptographic mechanisms by finding a trade-off between security and efficiency.

Multi-cloud Architectures and Surveys. The security of MCS has garnered significant attention in the academic community. For example, AlZain et al. [10] provide an early survey that motivates the transition to multi-cloud to mitigate insider threats, outages, and vendor lock-in, and reviews initial MCS systems such as RACS, HAIL, DepSky, and ICStore. Other conceptual works, e.g., Kathuria et al. [57] and Tupe [107], further motivate multi-cloud through replication and integrity verification. Bohli et al. [22] offer one of the first structured taxonomies of multi-cloud architectures, distinguishing replication of applications, partitioning of tiers, partitioning of logic, and partitioning of data, and analyzing trade-offs among confidentiality, integrity, availability, and compliance. Other overviews, such as [44,49], focus primarily on system-level aspects like resource provisioning, elasticity, and performance. These works remain architectural and do not systematize the underlying cryptographic building blocks for storage.

Cryptography in Multi-clouds. Closer to our focus, Naik and Kannan [53] reviewed cryptographic techniques in distributed and multi-cloud settings. They proposed the Multi-Cloud Security Technique (MCST), but their evaluation was limited to performance comparisons. The protocol SeDaSC [105] discusses attribute-based encryption and proxy re-encryption for multi-cloud data sharing, but does not extend to the wide range of primitives used in storage protocols. Beyond surveys, Kapusta's PhD thesis [54] explores efficient keyless fragmentation algorithms for secure storage, highlighting performance-oriented dispersal strategies, and Ukwandu's thesis, RESCUE [106], is limited to data sharing methods in its design methodology and does not discuss architectural constructions neither the presence of a proxy. In addition, Shor et al. [98] conduct a comparative performance study of encryption and secret-sharingbased confidentiality mechanisms in multi-cloud environments, analyzing schemes such as AONT-RS, and secure RAID techniques. Their evaluation remains performance-oriented rather than taxonomic. These contributions offer valuable insights, but they do not provide a unified systematization of MCS protocols across trust models and security goals, which remains the focus of our SoK.

Limitations of Prior Surveys. In summary, while the security of multi-cloud storage has garnered increasing attention, existing surveys either *(i)* focus on single-cloud threats, *(ii)* restrict themselves to a single primitive, *(iii)* analyze architectures without systematizing the cryptographic techniques underpinning MCS protocols, or *(iv)* discuss cryptography in multi-cloud without giving a unified systematization. Table 1 compares this SoK with the previous works. We include the most representative papers from the state of the art; additional references can be found in the relevant sections.

Table 1. Positioning of related work.

References	Type	Cloud computing	Multi-cloud architecture	Cryptography	Main contribution
[47,51]	Survey	●	○	◎	Architecture of a cryptographic storage service
[11,35]	Survey	◎	◎	●	Secret sharing and its variants
[41]	Thesis	◎	◎	●	AONTs and their applications for secure distributed storage
[14]	Survey	◎	◎	●	Erasure coding in MCS
[10]	Survey	●	◎	◎	Early survey of cloud storage schemes and limitations
[57,107]	Survey	●	●	○	Early motivation for multi-cloud approach
[22]	Survey	●	●	◎	Architectural taxonomy of multi cloud storage patterns
[44,49]	Survey	●	●	○	System-level aspects of multi cloud schemes
[53]	Survey	●	●	◎	System architecture over multi clouds with some focus on cryptography
[105]	Survey	●	◎	●	Data sharing with Attribute based encryption and Proxy reencryption
[54]	Thesis	◎	◎	●	Keyless fragmentation algorithms for secure distributed storage
[106]	Thesis	◎	●	◎	Data sharing methods in MCS architecture
[98]	Evaluation	●	◎	●	Performance-oriented comparison of MCS
Our work	SoK	●	●	●	Taxonomy on distributed storage by trust model and cryptographic primitives

Legend: ● substantial coverage ◎ partial coverage ○ not addressed

1.2 Our Contributions

In this SoK, we systematize the literature on Multi-Cloud Storage (MCS) along two complementary dimensions to provide a structured analysis. First, at the architectural level, we classify schemes according to their trust model, distinguishing between systems relying on a trusted proxy (or no proxy), and systems employing an untrusted proxy, and in each case, we further differentiate between keyless and key-leveraging protocols. Second, at the cryptographic level, we analyze the techniques used to achieve the core security objectives of confidentiality, availability, and integrity, while also covering additional properties such as access control and retrievability. This two-dimensional taxonomy enables us to: *(i)* highlight recurring design patterns, *(ii)* evaluate trade-offs between security, efficiency, and deployability, and *(iii)* identify trends, redundancies, and open problems in the current landscape.

To the best of our knowledge, this is the first SoK that offers a complete picture of the cryptographic concepts already deployed – or with strong potential to be deployed – in MCS. We do not claim to exhaust all cryptographic primitives and protocols explored in this context; rather, we focus on those we consider most relevant and beneficial to the scope of this paper.

Beyond surveying existing works, our goal is twofold: *(i)* to provide a unified terminology and framework for reasoning about MCS security, and *(ii)* to guide practitioners and system designers in selecting appropriate cryptographic mechanisms and architectures according to their deployment requirements and security needs.

In summary, our work provides a comprehensive SoK that not only surveys existing MCS schemes but also bridges their underlying cryptographic foundations. By connecting architectural trust models with secure primitives, analyzing how different techniques combine to achieve confidentiality, availability, and integrity, and incorporating state-of-the-art advances, we deliver a resource that informs future research and aids practical deployment of secure multi-cloud storage.

1.3 Organization of the Paper

The remainder of this paper is structured as follows. Section 2 presents a systematization from the MCS perspective, introducing our system model, design goals, trust-based taxonomy, and key management models, as well as the security objectives typically required in these settings. Section 3 surveys the cryptographic primitives underlying MCS schemes, organized according to the security goals they support. Section 4 systemizes existing multi-cloud storage protocols, classifying them according to the assumptions defined earlier, and analyzing their trade-offs, recurring patterns, and open challenges. Finally, Sect. 5 summarizes the key findings and insights of this study.

2 System Model and Design Goals

2.1 Multi-cloud Storage

A Multi-Cloud Storage (MCS) scheme involves three entities interacting as shown in Fig. 1.

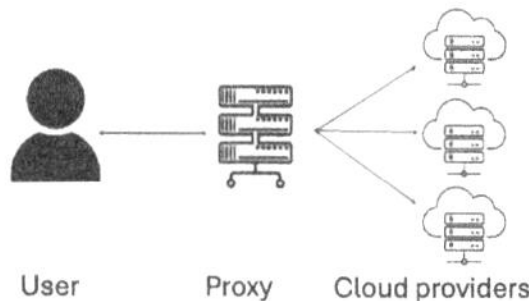

Fig. 1. Multi-Cloud Storage components.

1. *User.* An honest entity that wishes to store data securely on multiple clouds. This entity represents a logical role that may encompass data owners who upload data and authorized users who may access or retrieve stored data according to access control policies.
2. *Proxy (optional).* An optional intermediary responsible for managing cloud infrastructures, including selecting cloud providers, handling the Disperse operation, and coordinating the distribution of data across the storage network.
3. *Cloud Service Providers (CSPs).* n independent cloud providers who Receive the corresponding shares from the user or proxy and store them.

There are two phases: *upload*, where the user stores data $\mathcal{D}$ via the proxy (if present), and *download*, where the user retrieves shares from any subset of at least k CSPs and reconstructs $\mathcal{D}$.

2.2 MCS Assumptions

Trust Assumptions. Based on our research, we group MCS protocols into two main trust models that form the backbone of our taxonomy.

- *Trusted processor (user or trusted proxy).* All cryptographic operations (which aim to protect confidentiality, availability, integrity, etc.) are performed by a fully trusted entity. This entity may be the user himself (no proxy) or an external trusted proxy. It has access to plaintext data, and is trusted to behave honestly.
- *Untrusted proxy.* A middle proxy delegated the performance of heavy data processing and distribution, but is *not* trusted with plaintext or secret keys. It must be constrained by cryptographic mechanisms to prevent data exposure or tampering.

Key Management Assumptions. In addition to the trust placed in the proxy, MCS protocols differ in how they manage cryptographic secrets. We therefore distinguish two complementary key management models that cut across both trust settings.

- *Key-leveraging protocols.* These schemes assume that the trusted processor retains secret material – such as encryption keys, long-term hashes, or identity private keys.
- *Keyless protocols.* Also referred to as forgetful user models [60], where no long-term secrets are stored between upload and download by the trusted entity that handles the Process operation. During retrieval, the user may rely on transient or ephemeral secrets (e.g., short-lived tokens) to decrypt or reconstruct data.

These models determine where cryptographic responsibilities lie, and fundamentally shape how confidentiality, integrity, and availability are enforced.

2.3 Abstract MCS Interface

Based on these assumptions, we generalize a Multi-Cloud Storage (MCS) scheme with the following design goal: to modularize data preparation, distribution, and reconstruction, allowing flexibility in how roles are assigned to entities. As by the name, the system uses a single type of service provided by the CSPs: storage. Taking into account the previous literature, we define MCS as follows.

Definition 1. *A Multi-Cloud Storage (*MCS*) scheme is a tuple of probabilistic polynomial-time (ppt) algorithms,* $\Pi_{\mathsf{MCS}} = (\mathsf{Param}, \mathsf{Process}, \mathsf{Disperse}, \mathsf{Receive}, \mathsf{Retrieve}, \mathsf{Merge}, \mathsf{Rebuild})$*, that operates on data* $\mathcal{D}$*, where each function operates over system parameters and adapts based on the trust relationship between the user, the proxy, and the CSPs.*

Global Parameters

- $\mathcal{D} \in \{0,1\}^*$: *the original data to be stored.*
- *Param* $\rightarrow (\lambda, n, k)$: λ *is the security parameter and* $(k, n) \in \mathbb{N}^2$ *are the threshold parameters, where any* k *of* n *total fragments suffice for recovery. The threshold may range from minimal* ($k < n$) *to full threshold* ($k = n$) *depending on the desired confidentiality-availability trade-off.*

Upload Phase

- $\mathsf{Process}(\mathcal{D}, Param) \rightarrow (\mathcal{D}', \{s_i\}_{i=1}^n)$: *Transforms the input data* $\mathcal{D} \in \{0,1\}^*$ *into a processed form* $\mathcal{D}'$ *and auxiliary elements* $\{s_i\}$. *The* s_i *may include encrypted shares, MACs, signatures, or metadata depending on the scheme.*
- $\mathsf{Disperse}(\mathcal{D}', \{s_i\}_{i=1}^n, Param) \rightarrow \{c_i\}_{i=1}^n$: *Takes the processed data and outputs storage-specific payloads* c_i *destined for the cloud providers. Encapsulates redundancy and recoverability through secret sharing, erasure coding, or encryption.*
- $\mathsf{Receive}(c_i, aux_i) \rightarrow store_i$: *Defines how each CSP* i *handles the incoming data fragment* c_i *along with optional auxiliary metadata.*

Download Phase

- $\mathsf{Retrieve}(i) \rightarrow (c_i, aux_i)$: *Cloud provider* i *returns the stored fragment* c_i *along with auxiliary information* aux_i *(e.g., integrity metadata, encryption context, or audit proof).*
- $\mathsf{Merge}(\{c_i\}_{i\in I}, Param) \rightarrow (\mathcal{D}', \{s_i\}_{i\in I})$: *Takes any subset* $I \subseteq \{1, ..., n\}$ *with* $|I| \geq k$ *of returned fragments and reconstructs the intermediate processed data* $\mathcal{D}'$ *and associated elements* $\{s_i\}$.
- $\mathsf{Rebuild}(\mathcal{D}', \{s_i\}) \rightarrow \mathcal{D} \cup \perp$: *Recovers the original data* $\mathcal{D} \in \{0,1\}^*$ *from the merged view, or outputs* $\perp$ *in case of failure (e.g., due to corruption or insufficient fragments).*

2.4 Security Goals

Depending on the application and the protocol, the following security properties may be required.

- *Confidentiality.* No information about $\mathcal{D}$ is leaked to unauthorized sets of users.
- *Integrity.* Any modification of stored fragments is detectable during recovery.
- *Availability.* Data remains recoverable as long as at least k valid fragments remain accessible.
- *Accountability.* Faulty or malicious behavior can be traced and attributed.
- *Access Control.* Only authorized entities can get access to the data.
- *Retrievability/Auditability.* The system can prove that data is retrievable and has not been lost.

These security properties can vary depending on the tradeoffs that should be made. It is important to take into consideration both the computational security and the space efficiency parameters when implementing these solutions.

Among other properties, we can find Fork Consistency (users detect if a malicious CSP presents divergent views of the data [64,73]) and Authenticity, which allows users to verify the origin of the recovered data.

In multi-cloud settings, security guarantees are typically required to hold even when a subset of up to f cloud providers behaves arbitrarily or maliciously (i.e., under Byzantine faults). Rather than constituting a separate security goal, Byzantine Fault Tolerance $\mathsf{BFT}(f)$ characterizes the adversarial conditions under which confidentiality, integrity, availability, and accountability must be preserved, assuming a total of n providers and appropriate resilience bounds (e.g., $n \geq 3f + 1$).

Furthermore, the paper [24] introduces formal security notions for cloud storage which we do not discuss here. Other common threats in MCS environments include: data exposure or unauthorized access, data loss or manipulation, service level agreement (SLA) violations, malicious insiders at cloud providers, insecure APIs, shared-technology vulnerabilities in multi-tenant infrastructure, and weak registration processes enabling attacker-controlled accounts. We assume data is transmitted securely using encrypted channels such as TLS to prevent interception.

3 Cryptographic Primitives Used in MCS Schemes

In this section, we discuss the cryptographic primitives used in MCS schemes and we classify them based on their main security goals.

3.1 Confidentiality Primitives

We define confidentiality primitives as the building blocks that provide secrecy in an MCS scheme. The primary goal of any MCS scheme is to protect user data against untrusted proxies and cloud providers. This requires decoupling confidentiality from storage and placement decisions, ensuring that data secrecy holds regardless of how and where the data is stored. Confidentiality primitives are usually used in the Process phase of the upload (Definition 1).

Encryption. The most common method for ensuring confidentiality in MCS is encryption. The canonical choices for securing large volumes of data are Secret-Key Encryption (SKE) and Public-Key Encryption (PKE) schemes. Typical SKE algorithms include AES used with different modes of operation. For instance, CBC provides confidentiality only (and requires a separate mechanism for integrity), whereas AEADs modes such as EAX (or GCM) provide both confidentiality and integrity/authenticity, making them well-suited for modern cloud storage systems.

Earlier works also employed legacy ciphers such as 3DES; however, such constructions are no longer considered suitable for contemporary deployments due to efficiency and security limitations.

In the literature, the central challenge for SKE-based systems has consistently been the secure management and protection of the Data Encryption Key (DEK). In hybrid designs, PKE is often employed to protect these DEKs–typically through a Key Encapsulation Mechanism (KEM) that encapsulates a symmetric key, combined with a Data Encapsulation Mechanism (DEM) that encrypts the data itself [99].

Beyond conventional SKEPKE hybrids, more advanced cryptographic approaches have been explored to enhance confidentiality and flexibility, including proxy re-encryption and homomorphic encryption.

- *Proxy Re-Encryption (*PRE*).* This concept is very appealing for MCS [21] because it enables a data owner to delegate the decryption of the encrypted data to the authorized recipients by passing through a proxy. A semi-trusted proxy transforms a ciphertext for key A into one for key B without learning the plaintext. Certificate-based proxy re-encryption [71] is a new cryptographic primitive to effectively support the data confidentiality in public cloud storage, which enjoys the advantages of certificate-based encryption while providing the functionalities of proxy re-encryption.
- *Homomorphic Encryption (*HE*).* Another interesting concept in MCS [43] because it enables computations on encrypted data across different providers without revealing the underlying plaintext, thus preserving confidentiality even during processing. For example, [60] used HE to enable secure delegation of share generation and distribution to an untrusted proxy, eliminating the need for user-side keys while keeping data confidential across multiple clouds.

All-or-Nothing Transform. Introduced by Rivest in 1997 [92], an All-Or-Nothing Transform (AONT) is a keyless transformation that ensures no partial information about the input is accessible unless the entire output is available. Originally designed to increase resistance to brute-force attacks on symmetric encryption, AONTs have since been used as lightweight confidentiality layers in storage systems. A useful generalization of an AONT was introduced by [30], who suggested considering an AONT which has a two-part output: a public output that can be revealed to the adversary (similar to an encrypted data), and a secret output that has the exposure-resilience property and needs to be protected (similar to a DEK).

Definition 2. *An* AONT *is a randomized transformation* $f : \{0,1\}^* \rightarrow \{0,1\}^*$ *such that:*

- *For* $x_i \in \{0,1\}^\lambda, i = 0,\ldots,n$, *given the entire output* $f(x_0\|\cdots\|x_n) = d_0\|\cdots\|d_\ell$, $d_j \in \{0,1\}^\lambda, j = 0,\ldots,\ell$, *it is easy to recover the input* $\mathcal{D} = x_0\|\cdots\|x_n$.

- *Given all but one block of the output (the secret output), i.e., any* $\{d_j\} \in \{0,1\}^\lambda, j = 0, \ldots, \ell$ *missing, it is computationally hard to learn anything about any* $x_i \in \{0,1\}^\lambda, i = 0, \ldots, n$.

Among AONTs presented in the literature, we discuss those used to provide confidentiality in MCS.

1. AONTRP. Resch and Plank [90] introduced an AONT variant (we refer to it as AONTRP), which hides the data by encrypting it under a random key and binding the key to the ciphertext via a hash. Multiple variations of this AONT have been proposed in the literature. The secure version SAONT [120] adds stronger tags for short-plaintext security, while the convergent instantiation CAONT [65] adapts the transform for deduplication in MCS.
2. OAEP. Optimal Asymmetric Encryption Padding [16], widely used in RSA encryption, can also be viewed as an AONT. Its randomized encoding ensures that partial exposure yields no information. Boyko shows that OAEP satisfies strong AONT security notions (formalized via polynomial indistinguishability) in the random oracle model [25]. A convergent variant of OAEP has been adopted in MCS schemes such as CDStore [66].

Karame et al. [56] introduced bastion AONTs, as an extension of Stinson's information-theoretically secure AONTs [101]. This construction is fast and efficient but not keyless, it was designed to protect distributed encrypted data when the attacker has access to the encryption key. Other more general AONT constructions were presented by [41] in the context of distributed storage, with variations depending on the assumptions made about the input and output blocks. From a practical perspective, AONTs occupy an intermediate position between encryption and secret sharing. Unlike encryption, AONTs do not rely on a long-term secret key and therefore avoid key-management overhead; however, their confidentiality guarantees rely on the assumption that at least one output block remains unavailable to the adversary. Unlike secret sharing, AONTs incur minimal storage overhead and are computationally lightweight, but they do not tolerate the permanent loss of output blocks. As a result, AONTs are often combined with erasure coding to balance confidentiality, availability, and efficiency.

3.2 Confidentiality and Access Control Primitives

Some primitives, which are also usually used in the Process phase, simultaneously enforce confidentiality and fine-grained access control; we discuss them separately here.

1. *Attribute-Based Encryption (*ABE*).* It is a cryptographic primitive that enables fine-grained access control over encrypted data. Decryption succeeds only if the attributes associated with a user's secret key satisfy the policy embedded in the system.

   In CP-ABE (Ciphertext-Policy ABE), the user defines an attribute-based

access policy which is embedded into the ciphertext. In MCS, CP-ABE eases data sharing among cloud providers, as a user can specify whom they share the file with directly within the file using the access policy [42,121].
In contrast, KP-ABE (Key-Policy ABE) reverses this mapping by embedding access policies into users' keys rather than into the ciphertext [77].
MA-ABE (Multi-Authority ABE), removes the single point of trust by distributing attribute issuance across multiple authorities. This is especially important in multi-organizational scenarios, where no single entity should hold complete control over access management [77].
2. *Identity-Based Encryption (*IBE*).* It is a public-key encryption scheme in which public keys are arbitrary strings, such as email addresses, user roles, or time-bound tags. A Private Key Generator (PKG) issues secret keys corresponding to these identities. In MCS, IBE can be used to encrypt sensitive components directly to a user's identity, simplifying key management.
However, classical single-authority IBE schemes inherently exhibit a key escrow property, as the PKG can derive all users' private keys, which is undesirable in untrusted cloud settings. Variants based on distributed PKGs have been proposed to mitigate this limitation.
An extension of IBE is IBBE (Identity-Based Broadcast Encryption), where a symmetric secret is encrypted once to a set of identities (a group of authorized users), and each participant can independently decrypt using their identity-derived key [100].
3. *Multi-Key Encryption (*MKE*).* It allows a ciphertext encrypted under multiple public keys to be jointly decrypted only if all corresponding secret keys participate, thereby requiring collaborative cooperation for successful decryption [60].

The importance of using both ABE and PRE in MCS was discussed in detail in [105].

3.3 Confidentiality and Availability Primitives

This part focuses on cryptographic primitives that simultaneously ensure confidentiality and availability, typically through distributed trust. While such primitives offer strong guarantees, they are generally too expensive (computationally or storage) to be applied to entire datasets. Instead, they are most often used to protect small but critical components (and thus used in the Process phase) [8,70,98], such as DEKs or secret AONT outputs, which must remain both secret and recoverable even in the face of partial compromise or cloud outages [81]. When secure local storage is not feasible, distributing these secrets across multiple clouds using threshold mechanisms becomes a robust alternative.

Threshold Secret Sharing. A (k, n)-threshold secret sharing scheme distributes a secret into n shares, such that any k suffice to reconstruct the secret (*recoverability*), while any subset of fewer than k reveals negligible or no information (*privacy*).

Secret sharing can be broadly classified into perfect secret sharing (PSS), which offers information-theoretic privacy–unauthorized subsets learn no information about the secret–and computational secret sharing (CSS), which ensures privacy under standard cryptographic assumptions, allowing only negligible leakage.

In practice, most PSS-based MCS systems rely on a small set of well-established constructions. Shamir's secret sharing scheme (SSS) [95], based on polynomial interpolation, is by far the most widely used and commonly employed in practice (e.g., SSMS [59]) to protect DEKs. An alternative family of PSS schemes is based on the Chinese Remainder Theorem (CRT), such as the AsmuthBloom and Mignotte schemes [87], which offer different algebraic instantiations with comparable security guarantees. Blakley's scheme [20], which relies on hyperplane geometry, is less efficient and rarely used in practice.

Beyond these canonical constructions, a number of variants have been proposed to address specific optimizations or architectural concerns. Examples include PRESS [78], a recursive variant of Shamir's scheme that reduces storage overhead, and LASS (Latin-Square-Autotopism Secret Sharing) [117], which derives deterministically constructed keys to improve key management.

Secret sharing schemes offer strong security guarantees, but they incur high storage and computational costs, since each share is typically the size of the original secret. Consequently, they are applied in MCS primarily to protect small but critical secrets, while broader data availability is usually ensured via more efficient primitives such as information dispersal algorithms (discussed in the next section).

Secret sharing schemes can be generalized by Ramp Schemes [20] by introducing a tunable privacy threshold. A (ℓ, k, n) ramp scheme guarantees that: (1) the secret can be reconstructed from any k or more shares, and (2) any set of ℓ or fewer shares reveals no information about the secret. For sets of shares between ℓ and k, partial information leakage may occur, making ramp schemes suitable for applications where strict secrecy can be relaxed in favor of reduced share sizes or improved performance. These schemes interpolate between the two extremes:

- When $\ell = k$, we recover a standard perfect threshold secret sharing scheme.
- When $\ell = 0$, the scheme behaves like an information dispersal algorithm (IDA) with no secrecy guarantees.

3.4 Availability Primitives

Ensuring availability in MCS typically requires introducing redundancy, so that data remains accessible even in the presence of outages or failures. This is distinct from threshold secret sharing, which also guarantees availability but does so through distributed trust rather than redundancy. Redundancy can be achieved in different ways, the most common being replication, parity, and erasure codes.

A comparison of the main cryptographic primitives used to guarantee availability in MCS (PSS and IDA) is provided in Table 2.

Replication, Parity and RAID. Replication and parity-based schemes are fundamental techniques to ensure availability in storage systems. Replication duplicates data across multiple nodes or cloud providers, allowing retrieval as long as one copy remains accessible; it provides fast recovery and minimal decoding overhead but incurs significant storage costs. Parity-based methods, such as those used in RAID systems, achieve fault tolerance more efficiently by storing parity blocks–often computed as XOR combinations of data blocks–to enable error detection without full duplication. Originally designed for local disks, these mechanisms inspired early multi-cloud storage schemes, where parity offered lightweight redundancy with lower overhead than full replication.

More advanced approaches generalize these ideas by adding error correction into *information dispersal algorithms* (IDAs), which we discuss in the following section. Weatherspoon and Kubiatowicz [111] showed that erasure-coded storage achieves far greater durability than replication with roughly an order of magnitude less storage and bandwidth, motivating the adoption of coding-based redundancy in modern multi-cloud systems.

Information Dispersal Algorithms. To achieve stronger trade-offs between reliability and efficiency, Information Dispersal Algorithms (IDAs) were introduced, underpinned by erasure coding [84]. IDAs split data into n fragments such that any k suffice for reconstruction, offering configurable resilience with much lower storage overhead than replication. In MCS, they are particularly suited for distributing large datasets where confidentiality is ensured by other means, since IDAs by themselves do not provide secrecy as discussed in the previous section.

The first IDA was proposed by Rabin [88], and many variants have since been developed. Key families include:

- *ReedSolomon* (RS) *Codes* [90]. Classical Maximum Distance Separable (MDS) codes, guaranteeing recovery from any k fragments and achieving optimal storage efficiency for a given level of fault tolerance. Systematic RS codes are widely deployed; while partial collections of fragments may reveal linear information about the data (often described as a linear ramp leakage profile [36]).
- *Cauchy-ReedSolomon (*CRS*) Codes* [61]. An optimized RS variant replacing expensive finite-field multiplications with XOR operations, practical for storage systems.
- *Luby Transform (*LT*) and Raptor Codes* [15,31]. Beyond classical MDS codes, near-optimal erasure codes such as Tornado or Raptor codes reduce encoding cost at the expense of needing slightly more than k (i.e., $(1+\epsilon)k$) fragments for decoding. Rateless codes (LT, Raptor) are particularly suited for streaming or unpredictable environments, though with more complex decoding. They trade MDS guarantees for flexibility and low encoding cost, making them attractive in cooperative or large-scale MCS settings.

Beyond these, High-Speed Resilient Coding (HSRC) [68] and Privacy-Protecting Codes (PPC) [97] target fast encoding and repair but offer weak confidentiality; Zigzag (NZZD) codes [115] reduce decoding/repair complexity; XOR-based designs (e.g., WEAVER [1]) improve repair efficiency with reduced storage efficiency. In addition, LWE-based proposals [119] explore post-quantum dispersal using lattice-based constructions. Unlike classical IDAs, these schemes integrate confidentiality directly into the dispersal process by relying on the hardness of the Learning With Errors problem, while simultaneously providing availability through coding-based redundancy. We discuss them here since their primary mechanism is data dispersal for fault tolerance.

To curb repair bandwidth, regenerating codes [40] use network coding to minimize transfer during node repair – NCCloud [46] is a practical example. A recent work optimizes code parameters and placement across providers [45].

Another coding approach employed in multi-cloud storage is based on Redundant Residue Number Systems (RRNS). It splits data into residues with respect to multiple pairwise coprime moduli and introduces redundancy by adding extra moduli. This enables both error detection and correction in case some residues are corrupted or lost, thereby strengthening availability and even integrity. In MCS settings, RRNS has been combined with modular secret sharing [104] and hybrid storage systems [33] to provide resilience against malicious providers while maintaining efficient reconstruction.

Finally, coding techniques are often combined with other mechanisms – such as auditing, redundancy monitoring, and intruder detection – to provide a complete availability layer.

Table 2. Comparison between PSS and IDA.

Property	PSS	IDA
Trait	Information-theoretic confidentiality	Space efficiency
Purpose	Distribute shares of a secret	Disperse data blocks
Main methods	Polynomial interpolation, CRT, etc.	Erasure coding (e.g. RS codes)
Share size	$\lvert\mathcal{D}_i\rvert = \lvert\mathcal{D}\rvert$	$\lvert\mathcal{D}_i\rvert = \lvert\mathcal{D}\rvert/k$
Representative schemes	Shamir's (SSS) [95]	Rabin's IDA [88]

3.5 Integrity Primitives

To ensure that outsourced data has not been altered or tampered with, MCS schemes integrate cryptographic mechanisms for integrity verification. These primitives provide assurance that the data retrieved is exactly what was originally stored. The most common approaches include Message Authentication Codes (MAC) used in symmetric-key settings, and Digital Signature Algorithms (DSA), such as EdDSA, used in public-key settings.

Beyond these standard primitives, several lightweight techniques can also strengthen integrity guarantees. Examples include embedding canaries (known check values) inside the data [90], storing and verifying cryptographic hashes of data blocks or slices [66], and re-checking consistency by attempting reconstruction with $k+1$ shares instead of exactly k in threshold-based schemes [97]. Such approaches provide simple yet effective safeguards that complement stronger cryptographic mechanisms.

3.6 Integrity and Auditability Primitives

Integrity and auditability primitives enable the client to detect any data corruption or tampering by cloud providers and to verify that the stored data is still retrievable without downloading it in full. These primitives typically require the client to embed additional verification metadata into the data before outsourcing it, and then periodically challenge the servers to produce cryptographic proofs of correct storage. The three main classes are:

- *Proofs of Data Possession (*PDP*)* [23]. Allow a client to verify that a server still possesses the original data blocks without retrieving them, by checking the correctness of responses to random spot-check challenges.
- *Proofs of Retrievability (*POR*)* [23]. Extend PDP by ensuring not only that data blocks are present, but also that the entire file can be reconstructed with high probability from the challenged blocks.
- *Blockchain-based Protocols.* Recent approaches leverage smart contracts and distributed verifiers to remove reliance on a single third-party auditor (TPA). For example, Witanto et al. [113] use ZSS signatures and bilinear pairings for block-level proofs, with verification tasks distributed across multiple auditors coordinated through blockchain. This ensures transparency, batch verification, and stronger auditability guarantees in multi-cloud settings.

Such techniques are widely used in MCS schemes to provide strong integrity and retrievability guarantees without compromising efficiency.

Beyond the basic PDP and POR classes, several refinements have been proposed for multi-cloud settings. For example, Blockchain-Assisted Multi-Copy PDP [76] and Identity-Based Multi-Copy PDP [63] extend PDP to scenarios where multiple replicas of data are distributed across clouds.

In addition, several dedicated public auditing protocols enable integrity verification by external entities. A common setting introduces a trusted TPA that performs verification on behalf of the client. For instance, Wang et al. [96] propose a dynamic auditing scheme based on BLS homomorphic authenticators, allowing the TPA to verify data integrity without accessing its content. While such protocols provide strong auditability guarantees and relieve clients from performing integrity checks, they rely on pairing-based cryptography, which incurs non-trivial computational costs and is not considered post-quantum secure.

3.7 Integrity, Retrievability, and Accountability Primitives

Beyond ensuring that outsourced data remains intact and recoverable, different cryptographic primitives extend it to accountability by enabling attribution of misbehavior. While PDP and POR detect data loss or tampering, they do not by themselves provide binding evidence of which party misbehaved. Accountability requires primitives that allow such attribution:

- *Commitment Schemes.* Let a storage provider commit to specific data or metadata in a binding and verifiable way, ensuring any deviation can be cryptographically proven.
- *Blockchain Audit Logs.* As in [117], recording audit results on-chain enables transparent accountability, since misbehavior can be publicly verified and traced back to the responsible provider (Nap Checks).

3.8 Byzantine Fault Tolerance (BFT)

While redundancy, coding, and cryptographic proofs ensure data availability and integrity, they typically assume that most providers behave honestly. To resist fail-stop events or even active attacks without service interruption or loss of data integrity, secret sharing and other primitives should be combined with Byzantine agreement protocols [38,109]. Consensus protocols such as PBFT [32] or other quorum-based systems [72] guarantee consistency and liveness as long as a threshold of providers are honest, while SUNDR [73], introduced fork consistency for detecting equivocation in untrusted storage. While not a cryptographic primitive per se, BFT complements MCS security goals by ensuring consistency and availability in adversarial settings, often relying on digital signatures or threshold signatures to authenticate protocol messages.

4 MCS Protocols

In this part, we survey the state of the art across the main categories of trusted and untrusted proxy models, emphasizing how different works combine cryptographic primitives to achieve their respective security goals under their security model's trust assumptions.

The first subsection assumes the presence of a trusted processor, either the user himself or a trusted proxy, which represents the most extensively studied setting in the literature. We divide it into two parts: keyless and key-leveraging protocols. Within the keyless category, we further distinguish three categories: keyless by construction, keyless by separation, and keyless by masking. We then discuss key-leveraging protocols, which rely either on long-term secret keys, or on identity keys.

The second subsection explores systems involving an untrusted proxy, a model that remains less explored yet particularly relevant for practical MCS settings. We also divide this part into key-leveraging and keyless protocols and discuss the ambiguity often found in their underlying trust and security assumptions, proposing directions for extending them toward more realistic untrusted-processor settings. We summarize the advantages and limitations of each family.

As our SoK reveals, the majority of works assume a trusted processor; only a handful explore untrusted proxy models. Table 3 presents a comparative overview of representative protocols, where we specify for each scheme whether a proxy is used, if so whether it is trusted, what is its key management model, what mechanisms it uses to ensure confidentiality, availability, data integrity, as well as any additional security guarantees it provides.

Table 3. Comparison of cryptography in the most representative MCS schemes.

Paper	Protocol	Trusted	Keyless	Confidentiality	Availability	Integrity	Other security properties
[91]	Pond	-	✓	✗	IDA (CRS)	BFT protocols	BFT
[17]	Depsky	-	✓	SKE, PSS	IDA, PSS	Digests of slices	Accountability, BFT
[108]	Hybris	-	✗	SKE (AES)	IDA (RS)	Digests of slices	BFT
[112]	Tahoe	-	✗	SKE (AES)	IDA (RS)	Merkle Trees, DSA	Access Control
[121]	ABE-DSC	-	✗	CP-ABE	✗	✗	Access Control
[3]	RACS	✓	✓	✗	RAID or IDA (RS)	✗	-
[23]	HAIL	-	✓	✗	RAID	PDP, POR	Retrievability
[90]	AONT-RS	-	✓	AONT (AONTRP)	IDA (RS)	Canary	-
[28]	ICStore	-	✓	SKE, PSS	Replication or RAID	DSA on roots of hash trees	BFT
[50]	SecReS	✓	✓	CSKE, PSS	IDA (RS)	Merkle Trees	Access Control
[103]	SDSMC	-	✗	SKE (AES)	Replication	Index-based slices	-
[117]	Gecko	-	✗	CSKE, PSS (LASS)	IDA (RS)	Blockchain (NAP-check)	Accountability, Retrievability
[2]	POMS	✗	✓	SKE, CP-ABE	POR-encoded shares	IBS, POR	Access Control, Auditability, Retrievability
[77]	HealthShare	-	✗	KP-ABE, MA-ABE	Replication	DSA	Access Control
[42]	ABESS	✗	✗	CP-ABE, PSS	IDA, Replication	DSA, HMAC	Access Control, Accountability
[78]	SCUD	-	✓	PSS (PRESS)	PSS	DSA (ECDSA)	-
[66]	CDStore	-	✓	CAONT (COAEP)	IDA (RS)	Digests of slices	-
[46]	NCCloud	✓	✓	✗	IDA (F – MSR)	Redundancy checks	-
[116]	CloudSeal	✗	✗	SKE, PRE	-	-	Access Control, Broadcast revocation (SSS)
[31]	LTCS	✓	✗	SKE (AES)	IDA (LT)	Integrity check protocol	Auditability
[97]	CloudS	✓	✓	PCE	PPC	Redundancy checks	-
[119]	SWE	✓	✗	LWE hardness	LWE redundancy	Redundancy checks	-
[60]	KAPRE	✗	✓	SKE, HPRE, PKE, PSS	IDA, PSS	auth enc, commitment HPRF	Accountability
[60]	KAME	✗	✓	SKE, HMKE, PKE, PSS	IDA, PSS	auth enc, commitment HPRF	Accountability

4.1 Trusted Proxy

We consider two approaches which seem semantically similar: either the user trusts a third party delegate, the proxy, to perform the Process/Disperse operations during the upload, or the user himself performs these same operations. The goal of an MCS scheme in this case is to provide security against a coalition of $k-1$ cloud providers. Many protocols were proposed in the literature to achieve this goal.

Keyless Approaches. They are divided into three important categories: the first one focuses on protocols that are by construction keyless, we remark that they are generally based on only one primitive, the second category involves protocols that distribute the key separately from the ciphertext to give the keyless aspect to the scheme, and the third category discusses schemes that encapsulate and hide the key within the ciphertext.

Keyless by Construction. This first part discusses schemes that do not rely on encryption and thus are keyless by construction. We divide this category into two subcategories.

1. The first one involves MCS schemes that use IDAs, mainly focus on availability, and do not guarantee semantic security (weak to no confidentiality), e.g. [3,23,39,46,55,68,82,91,110].

   Representative schemes. The OceanStore prototype, known as Pond [91], was among the first multi-cloud storage systems to combine erasure coding (using CRS codes) with BFT consensus, ensuring durability and consistency even in hostile environments. Subsequently, the Redundant Array of Cloud Storage (RACS) system [3] demonstrated the feasibility of distributing erasure-coded data across multiple providers to mitigate vendor lock-in. In RACS, a trusted proxy splits objects into chunks, adds redundancy via RAID or RS coding, and disperses the resulting shares among providers; multiple cooperating proxies can also be deployed to avoid single points of failure. Building on this concept, the MCS Scalia [82] introduced optimization-driven orchestration, dynamically adapting data placement to meet cost, durability, and availability objectives through a hardwaresoftware integration running on customer premises. The High-Availability and Integrity Layer (HAIL) scheme [23] further extended the focus to integrity, combining replication with proofs of data possession and proofs of retrievability to verify that redundant fragments remain intact across clouds. The protocol CYRUS [39] is a client-operated MCS that chunks data using Rabin's fingerprinting and uses non systematic RS coding. They claim it is implemented as a (t, n) CSS scheme but the guarantees are only true for a limited number of colluding providers (because confidentiality is partial). This method adds adaptive CSP selection, and supports deduplication and multi-client synchronization. The Network-Coded Cloud (NCCloud) [46] improved repair efficiency through functional minimum-storage regenerating ($\mathsf{F}-\mathsf{MSR}$) codes, reducing repair bandwidth while maintaining double-fault tolerance via the MDS property. The DDFM scheme [110] introduces a Granular Data Fragmentation Strategy (based on Granular Computing) to split files into variable-sized fragments, which are then dispersed redundantly across clouds. In addition, DDFM integrates system-level access-control protocols (OpenID, OAuth) for authentication and authorization. The InterCloud RAIDer scheme [68] proposed a fully client-side design that employs High-Speed Resilient Coding (HSRC) for redundancy and a lightweight proof of data-possession mechanism derived from deduplication hashes, providing strong availability and moderate confidentiality without relying on a proxy. Finally, Katarzyna et al. [55] propose a fast fragmentation algorithm that combines ideas from secret sharing and information dispersal. This method emphasizes performance: it disperses, permutes and then encodes data, while availability is guaranteed through erasure codes.

Advantages and limitations. These protocols are typically lightweight and efficient, as they avoid expensive cryptographic operations such as encryption or key management. They achieve high availability and fault tolerance through erasure coding or replication. Such approaches highlight a trend toward optimizing MCS for speed and scalability rather than relying solely on heavy encryption or secret sharing techniques. The main drawback of these schemes is their lack of semantic confidentiality, since data fragments are only encoded, a subset of providers may still learn partial information. They assume an honest-but-curious or non-colluding model, which weakens protection against insider threats.

2. The second subcategory includes schemes that leverage secret sharing [5,8,9, 12,26,70,78,80,102,104] to jointly guarantee confidentiality and availability without relying on encryption keys.

   Representative schemes. Several MCS schemes [5,8,9] directly adopt Shamir's Secret Sharing (SSS) as their core primitive to ensure confidentiality, integrity, and availability. Protocols such as FVSS [12], Belisarius [80], ARCHISTAR [70] and the work of [118], extend basic secret sharing with efficient verifiability, Byzantine fault tolerance, access control, and trust-optimizing allocation respectively. The protocol SCUD [78] achieves information-theoretic confidentiality via PRESS – a recursive variant of SSS that reduces space inefficiency – complemented by ECDSA signatures for integrity and replication for availability. Potshards [102] combines a full threshold SSS with RAID-style striping for availability but is very inefficient. Other efforts attempt to address architectural enhancements. For instance, SAFE [26] performs share generation and renewal inside a Trusted Execution Environment (TEE) to improve security management. However, this approach reintroduces centralized trust in hardware, weakening the decentralization and openness that multi-cloud cryptographic designs typically aim to preserve. Tchernykh et al. [104] further explore the use of PSS by integrating modular secret sharing (Asmuth-Bloom and Mignotte) with Redundant Residue Number Systems (RRNS) for error detection and correction. Their framework combines threshold-based confidentiality with reliability, demonstrating how secret sharing can be augmented with redundancy to enhance integrity and fault tolerance.

   Advantages and Limitations. These schemes provide information-theoric confidentiality and high availability. They are also fast on small to medium files. While these systems demonstrate the simplicity of direct secret sharing, they suffer from significant storage overhead which limits scalability for large datasets.

Keyless by Separation. These protocols usually rely on a combination of encryption and IDA for guaranteeing the confidentiality and availability of the data, and rely on secret sharing for securing the key, which creates a tradeoff between security, computation and space.

Representative Schemes. The SSMS (Secret Sharing Made Short) cryptographic method, also known as HK1 [59] was introduced by Hugo Krawczyk and became a foundational design pattern for secure MCS, also called computational secret sharing (CSS). It combines SKE with PSS and IDAs to balance efficiency and security: data is first encrypted with a symmetric key, the key is secret-shared among the providers, and the ciphertext is erasure-coded. This hybrid approach minimizes the overhead of secret sharing while retaining its confidentiality guarantees. It was later extended to a robust version called RCSS [94] by using commitment schemes. It has been widely adopted in the world of cloud storage. The SSMS protocol was applied by Bessani et al. in DepSky [17] for fault-tolerant file storage, later extended in SCFS [18] as a file system abstraction adding deduplication and auditing, and redesigned for efficiency and retrievability in CHARON [75]. Variants of this design also appear in works like [79] for their privacy management system, which adds hash-based integrity checks and BFT security, and [52] which adds SSS for user authentication tokens. Another extension of the SSMS model is SecSFE [62], which targets medical data by adding a preliminary fragmentation step before encryption and secret sharing, and incorporates SHA $-$ 1 signatures with TPA-based auditing for integrity verification. In addition, [122] propose a framework to secure cloud computing by integrating Fully Homomorphic Encryption into Depsky's storage architecture. Its adds a parallelized processing dispatcher to perform computations directly on encrypted data without decryption. This approach enhances confidentiality by keeping data encrypted end-to-end, improves integrity through DepSky's Byzantine fault-tolerant design, and maintains high availability by replicating encoded blocks across multiple clouds. Unlike traditional SSMS schemes that generate keys randomly, the protocol Gecko [117] employs Latin-square Autotopism Secret Sharing (LASS) to secret-share a deterministically constructed key derived from an autotopism, providing a higher level of key protection, but without fault tolerance in the secret-sharing layer. To strengthen integrity, Gecko integrates a blockchain-based audit mechanism: a protocol called NAP-check verifies downloaded slices and pinpoints corrupted ones. SecReS [50] extends the SSMS design pattern in the same way by integrating convergent encryption. Integrity and proof of ownership are guaranteed using Merkle hash trees that allow block-level verification and secure deduplication. Cachin et al. proposed ICStore [28], a dependable intercloud storage system designed to provide confidentiality, integrity, reliability, and consistency (CIRC). ICStore encrypts data with SKE, protects the encryption key using SSS, and verifies integrity through DSA on the roots of per-file hash trees. For reliability, it employs a redundancy layer that can use either replication (high cost but simple) or erasure coding similar to RAID-5 as in RACS or HAIL. To tolerate arbitrary faults among providers, ICStore integrates BFT protocols to maintain consistency during updates, ensuring correct operation even if some clouds behave maliciously.

Advantages and Limitations. These schemes have been widely deployed in practice and offer significantly better performance than pure secret-sharingbased approaches for large datasets at the cost of relying on computational rather than information-theoretic security. However, they still require a trusted proxy or client to perform key generation, encryption, and dispersal correctly. Moreover, in order to retrieve the data, trusted processors must perform a 2-step reconstruction: they first reconstruct the key from distributed shares, then use it to decrypt the reconstructed ciphertext.

Keyless by Masking. This part discusses schemes that hide the key within the ciphertext and then ensure its availability via IDAs. The most common way to do that and ensure confidentiality of the data and the key is by using AONTs.

Representative Schemes. One of the earliest and most widely adopted AONT-based MCS systems is AONT-RS, it serves as the core of several industrial solutions (e.g., Astran, Cleversafe). The scheme was first introduced by Resch and Plank [90], who combined an All-Or-Nothing Transform (AONT) with ReedSolomon (RS) erasure coding to achieve an efficient and secure storage scheme: the AONT provides confidentiality while RS coding ensures availability. Over time, several variants have been proposed to improve different aspects of security and performance. Lahkar et al. [61] proposed AONT-CRS, replacing RS with Cauchy ReedSolomon (CRS) codes to improve encoding and decoding performance. Inspired by convergent encryption, [65] introduced CAONT-RS, which replaces the random key of the AONT with a deterministic hash of the data so that identical files produce identical encoded fragments, enabling cross-user deduplication–a property absent from random-key schemes. Similarly, CDStore [66] applied CAONT-RS by combining OAEP-based AONT with RS coding under the same convergent principle. To strengthen integrity and recoverability, Chen et al. [37] presented RAONT-RS, which integrates commitment schemes to detect corruption and support accountability, replacing the earlier canary-based approach. More recently, [120] proposed SAONT-RS, which introduces an improved AONT and couples it with erasure coding to securely and efficiently handle large data. SAONT-RS addresses several limitations of earlier designs. Other variants explore alternative coding layers. For example, the paper [15] proposed AONT-LT, which combines AONT with Luby Transform (LT) codes. As discussed earlier, LT codes offer high flexibility and low encoding cost, making them a strong alternative to RS, especially when the threshold parameter k is large. In 2019, [115] introduced AONT-NZZD, which pairs an AONT (similar to Rivest's but using hashing instead of encryption) with NZZD erasure coding. AONT-NZZD claims higher performance, while addressing several weaknesses of AONT-RS in terms of reliability, confidentiality, and recoverability.
As an alternative to AONT-IDA approaches, the article [97] introduced CloudS, which follows the same protocol semantic by using a primitive that hides the key within the cipher. It introduces Privacy Protecting Codes (PPC), and combines them with a novel Parallel Cyclic Encryption (PCE) scheme. PPC is first applied to disperse data and achieve availability with low storage and computational overhead, and PCE encrypts each chunk with a random key and hides this key inside another chunk, eliminating centralized key

management. The combined PCEPPC scheme achieves similar security to AONTRS and better performance depending on the threshold parameter k.

Advantages and limitations. AONT-based schemes provide computational confidentiality without requiring explicit key management as the encryption key is embedded within the transformed data. These schemes are efficient, stateless, and well-suited for large-scale storage, which explains their adoption in several industrial systems. However, they lack formal modeling of AONT constructions under rigorous adversarial settings, and do not address an untrusted proxy model.

Key-Leveraging Protocols. In this part, we present the protocols that assume the presence of a stored secret on the user's or proxy's side. These schemes generally assume that the user or proxy maintains secret information, including encryption keys, persistent hashes, or identity-proving private keys.

1. The first group of protocols assume that the data owner manages secrets like encryption keys or high value small data.

   Representative schemes. Early schemes like [19,83,103,121,123] focused solely on confidentiality, without providing availability guarantees. For instance, the schemes SDSMC [103] and the one in [83] employ simple data chunking with AES encryption, while integrity is ensured through index-based slicing and hashing, respectively. [123] introduces an authentication and confidentiality mechanism based on homomorphic encryption to protect outsourced data against unauthorized access.
   Other protocols combine encryption with IDAs to add availability. For example, Celesti et al. [34] demonstrate how multi-cloud systems can integrate client-side symmetric encryption with data fragmentation and dispersal to achieve both secrecy and availability. Similarly, Hybris [108] and Tahoe-LAFS [112] follow the SSMS design pattern, where the user retains full control of the encryption key. In Tahoe-LAFS, integrity is ensured through Merkle hash trees and RSA digital signatures, providing verifiable storage. Another cloud storage service that follows the SSMS design, but employs LT codes instead of RS codes is LTCS [31]. To ensure integrity, LTCS incorporates public verifiability mechanisms that enable third-party auditing of stored fragments without requiring their retrieval, balancing reliability, security, and cost-efficiency. Additionally, several frameworks combine block cipher encryption with deduplication to minimize storage overhead, such as DAC [114] and DupLESS [58]. Taking a different approach, Cao et al. [119] introduced the Storage with Errors (SWE) protocol, a secure and efficient dispersal scheme that integrates an IDA with lattice-based cryptography. As a post-quantum MCS system, SWE leverages the hardness of the Learning With Errors (LWE) problem to guarantee that even if all n fragments are compromised, the original data remains unrecoverable without the secret vector s held by the user. Availability is achieved through the redundancy inherent in LWE, while

integrity is verified via a lightweight consistency check using $(k+1)$ fragments.

A different class of schemes applies an invertible Discrete Wavelet Transform (DWT) to split files into fragments with varying levels of sensitivity. In [86], the small, high-value fragment is encrypted using AES, while the remaining fragments are masked via XOR with a SHA − 3 digest of the sensitive portion. Similarly, [85] stores the most sensitive fragment in a trusted local environment, while the larger, less critical fragments are outsourced to public clouds. Both approaches reduce encryption overhead while ensuring that no single fragment discloses meaningful information, thus achieving confidentiality through selective protection and availability through dispersal. Building on this concept, the paper [69] proposes an enhanced privacy-preserving data-splitting framework that further improves efficiency by reducing the number of generated fragments and storage operations. In their model, sensitive fragments are retained locally at the proxy, while less sensitive data portions are distributed across multiple CSPs.

Advantages and Limitations. Secret-leveraging protocols offer straightforward designs, as they rely on conventional encryption. Despite the fact that they provide strong computational confidentiality, this comes at the cost of explicit key management, which reintroduces a single point of failure, undesirable in MCS. In principle, most of these designs could become keyless by dispersing the secret alongside the data using secret sharing, or transform into untrusted-proxy schemes by assuming that the proxy only performs the Disperse operation.

2. Other schemes rely on users holding private identity keys [77,100,121].

   Representative Schemes. Zhang et al. [121] employ CP-ABE for confidentiality and fine-grained access control, where data is categorized into different sensitivity levels, and each level is encrypted under a unified access structure. However, this scheme focuses solely on confidentiality and does not address availability. HealthShare [77] is a client-centric MCS designed for secure electronic health record (EHR) sharing, combining KP-ABE and MA-ABE to provide decentralized trust and fine-grained authorization. Integrity is maintained through digital signatures, while availability is ensured via replication. Similarly, [100] introduces a hybrid framework that integrates symmetric encryption (SKE) with Identity-Based Broadcast Encryption (IBBE) for scalable group key management, in which the data encryption key (DEK) is encrypted once under a broadcast key and distributed across multiple clouds, achieving efficient access control and redundancy-based availability.

   Advantages and Limitations. These protocols provide strong confidentiality and fine-grained access control through identity- or attribute-based encryption mechanisms. However, they inherently rely on persistent private or master keys, making them difficult to adapt into fully keyless architectures. Such schemes could be extended to untrusted-proxy settings by delegating only the Disperse operation to the proxy.

4.2 Untrusted Proxy

This section discusses the presence of an untrusted proxy, which performs the Disperse operation, while the user carries out the Process phase. Considering an untrusted proxy in MCS settings is crucial, as fully trusting the proxy would undermine the very goal of multi-cloud architectures, which is to achieve distributed trust among independent parties. At the same time, employing a proxy remains practical, as it relieves users from the burden of interacting with multiple cloud providers simultaneously – especially when the user's primary goal is to ensure the availability of their data rather than to manage complex cryptographic or communication tasks. In MCS protocols, even when declared "untrusted", the proxy – by definition a mediator – retains a degree of implicit trust, since it must correctly transmit or transform information during the upload phase for the system to function at all.

Based on the state of the art, the proxy is most often modeled as semi-trusted (or honest-but-curious): it correctly follows the protocol but may attempt to infer confidential information from observed data flows. A stronger and less explored model is that of a malicious proxy operating under the covert adversarial model [13], also referred to as malicious with abort, where the proxy may deviate arbitrarily from the protocol as long as such deviation cannot be detected except with negligible probability. These are reasonable assumptions in the real world, as a proxy, often operated by a company, risks its reputation if caught misbehaving.

Key-Leveraging Protocols. The simplest way to preserve confidentiality against an untrusted proxy – whether semi-trusted or covert – is to retain a local encryption key, as done in key-leveraging protocols relying on a trusted processor. Such schemes can, in principle, be adapted to an untrusted-proxy setting by restricting the proxy's role to data distribution while keeping all key material inaccessible to it.

Representative Schemes. In [74], the authors present a model that emphasizes authentication and integrity rather than confidentiality. The system combines RSA-based user authentication, VPN-secured communication, and Proofs of Data Possession (PDP) for integrity verification. A semi-trusted proxy auditor monitors cloud activity and validates integrity proofs but never holds decryption keys. Availability is maintained through RAID-style redundancy, while users retain the credentials and hashes required for verification. The ABESS protocol [42] supports collaborative sharing of healthcare records across multiple clouds, using CP-ABE combined with SSMS to encrypt and disperse data across independent CSPs. Integrity and authenticity are ensured through Digital Signatures (DSA) on complete records and HMACs on individual shares to detect tampering at the cloud level. However, the scheme incurs substantial computational overhead and long waiting times for multi-party sharing operations. Users and health centers must manage CP-ABE master keys and private keys issued by a central or federated key authority, while each client locally stores DSA and ABE keys for encryption and signing. Rayudu et al. [89] integrate symmetric encryption, proxy re-encryption, and erasure coding to achieve confidentiality, availability, and secure data forwarding. Meanwhile, Lin and Tzeng [67] use threshold PRE combined with erasure coding in order to support secure data forwarding. Key material is distributed among independent key servers using SSS, which perform partial decryption collaboratively. In both designs, the proxy is semi-trusted and assumed non-colluding with key servers, and performs re-encryption without decryption. Users maintain long-term key pairs, and decryption is performed cooperatively through distributed key shares. Similarly, Alfassa et al. [6] propose a multi-cloud framework that combines symmetric encryption with Shamir's secret sharing for key protection and RSA for encrypting key fragments, alongside improved Proxy Re-Encryption (I-PRE) for controlled data sharing. The proxy re-encrypts data between users without accessing plaintext, while clouds store encrypted fragments of both the data and the key. The proxy is also considered honest-but-curious and non-colluding with CSPs. Users retain their own secret keys, making this another clear instance of a key-leveraging design. CloudSeal [116] is an end-to-end secure content storage and delivery framework providing confidentiality and dynamic access control. Data is encrypted under SKE, and a semi-trusted proxy applies PRE to delegate decryption rights without exposing plaintexts. Upon user revocation, new keys are distributed through threshold secret sharing with broadcast revocation. The proxy is semi-trusted–honest in operation but curious about cached or transiting content–and the scheme focuses on scalable confidentiality rather than integrity or availability.

Advantages and Limitations. This family of approaches is practical and realistic, particularly in enterprise or regulated contexts where a proxy naturally exists for coordination or auditing. They provide flexible delegation through re-encryption or attribute-based mechanisms. However, they merely shift the trust boundary: while the proxy no longer learns plaintext, the security now depends on protecting the DEK and other long-term secrets held by users. Key management can be expensive over the years as it requires key rotation. Moreover, an encryption key may be lost, making the data unrecoverable. These schemes also remain vulnerable to insider compromise or key leakage, and few provide formal security models for proxy misbehavior or collusion with cloud providers.

Keyless Protocols. We define keyless protocols as those in which the user does not retain any long-term secret keys or hashes during the upload phase. However, during the download phase, in the presence of an untrusted proxy, the user must possess some form of transient secret–such as an ephemeral decryption token–to retrieve data securely. Without this minimal secret material, the proxy would always be able to access the plaintext, even if acting only as an honest-but-curious intermediary.

Representative Schemes. In the MCS KAPRE (Keyless Archivage with Proxy Re-Encryption) [60], the user encrypts the data with authenticated SKE and protects the encryption key using SSS combined with homomorphic PRE to ensure its confidentiality. The proxy disperses encrypted data chunks of the data using an IDA. Integrity is verified through key-homomorphic PRF commitments, enabling the proxy to detect corrupted shares and hold providers accountable. KAPRE loses confidentiality if the proxy colludes with any provider. For that reason, the authors presented KAME (Keyless Archivage with Multikey Encryption), which extends KAPRE to tolerate collusion between the proxy and up to $(k-2)$ providers. It replaces proxy re-encryption with homomorphic multi-key encryption (MKE), so that each Shamir coefficient is encrypted under all parties' public keys. Decryption then requires partial decryptions from all participants, ensuring that no single entity – including the proxy – can reconstruct key shares alone. The scheme POMS [2] (Proxy Offloading for Multi-cloud) is an honest-but-curious proxy scheme that aims to improve efficiency while preserving confidentiality, integrity, and retrievability. The user encrypts data with a SKE, encrypts the DEK with CP-ABE for fine-grained access control, and generates a searchable ciphertext and a digital identity-based signature. These components are sent to the proxy, which applies a proof-of-retrievability (POR) encoding to generate and distribute storage shares across multiple clouds. The proxy acts as an auditor, verifying retrievability without learning plaintext or keys. While POMS is considered keyless, it assumes the existence of a trusted authority that issues temporary secret keys to users during the download phase.

Advantages and Limitations. These schemes offer strong security guarantees and practical applicability, particularly in scenarios requiring secure delegation and minimal key management. However, they incur significant computational and communication overhead on the user's side. Moreover, the current state of the art in this area remains limited, with only a few concrete constructions available, highlighting the need for further research into efficient and formally verified keyless designs.

5 Conclusion

This SoK has provided the first systematic study of cryptographic approaches for Multi-Cloud Storage. By classifying protocols along two dimensions – trust models and cryptographic primitives – we clarified how confidentiality, integrity, and availability are achieved under different assumptions and design choices.

Each approach offers distinct strengths: secret sharing achieves strong confidentiality at a high storage cost, erasure coding improves efficiency but leaks partial information, and hybrid constructions balance the two at the expense of complexity. Similarly, the use of trusted or untrusted proxies, keyless designs, or local client memory, introduces different trust assumptions, highlighting that no single model suffices for all settings. Our analysis shows that design trade-offs are unavoidable: stronger guarantees often come with higher storage, communication, or computation overheads.

At the same time, many schemes can be extended depending on security requirements. For example, protocols originally designed for trusted proxies can be adapted to untrusted ones, and keyless designs can be reinforced by secret-sharing or embedding keys inside the data. Likewise, access control, auditability, and robustness features can be layered on top of existing storage schemes. Ideally, a dispersed encryption key or sensitive fragment should enjoy stronger protection than the file it secures – a principle guiding future hybrid designs.

In summary, our systematization reveals that MCS security is not a solved problem but a rich design space where cryptography, distributed systems, and trust models intersect. We hope this SoK helps unify terminology, identify open challenges, and guide future designs toward secure, efficient, and trustworthy multi-cloud architectures.

We particularly encourage further research in this field, especially in the exploration of keyless and untrusted-proxy models, which remain among the least developed yet most promising directions for future MCS security. Another open avenue concerns the integration of post-quantum cryptography into multi-cloud settings, as exemplified by lattice-based schemes such as SWE, which illustrates the need for quantum-resilient yet efficient and creative integration of post-quantum techniques.

Acknowledgments. We would like to express our gratitude to Nigel Smart for his insightful comments and frequent discussions on the manuscript, and to the Astran Crypto team, specifically Gilles Seghaier, Elouan Gros, and Daoud Jahdou, for their comments, helpful advice, and valuable perspectives. We also thank the anonymous reviewers for their constructive feedback, which helped to improve the quality and clarity of this paper.

This work was supported by the joint research laboratory of EPITA and Astran, and by the France 2030 innovation program of Bpifrance and the French government.

References

1. WEAVER codes: Highly fault tolerant erasure codes for storage systems. In: 4th USENIX Conference on File and Storage Technologies (FAST 05). USENIX Association, San Francisco, CA (2005). https://www.usenix.org/conference/fast-05/weaver-codes-highly-fault-tolerant-erasure-codes-storage-systems
2. Abdel-Rahman, A.O., Azogagh, S., Birba, Z.A., Van, A.T.: POMS : Proxy offloading for multicloud storage with keyword search. Cryptology ePrint Archive, Paper 2024/1747 (2024). https://eprint.iacr.org/2024/1747

3. Abu-Libdeh, H., Princehouse, L., Weatherspoon, H.: RACS: a case for cloud storage diversity. In: Proceedings of the 1st ACM Symposium on Cloud Computing, pp. 229–240. SoCC 2010, Association for Computing Machinery, New York, NY, USA (2010). https://doi.org/10.1145/1807128.1807165
4. Adei, D., Orsini, C., Scafuro, A., Verber, T.: How to recover a cryptographic secret from the cloud. Cryptology ePrint Archive, Paper 2023/1308 (2023). https://eprint.iacr.org/2023/1308
5. Alam, M., Kather, S.: An approach to secret sharing algorithm in cloud computing security over single to multi clouds. Int. J. Sci. Res. Publ. **3** (2013)
6. Alfassa, S.M., Padmaveni, K.: Improved availability using i_rrect algorithm in cloud environment. In: 2018 Second International Conference on Intelligent Computing and Control Systems (ICICCS), pp. 625–630 (2018). https://doi.org/10.1109/ICCONS.2018.8663034
7. Alqahtani, H.: A novel approach to providing secure data storage using multi cloud computing. University of Bedfordshire (2019). https://books.google.fr/books?id=Mq-TzgEACAAJ
8. Alsolami, F., Boult, T.E.: CloudStash: using secret-sharing scheme to secure data, not keys, in multi-clouds. In: 2014 11th International Conference on Information Technology: New Generations, pp. 315–320 (2014). https://doi.org/10.1109/ITNG.2014.119
9. Althamary, I., Alkharobi, T.: Secure file sharing in multi-clouds using Shamir's secret sharing scheme. Trans. Netw. Commun. **4** (2016). https://doi.org/10.14738/tnc.46.2560
10. AlZain, M.A., Pardede, E., Soh, B., Thom, J.A.: Cloud computing security: from single to multi-clouds. In: 2012 45th Hawaii International Conference on System Sciences, pp. 5490–5499 (2012). https://doi.org/10.1109/HICSS.2012.153
11. Attasena, V., Darmont, J., Harbi, N.: Secret sharing for cloud data security: a survey. VLDB J.**26**(5), 657–681 (2017). https://doi.org/10.1007/s00778-017-0470-9
12. Attasena, V., Harbi, N., Darmont, J.: fVSS: a new secure and cost-efficient scheme for cloud data warehouses. In: ACM (ed.) Proceedings of the 17th International Workshop on Data Warehousing and OLAP (DOLAP 2014), Shangai, China, pp. 81–90. (2014). https://doi.org/10.1145/2666158.2666173, https://hal.science/hal-01081882
13. Aumann, Y., Lindell, Y.: Security against covert adversaries: Efficient protocols for realistic adversaries. Cryptology ePrint Archive, Paper 2007/060 (2007). https://eprint.iacr.org/2007/060
14. Balaji, S.B., Krishnan, M.N., Vajha, M., Ramkumar, V., Sasidharan, B., Kumar, P.V.: Erasure coding for distributed storage: an overview (2018). https://arxiv.org/abs/1806.04437
15. Baldi, M., Maturo, N., Montali, E., Chiaraluce, F.: AONT-LT: a data protection scheme for cloud and cooperative storage systems. In: 2014 International Conference on High Performance Computing & Simulation (HPCS), pp. 566–571 (2014). https://doi.org/10.1109/HPCSim.2014.6903736
16. Bellare, M., Rogaway, P.: Optimal asymmetric encryption. In: Santis, A.D. (ed.) EUROCRYPT 1994. LNCS, vol. 950, pp. 92–111. Springer, Heidelberg (1995). https://doi.org/10.1007/BFb0053428
17. Bessani, A., Correia, M., Quaresma, B., André, F., Sousa, P.: DepSky: dependable and secure storage in a cloud-of-clouds. ACM Trans. Storage **9**(4) (2013). https://doi.org/10.1145/2535929

18. Bessani, A., et al.: SCFS: a shared cloud-backed file system, pp. 169–180 (2014)
19. Bharot, N., Mehta, N., Breslin, J., Verma, P.: CloudLock: secure data sharing using a hybrid cryptosystem in multi-cloud data storage. Cluster Comput. **28** (2025). https://doi.org/10.1007/s10586-025-05433-7
20. Blakley, G.R., Meadows, C.: Security of ramp schemes. In: Blakley, G.R., Chaum, D. (eds.) CRYPTO 1984. LNCS, vol. 196, pp. 242–268. Springer, Heidelberg (1984). https://doi.org/10.1007/3-540-39568-7_20
21. Blaze, M., Bleumer, G., Strauss, M.: Divertible protocols and atomic proxy cryptography, vol. 1403, pp. 127–144 (1998). https://doi.org/10.1007/BFb0054122
22. Bohli, J.M., Gruschka, N., Jensen, M., Iacono, L.L., Marnau, N.: Security and privacy-enhancing multicloud architectures. IEEE Trans. Dependable Secure Comput. **10**(4), 212–224 (2013). https://doi.org/10.1109/TDSC.2013.6
23. Bowers, K.D., Juels, A., Oprea, A.: HAIL: a high-availability and integrity layer for cloud storage. Cryptology ePrint Archive, Paper 2008/489 (2008). https://eprint.iacr.org/2008/489
24. Boyd, C., Davies, G.T., Gjøsteen, K., Toorani, M., Raddum, H.: Security notions for cloud storage and deduplication. Cryptology ePrint Archive, Paper 2017/1208 (2017). https://eprint.iacr.org/2017/1208
25. Boyko, V.: On the security properties of OAEP as an all-or-nothing transform. In: Wiener, M. (ed.) CRYPTO 1999. LNCS, vol. 1666, pp. 503–518. Springer, Heidelberg (1999). https://doi.org/10.1007/3-540-48405-1_32
26. Buchmann, J., et al.: SAFE: a secure and efficient long-term distributed storage system. Cryptology ePrint Archive, Paper 2020/690 (2020). https://eprint.iacr.org/2020/690
27. Buyya, R., Ranjan, R., Calheiros, R.: Intercloud: utility-oriented federation of cloud computing environments for scaling of application services, vol. 6081 (2010). https://doi.org/10.1007/978-3-642-13119-6_2
28. Cachin, C., Haas, R., Vukolic, M.: Dependable storage in the intercloud. IBM Res. **3783**, 1–6 (2010)
29. Cachin, C., Keidar, I., Shraer, A.: Trusting the cloud. SIGACT News **40**(2), 81–86 (2009). https://doi.org/10.1145/1556154.1556173
30. Canetti, R., Dodis, Y., Halevi, S., Kushilevitz, E., Sahai, A.: Exposure-resilient functions and all-or-nothing transforms. In: Preneel, B. (ed.) EUROCRYPT 2000. LNCS, vol. 1807, pp. 453–469. Springer, Heidelberg (2000). https://doi.org/10.1007/3-540-45539-6_33
31. Cao, N., Yu, S., Yang, Z., Lou, W., Hou, Y.T.: Lt codes-based secure and reliable cloud storage service. In: 2012 Proceedings IEEE INFOCOM, pp. 693–701 (2012). https://doi.org/10.1109/INFCOM.2012.6195814
32. Castro, M., Liskov, B.: Practical byzantine fault tolerance. In: Proceedings of the Third Symposium on Operating Systems Design and Implementation, pp. 173–186. OSDI 1999, USENIX Association, USA (1999)
33. Celesti, A., Galletta, A., Fazio, M., Villari, M.: Towards hybrid multi-cloud storage systems: Understanding how to perform data transfer. Big Data Res. **16**, 1–17 (2019). https://doi.org/10.1016/j.bdr.2019.02.002, https://www.sciencedirect.com/science/article/pii/S2214579618302004
34. Celesti, A., Tusa, F., Villari, M., Puliafito, A.: Adding long-term availability, obfuscation, and encryption to multi-cloud storage systems. J. Netw. Comput. Appl. **34**(4), 1216–1227 (2011). https://doi.org/10.1016/j.jnca.2010.05.009
35. Chattopadhyay, A.K., Saha, S., Nag, A., Nandi, S.: Secret sharing: a comprehensive survey, taxonomy and applications. Comput. Sci. Rev. **51**, 100608

(2024). https://doi.org/10.1016/j.cosrev.2023.100608, https://www.sciencedirect.com/science/article/pii/S1574013723000758
36. Chen, H., Cramer, R.: Algebraic geometric secret sharing schemes and secure multi-party computations over small fields. In: Dwork, C. (ed.) CRYPTO 2006. LNCS, vol. 4117, pp. 521–536. Springer, Heidelberg (2006). https://doi.org/10.1007/11818175_31
37. Chen, L., Laing, T.M., Martin, K.M.: Revisiting and extending the AONT-RS scheme: a robust computationally secure secret sharing scheme. In: Joye, M., Nitaj, A. (eds.) AFRICACRYPT 17. LNCS, vol. 10239, pp. 40–57. Springer, Heidelberg (2017). https://doi.org/10.1007/978-3-319-57339-7_3
38. Chockler, G., Guerraoui, R., Keidar, I., Vukolic, M.: Reliable distributed storage. Computer **42** (2009). https://doi.org/10.1109/MC.2009.126
39. Chung, J.Y., Joe-Wong, C., Ha, S., Hong, J.W.K., Chiang, M.: Cyrus: towards client-defined cloud storage. In: Proceedings of the Tenth European Conference on Computer Systems. EuroSys 2015, Association for Computing Machinery, New York, NY, USA (2015). https://doi.org/10.1145/2741948.2741951
40. Dimakis, A.G., Godfrey, P.B., Wu, Y., Wainwright, M.J., Ramchandran, K.: Network coding for distributed storage systems. IEEE Trans. Inf. Theory **56**(9), 4539–4551 (2010). https://doi.org/10.1109/TIT.2010.2054295
41. Esfahani, A.: Generalizations of all-or-nothing transforms and their application in secure distributed storage. Phd thesis, University of Waterloo, Waterloo (2021)
42. Fabian, B., Ermakova, T., Junghanns, P.: Collaborative and secure sharing of healthcare data in multi-clouds. Inf. Syst. **48**, 132–150 (2014). https://doi.org/10.1016/j.is.2014.05.004
43. Gentry, C.: A fully homomorphic encryption scheme. Ph.D. thesis, Stanford University (2009). crypto.stanford.edu/craig
44. Hong, J., Dreibholz, T., Schenkel, J., Hu, J.: An overview of multi-cloud computing, pp. 1055–1068 (2019). https://doi.org/10.1007/978-3-030-15035-8_103
45. Hu, P., Sung, C.W., Ho, S.W., Chan, T.H.: Optimal coding and allocation for perfect secrecy in multiple clouds. IEEE Trans. Inf. Forensics Secur. **11**(2), 388–399 (2016). https://doi.org/10.1109/TIFS.2015.2500193
46. Hu, Y., Chen, H.C.H., Lee, P.P.C., Tang, Y.: NCCLOUD: applying network coding for the storage repair in a cloud-of-clouds. In: Proceedings of the 10th USENIX Conference on File and Storage Technologies, p. 21. FAST 2012, USENIX Association, USA (2012)
47. Hussein, N., Salih, A., Khanfar, K.: A survey of cryptography cloud storage techniques. Int. J. Comput. Sci. Mob. Comput. **52**, 186–191 (2016)
48. ImmuniWeb: Top 10 cloud security incidents in 2022 (2022). https://www.immuniweb.com/blog/top-10-cloud-security-incidents-in-2022.html
49. Imran, H.A., et al.: Multi-cloud: a comprehensive review. In: 2020 IEEE 23rd International Multitopic Conference (INMIC), pp. 1–5 (2020). https://doi.org/10.1109/INMIC50486.2020.9318176
50. Islam, T., Mistareehi, H., Manivannan, D.: SECRES: a secure and reliable storage scheme for cloud with client-side data deduplication. In: 2019 IEEE Global Communications Conference (GLOBECOM), pp. 1–6 (2019). https://doi.org/10.1109/GLOBECOM38437.2019.9013469
51. Kaaniche, N., Laurent, M.: Data security and privacy preservation in cloud storage environments based on cryptographic mechanisms. Comput. Commun. **111** (2017). https://doi.org/10.1016/j.comcom.2017.07.006

52. Kadam, M., Chaudhary, S., Carvalho, B.: Security approach for multi-cloud data storage. Int. J. Comput. Appl. **126**, 27–31 (2015). https://doi.org/10.5120/ijca2015906032
53. Kannan, M., Naik, H.: A survey on protecting confidential data over distributed storage in cloud. SSRN Electron. J. **5**, 1–7 (2021). https://doi.org/10.2139/ssrn.3740465
54. Kapusta, K.: Protecting data confidentiality combining data fragmentation, encryption, and dispersal over a distributed environment. Phd thesis, Télécom ParisTech, Paris, France (2018). english. NNT: 2018ENST0061. tel-03523671
55. Kapusta, K., Memmi, G.: A fast fragmentation algorithm for data protection in a multi-cloud environment (2018). https://arxiv.org/abs/1804.01886
56. Karame, G., Soriente, C., Lichota, K., Capkun, S.: Securing cloud data under key exposure. IEEE Trans. Cloud Comput. (2017). https://doi.org/10.1109/TCC.2017.2670559
57. Kathuria, S.: A survey on security provided by multi-clouds in cloud computing. Int. J. Sci. Res. Netw. Secur. Commun. **6**(1), 23–27 (2018). https://doi.org/10.26438/ijsrnsc/v6i1.2327, https://ijsrnsc.org/index.php/j/article/view/120/120
58. Keelveedhi, S., Bellare, M., Ristenpart, T.: DupLESS: server-aided encryption for deduplicated storage. In: 22nd USENIX Security Symposium (USENIX Security 13), pp. 179–194. USENIX Association, Washington, D.C. (2013). https://www.usenix.org/conference/usenixsecurity13/technical-sessions/presentation/bellare
59. Krawczyk, H.: Secret sharing made short. In: Stinson, D.R. (ed.) CRYPTO 1993. LNCS, vol. 773, pp. 136–146. Springer, Heidelberg (1994). https://doi.org/10.1007/3-540-48329-2_12
60. Lafourcade, P., Mallordy, L.B., Olivier-Anclin, C., Robert, L.: Secure keyless multi-party storage scheme. In: ESORICS : European Symposium On Research In Computer Security. Lecture Notes in Computer Science, vol. LNCS - 14984, pp. 279–298. Springer Nature Switzerland, Bydgoszcz, Poland (2024). https://doi.org/10.1007/978-3-031-70896-1_14, https://hal.science/hal-04540895
61. Lahkar, H., R., M.C.: Towards high security and fault tolerant dispersed storage system with optimized information dispersal algorithm. Int. J. Adv. Res. Comput. Sci. **5**(6), 167–172 (2014). https://www.ijarcs.info/index.php/Ijarcs/article/view/2205
62. Le, D.N., Seth, B., Dalal, S.: A hybrid approach of secret sharing with fragmentation and encryption in cloud environment for securing outsourced medical database: a revolutionary approach. J. Cyber Secur. Mob. **7**(4), 379–408 (2018). https://doi.org/10.13052/2245-1439.742, https://journals.riverpublishers.com/index.php/JCSANDM/article/view/5311
63. Li, J., Yan, H., Zhang, Y.: Efficient identity-based provable multi-copy data possession in multi-cloud storage. IEEE Trans. Cloud Comput. **10**(1), 356–365 (2022). https://doi.org/10.1109/TCC.2019.2929045
64. Li, J., Krohn, M., Mazières, D., Shasha, D.: Secure untrusted data repository (SUNDR). In: 6th Symposium on Operating Systems Design & Implementation (OSDI 04). USENIX Association, San Francisco, CA (2004). https://www.usenix.org/conference/osdi-04/secure-untrusted-data-repository-sundr
65. Li, M., Qin, C., Lee, P.P.C., Li, J.: Convergent dispersal: toward storage-efficient security in a cloud-of-clouds. In: Kozuch, M.A., Yu, M. (eds.) 6th USENIX Workshop on Hot Topics in Cloud Computing, HotCloud 2014, Philadelphia, PA, USA, June 17-18, 2014. USENIX Association (2014). https://www.usenix.org/conference/hotstorage14/workshop-program/presentation/li_mingqiang

66. Li, M., Qin, C., Li, J., Lee, P.: CDSTORE: toward reliable, secure, and cost-efficient cloud storage via convergent dispersal. IEEE Internet Comput. **20** (2016). https://doi.org/10.1109/MIC.2016.45
67. Lin, H.Y., Tzeng, W.G.: A secure erasure code-based cloud storage system with secure data forwarding. IEEE Trans. Parallel Distrib. Syst. **23**(6), 995–1003 (2012). https://doi.org/10.1109/TPDS.2011.252
68. Ling, C., Datta, A.: Intercloud raider: A do-it-yourself multi-cloud private data backup system, vol. 8314, pp. 453–468 (2014). https://doi.org/10.1007/978-3-642-45249-9_30
69. Loh, R., Thing, V.L.L.: Data privacy in multi-cloud: an enhanced data fragmentation framework. In: 2021 18th International Conference on Privacy, Security and Trust (PST), pp. 1–5 (2021). https://doi.org/10.1109/PST52912.2021.9647746
70. Loruenser, T., Happe, A., Slamanig, D.: ARCHISTAR: towards secure and robust cloud based data sharing. In: 2015 IEEE 7th International Conference on Cloud Computing Technology and Science (CloudCom), pp. 371–378 (2015). https://doi.org/10.1109/CloudCom.2015.71
71. Lu, Y., Li, J.: A pairing-free certificate-based proxy re-encryption scheme for secure data sharing in public clouds. Future Gener. Comput. Syst. **62**(C), 140–147 (2016). https://doi.org/10.1016/j.future.2015.11.012
72. Malkhi, D., Reiter, M.: Byzantine quorum systems. Distrib. Comput. **11**(4), 203–213 (1998). https://doi.org/10.1007/s004460050050
73. Mazières, D., Shasha, D.: Building secure file systems out of byzantine storage. In: Proceedings of the Twenty-First Annual Symposium on Principles of Distributed Computing, pp. 108–117. PODC 2002, Association for Computing Machinery, New York, NY, USA (2002). https://doi.org/10.1145/571825.571840
74. Megouache, L., Zitouni, A., Djoudi, M.: Ensuring user authentication and data integrity in multi-cloud environment. Hum. Centric Comput. Inf. Sci. **10** (2020). https://doi.org/10.1186/s13673-020-00224-y
75. Mendes, R., Oliveira, T., Cogo, V., Neves, N., Bessani, A.: Charon: a secure cloud-of-clouds system for storing and sharing big data. IEEE Trans. Cloud Comput. **9**(4), 1349–1361 (2021). https://doi.org/10.1109/TCC.2019.2916856
76. Miao, Y., Huang, Q., Xiao, M., Susilo, W.: Blockchain assisted multi-copy provable data possession with faults localization in multi-cloud storage. IEEE Trans. Inf. Forensics Secur. **17**, 3663–3676 (2022). https://doi.org/10.1109/TIFS.2022.3211642
77. Michalas, A., Weingarten, N.: HealthShare: using attribute-based encryption for secure data sharing between multiple clouds. In: 2017 IEEE 30th International Symposium on Computer-Based Medical Systems (CBMS), pp. 811–815 (2017). https://doi.org/10.1109/CBMS.2017.30
78. Niknia, A., Correia, M., Karimpour, J.: Secure cloud-of-clouds storage with space-efficient secret sharing. Cryptology ePrint Archive, Paper 2021/666 (2021). https://eprint.iacr.org/2021/666
79. Pachala, S., Rupa, C., Lingamgunta, S.: An improved security and privacy management system for data in multi-cloud environments using a hybrid approach. Evolutionary Intell. **14** (2021). https://doi.org/10.1007/s12065-020-00555-w
80. Padilha, R., Pedone, F.: Belisarius: BFT storage with confidentiality. In: Proceedings of the 2011 IEEE 10th International Symposium on Network Computing and Applications, pp. 9–16. NCA 2011, IEEE Computer Society, USA (2011). https://doi.org/10.1109/NCA.2011.15

81. Pal, D., Khethavath, P., Thomas, J.P., Chen, T.: Multilevel threshold secret sharing in distributed cloud. In: Abawajy, J.H., Mukherjea, S., Thampi, S.M., Ruiz-Martínez, A. (eds.) Security in Computing and Communications, pp. 13–23. Springer International Publishing, Cham (2015). https://doi.org/10.1007/978-3-319-22915-7_2
82. Papaioannou, T.G., Bonvin, N., Aberer, K.: Scalia: an adaptive scheme for efficient multi-cloud storage. In: SC 2012: Proceedings of the International Conference on High Performance Computing, Networking, Storage and Analysis, pp. 1–10 (2012). https://doi.org/10.1109/SC.2012.101
83. Pathak, N.N., Nagori, M.: Enhanced security for multi cloud storage using AES algorithm (2015). https://api.semanticscholar.org/CorpusID:203689128
84. Plank, J.S.: Erasure codes for storage systems (2013). https://api.semanticscholar.org/CorpusID:3238809
85. Qiu, H., Memmi, G., Noura, H.: An efficient secure storage scheme based on information fragmentation. In: 2017 IEEE 4th International Conference on Cyber Security and Cloud Computing (CSCloud), pp. 108–113 (2017). https://doi.org/10.1109/CSCloud.2017.44
86. Qiu, H., Noura, H., Qiu, M., Ming, Z., Memmi, G.: A user-centric data protection method for cloud storage based on invertible DWT. IEEE Trans. Cloud Comput. **9**(4), 1293–1304 (2021). https://doi.org/10.1109/TCC.2019.2911679
87. Quisquater, M., Preneel, B., Vandewalle, J.: On the security of the threshold scheme based on the Chinese remainder theorem. In: Proceedings of the 5th International Workshop on Practice and Theory in Public Key Cryptosystems: Public Key Cryptography, pp. 199–210. PKC 2002, Springer-Verlag, Berlin, Heidelberg (2002). https://doi.org/10.1007/3-540-45664-3_14
88. Rabin, M.O.: Efficient dispersal of information for security, load balancing, and fault tolerance. J. ACM **36**(2), 335–348 (1989). https://doi.org/10.1145/62044.62050
89. Rayudu, V.D., Vazralu, M., Sandeep, M.: A secure erasure code-based cloud storage system with secure data forwarding. Int. J. Comput. Sci. Mob. Comput. (IJCSMC) **3**(8), 337–344 (2014). https://www.ijcsmc.com/docs/papers/August2014/V3I8201422.pdf
90. Resch, J.K., Plank, J.S.: AONT-RS: blending security and performance in dispersed storage systems. In: Ganger, G.R., Wilkes, J. (eds.) 9th USENIX Conference on File and Storage Technologies, San Jose, CA, USA, February 15-17, 2011, pp. 191–202. USENIX (2011). http://www.usenix.org/events/fast11/tech/techAbstracts.html#Resch
91. Rhea, S., Eaton, P., Geels, D., Weatherspoon, H., Zhao, B., Kubiatowicz, J.: Pond: the OceanStore prototype. In: 2nd USENIX Conference on File and Storage Technologies (FAST 03). USENIX Association, San Francisco, CA (2003). https://www.usenix.org/conference/fast-03/pond-oceanstore-prototype
92. Rivest, R.L.: All-or-nothing encryption and the package transform. In: Biham, E. (ed.) FSE 1997. LNCS, vol. 1267, pp. 210–218. Springer, Heidelberg (1997). https://doi.org/10.1007/BFb0052348
93. Rocha, F.L., Correia, M.P.: Lucy in the sky without diamonds: stealing confidential data in the cloud. In: 2011 IEEE/IFIP 41st International Conference on Dependable Systems and Networks Workshops (DSN-W), pp. 129–134 (2011). https://api.semanticscholar.org/CorpusID:11517338
94. Rogaway, P., Bellare, M.: Robust computational secret sharing and a unified account of classical secret-sharing goals. In: Ning, P., De Capitani di Vimercati, S.,

Syverson, P.F. (eds.) ACM CCS 2007, pp. 172–184. ACM Press (2007). https://doi.org/10.1145/1315245.1315268
95. Shamir, A.: How to share a secret. Commun. Assoc. Comput. Mach. **22**(11), 612–613 (1979). https://doi.org/10.1145/359168.359176
96. Shen, J., Shen, J., Chen, X., Huang, X., Susilo, W.: An efficient public auditing protocol with novel dynamic structure for cloud data. IEEE Trans. Inf. Forensics Secur. **12**(10), 2402–2415 (2017). https://doi.org/10.1109/TIFS.2017.2705620
97. Shen, L., Feng, S., Sun, J., Li, Z., Wang, G., Liu, X.: Clouds: a multi-cloud storage system with multi-level security. In: Wang, G., Zomaya, A., Martinez, G., Li, K. (eds.) Algorithms and Architectures for Parallel Processing, pp. 703–716. Springer International Publishing, Cham (2015). https://doi.org/10.1007/978-3-642-31909-9_30
98. Shor, R., Yadgar, G., Huang, W., Yaakobi, E., Bruck, J.: How to best share a big secret. In: Proceedings of the 11th ACM International Systems and Storage Conference, pp. 76–88. SYSTOR 2018, Association for Computing Machinery, New York, NY, USA (2018). https://doi.org/10.1145/3211890.3211896
99. Smart, N.P.: Cryptography made simple. ISC, Springer, Heidelberg (2016). https://doi.org/10.1007/978-3-319-21936-3
100. Sohal, M., Bharany, S., Sharma, S., Maashi, M.S., Aljebreen, M.: A hybrid multi-cloud framework using the IBBE key management system for securing data storage. Sustainability **14**(20) (2022). https://doi.org/10.3390/su142013561, https://www.mdpi.com/2071-1050/14/20/13561
101. Stinson, D.: Something about all or nothing (transforms). Des. Codes Cryptography **22**, 133–138 (2001). https://doi.org/10.1023/A:1008304703074
102. Storer, M.W., Greenan, K.M., Miller, E.L., Voruganti, K.: Potshards—a secure, recoverable, long-term archival storage system. ACM Trans. Storage **5**(2) (2009). https://doi.org/10.1145/1534912.1534914
103. Subramanian, K., John, F.: Enhanced security for data sharing in multi cloud storage (SDSMC). Int. J. Adv. Comput. Sci. Appl. **8** (2017). https://api.semanticscholar.org/CorpusID:5675637
104. Tchernykh, A., et al.: Performance evaluation of secret sharing schemes with data recovery in secured and reliable heterogeneous multi-cloud storage. Cluster Comput. **22** (2019). https://doi.org/10.1007/s10586-018-02896-9
105. Thilakanathan, D., Chen, S., Nepal, S., Calvo, R.: Secure data sharing in the cloud (2014). https://doi.org/10.1007/978-3-642-38586-5_2
106. Ukwandu, E.: RESCUE: evaluation of a fragmented secret share system in distributed-cloud architecture. Ph.D. thesis, Edinburgh Napier University, UK (2019)
107. Vaishali Tupe, V.D.: Data security in multi-cloud environment a survey. In: International Conference and Workshop on Communication, Computing and Virtualization **ICWCCV2015**(1) (2015). /proceedings/icwccv2015/number1/785-1552/
108. Viotti, P., Dobre, D., Vukolić, M.: Hybris: robust hybrid cloud storage. ACM Trans. Storage **13**(3) (2017). https://doi.org/10.1145/3119896
109. Vukolić, M.: The byzantine empire in the intercloud. SIGACT News **41**(3), 105–111 (2010). https://doi.org/10.1145/1855118.1855137
110. Wang, L., Liu, L., Liu, S., Chen, D., Chen, Y.: A secured distributed and data fragmentation model for cloud storage. Appl. Mech. Mater. **347-350**, 2693–2699 (2013). https://doi.org/10.4028/www.scientific.net/AMM.347-350.2693

111. Weatherspoon, H., Kubiatowicz, J.D.: Erasure coding vs. replication: a quantitative comparison. In: Druschel, P., Kaashoek, F., Rowstron, A. (eds.) Peer-to-Peer Systems. pp. 328–337. Springer Berlin Heidelberg, Berlin, Heidelberg (2002). https://doi.org/10.1007/978-3-642-31909-9_30
112. Wilcox-O'Hearn, Z., Warner, B.: Tahoe – the least-authority filesystem. Cryptology ePrint Archive, Paper 2012/524 (2012). https://eprint.iacr.org/2012/524
113. Witanto, E.N., Stanley, B., Lee, S.G.: Distributed data integrity verification scheme in multi-cloud environment. Sensors **23**(3) (2023). https://doi.org/10.3390/s23031623, https://www.mdpi.com/1424-8220/23/3/1623
114. Wu, S., Li, K.C., Mao, B., Liao, M.: DAC: improving storage availability with deduplication-assisted cloud-of-clouds. Future Gener. Comput. Syst. **74**, 190–198 (2017). https://doi.org/10.1016/j.future.2016.02.001, https://www.sciencedirect.com/science/article/pii/S0167739X16300073
115. Xie, P., Li, H., Yu, H., Chen, Z.: AONT-NZZD: a secure and efficient dispersal scheme in distributed storage systems . In: 2019 IEEE International Conference on Big Data (Big Data), pp. 6232–6239. IEEE Computer Society, Los Alamitos, CA, USA (2019). https://doi.org/10.1109/BigData47090.2019.9005571, https://doi.ieeecomputersociety.org/10.1109/BigData47090.2019.9005571
116. Xiong, H., Zhang, X., Zhu, W., Yao, D.: Cloudseal: end-to-end content protection in cloud-based storage and delivery services. In: Rajarajan, M., Piper, F., Wang, H., Kesidis, G. (eds.) Security and Privacy in Communication Networks, pp. 491–500. Springer, Berlin Heidelberg, Berlin, Heidelberg (2012). https://doi.org/10.1007/978-3-642-31909-9_30
117. Yan, M., Feng, J., Marbach, T., Stones, R., Wang, G., Liu, X.: Gecko: a resilient dispersal scheme for multi-cloud storage. IEEE Access (2019). https://doi.org/10.1109/ACCESS.2019.2920405
118. Yang, J., Zhu, H., Liu, T.: Secure and economical multi-cloud storage policy with NSGA-II-C. Appl. Soft Comput. **83**, 105649 (2019). https://doi.org/10.1016/j.asoc.2019.105649, https://www.sciencedirect.com/science/article/pii/S1568494619304296
119. Yang, L., et al.: A secure and fast dispersal storage scheme based on the learning with errors problem. In: Security and Privacy in Communication Networks (SecureComm 2016). Lecture Notes of the Institute for Computer Sciences, Social Informatics and Telecommunications Engineering, vol. 198, pp. 392–411. Springer (2016). https://doi.org/10.1007/978-3-319-59608-2_23
120. Yao, L., Lu, J., Liu, J., Wang, D., Meng, B.: A secure and efficient distributed storage scheme SAONT-RS based on an improved AONT and erasure coding. IEEE Access **6**, 55126–55138 (2018). https://doi.org/10.1109/ACCESS.2018.2872749
121. Zhang, W., Zhang, Y., Shi, Q., Liu, Q., Liao, X.: An efficient attribute-based encryption scheme with data security classification in the multi-cloud environment. Electronics **12**(20), 4237 (2023). https://doi.org/10.3390/electronics12204237, https://www.mdpi.com/2079-9292/12/20/4237
122. Zibouh, O., Dalli, A., Drissi, H.: Cloud computing security through parallelizing fully homomorphic encryption applied to multi-cloud approach (2016). https://api.semanticscholar.org/CorpusID:27115275
123. Zkik, K., Orhanou, G., Hajji, S.: Secure mobile multi cloud architecture for authentication and data storage. Int. J. Cloud Appl. Comput. (IJCAC) **7**, 62–76 (2017). https://doi.org/10.4018/IJCAC.2017040105

SoK: A Generalized Attack on RSA and Its Variants

Mengce Zheng[1(✉)], Abderrahmane Nitaj[2], Maher Boudabra[3], Michel Seck[4], Oumar Niang[4], and Djiby Sow[5]

[1] Zhejiang Wanli University, Ningbo, China
mengce.zheng@gmail.com, mczheng@zwu.edu.cn
[2] Université Caen Normandie, CNRS, Normandie Univ, LMNO UMR6139, 14000 Caen, France
abderrahmane.nitaj@unicaen.fr
[3] King Fahd University of Petroleum and Minerals, Dhahran, Saudi Arabia
[4] LTISI, CRISIN'2D, Ecole Polytechnique de Thies, Thies, Senegal
[5] Department of Mathematics and Computer Science, FST, UCAD, Dakar, Senegal

Abstract. This paper introduces a generalized cryptanalytic framework for RSA and its variants, systematizing existing attacks while revealing a wide class of structural weaknesses independent of the private exponent's size. While traditional analyses exploit the key equation $ed \equiv 1 \pmod{(p-1)(q-1)}$ or its extensions like $ed \equiv 1 \pmod{(p^n-1)(q^n-1)}$ for a given RSA modulus $N = pq$ and its public exponent e, we unify these approaches by investigating the more general algebraic property defined by the congruence $eu \equiv 1 \pmod{(p^n - a)(q^n - b)}$, where a, b, and u are unknown small integer parameters. Using Coppersmith's method with unravelled linearization, we demonstrate that the modulus N can be factored in polynomial time if such a relation exists for parameters within a new, rigorously derived bound. Our framework not only unifies and generalizes several well-known attacks (retrieving their bounds as special cases when $a = b = 1$) but also significantly expands the set of weak keys. We show that an RSA instance secure against all previous small private exponent attacks may still be broken if its public key possesses this hidden algebraic structure. This work serves as a comprehensive security analysis, highlighting a new family of weak keys that future cryptographic designs should avoid.

Keywords: Coppersmith's method · Factorization · Lattice · RSA · Weak key

1 Introduction

In 1978, Rivest, Shamir, and Adleman [22] proposed the RSA cryptosystem, which remains popular and widely used in various applications. The core arithmetic of RSA consists of modular exponentiation, modulo a public integer $N = pq$, where p and q are private large prime numbers of the same bit-size, typically satisfying $q < p < 2q$. The public exponent is an integer e satisfying $\gcd(e, \phi(N)) = 1$, where $\phi(N) = (p-1)(q-1)$ is Euler's totient function. The

F. -H. Liu (Ed.): CT-RSAC 2026, LNCS 16496, pp. 100–123, 2026.
https://doi.org/10.1007/978-3-032-22931-1_4

private exponent is an integer d satisfying the key equation $ed \equiv 1 \pmod{\phi(N)}$. In RSA, to encrypt a plaintext message $m < N$, one uses the public key (N, e) and computes the ciphertext $c \equiv m^e \pmod{N}$. To decrypt, one uses the private key (N, d) and computes $m \equiv c^d \pmod{N}$. The security of RSA primarily relies on the presumed difficulty of the integer factorization problem and the key equation problem. Specifically, these are: the problem of factoring the modulus $N = pq$; and the problem of solving the key equation $ed \equiv 1 \pmod{\phi(N)}$ to find the private exponent d where $\phi(N)$ is also unknown.

These problems are considered computationally infeasible for classical computers. Nevertheless, RSA has been intensively cryptanalyzed by exploiting vulnerabilities related to the key equation [1,10,17,27]. In 1990, Wiener [26] proposed an attack based on the continued fraction method, proving that the key equation can be solved, and thus the modulus N can be factored if $d < \frac{1}{3}N^{1/4}$. In 1999, Boneh and Durfee [2] improved this bound, demonstrating that N can be factored if $d < N^{0.292}$. The Boneh-Durfee method is based on Coppersmith's technique [6] and lattice basis reduction. Subsequently, in 2010, Herrmann and May [9] simplified the Boneh-Durfee method and achieved the same bound using the unravelled linearization technique.

Over the last three decades, several variants of RSA have been proposed, often based on different moduli or different arithmetic operations. The primary motivation behind these variants is to enhance security or improve efficiency. Some of these variants retain the modulus $N = pq$ but employ different algebraic structures, such as elliptic curves [13,14], Edwards curves [3], Gaussian integers [8], number fields [5,19,24,29], cubic Pell curves [18,23], and high-dimension curves [7].

For instance, in the RSA variants proposed in [5,8,14], while the modulus remains $N = pq$, Euler's totient function $\phi(N) = (p-1)(q-1)$ is replaced by $\psi_2(N) = (p^2-1)(q^2-1)$. This modification leads to a variant key equation $ed \equiv 1 \pmod{\psi_2(N)}$. These schemes have been subject to intensive cryptanalysis in [4,21,28]. To be concrete, Peng et al. [21] and Zheng et al. [28] demonstrated that if $e = N^\alpha$ and $d < N^\delta$, such key equation $ed \equiv 1 \pmod{\psi_2(N)}$ can be solved, and consequently N can be factored, if $\delta < 2 - \sqrt{\alpha}$.

In other variants, such as those described in [7,19,24,29], the key equation takes the form $ed \equiv 1 \pmod{\psi_n(N)}$, where $\psi_n(N) = (p^n - 1)(q^n - 1)$ for a fixed integer $n \geq 2$. The cryptanalysis of this variant key equation, presented in [25], yielded an attack threshold where $d < N^\delta$ with $\delta < n - \sqrt{\alpha n/2}$ assuming $e = N^\alpha$ and $n/2 \leq \alpha \leq (n+1)^2/(2n)$. This result generalizes previous findings, specifically for $n = 1$ (effectively $\phi(N)$ if $a = b = 1$ were used in a ψ_1 context, leading to $\delta < 1 - \sqrt{\alpha/2}$, which recovers the Boneh-Durfee bound [2] for $\alpha \approx 1$) and for $n = 2$ (leading to $\delta < 2 - \sqrt{\alpha}$ given in [21,28]).

The aforementioned attacks primarily exploit the arithmetic relationships involving e, $N = pq$, and specific functions like $\phi(N) = (p-1)(q-1)$ or its generalization $\psi_n(N) = (p^n - 1)(q^n - 1)$ for $n \geq 2$. However, these approaches are based on the assumption that a vulnerability, if one exists, must be tied to a small private exponent d. A fundamental question is whether other, more subtle algebraic structures could render a public key insecure. Could an RSA public key (N, e) be weak even if the corresponding private exponent d is large and safe from all known attacks? This paper answers that question in the affirmative.

We move beyond the paradigm of small private exponents and introduce a new vulnerability model based on a generalized algebraic property of the public key. This paper investigates a more generalized relationship involving e, N, and a novel function $\psi_n(N, a, b)$, defined as

$$\psi_n(N, a, b) = (p^n - a)(q^n - b),$$

where a and b are positive integers. Hence, the standard Euler's totient function $\phi(N)$ (corresponding to $\psi_1(N, 1, 1)$) and the generalized function $\psi_n(N)$ (corresponding to $\psi_n(N, 1, 1)$) are special instances of $\psi_n(N, a, b)$.

We analyze a new modified key equation

$$eu \equiv 1 \pmod{\psi_n(N, a, b)},$$

where u (a parameter may be related to the private exponent), a, and b are unknown but sufficiently small. Employing Coppersmith's method [6] in conjunction with the Herrmann-May linearization technique [9], we demonstrate that N can be factored if u, a, and b are suitably small. Specifically, assuming $e = N^\alpha$, $u < N^\delta$, and $a, b \le N^\beta$ (with $|aq^n - bp^n| < 2N^{n/2}$), we establish that the modified equation $eu \equiv 1 \pmod{\psi_n(N, a, b)}$ can be solved. leading to the factorization of N, provided the following conditions hold

$$\alpha > \frac{n}{2} + \beta, \quad \beta < \frac{n}{6}, \quad \text{and} \quad \delta < n - \sqrt{\frac{\alpha(2\beta + n)}{2}}.$$

We argue that the existence of such a relation for any small (u, a, b) constitutes a new type of weak key, independent of the size of the standard private exponent d. While no current system intentionally uses this structure, our work serves as a crucial security analysis for both existing and future RSA-like schemes, identifying a potential weakness that could arise from faulty key generation, hardware errors, or unforeseen design choices.

We develop a complete cryptanalytic attack using Coppersmith's method to solve for the unknowns and factor the modulus N. We rigorously derive the conditions for our attack's success, establishing the above new bound. Our technical novelty lies in identifying this congruence as an attack surface and developing the algebraic method (see Lemma 1) to recover the necessary parameters from Coppersmith's method. Furthermore, our proposed attacks offer several advantages over the known methods. In terms of concreteness, the following facts are derived.

- Setting $n = 1$ and $\beta = 0$ (corresponding to $a = b = 1$), our bound becomes $\delta < 1 - \sqrt{\alpha/2}$. This retrieves the Boneh-Durfee bound $d < N^{0.292}$ when the public exponent e is full-size (i.e., $\alpha \approx 1$, resulting in $\delta < 1 - \sqrt{2}/2 \approx 0.292$).
- Setting $n = 2$ and $\beta = 0$ (corresponding to $a = b = 1$), our bound $\delta < 2 - \sqrt{\alpha}$ matches the one reported in [21,28].

- For any positive integer n and $\beta = 0$ (corresponding to $a = b = 1$), our bound is $\delta < n - \sqrt{\alpha n/2}$, which is consistent with the bound from [25].
- Our approach leads to the factorization of N even if the private exponent d (satisfying the standard key equation $ed \equiv 1 \pmod{\phi(N)}$ or $ed \equiv 1 \pmod{\psi_n(N)}$ with $a = b = 1$) is larger than the attack thresholds of previous methods. This is because our attack targets a different parameter u related to the generalized congruence $eu \equiv 1 \pmod{\psi_n(N, a, b)}$ for appropriately small a, b (potentially different from 1).

We demonstrate that our framework is a true generalization. By setting $a = b = 1$, our attack bound precisely reduces to the bounds of several existing attacks.

Moreover, the collection of public exponents e that are vulnerable to our proposed attacks is potentially much larger than those susceptible to attacks on standard RSA and its variants. In the standard attacks with $a = b = 1$, the number of weak public exponents e of full-size (i.e., $e \approx N^n$, implying $\alpha \approx n$) is related to the number of private exponents d such that

$$d < N^{(1-\frac{\sqrt{2}}{2})n} \quad \text{and} \quad \gcd\left(d, (p^n - 1)(q^n - 1)\right) = 1.$$

With our approach, for each pair of positive integers (a, b) with $a, b \leq N^\beta$ and $\beta < n/6$, a full-size public exponent e with $\alpha \approx n$ is vulnerable if there exists small u such that

$$u < N^{n-\sqrt{\frac{n(2\beta+n)}{2}}} \quad \text{and} \quad \gcd\left(u, (p^n - a)(q^n - b)\right) = 1.$$

Therefore, the existence of many such pairs (a, b) significantly increases the vulnerable scenarios under which an exponent e might be found weak.

This work systematizes the security landscape of RSA and its variants by introducing a generalized cryptanalytic framework. Our contributions are three-fold:

1. **Unification of Existing Attacks:** We show that the standard RSA key equation and its known variants are all special instances of a single generalized congruence $eu \equiv 1 \pmod{\psi_n(N, a, b)}$. This provides a unified algebraic explanation for why previous attacks succeed.
2. **Expansion of the Weak Key Space:** By relaxing the structural parameters a and b beyond unity, we define a continuous *Security Polytope*. We demonstrate that an RSA instance secure against all previous small private exponent attacks may still be vulnerable if its public key possesses this hidden generalized structure.
3. **A New Generalized Bound:** We rigorously derive a new attack bound that subsumes previous results. Specifically, we prove that for parameters within the derived bound, the modulus N can be factored in polynomial time using Coppersmith's method.

To facilitate reproducibility, the open-source `SageMath` implementation of the proposed attack is available at https://github.com/MengceZheng/RSA_GAF.

The remainder of this paper is organized as follows. In Sect. 2, we introduce the main tools and useful lemmas used in our proposed attack. In Sect. 3, we detail the new generalized attack strategy. In Sect. 4, we provide a comprehensive comparison of our proposed attack with previous ones and show a numerical example. We conclude this paper in Sect. 5.

2 Preliminaries

In this section, we review the fundamental concepts and tools that support our attack, primarily focusing on lattice basis reduction and Coppersmith's method. Additionally, we introduce several new or specifically adapted lemmas crucial for our attack.

2.1 Lattice Basis Reduction

Let ω be a positive integer, and let $\boldsymbol{b}_1, \ldots, \boldsymbol{b}_\omega$ be ω linearly independent vectors in $\mathbb{R}^k$, where $k \geq \omega$. A lattice $\mathcal{L}$, spanned by the basis vectors $\boldsymbol{b}_1, \ldots, \boldsymbol{b}_\omega$, is the discrete subgroup defined by

$$\mathcal{L} = \left\{ \sum_{i=1}^{\omega} \lambda_i \boldsymbol{b}_i \mid \lambda_i \in \mathbb{Z} \right\}.$$

The integer ω is the rank of the lattice $\mathcal{L}$, and k is the dimension of the ambient space $\mathbb{R}^k$. If $\omega = k$, then $\mathcal{L}$ is a full-rank lattice. An important invariant of the lattice is its determinant (also known as its volume). It is defined by $\det(\mathcal{L}) = \sqrt{\det(BB^\top)}$, where B is the matrix whose rows are the basis vectors $\boldsymbol{b}_1, \ldots, \boldsymbol{b}_\omega$ and $B^\top$ denotes its matrix transpose. If $\omega = k$, this simplifies to $|\det(B)|$.

A lattice possesses infinitely many bases. Among them, certain bases consisting of relatively short and nearly orthogonal vectors, are particularly useful for solving various Diophantine problems arising in cryptanalysis. In general, finding such a good basis (e.g., one containing the shortest possible non-zero vector) is a computationally hard problem, known as the lattice reduction problem. In 1982, Lenstra, Lenstra, and Lovász [15] introduced the LLL algorithm, which provides an efficient polynomial-time solution for finding a reduced basis. This reduced basis contains vectors that are short in a well-defined sense. The following theorem provides upper bounds on the output vectors of the LLL algorithm, as often used in practice (e.g., see [16]).

Theorem 1 (LLL). *Let $\mathcal{L}$ be a lattice with a basis $(\boldsymbol{b}_1, \ldots, \boldsymbol{b}_\omega)$. The LLL algorithm, applied to $(\boldsymbol{b}_1, \ldots, \boldsymbol{b}_\omega)$, outputs a reduced basis $(\boldsymbol{u}_1, \ldots, \boldsymbol{u}_\omega)$ such that, for $i = 1, \ldots, \omega$,*

$$\|\boldsymbol{u}_1\| \leq \ldots \leq \|\boldsymbol{u}_i\| \leq 2^{\frac{\omega(\omega-1)}{4(\omega+1-i)}} \det(\mathcal{L})^{\frac{1}{\omega+1-i}},$$

where $\|\boldsymbol{u}_i\|$ denotes the Euclidean norm of a vector $\boldsymbol{u}_i$.

2.2 Coppersmith's Method

In 1997, Coppersmith [6] presented a method to find small integer solutions of modular polynomial equations of the form $f_1(x) \equiv 0 \pmod{R}$, where $f_1(x)$ is a univariate polynomial with integer coefficients and R is an integer modulus. He also presented a method to find small integer roots of bivariate polynomial equations $f_2(x, y) = 0$. Since its introduction, Coppersmith's method has become a cornerstone technique for solving various types of Diophantine equations encountered in cryptanalysis. It has also been generalized to find small roots of multivariate polynomial equations [12]. Coppersmith's method and its variants fundamentally rely on lattice reduction techniques. Another key concept is the Euclidean norm of a polynomial, used in Howgrave-Graham's reformulation of Coppersmith's original method.

The Euclidean norm of a polynomial $g(x_1, \ldots, x_k) = \sum a_{i_1,\ldots,i_k} x_1^{i_1} \cdots x_k^{i_k}$ is defined by

$$\|g(x_1, \ldots, x_k)\| = \sqrt{\sum a_{i_1,\ldots,i_k}^2}.$$

In 1997, Howgrave-Graham [11] presented an elegant reformulation of Coppersmith's method for finding small roots of modular polynomial equations. It is later reformulated as the following theorem (see [16]).

Theorem 2 (Howgrave-Graham). *Let e and m be two positive integers. Let $g(x_1, \ldots, x_k) \in \mathbb{Z}[x_1, \ldots, x_k]$ be a multivariate polynomial with at most ω monomials ($\omega \geq k$). If the conditions*

$$g(z_1, \ldots, z_k) \equiv 0 \pmod{e^m} \quad \text{and} \quad \|g(x_1X_1, \ldots, x_kX_k)\| < \frac{e^m}{\sqrt{\omega}}$$

are satisfied for integers $(z_1, \ldots, z_k)$ with $|z_i| < X_i$ and known upper bounds X_i, then $g(z_1, \ldots, z_k) = 0$ holds over the integers.

To solve a given modular polynomial equation $f(x_1, \ldots, x_k) \equiv 0 \pmod{e}$, Coppersmith's method typically starts by constructing a set of ω polynomials $f_1, \ldots, f_\omega$ related to f. These polynomials f_j are constructed such that they share the desired roots $(z_1, \ldots, z_k)$ modulo e^m for some optimized integer m. Using the coefficient vectors of these ω polynomials (scaled appropriately with the bounds X_i), one constructs a basis B for a lattice $\mathcal{L}$ of dimension ω. Applying the LLL algorithm via Theorem 1 to this basis yields a reduced basis, corresponding to ω new polynomials $g_1, \ldots, g_\omega$. These polynomials are integer linear combinations of the coefficient vectors of the f_j's and thus also have the desired roots $(z_1, \ldots, z_k)$ modulo e^m. One or more of these g_i polynomials (particularly those corresponding to first short vectors in the reduced basis) are then tested using Howgrave-Graham's theorem. If Theorem 2 applies, these selected g_i polynomials vanish over the integers for the roots $(z_1, \ldots, z_k)$.

The common integer solution $(z_1, \ldots, z_k)$ can then often be found by computing a Gröbner basis or using resultant computations. A common heuristic condition for the success of Coppersmith's method, ensuring that at least k short vectors from LLL algorithm will likely satisfy the Howgrave-Graham bound, is related to the determinant of the lattice.

$$2^{\frac{\omega(\omega-1)}{4(\omega+1-k)}} \det(\mathcal{L})^{\frac{1}{\omega+1-k}} < \frac{e^m}{\sqrt{\omega}}.$$

Analyzing this inequality allows one to determine the maximum size of the roots (i.e., the X_i bounds) that can be found for a given polynomial and its modulus. For multivariate cases ($k \geq 2$), Coppersmith's method relies on heuristic arguments, including the following common assumption.

Assumption 1. *The first k polynomials $g_1, \ldots, g_k$ (or a suitable subset of k polynomials) obtained from the reduced basis that satisfy Theorems 1 and 2 are algebraically independent.*

2.3 Useful Lemmas

If $N = pq$ is an RSA modulus with $q < p < 2q$, then one has the following inequalities (see [20]),

$$\frac{\sqrt{2}}{2} N^{\frac{1}{2}} < q < N^{\frac{1}{2}} < p < \sqrt{2} N^{\frac{1}{2}}. \tag{1}$$

Next, we present an important lemma that will be instrumental in our proposed attack.

Lemma 1. *Let $N = pq$ be an RSA modulus with $q < p < 2q$, and let M be an integer such that $M = aq^n + bp^n - ab$, where a and b are two unknown positive integers. If $a, b < N^{n/6}/2$ and $|aq^n - bp^n| < 2N^{n/2}$, then*

$$aq^n + bp^n = M + \left\lfloor \frac{M^2}{4N^n} \right\rfloor,$$

and

$$|aq^n - bp^n| = \sqrt{\left(M + \left\lfloor \frac{M^2}{4N^n} \right\rfloor\right)^2 - 4N^n \left\lfloor \frac{M^2}{4N^n} \right\rfloor}.$$

Proof. Suppose that $M = aq^n + bp^n - ab$, $|aq^n - bp^n| < 2N^{n/2}$, and $a, b < N^{n/6}/2$. Since $a, b \geq 1$, we have $ab \geq 1$. Then

$$(aq^n + bp^n)^2 = (aq^n - bp^n)^2 + 4abN^n < \left(2N^{\frac{n}{2}}\right)^2 + 4abN^n = 4N^n + 4abN^n.$$

Since $1 \leq ab$, we have $4N^n \leq 4abN^n$. Thus, $4N^n + 4abN^n \leq 8abN^n$. Given $ab < \left(N^{n/6}/2\right)^2 = N^{n/3}/4$, it follows that

$$(aq^n + bp^n)^2 < 8 \cdot \frac{1}{4} N^{\frac{n}{3}} \cdot N^n = 2N^{\frac{4n}{3}}.$$

Hence, $aq^n + bp^n < 2^{1/2}N^{2n/3}$. On the other hand, we have[1]

$$4abN^n < (aq^n + bp^n)^2 = (M + ab)^2 = (aq^n - bp^n)^2 + 4abN^n < 4N^n + 4abN^n.$$

Then

$$ab < \frac{(M + ab)^2}{4N^n} < 1 + ab,$$

and

$$ab = \left\lfloor \frac{(M + ab)^2}{4N^n} \right\rfloor = \left\lfloor \frac{M^2 + 2abM + (ab)^2}{4N^n} \right\rfloor.$$

The term $2abM + (ab)^2$ satisfies

$$2abM + (ab)^2 = 2ab\,(aq^n + bp^n) - (ab)^2 < \frac{1}{2}N^{\frac{n}{3}} \cdot 2^{\frac{1}{2}}N^{\frac{2n}{3}} = 2^{-\frac{1}{2}}N^n.$$

This implies that

$$\frac{M^2 + 2abM + (ab)^2}{4N^n} < \frac{M^2}{4N^n} + 2^{-\frac{5}{2}},$$

and hence

$$ab = \left\lfloor \frac{M^2 + 2abM + (ab)^2}{4N^n} \right\rfloor = \left\lfloor \frac{M^2}{4N^n} \right\rfloor.$$

From this, we deduce

$$aq^n + bp^n = M + ab = M + \left\lfloor \frac{M^2}{4N^n} \right\rfloor,$$

and

$$|aq^n - bp^n| = \sqrt{(aq^n + bp^n)^2 - 4abN^n} = \sqrt{\left(M + \left\lfloor \frac{M^2}{4N^n} \right\rfloor\right)^2 - 4N^n \left\lfloor \frac{M^2}{4N^n} \right\rfloor}.$$

This terminates the proof. □

The following simple result guarantees that, for any given b, the inequality $|aq^n - bp^n| < 2N^{n/2}$ (a condition in Lemma 1) always holds for a certain choice of integer a.

Lemma 2. *Let $N = pq$ be an RSA modulus with $q < p < 2q$. Let b be a positive integer, and let $a = [bp^n/q^n]$, where $[\zeta]$ denotes the nearest integer to ζ. Then*

$$|aq^n - bp^n| < 2N^{\frac{n}{2}}.$$

[1] This inequality is strict since the equality $aq^n = bp^n$ never occurs for distinct random large primes $p, q \approx N^{1/2}$ and small integers $a, b < N^{n/6}/2 \approx p^{n/3}$ (or $\approx q^{n/3}$).

Proof. Suppose $a = [bp^n/q^n]$. By definition of the nearest integer, we have

$$\left| a - \frac{bp^n}{q^n} \right| \leq \frac{1}{2}.$$

Multiplying by q^n (which is positive), we get

$$|aq^n - bp^n| \leq \frac{1}{2} q^n.$$

Using the inequality $q < N^{1/2}$ from (1), we have $q^n < (N^{1/2})^n = N^{n/2}$. Therefore,

$$|aq^n - bp^n| \leq \frac{1}{2} q^n < \frac{1}{2} N^{\frac{n}{2}} < N^{\frac{n}{2}}.$$

Since it is obvious that $N^{n/2} < 2N^{n/2}$, this terminates the proof. □

3 The Generalized Attack

In this section, we present a new generalized attack on RSA and its variants applicable when there exist two positive integers a and b such that the public exponent e satisfies the congruence $eu \equiv 1 \pmod{(p^n - a)(q^n - b)}$ for a small integer u.[2]

Theorem 3. *Let $N = pq$ be an RSA modulus with $q < p < 2q$. Let a, b be two unknown positive integers such that $a, b \leq N^\beta$ for some $\beta < n/6 - \log_N 2$, and let them also satisfy $|aq^n - bp^n| < 2N^{n/2}$. Let $e = N^\alpha$ be a public exponent satisfying the equation $eu \equiv 1 \pmod{(p^n - a)(q^n - b)}$ with an unknown $u < N^\delta$. If $\alpha > n/2 + \beta$, and*

$$\delta < n - \sqrt{\frac{\alpha(2\beta + n)}{2}}, \tag{2}$$

then N can be factored in polynomial time.

Proof. The equation $eu \equiv 1 \pmod{(p^n - a)(q^n - b)}$ implies the existence of an integer v such that

$$eu - v(p^n - a)(q^n - b) = 1.$$

Expanding the product term gives $(p^n - a)(q^n - b) = N^n - (aq^n + bp^n - ab)$. Let y_0 denote $-(aq^n + bp^n - ab)$. Then the equation becomes $eu - v(N^n + y_0) = 1$, which leads to the congruence $v(N^n + y_0) + 1 \equiv 0 \pmod{e}$.

We can therefore define a polynomial

$$f(x, y) = x(A + y) + 1 \quad \text{with} \quad A = N^n,$$

[2] In this generalized framework, the parameter u acts as a "generalized private exponent." Unlike the standard private exponent d, u is the modular inverse of e with respect to the hidden structure $\psi_n(N, a, b)$.

which has a small integer root $(x_0, y_0) = (v, -(aq^n + bp^n - ab))$ modulo e. To find this root, we apply the linearization method of Herrmann and May [9]. The relation $f(x, y) \equiv 0 \pmod{e}$ can be expressed as $Ax + xy + 1 \equiv 0 \pmod{e}$. Let $z = xy + 1$. This introduces a new variable z and a new polynomial relation

$$g(x, z) = Ax + z \equiv 0 \pmod{e}.$$

The goal is to find the small integer roots (x_0, y_0) by finding the roots of a system of polynomials in variables x, y and z.

Let m and t be two positive integer parameters to be optimized later. We define two sets of indices (k, i, j) as follows.

$$\mathcal{I} = \{(k, i, j) \mid j = 0, \ k = 0, \dots, m, \ i = 0, \dots, m - k\},$$
$$\mathcal{J} = \{(k, i, j) \mid j = 1, \dots, t, \ k = \lfloor m/t \rfloor j, \dots, m, \ i = 0\}.$$

From the relationship

$$v = \frac{eu - 1}{(p^n - a)(q^n - b)} \approx \frac{eu}{N^n},$$

and given the sizes $e = N^\alpha$ and $u < N^\delta$, we can establish bounds for the roots. For the solution $(x_0, y_0) = (v, -(aq^n + bp^n - ab))$, we have

- $|x_0| = |v| < N^{\alpha+\delta-n}$ and we set the bound $X = N^{\alpha+\delta-n}$.
- $|y_0| = |aq^n + bp^n - ab| < (a + b)p^n < 2N^\beta(2^{1/2}N^{1/2})^n = 2^{1+n/2}N^{\beta+n/2}$ and we set the bound $Y = 2^{1+n/2}N^{\beta+n/2}$.
- $|z_0| = |x_0 y_0 + 1| < XY + 1$ and we set the bound $Z = 2^{1+n/2}N^{\alpha+\beta+\delta-n/2}$.

Since $N \gg 2$ for standard RSA and its variants, we omit constant factors for simplicity in the asymptotic analysis. These bounds can be formally written as

$$X = N^{\alpha+\delta-n}, \ Y = N^{\beta+\frac{n}{2}}, \ Z = N^{\alpha+\beta+\delta-\frac{n}{2}}. \quad (3)$$

Remark 1. In the above bounds for $|x_0|, |y_0|, |z_0|$, we omit small constant factors to simplify the asymptotic analysis, which is also a common treatment used in Coppersmith's method. In a finite-dimensional implementation, these constants imply a negligible reduction in the bound δ, which does not affect the polynomial-time solvability.

To apply Coppersmith's method, we construct a lattice $\mathcal{L}$ from the following set of polynomials, which all have the root (x_0, y_0, z_0) modulo e^m.

$$G_{k,i,j}(x, y, z) = x^i y^j g(x, z)^k e^{m-k} \quad \text{for} \quad (k, i, j) \in \mathcal{I} \cup \mathcal{J},$$

where $g(x, z) = Ax + z$ and the relation $xy = z - 1$ is used. The lattice is built by constructing a basis matrix where the rows are the coefficients of the polynomials $G_{k,i,j}(xX, yY, zZ)$, ordered following the lexical order of $(k, i, j) \in \mathcal{I} \cup \mathcal{J}$, and the columns are the coefficients of the monomials $x^i y^j z^k$, ordered in the same way. A toy example of the resulting lattice basis matrix for $m = 3$ and $t = 1$ is shown in Table 1.

Table 1. A toy example of lattice basis matrix for $m = 3$ and $t = 1$.

$G_{k,i,j}$	1	x	x^2	x^3	z	xz	x^2z	z^2	xz^2	z^3	yz^3
$G_{0,0,0}$	e^3	0	0	0	0	0	0	0	0	0	0
$G_{0,1,0}$	0	Xe^3	0	0	0	0	0	0	0	0	0
$G_{0,2,0}$	0	0	X^2e^3	0	0	0	0	0	0	0	0
$G_{0,3,0}$	0	0	0	X^3e^3	0	0	0	0	0	0	0
$G_{1,0,0}$	0	AXe^2	0	0	Ze^2	0	0	0	0	0	0
$G_{1,1,0}$	0	0	AX^2e^2	0	0	XZe^2	0	0	0	0	0
$G_{1,2,0}$	0	0	0	AX^3e^2	0	0	X^2Ze^2	0	0	0	0
$G_{2,0,0}$	0	0	A^2X^2e	0	0	$2AXZe$	0	Z^2e	0	0	0
$G_{2,1,0}$	0	0	0	A^2X^3e	0	0	$2AX^2Ze$	0	XZ^2e	0	0
$G_{3,0,0}$	0	0	0	A^3X^3	0	0	$3A^2X^2Z$	0	$3AXZ^2$	Z^3	0
$G_{3,0,1}$	0	0	$-A^3X^2$	0	0	$-3A^2XZ$	A^3X^2Z	$-3AZ^2$	$3A^2XZ^2$	$3AZ^3$	YZ^3

By construction, the matrix of the lattice is upper triangular, and its determinant is the product of its diagonal entries, that is

$$\det(\mathcal{L}) = X^{n_X} Y^{n_Y} Z^{n_Z} e^{n_e}, \tag{4}$$

where the exponents n_X, n_Y, n_Z, n_e and the lattice dimension ω are sums over the index set $I \cup J$. More precisely,[3]

$$\begin{aligned}
n_X &= \sum_{k=0}^{m}\sum_{i=0}^{m-k} i + \sum_{j=1}^{t}\sum_{k=\lfloor m/t \rfloor j}^{m} 0 \\
&= \frac{1}{6}m(m+1)(m+2), \\
n_Y &= \sum_{k=0}^{m}\sum_{i=0}^{m-k} 0 + \sum_{j=1}^{t}\sum_{k=\lfloor m/t \rfloor j}^{m} j \\
&= \frac{1}{6}(t+1)(mt-m+3t), \\
n_Z &= \sum_{k=0}^{m}\sum_{i=0}^{m-k} k + \sum_{j=1}^{t}\sum_{k=\lfloor m/t \rfloor j}^{m} k \\
&= \frac{1}{6}m(m+1)(m+2) + \frac{m}{12t}(4mt^2 - 3mt - m + 9t^2 + 3t), \\
n_e &= \sum_{k=0}^{m}\sum_{i=0}^{m-k} (m-k) + \sum_{j=1}^{t}\sum_{k=\lfloor m/t \rfloor j}^{m} (m-k) \\
&= \frac{1}{3}m(m+1)(m+2) + \frac{m}{12t}(t-1)(2mt-m+3t), \\
\omega &= \sum_{k=0}^{m}\sum_{i=0}^{m-k} 1 + \sum_{j=1}^{t}\sum_{k=\lfloor m/t \rfloor j}^{m} 1 \\
&= \frac{1}{2}(m+1)(m+2) + \frac{1}{2}m(t-1) + t.
\end{aligned}$$

[3] For asymptotic simplicity, we assume m is a multiple of t and then omit the floor function $\lfloor m/t \rfloor$.

Setting $t = \tau m$ for $\tau > 0$ and considering the dominant terms for sufficiently large m, the above quantities can be approximated by

$$n_X = \frac{1}{6}m^3,\ n_Y = \frac{\tau^2}{6}m^3,\ n_Z = \frac{2\tau+1}{6}m^3,\ n_e = \frac{\tau+2}{6}m^3,\ \omega = \frac{\tau+1}{2}m^2. \quad (5)$$

For the attack to succeed, we need to find at least three algebraically independent polynomials that are short enough to satisfy the conditions in Theorem 2. Using the LLL bound for the third vector ($i = 3$ in Theorem 1), the resulting condition is

$$2^{\frac{\omega(\omega-1)}{4(\omega-2)}} \det(\mathcal{L})^{\frac{1}{\omega-2}} < \frac{e^m}{\sqrt{\omega}},$$

which can be transformed into

$$\det(\mathcal{L}) < 2^{\frac{-\omega(\omega-1)}{4}} \omega^{\frac{-(\omega-2)}{2}} e^{m(\omega-2)} < e^{m\omega}.$$

Asymptotically, for large ω, this simplifies to $\det(\mathcal{L}) < e^{m\omega}$. Combining this with (4) yields the inequality

$$X^{n_X} Y^{n_Y} Z^{n_Z} e^{n_e} < e^{m\omega}.$$

Using the derived exponents (5), and neglecting the lower-order terms, we have

$$X^{\frac{1}{6}m^3} Y^{\frac{\tau^2}{6}m^3} Z^{\frac{2\tau+1}{6}m^3} e^{\frac{\tau+2}{6}m^3} < e^{\frac{\tau+1}{2}m^3}.$$

Then, substituting the bounds from (3), we obtain

$$N^{\frac{1}{6}m^3\cdot(\alpha+\delta-n)} N^{\frac{\tau^2}{6}m^3\cdot(\beta+\frac{n}{2})} N^{\frac{2\tau+1}{6}m^3\cdot(\alpha+\beta+\delta-\frac{n}{2})} N^{\frac{\tau+2}{6}m^3\cdot\alpha} < N^{\frac{\tau+1}{2}m^3\cdot\alpha}.$$

Taking the logarithm and simplifying, we get

$$\alpha + \delta - n + \tau^2\left(\beta + \frac{n}{2}\right) + (2\tau+1)\left(\alpha + \beta + \delta - \frac{n}{2}\right) + (\tau+2)\alpha < 3(\tau+1)\alpha,$$

which leads to

$$(2\beta + n)\tau^2 + (4\beta + 4\delta - 2n)\tau + 2\alpha + 2\beta + 4\delta - 3n < 0.$$

This quadratic expression in τ on the left side can be minimized at

$$\tau_0 = \frac{n - 2\beta - 2\delta}{2\beta + n}.$$

Substituting this value into the inequality yields

$$-2\delta^2 + 4n\delta + 2\alpha\beta + n\alpha - 2n^2 < 0.$$

This is a quadratic inequality in δ, which holds if δ is less than the smallest root, leading to the condition

$$\delta < n - \sqrt{\frac{\alpha(2\beta + n)}{2}}.$$

Furthermore, the optimization requires $\tau_0 > 0$, which implies $n - 2\beta - 2\delta > 0$, or $\delta < n/2 - \beta$. The condition $\alpha > n/2 + \beta$ given in the theorem ensures that

$$\delta < \min\left\{n - \sqrt{\frac{\alpha(2\beta+n)}{2}},\ \frac{n}{2} - \beta\right\} = n - \sqrt{\frac{\alpha(2\beta+n)}{2}}.$$

Under this condition on δ, the LLL algorithm will produce sufficiently short vectors corresponding to at least three algebraically independent polynomials that hold over the integers. Using resultants or Gröbner basis computations, one can solve for the integer root $(x_0, y_0) = (v, -(aq^n + bp^n - ab))$. Let $M = -y_0 = aq^n + bp^n - ab$. Using Lemma 1 with $a, b < N^{n/6}/2$, one computes

$$S = M + \left\lfloor \frac{M^2}{4N^n} \right\rfloor = aq^n + bp^n$$

and

$$D = \sqrt{S^2 - 4N^n \left\lfloor \frac{M^2}{4N^n} \right\rfloor} = |aq^n - bp^n|.$$

This allows one to recover $S = aq^n + bp^n$ and $D = |aq^n - bp^n|$. From these two values, one can determine $2aq^n$ and $2bp^n$ and compute prime factors using greatest common divisors with N through $\gcd(N, S + D)$ and $\gcd(N, S - D)$. This finally reveals the prime factors

$$p = \max\{\gcd(N, S + D),\ \gcd(N, S - D)\},$$

and

$$q = \min\{\gcd(N, S + D),\ \gcd(N, S - D)\},$$

thus factoring $N = pq$. This completes the proof. □

For completeness, we present the following algorithm that outputs the prime factors of a given RSA modulus satisfying Theorem 3.

We briefly describe the post-factorization parameter recovery of u, a, b. Once the modulus N is factored into p and q, the parameters a and b can be efficiently recovered to run the decryption algorithm. Recall that $S = aq^n + bp^n$ and $D = |aq^n - bp^n|$ are recovered using Algorithm 1. Then, aq^n and bp^n can be easily determined. Since p, q are known, we compute p^n and q^n. With aq^n and bp^n known, we can efficiently derive values for a, b using divisions. Finally, we can recover $u = e^{-1} \bmod (p^n - a)(q^n - b)$.

Algorithm 1. Factoring Algorithm Based on the Generalized Attack

Input: An RSA modulus N, a public exponent e, an integer n, and reals α, β, δ.
Output: The factorization of $N = pq$ with its prime factors p and q.

1: Define a modular polynomial $f(x, y)$ with unknown variables x, y:

$$f(x, y) = x(N^n + y) + 1 \pmod{e}.$$

2: Let $z = xy + 1$ and define a linear polynomial $g(x, z)$ with unknown variables x, z:

$$g(x, z) = N^n x + z \pmod{e}.$$

3: Set the estimated bounds X, Y, Z on unknown variables x, y, z:

$$X = \left\lfloor N^{\alpha+\delta-n} \right\rfloor, \; Y = \left\lfloor 2^{1+\frac{n}{2}} N^{\beta+\frac{n}{2}} \right\rfloor, \; Z = XY + 1.$$

4: Choose a suitable integer m and compute the relevant optimized integer t:

$$t = \left\lceil \frac{n - 2\beta - 2\delta}{2\beta + n} \cdot m \right\rceil$$

5: Extract root $y_0 = -(aq^n + bp^n - ab)$ using Coppersmith's method via Theorem 3.
6: Let $M = -y_0$ and compute S (i.e., $aq^n + bp^n$) and D (i.e., $|aq^n - bp^n|$):

$$S = M + \left\lfloor \frac{M^2}{4N^n} \right\rfloor, \; D = \sqrt{S^2 - 4N^n \left\lfloor \frac{M^2}{4N^n} \right\rfloor}$$

7: Compute $\gcd(N, S + D)$, $\gcd(N, S - D)$ and return the factorization of $N = pq$:

$$\{p, \; q\} = \{\gcd(N, S + D), \; \gcd(N, S - D)\}$$

4 Comparison and Discussion

In this section, we compare the generalized attack with several existing methods that target the standard RSA key equation or its variants (see Table 2). We demonstrate that our result covers previous bounds as special cases. Furthermore, we visualize the attack bounds and provide a detailed numerical example to illustrate the practical application of the generalized attack.

4.1 Comparison with Existing Attacks

Comparison with Boneh-Durfee Attack. A landmark attack on RSA with small private exponents is the one by Boneh and Durfee [2]. It exploits the key equation $ed \equiv 1 \pmod{(p-1)(q-1)}$, where $d < N^{\delta_0}$ is the private exponent. For a public exponent of full-size $e \approx N$ (i.e., $\alpha = 1$), the attack is effective for $\delta_0 < 1 - \sqrt{2}/2 \approx 0.292$.

This bound can be retrieved as a special case of our result in Theorem 3. By setting the parameters to match standard RSA (i.e., $n = 1$, $a = b = 1$, which

Table 2. Comparison of attacks on RSA and its variants with $e = N^\alpha$, $a, b \leq N^\beta$.

Attack	Target Equation	Attack Condition	Parameters (n, α, β)
Wiener [26]	$ed \equiv 1 \pmod{\phi(N)}$	$d < \frac{1}{3}N^{0.25}$	$(1, 1, 0)$
Boneh-Durfee [2]	$ed \equiv 1 \pmod{\phi(N)}$	$d < N^{0.292}$	$(1, 1, 0)$
Peng et al. [21] Zheng et al. [28]	$ed \equiv 1 \pmod{\psi_2(N)}$	$d < N^{2-\sqrt{\alpha}}$	$(2, \alpha, 0)$
Teleşeanu [25]	$ed \equiv 1 \pmod{\psi_n(N)}$	$d < N^{n-\sqrt{\alpha n/2}}$	$(n, \alpha, 0)$
This Work	$eu \equiv 1 \pmod{\psi_n(N, a, b)}$	$u < N^{n-\sqrt{\alpha(2\beta+n)/2}}$	(n, α, β)

implies $\beta = 0$) and assuming a full-size public exponent (i.e., $\alpha = 1$), the bound from (2) becomes

$$\delta < n - \sqrt{\frac{\alpha(2\beta + n)}{2}} = 1 - \sqrt{\frac{1}{2}} = 1 - \frac{\sqrt{2}}{2}.$$

This exactly matches the Boneh-Durfee bound.

Discussion on Standard RSA with Implicit Perturbation $(n = 1, \beta > 0)$.

Our framework extends to standard RSA where the prime factors satisfy a perturbed relation $eu \equiv 1 \pmod{(p - a)(q - b)}$ with $a, b \approx N^\beta > 1$. This corresponds to RSA with shifted primes. Our bound becomes $\delta < 1 - \sqrt{\alpha/2 + \alpha\beta}$. As the perturbation size β increases, the attack range for d decreases continuously.

Comparison with Attacks on RSA Variants $(n = 2)$.

In [21,28], Peng et al. and Zheng et al. proposed methods to attack RSA variants where the key equation is $ed \equiv 1 \pmod{(p^2 - 1)(q^2 - 1)}$. Both works showed that their attacks can factor the modulus $N = pq$ if $e = N^\alpha$ and the private key $d < N^{\delta_0}$ satisfies $\delta_0 < 2 - \sqrt{\alpha}$.

Our generalized result also covers this bound. By setting $n = 2$ and $a = b = 1$ (implying $\beta = 0$), the bound from Theorem 3 becomes

$$\delta < n - \sqrt{\frac{\alpha(2\beta + n)}{2}} = 2 - \sqrt{\frac{2\alpha}{2}} = 2 - \sqrt{\alpha}.$$

This exactly matches the bound reported in [21,28].

Comparison with Teleşeanu's Attack. Recently, Teleşeanu [25] presented an attack on RSA-like schemes with a key equation of the form

$$ed \equiv 1 \pmod{(p^n - 1)(q^n - 1)}$$

for $n \geq 2$. The attack succeeds if $d < N^{\delta_0}$ with $\delta_0 < n - \sqrt{\alpha n/2}$, for a public exponent $e = N^\alpha$ in a certain range.

Once again, our generalized attack retrieves this bound. Setting $a = b = 1$ (which means $\beta = 0$), the condition from Theorem 3 gives

$$\delta < n - \sqrt{\frac{\alpha(2\beta + n)}{2}} = n - \sqrt{\frac{\alpha n}{2}}.$$

matching the bound from [25].

4.2 Visualizing the Attack Surface

To highlight the improvement of our method, we further visualize the attack bounds. Figure 1 plots the attack threshold δ as a function of the public exponent size α and a structural parameter β for the case $n = 2$. The solid line represents the bound for previous attacks on the $\psi_2(N)$ variant (i.e., $\delta < 2 - \sqrt{\alpha}$), which assumes $a = b = 1$ (i.e., $\beta = 0$). The dashed lines represent the bounds on our parameter u for different choices of $\beta > 0$.

While the bound on u becomes stricter as β grows, our attack opens up a new multi-dimensional surface of vulnerability. An adversary is no longer limited to attacking a single line (i.e., $\beta = 0$), but can now search for weaknesses across the entire area under the curves. Any public key (N, e) is vulnerable if it satisfies our generalized relation for *any* combination of small (δ, β) that falls below the corresponding curve.

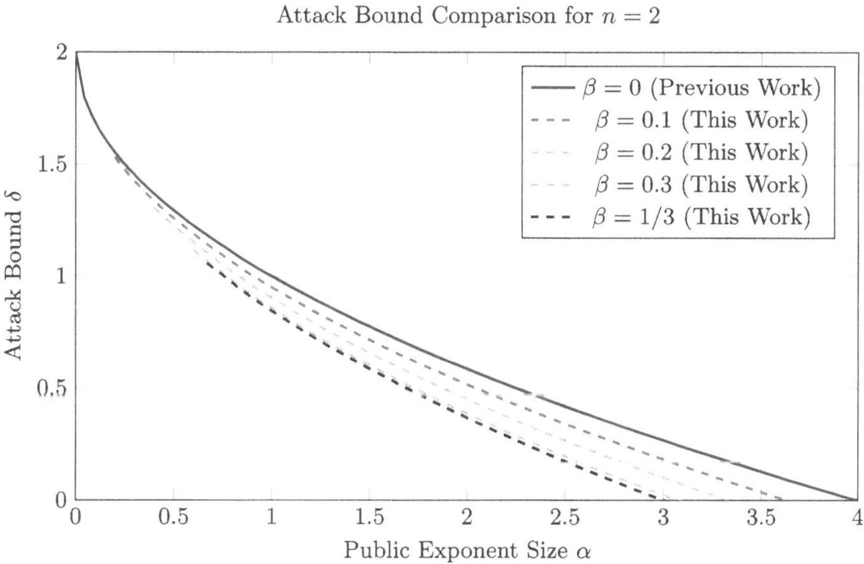

Fig. 1. Comparison of the attack bound δ as a function of α, β for $n = 2$. The curves represent the security threshold for different parameters β. The area *below* each curve indicates the *Insecure Region* corresponding to that β. Note that our framework reveals a multi-dimensional attack surface (parameterized by $\beta > 0$), whereas previous attacks are restricted to the single curve where $\beta = 0$ (i.e., $a = b = 1$).

4.3 A Numerical Example

We show a detailed numerical example below to illustrate the practical application of our generalized attack. Consider an attack scenario with parameters

$n = 2$, a 200-bit modulus N, and a 400-bit public exponent e. Suppose we are given the following known values.

$$\begin{aligned} N &= 1223852682569144461759988126766200863829976896432051027669117, \\ e &= 3215127331379995171260794981442320178984588355909234391254 46\backslash \\ &\quad 2091762455897819827135854294788029132909777334023243884982 59. \end{aligned}$$

Here, $e = N^{\alpha}$ with $\alpha \approx 1.9888$. The standard attacks mentioned above are ineffective, as we will show later. To apply our method as described in Algorithm 1, we take attack parameters $\delta = 0.35$ and $\beta = 0.25$, which satisfy the condition $\delta < n - \sqrt{\alpha(2\beta + n)/2} \approx 0.423$. The estimated bounds for the factoring algorithm are

$$\begin{aligned} X &= \lfloor N^{\alpha+\delta-n} \rfloor = 230425029816594033263, \\ Y &= \lfloor 2^{1+\frac{n}{2}} N^{\beta+\frac{n}{2}} \rfloor \\ &= 514898256753110504766215294701696155526633164678617068924491\backslash \\ &\quad 6943569617861620, \\ Z &= XY + 1 \\ &= 118645446164847778103070031409659415386669175332066817546790\backslash \\ &\quad 5809686279902253667309027921211066061. \end{aligned}$$

We construct the lattice $\mathcal{L}$ as described in Sect. 3 with parameters $m = 5$ and $t = 1$, resulting in a lattice of dimension $\omega = 22$. After applying the LLL algorithm and extracting the integer root $(x_0, y_0) = (v, -(aq^n - bp^n + ab))$ of the resulting polynomial system, we obtain

$$\begin{aligned} x_0 &= 545662057038567280891 0, \\ y_0 &= -171810640254871482249218003757737130702123357988858634565108\backslash \\ &\quad 06276539393443929. \end{aligned}$$

Setting $M = -y_0$ and applying Lemma 1, we obtain

$$\begin{aligned} S &= M + \left\lfloor \frac{M^2}{4N^n} \right\rfloor \\ &= 171810640254871482249218003757737130702123358481557807120603\backslash \\ &\quad 23650505499574146, \\ D &= \sqrt{S^2 - 4N^n \left\lfloor \frac{M^2}{4N^n} \right\rfloor} \\ &= 8811982824535315129733462492259506995404637639050451438687 92. \end{aligned}$$

From S and D, we can find the prime factors of N by computing

$$\begin{aligned} p = \gcd(N, S - D) &= 1267370237553798131313152809849, \\ q = \gcd(N, S + D) &= 965663107989147165902355920933. \end{aligned}$$

The product of p and q correctly yields the original modulus N.

Moreover, u, a, b can be efficiently computed as well. We first obtain aq^n and bp^n using S and D.

$$\begin{aligned} aq^n &= \frac{S+D}{2} \\ &= 859053201274357455306004141465261302177929253705324012626204\backslash \\ &\quad 3777775321721469, \\ bp^n &= \frac{S-D}{2} \\ &= 859053201274357367186175896112110004843304331110254058579827\backslash \\ &\quad 9872730177852677. \end{aligned}$$

With p and q known for $n = 2$, we compute

$$a = \frac{aq^2}{q^2} = 9212315021370821, \quad b = \frac{bp^2}{p^2} = 5348266656237077.$$

Finally, u can be computed as

$$u = e^{-1} \bmod (p^2 - a)(q^2 - b) = 254204870223285415405339.$$

With p and q known, we can analyze why previous attacks in [2,21,25,28] would fail. The standard RSA private exponent d_1 under the standard RSA key equation $ed_1 \equiv 1 \pmod{(p-1)(q-1)}$ corresponding to e is

$$d_1 = 2475465207032184646603411338062463641065507532126974628172211.$$

Therefore, we know

$$d_1 \approx N^{0.988}, \text{ and } 0.988 \gg 1 - \frac{\sqrt{2}}{2} \approx 0.292.$$

This value is far too large for the Boneh-Durfee attack.

Similarly, for the RSA variant with $n = 2$, the corresponding private exponent d_2 in the equation $ed_2 \equiv 1 \pmod{\left(p^2 - 1\right)\left(q^2 - 1\right)}$ is

$$\begin{aligned} d_2 &= 2501486750528548535297703714851475675173415850246964445336l3\backslash \\ &\quad 02378788262369644878327563723429475101032365690797377601l739. \end{aligned}$$

Therefore, we know

$$d_2 \approx N^{1.987}, \text{ and } 1.987 \gg 2 - \sqrt{\alpha} \approx 0.589.$$

This value is much larger than the bound required by the attacks in [21,25,28]. This numerical example demonstrates that our generalized attack can succeed even when the private exponents for RSA key equations are large.

4.4 Estimating the Number of Weak Exponents

Our generalized attack significantly increases the set of public exponents that can be considered weak. In standard attacks, a public exponent e is deemed vulnerable only if its corresponding private exponent d is small. In our method, however, e is vulnerable if there exists a certain set of small parameters (u, a, b) that satisfies the generalized key equation $eu \equiv 1 \pmod{\psi_n(N, a, b)}$.

It is important to distinguish between targeted variants and standard RSA instances. For a cryptosystem explicitly designed with parameters satisfying $\psi_n(N, a, b)$ for specific $a, b > 1$, our attack is deterministic. However, for a standard RSA key generated with random primes, the probability that there exist small a, b satisfying the relation is determined by the density of such algebraic structures. While this probability may be low for random keys, our analysis proves that the class of weak keys is larger than previously understood.

A heuristic estimate can quantify this increase. For a full-size public exponent $e \approx N^n$ (i.e., $\alpha = n$), the number of standard weak exponents is determined by the number of private exponents d that fall below the attack bound [25]. This quantity is on the order of $\mathcal{O}(N^{(1-\sqrt{2}/2)n-\epsilon})$. To formalize this, we analyze such a full-size case when the corresponding private exponent d in the equation $ed \equiv 1 \pmod{(p^n-1)(q^n-1)}$ satisfies $d < N^{(1-\sqrt{2}/2)n}$. The number of such weak exponents corresponds to the cardinality of the set

$$\mathcal{D}_n = \left\{ d \mid d < N^{(1-\frac{\sqrt{2}}{2})n} \text{ and } \gcd\left(d, (p^n-1)(q^n-1)\right) = 1 \right\}.$$

Thus, the cardinality of $\mathcal{D}_n$ can be approximated by considering the density of integers that are coprime to $\psi_n(N)$. We have $|\mathcal{D}_n| \approx \rho \cdot N^{(1-\sqrt{2}/2)n}$, where the density ratio $\rho = \varphi(\psi_n(N))/\psi_n(N)$ is a value bounded between two positive constants for sufficiently large N. As a consequence, the number of weak exponents is extremely close to $N^{(1-\sqrt{2}/2)n}$, which can be written as $\mathcal{O}(N^{(1-\sqrt{2}/2)n-\epsilon})$, that is $\mathcal{O}(N^{0.292n-\epsilon})$.

Moreover, our approach introduces new parameters $a, b < N^{n/6}/2$. The availability of approximately $N^{n/6}/2$ choices for parameter a (and b of nearly the same size) can be viewed as expanding the dimensions of vulnerability. This leads to a simplified estimate for the number of weak instances on the order of

$$\mathcal{O}\left(N^{\frac{n}{6}}\right) \cdot \mathcal{O}\left(N^{n-\sqrt{\frac{(2\cdot\frac{n}{6}+n)\cdot n}{2}}-\epsilon}\right) = \mathcal{O}\left(N^{\frac{n}{6}} \cdot N^{(1-\frac{\sqrt{6}}{3})n-\epsilon}\right) = \mathcal{O}\left(N^{(\frac{7}{6}-\frac{\sqrt{6}}{3})n-\epsilon}\right),$$

that is $\mathcal{O}\left(N^{0.350n-\epsilon}\right)$. This leads to a considerable increase $\mathcal{O}(N^{0.350n-0.292n}) \approx \mathcal{O}(N^{0.057n})$ in the number of potentially weak exponents compared to previous attacks.

Remark 2. The attack strategy is not restricted to the integer n and can be mounted for any integer r such that $1 \leq r \leq n$. This means that a public exponent e is vulnerable if a relation of $eu \equiv 1 \pmod{(p^r-a)(q^r-b)}$ exists for *any* such r with small parameters.

A common critique regarding small exponent attacks is the perceived sparsity of weak keys. Indeed, for a randomly chosen modulus N, the probability that the private exponent d falls below the Boneh-Durfee bound is low. However, this observation presents a narrow view, limited of the vulnerability space.

Our generalized framework reveals that such scarcity of weak keys is an artifact of fixing the structural parameters to unity. By introducing the generalized attack along with a unified bound, we define a continuous *Security Polytope* in the parameter space $(n, \alpha, \beta, \delta)$. Within this polytope:

- While standard weak keys may be rare, the universe of RSA variants (characterized by $\beta > 0$) is vast. Our result demonstrates that as the structural complexity of a variant increases with various a, b, the secure region for the private exponent δ shrinks. This implies that many RSA variants proposed in the literature might be inherently more fragile than standard RSA.
- If a protocol designer chooses parameters that satisfy a perturbed key equation (e.g., to enable faster decryption or other properties), they essentially move the cryptosystem along the β-axis of our polytope. Our analysis serves as a rigorous impossibility result: it quantifies exactly how much algebraic structure can be added before the system becomes insecure, regardless of the randomness of d.

4.5 Further Generalization for Intermediate Powers

The attack presented in Theorem 3 can be generalized for any intermediate power r where $1 \leq r \leq n$. This significantly broadens the applicability of the attack, as a single public key must be secure against a family of potential congruences.

Corollary 1. *Let $N = pq$ be an RSA modulus using the variant Euler function $\psi_n(N, 1, 1)$ with $q < p < 2q$. Let $1 \leq r \leq n - 1$ be a positive integer. Suppose that a, b are two unknown positive integers such that $a, b \leq N^{\beta}$ for some $\beta < r/6 - \log_N 2$, and a, b also satisfy $|aq^r - bp^r| < 2N^{r/2}$. Suppose that $e = N^{\alpha}$ is a public exponent satisfying the equation $eu \equiv 1 \pmod{(p^r - a)(q^r - b)}$ with an unknown $u < N^{\delta}$. If $\alpha > r/2 + \beta$, and*

$$\delta < r - \sqrt{\frac{\alpha(2\beta + r)}{2}},$$

then N can be factored in polynomial time.

Proof. The proof follows directly from the proof of Theorem 3 by substituting n with r. □

This corollary implies that the total number of weak instances for an RSA variant based on $\psi_n(N, 1, 1)$ is not just the number of vulnerable exponents related to $(p^n - 1)(q^n - 1)$, but the union of vulnerable exponents across all intermediate structures $(p^r - a)(q^r - b)$ defined by $r = 1, 2, \ldots, n-1$ and potential a, b.

Moreover, a direct consequence of this corollary is that one can test for vulnerabilities related to the simpler structure $\psi_r(N,1,1) = (p^r - 1)(q^r - 1)$ for $r = 1$ and 2.

Corollary 2. *Let $N = pq$ be an RSA modulus using the variant Euler function $\psi_n(N,1,1)$ with $q < p < 2q$. Let $r = 1, 2$ and suppose given a public exponent $e = N^\alpha$ satisfying the equation $eu \equiv 1 \pmod{(p^r - 1)(q^r - 1)}$ with an unknown $u < N^\delta$. If $\alpha > r/2$, and*

$$\delta < r - \sqrt{\frac{\alpha r}{2}},$$

then N can be factored in polynomial time.

Proof. This is a direct application of Corollary 1 with parameters $a = b = 1$, which implies $\beta = 0$. Note that $|aq^r - bp^r| < 2N^{r/2}$, i.e., $p^r - q^r < 2p^{r/2}q^{r/2}$ must be ensured. Therefore, we have

$$\left(\frac{p}{q}\right)^r - 1 < 2\left(\frac{p}{q}\right)^{\frac{r}{2}},$$

which leads to

$$\left(\frac{p}{q}\right)^r - 2\left(\frac{p}{q}\right)^{\frac{r}{2}} - 1 < 0.$$

Focusing on the resulting quadratic inequality with respect to $(p/q)^{r/2}$, we have

$$1 - \sqrt{2} < \left(\frac{p}{q}\right)^{\frac{r}{2}} < 1 + \sqrt{2}.$$

Note that p and q are positive primes; we shall ensure that

$$0 < \left(\frac{p}{q}\right)^{\frac{r}{2}} < 1 + \sqrt{2}.$$

Since we have $q < p < 2q$, i.e., $1 < p/q < 2$, it follows that $r = 1$ or $r = 2$ will fulfill the required constraint. To be specific, we obtain $1 < (p/q)^{1/2} < \sqrt{2}$ for $r = 1$, which falls within the above interval. For $r = 2$, we obtain $1 < (p/q)^{2/2} < 2$, which still falls within the above interval. The existence of such a relation for $r = 1, 2$ is sufficient for the generalized attack to succeed, which covers the previous attacks [2,21,28]. □

5 Conclusion

We introduced a generalized attack framework on RSA and its variants in this research. The attack is based on the new key equation $eu \equiv 1 \pmod{\psi_n(N,a,b)}$, where $\psi_n(N,a,b) = (p^n - a)(q^n - b)$ for an RSA modulus $N = pq$ and $n \geq 1$ with small unknown integers a and b. We demonstrated that if this equation holds for a sufficiently small parameter u, the modulus N can be efficiently factored (subject to a standard assumption within Coppersmith's method).

This result significantly expands the class of weak exponents beyond those covered by former small private exponent attacks. It also subsumes previous cryptanalytic work as special cases, since our attack bounds reduce to the well-known bounds of earlier methods when setting $a = b = 1$. Our findings suggest that the security of RSA-like cryptosystems relies on more complex algebraic relationships than previously considered.

Acknowledgments. The authors would like to thank the anonymous reviewers for their detailed comments and impressive suggestions, which improved this paper in terms of both technical and editorial quality. Mengce Zheng gratefully acknowledges the financial support for academic visiting provided by the China Scholarship Council (CSC No. 202308330390). This work was partially supported by the National Natural Science Foundation of China (No. 62002335), and Ningbo Young Science and Technology Talent Cultivation Program (No. 2023QL007).

Disclosure of Interests. The authors have no competing interests.

References

1. Boneh, D.: Twenty years of attacks on the RSA cryptosystem. Not. AMS **46**(2), 203–213 (1999)
2. Boneh, D., Durfee, G.: Cryptanalysis of RSA with Private Key d Less than $N^{0.292}$. In: Stern, J. (ed.) EUROCRYPT 1999. LNCS, vol. 1592, pp. 1–11. Springer, Heidelberg (1999). https://doi.org/10.1007/3-540-48910-X_1
3. Boudabra, M., Nitaj, A.: A new public key cryptosystem based on Edwards curves. J. Appl. Math. Comput. **61**(1–2), 431–450 (2019). https://doi.org/10.1007/S12190-019-01257-Y
4. Bunder, M., Nitaj, A., Susilo, W., Tonien, J.: A New Attack on Three Variants of the RSA Cryptosystem. In: Liu, J.K., Steinfeld, R. (eds.) ACISP 2016. LNCS, vol. 9723, pp. 258–268. Springer, Cham (2016). https://doi.org/10.1007/978-3-319-40367-0_16
5. Castagnos, G.: An efficient probabilistic public-key cryptosystem over quadratic fields quotients. Finite Fields Appl. **13**(3), 563–576 (2007). https://doi.org/10.1016/J.FFA.2006.05.004
6. Coppersmith, D.: Small Solutions to Polynomial Equations, and Low Exponent RSA Vulnerabilities. J. Cryptol. **10**(4), 233–260 (1997). https://doi.org/10.1007/s001459900030
7. Cotan, P., Teşeleanu, G.: Small private key attack against a family of RSA-like cryptosystems. In: Fritsch, L., Hassan, I., Paintsil, E. (eds.) Secure IT Systems - 28th Nordic Conference, NordSec 2023, Proceedings. Lecture Notes in Computer Science, Oslo, Norway, 16–17 November 2023, vol. 14324, pp. 57–72. Springer, Heidelberg (2023). https://doi.org/10.1007/978-3-031-47748-5_4
8. Elkamchouchi, H., Elshenawy, K., Shaban, H.: Extended RSA cryptosystem and digital signature schemes in the domain of Gaussian integers. In: The 8th International Conference on Communication Systems, 2002, ICCS 2002, vol. 1, pp. 91–95. IEEE (2002)

9. Herrmann, M., May, A.: Maximizing Small Root Bounds by Linearization and Applications to Small Secret Exponent RSA. In: Nguyen, P.Q., Pointcheval, D. (eds.) PKC 2010. LNCS, vol. 6056, pp. 53–69. Springer, Heidelberg (2010). https://doi.org/10.1007/978-3-642-13013-7_4
10. Hinek, M.J.: Cryptanalysis of RSA and Its Variants, CRC Press (2009)
11. Howgrave-Graham, N.: Finding small roots of univariate modular equations revisited. In: Darnell, M. (ed.) Cryptography and Coding 1997. LNCS, vol. 1355, pp. 131–142. Springer, Heidelberg (1997). https://doi.org/10.1007/BFb0024458
12. Jochemsz, E., May, A.: A Strategy for Finding Roots of Multivariate Polynomials with New Applications in Attacking RSA Variants. In: Lai, X., Chen, K. (eds.) ASIACRYPT 2006. LNCS, vol. 4284, pp. 267–282. Springer, Heidelberg (2006). https://doi.org/10.1007/11935230_18
13. Koyama, K., Maurer, U.M., Okamoto, T., Vanstone, S.A.: New Public-Key Schemes Based on Elliptic Curves over the Ring Z¡Subscript¿n¡/Subscript¿. In: Feigenbaum, J. (ed.) CRYPTO 1991. LNCS, vol. 576, pp. 252–266. Springer, Heidelberg (1992). https://doi.org/10.1007/3-540-46766-1_20
14. Kuwakado, H., Koyama, K., Tsuruoka, Y.: New RSA-type scheme based on singular cubic curves $y^2 \equiv x^3 + bx^2 \pmod{n}$. IEICE Trans. Fundam. Electron. Commun. Comput. Sci. **E78-A**(1), 27–33 (1995)
15. Lenstra, A., Lenstra, H., Lovász, L.: Factoring polynomials with rational coefficients. Math. Ann. **261**(4), 515–534 (1982)
16. May, A.: New RSA vulnerabilities using lattice reduction methods, University of Paderborn (2003). Ph.D. thesis
17. May, A.: Using LLL-reduction for solving RSA and factorization problems. In: Nguyen, P.Q., Vallée, B. (eds.) The LLL Algorithm - Survey and Applications, pp. 315–348. Information Security and Cryptography, Springer, Heidelberg (2010).https://doi.org/10.1007/978-3-642-02295-1_10
18. Murru, N., Saettone, F.M.: A Novel RSA-Like Cryptosystem Based on a Generalization of the Rédei Rational Functions. In: Kaczorowski, J., Pieprzyk, J., Pomykała, J. (eds.) NuTMiC 2017. LNCS, vol. 10737, pp. 91–103. Springer, Cham (2018). https://doi.org/10.1007/978-3-319-76620-1_6
19. Nasrutdinov, M., Tronin, S.: RSA cryptosystem for rings with commuting ideals. Lobachevskii J. Math. **43**(12), 3591–3596 (2022)
20. Nitaj, A.: Another Generalization of Wiener's Attack on RSA. In: Vaudenay, S. (ed.) AFRICACRYPT 2008. LNCS, vol. 5023, pp. 174–190. Springer, Heidelberg (2008). https://doi.org/10.1007/978-3-540-68164-9_12
21. Peng, L., Hu, L., Lu, Y., Wei, H.: An Improved Analysis on Three Variants of the RSA Cryptosystem. In: Chen, K., Lin, D., Yung, M. (eds.) Inscrypt 2016. LNCS, vol. 10143, pp. 140–149. Springer, Cham (2017). https://doi.org/10.1007/978-3-319-54705-3_9
22. Rivest, R., Shamir, A., Adleman, L.: A method for obtaining digital signatures and public-key cryptosystems. Commun. ACM **21**(2), 120–126 (1978). https://doi.org/10.1145/359340.359342
23. Seck, M., Nitaj, A.: A new public key cryptosystem based on the cubic Pell curve. In: Dabrowski, A., Pieprzyk, J., Pomykala, J. (eds.) 4th International Conference on Number-Theoretic Methods in Cryptology , NuTMiC 2024. LNCS, Szczecin, Poland, 24–26 June 2024, Revised Selected Papers, vol. 14966, pp. 239–261. Springer, Heidelberg (2024). https://doi.org/10.1007/978-3-031-82380-0_8
24. Takagi, T., Naito, S.: Construction of RSA cryptosystem over the algebraic field using ideal theory and investigation of its security. Electron. Commun. Japan (Part III: Fundam. Electron. Sci.) **83**(8), 19–29 (2000)

25. Teşeleanu, G.: A lattice attack against a family of RSA-like cryptosystems. In: Dolev, S., Elhadad, M., Kutylowski, M., Persiano, G. (eds.) 8th International Symposium on Cyber Security, Cryptology, and Machine Learning, CSCML 2024, Proceedings. LNCS, Be'er Sheva, Israel, 19–20 December 2024, vol. 15349, pp. 343–355. Springer, Heidelberg (2024).https://doi.org/10.1007/978-3-031-76934-4_25
26. Wiener, M.: Cryptanalysis of short RSA secret exponents. IEEE Trans. Inf. Theor. **36**(3), 553–558 (1990). https://doi.org/10.1109/18.54902
27. Zheng, M., Kang, H.: Lattice-based cryptanalysis of RSA-type cryptosystems: a bibliometric analysis. Cybersecurity **7**(1), 74 (2024). https://doi.org/10.1186/s42400-024-00289-7
28. Zheng, M., Kunihiro, N., Hu, H.: Cryptanalysis of RSA Variants with Modified Euler Quotient. In: Joux, A., Nitaj, A., Rachidi, T. (eds.) AFRICACRYPT 2018. LNCS, vol. 10831, pp. 266–281. Springer, Cham (2018). https://doi.org/10.1007/978-3-319-89339-6_15
29. Zheng, Z., Liu, F.: On the high dimensional RSA algorithm - a public key cryptosystem based on lattice and algebraic number theory. CoRR abs/2202.02675 (2022). https://arxiv.org/abs/2202.02675

Post-Quantum Cryptography

HIC Is All You Need: Practical Post-Quantum Password-Authenticated Public-Key Encryption

Afonso Arriaga[1], David Mestel[2], Jan Oupický[1(✉)], Peter Browne Rønne[1], and Marjan Škrobot[1]

[1] University of Luxembourg, Esch-sur-Alzette, Luxembourg
{afonso.delerue,jan.oupicky,peter.roenne}@uni.lu
[2] Maastricht University, Maastricht, The Netherlands
david.mestel@maastrichtuniversity.nl

Abstract. Password-Authenticated Public-Key Encryption (PAPKE) enables secure encryption using only a shared, human-memorable password—eliminating the need for trusted intermediaries or pre-established infrastructure. It allows a sender to encrypt a message for a recipient, using the recipient's password-authenticated public key and a shared password, while provably resisting man-in-the-middle and offline dictionary attacks. PAPKE's support for reusable password-authenticated public keys makes it especially suitable for asynchronous, PKI-free communication scenarios.

An important open problem is to construct PAPKE schemes that are secure against quantum adversaries, as existing instantiations rely on Diffie-Hellman assumptions. The PAPKE-IC construction (ACNS 2019) is generic and admits integration with post-quantum PKE schemes. However, the scheme assumes an Ideal Cipher (IC) over the public key domain, which is large for most post-quantum PKE schemes. While an IC is typically instantiated using a block cipher, standard block ciphers operate over much smaller domains (e.g., 128 or 256 bits). Alternatively, one can use an 8-round Feistel network, which achieves indifferentiability from an ideal cipher, or domain extenders. The latter are inefficient at the domain sizes required, making the efficient and secure instantiation of the IC in PAPKE-IC, in combination with post-quantum PKE, particularly challenging.

In this paper, we propose PAPKE-HIC, a UC-secure PAPKE scheme built from a PKE scheme and a Half-Ideal Cipher (HIC, introduced at EUROCRYPT 2023), which circumvents the challenges of instantiating ideal ciphers over large domains. We provide a detailed security proof of PAPKE-HIC and establish precise requirements for the underlying PKE: strong robustness, one-wayness, ciphertext anonymity, and pseudo-uniformity of public keys. Our analysis identifies a gap in the original PAPKE-IC security proof, motivating the introduction of a novel property, which we denote Decryption Robustness (DROB-CCA). Although DROB-CCA is implied by strong robustness (SROB-CCA), the reduction is not tight and incurs a quadratic security loss. We analyze which PKE schemes directly satisfy DROB-CCA, and conclude by presenting con-

F. -H. Liu (Ed.): CT-RSAC 2026, LNCS 16496, pp. 127–154, 2026.
https://doi.org/10.1007/978-3-032-22931-1_5

crete instantiations of PAPKE-HIC. To our knowledge, this is the first practical, post-quantum instantiation of the PAPKE primitive.

Keywords: Password-Authenticated Public-Key Encryption (PAPKE) · Post-Quantum PAPKE · PAKE · Decryption Robustness (DROB-CCA)

1 Introduction

Password-based authentication remains an important and widely deployed mechanism in modern cryptographic systems. While traditional Authenticated Key Exchange (AKE) protocols rely on long-term private keys managed through Public Key Infrastructures (PKI), such frameworks assume stable device identity and secure key storage—assumptions that do not hold universally. Advances such as passkeys, secure enclaves, and biometric authentication have improved key management on end-user devices, but these solutions depend on proprietary hardware and platform support, and remain inaccessible in many contexts. In contrast, numerous real-world scenarios—such as onboarding in IoT protocols like Thread [33], ePassport inspection [25], peer-to-peer file transfers [35], and ephemeral wireless network sessions [36]—lack the infrastructure or trust anchors required for PKI-based schemes. In these settings, password-based authentication remains a practical and cryptographically meaningful tool as it enables secure communication using pre-shared low-entropy secrets without requiring persistent credentials, trusted intermediaries, or pre-established infrastructure.

PAKE. Password-Authenticated Key Exchange (PAKE) protocols address the core limitations of traditional password-based authentication, e.g., sending a password over a server-authenticated TLS channel. A PAKE enables two parties, who only share a low-entropy password, to establish a high-entropy session key, while provably resisting offline dictionary attacks. This is a core security guarantee: an adversary must interact with an honest party to test each password guess. Passive eavesdropping yields no advantage, even under full transcript access. This interaction-bound guessing constraint makes PAKE significantly more robust than simple password transmission schemes, and mutual authentication offers the additional benefit of protecting against phishing attacks.

PAPKE. Password-Authenticated Public-Key Encryption (PAPKE) [12] is a cryptographic primitive that combines password authentication and CCA-secure encryption into a single mechanism, unifying two core security objectives: secrecy and authenticity. It enables a sender to encrypt a message for a recipient, using the recipient's password-authenticated public key and a shared password. The resulting ciphertext enforces password-based access control over the message, provides chosen-ciphertext security, and resists man-in-the-middle attacks, assuming the password remains unknown to the adversary.

Unlike PAKE, which derives a shared session key through mutual interaction, PAPKE supports *unilateral* encryption, enabling secure message delivery without requiring real-time interaction or composition with a symmetric key scheme. PAPKE also provides a theoretically stronger abstraction than PAKE: a UC-secure PAKE protocol can be derived from a UC-secure PAPKE instance by encrypting a session key rather than an arbitrary message. The inverse, however, does not hold due to a defining feature of PAPKE: the use of a reusable authenticated public key.[1] Such reusability enables any sender, who holds an authenticated public key from the receiver and the corresponding password, to generate multiple valid ciphertexts without fresh interaction or per-session key derivation. The reusability of public keys makes PAPKE especially well-suited for scenarios requiring asynchronous communication, credential recovery, and one-to-many password-authenticated key exchange protocols such as SweetPAKE [6] and Oblivious PAKE [6,27], where scalability and minimal communication overhead are essential. These PAPKE-based protocols are natural candidates for extending WPA3 to support multi-password authentication [34]. Importantly, such an extension should ensure post-quantum security with minimal communication and interaction overhead.

Two Existing Approaches to PAPKE and their Limitations. PAPKE has been realized using two main approaches [12]. The first is a generic construction, PAPKE-IC, which relies on the Ideal Cipher (IC) model. The second, PAPKE-FO, is a direct construction based on the Decisional Diffie-Hellman (DDH) assumption and applies the Fujisaki-Okamoto (FO) transform, thus relying on the Random Oracle (RO) model instead.

When comparing the two approaches, PAPKE-IC is conceptually simpler and reflects the design of the classic Encrypted Key Exchange (EKE) protocol. However, it presents IC instantiability challenges. A poor IC instantiation may enable offline dictionary attacks. For example, if the IC is instantiated using a block cipher whose block size does not match the public key space, an adversary can decrypt the password-authenticated ciphertext under candidate passwords and discard those that do not yield a plaintext within the valid public key space.

To instantiate the ideal cipher over larger domains in PAPKE-IC, one may employ an 8-round Feistel network [17] or a domain extender from [15], both shown to achieve indifferentiability from an ideal cipher. These constructions are costly to implement over large algebraic domains (and in constant time). Consequently, practical and efficient instantiations of PAPKE-IC remain elusive in the post-quantum setting, underscoring the need for alternative designs.

1.1 Our Contributions

Main Contribution: PAPKE-HIC with Precise Security Requirements. We introduce a new UC-secure Password-Authenticated Public-Key Encryption scheme, PAPKE-HIC, using the Half-Ideal Cipher (HIC) from [32]. Concretely, we show how to generically construct a PAPKE scheme from a Public-Key Encryption (PKE) scheme and a Half-Ideal Cipher (HIC) that can

[1] A recent notion, Bare PAKE [7], captures a form of reusability within PAKEs.

be instantiated using a modified 2-round Feistel construction m2F. The main advantage of m2F is that it employs an Ideal Cipher defined over a fixed-length bitstring domain, rather than over large algebraic domains required in prior IC-based constructions such as PAPKE-IC, making it significantly easier to instantiate efficiently. As a result, our design resolves a key open question: how to efficiently realize PAPKE in the post-quantum setting without sacrificing concrete security or performance.

We provide a detailed and rigorous proof that PAPKE-HIC realizes the UC-PAPKE functionality in the Universal Composability (UC) framework (Theorem 1). In doing so, we formally establish precise security requirements for the underlying Public-Key Encryption scheme. As in the PAPKE-IC proof [12], we identify three necessary properties: *anonymity and indistinguishability security* (AI-CCA), *strong robustness* (SROB-CCA), and *pseudo-uniformity of public keys* (UNI-PK). We further generalize the proof to accommodate Public-Key Encryption schemes with imperfect correctness and pseudo-uniform public key distributions (UNI-PK)—features that are relevant for several post-quantum Public-Key Encryption schemes.

Second Contribution: Security Gap in the Original PAPKE-IC Proof and New Public-Key Encryption Property—Decryption Robustness. Our analysis reveals a subtle gap in the original analysis of PAPKE-IC [12]: the proof must ensure that an adversary, without access to the public key, cannot forge a ciphertext that decrypts successfully. We formalize this requirement as a new property called *decryption robustness* (DROB-CCA). While DROB-CCA is implied by strong robustness (SROB-CCA), as shown in Theorem 2, the reduction is not tight and incurs a quadratic security loss. Critically, when applying Theorem 2 to derive the concrete bound of PAPKE-HIC in Theorem 1, the DROB-CCA-related advantage becomes the dominant term, significantly weakening the overall security guarantee. In addition, we identify a further minor omission in the original analysis: the "badkeys abort" mechanism in the $\mathcal{F}_{\mathsf{PAPKE}}$ functionality was not accounted for in the proof.

Third Contribution: Concrete Instantiations of PAPKE-HIC with Post-quantum PKE. Motivated by the limitations of the reduction in Theorem 2, we investigate which Public-Key Encryption schemes satisfy DROB-CCA directly with tighter bounds. We show that any PKE built using the standard KEM+DEM paradigm, where the KEM employs a variant of the *prefix-hashing* Fujisaki-Okamoto (FO) transform [19] and the DEM satisfies ciphertext integrity (INT-CTXT), achieves DROB-CCA without relying on the generic reduction (Theorem 5). This applies to post-quantum PKEs built from ML-KEM [30], or FrodoKEM [29].

We further show how to build DROB-CCA-secure PKE from KEMs that do not employ the prefix-hashing FO transform, such as Classic McEliece [2]. We also prove that the DHIES* [1], the hybrid PKE that was originally used to instantiate PAPKE-IC [12], also satisfies DROB-CCA with a tighter bound.

Finally, we implement and benchmark post-quantum $\mathsf{PAPKE\text{-}IC}$ and $\mathsf{PAPKE\text{-}HIC}$ using ML-KEM [30], FrodoKEM [29] and Classic McEliece [2] in various configurations.

2 Preliminaries

In this section, we present the cryptographic primitives relevant to our work. We begin with standard definitions of Public-Key Encryption (PKE), Key Encapsulation Mechanism (KEM), and Data Encapsulation Mechanism (DEM). We then introduce Password-Authenticated Public-Key Encryption (PAPKE) [12], followed by the Half-Ideal Cipher (HIC) [32], which forms the foundation of our construction.

All relevant PKE and DEM security definitions are provided in Fig. 1. Let SCH be a scheme and EXP be a security experiment. For experiments where the adversary's $(\mathcal{A})$ goal is to guess the challenger's bit, we define its advantage as $\mathsf{Adv}^{\mathsf{EXP}}_{\mathcal{A},\mathsf{SCH}}(\lambda) := \left|\Pr\left[\mathsf{Exp}^{\mathsf{EXP}}_{\mathcal{A},\mathsf{SCH}}(\lambda) = 1\right] - \frac{1}{2}\right|$, and $\mathsf{Adv}^{\mathsf{EXP}}_{\mathcal{A},\mathsf{SCH}}(\lambda) := \Pr\left[\mathsf{Exp}^{\mathsf{EXP}}_{\mathcal{A},\mathsf{SCH}}(\lambda) = 1\right]$ otherwise. We say that SCH is EXP-secure if $\mathsf{Adv}^{\mathsf{EXP}}_{\mathcal{A},\mathsf{SCH}}(\lambda)$ is negligible for any PPT adversary $\mathcal{A}$.

2.1 Public-Key Encryption (PKE)

We present the definition of a Public-Key Encryption scheme (PKE) and relevant security notions.

Definition 1. *A Public-Key Encryption scheme (PKE) is a triple of PPT algorithms* $(\mathsf{Keygen}, \mathsf{Enc}, \mathsf{Dec}) : \mathsf{Keygen} : \mathbb{N} \to \mathcal{PK} \times \mathcal{SK}$, $\mathsf{Enc} : \mathcal{PK} \times \mathcal{M} \times \mathcal{R} \to \mathcal{C}$, $\mathsf{Dec} : \mathcal{SK} \times \mathcal{C} \to \mathcal{M} \cup \{\perp\}$, *where* $\mathcal{PK}$ *is the public key space,* $\mathcal{SK}$ *is the private key space,* $\mathcal{M}$ *is the message space,* $\mathcal{R}$ *is the randomness space and* $\mathcal{C}$ *is the ciphertext space.*

Correctness. [23] We say a Public-Key Encryption scheme is δ-correct if

$$\mathbb{E}_{(pk,sk) \leftarrow \$\mathsf{Keygen}(\lambda)}\left[\max_{m \in \mathcal{M}} \Pr_{r \leftarrow \$\mathcal{R}}\left[\mathsf{Dec}(sk, \mathsf{Enc}(pk, m, r)) \neq m\right]\right] \leq \delta(\lambda).$$

PKE Security Properties. The standard security requirement for Public-Key Encryption is *indistinguishability under chosen-ciphertext attacks* ($\mathsf{IND\text{-}CCA}$). Another crucial property is *public key anonymity under chosen-ciphertext attacks* ($\mathsf{ANO\text{-}CCA}$), which ensures that ciphertexts reveal no information about the specific public key used during encryption. These properties can be combined into the *anonymity and indistinguishability under chosen-ciphertext attacks* ($\mathsf{AI\text{-}CCA}$), as done in [12].[2] A more recent property that has proven essential for the construction of PAKE from KEM is the *pseudo-uniformity of public keys*

[2] Note that the notions are equivalent: $\mathsf{AI\text{-}CCA} \iff \mathsf{IND\text{-}CCA} + \mathsf{ANO\text{-}CCA}$.

(UNI-PK), which captures the notion that public keys produced by the key generation algorithm are (computationally) indistinguishable from uniformly random elements of the public key space $\mathcal{PK}$ (called *fuzziness* in [8]; see also [4] for reference). Another important property of a PKE is *strong robustness under chosen-ciphertext attacks* (SROB-CCA), which ensures that it is computationally hard to create a ciphertext that decrypts successfully under two distinct secret keys, both honestly generated via Keygen. All of these properties are defined in Fig. 1.

In this work, we introduce two novel properties: *decryption robustness* (DROB) and its chosen-ciphertext analogue, *decryption robustness under chosen-ciphertext attacks* (DROB-CCA). These properties formalize the requirement that it should be hard to craft a ciphertext that decrypts correctly *without knowledge of the public key.* While unconventional in standard PKE settings—where public keys are, by definition, public—this property becomes essential in PAPKE, where the public key is treated as secret. We provide exact definitions in Fig. 1 and a detailed discussion in Sect. 4, including its relationship to SROB-CCA.

2.2 Key Encapsulation Mechanism (KEM)

We define a Key Encapsulation Mechanism (KEM). See the full version of the paper [5] for definitions of KEM security properties.

Definition 2. *A Key Encapsulation Mechanism (KEM) is a triple of PPT algorithms* (Keygen, Encap, Decap) *defined as:* Keygen : $\mathbb{N} \to \mathcal{PK} \times \mathcal{SK}$, Encap : $\mathcal{PK} \to \mathcal{K} \times \mathcal{C}$, Decap : $\mathcal{SK} \times \mathcal{C} \to \mathcal{K} \cup \{\perp\}$, *where $\mathcal{PK}$ is the public key space, $\mathcal{SK}$ is the private key space, $\mathcal{K}$ is the symmetric key space, and $\mathcal{C}$ is the ciphertext space.*

We say a KEM is implicitly rejecting *if* Decap *never outputs the symbol $\perp$; otherwise, it is called* explicitly rejecting.

2.3 Data Encapsulation Mechanism (DEM)

We present the definition of a Data Encapsulation Mechanism (DEM) and relevant security notions.

Definition 3. *A DEM is a triple of PPT algorithms* (Keygen, Enc, Dec) *defined as:* Keygen : $\mathbb{N} \to \mathcal{K}$, Enc : $\mathcal{K} \times \mathcal{M} \to \mathcal{C}$, Dec : $\mathcal{K} \times \mathcal{C} \to \mathcal{M} \cup \{\perp\}$, *where $\mathcal{K}$ is the symmetric key space, $\mathcal{M}$ is the message space, and $\mathcal{C}$ is the ciphertext space.*

A DEM is typically an authenticated symmetric-key encryption scheme used in hybrid encryption. We assume that the symmetric key space $\mathcal{K}$, resp. the message space $\mathcal{M}$, is the same in the DEM and the KEM, resp. PKE, definitions.

DEM Security Properties. In our proofs, we only directly work with the *integrity of ciphertexts* (INT-CTXT) property of DEM from [10] (Fig. 1). This property captures the difficulty of generating a valid ciphertext (that decrypts to a valid message, i.e., $m \neq \perp$) without knowledge of the corresponding symmetric key.

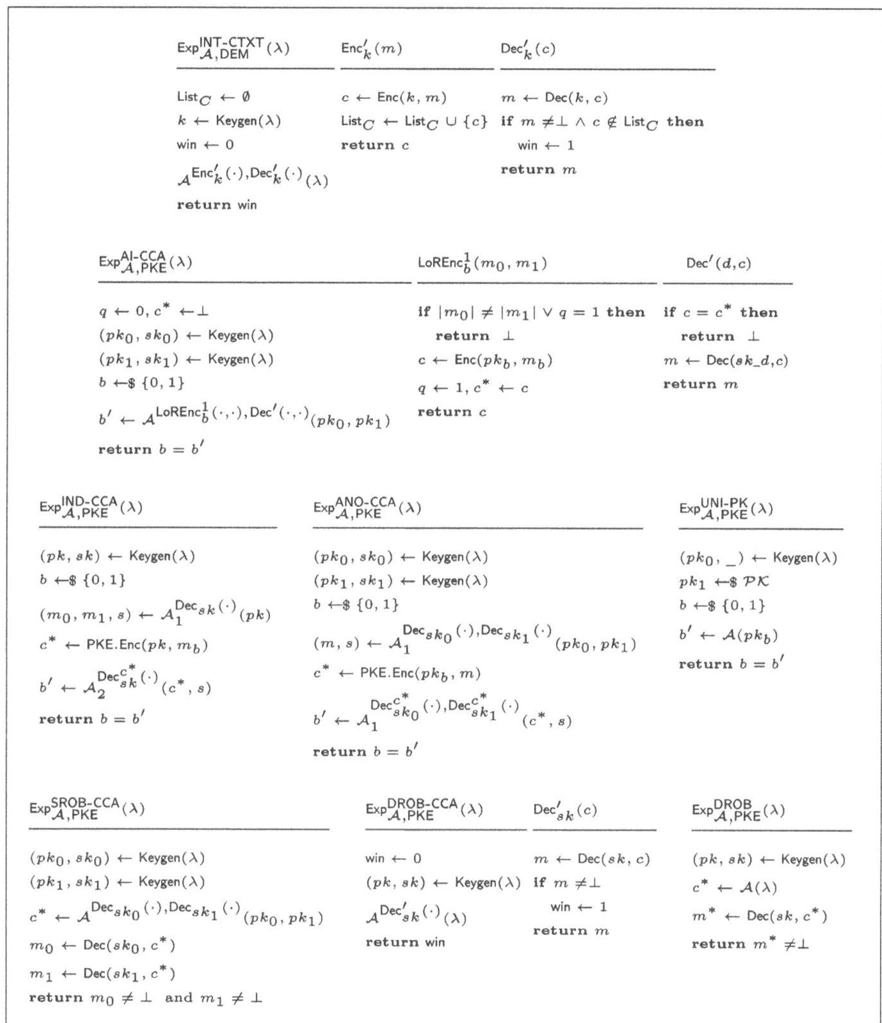

Fig. 1. Security experiments defining properties of PKEs and DEMs. (1) INT-CTXT is the standard *ciphertext integrity* from [10]; (2) AI-CCA is the *anonymity and indistinguishability* from [1,12] which is equivalent to IND-CCA + ANO-CCA; (3) IND-CCA is the standard *indistinguishability under chosen-ciphertext attacks*; (4) ANO-CCA for is the *anonymity under chosen-ciphertext attacks* from [9]; (5) UNI-PK is the *pseudo-uniformity of public keys* similar to the one from [4] and *fuzziness* from [8]; (6) SROB-CCA is the *strong-robustness* from [12]; (7) DROB-CCA is the *decryption robustness under chosen-ciphertext attacks*; (8) DROB is the *decryption robustness.* $\mathsf{Dec}^{c^*}_{sk}(\cdot)$ is a decryption oracle with a private key sk which returns $\perp$ if c^* is queried.

2.4 Password-Authenticated Public-Key Encryption (PAPKE)

A Password-Authenticated Public-Key Encryption scheme (PAPKE) is a relatively recent primitive introduced in [12]. PAPKE extends Public-Key Encryption with password-based authentication.

Definition 4. *A Password-Authenticated Public-Key Encryption (PAPKE) is a triple of PPT algorithms* $(\mathsf{Keygen}, \mathsf{Enc}, \mathsf{Dec})$ *defined as:* $\mathsf{Keygen} : \mathbb{N} \times \mathcal{PW} \rightarrow \mathcal{SK} \times \mathcal{APK}$, $\mathsf{Enc} : \mathcal{APK} \times \mathcal{PW} \times \mathcal{M} \rightarrow \mathcal{C}$, $\mathsf{Dec} : \mathcal{SK} \times \mathcal{C} \rightarrow \mathcal{M} \cup \{\perp\}$, *where* $\mathcal{PW}$ *is the password dictionary,* $\mathcal{SK}$ *is the private key space,* $\mathcal{APK}$ *is the authenticated public key space,* $\mathcal{M}$ *is the message space, and* $\mathcal{C}$ *is the ciphertext space.*

PAPKE Security Properties. The PAPKE paper [12] defines two game-based security definitions: *indistinguishability against chosen-ciphertext and chosen-key attacks* (IND-CCKA) and *ciphertext authenticity* (AUTH-CTXT). IND-CCKA captures resistance against offline dictionary attacks, secrecy of messages under chosen-ciphertext attacks, security against man-in-the-middle attacks, and long-term security. AUTH-CTXT ensures that an adversary cannot create a valid ciphertext without knowing the password.

We do not detail these game-based definitions, as we work within the Universal Composability (UC) framework [13], which implies both definitions. The ideal functionality of PAPKE ($\mathcal{F}_{\mathsf{PAPKE}}$) is defined in Fig. 2.

Compared to the original functionality in [12], we slightly modify $\mathcal{F}_{\mathsf{PAPKE}}$ to ensure that the messages ENC-M and ENC-L also send apk' to $\mathcal{A}$ together with m and $|m|$, respectively. We believe this is an accidental omission in the original definition, since in the proofs of PAPKE-IC and PAPKE-FO the authors write "... $(\mathsf{ENC\text{-}M}, sid, apk', m)$ from $\mathcal{F}_{\mathsf{PAPKE}}$ ...". In our proof of PAPKE-HIC (Theorem 1), we found that sending apk' in ENC-M is necessary because the simulator must encrypt the message "honestly" and otherwise cannot determine the correct apk' to use with certainty.

2.5 Half-Ideal Cipher (HIC)

The (randomized) Half-Ideal Cipher (HIC) is a Universal Composability (UC) security notion recently proposed in [32]. It serves as a relaxation of the Ideal Cipher (IC) notion with application to PAKEs. The HIC security model is formalized by an ideal functionality $\mathcal{F}_{\mathsf{HIC}}$ (Fig. 4), which is parameterized by the domain $\mathcal{D} = \mathcal{R} \times \mathcal{G}$. Note that in our use case, $\mathcal{G} = \mathcal{PK}$, where $\mathcal{PK}$ is the public key space of a PKE. The HIC abstraction offers a practical alternative to ideal ciphers in the design of EKE-like protocols, eliminating the need for direct application of an IC over groups, which can be complex to instantiate [32].

Notably, HIC provides an *honest interface* accessible to honest parties, and an *adversarial interface* accessible to the adversary. The adversarial interface is more powerful because it allows the adversary to choose 1) the encryption randomness $r \in \mathcal{R}$ and half of the ciphertext $T \in \mathcal{G}$ during encryption and 2) the adversary also receives $r \in \mathcal{R}$ (compared to only $M \in \mathcal{G}$) during decryption.

1. **Key Generation**. On input $(\mathsf{KEYGEN}, sid, pwd)$ from party $\mathcal{P}$:
   - If $sid \neq (\mathcal{P}, sid')$ or a record $(\mathsf{keyrec}, sid, \cdot, \cdot)$ exists, ignore.
   - Send (KEYGEN, sid) to $\mathcal{A}$ and wait for $(\mathsf{KEYCONF}, sid, apk, \mathcal{M})$ from $\mathcal{A}$.
   - If a record $(\mathsf{badkeys}, sid, apk', \cdot)$ with $apk' = apk$ exists, abort.
   - Create a record $(\mathsf{keyrec}, sid, apk, pwd)$ and output $(\mathsf{KEYCONF}, sid, apk)$ to $\mathcal{P}$.

2. **Encryption**. On input $(\mathsf{ENCRYPT}, sid, apk', pwd', m)$ from party $\mathcal{Q}$ where $m \in \mathcal{M}$:
   - If a record $(\mathsf{keyrec}, sid, apk, pwd)$ with $apk = apk'$ exists and $\mathcal{P}$ (from $(\mathcal{P}, sid') \leftarrow sid$) is honest, then:
     - Send $(\mathsf{ENC\text{-}L}, sid, apk', |m|)$ to $\mathcal{A}$ and wait for $(\mathsf{CIPHERTEXT}, sid, c)$ from $\mathcal{A}$.
     - Abort if a record $(\mathsf{enrec}, sid, \cdot, c)$ for c already exists.
     - Create a record $(\mathsf{enrec}, sid, m', c)$ with $m' \leftarrow m$ if $pwd' = pwd$, and $m \leftarrow \perp$, else.
   - Else:
     - If a record $(\mathsf{badkeys}, sid, apk_j, pwd_j)$ with $apk_j = apk'$ exists, set $pwd^* \leftarrow pwd_j$.
     - Else, send $(\mathsf{GUESS}, sid, apk')$ to $\mathcal{A}$, wait for $(\mathsf{GUESS}, sid, pwd^*)$ from $\mathcal{A}$ and create record $(\mathsf{badkeys}, sid, apk', pwd^*)$.
     - If $pwd' = pwd^*$, send $(\mathsf{ENC\text{-}M}, sid, apk', m)$ to $\mathcal{A}$, and wait for $(\mathsf{CIPHERTEXT}, sid, c)$ from $\mathcal{A}$.
     - If $pwd' \neq pwd^*$, send $(\mathsf{ENC\text{-}L}, sid, apk', |m|)$ to $\mathcal{A}$, and wait for $(\mathsf{CIPHERTEXT}, sid, c)$ from $\mathcal{A}$.
   - Output $(\mathsf{CIPHERTEXT}, sid, c)$ to $\mathcal{Q}$.
3. **Decryption**. On input $(\mathsf{DECRYPT}, sid, c)$ from party $\mathcal{P}$:
   - If $sid \neq (\mathcal{P}, sid')$ or no record $(\mathsf{keyrec}, sid, apk, pwd)$ exists, ignore.
   - If a record $(\mathsf{enrec}, sid, m, c)$ for c exists, where $m \in \mathcal{M} \cup \{\perp\}$:
     - Output $(\mathsf{PLAINTEXT}, sid, m)$ to $\mathcal{P}$.
   - Else:
     - Send $(\mathsf{DECRYPT}, sid, c)$ to $\mathcal{A}$ and wait for $(\mathsf{PLAINTEXT}, sid, m, pwd^*)$ from $\mathcal{A}$.
     - If $pwd^* = pwd$, set $m' \leftarrow m$ and $m' \leftarrow \perp$ otherwise.
     - Create a record $(\mathsf{enrec}, sid, m', c)$.
     - Output $(\mathsf{PLAINTEXT}, sid, m')$ to $\mathcal{P}$.

Fig. 2. Patched ideal functionality $\mathcal{F}_{\mathsf{PAPKE}}$ from [12]—the functionality additionally sends apk' for messages ENC-M and ENC-L. The functionality is parametrized by the message space $\mathcal{M}$.

It was shown in [32] that the *Modified 2-Feistel* (m2F) construction (Definition 5) realizes $\mathcal{F}_{\mathsf{HIC}}$ in the Random Oracle (RO) and Ideal Cipher (IC) model. Although m2F internally uses an ideal cipher, it is an ideal cipher over bitstrings of small size, which is easy to instantiate using a regular block cipher.

Definition 5. *Let* $\mathsf{H} : \mathcal{PW} \times \mathcal{R} \to \mathbb{G}$ *and* $\mathsf{G} : \mathcal{PW} \times \mathbb{G} \to \mathcal{K}$ *be random oracles and let* $\mathsf{IC} = (\mathsf{IC.Enc}, \mathsf{IC.Dec})$ *be an ideal cipher over* $\mathcal{R}$. *A Modified 2-Feistel construction* $\mathsf{m2F} = \mathsf{m2F}[\mathsf{H}, \mathsf{G}, \mathsf{IC}]$ *is a tuple of PPT algorithms* $\mathsf{m2F.Enc}/\mathsf{m2F.Dec} : \mathcal{PW} \times \mathcal{R} \times \mathbb{G} \to \mathcal{R} \times \mathbb{G}$ *where* $\mathcal{PW}$ *is the dictionary of possible passwords,* $\mathcal{R} = \{0,1\}^n$, $\mathbb{G}$ *is a group and* $\mathcal{K}$ *is the keyspace of* IC. *The descriptions of* m2F.Enc *and* m2F.Dec *are in Fig. 3.*

$\mathsf{m2F.Enc}(pw, r, M)$	$\mathsf{m2F.Dec}(pw, s, T)$
$R \leftarrow \mathsf{H}(pw, r)$	$t \leftarrow \mathsf{G}(pw, T)$
$T \leftarrow M \odot R$	$r \leftarrow \mathsf{IC.Dec}(t, s)$
$t \leftarrow \mathsf{G}(pw, T)$	$R \leftarrow \mathsf{H}(pw, r)$
$s \leftarrow \mathsf{IC.Enc}(t, r)$	$M \leftarrow T \odot R^{-1}$
return (s, T)	**return** (r, M)

Fig. 3. The modified 2-Feistel ($\mathsf{m2F}[\mathsf{H}, \mathsf{G}, \mathsf{IC}]$) [32], $\odot$ is the group operation in $\mathbb{G}$ and $(\cdot)^{-1}$ is the inverse in $\mathbb{G}$.

3 PAPKE-HIC—Practical Post-quantum PAPKE

In this section, we present a new practical PAPKE construction, PAPKE-HIC (Fig. 5), which achieves the UC-PAPKE notion, offers strong security guarantees, and avoids the need to instantiate an ideal cipher over groups or large domains. We show how to instantiate PAPKE-HIC using any AI-CCA, SROB-CCA, UNI-PK, and DROB-CCA-secure Public-Key Encryption scheme and a half-ideal

Interface for honest parties:

1. **Encryption.** On query $(\mathsf{Enc}, sid, pw, M)$ from $\mathcal{P}$ where $M \in \mathcal{G}$:
   - $r \leftarrow\!\!\$\ \mathcal{R}$
   - If $\exists c$ s.t. $(sid, pw, (r, M), c) \in \mathsf{List_{HIC}}$, then:
     - Output c to $\mathcal{P}$
   - Else:
     - $c \leftarrow\!\!\$\ \mathcal{D} \setminus \{c' \in \mathcal{D} : \exists (sid, pw, *, c') \in \mathsf{List_{HIC}}\}$
     - $\mathsf{List_{HIC}} \leftarrow \{(sid, pw, (r, M), c)\} \cup \mathsf{List_{HIC}}$
     - Output c to $\mathcal{P}$
2. **Decryption.** On query $(\mathsf{Dec}, sid, pw, c)$ from $\mathcal{P}$ where $c \in \mathcal{D}$:
   - Query $(r, M) \leftarrow \mathcal{F}_{\mathsf{HIC}}.\mathsf{AdvDec}(sid, pw, c)$
   - Output M to $\mathcal{P}$.

Interface for Adversary $\mathcal{A}$ (or corrupt parties):

1. **Encryption.** On query $(\mathsf{AdvEnc}, sid, pw, (r, M), T)$ from $\mathcal{A}$ where $(r, M) \in \mathcal{D}$ and $T \in \mathcal{G}$:
   - If $\exists c$ s.t. $(sid, pw, (r, M), c) \in \mathsf{List_{HIC}}$, then:
     - Output c to $\mathcal{A}$
   - Else:
     - $s \leftarrow\!\!\$\ \mathcal{R} \setminus \{s' \in \mathcal{R} : \exists (sid, pw, *, (s', T)) \in \mathsf{List_{HIC}}\}$
     - $c \leftarrow (s, T)$
     - $\mathsf{List_{HIC}} \leftarrow \{(sid, pw, (r, M), c)\} \cup \mathsf{List_{HIC}}$
     - Output c to $\mathcal{A}$
2. **Decryption.** On query $(\mathsf{AdvDec}, sid, pw, c)$ from $\mathcal{A}$ where $c \in \mathcal{D}$:
   - If $\exists m$ s.t. $(sid, pw, m, c) \in \mathsf{List_{HIC}}$, then:
     - Output m to $\mathcal{A}$
   - Else:
     - $m \leftarrow\!\!\$\ \mathcal{D} \setminus \{m' \in \mathcal{D} : \exists (sid, pw, m', *) \in \mathsf{List_{HIC}}\}$
     - $\mathsf{List_{HIC}} \leftarrow \{(sid, pw, m, c)\} \cup \mathsf{List_{HIC}}$
     - Output m to $\mathcal{A}$

Fig. 4. Ideal functionality $\mathcal{F}_{\mathsf{HIC}}$ for the Half-Ideal Cipher from [32]. The functionality is parametrized by the domain $\mathcal{D} = \mathcal{R} \times \mathcal{G}$.

Setup. Let PKE = (Keygen, Enc, Dec) be a public key encryption scheme with a public key space $\mathcal{PK}$ and let HIC = (HIC.Enc, HIC.Dec) be a half-ideal cipher with the domain $\mathcal{D} = \mathcal{R} \times \mathcal{PK}$.

PAPKE.Keygen(λ, pw).
Compute $(sk, pk) \leftarrow\$$ PKE.Keygen(λ) and $apk \leftarrow$ HIC.Enc(pw, pk). Output (sk, apk).

PAPKE.Enc(apk', pw', m).
Compute a public key $pk' \leftarrow$ HIC.Dec(pw', apk'), and output $c \leftarrow$ PKE.Enc(pk', m).

PAPKE.Dec(sk, c').
Decrypt $m \leftarrow$ PKE.Dec(sk, c') and output m.

Fig. 5. The generic PAPKE-HIC construction.

cipher. Furthermore, we discuss subtle issues overlooked in the original proof of PAPKE-IC in [12].

3.1 Benefits of PAPKE-HIC

PAPKE-HIC, depicted in Fig. 5, is inspired by the original PAPKE-IC construction from [12], with the difference that a half-ideal cipher (HIC) [32] is used instead of an ideal cipher (IC). The main benefit of a HIC, or more precisely its instantiation m2F (Sect. 2.5), is that it avoids the need for an IC over the public key space. Constructing a post-quantum PAPKE requires a post-quantum PKE, and such schemes typically involve large public keys. As a result, instantiating a post-quantum PAPKE-IC in practice is challenging, making the HIC-based approach a more practical alternative.

Recall that m2F uses an ideal cipher internally, but this cipher operates over bitstrings of length 256 (assuming a 128-bit security), which can be instantiated using a regular block cipher. Even though some post-quantum KEMs, such as Classic McEliece [2], have public keys that are indistinguishable from random bitstrings, and there exist methods for encoding public keys as random bitstrings (e.g., Kemeleon for ML-KEM [22]), the main challenge remains their size. For instance, the size of a Kemeleon-encoded ML-KEM public key is 781 *bytes*, and for Classic McEliece it is 261120 *bytes* at NIST security level 1.

There are techniques to instantiate an ideal cipher over bitstrings > 256 [15, 17]; however, these are practically inefficient for large domains.

While m2F requires a *hash-to-group* function, hashing into the group—which in this case is the public key space—is easy in our setting, as most of the post-quantum KEMs derive their keys from a seed. This derivation mechanism can be used to implement the required hash-to-group function.

3.2 Proof of PAPKE-HIC and Issues with the PAPKE-IC Proof

We now explain why substituting an ideal cipher (IC) with a half-ideal cipher (HIC) in the PAPKE construction does not compromise security. First, a HIC ciphertext generated via the $\mathsf{HIC.Enc}$ interface effectively commits the adversary to a unique key (password) used to produce that ciphertext (authenticated public key). This commitment property holds just as it does in the IC setting, despite the adversary having additional power to specify part of a ciphertext using the adversarial $\mathsf{HIC.AdvEnc}$ interface. Crucially, the simulator can straight-line extract the associated key (password), ensuring that only a single password guess is possible per adversarially generated authenticated public key. Furthermore, as with IC, decrypting a HIC ciphertext (authenticated public key) using a key (password) different from the one used in encryption yields a random element in the HIC domain. This allows the simulator to embed a public key of its choice when simulating $\mathsf{HIC.Dec}$ responses.

In Theorem 1, we prove that $\mathsf{PAPKE\text{-}HIC}$ (Fig. 5) securely realizes the PAPKE UC functionality (Fig. 2) by leveraging the HIC functionality (Fig. 4) and several security properties of the underlying PKE scheme.

Theorem 1. *The scheme* $\mathsf{PAPKE\text{-}HIC}$ *(Fig. 5) UC-realizes* $\mathcal{F}_{\mathsf{PAPKE}}$ *(Fig. 2) in the* $\mathcal{F}_{\mathsf{HIC}}$*-hybrid model, if the Public-Key Encryption scheme* PKE *is* $\mathsf{AI\text{-}CCA}$, $\mathsf{SROB\text{-}CCA}$, $\mathsf{UNI\text{-}PK}$, $\mathsf{DROB\text{-}CCA}$*-secure and* δ*-correct. Specifically, there exists a simulator* SIM*, such that for all environments* $\mathcal{Z}$ *controlling a dummy adversary* $\mathcal{A}$*, its distinguishing advantage,* Adv*, between the real and ideal world is*

$$\begin{aligned}\mathsf{Adv}(\lambda) \leq\ & \frac{q_{\mathsf{HIC}}^2}{2\cdot|\mathcal{R}|} + \frac{q_{\mathsf{HIC}}^2}{2\cdot|\mathcal{PK}|} + \frac{q_{\mathsf{PAPKE}}}{|\mathcal{R}\times\mathcal{PK}|} + q_{\mathsf{PAPKE}}\cdot\delta(\lambda) \\ & + 2\cdot q_{\mathsf{HIC}}\cdot(q_{\mathsf{HIC}}+1)\cdot\mathsf{Adv}^{\mathsf{SROB\text{-}CCA}}_{\mathcal{B},\mathsf{PKE}}(\lambda) \\ & + 2\cdot(q_{\mathsf{HIC}}+1)\cdot q_{\mathsf{PAPKE,Enc}}\cdot\mathsf{Adv}^{\mathsf{AI\text{-}CCA}}_{\mathcal{B},\mathsf{PKE}}(\lambda) \\ & + q_{\mathsf{HIC}}\cdot\mathsf{Adv}^{\mathsf{UNI\text{-}PK}}_{\mathcal{B},\mathsf{PKE}}(\lambda) + \mathsf{Adv}^{\mathsf{DROB\text{-}CCA}}_{\mathcal{B},\mathsf{PKE}}(\lambda).\end{aligned}$$

Here q_{HIC} *and* q_{PAPKE} *represent upper bounds on the number of queries to* $\mathcal{F}_{\mathsf{HIC}}$ *and* $\mathcal{F}_{\mathsf{PAPKE}}$*, respectively.* $\mathcal{R}$ *is the* HIC *randomness space and* $\mathcal{PK}$ *is the public key space of* PKE.

The proof of Theorem 1 is provided in the full version of the paper [5]. Given the similarities between the IC and the HIC, our proof is inspired by the original proof of $\mathsf{PAPKE\text{-}IC}$ (Theorem 3, [12]). However, we identified and addressed several subtle issues in the original proof.

The main issue concerns the treatment of the event bad_5 in Game_5 (using numbering from [12]). The original proof claims that this event cannot occur because there always exists a row in $\mathbf{L}$ for the honest apk such that $sk \neq \perp$. However, under the simulator's decryption procedure in Game_5, the corresponding row in $\mathbf{L}$ is generated via a call to $\mathsf{IC.Enc}(pw, pk)$ and therefore contains $sk = \perp$. One could alter the simulation of the key generation process to avoid this issue—for example, by sampling apk, querying $\mathsf{IC.Dec}(pw, apk)$, and retrieving (pk, sk) from $\mathbf{L}$ to ensure $sk \neq \perp$. While this would prevent bad_5 in Game_5, it does not extend to later games such as Game_8, where the generated (pk, sk) pair becomes independent of apk, and the simulator cannot rely on knowing the password. In such settings, the environment could potentially craft a valid ciphertext without knowing the public key, which reintroduces bad_5.

This motivates our *decryption robustness* property DROB-CCA (Sect. 4), which formalizes the requirement that an adversary cannot forge a valid ciphertext under a public key it does not know, even with access to a decryption oracle. In our proof, we argue the equivalent of the bad_5 event (in our proof referred to as bad_9) using the DROB-CCA-security of the PKE. This corresponds to the final term in the bound stated in Theorem 1.

We also observed that the "badkeys" abort (3rd line in the key generation of $\mathcal{F}_{\mathsf{PAPKE}}$) is not mentioned in the original proof. Although minor, this omission is relevant. The event occurs with negligible probability, assuming a large *apk* keyspace. In our proof, it contributes the $q_{\mathsf{PAPKE}} \cdot |\mathcal{R} \times \mathcal{PK}|^{-1}$ term in Theorem 1.

Additionally, we generalize the proof to consider non-perfectly correct Public-Key Encryption schemes with non-perfectly uniform public keys (UNI-PK). This is important when instantiating PAPKE-HIC with a post-quantum PKE, as most available schemes are neither perfectly correct nor have perfectly uniform public keys. Note that our proof of PAPKE-HIC can be adapted into a PAPKE-IC proof by modifying our Game_2 to accommodate for an IC instead of a HIC.

3.3 Why DROB-CCA Matters for the Security of UC-PAPKE?

Let us first explain why the DROB-CCA property is necessary in the context of PAPKE within the Universal Composability (UC) framework. Consider the following PAPKE attack in the UC framework. The environment $\mathcal{Z}$ initiates a party $\mathcal{P}$ with a *high-entropy password* pw by sending the message $(\mathsf{KEYGEN}, sid, pw)$. The simulator, upon receiving the message (KEYGEN, sid), must choose a (random) apk, without knowing the actual password pw.

Later, $\mathcal{Z}$ instructs $\mathcal{P}$ to decrypt a randomly chosen ciphertext c by sending $(\mathsf{DECRYPT}, sid, c)$. Since $\mathcal{P}$ was honestly initiated, there exists a key record $(sid, apk, pw) \in \mathsf{List}_{\mathsf{keyrec}}$. However, there is no corresponding encryption record in $\mathsf{List}_{\mathsf{encrec}}$, because the ciphertext c was chosen independently by the environment.

The simulator, upon receiving query $(\mathsf{DECRYPT}, sid, c)$, must respond with $(\mathsf{PLAINTEXT}, sid, m, pw^*)$. The probability that $pw^* = pw$, i.e., that the simulator guesses the correct password, is negligible because pw is hidden from the simulator and was chosen from a high-entropy distribution. Thus, with overwhelming probability, the response sent to $\mathcal{P}$ must be $\perp$, i.e., decryption fails.

At first glance, this may seem like an artificial attack: the environment is not even trying to learn the underlying public key, but rather to exploit behavioral inconsistencies between the real world and the simulated ideal world. Nevertheless, it pinpoints an important observation: we can only ensure a sound simulation if ciphertexts selected before key generation are also rejected in the real world. This motivates the need for our DROB-CCA property.

4 Decryption Robustness of Public-Key Encryption

Motivated by the requirements of the proof of PAPKE-(H)IC (Sect. 3.2), we defined in Sect. 2 a new Public-Key Encryption property, called *decryption robustness under chosen ciphertext-attacks* (DROB-CCA). In this section, we examine how it relates the existing *strong robustness* (SROB-CCA) property and also which schemes satisfy DROB-CCA directly. To the best of our knowledge, this is a new property, relevant in a setting where the public key is not yet known—an atypical situation in public-key encryption security modeling, where public keys are generally assumed to be known to all parties.

First, we show that DROB-CCA is implied by SROB-CCA in Sect. 4.1. However, the reduction is not tight, with at least a quadratic security loss. A direct proof with a tighter bound is therefore preferable for concrete security analyses.

In Sect. 4.2, we show that a hybrid PKE constructed from a KEM and a DEM satisfies DROB-CCA if 1) the DEM is INT-CTXT-secure and 2) the KEM is constructed using a variant of an FO transform that is contributory, i.e., that utilizes the public key during the symmetric key derivation. Note that many post-quantum KEMs satisfy condition 2), e.g., ML-KEM [30] or FrodoKEM [29]. We prove the result for a specific variant of the FO transform introduced in [19] called *Fujisaki-Okamoto Transformation with Prefix Hashing*. The transform is described in Fig. 7.

It's also worth noting that not all KEMs satisfy condition 2). For example, Classic McEliece [2] does not involve the public key during the symmetric key derivation. More importantly, as observed in [20], there exist ciphertexts that decapsulate to the same key under any keypair. This implies that a hybrid PKE using Classic McEliece cannot satisfy DROB-CCA since an adversary can select one of these ciphertexts and use its decapsulated value as the DEM key.

This motivates our *hashed public key* KEM transform (HPK), presented in the full version of the paper [5], which transforms any KEM into one that can be used to build a DROB-CCA-secure PKE scheme.

In the full version [5], we show that DHIES*, originally used to instantiate PAPKE-IC in [12], also directly satisfies DROB-CCA.

4.1 Strong Robustness Implies Decryption Robustness

We separate the proof SROB-CCA $\implies$ DROB-CCA into two steps. First, in Theorem 2, we prove that SROB-CCA $\implies$ DROB, where DROB (Fig. 1) is a weaker variant of DROB-CCA in which the adversary does not have access to the Dec oracle. Then, we prove that DROB is equivalent to DROB-CCA, albeit with a $q \in \mathsf{poly}(\lambda)$ security loss. The relationships are visualized in Fig. 6.

Theorem 2. *If a Public-Key Encryption scheme* PKE *satisfies* SROB-CCA, *then it also satisfies* DROB. *In other words, for any PPT adversary* $\mathcal{A}$ *against* DROB, *there exists a PPT adversary* $\mathcal{B}$ *against* SROB-CCA *such that*

$$\mathsf{Adv}^{\mathsf{DROB}}_{\mathcal{A},\mathsf{PKE}}(\lambda) \leq \sqrt{\mathsf{Adv}^{\mathsf{SROB\text{-}CCA}}_{\mathcal{B},\mathsf{PKE}}(\lambda)}.$$

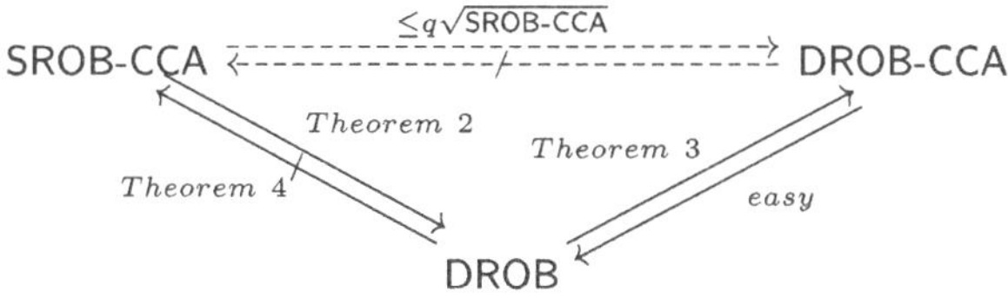

Fig. 6. Relations among SROB-CCA, DROB-CCA and DROB.

Proof. We prove the contrapositive: if there is an efficient adversary $\mathcal{A}$ against DROB, then there is an efficient adversary $\mathcal{B}$ against SROB-CCA.

The SROB-CCA adversary $\mathcal{B}$ receives the security parameter λ, two public keys pk_0, pk_1 corresponding to the private keys sk_0, sk_1, and access to two decryption oracles $\mathsf{Dec}(sk_0, \cdot), \mathsf{Dec}(sk_1, \cdot)$. $\mathcal{B}$ simply runs $\mathcal{A}$ with λ as input and once $\mathcal{A}$ outputs c^*, $\mathcal{B}$ submits it to the challenger. Let us analyze the advantage of $\mathcal{B}$.

We need to show that $f(\lambda) := \Pr\left[\mathsf{Exp}^{\mathsf{SROB\text{-}CCA}}_{\mathcal{B},\mathsf{PKE}}(\lambda) = 1\right]$ is non-negligible; specifically that

$$\exists d \in \mathbb{N}, \forall n_0 \in \mathbb{N}, \exists \lambda \geq n_0 : f(\lambda) > \frac{1}{\lambda^d}.$$

By assumption, $g(\lambda) := \Pr\left[\mathsf{Exp}^{\mathsf{DROB}}_{\mathcal{A},\mathsf{PKE}}(\lambda) = 1\right]$ is non-negligible, i.e., there exists $d_{\mathsf{DROB}} \in \mathbb{N}$ s.t. for any $n_0 \in \mathbb{N}$ there exists $\lambda \geq n_0$ for which $g(\lambda) > \frac{1}{\lambda^{d_{\mathsf{DROB}}}}$. Note that

$$\begin{aligned} g(\lambda) &= \Pr_{\substack{(pk,sk)\sim\mathsf{Keygen}(\lambda)\\ r\sim U}}\left[\mathsf{Dec}(sk, \mathcal{A}(\lambda, r)) \neq \perp\right] \\ &= \sum_{c\in\mathcal{C}}\left(\Pr_{r\sim U}\left[\mathcal{A}(\lambda, r) = c\right] \Pr_{(pk,sk)\sim\mathsf{Keygen}(\lambda)}\left[\mathsf{Dec}(sk, c) \neq \perp\right]\right) \\ &> \frac{1}{\lambda^{d_{\mathsf{DROB}}}}, \end{aligned}$$

where $\mathcal{C}$ is the set of ciphertexts and r denotes the random coins for $\mathcal{A}$ from the uniform distribution over $\{0,1\}^{\mathsf{poly}(\lambda)}$ (denoted as U). By explicit definition of $\mathcal{B}$ in terms of $\mathcal{A}$, we have

$$\begin{aligned} f(\lambda) &= \Pr\left[\mathsf{Exp}^{\mathsf{SROB\text{-}CCA}}_{\mathcal{B},\mathsf{PKE}}(\lambda) = 1\right] \\ &= \Pr_{\substack{(pk_0,sk_0)\sim\mathsf{Keygen}(\lambda)\\ (pk_1,sk_1)\sim\mathsf{Keygen}(\lambda)\\ r\sim U}}\left[\mathsf{Dec}(sk_0, \mathcal{A}(\lambda, r)) \neq \perp \wedge \mathsf{Dec}(sk_1, \mathcal{A}(\lambda, r)) \neq \perp\right] \\ &= \sum_{c\in\mathcal{C}}\left(\Pr_{r\sim U}\left[\mathcal{A}(\lambda, r) = c\right] \cdot \Pr_{\substack{(pk_0,sk_0)\sim\mathsf{Keygen}(\lambda)\\ (pk_1,sk_1)\sim\mathsf{Keygen}(\lambda)}}\left[\mathsf{Dec}(sk_0, c) \neq \perp \wedge \mathsf{Dec}(sk_1, c) \neq \perp\right]\right). \end{aligned}$$

For a fixed c, the probabilities that $\mathsf{Dec}(sk_0, c) \neq \perp$ and $\mathsf{Dec}(sk_1, c) \neq \perp$ are independent since sk_0 and sk_1 are independently sampled, therefore

$$f(\lambda) = \sum_{c \in C} \left(\Pr_{r \sim U} [\mathcal{A}(\lambda, r) = c] \cdot \left(\Pr_{(pk,sk) \sim \mathsf{Keygen}(\lambda)} [\mathsf{Dec}(sk, c) \neq \perp] \right)^2 \right). \quad (1)$$

Jensen's inequality gives us that $\psi(\mathbb{E}[X]) \leq \mathbb{E}(\psi(X))$ where ψ is a real convex function and $X : \Omega \to \mathcal{X}$ a random variable. Furthermore, for any $h : \mathcal{X} \to \mathbb{R}$, $h(X)$ is a random variable and $\mathbb{E}[h(X)] = \sum_{x \in \mathcal{X}} h(x) \Pr[X = x]$. In our case $\psi(x) := x^2$, $X := \mathcal{A}(\lambda, r)$ where r is sampled uniformly at random from the appropriate domain and

$$h(c) := \Pr_{(sk,pk) \sim \mathsf{Keygen}(\lambda)} [\mathsf{Dec}(sk, c) \neq \perp].$$

Therefore, by applying Jensen's inequality to Eq. (1) we get

$$\begin{aligned} f(\lambda) &\geq \left(\sum_{c \in C} \Pr_{r \sim U} [\mathcal{A}(\lambda, r) = c] \cdot \Pr_{(sk,pk) \sim \mathsf{Keygen}(\lambda)} [\mathsf{Dec}(sk, c) \neq \perp] \right)^2 \\ &= g(\lambda)^2 > \frac{1}{\lambda^{2d_{\mathsf{DROB}}}}. \end{aligned}$$

In other words, we have found $d := 2d_{\mathsf{DROB}}$ which proves that $f(\lambda)$ is non-negligible.

Next, we show that DROB is nearly equivalent to DROB-CCA. The implication DROB-CCA $\implies$ DROB is clear as any successful DROB adversary always wins the DROB-CCA game by submitting its output c^* to the Dec oracle at the end. So, $\mathsf{Adv}^{\mathsf{DROB}}_{\mathcal{A},\mathsf{PKE}}(\lambda) \leq \mathsf{Adv}^{\mathsf{DROB\text{-}CCA}}_{\mathcal{B},\mathsf{PKE}}(\lambda)$. We prove the other implication in Theorem 3.

Theorem 3. *If a Public-Key Encryption scheme* PKE *satisfies* DROB, *then it also satisfies* DROB-CCA. *Specifically, for any PPT adversary $\mathcal{A}$ against* DROB-CCA, *there exists a PPT adversary $\mathcal{B}$ against* DROB *such that*

$$\mathsf{Adv}^{\mathsf{DROB\text{-}CCA}}_{\mathcal{A},\mathsf{PKE}}(\lambda) \leq q_D \cdot \mathsf{Adv}^{\mathsf{DROB}}_{\mathcal{B},\mathsf{PKE}}(\lambda).$$

where q_D is the number of $\mathcal{A}$'s Dec *oracle queries.*

Theorem 3 is proven in the full version of the paper [5].

Corollary 1. *If a Public-Key Encryption scheme* PKE *satisfies* SROB-CCA, *then it also satisfies* DROB-CCA. *More precisely, for any PPT adversary $\mathcal{A}$ against* DROB-CCA *there exists a PPT adversary $\mathcal{B}$ against* SROB-CCA *such that*

$$\mathsf{Adv}^{\mathsf{DROB\text{-}CCA}}_{\mathcal{A},\mathsf{PKE}}(\lambda) \leq q_D \cdot \sqrt{\mathsf{Adv}^{\mathsf{SROB\text{-}CCA}}_{\mathcal{B},\mathsf{PKE}}(\lambda)}.$$

where q_D is the number of $\mathcal{A}$'s Dec *oracle queries.*

Theorem 4. *There exists a Public-Key Encryption scheme that is* DROB-*secure, but is not* SROB-CCA-*secure. In other words,* DROB *does not imply* SROB-CCA.

Theorem 4 is proven in the full version of the paper [5]. Note that Theorem 4 shows that DROB-CCA and SROB-CCA are not equivalent notions.

4.2 Building a DROB-CCA PKE from a Prefix-Hashing FO KEM

In Sect. 4.1, we have shown that SROB-CCA implies DROB-CCA. However, the reduction is not tight. Specifically, there is at least a quadratic security loss. This motivates Theorem 5, which shows that the standard hybrid (KEM+DEM) Public-Key Encryption construction (PKE^{hy} in Fig. 8) directly satisfies DROB-CCA, provided that 1) the DEM is INT-CTXT-secure and 2) the KEM is constructed using the prefix-hashing Fujisaki-Okamoto transform pFO (Fig. 7).

The pFO transform is a modified version of the transform introduced in [19, Figure 4]—this transform does not derive the "rejection key" $\bar{K}$ from $\mathsf{ID}(pk)$, which exactly models KEMs such as ML-KEM [30]. Note that in the proof and the description of the transform (Fig. 7) we use Python-like syntax to indicate truncated outputs, e.g., the first 128 bits of the value $\mathsf{F}(x)$ is denoted as $\mathsf{F}(x)[0:128]$.

```
pFO[PKE1, ID, F].Keygen(λ)
  (pk, sk') ← PKE1.Keygen(λ)
  s ←$ M
  sk ← (sk', s, pk)
  return (pk, sk)

pFO[PKE1, ID, F].Encap(pk)
  m ←$ M
  (K, r) ← F(ID(pk), m)
  c ← PKE1.Enc(pk, m, r)
  return (K, c)

pFO[PKE1, ID, F].Decap(sk, c)
  (sk', s, pk) ← sk
  m' ← PKE1.Dec(sk', c)
  (K, r) ← F(ID(pk), m')
  K̄ ← F(s, c)[0 : k]
  if m' = ⊥ ∨ PKE1.Enc(pk, m', r) ≠ c
    return K̄ [/⊥]
  return K
```

Fig. 7. $\mathsf{pFO}[\mathsf{PKE}_1, \mathsf{ID}, \mathsf{F}]$ is the prefix-hashing FO transform inspired by [19, Figure 4]. PKE_1 is a PKE, ID is a fixed-length output function and F is a random oracle. The inclusion of the [boxed code] defines the explicitly rejecting transform.

We prove Theorem 5 in the QROM model [11] using the following lemma from [31, Lemma 2.2] which shows that a quantum random oracle can be used as a PRF.

Lemma 1. *Let $l \in \mathbb{N}$. Let $\mathsf{F} : \{0,1\}^l \times \mathcal{X} \to \mathcal{Y}$ and $\mathsf{H} : \mathcal{X} \to \mathcal{Y}$ be two independent random oracles. If an unbounded-time quantum adversary $\mathcal{D}$ makes at most q queries to its quantum-accessible random oracles, then we have*

$$\left|\Pr\left[1 \leftarrow \mathcal{D}^{\mathsf{F},\mathsf{F}(t,\cdot)}() | t \leftarrow\!\$\, \{0,1\}^l\right] - \Pr\left[1 \leftarrow \mathcal{D}^{\mathsf{F},\mathsf{H}}()\right]\right| \leq \frac{2 \cdot q}{\sqrt{2^l}}.$$

Theorem 5. *Let $\mathsf{PKE} = \mathsf{PKE}^{hy}[\mathsf{KEM}, \mathsf{DEM}]$ be a hybrid Public-Key Encryption scheme constructed from an implicitly rejecting key encapsulation mechanism* KEM *and a data encapsulation mechanism* DEM. *If* KEM *is constructed using the prefix-hashing FO transform* pFO *(Fig. 7), i.e.,* $\mathsf{KEM} = \mathsf{pFO}[\mathsf{PKE}_1, \mathsf{ID}, \mathsf{F}]$ *where*

$\mathsf{PKE}^{hy}[\mathsf{KEM},\mathsf{DEM}].\mathsf{Keygen}(\lambda)$	$\mathsf{PKE}^{hy}[\mathsf{KEM},\mathsf{DEM}].\mathsf{Enc}(pk,m)$	$\mathsf{PKE}^{hy}[\mathsf{KEM},\mathsf{DEM}].\mathsf{Dec}(sk,c)$
$(pk,sk) \leftarrow \mathsf{KEM.Keygen}(\lambda)$ **return** (pk,sk)	$(c_1,k) \leftarrow \mathsf{KEM.Encap}(pk)$ $c_2 \leftarrow \mathsf{DEM.Enc}(k,m)$ $c \leftarrow (c_1,c_2)$ **return** c	$(c_1,c_2) \leftarrow c$ $k \leftarrow \mathsf{KEM.Decap}(sk,c_1)$ [**if** $k = \perp$ **then** **return** $\perp$] (boxed) $m \leftarrow \mathsf{DEM.Dec}(k,c_2)$ **return** m

Fig. 8. Description of the standard hybrid PKE construction using a KEM and a DEM. The inclusion of the boxed code defines the construction for explicitly rejecting KEMs.

PKE_1 *is a Public-Key Encryption scheme,* $\mathsf{ID} : \mathcal{PK} \to \{0,1\}^n$ *is a fixed-length output function,* $\mathsf{F} : \{0,1\}^* \to \{0,1\}^k \times \{0,1\}^{\overline{r}}$ *is a quantum random oracle and* DEM *is* INT-CTXT*-secure, then for any QPT adversary* $\mathcal{A}$ *against* DROB-CCA *of* PKE *there exists a QPT adversary* $\mathcal{B}$ *against* INT-CTXT *of* DEM *such that*

$$\mathsf{Adv}^{\mathsf{DROB\text{-}CCA}}_{\mathcal{A},\mathsf{PKE}}(\lambda) \leq \frac{4 \cdot q_{\mathsf{F}}}{\sqrt{2^{\min(m,k)}}} + q_D \cdot \mathsf{Adv}^{\mathsf{INT\text{-}CTXT}}_{\mathcal{B},\mathsf{DEM}}(\lambda),$$

for $(pk,sk) \leftarrow \mathsf{PKE}_1.\mathsf{Keygen}(\lambda)$*, where* $m = H_\infty(\mathsf{ID}(pk))$ *is the min-entropy of* $\mathsf{ID}(pk)$*,* q_{F} *denotes the number of queries to the quantum random oracle* F *and* q_D *denotes the number of queries to the (classical) oracle* Dec.

Proof. Let $\mathcal{A}$ be an adversary against DROB-CCA of PKE. Denote by $\Pr[\mathsf{Game_i}]$ the probability that $\mathcal{A}$ wins the i-th game. See the full version of the paper [5] for a detailed description of the games.

$\mathsf{Game_0}$. This is the unmodified DROB-CCA game with an unpacked PKE, i.e.,

$$\mathsf{Adv}^{\mathsf{DROB\text{-}CCA}}_{\mathcal{A},\mathsf{PKE}}(\lambda) = \Pr[\mathsf{Game_0}].$$

$\mathsf{Game_1}$. In $\mathsf{Game_1}$, we replace the KEM key and randomness derivation in the decryption oracle $(K,r) \leftarrow \mathsf{F}(\mathsf{ID}(pk),m_1)$ with $(K,r) \leftarrow \mathsf{H}_1(m_1)$ where H_1 is an internal random oracle. This change is undetectable by $\mathcal{A}$ with probability given by Lemma 1.

We build a distinguisher $\mathcal{D}$ from Lemma 1 as follows. $\mathcal{D}$ has access to two quantum random oracles F,F' where $\mathsf{F}'(\cdot) = \mathsf{F}(t,\cdot)$ for $t \leftarrow\$ \{0,1\}^m$, or $\mathsf{F}'(\cdot) = \mathsf{H}_1(\cdot)$. $\mathcal{D}$ runs $\mathcal{A}$ in a modified $\mathsf{Game_0}$ where $(K,r) \leftarrow \mathsf{F}(\mathsf{ID}(pk),m_1)$ in the decryption oracle is replaced with $(K,r) \leftarrow \mathsf{F}'(m_1)$. $\mathcal{D}$ outputs 1 if $\mathcal{A}$ wins the game, i.e., submits a decrypting ciphertext. Clearly, if $\mathsf{F}'(\cdot) = \mathsf{F}(t,\cdot)$ then the game corresponds to $\mathsf{Game_0}$ since t has the same min-entropy as $\mathsf{ID}(pk)$ and if $\mathsf{F}'(\cdot) = \mathsf{H}_1(\cdot)$, then it corresponds to $\mathsf{Game_1}$.

By Lemma 1, $|\Pr[\mathsf{Game_0}] - \Pr[\mathsf{Game_1}]| =$

$$\left|\Pr\left[1 \leftarrow \mathcal{D}^{\mathsf{F},\mathsf{F}(t,\cdot)}() | t \leftarrow\$ \{0,1\}^m\right] - \Pr\left[1 \leftarrow \mathcal{D}^{\mathsf{F},\mathsf{H}_1}()\right]\right| \leq \frac{2 \cdot q_{\mathsf{F}}}{\sqrt{2^m}}.$$

Game_2. In Game_2, we replace the rejection KEM key derivation in the decryption oracle $K' \leftarrow \mathsf{F}(s, c_1)$ with $K' \leftarrow \mathsf{H}_2(c_1)$ where H_2 is an internal random oracle. Analogously to the previous game hop, by Lemma 1 we get

$$|\Pr[\mathsf{Game}_1] - \Pr[\mathsf{Game}_2]| \leq \frac{2 \cdot q_\mathsf{F}}{\sqrt{2^k}}.$$

Game_3. In Game_3, we reorganize the decryption oracle code. K is sampled from the same distribution regardless of whether H_1 or H_2 is called. Therefore, we can "unroll" H_1 and H_2 and replace them with sampling of $K \leftarrow \$ \{0,1\}^k$ with record keeping. We also remove the "rejection if branch."

We keep a list List_C with pairs (c_1, K) where c_1 is the queried KEM ciphertext. Observe that keeping the list indexed by c_1 is enough to preserve consistency. Consider that $\mathcal{A}$ queries $c = (c_1, c_2)$ and $c' = (c_1', c_2')$ to the Dec oracle:

- If $c_1 = c_1'$, then the lookup in List_C assures consistency.
- If $c_1 \neq c_1'$ and $\mathsf{PKE}_1.\mathsf{Dec}(sk, c_1) \neq \mathsf{PKE}_1.\mathsf{Dec}(sk, c_1')$, then Game_2 also derives independent DEM keys.
- If $c_1 \neq c_1'$ and $\mathsf{PKE}_1.\mathsf{Dec}(sk, c_1) = m' = \mathsf{PKE}_1.\mathsf{Dec}(sk, c_1')$, then observe that the derived DEM keys are also independent because c_1 or c_1' must fail the FO re-encryption check given that $\mathsf{PKE}_1.\mathsf{Enc}(pk, m', r)$ is deterministic.

Since this game is just a code reorganization, we have $\Pr[\mathsf{Game}_2] = \Pr[\mathsf{Game}_3]$.

Observe that $\mathcal{A}$ wins Game_3 iff it queries $c = (c_1, c_2)$ where $\mathsf{DEM}.\mathsf{Dec}(K, c_2) \neq \perp$ where $K \leftarrow\$ \{0,1\}^k$. We show that we can build an $\mathsf{INT\text{-}CTXT}$ adversary $\mathcal{B}$ using $\mathcal{A}$ in Game_3.

Let $i \in \{1, \ldots, q_D\}$ be the index of the first query from $\mathcal{A}$ that decrypts. $\mathcal{B}$ guesses $i \in \{1, \ldots, q_D\}$ and runs $\mathcal{A}$ in a modified Game_3 where $\mathcal{B}$ answers with $\perp$ to the first $i-1$ queries. During the i-th query, it uses its Dec oracle from the $\mathsf{INT\text{-}CTXT}$ challenger instead of calling $\mathsf{DEM}.\mathsf{Dec}(K, \cdot)$ with $K \leftarrow\$ \{0,1\}^k$. Observe that K is sampled from the same distribution in Game_3 and in the $\mathsf{INT\text{-}CTXT}$ game and $\mathcal{B}$ perfectly simulates Game_3 if it guessed i. Therefore, $\mathcal{B}$ always wins if it correctly guessed i and $\mathcal{A}$ wins. In other words,

$$\Pr[\mathsf{Game}_3] \leq q_D \cdot \mathsf{Adv}^{\mathsf{INT\text{-}CTXT}}_{\mathcal{B},\mathsf{DEM}}(\lambda).$$

In total, we have

$$\mathsf{Adv}^{\mathsf{DROB\text{-}CCA}}_{\mathcal{A},\mathsf{PKE}}(\lambda) \leq \frac{4 \cdot q_\mathsf{F}}{\sqrt{2^{\min(m,k)}}} + q_D \cdot \mathsf{Adv}^{\mathsf{INT\text{-}CTXT}}_{\mathcal{B},\mathsf{DEM}}(\lambda).$$

Explicitly Rejecting pFO. Note that a variant of Theorem 5 also holds for a PKE constructed from an explicitly rejecting pFO KEM. The proof is almost identical except we do not need to consider the rejection key. As a consequence there is no $s \in \{0,1\}^k$ and the bound is $\mathsf{Adv}^{\mathsf{DROB\text{-}CCA}}_{\mathcal{A},\mathsf{PKE}}(\lambda) \leq \frac{2 \cdot q_\mathsf{F}}{\sqrt{2^m}} + q_D \cdot \mathsf{Adv}^{\mathsf{INT\text{-}CTXT}}_{\mathcal{B},\mathsf{DEM}}(\lambda)$.

Application of Theorem 5 *to Existing KEMs.* Recall that compared to prefix-hashing FO transform from [19], the pFO transform is slightly modified so that it directly models KEMs such as ML-KEM [30] and FrodoKEM [29]. However, the inclusion of $\mathsf{ID}(pk)$ in rejection key derivation only tightens the bound from Theorem 5—we get $4 \cdot q_{\mathsf{F}} \cdot \sqrt{2^{-m}}$ instead of $4 \cdot q_{\mathsf{F}} \cdot \sqrt{2^{-\min(m,k)}}$.

As discussed in [19], the function ID may either be a hash function or a function that selects the random portion of the public key. For instance, in ML-KEM, ID is instantiated as SHA3-256, meaning the entire public key is hashed—including a 256-bit random seed. In FrodoKEM, the key derivation is more involved, however, it still incorporates a hash of the entire public key.

Impact of Theorem 5 *on Concrete Security.* We compare the concrete DROB-CCA security bounds implied by Theorem 2 and by Theorem 5 considering a hybrid PKE instantiated with ML-KEM [30].

From [20, Theorem 2 + Theorem 12], we have $\mathsf{Adv}^{\mathsf{SROB\text{-}CCA}}_{\mathcal{A},\mathsf{PKE}}(\lambda) \leq \frac{4 \cdot q_{\mathsf{F}}}{2^{128}} + \epsilon$, where q_{F} denotes the number of queries to the quantum-accessible random oracle and $\epsilon \ll 2^{-128}$ a negligible term. By Corollary 1, we have $\mathsf{Adv}^{\mathsf{DROB\text{-}CCA}}_{\mathcal{A},\mathsf{PKE}}(\lambda) \leq q_D \cdot \sqrt{\mathsf{Adv}^{\mathsf{SROB\text{-}CCA}}_{\mathcal{B},\mathsf{PKE}}(\lambda)}$, where q_D is the number of decryption queries. Replacing $\mathsf{Adv}^{\mathsf{SROB\text{-}CCA}}_{\mathcal{A},\mathsf{PKE}}(\lambda)$ term with the bound above, we get $\mathsf{Adv}^{\mathsf{DROB\text{-}CCA}}_{\mathcal{A},\mathsf{PKE}}(\lambda) \leq q_D \cdot \sqrt{\frac{4 \cdot q_{\mathsf{F}}}{2^{128}} + \epsilon}$. While Corollary 1 shows that DROB-CCA and SROB-CCA are asymptotically equivalent, a concrete security analysis reveals that even for arguably modest upper bounds on q_{F} and q_D (say $q_{\mathsf{F}} = 2^{40}$ and $q_D = 2^{16}$), the combination of [20, Theorem 2 + Theorem 12] and Corollary 1 provides limited insight into the actual security guarantees that ML-KEM delivers in terms of *decryption robustness*, as it does not yield an upper bound that would be regarded as meaningful under modern security standards.

In contrast, the direct analysis of the prefix-hashing FO transform allows us to establish security bounds via Theorem 5 that remain meaningful in practical settings, i.e., we have that $\mathsf{Adv}^{\mathsf{DROB\text{-}CCA}}_{\mathcal{A},\mathsf{PKE}}(\lambda) \leq \frac{4 \cdot q_{\mathsf{F}}}{\sqrt{2^{\min(m,k)}}} + q_D \cdot \mathsf{Adv}^{\mathsf{INT\text{-}CTXT}}_{\mathcal{B},\mathsf{DEM}}(\lambda)$, where $m = k = 256$ for ML-KEM. Since the DEM can be selected such that $\mathsf{Adv}^{\mathsf{INT\text{-}CTXT}}_{\mathcal{B},\mathsf{DEM}}(\lambda)$ becomes the non-dominant term, this gives a meaningful upper bound on the decryption-robustness advantage against PKE from ML-KEM in practical settings.

5 Implementation and Performance

In this section, we discuss which KEMs are suitable to build a post-quantum PAPKE-HIC. The main advantage of PAPKE-HIC compared to PAPKE-IC is the fact that it does not require an ideal cipher over large algebraic domains, which affects performance. To demonstrate the concrete advantage of our HIC-based approach, we implemented post-quantum PAPKE-HIC and PAPKE-IC using ML-KEM [30], FrodoKEM [29] and Classic McEliece [2]. We focus on ML-KEM implementation details and performance results in this section, while further results for FrodoKEM and Classic McEliece are provided in the full version [5].

5.1 Possible PAPKE-HIC Instantiations

We consider three post-quantum KEMs: ML-KEM [30], FrodoKEM [29] and Classic McEliece [2] as candidates for PAPKE-HIC instantiation. Recall that PAPKE-HIC requires a PKE scheme that is IND-CCA, ANO-CCA, SROB-CCA, UNI-PK, and DROB-CCA (Theorem 1). We construct a post-quantum PKE using the standard KEM+DEM construction (Fig. 8). Note that IND-CCA-security of the PKE is easily achievable since each mentioned KEM is IND-CCA. As shown in Sect. 4.1, deriving DROB-CCA from SROB-CCA incurs a quadratic security degradation, which then becomes the dominant term in the security bound of Theorem 1. Considering concrete security, this may require choosing larger security parameters for PAPKE-HIC instantiations. However, as shown in Sect. 4.2, this is unnecessary for KEMs with the prefix-hashing FO transform (pFO) described in Fig. 7. We now analyze each KEM separately.

ML-KEM. The hybrid PKE with ML-KEM is ANO-CCA [28] and SROB-CCA [20]. Moreover, in ML-KEM, the public key is computationally indistinguishable from uniform under the MLWE assumption [8], thus supporting the UNI-PK property in practice. ML-KEM uses the pFO transform, and thus directly satisfies DROB-CCA with the bound from Theorem 5.

FrodoKEM. The hybrid PKE with FrodoKEM is ANO-CCA and SROB-CCA as shown in [37]. FrodoKEM uses the pFO transform, so it satisfies DROB-CCA with the bound from Theorem 5. FrodoKEM satisfies UNI-PK under the LWE assumption by an analogous argument as for ML-KEM in [8].

Classic McEliece. It was shown in [37] that Classic McEliece satisfies ANO-CCA under additional assumptions. UNI-PK is considered a standard assumption for Classic McEliece [2]. However, [20] demonstrated that Classic McEliece does not satisfy SCFR-CCA, which means that the hybrid PKE with Classic McEliece is not SROB-CCA. A modified variant of Classic McEliece, proposed in [37], yields a hybrid PKE that satisfies SROB-CCA. This modified variant essentially integrates the pFO transform internally into Classic McEliece, thus directly satisfying DROB-CCA per Theorem 5.

Still, modifying the internals of an existing scheme can be impractical. That is why we introduce the *hashed public key* (HPK) KEM transform in the full version of the paper [5], a simpler black-box modification resulting in a DROB-CCA-secure scheme. We show that HPK preserves anonymity and that any HPK-transformed KEM is SCFR-CCA and consequently the hybrid PKE is SROB-CCA.

5.2 ML-KEM PAPKE Implementation

The crux of implementing PAPKE-IC is the instantiation of the ideal cipher over the ML-KEM public key space, which is a group. There exist two approaches to implement an ideal cipher over the ML-KEM public key space. The first approach is to combine an ideal cipher over bitstrings with a quasi-bijective encoding of the public keys to bitstrings [21]. This requires an ideal cipher over a large bitstring domain, which can be realized either via domain extenders [15] or via an 8-round Feistel network [17]. The second approach is to use the 8-round Feistel construction [17] to build an ideal cipher over the public key space directly, which in turn requires 4 hash-to-group operations.[3]

Regarding the PAPKE-HIC implementation, there currently exists only one HIC construction, m2F (Fig. 3), which requires one hash-to-group operation, i.e., hashing to the ML-KEM public key space. To realize this, we implemented two hash-to-group approaches. The first one employs the SampleNTT subroutine from [30, Algorithm 7], the same rejection sampling routine used by ML-KEM key generation. The second approach is to use Kemeleon [22], specifically Kemeleon decoding, which maps bitstrings to ML-KEM public keys.

To summarize, we have implemented and benchmarked the following implementations of post-quantum PAPKE with ML-KEM:

(a) PAPKE-IC is implemented by combining Kemeleon—used to encode ML-KEM as a pseudo-uniform bitstring—with an ideal cipher instantiated over bitstrings, either via a domain extender or an 8-round Feistel network.
(b) PAPKE-IC is also implemented by directly employing an 8-round Feistel, in which four of the hashing operations are hash-to-group operations realized using either SampleNTT or Kemeleon decoding.
(c) PAPKE-HIC is implemented with a 2-round modified Feistel m2F, in which the single hash-to-group operation is implemented either via SampleNTT or Kemeleon decoding.

Note that the underlying Public-Key Encryption scheme is the KEM+DEM hybrid construction PKE^{hy} (Fig. 8) with ML-KEM serving as the KEM. Recall from Sect. 3 that we require the PKE to be SROB-CCA-secure, which in this case requires the DEM to be FROB-secure [20, Theorem 2]. Standard AEAD constructions, such as AES-GCM, are typically not FROB-secure [18], therefore, we use the CTX construction introduced in [14, Figure 2] which builds an FROB-secure[4] DEM from an AEAD and a collision-resistant hash function. We use AES-256-GCM as the underlying AEAD and SHA-256 as the hash function.

Our C++ implementation uses libraries Botan (https://botan.randombit.net/) and Catch2 (https://github.com/catchorg/Catch2). Specifically, we use Botan for cryptographic primitives, such as ML-KEM and AES-256-GCM, and Catch2 for benchmarking. More details and the full code is available at https://github.com/PAPKE-HIC/benchmarks.

5.3 ML-KEM PAPKE Performance Results

We executed the benchmarks on a machine with AMD EPYC 7543 (2,8 GHz) as a CPU, running Ubuntu 24.04 and compiled using GCC 13. We used the `--benchmark-samples 1000` Catch2 parameter during benchmarking.

[3] One wire carries the group element while the second carries a random bitstring.
[4] The paper in question [14] uses a different security notion ($\mathsf{CAE}_{\mathsf{XX}}$) which implies FROB from [20].

Table 1 provides performance results of our PAPKE-IC and PAPKE-HIC implementations with ML-KEM-512. For ML-KEM-768, ML-KEM-1024 see Tables 2 and 3.

Table 1. ML-KEM-512 PAPKE performance. Values are in microseconds in the format: `mean ± std. dev.`; "bitstring Extender/Feistel" refers to variants (a), "Feistel+H2G" refers to variants (b) from Sect. 5.2.

Variant	Key Gen.	Encryption	Decryption
PAPKE-HIC, SampleNTT	116 ± 8	116 ± 11	98 ± 7
PAPKE-IC, Feistel+H2G, SampleNTT	170 ± 6	189 ± 15	98 ± 10
PAPKE-IC, bitstring Feistel	417 ± 258	14 606 ± 126	103 ± 13
PAPKE-IC, bitstring Extender	974 ± 227	14 816 ± 114	99 ± 10
PAPKE-HIC, Kemeleon	14 572 ± 222	14 534 ± 185	100 ± 10
PAPKE-IC, Feistel+H2G, Kemeleon	56 932 ± 503	57 449 ± 864	98 ± 9

Table 2. ML-KEM-768 PAPKE performance. Values are in microseconds in the format: `mean ± std. dev.`; "bitstring Extender/Feistel" refer to variants (a), "Feistel+H2G" refer to variants (b) from Sect. 5.2.

Variant	Key Gen.	Encryption	Decryption
PAPKE-HIC, SampleNTT	162 ± 9	163 ± 10	171 ± 13
PAPKE-IC, Feistel+H2G, SampleNTT	248 ± 10	257 ± 11	170 ± 9
PAPKE-IC, bitstring Feistel	471 ± 174	40 628 ± 308	179 ± 10
PAPKE-IC, bitstring Extender	2 183 ± 181	43 534 ± 431	178 ± 13
PAPKE-HIC, Kemeleon	40 480 ± 268	41 082 ± 632	183 ± 15
PAPKE-IC, Feistel+H2G, Kemeleon	166 040 ± 1 810	163 714 ± 2 374	197 ± 19

We found that the Kemeleon-based hash-to-group is the bottleneck in variants that use it. This is because Kemeleon decoding requires division of large integers (around 6000 bits for ML-KEM-512). Note that PAPKE-IC with bitstring ideal cipher constructions use Kemeleon *encoding* during key generation and *decoding* during encryption. This explains why those instantiations perform better than PAPKE-HIC (Kemeleon variant), which relies on Kemeleon decoding for the hash-to-group, at key generation, but perform essentially the same at encryption.

Overall, the best performing constructions rely on the SampleNTT-based hashing to group, and of those, PAPKE-HIC performs better than PAPKE-IC. This is to be expected when we trade four hash-to-group operations for one hash-to-group operation and a block cipher.

Table 3. ML-KEM-1024 PAPKE performance. Values are in microseconds in the format: `mean ± std. dev.`; "bitstring Extender/Feistel" refer to variants (a), "Feistel+H2G" refer to variants (b) from Sect. 5.2.

Variant	Key Gen.	Encryption	Decryption
PAPKE-HIC, SampleNTT	215 ± 9	222 ± 14	269 ± 18
PAPKE-IC, Feistel+H2G, SampleNTT	327 ± 10	345 ± 13	266 ± 14
PAPKE-IC, bitstring Feistel	984 ± 577	$88\,959 \pm 1\,228$	280 ± 21
PAPKE-IC, bitstring Extender	$2\,767 \pm 657$	$89\,841 \pm 972$	282 ± 20
PAPKE-HIC, Kemeleon	$87\,908 \pm 372$	$89\,760 \pm 1\,157$	284 ± 21
PAPKE-IC, Feistel+H2G, Kemeleon	$354\,004 \pm 4\,455$	$353\,089 \pm 3\,801$	290 ± 16

It's also worth noting that the (relative) high variance of PAPKE-IC variants with bitstring ideal cipher is caused by rejection of keypairs—only certain ML-KEM public keys can be Kemeleon-encoded. For ML-KEM-512 the success probability is $\approx 56\%$ [22], but for ML-KEM-768 it is $\approx 83\%$, which explains the smaller relative variance for ML-KEM-768 in Table 2.

6 Conclusion

Why was DROB-CCA Not Needed in KEM-to-PAKE Compilers? The new DROB notion introduced here targets PKE schemes, but a similar property could trivially be adapted for explicitly rejecting KEMs. One might even consider an analogue for implicitly rejecting KEMs, although this would require examining the internal workings of the KEM to identify the winning condition in decapsulation and determine when the decapsulation did not fail. Given the long line of work compiling KEMs to PAKE in the UC framework [3,4,8,26,32], why has decryption robustness (or another similar property) not previously emerged as a required property in the PAKE setting?

In OEKE-style protocols (e.g., OCAKE, EKE-KEM, CHIC, and NoIC [3,4, 8,32]), the simulator can reject ciphertexts based on authentication tags derived from a random oracle. This effectively forces the adversary to commit to a specific password, which can then be extracted by the simulator. This password allows the simulator to associate an *apk* to a unique public key with knowledge of the secret key; a tag not returned by the random oracle will only be valid with negligible probability over the oracle's output space.

In EKE-style compilers (e.g., CAKE, EKE-PRF [8,26]), the KEM ciphertext is further encrypted with an ideal cipher (with domain separation from the session identifier and the password attributed to the party). As a result, if the adversary submits a ciphertext that was never queried to the IC, it is impossible to extract a valid password. (Due to the IC's behavior, the underlying KEM ciphertext is also completely random.) This appears to be precisely what [26] identified as being overlooked in CAKE [8], which they fix by requiring "strong pseudorandomness" from the underlying key agreement (KA). According to the authors, this property on the KA is satisfied when the KA is built from KEM satisfying both SPR-CCA and SMT-CCA security properties [37].

We leave it as future work to investigate whether DROB-CCA (or a variant thereof) would be sufficient for EKE-style compilers from KEMs. The issues appear related, and strong pseudorandomness may be unnecessarily strong if DROB-CCA alone suffices to prevent such attacks, provided the session key is derived from a KDF that binds the full communication transcript and the underlying common secrets (i.e. the password and the KEM key).

It is also worth noting that the standard $\mathcal{F}_{\mathsf{PAKE}}$ functionality is implicitly rejecting, whereas $\mathcal{F}_{\mathsf{PAPKE}}$ explicitly rejects. This means that in PAPKE, the simulator must decide whether decryption fails, while in PAKE, the simulator can output a random session key and defer consistency of the simulation to a later stage. Another important difference is that PAPKE allows reuse of the authenticated public key and supports multiple decryption queries, whereas PAKE built from KEM demands only a single decryption/decapsulation per party (assuming the appropriate domain separation in idealized objects is in place).

Quantum Adversaries. Although we have lifted some simpler theorems to the QROM (Theorem 5 and Theorem 6 in the full version [5]), the analysis of the main PAPKE-HIC construction remains in the classical setting, as we do not consider a quantum-accessible Half Ideal Cipher. Currently we have a somewhat limited set of techniques for lifting proofs to the QROM and even fewer for the QICM. The lack of perfect independence between input-output pairs and the possibility of quantum queries to the inverse permutation makes the analysis of quantum-accessible ideal ciphers usually a challenging barrier to overcome. (The same applies to the Half Ideal Cipher.) This is likely why lifting the security proofs of generic PAKE compilers from KEMs remains an open problem and an active area of research. New efforts in this direction are emerging, namely with a partial quantum proof for OCAKE protocol [24] and a generic compiler that avoids the IC [3]. Since PAPKE implies PAKE, a generic PAPKE construction proven secure in the quantum setting would also resolve the open problem for PAKE. We leave this as an interesting direction for future work.

Benefits of Contributory KEMs. KEMs that incorporate the public key into the symmetric key derivation are typically referred to as *contributory* [16, 19] meaning that both parties contribute to the derived symmetric key during a key exchange. In this paper, we identify an additional benefit: contributory KEMs naturally give rise to hybrid Public-Key Encryption schemes that satisfy DROB-CCA when paired with an integrity-protecting DEM.

Acknowledgments. Jan Oupický was supported by the industrial partnership project between the interdisciplinary research center SnT and LuxTrust. Afonso Arriaga and Peter Rønne received support from the Luxembourg National Research Fund (FNR) under the CORE project (C21/IS/16221219/ImPAKT). Afonso Arriaga and Marjan Škrobot also received support from FNR Core Junior project (C21/IS/16236053/FuturePass).

References

1. Abdalla, M., Bellare, M., Neven, G.: Robust encryption. In: Micciancio, D. (ed.) TCC 2010. LNCS, vol. 5978, pp. 480–497. Springer, Heidelberg (2010). https://doi.org/10.1007/978-3-642-11799-2_28
2. Albrecht, M.R., et al.: Classic McEliece. Technical report, National Institute of Standards and Technology (2022). https://csrc.nist.gov/projects/post-quantum-cryptography/round-4-submissions
3. Arriaga, A., Barbosa, M., Jarecki, S.: NoIC: PAKE from KEM without ideal ciphers. Cryptology ePrint Archive, Report 2025/231 (2025). https://eprint.iacr.org/2025/231
4. Arriaga, A., Barbosa, M., Jarecki, S., Skrobot, M.: C'est Très CHIC: a compact password-authenticated key exchange from lattice-based KEM. In: Chung, K.M., Sasaki, Y. (eds.) Advances in Cryptology – ASIACRYPT 2024, Part V. LNCS, vol. 15488, pp. 3–33. Springer, Singapore (2024). https://doi.org/10.1007/978-981-96-0935-2_1
5. Arriaga, A., Mestel, D., Oupický, J., Rønne, P.B., Škrobot, M.: HIC is all you need: Practical Post-Quantum Password-Authenticated Public-Key Encryption. Cryptology ePrint Archive, Report 2026/020 (2026). https://eprint.iacr.org/2026/020
6. Arriaga, A., Ryan, P.Y.A., Skrobot, M.: SweetPAKE: key exchange with decoy passwords. In: Zhou, J., Quek, T.Q.S., Gao, D., Cárdenas, A.A. (eds.) ASIACCS 24: 19th ACM Symposium on Information, Computer and Communications Security. ACM Press, Singapore (2024). https://doi.org/10.1145/3634737.3645009
7. Barbosa, M., Gellert, K., Hesse, J., Jarecki, S.: Bare PAKE: universally composable key exchange from just passwords. In: Reyzin, L., Stebila, D. (eds.) Advances in Cryptology – CRYPTO 2024, Part II. LNCS, vol. 14921, pp. 183–217. Springer, Cham (2024). https://doi.org/10.1007/978-3-031-68379-4_6
8. Beguinet, H., Chevalier, C., Pointcheval, D., Ricosset, T., Rossi, M.: GeT a CAKE: generic transformations from key encaspulation mechanisms to password authenticated key exchanges. In: Tibouchi, M., Wang, X. (eds.) ACNS 2023, Part II. LNCS, vol. 13906, pp. 516–538. Springer, Cham (2023). https://doi.org/10.1007/978-3-031-33491-7_19
9. Bellare, M., Boldyreva, A., Desai, A., Pointcheval, D.: Key-privacy in public-key encryption. In: Boyd, C. (ed.) Advances in Cryptology – ASIACRYPT 2001. LNCS, vol. 2248, pp. 566–582. Springer, Heidelberg (2001). https://doi.org/10.1007/3-540-45682-1_33
10. Bellare, M., Namprempre, C.: Authenticated encryption: relations among notions and analysis of the generic composition paradigm. J. Cryptol. **21**(4), 469–491 (2008). https://doi.org/10.1007/s00145-008-9026-x
11. Boneh, D., Dagdelen, Ö., Fischlin, M., Lehmann, A., Schaffner, C., Zhandry, M.: Random oracles in a quantum world. In: Lee, D.H., Wang, X. (eds.) Advances in Cryptology – ASIACRYPT 2011. LNCS, vol. 7073, pp. 41–69. Springer, Heidelberg (2011). https://doi.org/10.1007/978-3-642-25385-0_3
12. Bradley, T., Camenisch, J., Jarecki, S., Lehmann, A., Neven, G., Xu, J.: Password-authenticated public-key encryption. Cryptology ePrint Archive, Report 2019/199 (2019). https://eprint.iacr.org/2019/199
13. Canetti, R., Halevi, S., Katz, J., Lindell, Y., MacKenzie, P.D.: Universally composable password-based key exchange. In: Cramer, R. (ed.) Advances in Cryptology – EUROCRYPT 2005. LNCS, vol. 3494, pp. 404–421. Springer, Heidelberg (2005). https://doi.org/10.1007/11426639_24

14. Chan, J., Rogaway, P.: On committing authenticated-encryption. In: Atluri, V., Di Pietro, R., Jensen, C.D., Meng, W. (eds.) ESORICS 2022, Part II. LNCS, vol. 13555, pp. 275–294. Springer, Cham (2022). https://doi.org/10.1007/978-3-031-17146-8_14
15. Coron, J.S., Dodis, Y., Mandal, A., Seurin, Y.: A domain extender for the ideal cipher. In: Micciancio, D. (ed.) TCC 2010. LNCS, vol. 5978, pp. 273–289. Springer, Heidelberg (2010). https://doi.org/10.1007/978-3-642-11799-2_17
16. Cremers, C., Dax, A., Medinger, N.: Keeping up with the KEMs: stronger security notions for KEMs and automated analysis of KEM-based protocols. In: Luo, B., Liao, X., Xu, J., Kirda, E., Lie, D. (eds.) ACM CCS 2024: 31st Conference on Computer and Communications Security, pp. 1046–1060. ACM Press, Salt Lake City, UT, USA (2024). https://doi.org/10.1145/3658644.3670283
17. Dai, Y., Steinberger, J.P.: Indifferentiability of 8-round Feistel networks. In: Robshaw, M., Katz, J. (eds.) Advances in Cryptology – CRYPTO 2016, Part I. LNCS, vol. 9814, pp. 95–120. Springer, Heidelberg (2016). https://doi.org/10.1007/978-3-662-53018-4_4
18. Dodis, Y., Grubbs, P., Ristenpart, T., Woodage, J.: Fast message franking: from invisible salamanders to encryptment. In: Shacham, H., Boldyreva, A. (eds.) Advances in Cryptology – CRYPTO 2018, Part I. LNCS, vol. 10991, pp. 155–186. Springer, Cham (2018). https://doi.org/10.1007/978-3-319-96884-1_6
19. Duman, J., Hövelmanns, K., Kiltz, E., Lyubashevsky, V., Seiler, G.: Faster lattice-based KEMs via a generic Fujisaki-Okamoto transform using prefix hashing. In: Vigna, G., Shi, E. (eds.) ACM CCS 2021: 28th Conference on Computer and Communications Security, pp. 2722–2737. ACM Press, Virtual Event, Republic of Korea (2021). https://doi.org/10.1145/3460120.3484819
20. Grubbs, P., Maram, V., Paterson, K.G.: Anonymous, robust post-quantum Public-Key Encryption. In: Dunkelman, O., Dziembowski, S. (eds.) Advances in Cryptology – EUROCRYPT 2022, Part III. LNCS, vol. 13277, pp. 402–432. Springer, Cham (2022). https://doi.org/10.1007/978-3-031-07082-2_15
21. Gu, Y., Jarecki, S., Krawczyk, H.: KHAPE: asymmetric PAKE from key-hiding key exchange. In: Malkin, T., Peikert, C. (eds.) Advances in Cryptology – CRYPTO 2021, Part IV. LNCS, vol. 12828, pp. 701–730. Springer, Cham (2021). https://doi.org/10.1007/978-3-030-84259-8_24
22. Günther, F., Stebila, D., Veitch, S.: Obfuscated key exchange. In: Luo, B., Liao, X., Xu, J., Kirda, E., Lie, D. (eds.) ACM CCS 2024: 31st Conference on Computer and Communications Security, pp. 2385–2399. ACM Press, Salt Lake City, UT, USA (2024). https://doi.org/10.1145/3658644.3690220
23. Hofheinz, D., Hövelmanns, K., Kiltz, E.: A modular analysis of the Fujisaki-Okamoto transformation. In: Kalai, Y., Reyzin, L. (eds.) TCC 2017, Part I. LNCS, vol. 10677, pp. 341–371. Springer, Cham (2017). https://doi.org/10.1007/978-3-319-70500-2_12
24. Hövelmanns, K., Hülsing, A., Kudinov, M., Ritsch, S.: CAKE requires programming - on the provable post-quantum security of (O)CAKE. Cryptology ePrint Archive, Report 2025/458 (2025). https://eprint.iacr.org/2025/458
25. International Civil Aviation Organization (ICAO): Doc 9303: Machine readable travel documents (2021). https://www.icao.int/publications/Documents/9303_p11_cons_en.pdf
26. Januzelli, J., Roy, L., Xu, J.: Under what conditions is encrypted key exchange actually secure? In: Fehr, S., Fouque, P.A. (eds.) Advances in Cryptology – EUROCRYPT 2025, Part II. LNCS, vol. 15602, pp. 451–481. Springer, Cham (2025). https://doi.org/10.1007/978-3-031-91124-8_16

27. Kiefer, F., Manulis, M.: Oblivious PAKE: efficient handling of password trials. In: Lopez, J., Mitchell, C.J. (eds.) ISC 2015. LNCS, vol. 9290, pp. 191–208. Springer, Cham (2015). https://doi.org/10.1007/978-3-319-23318-5_11
28. Maram, V., Xagawa, K.: Post-quantum anonymity of Kyber. In: Boldyreva, A., Kolesnikov, V. (eds.) PKC 2023, Part I. LNCS, vol. 13940, pp. 3–35. Springer, Cham (2023). https://doi.org/10.1007/978-3-031-31368-4_1
29. Naehrig, M., et al.: FrodoKEM. Technical report, National Institute of Standards and Technology (2020). https://csrc.nist.gov/projects/post-quantum-cryptography/post-quantum-cryptography-standardization/round-3-submissions
30. NIST: Module-Lattice-Based Key-Encapsulation Mechanism Standard. Technical report, Federal Information Processing Standard (FIPS) 203, U.S. Department of Commerce (2024). https://doi.org/10.6028/NIST.FIPS.203
31. Saito, T., Xagawa, K., Yamakawa, T.: Tightly-secure key-encapsulation mechanism in the quantum random oracle model. Cryptology ePrint Archive, Report 2017/1005 (2017). https://eprint.iacr.org/2017/1005
32. Santos, B.F.D., Gu, Y., Jarecki, S.: Randomized half-ideal cipher on groups with applications to UC (a)PAKE. In: Hazay, C., Stam, M. (eds.) Advances in Cryptology - EUROCRYPT 2023, Part V. LNCS, vol. 14008, pp. 128–156. Springer, Cham (2023). https://doi.org/10.1007/978-3-031-30589-4_5
33. Thread Group: Thread Networking Protocol (2020). https://www.threadgroup.org/
34. Vanhoef, M.: Multiple Passwords in WPA3: Use Cases & Initial Proposals (2025). https://papers.mathyvanhoef.com/pake2025-slides.pdf
35. Warner, B.: Magic Wormhole: Simple Secure File Transfer. In: PyCon US (2016). https://magic-wormhole.readthedocs.io/
36. Wi-Fi Alliance: Wi-Fi Certified WPA3 Security (2021). https://www.wi-fi.org/discover-wi-fi/security
37. Xagawa, K.: Anonymity of NIST PQC round-3 KEMs. Cryptology ePrint Archive, Report 2021/1323 (2021). https://eprint.iacr.org/2021/1323

A Novel Masking Scheme with Low Additional Overhead for LWE-Based PQC Family

Jian Lu, Zhuang Xu(✉), Shunxian Gao, Bin Wei, Jianyang Li, Meng Li, Linpeng Wang, Juan Ren, and Yun Wang

Beijing Smartchip Microelectronics Technology Co., Ltd., Beijing, China
xuzhuang@sgchip.sgcc.com.cn

Abstract. Lattice-based public-key cryptography is widely recognized as a highly competitive branch of post-quantum cryptography (PQC). In this work, we present a novel masking scheme with broad applicability to public-key encryption schemes based on the learning with errors problem or its variants, which requires only two core modules (i.e., CF-Decode and Rec-msg) to build the masked decoder. This design ensures both simplicity and scalability, making it suitable for a wide range of lattice-based protocols. We illustrate the practical use of the generalized masking scheme by instantiating it for two prominent candidates in the NIST PQC competition—Kyber and SABER. Additionally, we perform a comprehensive security analysis and evaluate the software/hardware co-design implementation of masked Kyber decryption. Performance evaluations reveal that masked decryption incurs a 1.53× clock cycle overhead compared to the unmasked version. In terms of hardware costs, the design has resulted in only a 2% increase in look-up table (LUT) utilization, with almost no additional flip-flop (FF) consumption. Notably, the CF-Decode and Rec-msg modules contribute minimally to area overhead, adding only 90 LUTs and 4 FFs. Experimental results of practical side-channel analysis and leakage assessment confirm that the proposed scheme effectively mitigates first-order power analysis attacks, demonstrating its feasibility for secure PQC implementations.

Keywords: Post-quantum cryptography · Lattice-based cryptography · Masking · Side-channel analysis · Software/hardware co-design

1 Introduction

The rapid development of quantum computing technology poses serious challenges in classical Public-Key Cryptography (PKC), such as RSA and elliptic curve cryptography. In 2016, the National Institute of Standards and Technology (NIST) initialized a global competition for quantum-resistant public-key cryptographic schemes, i.e., Post-Quantum Cryptography (PQC) standardization [1]. After three rounds of evaluation, NIST announced the first

F. -H. Liu (Ed.): CT-RSAC 2026, LNCS 16496, pp. 155–177, 2026.
https://doi.org/10.1007/978-3-032-22931-1_6

batch of PQC algorithms to be standardized: CRYSTALS-Kyber for Public-Key Encryption(PKE)/Key-Encapsulation Mechanism (KEM), CRYSTALS-Dilithium, SPHINCS$^+$ and Falcon for digital signatures in 2022 [2]. Notably, three out of seven finalists in Round 3 (i.e., Kyber, Dilithium and SABER) derive their hardness from Learning with Errors (LWE) [27] or Learning with Rounding (LWR) [6] problems operating on structured lattices. In addition, FrodoKEM [15], whose security is closely related to the hardness of LWE problem on unstructured lattice, is considered for standardization by the International Organization for Standardization (ISO) and has already entered the approval phase [18].

Regev's LWE problem [27] and its algebraic variants, known as the Ring Learning with Errors (RLWE) problem [23] and Module Learning with Errors (MLWE) problem [22], have become very popular in the design of PKE, key exchange, digital signature and homomorphic encryption schemes [9]. Theoretical quantum-resistant security guarantees and implementation performance on different Hardware (HW) and Software (SW) platforms served as the primary criteria for selection in the initial rounds of the NIST PQC standardization. However, when it comes to actual deployment and implementation, there is a notable limitation: Although LWE-based cryptography demonstrates security against quantum computing threats, it provides no inherent protection against Side-Channel Analysis (SCA). A particularly effective method to extract secrets (e.g., cryptographic key and plaintext) from cryptographic devices is Correlation Power Analysis (CPA) [10], which can be regarded as an efficient variant of traditional Differential Power Analysis (DPA) [21].

Masking [11,17] is a sound algorithmic-level countermeasure against passive physical attacks such as power analysis, electromagnetic analysis, etc. Generally, the masking scheme works by splitting the secret value into multiple random shares and performing subsequent computations on each share independently. Masking can provide provable security against side-channel attacks under certain formal security models (such as the probing model [19]). Nevertheless, due to the duplication of computations, the runtime of a masked implementation theoretically grows significantly with the increase in the order of masking. In public-key cryptosystems, the decryption operation typically requires the most careful consideration for countermeasure against CPA/DPA attacks, as it is the component that manipulates long-term secrets.

1.1 Related Works

A masked implementation of RLWE decryption was initially presented in the pioneering work by Reparaz *et al.* [29]. The core idea is to split the secret key into two shares, multiply each share by one ciphertext component c_1, and then add the other ciphertext component c_2 to one of these shares. For the non-linear part (i.e., message decoder), the authors design a probabilistic masked decoder that outputs message bits by evaluating whether the input shares fulfill predefined rules. In their design, the decoding process is executed 16 times, with each iteration introducing a specific small offset Δ_i to the shares, thereby approaching a satisfactory decoding success rate. However, this iterative decoding process leads to higher decryption latency.

In subsequent work, Reparaz *et al.* [28] proposed an alternative masking scheme that takes advantage of the almost additive homomorphism of the RLWE encryption. Their technique exploits that, for two ciphertexts (c_1, c_2) and (c'_1, c'_2) encrypting m and m' under the same public key, the component-wise sum $(c_1 + c'_1, c_2 + c'_2)$ constitutes a valid encryption of $m \oplus m'$. Notably, even though no complex decoder is involved, the decryption process requires an extra encryption of m', which in turn lowers its overall efficiency. Another disadvantage is that the accumulation of noise from two ciphertexts increases the decryption failure rate.

In [26], Oder *et al.* designs a first-order full masking scheme for the RLWE-based scheme satisfying Indistinguishability under Chosen-Ciphertext Attack (IND-CCA). In the masked decoder used for decryption with Indistinguishability under Chosen-Plaintext Attack (IND-CPA), their construction transforms arithmetic masking shares over modulo q into shares over modulo 2^k, followed by an Arithmetic-to-Boolean (A2B) conversion. However, when applied to a specific algorithm—NewHope [4], masked IND-CPA-secure decryption requires significantly more clock cycles than its unmasked version, with an overhead factor of approximately 3.36. Subsequent research works [20,33] extend the work of [26] to masked hardware implementations of Kyber that utilize efficient pipelined or parallelized architectures.

Bos *et al.* [8] also employ an A2B-based masking strategy to obtain first-order and higher-order masked Kyber. They introduce a masked one-bit compression technique that relies on a bit-sliced binary search over prime moduli. The implementation is evaluated on an Arm Cortex-M0+ processor, showing a 1.6× performance overhead for first-order masked decryption compared to an unprotected version.

In summary, current masking schemes for LWE-based cryptography still have problems such as high implementation complexity, high performance overhead, and high resource requirements. In addition, the conversion between different types of masks also incurs performance and resource overhead. For example, regarding the conversion from arithmetic masking to Boolean masking, both the lookup-table-based method and the algebra-based conversion method have certain performance and resource bottlenecks. This paper proposes a masking scheme that is concise, easy to implement, and has low additional resource overhead. Furthermore, this scheme features good scalability and is applicable to the LWE-based PQC family.

1.2 Contributions

In this work, we consider the masking scheme in the case where the decryption error range is $\left(-\frac{3q}{16}, \frac{q}{4}\right)$. Then we summarize our specific contributions as follows.

1) Concise framework. We propose a novel first-order masking scheme for PKE based on LWE or its variant. Compared to related works, this scheme does

not require lookup tables or mask conversion, just utilizes two modules named CF-Decode and Rec-msg to construct the core decoder.
2) Easy to implement. The Rec-msg module can be seen as a binary function that can be implemented by bit addition and shift. When the modulus q is a power of 2, CF-Decode can also be achieved by multiplication and shift. If the modulus q is a prime number, the division by q can be replaced by an approximation, that is $1/q \approx \mathrm{A}/2^{\mathrm{B}}$, where A and B are integers.
3) Wide applicability. Our proposed scheme supports arbitrary moduli and can be adopted by various NIST PQC submissions, such as Kyber [25], SABER [7], FrodoKEM [15] and NewHope [3].
4) We implement the masked Kyber in Software/Hardware (SW/HW) co-design way and evaluate its side-channel resistance by both realistic attack and leakage assessment. Evaluation results show that the masking scheme achieves first-order security under power analysis attack with low additional overhead in the aspect of Look-Up Table (LUT) and Flip-Flop (FF) consumption.

1.3 Organization

The remainder of this paper is organized as follows. In Sect. 2, we introduce the necessary notations and mathematical background. In Sect. 3, we present our masking scheme for LWE-style PKE, while in Sect. 4 we instantiate the generalized scheme into two algorithms—Kyber and SABER. In Sect. 5, we evaluate the performance of the masked Kyber. In Sect. 6, we evaluate the resistance of the masked Kyber to SCA by actual attack and statistical tool. We conclude in Sect. 7, discussing extension and future work.

2 Preliminaries

2.1 Notations

Let $\mathbb{Z}_q$ be the ring of integers modulo q, where q is a prime. Vectors and matrices over $\mathbb{Z}_q$ (i.e., elements of $\mathbb{Z}_q^k$ and $\mathbb{Z}_q^{k\times l}$) are denoted by lower-case bold letters and upper-case bold letters, respectively. The polynomial ring $\mathbb{Z}_q[x]/(x^n+1)$ is denoted by R_q. Polynomials in R_q are denoted by normal lowercase letters (e.g., a). Vectors of polynomials and matrices of polynomials in R_q are denoted by lower-case bold letters (e.g., $\mathbf{a}$) and capital bold letters (e.g., $\mathbf{A}$), respectively. The transpose of a vector or a matrix is represented using the superscript $^\top$. The i-th coefficient of a polynomial $a \in R_q$ is denoted by $a[i]$ and the j-th polynomial of a given $\mathbf{x}$ in module R_q^k is represented as x_j. For a polynomial $f \in R_q$, its representation after Number-Theoretic Transform (NTT) is denoted by $\hat{f}$ for short. The multiplication in $\mathbb{Z}_q$ or R_q is denoted by the operator "$\cdot$". Point-wise Multiplication (PWM) of two polynomials $\hat{a}$, $\hat{b} \in R_q$ is denoted by $\hat{c} = \hat{a} \circ \hat{b}$. Byte arrays of length n are denoted by $\mathcal{B}^n$. The discrete Gaussian distribution is denoted by $\mathcal{D}_\sigma(\cdot)$, where σ is the standard deviation. A Centered Binomial Distribution (CBD) on $[-\eta, \eta]$ is defined as B_η. The uniform distribution is denoted by $\mathcal{U}$. Given a distribution $\mathcal{S}$, let $s \leftarrow \mathcal{S}$ denote that s is chosen according to $\mathcal{S}$. $\#G$ denotes the cardinality of the set G. $P(A)$ denotes the probability that event A occurs. $P(A, B)$ is the joint probability, i.e., the probability that events A and B occur simultaneously.

2.2 Basic Background of LWE-Based PQC

LWE Problems. Before introducing LWE problems, we first provide the definition of LWE instance below.

Definition 1 (LWE Instance). *For a given dimension $n \geq 1$, elements in $\mathbb{Z}_q$ with $q > 2$ and a Gaussian error distribution $\mathcal{D}_\sigma(\cdot)$, an LWE instance is defined as the pair $(\mathbf{a}, t) \in \mathbb{Z}_q^n \times \mathbb{Z}_q$ where $\mathbf{a} \leftarrow \mathcal{U}(\mathbb{Z}_q^n)$, and $t = \mathbf{a}^\top \cdot \mathbf{s} + e$ with $\mathbf{s} \leftarrow \mathcal{D}_\sigma(\mathbb{Z}_q^n)$ and $e \leftarrow \mathcal{D}_\sigma(\mathbb{Z}_q)$.*

There are two basic versions of the LWE problem: search and decisional problems. Search-LWE problem requires to recover the vector $\mathbf{s} \in \mathbb{Z}_q^n$ from a collection of LWE instances $\{(\mathbf{a}_i, t_i)\}_{i=1}^m$. Decision-LWE problem asks to distinguish valid LWE instances from uniformly random instances drawn from $\mathbb{Z}_q^n \times \mathbb{Z}_q$.

Cryptographic schemes constructed based on the (decisional) plain LWE problem incur quadratic overheads in both key size and computational complexity [27]. Thus, most of the lattice-based schemes, especially those in the NIST standardization process, are based on algebraically structured variants of LWE problem. Expanding on the idea of LWE, related problems with a similar structure have been proposed. The ring variant of the LWE problem [23] deals with computation over polynomials in polynomial rings $R_q = \mathbb{Z}_q[x]/(x^n + 1)$ with $s, e \leftarrow \mathcal{D}_\sigma(R_q)$ such that the corresponding RLWE instance is defined as $(a, t = a \cdot s + e) \in R_q \times R_q$. More generally, in the MLWE [22] problem, the vectors (of polynomials) $\mathbf{a}_i$, $\mathbf{s}$ and polynomials e_i are drawn from $R_q^{k_1}$ and R_q, respectively. Search-MLWE is the problem of recovering $\mathbf{s}$ from a set $\{(\mathbf{a}_i, {\mathbf{a}_i}^\top \cdot \mathbf{s} + e_i)\}_{i=i}^m$, while Decision-MLWE is the problem of distinguishing such a set from a set uniformly sampled from $R_q^{k_1} \times R_q$.

There is also a class of LWE-like problems that replace the addition of a noise term by a deterministic rounding process. For example, an instance of the LWR [6] problem is of the form $\left(\mathbf{a}, t := \lfloor \frac{p}{q}(\mathbf{a}^\top \cdot \mathbf{s}) \rceil\right) \in \mathbb{Z}_q^n \times \mathbb{Z}_p$. The same ideas apply to the other variants of LWE that use deterministic rounding error, such as Ring-Learning with Rounding (LWR) and Module-Learning with Rounding (LWR).

LWE-Based PKE. The LWE encryption scheme is described as follows (For simplicity, we only describe the public-key encryption architecture for 1-bit plaintext encryption here).

- In the key generation phase, the private key $\mathbf{s}$ and the error $\mathbf{e}$ are sampled from the discrete Gaussian distribution $\mathcal{D}_\sigma(\mathbb{Z}_q^n)$ and $\mathcal{D}_\sigma(\mathbb{Z}_q^m)$, respectively. The public key is a pair $(\mathbf{A}, \mathbf{t})$, where the matrix $\mathbf{A} \leftarrow \mathcal{U}(\mathbb{Z}_q^{m\times n})$ and $\mathbf{t} = (\mathbf{A} \cdot \mathbf{s} + \mathbf{e}) \bmod q$.

- In the encryption operation of the 1 bit message m, the ciphertext is computed as a pair $(\mathbf{u}, v)$, where $\mathbf{u} = (\mathbf{A}^\top \cdot \mathbf{r} + \mathbf{e}_1) \bmod q$ and $v = (\mathbf{t}^\top \cdot \mathbf{r} + e_2 + \lceil q/2 \rfloor m) \bmod q$. The encryption operation requires generation of three error vectors $\mathbf{r}$, $\mathbf{e}_1$ and e_2.
- The decryption operation uses the private key $\mathbf{s}$ to compute the message as $m = th(w)$, where $w = (v - \mathbf{s}^\top \cdot \mathbf{u}) \bmod q$. The function $th(x)$ is simply defined as

$$th(x) = \begin{cases} 0, & \text{if } x \in [0, q/4) \cup (3q/4, q); \\ 1, & \text{if } x \in (q/4, 3q/4). \end{cases} \tag{1}$$

Likewise, we can get encryption schemes for LWR and algebraically structured variants of LWE/LWR from the scheme above by just fixing the field of elements to the algebraic field. For example, R_q substitutes $\mathbb{Z}_q$ or $\mathbb{Z}_q^n$ in RLWE, $R_q^{k_1 \times k_2}$ and $R_q^{k_2}$ substitute $\mathbb{Z}_q^{n \times n}$ and $\mathbb{Z}_q^n$ in MLWE. For efficiency, most of LWE cryptographic schemes use the central binomial distribution B_η instead of the discrete Gaussian distribution $\mathcal{D}_\sigma(\cdot)$, where $q \gg \eta$.

2.3 Masking Related Notions

Masking is an effective countermeasure against power side-channel attacks, using randomization to break the statistical dependence between sensitive data and related power consumption. The definition of dth-order masking is given below.

Definition 2 (d^{th}-order masking [12]). *The dth-order masking scheme works by splitting each sensitive intermediate variable into $d+1$ random shares such that no combination of up to d shares can reveal information about the original sensitive value.*

The dth-order masking scheme is aimed at defending Side-Channel Analysis (SCA) that utilizes leaks of at most d intermediates. However, secret-related bias in the distribution of masking shares or insufficient compositional security can weaken resistance to SCA. A widely used idealized security model to evaluate the security level against SCA, known as the probing model, is defined as follows.

Definition 3 (t-probing model and t-probing security [14,19]). *In the t-probing model, an attacker's capability is constrained to observing at most t intermediate wires within the target circuit. We call an implementation scheme t-probing secure if it is secure under the t-probing model, i.e., every t-tuple of intermediate variables is statistically independent of any sensitive variable.*

The t-probing model envisages a powerful adversary who can directly read intermediate values. The probing security is also a necessary prerequisite for resistance against practical SCA, such as DPA and CPA.

In this work, we restrict attention to the first-order masking scheme (i.e., d^{th}-order masking with $d = 1$) for LWE-based PKE, and the corresponding security under the 1-probing model (i.e., t-probing security with $t = 1$).

3 Masked Lattice-Based PQC

In this section, we will introduce our masking scheme for the decryption process. As shown in Fig. 1, we first use the most natural way to split the calculation process of decryption, that is, to split the secret $\mathbf{s}$ additively into two shares $\mathbf{s}_1$ and $\mathbf{s}_2$ such that $\mathbf{s} = (\mathbf{s}_1 + \mathbf{s}_2) \bmod q$, where $\mathbf{s}_1 \leftarrow \mathcal{U}(\mathbb{Z}_q^{n\times 1})$ and $\mathbf{s}_2 = (\mathbf{s} - \mathbf{s}_1) \bmod q$. Next, the bulk of the computation of w is amenable to splitting, we have $w_1 = v - \mathbf{s}_1^\top \cdot \mathbf{u}$ and $w_2 = -\mathbf{s}_2^\top \cdot \mathbf{u}$. Then we need a mask decoder to perform mask decoding, and this function is named CF-Decode (since its computation involves compression and floored rounding) and is defined as $m_1 = \text{CF-Decode}(w_1)$ and $m_2 = \text{CF-Decode}(w_2)$. Lastly, we will reconstruct the message using a function called Rec-msg and denoted by $m' = \text{Rec-msg}(m_1, m_2)$.

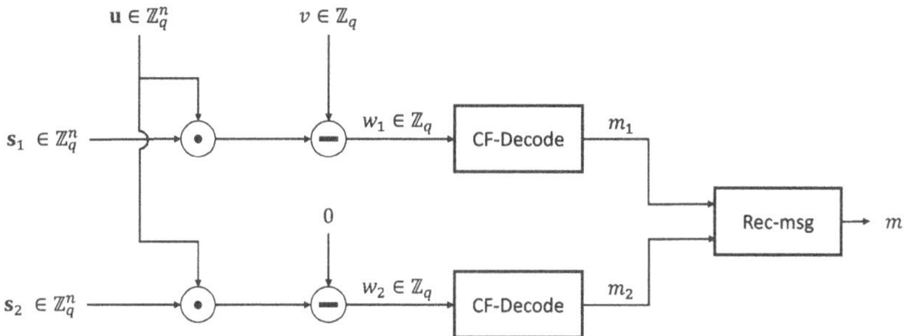

Fig. 1. Calculation process of masked decryption for LWE-based PQC.

The functions CF-Decode and Rec-msg are defined as follows:

$$\text{CF-Decode}(x) := \left\lfloor \frac{2^4}{q} \cdot x \right\rfloor \bmod 2^4, \tag{2}$$

$$\text{Rec-msg}(m_1, m_2) := \left\lceil \frac{m_1 + m_2}{2^3} \right\rfloor \bmod 2, \tag{3}$$

where $x \in \mathbb{Z}_q$, $m_1, m_2 \in \mathbb{Z}_{2^4}$.

For LWE-based cryptography, the parameter u represents a matrix, while v, w_1, and w_2 are vectors. In this scheme, both the CF-Decode and the Rec-msg functions are computed element-wise for vectors. In the RLWE-based variant, these operations are performed coefficient-wise on polynomials. For MLWE-based cryptography, the computations are similarly executed coefficient-wise, but for polynomial vectors.

Proposition 1. *Let Error* $= v - \mathbf{s}^\top \cdot \mathbf{u} - \lceil q/2 \rfloor \cdot m$. *Then, the masking scheme can decrypt the ciphertext correctly (i.e.,* $m' = m$*) when* $-\frac{3q}{16} < Error < \frac{q}{4}$.

Proof. From the decryption operation, one share is $\mathbf{s}_1 \leftarrow \mathcal{U}(\mathbb{Z}_q^{n\times 1})$, and $w_1 = v - \mathbf{s}_1^\top \cdot \mathbf{u}$. The other share is $\mathbf{s}_2 = (\mathbf{s} - \mathbf{s}_1) \bmod q$ and $w_2 = -\mathbf{s}_2^\top \cdot \mathbf{u}$. Then we have $w = (w_1 + w_2) \bmod q = (m \cdot \lceil \frac{q}{2} \rfloor + \mathbf{e}^\top \cdot \mathbf{r} + e_2 - \mathbf{s}^\top \cdot \mathbf{e}_1) \bmod q$, where elements of $\mathbf{s}$, $\mathbf{e}$, $\mathbf{r}$, $\mathbf{e}_1$ and e_2 are all sampled from B_η ($q \gg \eta$).

For the sake of convenience, the interval $[0, q)$ is divided into 16 parts as shown in Fig. 2, i.e., each quadrant is evenly divided into four parts.

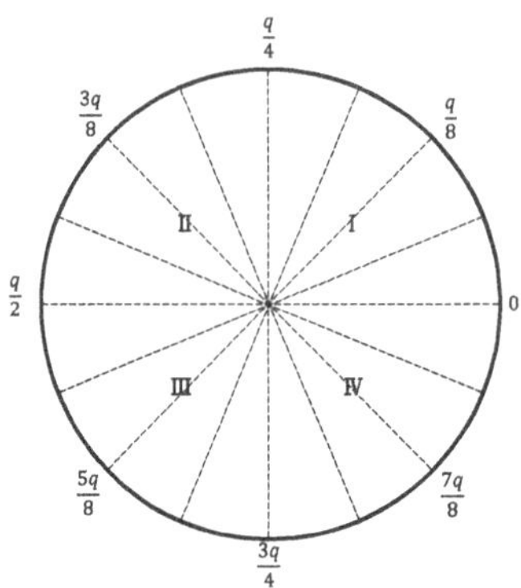

Fig. 2. Sixteen equal divisions of the value range $[0, q)$.

We suppose $w_1 \in [\frac{i}{16}q, \frac{i+1}{16}q)$ and $w_2 \in [\frac{j}{16}q, \frac{j+1}{16}q)$, where i, j are integers in $[0, 15]$. Then $w_1 + w_2 \in [\frac{i+j}{16}q, \frac{i+j+2}{16}q) := U$ (before modulo q). After modulo q, we get the value range of w: $U_w = U_w{}' \cup U_w{}''$. The definitions of $U_w{}'$ and $U_w{}''$ are as follows:

$$U_w{}' = \begin{cases} [\frac{15}{16}q,\ q), & \text{if } (i+j) \bmod 16 = 15; \\ [\frac{(i+j) \bmod 16}{16}q,\ \frac{(i+j+1) \bmod 16}{16}q), & \text{otherwise.} \end{cases} \quad (4)$$

$$U_w{}'' = \begin{cases} [\frac{15}{16}q,\ q), & \text{if } (i+j) \bmod 16 = 14; \\ [\frac{(i+j+1) \bmod 16}{16}q,\ \frac{(i+j+2) \bmod 16}{16}q), & \text{otherwise.} \end{cases} \quad (5)$$

According to the positions of $U_w{}'$ and $U_w{}''$, there are two cases for the range U_w :

(a) $U_w{}'$ and $U_w{}''$ are on the same side of the straight line between $\frac{q}{4}$ and $\frac{3q}{4}$, i.e., $(i+j) \bmod 16 \notin \{3, 11\}$;
(b) $U_w{}'$ and $U_w{}''$ are on different sides of the straight line between $\frac{q}{4}$ and $\frac{3q}{4}$, i.e., $(i+j) \bmod 16 \in \{3, 11\}$.

As $-\frac{3q}{16} < Error < \frac{q}{4}$, we know $w \notin [\frac{q}{4}, \frac{5}{16}q) \cup [\frac{3}{4}q, \frac{13}{16}q)$. Therefore, for case (a), we have $th(w) = th(\frac{(i+j) \bmod 16}{16}q)$ trivially, even for $(i+j) \bmod 16 \in$

$\{4, 12\}$. For case (b), the range U_w'' is invalid, so $w \in U_w'$. Then $th(w) = th(\frac{(i+j) \bmod 16}{16}q)$ for all cases. So, the decryption equation

$$m = th(w) = \begin{cases} 0, & \text{if } w \in [0, q/4) \cup [13q/16, q); \\ 1, & \text{if } w \in [5q/16, 3q/4). \end{cases} \quad (6)$$

is equivalent to

$$m = \begin{cases} 0, & \text{if } (i+j) \bmod 16 \in \{0, 1, 2, 3, 13, 14, 15\}; \\ 1, & \text{if } (i+j) \bmod 16 \in \{5, 6, 7, 8, 9, 10, 11\}. \end{cases} \quad (7)$$

On the other hand, we have $m_1 = \mathsf{CF\text{-}Decode}(w_1) = i$, $m_2 = \mathsf{CF\text{-}Decode}(w_2) = j$.

$$m' = \mathsf{Rec\text{-}msg}(m_1, m_2) = \begin{cases} 0, & \text{if } (i+j) \bmod 16 \in \{0, 1, 2, 3, 13, 14, 15\}; \\ 1, & \text{if } (i+j) \bmod 16 \in \{5, 6, 7, 8, 9, 10, 11\}. \end{cases} \quad (8)$$

So $m = m'$, Proposition 1 has been proven correct. □

Proposition 2. *The masking scheme shown in Fig. 1 is 1-probing secure.*

Proof. According to Definition 3, the core task is to demonstrate that each individual intermediate variable is statistically independent of any sensitive variable.

In our masking scheme, we consider two sensitive variables, i.e., $\mathbf{s}$ and m, along with six critical intermediate variables: $\mathbf{s}_1$, $\mathbf{s}_2$, w_1, w_2, m_1 and m_2.

Since $\mathbf{s}_1 \leftarrow \mathcal{U}(\mathbb{Z}_q^{n\times 1})$ is uniformly distributed, it follows that $\mathbf{s}_2 = (\mathbf{s}-\mathbf{s}_1) \bmod q$ is also uniformly distributed. For any $\mathbf{x}_1, \mathbf{x}_2, \mathbf{x} \in \mathbb{Z}_q^{n\times 1}$, we have $P(\mathbf{s}_1 = \mathbf{x}_1, \mathbf{s} = \mathbf{x}) = P(\mathbf{s}_1 = \mathbf{x}_1) \cdot P(\mathbf{s} = \mathbf{x}) = \frac{1}{q^n}P(\mathbf{s} = \mathbf{x})$, and $P(\mathbf{s}_2 = \mathbf{x}_2, \mathbf{s} = \mathbf{x}) = P(\mathbf{s}_1 = (\mathbf{x} - \mathbf{x}_2) \bmod q, \mathbf{s} = \mathbf{x}) = P(\mathbf{s}_1 = (\mathbf{x} - \mathbf{x}_2) \bmod q) \cdot P(\mathbf{s} = \mathbf{x}) = \frac{1}{q^n}P(\mathbf{s} = \mathbf{x}) = P(\mathbf{s}_2 = \mathbf{x}_2) \cdot P(\mathbf{s} = \mathbf{x})$. So $\mathbf{s}_1$ (or $\mathbf{s}_2$) is statistically independent of secret $\mathbf{s}$. This ensures that neither $\mathbf{s}_1$ nor $\mathbf{s}_2$ alone reveals information about $\mathbf{s}$. Similarly, the independence from m can be proven.

w_1 and w_2 are arithmetic shares of the original intermediate variable w. Since $w_1 = v - \mathbf{s}_1^\top \cdot \mathbf{u}$ (or $w_2 = -\mathbf{s}_2^\top \cdot \mathbf{u}$) can be viewed as the result of applying a linear transformation to the uniformly random vector $\mathbf{s}_1$ (or $\mathbf{s}_2$), then w_1 (or w_2) remains uniformly random (except for the rare case where $\mathbf{u} = \mathbf{0}$). Consequently, adversaries probing w_1 (or w_2) gain no information about w, $\mathbf{s}$, or m.

Lastly, we consider the case in which an attacker places the "probe" on m_1 or m_2. Since m_1 (or m_2) is entirely determined by w_1 (or w_2), it does not depend on the secret $\mathbf{s}$. m_1 and m_2 can also be considered as shares of m. Let $U_i := [\frac{i}{16}q, \frac{i+1}{16}q)$, where $0 \le i \le 15$, $G_1 := \bigcup_{i=5}^{11} U_i$, $G_0 := (\bigcup_{i=0}^{3} U_i) \cup (\bigcup_{j=13}^{15} U_j)$. Then $P(m_1 = i) = P(m_2 = i) = \frac{\#U_i}{q}$. For any $i \in \{0, 1, 2, \cdots, 15\}$ and $b \in \{0, 1\}$, by the independence of w_1 and w, we obtain $P(m_1 = i, m = b) = P(w_1 \in U_i, w \in G_b) = P(w_1 \in U_i) \cdot P(w \in G_b) = \frac{\#U_i}{q}P(w \in G_b) = P(m_1 = i) \cdot P(m = b)$. This implies that m_1 (and similarly m_2) is independent of m, so an adversary observing only a single share cannot learn any information about m. □

4 Masking Kyber and SABER

In this section, we will take Kyber and SABER as examples to illustrate how the aforementioned masking scheme can be applied to the cryptographic algorithm.

4.1 Masking Kyber

The latest version of Kyber [5] has been standardized by NIST, with minor modifications, as FIPS 203 Module-Lattice-Based Key-Encapsulation Mechanism (ML-KEM) [25]. The Kyber-PKE decryption algorithm is presented in Algorithm 1.

Algorithm 1. Kyber.CPAPKE.Dec (sk, c) [5]

1: $\mathbf{u} = \text{Decompress}_q\left(\text{Decode}_{d_u}(c_1)\right)$
2: $v = \text{Decompress}_q\left(\text{Decode}_{d_v}(c_2)\right)$
3: $\hat{\mathbf{s}} = \text{Decode}(sk)$
4: $m = \text{Encode}_1\left(\text{Compress}_q\left(v - \text{INTT}\left(\hat{\mathbf{s}}^\top \circ \text{NTT}(\mathbf{u})\right), 1\right)\right)$
5: **return** m

The decryption procedure receives the secret key sk and a ciphertext c. Decode and Decompress functions convert the ciphertext $c = (c_1, c_2)$ from a byte array to a vector of polynomials $\mathbf{u}$ and a polynomial v. In addition, the secret key is deserialized as a vector of polynomials $\hat{\mathbf{s}}$. Then, the inner product between the polynomial vectors $\hat{\mathbf{s}}$ and $\hat{\mathbf{u}}$ is calculated. Thereafter, the Inverse Number-Theoretic Transform (INTT) maps the result $\hat{\mathbf{s}}^\top \circ \text{NTT}(\mathbf{u})$ back to the time domain, i.e., $\mathbf{s}^\top \mathbf{u}$. Finally, the message is restored in the form of a binary string by Compress and Encode functions. The first input, i.e., secret key sk, is created by the key generation procedure, where $sk = \mathit{Encode}(\text{NTT}(\mathbf{s}))$. Each coefficient of the polynomials in $\mathbf{s}$ is drawn from the CBD B_η, where the sampling parameter η is set to 2 or 3. In Kyber, $q = 3329$ serves as the modulus. d_u and d_v represent the compressed sizes of the polynomial coefficients of the ciphertexts $\mathbf{u}$ and v, respectively. Depending on different security levels, they have the following value options: $d_u = 10$ or 11, and $d_v = 4$ or 5.

According to the prototype scheme shown in Fig. 1, a masked Kyber decryption process is instantiated as Fig. 3. Since the operands in Kyber are polynomials (or polynomial vectors), CF-Decode and Rec-msg operate on the individual coefficients of these polynomials.

4.2 Masking SABER

The SABER decryption procedure (see Algorithm 2) takes the secret key sk and the ciphertext c as inputs. Since moduli p, q and T in SABER are all powers of 2, denoted by $q = 2^{\epsilon_q}$, $p = 2^{\epsilon_p}$ and $T = 2^{\epsilon_T}$ (refer to [7] for concrete parameter choices), the modulo operation works as a simple low-bit truncation.

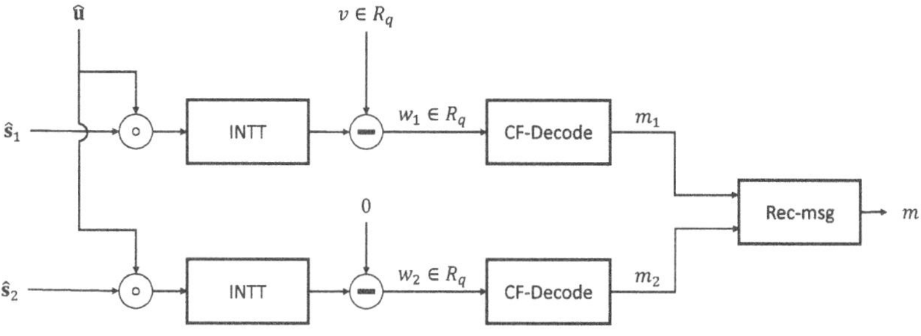

Fig. 3. Diagram of masked Kyber-PKE decryption.

First, v is obtained by multiplying the polynomial vectors $\mathbf{b}'$ and $(\mathbf{s} \bmod p)$, and then subtracting "c_m" from v. Since "c_m" was compressed into R_T as c_m during encryption, c_m needs to be multiplied by $2^{\epsilon_p - \epsilon_T}$ to map it back to R_p for calculation in decryption. In the algorithm, the constant polynomial $h_2 \in R_q$ is defined so that every coefficient is equal to $(2^{\epsilon_p - 2} - 2^{\epsilon_p - \epsilon_T - 1} + 2^{\epsilon_q - \epsilon_p - 1})$. This constant allows rounding operations to be replaced with a simple bit-shift. After rounding to R_2, we obtain the output message m'. It can be shown that the original message m and the resulting m' coincide with a high probability.

Algorithm 2. SABER.CPAPKE.Dec $(\mathbf{s}, c = (c_m, \mathbf{b}'))$ [7]

1: $v = \mathbf{b}'^{\top} \cdot (\mathbf{s} \bmod p) \in R_p$
2: $m' = \left(\left(v - 2^{\epsilon_p - \epsilon_T} c_m + h_2\right) \bmod p\right) \gg (\epsilon_p - 1) \in R_2$
3: **return** m'

Based on the masking framework presented in Fig. 1, the masked version of SABER decryption is depicted in Fig. 4. Since both w_1 and w_2 lie in R_p, CF-Decode in SABER is instantiated as $\mathsf{CF\text{-}Decode}(x) := \left\lfloor \frac{2^4}{p} \cdot x \right\rceil \bmod 2^4$.

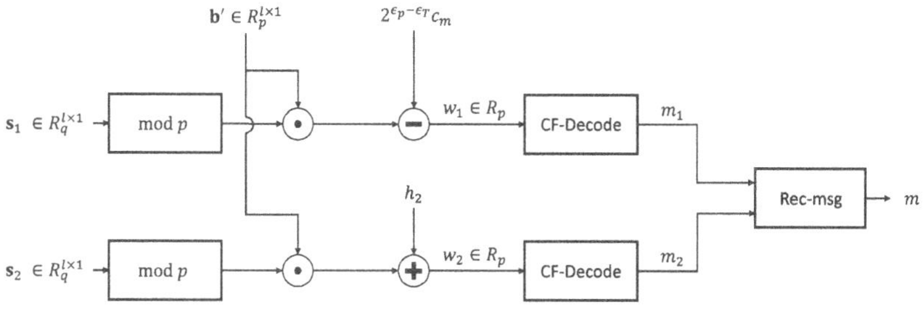

Fig. 4. Diagram of masked SABER-PKE decryption.

5 Performance Evaluation of Masked Kyber

We perform a case study on a SW/HW co-designed implementation of Kyber1024. The design on a FPGA platform using the Xilinx Artix-7 series device XC7A200T-FBG676-3. The software platform utilized is Vivado (version 2018.2). The highest frequency achieved in the synthesis is 172.41 MHz.

The high-level hierarchy of the processor is illustrated in Fig. 5. The hardware implements basic operators such as modular reduction, modular addition, modular subtraction, butterfly units, PWM0 and PWM1[1]. Based on these basic operators, it further implements advanced operators including NTT, INTT, PWM, polynomial addition and subtraction, encoding/decoding, and sampling. In addition, the hash operators required in Kyber are also implemented in hardware. The software part forms an algorithm protocol layer by calling hardware operators, supporting the implementation of key generation, encapsulation, and decapsulation algorithms for three security levels.

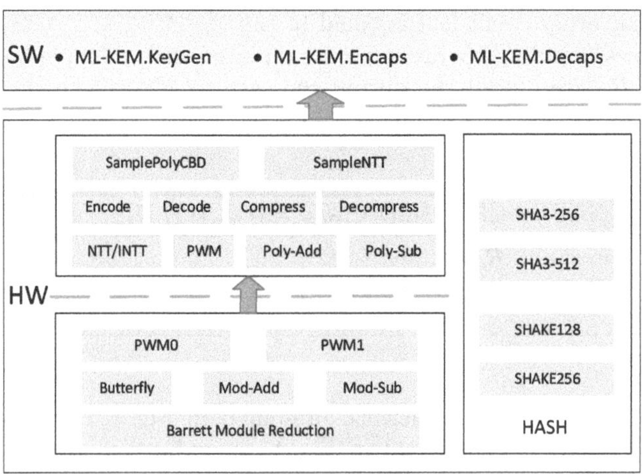

Fig. 5. Kyber SW and HW division block diagram.

In this implementation, the submodules Compress, Encode, Decode and Decompress are integrated into a single module termed Codepress, whose structural block diagram is shown in Fig. 6. The software determines parameters and operating modes and, via the Control Module, selects the appropriate operation module. The operation modules are divided into two parts: Encode_Compress (including Encode() and Encode(Compress()) operations) and Decode_Decompress (including Decode() and Decompress(Decode()) operations). The RAM interface (ram_if) is responsible for reading and writing input/output data by interacting with RAM1.

[1] Referring to [32], PWM0 and PWM1 are building blocks of PWM in the Number-Theoretic Transform (NTT) domain.

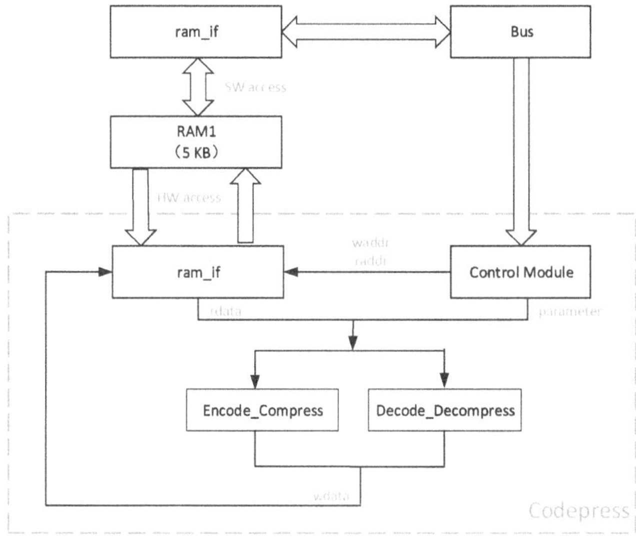

Fig. 6. Structural block diagram of Codepress.

Given the functional similarity between the CF-Decode function and the Compress function in Kyber when $d_v = 4$, we incorporated CF-Decode as a selectable branch within the compression logic for hardware implementation. Furthermore, since the Rec-msg function replaces the compression computation of m in Kyber, it is also included as part of the Codepress module. The hardware design workflow during mask decoding is depicted in Fig. 7.

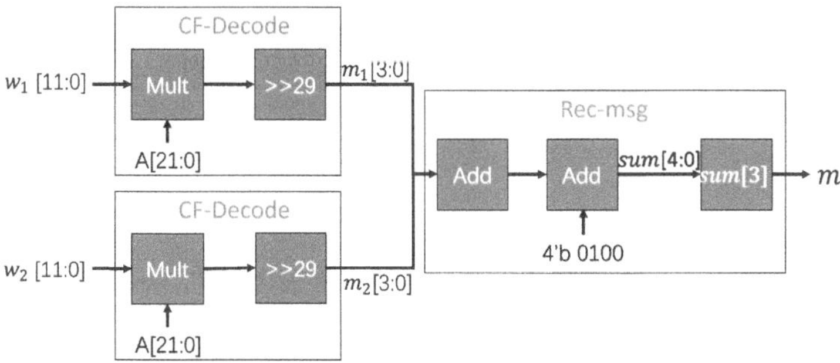

Fig. 7. Hardware design architecture of masked decoder (constant A = 2 580 335).

In this implementation, we implement CF-Decode by multiplying with 2 580 335 and then performing a right shift by 29 bits, which effectively avoids the division operation.[2] After that, we add the two obtained results and truncate the valid bits to implement Rec-msg. The addition of "4'b 0100" in Fig. 7 is intended to realize rounding, and thereafter only the third bit needs to be truncated.

By comparing the area overhead of the Codepress module before and after the incorporation of masking, we were able to determine the additional area resources required for CF-Decode and Rec-msg, which only added 90 Look-Up Tables (LUTs) and 4 Flip-Flops (FFs).

Performance comparison with related works is shown in Table 1. Because the underlying algorithms or parameter sets among these schemes are slightly different, we mainly focus on the comparison of overhead factor after applying the masking scheme. The results show that our design achieves a smaller overhead factor in cycle count compared with the SW implementation and the lowest overhead factor in hardware utilization (in terms of LUT, FF, etc.) among the listed works.

Table 1. Comparison with related works

Scheme	Algorithm	Architecture	Mode	Cycle	Overhead	LUTs	Overhead	FFs	Overhead	BRAMs	Overhead	DSPs	Overhead
This work	Kyber1024	SW/HW	Unmasked	23 886	-	5307	-	1110	-	20	-	2	-
			Masked [A]*	36 652	×1.53	5417	×1.02	1123	×1.01	20	×1	2	×1
[29]	RLWE	HW	Unmasked	2800	-	1713	-	830	-	-	-	1	-
			Masked [A]	7500	×2.68	2014	×1.18	959	×1.16	-	-	1	×1
[26]	RLWE	SW	Unmasked	163 887	-	-	-	-	-	-	-	-	-
			Masked [A2B]†	550 038	×3.36	-	-	-	-	-	-	-	-
[8]	Kyber768	SW	Unmasked	703 000	-	-	-	-	-	-	-	-	-
			Masked [A2B]	1 096 000	×1.6	-	-	-	-	-	-	-	-
[20]	Kyber512	HW	Unmasked	126 619	-	143 112	-	-	-	294	-	60	-
			Masked [A2B]	137 738	×1.08	152 860	×1.07	-	-	489.5	×1.66	76	×1.27
[33]	Kyber768	HW	Unmasked	10 000	-	7653	-	5074	-	11	-	-	-
			Masked [A2B]	10 000	×1‡	9204	×1.2	6452	×1.27	16	×1.45	-	-

* Arithmetic masking.

†A2B mask decoder technology is used for masking protection.

‡[33] duplicates not only the arithmetic unit but also the storage unit used to store multiplicative intermediate values and shares.

6 Side-Channel Resistance Evaluation of Masked Kyber

To evaluate the effectiveness of our masking scheme and demonstrate Proposition 2 experimentally, we implement the above mentioned SW/HW co-designed Kyber on a SAKURA board and conduct SCA evaluation.

[2] In our Compress function design, $\frac{1}{3329}$ is approximated as $\frac{A}{2^B}$. We set (A, B) to (2 580 335, 33), which is the smallest pair of integers that ensures the correctness of the final compression result under all compression parameters (i.e., $d \in \{1, 4, 5, 10, 11\}$). The constant A is reused in the design of CF-Decode. Here, multiplication $A \cdot x$ is achieved by bit shifting, addition, and subtraction.

For the most commonly targeted point of SCA—polynomial multiplication, we mount simplified CPA on unmasked and masked implementations. For our designed decoding function—CF-Decode, we utilize a Test Vector Leakage Assessment (TVLA) to evaluate the leakage.

6.1 CPA on PWM

Experimental Setup. A block diagram of the test setup is illustrated in Fig. 8. For all subsequent experiments, the mcs file (a non-volatile memory configuration settings file) of unmasked or masked Kyber is written into the flash of Kintex-7 chip. The test board is powered by a direct current power supply at 5 V. The work frequency is set to 5 MHz. The power traces are amplified by 30 dB via a preamplifier and sampled at 500 MHz using an oscilloscope. Communication (e.g., execution commands, response data, etc.) between the test board and the workstation is established through a Universal Asynchronous Receiver Transmitter (UART) interface. To simplify trace acquisition, we preset a trigger for some specific function, such as PWM.

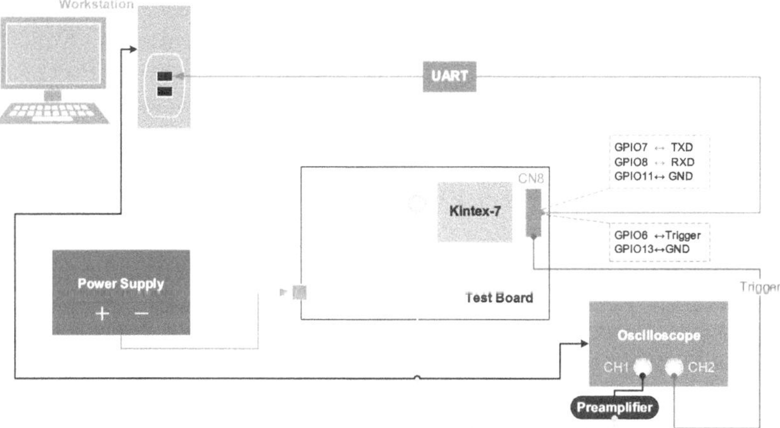

Fig. 8. Experimental environment.

CPA Target. The secret polynomial vector $\mathbf{s}$, the core of the long-term secret key, is the target of CPA. According to line 4 in Algorithm 1, the inner product of $\hat{\mathbf{s}}$ and NTT ($\mathbf{u}$) is an appropriate point for CPA. In the Kyber1024 parameter set (dimension $k = 4$), we have the following.

$$\hat{\mathbf{s}}^{\top} \circ \mathrm{NTT}(\mathbf{u}) = (\hat{s_0}, \hat{s_1}, \hat{s_2}, \hat{s_3}) \circ \begin{pmatrix} \hat{u_0} \\ \hat{u_1} \\ \hat{u_2} \\ \hat{u_3} \end{pmatrix} = \sum_{i=0}^{3} \hat{s}_i \circ \hat{u}_i, \tag{9}$$

where

$$\hat{s_i} = \left(\hat{s_i}[0] + \hat{s_i}[1]X, \hat{s_i}[2] + \hat{s_i}[3]X, \ldots, \hat{s_i}[254] + \hat{s_i}[255]X\right), \quad (10)$$

$$\hat{u_i} = \left(\hat{u_i}[0] + \hat{u_i}[1]X, \hat{u_i}[2] + \hat{u_i}[3]X, \ldots, \hat{u_i}[254] + \hat{u_i}[255]X\right). \quad (11)$$

The PWM between $\hat{s_i}$ and $\hat{u_i}$ is implemented in a similar way to that specified in [32]. The complete process of PWM is as follows (take $\hat{h_0} = \hat{s_0} \circ \hat{u_0}$ as an example, $i \in \{0, 1, \ldots, 127\}$).

PWM0:

$$f_0 = \hat{s_0}[2i] + \hat{s_0}[2i+1], \ f_1 = \hat{u_0}[2i] + \hat{u_0}[2i+1]; \quad (12)$$

$$g_0 = \hat{s_0}[2i] \cdot \hat{u_0}[2i], \ g_1 = \hat{s_0}[2i+1] \cdot \hat{u_0}[2i+1]. \quad (13)$$

PWM1:

$$f_2 = g_0 + g_1; \quad (14)$$

$$g_2 = f_0 \cdot f_1, \ g_3 = g_1 \cdot \zeta^{2br_7(i)+1}; \quad (15)$$

$$\hat{h_0}[2i] = g_0 + g_3, \ \hat{h_0}[2i+1] = g_2 - f_2. \quad (16)$$

Most of the CPA schemes [30,33] have focused on the last half of PWM0, i.e., Eq. (13). However, the parallel calculation of two multiplications in Eq. (13) has a negative impact on the efficiency of secret information recovery. Previous CPA dealt with this issue with two strategies: one is to guess two secret values $\hat{s_0}[2i]$ and $\hat{s_0}[2i+1]$ together [24], the other is to guess one secret value each time and treat the power consumption related to the other secret value as noise [30].

Unlike existing CPA works on PWM, we do not intend to carry out a complete attack that can reveal the entire secret key, but rather conduct a simplified CPA to verify the effectiveness of the masking scheme. Specifically, we focus solely on the recovery of the penultimate coefficient of the first component in the secret polynomial vector, i.e., $\hat{s_0}[254]$. We choose random ciphertexts with a special structure to minimize the impact of the parallel computation as much as possible[3]. The methodology developed for recovering this single coefficient is in fact generic and can be extended to other coefficients of the same polynomial, as well as to coefficients of the remaining component polynomials.

Special Structure of Random Ciphertexts. We chose the ciphertext-related polynomial vector $\hat{\mathbf{u}}$ with the following structure:

$$\hat{\mathbf{u}}^\top = \left(\hat{u_0^e}, 0, 0, 0\right), \text{where the coefficients of the odd terms in } \hat{u_0^e} \text{ are all } 0. \quad (17)$$

In other words, $\hat{u_0^e}[2i+1] = 0$ for $i \in \{0, 1, \cdots, 127\}$.
Then the intermediate results of PWM can be represented as follows:
PWM0:

$$f_0 = \hat{s_0}[2i] + \hat{s_0}[2i+1], \ f_1 = \hat{u_0}[2i]; \quad (18)$$

[3] We expect that the masked implementation remains secure under normal CPA if it is secure under this specialized CPA.

$$g_0 = \hat{s_0}[2i] \cdot \hat{u_0}[2i], \ g_1 = 0. \tag{19}$$

PWM1:

$$f_2 = g_0 + g_1 = \hat{s_0}[2i] \cdot \hat{u_0}[2i]; \tag{20}$$

$$g_2 = (\hat{s_0}[2i] + \hat{s_0}[2i+1]) \cdot \hat{u_0}[2i], \ g_3 = 0; \tag{21}$$

$$\hat{h_0}[2i] = \hat{s_0}[2i] \cdot \hat{u_0}[2i], \ \hat{h_0}[2i+1] = \hat{s_0}[2i+1] \cdot \hat{u_0}[2i]. \tag{22}$$

Based on hardware implementation details, i.e., the register that stores g_0 will be set to 0 under our chosen ciphertexts, we choose the Hamming weight of $\hat{s_0}[254] \cdot \hat{u_0}[254]$ as the leakage model for CPA.

CPA Experimental Results. First, we mount the foresaid CPA on an unmasked implementation of Kyber decryption. For a given number of random ciphertexts/traces, Pearson's correlation coefficient is calculated for each guess of $\hat{s_0}[254] \in \{0, 1, 2, \ldots, 3328\}$. The results obtained with 95 000 traces are shown in Fig. 9. The most significant peak exactly corresponds to the correct secret value. This shows that our CPA scheme works and that the unmasked implementation is vulnerable to Correlation Power Analysis (CPA). As shown in Fig. 9, after accumulating 2×2500 traces, the highest absolute value of the correlation corresponding to the correct guess occupies the top position.

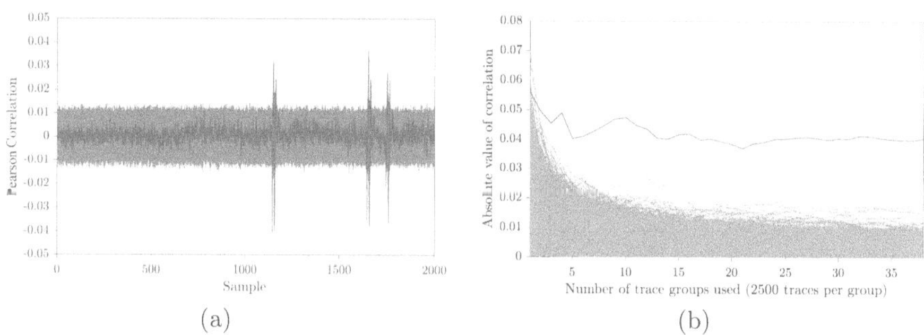

Fig. 9. Results of CPA on PWM (unmasked implementation): (a) Correlation coefficient curves for all possible values of $\hat{s_0}[254]$; (b) Highest absolute value of correlation for each key guess in function of the number of groups of traces used for $\hat{s_0}[254]$, blue curve indicates the correct guess.

Then we apply the same strategy to our designed masked Kyber. The result for 500 000 traces is shown in Fig. 10. As expected, the random mask in each execution breaks the correlation between the original secret coefficient and the target intermediate value. Even with 500 000 traces, no distinct peak appears.

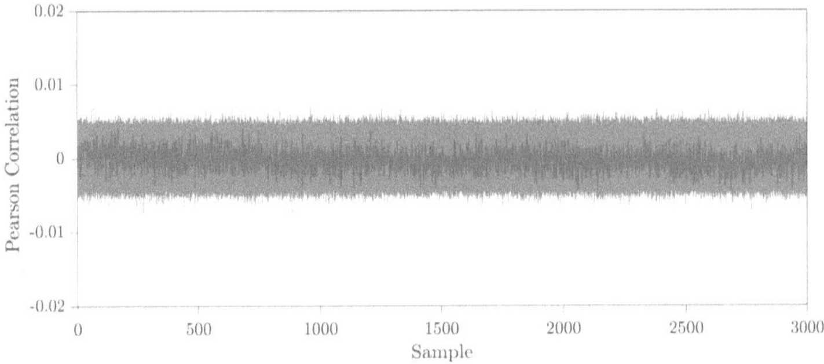

Fig. 10. Correlation coefficient curves for all possible values of $\hat{s_0}$ [254] (masked implementation).

6.2 Test Vector Leakage Assessment (TVLA) on Masked Decoding Function

The TVLA [16] is a well-known evaluation methodology for side-channel resistance validation that requires little knowledge about the details of the cryptographic implementation. We utilized it to evaluate the leakage of the newly designed decoder CF-Decode.

Experimental Setup. The experimental setup is similar to the configuration in Sect. 6.1. The only difference is in the sample rate. For TVLA, we set the sample frequency to 250 MHz, which means 50 sample points per clock cycle.

Non-specific TVLA: Fixed-Vs.-Random Data. Generally, a TVLA requires two trace datasets: one generated with a fixed input and the other obtained from random inputs. We build these trace datasets as follows:

1. Generate a random pair of public key and secret key and keep them unchanged in the whole test;
2. Set a total number of traces N_t, repeat below Step 3 to Step 4 N_t times;
3. Use a pseudo-random bit rng_b[4] to decide the subsequent actions in each individual trace collection event:
   (a) If rng_b = 0, a fixed ciphertext C_{fixed} is fed to be decrypted later, i.e., $C_{test} = C_{fixed}$;
   (b) Else, i.e., rng_b = 1, a random ciphertext C_{random} is generated via PKE.Encryption, $C_{test} = C_{random}$.
4. Run PKE.Decryption on the aforementioned ciphertext C_{test} and collect the triggered part trace;
5. Finally, separate the whole trace set into two datasets DS_{fixed} and DS_{random} according to the value of rng_b.

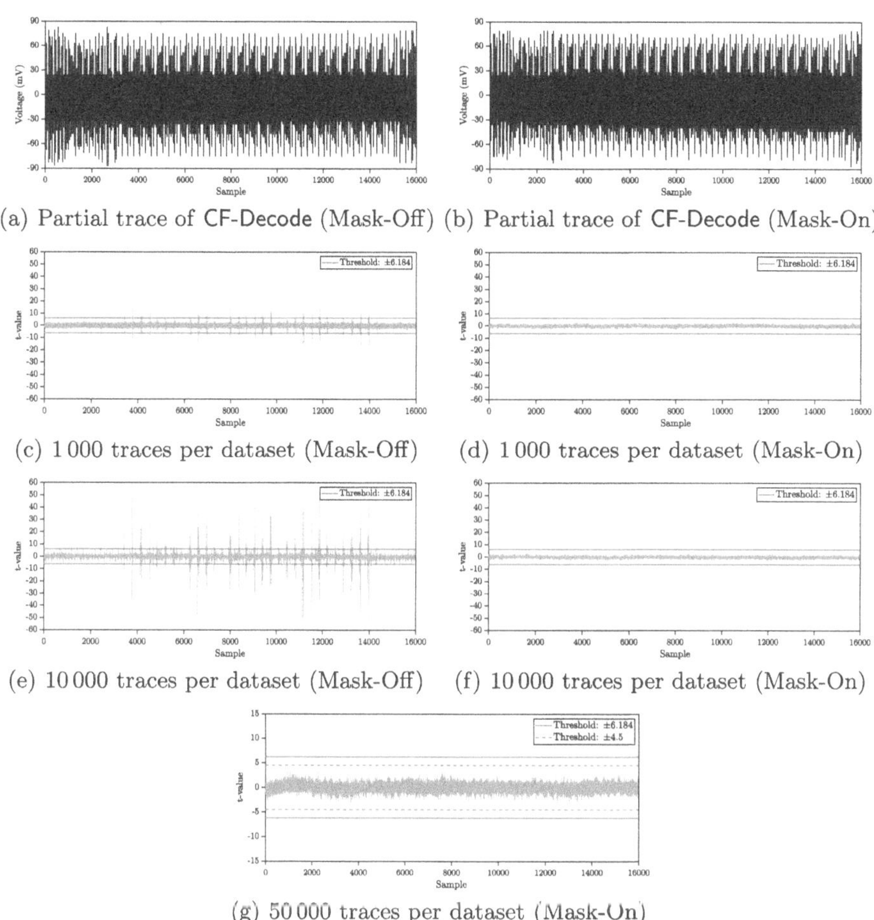

(a) Partial trace of CF-Decode (Mask-Off) (b) Partial trace of CF-Decode (Mask-On)

(c) 1 000 traces per dataset (Mask-Off) (d) 1 000 traces per dataset (Mask-On)

(e) 10 000 traces per dataset (Mask-Off) (f) 10 000 traces per dataset (Mask-On)

(g) 50 000 traces per dataset (Mask-On)

Fig. 11. Results of TVLA targeting CF-Decode function: the three sub-figures in the left column show one raw trace and TVLA results using different number of traces under "Mask-Off" condition, while the three sub-figures in the right column and the one at the bottom show one raw trace and TVLA results using different number of traces under "Mask-On" condition.

As $P(\text{rng\_b} = 0) = 1 - P(\text{rng\_b} = 1) \approx 1/2$, we expect to get two datasets, each with approximately $N_t/2$ traces (i.e., $N_t/2+\varepsilon$ traces for one dataset, $N_t/2-\varepsilon$ traces for the other dataset, where ε is an integer that may vary in different experiments). So, if we expect to build two datasets both with n traces, a N_t slightly bigger than $2n$ should be set experimentally in Step 2.

[4] In order to avoid bias due to order of collection, we collect traces in a random order determined by rng_b.

T-Value and Threshold. The t-value is calculated point-wise according to the Welch's t-test as:

$$t = \frac{\mu_{fixed} - \mu_{random}}{\sqrt{\frac{\sigma^2_{fixed}}{N_{fixed}} + \frac{\sigma^2_{random}}{N_{random}}}}, \tag{23}$$

where μ_{fixed} and μ_{random} are means of each set, σ^2_{fixed} and σ^2_{random} denote the variances, and N_{fixed}, N_{random} represent the cardinalities of the two sets. In line with [8], we set $N_{fixed} = N_{random}$.

In the original TVLA, the threshold is usually set to 4.5. If the t-value exceeds the range (−4.5, 4.5), then one can reject the null-hypothesis (i.e., two datasets were drawn from the same distribution) with a 99.999% confidence. While for long traces (i.e., a large number of sample points), a higher threshold should be adopted to avoid false positives [13]. In our test, there are 16 000 samples in trace corresponding to CF-Decode, so a threshold 6.184 is set according to the method in [13].

TVLA Results. We tested both masked implementation and implementation with "Mask-off" setting (i.e., the RNG related to mask is off). The TVLA results are shown in Fig. 11. For "Mask-Off" implementation, peaks which exceed threshold appear with just 1000 traces per dataset. The peaks of the t-value become more significant under 10 000 traces per dataset. In contrast, for "Mask-On" version, there is no t-value exceeding neither the modified threshold 6.184 nor the frequently used threshold 4.5 even when using 50 000 traces per dataset.

7 Conclusion

Summary. In this paper, we propose a first-order decryption masking scheme for Regev-based encryption, applicable to multiple LWE/LWR variants. The scheme employs two core functions, CF-Decode and Rec-msg, to perform a masked decoder that is not only concise and intuitive, but also highly practical for implementation. By adjusting the functional variables, our scheme enables flexible masking protection across different cryptographic schemes. We apply the proposed scheme to Kyber and SABER as case studies, with a particular focus on evaluating masked Kyber in terms of its performance achieved through SW/HW co-design and its resistance to side-channel attacks. Performance analysis shows that the masked version completes the decryption in 1.53× the clock cycles of the unmasked implementation. The resource utilization data indicates a marginal 2% increase in Look-Up Table (LUT) usage and a 1% increase in Flip-Flop (FF) usage after applying the masking scheme. Experimental results in aspect of SCA confirm that our method effectively resists first-order CPA.

Limitation. In the original unmasked LWE-based PKE, the error tolerance is broader, but the use of this masking scheme could theoretically increase the decryption failure rate. Taking Kyber1024 as an example, the decryption failure rate will increase from $2^{-174.96}$ (the accurate estimation result of [31]) to $2^{-96.1}$.

Extension. The scheme can also offer adaptability to handle different error ranges: By fine-tuning the parameters in CF-Decode and Rec-msg, we can derive masked decoding functions tailored to specific error bounds. For example, one may define $\mathsf{CF\text{-}Decode}(x) = \left\lfloor \frac{2^d}{q} \cdot x \right\rfloor \bmod 2^d$, $\mathsf{Rec\text{-}msg}(m_1, m_2) = \left\lceil \frac{m_1+m_2}{2^{d-1}} \right\rfloor \bmod 2$, which can be used to correctly output the message if the decryption error satisfies $-\left(\frac{q}{4} - \frac{q}{2^d}\right) < Error < \frac{q}{4}$.

Future Work. In the future, we will focus on the following three perspectives. First, we will address the residual error range by leveraging analogous formulas, thereby extending the solution to the interval $-\frac{q}{4} < Error < \frac{q}{4}$. Second, we will investigate high-order masking schemes for lattice-based PQC. Finally, we will explore masking schemes for complete KEM.

Acknowledgments. This work is supported by the National Natural Science Foundation of China under grant 62474092. We thank Huizhi Liu for providing guidance on the operation of the experimental instruments and the anonymous reviewers for their constructive comments. Our thanks also go to Sitong Zong for her proofreading contribution.

References

1. Alagic, G., et al.: Status report on the first round of the NIST post-quantum cryptography standardization process. Rep. NIST IR 8240, US Department of Commerce, NIST (2019). https://doi.org/10.6028/NIST.IR.8240
2. Alagic, G., et al.: Status report on the third round of the NIST post-quantum cryptography standardization process. Rep. NIST IR 8413-upd1, US Department of Commerce, NIST (2022). https://doi.org/10.6028/NIST.IR.8413-upd1
3. Alkim, E., et al.: NewHope algorithm specifications and supporting documentation. Submission to Round 1 of NIST post-quantum cryptography competition (2017). https://newhopecrypto.org/data/NewHope_2017_12_21.pdf
4. Alkim, E., Ducas, L., Pöppelmann, T., Schwabe, P.: NewHope without reconciliation. Cryptology ePrint Archive, Paper 2016/1157 (2016). https://eprint.iacr.org/2016/1157
5. Avanzi, R., et al.: CRYSTALS-Kyber algorithm specifications and supporting documentation (version 3.02). Submission to Round 3 of the NIST post-quantum project (2021). https://pq-crystals.org/kyber/data/kyber-specification-round3-20210804.pdf
6. Banerjee, A., Peikert, C., Rosen, A.: Pseudorandom functions and lattices. In: Pointcheval, D., Johansson, T. (eds.) EUROCRYPT 2012. LNCS, vol. 7237, pp. 719–737. Springer, Heidelberg (2012). https://doi.org/10.1007/978-3-642-29011-4_42
7. Basso, A., et al.: SABER: Mod-LWR based KEM (Round 3 Submission). Submission to NIST post-quantum cryptography competition (2023). https://www.esat.kuleuven.be/cosic/pqcrypto/saber/files/saberspecround3.pdf

8. Bos, J.W., Gourjon, M., Renes, J., Schneider, T., van Vredendaal, C.: Masking Kyber: first- and higher-order implementations. IACR Trans. Cryptogr. Hardw. Embed. Syst. **2021**(4), 173–214 (2021). https://doi.org/10.46586/tches.v2021.i4.173-214
9. Brakerski, Z., Gentry, C., Vaikuntanathan, V.: (Leveled) fully homomorphic encryption without bootstrapping. In: Goldwasser, S. (ed.) Proceedings of the 3rd Innovations in Theoretical Computer Science Conference (ITCS '12), pp. 309–325. ACM (2012). https://doi.org/10.1145/2090236.2090262
10. Brier, E., Clavier, C., Olivier, F.: Correlation power analysis with a leakage model. In: Joye, M., Quisquater, J.-J. (eds.) CHES 2004. LNCS, vol. 3156, pp. 16–29. Springer, Heidelberg (2004). https://doi.org/10.1007/978-3-540-28632-5_2
11. Chari, S., Jutla, C.S., Rao, J.R., Rohatgi, P.: Towards sound approaches to counteract power-analysis attacks. In: Wiener, M. (ed.) CRYPTO 1999. LNCS, vol. 1666, pp. 398–412. Springer, Heidelberg (1999). https://doi.org/10.1007/3-540-48405-1_26
12. Coron, J.-S., Prouff, E., Rivain, M., Roche, T.: Higher-order side channel security and mask refreshing. In: Moriai, S. (ed.) FSE 2013. LNCS, vol. 8424, pp. 410–424. Springer, Heidelberg (2014). https://doi.org/10.1007/978-3-662-43933-3_21
13. Ding, A.A., Zhang, L., Durvaux, F., Standaert, F.-X., Fei, Y.: Towards sound and optimal leakage detection procedure. In: Eisenbarth, T., Teglia, Y. (eds.) CARDIS 2017. LNCS, vol. 10728, pp. 105–122. Springer, Cham (2018). https://doi.org/10.1007/978-3-319-75208-2_7
14. Faust, S., Grosso, V., Merino Del Pozo, S., Paglialonga, C., Standaert, F.X.: Composable masking schemes in the presence of physical defaults & the robust probing model. IACR Trans. Cryptogr. Hardw. Embed. Syst. **2018**(3), 89–120 (2018). https://doi.org/10.13154/tches.v2018.i3.89-120
15. Glabush, L., Longa, P., Naehrig, M., Peikert, C., Stebila, D., Virdia, F.: FrodoKEM: a CCA-secure learning with errors key encapsulation mechanism. IACR Commun. Cryptol. **2**(3) (2025). https://doi.org/10.62056/ayivom2hd
16. Goodwill, G., Jun, B., Jaffe, J., Rohatgi, P.: A testing methodology for side-channel resistance validation. In: NIST Non-Invasive Attack Testing Workshop (2011). https://csrc.nist.gov/CSRC/media/Events/Non-Invasive-Attack-Testing-Workshop/documents/08_Goodwill.pdf
17. Goubin, L., Patarin, J.: DES and differential power analysis the "Duplication" method. In: Koç, Ç.K., Paar, C. (eds.) CHES 1999. LNCS, vol. 1717, pp. 158–172. Springer, Heidelberg (1999). https://doi.org/10.1007/3-540-48059-5_15
18. International Organization for Standardization: Information technology – Security techniques – Encryption algorithms – Part 2: Asymmetric ciphers – Amendment 2. ISO/IEC 18033-2:2006/FDAmd 2, ISO (2025). https://www.iso.org/standard/86890.html
19. Ishai, Y., Sahai, A., Wagner, D.: Private circuits: securing hardware against probing attacks. In: Boneh, D. (ed.) CRYPTO 2003. LNCS, vol. 2729, pp. 463–481. Springer, Heidelberg (2003). https://doi.org/10.1007/978-3-540-45146-4_27
20. Kamucheka, T., Nelson, A., Andrews, D., Huang, M.: A masked pure-hardware implementation of Kyber cryptographic algorithm. Cryptology ePrint Archive, Paper 2022/1547 (2022). https://eprint.iacr.org/2022/1547
21. Kocher, P., Jaffe, J., Jun, B.: Differential power analysis. In: Wiener, M. (ed.) CRYPTO 1999. LNCS, vol. 1666, pp. 388–397. Springer, Heidelberg (1999). https://doi.org/10.1007/3-540-48405-1_25

22. Langlois, A., Stehlé, D.: Worst-case to average-case reductions for module lattices. Des. Codes Cryptogr. **75**(3), 565–599 (2015). https://doi.org/10.1007/S10623-014-9938-4
23. Lyubashevsky, V., Peikert, C., Regev, O.: On ideal lattices and learning with errors over rings. In: Gilbert, H. (ed.) EUROCRYPT 2010. LNCS, vol. 6110, pp. 1–23. Springer, Heidelberg (2010). https://doi.org/10.1007/978-3-642-13190-5_1
24. Mujdei, C., Wouters, L., Karmakar, A., Beckers, A., Bermudo Mera, J.M., Verbauwhede, I.: Side-channel analysis of lattice-based post-quantum cryptography: Exploiting polynomial multiplication. ACM Trans. Embed. Comput. Syst. **23**(2) (2024). https://doi.org/10.1145/3569420
25. National Institute of Standards and Technology: Module-lattice-based key-encapsulation mechanism standard. Federal Information Processing Standards Publications (FIPS) FIPS 203, NIST (2024). https://doi.org/10.6028/NIST.FIPS.203
26. Oder, T., Schneider, T., Pöppelmann, T., Güneysu, T.: Practical CCA2-secure and masked ring-LWE implementation. IACR Trans. Cryptogr. Hardw. Embed. Syst. **2018**(1), 142–174 (2018). https://doi.org/10.13154/TCHES.V2018.I1.142-174
27. Regev, O.: On lattices, learning with errors, random linear codes, and cryptography. J. ACM **56**(6), 1–40 (2009). https://doi.org/10.1145/1568318.1568324
28. Reparaz, O., de Clercq, R., Sinha Roy, S., Vercauteren, F., Verbauwhede, I.: Additively homomorphic ring-LWE masking. In: Takagi, T. (ed.) PQCrypto 2016. LNCS, vol. 9606, pp. 233–244. Springer, Cham (2016). https://doi.org/10.1007/978-3-319-29360-8_15
29. Reparaz, O., Sinha Roy, S., Vercauteren, F., Verbauwhede, I.: A masked ring-LWE implementation. In: Güneysu, T., Handschuh, H. (eds.) CHES 2015. LNCS, vol. 9293, pp. 683–702. Springer, Heidelberg (2015). https://doi.org/10.1007/978-3-662-48324-4_34
30. Rodriguez, R.C., Bruguier, F., Valea, E., Benoit, P.: Correlation electromagnetic analysis on an FPGA implementation of CRYSTALS-Kyber. In: 2023 18th Conference on Ph.D Research in Microelectronics and Electronics (PRIME). pp. 217–220. IEEE (2023). https://doi.org/10.1109/PRIME58259.2023.10161764
31. Wang, L., Wang, Y., Jia, H.: On accuracy of testing decryption failure rate for encryption schemes under the LWE assumption. IET Inf. Secur. **2024**(1), 1–20 (2024). https://doi.org/10.1049/2024/2786399
32. Xing, Y., Li, S.: A compact hardware implementation of CCA-secure key exchange mechanism CRYSTALS-Kyber on FPGA. IACR Trans. Cryptogr. Hardw. Embed. Syst. **2021**(2), 328–356 (2021). https://doi.org/10.46586/TCHES.V2021.I2.328-356
33. Zhao, Y., et al.: Side channel security oriented evaluation and protection on hardware implementations of Kyber. IEEE Trans. Circuits Syst. I Regul. Pap. **70**(12), 5025–5035 (2023). https://doi.org/10.1109/TCSI.2023.3288600

Side-Channel and AI Security

A New Multiscalar Multiplication Method Resistant to Timing Attacks

Abhraneel Dutta[1](✉), Veronika Kuchta[2], and Francesco Sica[2]

[1] Department of Mathematics and Statistics, Florida International University, Miami, USA
abdutta@fiu.edu

[2] Department of Mathematics and Statistics, Florida Atlantic University, Boca Raton, USA

Abstract. Multiscalar multiplication (MSM) is a core operation in modern cryptographic systems, commonly used in various applications such as Zero-Knowledge Succinct Non-Interactive Arguments of Knowledge (ZK-SNARKs) and Homomorphic Encryption. In elliptic curve–based ZK-SNARK constructions, MSM accounts for up to 80–90% of the total proof generation time, making its optimization critical to improving overall protocol performance. Despite significant progress in accelerating MSM through algorithmic techniques such as Pippenger's method, existing implementations remain vulnerable to timing attacks due to irregular scalar representations and conditional operations on zero digits.

In this paper, we revisit the original Pippenger's MSM algorithm, proposing novel modifications that achieve resistance to timing attacks while at the same time increasing its performance by almost 25%. Our main contribution is a new scalar recoding algorithm that transforms conventional q-ary representations containing zero digits into equivalent non-zero representations. This ensures that all scalar digits are processed uniformly, eliminating timing-based side-channel leaks. Building on this recoding technique, we introduce a secure variant of Pippenger's bucket method, that avoids zero digits. Finally, we demonstrate that employing an endomorphism-based splitting yields shorter digit expansions and further efficiency gains. To the best of our knowledge, this is the first MSM algorithm explicitly designed to mitigate timing attacks within the Pippenger bucket method framework.

1 Introduction

Multiscalar multiplication is a fundamental operation in modern cryptographic systems, playing a critical role in applications such as Zero-Knowledge Succinct Non-Interactive Arguments of Knowledge (ZK-SNARKs) and Homomorphic Encryption. In ZK-SNARKs, which enable verifiable computations with minimal data revelation, multiscalar multiplication is often employed within elliptic curve-based constructions, such as [5]. Similarly, Homomorphic Encryption schemes, which allow computations on encrypted data, use multiscalar

F. -H. Liu (Ed.): CT-RSAC 2026, LNCS 16496, pp. 181–197, 2026.
https://doi.org/10.1007/978-3-032-22931-1_7

multiplication for efficient algebraic operations. The multiscalar multiplication problem is defined as follows: given a set of elliptic curve points P_i for $i \in \{1, \ldots, n\}$ and the corresponding scalars $a_i \in \mathbb{Z}$, compute the linear combination $\sum_{i=1}^{n} a_i P_i$. This operation is computationally intensive, particularly for large n, and optimizing it is crucial for the performance of cryptographic protocols which are based on elliptic curves.

In the implementation of ZK-SNARKs, approximately 80% of the proof generation time is dedicated to multiscalar multiplication (MSM). Consequently, optimizing MSM is essential for enhancing the performance of ZK-SNARK protocols.

The primary challenges in multiscalar multiplication (MSM) zk-SNARKs include computational complexity, memory overhead, and scalability. MSM, defined as computing $\sum_{i=1}^{n} a_i P_i$ for elliptic curve points P_i and scalars a_i, exhibits a computational complexity of $O(n)$ for n points. Each operation involves computationally expensive elliptic curve point additions and doublings, making MSM a significant bottleneck in zk-SNARK proof generation, often accounting for 80–90% of the total time [15]. Additionally, MSM requires storing large sets of elliptic curve points and scalars, leading to substantial memory overhead, particularly in zk-SNARK constructions with high-dimensional arithmetic circuits. Regarding scalability, traditional MSM algorithms, such as the Pippenger algorithm, are inherently serial and fail to exploit modern parallel computing architectures like GPUs or distributed systems, limiting their efficiency for large-scale applications.

Recent research has focused on optimizing MSM to improve the performance of zk-SNARKs, particularly through algorithmic improvements and hardware acceleration. Key advancements include Pippenger's algorithm, a new parallel MSM algorithm [9], elastic MSM [16]. A GPU-based implementation of zk-SNARKs that accelerates MSM using a novel parallel algorithm (cuZK) was proposed in [9]. Unlike traditional methods that decompose MSM into smaller independent computations, cuZK treats MSM as a unified task, storing elements in a sparse matrix to achieve near-linear speedup over the Pippenger's algorithm.

Deployment of MSM Methods in ZK-SNARK Implementation. To demonstrate the role of MSM and the security requirements we briefly review the proof generation process of Groth16 [6]. A ZK-SNARK protocol consists of three algorithms Setup, Prove, Verify For a given circuit C, the Setup algorithm translates it to a Quadratic Arithmetic Program (QAP) instance, which consists of three sets of polynomials, denoted $\boldsymbol{A}(z) = \{A_i(z)\}, \boldsymbol{B}(z) = \{B_i(z)\}, \boldsymbol{C}(z) = \{C_i(z)\}, i \in [1, m]$ with coefficients in a finite field $\mathbb{F}$, and a target polynomial $Z(z) \in \mathbb{F}[z]$. Suppose F is a function describing the QAP, by taking as input n elements of $\mathbb{F}$ and outputting n' elements, i.e. in total there are $N = n + n'$ input/output elements. Then a QAP computes this function F if for a valid assignment $(x_1, \ldots, x_N) \in \mathbb{F}^N$ of inputs and outputs there exist coefficients $(x_{N+1}, \ldots, x_m)$ such that the target polynomial $Z(z)$ divides the polynomial

$P(z) := \boldsymbol{A}(z) \cdot \boldsymbol{B}(z) - \boldsymbol{C}(z)$, i.e.

$$P(z) = \Big(A_0(z) + \sum_{i=1}^{m} x_i A_i(z)\Big) \cdot \Big(B_0(z) + \sum_{i=1}^{m} x_i B_i(z)\Big) - \Big(C_0(z) + \sum_{i=1}^{m} x_i C_i(z)\Big).$$

In other words this means that the target polynomial $Z(z)$ satisfies the following equation $\boldsymbol{A}(z) \cdot \boldsymbol{B}(z) - \boldsymbol{C}(z) = \boldsymbol{H}(z) \cdot \boldsymbol{Z}(z)$ for some polynomial $H(z) \in \mathbb{F}[z]$. The size of the QAP is m and the degree is the degree of $Z(z)$.

In the Prove algorithm, the prover knows a valid assignment for the circuit C, which is denoted as $(\boldsymbol{x}, \boldsymbol{w})$, where $\boldsymbol{x} = (x_1, \ldots, x_N)$ is public input and the secret part $\boldsymbol{w} = (x_{N+1}, \ldots, x_m)$. The prover evaluates the polynomials $\{A_i(z)\}_{i \in [N+1,m]}, \{B_i(z)\}_{i \in [N+1,m]}, \{C_i(z)\}_{i \in [N+1,m]}$ for $i \in [N+1, m]$ at a random value s, which is provided by the `Setup` algorithm and computes $\tilde{A}(s) = \sum_{i=N+1}^{m} x_i A_i(s)$, $\tilde{B}(s) = \sum_{i=N+1}^{m} x_i B_i(s)$ and $\tilde{C}(s) = \sum_{i=N+1}^{m} x_i C_i(s)$. Finally, the prover encodes these values into elliptic curve points $g^{\tilde{A}(s)}$, $g^{\tilde{B}(s)}$, $g^{\tilde{C}(s)}$. The proof then contains these points and is output by the prover.
In the Verify algorithm, the verifier evaluates the polynomials $\boldsymbol{A}(z), (z), \boldsymbol{C}(z)$ at a randomly sampled value s, i.e. computes $\{A_i(s)\}_{i \in [1,N]}, \{B_i(s)\}_{i \in [1,N]}$, and $\{C_i(s)\}_{i \in [1,N]}$ for $i \in [1, N]$ and the corresponding polynomials $\bar{A}(s) = \sum_{i=1}^{N} x_i A_i(s)$, $\bar{B}(s) = \sum_{i=1}^{N} x_i B_i(s)$ and $\bar{C}(s) = \sum_{i=1}^{N} x_i C_i(s)$. Finally, the verifier encodes these values into elliptic curve points $g^{\bar{A}(s)}$, $g^{\bar{B}(s)}$, $g^{\bar{C}(s)}$ and checks the verification equations by performing computations over an elliptic curve. A major task of the proof generation algorithm Prove and the verification algorithm `Verify` is to encode the public key with the witness vector $(\boldsymbol{x}, \boldsymbol{w})$, which is essentially an MSM instance with the witness vector serving as scalars.

Our Contribution. In this paper, we explore generalizations of Pippenger's MSM method. We propose thorough modifications of the Pippenger's method to avoid timing attacks. In [7] the authors present a new scalar recoding algorithm which allows for regular implementation of multiscalar multiplication algorithm. This recoding algorithm transforms conventional q-ary representation of scalars containing zeros into equivalent non-zero representations. It is important to note that the protocol in [7] only works for odd scalars. Given an odd integer of width c we map it into a non-zero, signed q-ary expansion $a = \sum_{j=0}^{L-1} d_j q^j$ with $d_j \in \{\pm 1, \pm 3, \pm 5, \ldots, \pm(2^c - 1)\}$. To deal with even scalars, we adapt our multiscalar multiplication by replacing each even a_i by $(a_i + 1)$. This modification leads to an additional sum $\sum_{a_i \in \mathcal{M}_e} P_i$, which will be computed separately and subtracted at the end of the computation. This specification is described in the preamble of Sect. 3. This non-zero digit representation for odd integers is described in Sect. 2.1. After completing this procedure, we present a new algorithm which is based on the basic idea of Pippenger's bucket method; however, the new recoding algorithm provides security guarantees against timing attacks, that, to the best of our knowledge, has not been considered before. The main idea behind Pippenger's bucket method is to organize the points into buckets according to the digit values of their corresponding scalars. The scalars are represented in base q and points with even scalars are modified to get instead odd scalars which are then expanded using the JT algorithm [7]. This is the moment where we apply our recoding algorithm from Sect. 3 to avoid timing attacks. In the end instead of skipping zero digits as it happens in Pippenger's bucket method, we process every scalar digit in a regular fashion. The new bucket filling algorithm with non-zero digits is derived and we show that it is possible to get a shorter digit expansion representation if we use a fast endomorphism ω attached to the usual j-invariant zero elliptic curve used in most applications; this is described in Sect. 3.1. Finally we provide a comparison of our algorithm with Pippenger's method and conclude that we achieve an improvement of 25%.

Organization of the Paper. Section 2 reviews MSM preliminaries, a brief introduction to the Straus' [13] and Pippenger MSM [12] techniques. Section 2.1 surveys briefly zero-free signed-digit recoding methods for timing attack resistant MSM, introduces branchless bucketing templates, and explains the recoding choice we adopt to harden our MSM against timing attacks. In Sect. 3 we construct a new MSM algorithm resistant against timing attacks. Section 3.1 then leverages an efficient curve endomorphism to group bases and shorten digit expansions, yielding a $2n$-base, single-scan variant. Section 4 summarizes our contributions and situates them against classical Pippenger, emphasizing zero-free recoding, the endomorphism based grouping, and their combined effect on MSM cost. Section 4.1 provides an asymptotic cost comparison accounting for halved digit length, doubled bases, and even scalar compensation. Section 4.2 outlines next research steps and our rationale for implementing the method across multiple platforms.

1.1 Notations

In this section we collect the symbols and notations used throughout the paper. We provide a quick reference so readers can map the goals to the formal algorithms and analyses that follow.

$E/\mathbb{F}_p$ (curve) Elliptic curve over the prime field $\mathbb{F}_p$.
$\mathbb{F}_p$ (field) Prime field.
r (integer) Order of the subgroup $\mathcal{G}$.
$\mathcal{G} \subseteq E(\mathbb{F}_p)$ (group) Cyclic subgroup of order r used for MSM.
P_i (point) i-th base point (from the CRS/SRS).
n (integer) Number of base points (per MSM).
$a_i \in [0, r)$ (scalar) i-th scalar.
c (integer) Window width (bits).
$q = 2^c$ (integer) Radix for windowed recoding.
h (integer) Number of windows (typically $\lceil \log_q r \rceil$).
L (integer) Digit length used by algorithms (often $L = h$).

$d_{i,j}$ (digit) Zero-free signed digit at position j for scalar a_i.
B (set) Allowed absolute digit values (default $\{1, 3, \ldots, q-1\}$).
$B[k]$ (point) Bucket accumulating points with $|d_{i,j}| = k$.
S_j (point) Reverse-accumulated sum for window j.
ϕ (endomorphism) Efficient curve endomorphism on $\mathcal{G}$.
$\mathcal{O}(P)$ (set) ϕ-orbit of P: $\{P, \phi(P), \phi^2(P), \ldots\}$.
ω (constant) Cube root of unity with $\omega^2 + \omega + 1 = 0$.
$\nu \in \mathbb{Z}[\omega]$ (element) Eisenstein divisor used in scalar splitting.
JT Recoding($\cdot$) (map) Zero-free signed-digit recoding (e.g., Joye–Tunstall).

2 Preliminaries

We provide a concise overview of Pippenger's algorithm for multiscalar multiplication (MSM), building upon the foundational Straus method, which we briefly introduce first.

Straus' Method. Let $\mathcal{G}$ be an elliptic curve subgroup of prime order r, $n \geqslant 1$, and $S_{n,r}$ be the following n-scalar multiplication over fixed points $P_1, \ldots, P_n \in E$,

$$S_{n,r} = \sum_{i=1}^{n} a_i P_i \ , \tag{1}$$

To compute $S_{n,r}$, the Straus method precomputes 2^{nc} points

$$\Big\{ \sum_{i=1}^{n} b_i P_i | \forall b_i \in [0, 2^c - 1], i \in [1, n] \Big\} \ ,$$

where c is a small integer. Next, the algorithm divides each a_i from (1) into segments of length c, i.e.

$$a_i = a_{i,h-1} \| a_{i,h-2} \| \cdots \| a_{i,1} \| a_{i,0} = \sum_{j=0}^{h-1} a_{i,j} 2^{jc}, i \in [1, n] \ ,$$

where $h = \lceil \log_2(r)/c \rceil$ and $0 \leqslant a_{ij} < 2^c$ for $j \in [1, h-1]$. The algorithm retrieves the point

$$S_{n,2^c} = \sum_{i=1}^{n} a_{i,h-1} P_i$$

from the precomputation table, doubles it c times, adds the precomputed point $\sum_{i=1}^{n} a_{i,h-2} P_i$ to obtain

$$S_{n,2^{2c}} = \sum_{i=1}^{n} (a_{i,h-1} \| a_{i,h-2}) P_i \ .$$

After $h-1$ repetitions, we obtain

$$S_{n,2^{hc}} = \sum_{i=1}^{n} (a_{i,h-1} \| a_{i,h-2} \| \dots \| a_{i,0}) P_0 \ . \tag{2}$$

Pippenger's Bucket Method. This method follows the same approach as the Straus method, differing only in the computation of

$$S_{n,2^c} = \sum_{i=1}^{n} a_{i,j} P_i \ ,$$

where $j \in [0, h-1], h = \lceil \log_2(r)/c \rceil$. Let $B = \{b_1, \dots, b_{|B|}\}$ be a set of non-negative integers containing zero. Given scalars $a_i, 0 \leqslant a_i < r$, the Pippenger method first computes [10, Algorithm 6] a signed radix-q representation

$$a_i = \sum_{j=0}^{h-1} a_{ij} q^j \ ,$$

where $h = \lceil \log_q r \rceil$, $-q/2 \leqslant a_{ij} < q/2$ and for every $i \in [1, n], j \in [0, h-1]$,

$$a_{ij} = \epsilon_{ij} b_{ij}, \text{ where } \epsilon_{ij} \in \{\pm 1\}, b_{ij} \in B = \{0, 1, \dots, q/2\}. \tag{3}$$

Then,

$$\begin{aligned} S_{n,r} &= \sum_{i=0}^{n} a_i P_i = \sum_{j=0}^{h-1} q^j \sum_{i=1}^{n} a_{ij} P_i \\ &= \sum_{j=0}^{h-1} q^j \sum_{i=1}^{n} b_{ij} \epsilon_{ij} P_i \\ &= \sum_{j=0}^{h-1} q^j \sum_{i=1}^{n} \Big(\sum_{k=1}^{|B|} b_k \cdot \sum_{i \text{ s.t. } b_{ij} = b_k} \epsilon_{ij} P_i \Big) \\ &= \sum_{j=0}^{h-1} q^j \sum_{k=1}^{|B|} b_k S_k^{(j)} \\ &= \sum_{j=0}^{h-1} q^j \mathfrak{S}_j \ , \end{aligned}$$

where

$$S_k^{(j)} = \sum_{\substack{i \text{ s.t.} \\ b_{ij} = b_k}} \epsilon_{ij} P_i, \quad b_k \in B \ ,$$

and

$$\mathfrak{S}_j = \sum_{k=1}^{|B|} b_k S_k^{(j)} \ .$$

Algorithm 1 . Subsum accumulation algorithm [10]

Input: $B = \{b_1, b_2, \ldots, b_{|B|}\}, S_1, S_2, \ldots, S_{|B|}$
Output: $S = b_1 S_1 + \cdots + b_{|B|} S_{|B|}$
1: Define a length-$(d+1)$ array $\mathsf{tmp} = [0] \times (d+1)$ ▷ $d = \max |b_i - b_{i-1}|$
2: **for** $i = |B|$ to 1 by -1 **do**
3: $\mathsf{tmp}[0] = \mathsf{tmp}[0] + S_i$ ▷ $\mathsf{tmp}[0] = \Sigma_i$
4: $k = b_i - b_{i-1}$
5: $\mathsf{tmp}[k] = \mathsf{tmp}[k] + \mathsf{tmp}[0]$ ▷ $\mathsf{tmp}[k] = \sum_{\substack{j \geqslant i \\ \beta_j = k}} \Sigma_j$
6: **return** $\sum_{k:\ |k| \leqslant d} k \cdot \mathsf{tmp}[k]$

All $S_k^{(j)}$'s can be computed with at most $n - (|B| - 1)$ additions; $\mathfrak{S}_j$ is then computed using Algorithm 1 with at most $2(|B| - 1) + d - 3$ additions, where d is the maximum difference between the two neighboring elements in B. The total cost of computing, via Horner's rule, of

$$S_{n,r} = \sum_{j=0}^{h-1} q^j \mathfrak{S}_j$$

is therefore at most

$$(h-1)(n + |B| + d - 3) + (h-1)(c+1) \approx (h-1)(n + |B|) \tag{4}$$

elliptic curve additions, where $q = 2^c$. Optimal choice of parameters are when $|B| = q/2 = 2^{c-1} \approx n$.

We justify that Algorithm 1 works by the following analysis. Let $b_0 = 0$ and $\beta_i = b_i - b_{i-1}$ for $1 \leqslant i \leqslant |B|$. Define

$$\Sigma_i = \sum_{j=i}^{|B|} S_j \ ,$$

with $\Sigma_{|B|+1} = 0$. Then

$$\begin{aligned} \sum_{i=1}^{|B|} b_i S_i &= \sum_{i=1}^{|B|} b_i (\Sigma_i - \Sigma_{i+1}) = \sum_{i=1}^{|B|} b_i \Sigma_i - \sum_{i=0}^{|B|-1} b_i \Sigma_{i+1} \\ &= \sum_{i=1}^{|B|} (b_i - b_{i-1}) \Sigma_i = \sum_{i=1}^{|B|} \beta_i \Sigma_i \ . \end{aligned}$$

Remark. Pippenger's algorithm does not require any precomputation, only the storage of $P_1, \ldots, P_n$. Improvements by Luo, Fu and Gong [10] and Fan, Kuchta, Sica and Xu [3] have been presented requiring additional precomputation and storage. Therefore, our work should be compared to the original Pippenger algorithm. Moreover, previous cited work is still vulnerable to timing attacks.

2.1 Regular Recoding for MSM: Methods and Our Selection

When choosing a scalar-multiplication routine for ECC, the implementation must be regular *i.e* each loop iteration performing the same sequence of operations, so that trivial "skip vs. add" patterns do not leak scalar bits to simple power analysis; see the surveys in [1,8]. A common way to enforce regularity is to recode the scalar so that there is no zero window in the digit matrix scanned by the main loop. Signed-digit recodings are natural here because point negation is essentially free on elliptic curves. Notable examples include Möller's nonzero base-q recoding, replacing any zero digit by $-q$ and propagating a carry to higher positions, in [11], Okeya and Takagi's windowed recoding that yields SPA-resistant addition chains in [14], generalized signed digit recoding for all bases by Dutta, Hutchinson and Karabina in [2], and Joye–Tunstall's (JT-Recoding) base-$q = 2^c$ with $c \geq 1$ methods that produce either unsigned digits in $\{1, \ldots, q-1\}$ for all scalars or signed odd digits in $\{\pm 1, \pm 3, \ldots, \pm(q-1)\}$ for odd scalars, leading to regular single-dimensional loops [7].

In our grouped MSM, we can apply JT recoding to the GLV components α_i and β_i and then process a single list of $2n$ bases $(P_1, \ldots, P_n, \ \omega P_1, \ldots, \omega P_n)$. For each window j and each nonzero odd digit d, we perform a branchless bucket fill by adding $\text{sgn}(d) \cdot \tilde{P}$ to bucket $u = (|d| + 1)/2$; since $|d|$ is odd, u ranges only over $\{1, \ldots, q/2\}$. Thus, compared to using all magnitudes $\{1, \ldots, q-1\}$, the odd-digit recoding halves the number of buckets per window, and grouping (α, β) into one pass means we do one scan instead of two. The net effect is branchless fills (no zero digits), a single cumulative scan over only $q/2$ buckets, and therefore a substantial reduction in bucket work and point-addition cost per window.

Given an odd integer a and a window width c (so the radix is $q = 2^c$), this routine maps the input to a zero-free, signed q-ary expansion

$$a = \sum_{j=0}^{L-1} d_j \, q^j,$$

where every output digit lies in the odd set $d_j \in \{\pm 1, \pm 3, \ldots, \pm(2^c - 1)\}$. In other words, it takes a single scalar and produces a vector of nonzero, odd-magnitude digits that exactly reconstruct the input under radix q, with length $L \approx \lceil \text{bitlen}(a)/c \rceil$. The procedure is designed to be regular (branch-free) and constant-shape. If the caller holds an even scalar s, one typically converts it to an odd input (e.g., $a = s + 1$) and carries a one-time final compensation in the target group; the recoder itself always consumes odd inputs and outputs only odd signed digits.

3 A New Multiscalar Multiplication Algorithm Resistant Against Timing Attacks

In this section, we propose a new multiscalar multiplication algorithm in the context of zkSNARKs. The objective of the algorithm is to compute a multiscalar multiplication of the form

Algorithm 2 . Odd Signed-Digit Recoding (JT Recooding) [7]

Input: Odd integer $a \in \mathbb{Z} \setminus \{0\}$; window width $c \geq 1$; set $q \leftarrow 2^c$
Output: A digit vector $(d_0, \ldots, d_{L-1})$ with $d_j \in \{\pm 1, \pm 3, \ldots, \pm(2^c - 1)\}$ and $a = \sum_{j=0}^{L-1} d_j\, q^j$
1: $j \leftarrow 0$
2: **while** $a \neq 0$ **do**
3: $\quad t \leftarrow a \bmod 2^{c+1}$ $\quad \triangleright\ t \in \{0, 1, \ldots, 2^{c+1} - 1\}$
4: $\quad d \leftarrow t - 2^c$ $\triangleright$ centered odd residue in $(-2^c, 2^c)$; since a is odd, $d \neq 0$ and is odd
5: $\quad d_j \leftarrow d$
6: $\quad a \leftarrow \dfrac{a-d}{2^c}$ $\quad \triangleright$ exact integer division; the new a remains odd
7: $\quad j \leftarrow j + 1$
8: $L \leftarrow j$
9: **return** $(d_0, \ldots, d_{L-1})$

$$S_{n,r} = \sum_{i=1}^{n} a_i P_i,$$

where each scalar $a_i < r$. The scalars a_i are first expressed in base $q = 2^c$ where c is a small positive integer i.e. the scalars are decomposed into a q-ary form

$$a_i = \sum_{j=0}^{h-1} a_{i,j} q^j, \ 0 \leqslant a_{i,j} < q,$$

where $h = \lceil \log_q r \rceil$. Consequently, it follows

$$S_{n,r} = \sum_{i=1}^{n} a_i P_i = \sum_{i=1}^{n} \sum_{j=0}^{h-1} a_{i,j} q^j P_i = \sum_{j=0}^{h-1} q^j \sum_{i=1}^{n} a_{i,j} P_i.$$

In the bucket filling phase shown in the Algorithm 3 just like in the Pippenger's algorithm, the objective is to organize the points of the elliptic curve according to the digit values of their corresponding scalars in a fixed base-q representation. For a given digit position j, each scalar digit $a_{i,j} \in \{0, 1, \ldots, q-1\}$ determines which of the $q-1$ available buckets the associated point P_i should be placed into. Specifically, if $a_{i,j} = k \neq 0$, then P_i is added to bucket B_k. Points with zero digits are ignored in this step. This process groups all points sharing the same digit value, creating partial sums that are later used in the accumulation phase. The output of this phase is a set of buckets $B[1], \ldots, B[q-1]$, where each bucket contains the sum of points with the same digit value.

In Algorithm 3 there is a conditional branch in step 3 that says whenever $a_{i,j}$ is non-zero then the points P_i's are added to the bucket, otherwise this step is skipped. This leaves this algorithm vulnerable to side channel attacks like timing attack, and simple power analysis. To overcome this challenge, we can recode the scalars with the help of Algorithm 2 as follows:

$$a_i = (a_{i,h-1}, a_{i,h-2}, \ldots, a_{i,1}, a_{i,0})_q \xrightarrow{\text{JT Recoding}} (d_{i,h-1}, \ldots, d_{i,1}, d_{i,0})_q$$

where $q = 2^c$ for some integer $c \geq 1$ and $d_{i,j} \in \{\pm 1, \pm 3, \ldots, \pm(q-1)\}$. After this recoding, the bucket filling stage is modified to be uniform and resistant to timing attacks. Instead of conditionally skipping zero digits, we can process every scalar digit $d_{i,j} \in \{\pm 1, \pm 3, \ldots, \pm(q-1)\}$ in a regular fashion. For each digit, we add either P_i or its negation $-P_i$ to the bucket $B[d_{i,j}]$, depending on the sign. This ensures that all bucket accesses and additions follow a fixed pattern, independent of the scalar values, thereby eliminating data-dependent branches. Importantly, the cost of computing $-P_i$ is negligible, as elliptic curve point negation involves only inverting the y-coordinate, making the method both secure and efficient.

As the JT signed recoding works only on odd scalars we need to perform a certain modification for our algorithm. Let $\mathcal{S}$ be the set of scalars used in multiscalar algorithm. While considering using the scalar recoding algorithm, it should be noted that the scalars should not be even i.e. having a 0 in its least significant entry. Therefore, we divide the scalars into two different groups

The set of all even scalars denoted as $\mathcal{M}_e := \{a_i \in \mathcal{S} : a_i \bmod 2 = 0\}$
The set of all scalars that are odd denoted as $\mathcal{M}_o := \{a_i \in \mathcal{S} : a_i \bmod 2 = 1\}$

Therefore, we partition the scalar set as $\mathcal{S} = \mathcal{M}_e \cup \mathcal{M}_o$ with $\mathcal{M}_e \cap \mathcal{M}_o = \emptyset$. For scalars in $\mathcal{M}_o$, we can apply JT recoding technique directly to compute the partial sum:

$$S_{\mathcal{M}_o} = \sum_{a_i \in \mathcal{M}_o} a_i P_i.$$

On the other hand, for the scalars in $\mathcal{M}_e$ we add 1 to each $a_i \in \mathcal{M}_e$ to make them odd, updating the set to $\mathcal{M}_e + 1 := \{a_i + 1 : a_i \in \mathcal{M}_e\}$, which eliminates zero in the least significant digit. We then apply JT signed recoding method to generate a non-zero q-ary representation for each $a_i \in \mathcal{M}_q + 1$ and compute the partial sum

$$S_{\mathcal{M}_e+1} = \sum_{a_i \in \mathcal{M}_e} (a_i + 1) P_i.$$

This introduces an extra partial sum $\sum_{a_i \in \mathcal{M}_e} P_i$, which we compute separately. Finally, we recover the desired total scalar multiplication as

$$S_{n,r} = \sum_{i=1}^{n} a_i P_i = S_{\mathcal{M}_o} + S_{\mathcal{M}_e+1} - \sum_{a_i \in \mathcal{M}_e} P_i.$$

The partial sum $\sum_{a_i \in \mathcal{M}_e} P_i$ we call the compensation sum of $S_{n,r}$.

Algorithm 3 . BucketFill (Unsigned) for window j

Input: Points $P_1, \ldots, P_n$; digits $a_{i,j} \in \{0, \ldots, q-1\}$; base $q = 2^w$
Output: Array $B[1..q-1]$ where $B[k] = \sum_{i:\, a_{i,j}=k} P_i$

```
1: for k = 1 to q − 1 do
2:     B[k] ← O
3: for i = 1 to n do
4:     k ← a_{i,j}
5:     if k ≠ 0 then
6:         B[k] ← B[k] + P_i
7: return B
```

The Bucket Accumulation Algorithm. After the bucket filling phase, we obtain a set of buckets $B[1], B[2], \ldots, B[q-1]$, where each bucket $B[k]$ contains the sum of all points P_i whose scalar digit $a_{i,j}$ at position j equals k. The objective of the bucket accumulation algorithm is to compute the partial sum

$$S_j = \sum_{k=1}^{q-1} k \cdot B[k],$$

but without explicitly multiplying buckets by scalars. To achieve this, the algorithm proceeds in reverse order from $k = q-1$ down to $k = 1$ and uses a temporary accumulator `tmp` to keep track of the cumulative sum of buckets. In each iteration, the current bucket $B[k]$ is added to `tmp`, and then `tmp` is added to the running result S_j.
This approach guarantees that each bucket $B[k]$ contributes exactly k times to the final result. For example:

Example 1 (Bucket accumulation with $q = 4$). Assume at window j the only nonempty buckets are $B[1] = P_{a_1}$, $B[2] = P_{a_2}+P_{a_3}$, and $B[3] = \mathcal{O}$. Initialize $\mathtt{tmp} \leftarrow \mathcal{O}$ and $S_j \leftarrow \mathcal{O}$, then sweep $k = 3, 2, 1$:

$$\begin{aligned} k = 3:&\quad \mathtt{tmp} \leftarrow \mathcal{O}+B[3] = \mathcal{O}, \quad S_j \leftarrow \mathcal{O}+\mathcal{O} = \mathcal{O}, \\ k = 2:&\quad \mathtt{tmp} \leftarrow \mathcal{O}+B[2] = P_{a_2}+P_{a_3}, \quad S_j \leftarrow \mathcal{O}+(P_{a_2}+P_{a_3}) = P_{a_2}+P_{a_3}, \\ k = 1:&\quad \mathtt{tmp} \leftarrow (P_{a_2}+P_{a_3})+B[1] = P_{a_2}+P_{a_3}+P_{a_1}, \\ &\quad S_j \leftarrow (P_{a_2}+P_{a_3})+(P_{a_2}+P_{a_3}+P_{a_1}) = 2(P_{a_2}+P_{a_3}) + P_{a_1}. \end{aligned} \tag{5}$$

Thus $S_j = 2 \cdot B[2] + 1 \cdot B[1] = \sum_{k=1}^{3} k \cdot B[k]$, and the bucket $B[2]$ appears exactly two times (once when $k = 2$ and again when $k = 1$), as desired.

3.1 Scalar Decomposition and Recoding in the Endomorphism Case

In proving systems the MSM $\sum_{i=1}^{n} a_i P_i$ dominates prover time, so any reduction in per-window bucket work or passes over the points has a significant impact.

Algorithm 4 . Bucket Accumulation Phase for Digit Position j

Input: Buckets $B[1 \dots q-1]$ where $B[k]$ stores the sum of points with digit value k at position j
Output: Partial sum $S_j = \sum_{k=1}^{q-1} k \cdot B[k]$
1: $S_j \leftarrow \mathcal{O}$ ▷ Initialize result to the identity point
2: tmp $\leftarrow \mathcal{O}$ ▷ Temporary accumulator
3: **for** $k \leftarrow q-1$ **to** 1 **by** -1 **do**
4: tmp $\leftarrow$ tmp $+ B[k]$
5: $S_j \leftarrow S_j +$ tmp
6: **return** S_j

Implementations of MSM mostly use the j-invariant zero elliptic curve $y^2 = x^3 + b$ for some constant $b \in \mathbb{F}_p$. It comes equipped with an endomorphism ϕ defined by $\phi(x, y) = (\zeta_3 x, y)$, where $\zeta_3 \neq 1 \in \mathbb{F}_p$ is a cube root of unity. Hence $\phi^3 =$ id and the endomorphism ring of our elliptic curve is isomorphic to $\mathbb{Z}[\omega]$, where $1 \neq \omega \in \mathbb{C}$ is a cube root of unity. In the endomorphism setting we can first shorten scalars by applying a Euclidean division in $\mathbb{Z}[\omega]$ to obtain $a_i \equiv \alpha_i + \omega\beta_i \bmod \nu$ with roughly half-size components. This already reduces the window count. We then recode α_i, β_i in base $q = 2^c$ using a regular (branch-free) signed-digit recoding in [7] that eliminates zero digits and supports constant-time bucket filling. Crucially, we group the two halves into a single windowed MSM over the unified bases $(P_1, \dots, P_n, \omega P_1, \dots, \omega P_n)$, so each window requires only one cumulative scan of the buckets instead of two. Intuitively, this design compresses the amount of work per window, keeping the fill linear in the number of bases while cutting the scan phase, and preserves a uniform control flow amenable to side-channel resistant implementations.

Firstly, we provide a step-by-step description of our MSM technique. Let the cyclic subgroup E have large order r. As shown in [3], $r \equiv 1 \pmod 3$ so that r splits in the Eisenstein ring $\mathbb{Z}[\omega]$:

$$r = \nu\bar{\nu} \ .$$

Therefore one of $\nu, \bar{\nu}$ (WLOG, ν) annihilates $\mathcal{G}$. Reduction modulo ν gives $\mathbb{Z}[\omega]/(\nu) \cong \mathbb{F}_r$ and sends $\omega \mapsto \lambda \in \mathbb{F}_r$ with $\lambda^2 + \lambda + 1 \equiv 0 \pmod r$. Performing Euclidean division in $\mathbb{Z}[\omega]$ to each scalar:

$$(\delta_i, \rho_i) \leftarrow \text{Euclidean Division}(a_i, \nu), \qquad a_i = \nu\delta_i + \rho_i, \quad |\rho_i|^2 \leqslant r/3.$$

We write $\rho_i \in \mathbb{Z}[\omega]$ in the $\{1, \omega\}$ basis,

$$\rho_i = \alpha_i + \omega\beta_i, \qquad \max(|\alpha_i|, |\beta_i|) \leqslant \sqrt{r} \ .$$

Consequently,

$$a_i \equiv \alpha_i + \lambda\beta_i \quad (\text{mod }) \text{r} \quad \Longrightarrow \quad a_i P_i = \alpha_i P_i + \beta_i \phi(P_i) \ ,$$

yielding the GLV-style [4] decomposition over the two bases P_i and ωP_i with short integer coefficients (α_i, β_i) determined by Euclidean division in $\mathbb{Z}[\omega]$.

1. **Step 1 (Parameters and Decomposition).** Fix a radix $q = 2^c$ and an efficiently computable endomorphism ω on the curve (e.g., $\omega^3 = \mathrm{id}$). For each scalar a_i, choose a decomposition

$$a_i \equiv \alpha_i + \omega\beta_i \pmod{\nu} ,$$

and expand the two parts in base q using $L = h/2$ windows. Each α_i and β_i are given a q-ary expansion by the JT recoding method in [7]:

$$\alpha_i = \sum_{j=0}^{L-1} a_{i,j} q^j, \qquad \beta_i = \sum_{j=0}^{L-1} b_{i,j} q^j, \qquad a_{i,j}, b_{i,j} \in \{\pm1, \pm3 \ldots, \pm q - 1\}.$$

The multi-scalar multiplication (MSM) target is

$$S = \sum_{i=1}^{n} a_i P_i = \sum_{j=0}^{L-1} q^j \left(\sum_{i=1}^{n} a_{i,j} P_i + \sum_{i=1}^{n} b_{i,j}\, \omega P_i \right). \tag{6}$$

For signed digits, write $d = \mathrm{sgn}(d)\,|d|$ with $|d| \in \{0, \ldots, q-1\}$ and $\mathrm{sgn}(0) = 0$.

2. **Step 2 (Grouping into a Single Windowed MSM).** For each window j, define $2n$ bases and digits by

$$\begin{aligned} (Q_1, \ldots, Q_{2n}) &:= (P_1, \ldots, P_n,\ \omega P_1, \ldots, \omega P_n), \\ (d_{1,j}, \ldots, d_{2n,j}) &:= (a_{1,j}, \ldots, a_{n,j},\ b_{1,j}, \ldots, b_{n,j}). \end{aligned}$$

The j-th window contribution is

$$W_j = \sum_{k=1}^{2n} d_{k,j}\, Q_k, \tag{7}$$

and (6) becomes $S = \sum_{j=0}^{L-1} q^j W_j$.

3. **Step 3 (Bucket Filling).** For each $t \in \{1, \ldots, q-1\}$, define the bucket sum

$$B_t^{(j)} := \sum_{\substack{1 \le k \le 2n \\ |d_{k,j}| = t}} \mathrm{sgn}(d_{k,j})\, Q_k. \tag{8}$$

Then the window sum (7) can be rewritten as

$$W_j = \sum_{t=1}^{q-1} t\, B_t^{(j)}. \tag{9}$$

4. **Step 4 (Bucket Scan via Cumulative-Sum Identity).** Define cumulative buckets for $t = 1, \ldots, q-1$ by

$$C_t^{(j)} := \sum_{u=t}^{q-1} B_u^{(j)}. \tag{10}$$

Then the running-sum identity yields

$$\sum_{t=1}^{q-1} C_t^{(j)} = \sum_{t=1}^{q-1}\sum_{u=t}^{q-1} B_u^{(j)} = \sum_{u=1}^{q-1}\sum_{t=1}^{u} B_u^{(j)} = \sum_{u=1}^{q-1} u\, B_u^{(j)} = W_j. \tag{11}$$

Equivalently, define the backward partials $A_q^{(j)} := \mathcal{O}$ and

$$A_t^{(j)} := A_{t+1}^{(j)} + B_t^{(j)} \qquad (t = q-1, \ldots, 1), \tag{12}$$

so that $C_t^{(j)} = A_t^{(j)}$ and

$$W_j = \sum_{t=1}^{q-1} A_t^{(j)}. \tag{13}$$

5. **Step 5 (Radix-q Stitching Across Windows).** Process windows from most significant to least significant. Define $S_L := \mathcal{O}$ and

$$S_j := q\, S_{j+1} + W_j \qquad (j = L-1, \ldots, 0), \tag{14}$$

so that the final result is $S = S_0$. Since $q = 2^c$, multiplication by q is realized by c doublings:

$$q\, S_{j+1} = [2]^c S_{j+1}.$$

i.e per window: c doublings for the radix shift, plus one addition to add W_j.

4 Conclusion

Our goal here is to show, in simple terms, how our MSM algorithm performs over classical Pippenger's method and where it can go next. We first give an asymptotic cost comparison that isolates the three effects, shorter digit expansions, twice as many bases from the endomorphism split, resistance against timing attacks and small even-scalar fixups and show when the method is faster, tending toward a 25% saving as h grows. We then point to immediate next steps towards tighter non-asymptotic bounds, constant-time memory behavior, and portable implementations to guide adoption and further optimization.

4.1 Comparison

We provide a theoretical comparison of the savings incurred by our improvement of the Pippenger algorithm. From (4) we see that the cost of the original Pippenger algorithm is about

$$h(n + |B|)$$

with $n \approx |B| = q/2$. Our algorithm has the net effect of halving size of scalars at the cost of doubling the number of points to $2n$. Our new set $B = \{1, 3, \ldots, q-1\}$ has unchanged size $|B| = q/2$. However, the JT recoding only works for odd

Algorithm 5 . Split and Recode with merged digit packing and divisibility screening (updated)

Input: Scalars $a_1, \ldots, a_n \in [0, r)$; points $P_1, \ldots, P_n \in \mathcal{G}$; endomorphism $\phi(P)=\omega P$ with $\omega^3=1$, $\omega^2+\omega+1=0$; divisor $\nu \in \mathbb{Z}[\omega]$; window size c with $q=2^c$; nonzero signed-digit recoder Recode
Output: Unified digits $D_{k,j} \in \{\pm 1, \ldots, \pm(q-1)\}$ for $k \in \{1, \ldots, 2n\}$, $j \in \{0, \ldots, L-1\}$ (no zeros); window count L; compensation sum $\mathsf{Comp} \in \mathcal{G}$

1: $L \leftarrow 0$; $\mathsf{Comp} \leftarrow \mathcal{O}$
2: **for** $i \leftarrow 1$ **to** n **do**
3: $(\delta_i, \rho_i) \leftarrow \text{EuclideanDivision}(a_i, \nu)$ ▷ $a_i = \nu\delta_i + \rho_i$, ρ_i short
4: Write $\rho_i = \alpha_i + \omega\beta_i$ with $(\alpha_i, \beta_i) \in \mathbb{Z}^2$
5: $Q_i \leftarrow \phi(P_i) = \omega P_i$ ▷ no EC additions (endomorphism map)
6: **(Divisibility screen to ensure odd positive integer for recoding)**
7: **if** $\alpha_i \bmod 2 = 0$ **then**
8: $\alpha_i \leftarrow \alpha_i + 1$; $\mathsf{Comp} \leftarrow \mathsf{Comp} + P_i$ ▷ store $+P_i$ to add/subtract at the end
9: **if** $\beta_i \bmod 2 = 0$ **then**
10: $\beta_i \leftarrow \beta_i + 1$; $\mathsf{Comp} \leftarrow \mathsf{Comp} + Q_i$ ▷ store $+\omega P_i$
11: **(Nonzero signed recoding in base q)**
12: $(A_{i,0}, A_{i,1}, \ldots) \leftarrow$ JT Recoding(q, α_i) with $A_{i,j} \in \{\pm 1, \pm 3, \ldots, \pm(q-1)\}$
13: $(B_{i,0}, B_{i,1}, \ldots) \leftarrow$ JT Recoding(q, β_i) with $B_{i,j} \in \{\pm 1, \pm 3 \ldots, \pm(q-1)\}$
14: $L \leftarrow \max\big(L, \mathsf{len}(A_{i,\cdot}), \mathsf{len}(B_{i,\cdot})\big)$
15: **(Merge into unified digit matrix rows $1..2n$)**
16: **for** $j \leftarrow 0$ **to** $\mathsf{len}(A_{i,\cdot})-1$ **do**
17: $D_{i,j} \leftarrow A_{i,j}$
18: **for** $j \leftarrow 0$ **to** $\mathsf{len}(B_{i,\cdot})-1$ **do**
19: $D_{n+i,j} \leftarrow B_{i,j}$
20: **return** $D_{k,j}$, L, Comp

scalars. Our workaround was to adjust the even scalars in each half, after division by ν, by adding one and subtracting the corresponding base point. On average, we would have to do this for n of the $2n$ points, resulting in a final addition of n points. Hence, our method has an average cost of

$$\frac{h}{2}\left(2n + \frac{q}{2}\right) + n \ ,$$

which, compared to $h(n + q/2)$, gives a relative improvement of

$$\frac{qh/4 - n}{nh + qh/2} \approx \frac{1}{4} - \frac{n}{qh} \approx \frac{1}{4} - \frac{1}{2h} \ ,$$

which, as h grows, approaches 25%.

4.2 Future Work

As a projected future work we can strengthen the theory with deriving tight and non-asymptotic bounds for the average and worst case costs under zero-free

Algorithm 6 . Grouped bucket MSM with endomorphism (single pass over $2n$ bases) + final compensation add

Input: Base points $P_1, \ldots, P_n \in \mathcal{G}$; endomorphism $\phi(P)=\omega P$; window size c with $q=2^c$; unified digits $D_{k,j}$, window count L, and compensation sum Comp from Alg. 5

Output: $S = \sum_{i=1}^{n} a_i P_i$

1: **Build** $2n$**-point array (no EC additions)**: $\tilde{P}_k \leftarrow P_k$ for $k \leq n$; $\tilde{P}_k \leftarrow \phi(P_{k-n})$ for $k > n$
2: $S \leftarrow \mathcal{O}$
3: **for** $j \leftarrow L-1$ **down to** 0 **do** ▷ windows MSB→LSB
4: **Initialize** $B[1, 3, \ldots, q-1] \leftarrow \mathcal{O}$
5: **for** $k \leftarrow 1$ **to** $2n$ **do** ▷ branchless fill (nonzero digits)
6: $d \leftarrow D_{k,j}$; $t \leftarrow |d|$; $X \leftarrow \mathrm{sgn}(d) \cdot \tilde{P}_k$; $B[t] \leftarrow B[t] + X$
7: $A \leftarrow \mathcal{O}$; $W \leftarrow \mathcal{O}$ ▷ scan (running sum)
8: **for** $t \leftarrow q-1, q-3, \ldots, 1$ **do**
9: $A \leftarrow A + B[t]$; $W \leftarrow W + A$
10: **for** $\ell \leftarrow 1$ **to** c **do**
11: $S \leftarrow 2S$
12: $S \leftarrow S + W$
13: **Final compensation add:** $S \leftarrow S - \mathsf{Comp}$
14: **return** S

recoding, including the exact overhead of even scalar adjustments after division by ν. Furthermore, we expect to optimize window size c (hence $q = 2^c$) jointly with h and endomorphism parameters to minimize the full cost model. We can also extend the uniform or constant-time model to cover memory-access obliviousness and microarchitectural leakage. Finally, we aim to deliver portable, verified implementations on different platforms like AVX2/AVX-512, CUDA/HIP, FPGA etc. benchmarked on BLS12-381, BN254, and to measure end-to-end impact in zkSNARK/zkVM pipelines (arkworks, gnark, Halo2), including CRS orbit partitioning, MSM scheduling with FFT/NTT, and fixed-base or general-group extensions.

References

1. Avanzi, R.M., et al (eds.): Handbook of Elliptic and Hyperelliptic Curve Cryptography. Discrete Mathematics and Its Applications, 2nd edn. Chapman & Hall/CRC, Boca Raton, FL (2012)
2. Dutta, A., Hutchinson, A., Karabina, K.: Extending the signed non-zero bit and sign-aligned columns methods to general bases for use in cryptography. In: Bhargavan, K., Oswald, E., Prabhakaran, M. (eds.) INDOCRYPT 2020. LNCS, vol. 12578, pp. 248–270. Springer, Cham (2020). https://doi.org/10.1007/978-3-030-65277-7_11
3. Fan, X., Kuchta, V., Sica, F., Xu, L.: Speeding up multi-scalar multiplications for pairing-based zkSNARKs. J. Cryptol. **38**(21) (2025). https://doi.org/10.1007/s00145-025-09540-x

4. Gallant, R.P., Lambert, R.J., Vanstone, S.A.: Faster point multiplication on elliptic curves with efficient endomorphisms. In: Kilian, J. (ed.) CRYPTO 2001. LNCS, vol. 2139, pp. 190–200. Springer, Heidelberg (2001). https://doi.org/10.1007/3-540-44647-8_11
5. Gennaro, R., Gentry, C., Parno, B., Raykova, M.: Quadratic span programs and succinct NIZKs without PCPs. In: Johansson, T., Nguyen, P.Q. (eds.) EUROCRYPT 2013. LNCS, vol. 7881, pp. 626–645. Springer, Heidelberg (2013). https://doi.org/10.1007/978-3-642-38348-9_37
6. Groth, J.: On the size of pairing-based non-interactive arguments. In: Fischlin, M., Coron, J.-S. (eds.) EUROCRYPT 2016. LNCS, vol. 9666, pp. 305–326. Springer, Heidelberg (2016). https://doi.org/10.1007/978-3-662-49896-5_11
7. Joye, M., Tunstall, M.: Exponent recoding and regular exponentiation algorithms. In: Preneel, B. (ed.) AFRICACRYPT 2009. LNCS, vol. 5580, pp. 334–349. Springer, Heidelberg (2009). https://doi.org/10.1007/978-3-642-02384-2_21
8. Karabina, K.: A survey of scalar multiplication algorithms, chap. 20. In: Chung, F., Graham, R., Hoffman, F., Mullin, R.C., Hogben, L., West, D.B. (eds.) 50 Years of Combinatorics, Graph Theory, and Computing. Discrete Mathematics and Its Applications, pp. 359–386. Chapman and Hall/CRC, Boca Raton, FL (2019). https://doi.org/10.1201/9780429280092-20
9. Lu, T., et al.: cuZK: accelerating zero-knowledge proof with a faster parallel multi-scalar multiplication algorithm on GPUs. IACR Trans. Cryptographic Hardware Embedded Syst., 194–220 (2023). https://doi.org/10.46586/tches.v2023.i3.194-220
10. Luo, G., Fu, S., Gong, G.: Speeding up multi-scalar multiplication over fixed points towards efficient zkSNARKs. IACR Trans. Cryptogr. Hardw. Embed. Syst. **2023**(2), 358–380 (2023). https://doi.org/10.46586/tches.v2023.i2.358-380
11. Möller, B.: Securing elliptic curve point multiplication against side-channel attacks. In: Davida, G.I., Frankel, Y. (eds.) ISC 2001. LNCS, vol. 2200, pp. 324–334. Springer, Heidelberg (2001). https://doi.org/10.1007/3-540-45439-X_22
12. Pippenger, N.: On the evaluation of powers and related problems. In: Proceedings of the 17th Annual Symposium on Foundations of Computer Science, FOCS 1976, Houston, TX, USA, October 1976, pp. 258–263. IEEE Computer Society (1976). https://doi.org/10.1109/SFCS.1976.21, preliminary version
13. Straus, E.G.: Addition chains of vectors (problem 5125). Am. Math. Mon. **71**(7), 806–808 (1964). https://doi.org/10.2307/2310929, problems and Solutions
14. Okeya, K., Takagi, T.: The width-w NAF method provides small memory and fast elliptic scalar multiplications secure against side channel attacks. In: Joye, M. (ed.) CT-RSA 2003. LNCS, vol. 2612, pp. 328–343. Springer, Heidelberg (2003). https://doi.org/10.1007/3-540-36563-X_23
15. Xavier, C.F.: PipeMSM: hardware acceleration for multi-scalar multiplication. Cryptology ePrint Archive, Paper 2022/999 (2022). https://eprint.iacr.org/2022/999
16. Zhu, X., He, H., Yang, Z., Deng, Y., Zhao, L., Hou, R.: Elastic MSM: a fast, elastic and modular preprocessing technique for multi-scalar multiplication algorithm on GPUs. Cryptology ePrint Archive, Paper 2024/057 (2024). https://eprint.iacr.org/2024/057

Enhancing Scale and Shift Invariance in Deep Learning-Based Side-Channel Attacks Through Equivariant Convolutional Neural Networks

David Perez[1,4], Sengim Karayalcin[2], Stjepan Picek[1,3](✉), and Servio Paguada[4]

[1] Radboud University, Nijmegen, The Netherlands
{david.perezperez,stjepan.picek}@ru.nl
[2] Leiden University, Leiden, The Netherlands
karayalcins@vuw.leidenuniv.nl
[3] Faculty of Electrical Engineering and Computing, University of Zagreb, Zagreb, Croatia
[4] Ikerlan, Gipuzkoa, Spain
slpaguada@ikerlan.es

Abstract. Deep learning-based side-channel analysis (DLSCA) has demonstrated remarkable performance over the past few years. Even with limited preprocessing and feature engineering, DLSCA can break protected targets, sometimes requiring only a single attack trace. In the DLSCA context, the commonly investigated countermeasures are Boolean masking and desynchronization. While the exact mechanisms of how DLSCA breaks masking are less understood, the core idea behind handling desynchronization is simple. Convolutional neural networks (CNNs) are shift invariant, allowing them to overcome desynchronization. However, considering the importance and practicality of desynchronization countermeasures, we know remarkably little about the limits of CNNs or how to enhance their capabilities when dealing with desynchronization.

In this work, we begin with the theoretical foundations of shift and temporal scale equivariance. Afterward, we build a neural network model allowing such equivariance and test it against several commonly considered targets. Our results demonstrate that equivariant CNNs are robust, easy to design, and achieve excellent attack performance. More precisely, we showcase how such a simple model can even outperform recent transformer-based neural networks. Finally, we demonstrate the practical relevance of scale equivariance by showing how an equivariant CNN can learn leakage from a device operating at one clock frequency and generalize to a device with a different clock frequency, a result not previously demonstrated in DLSCA.

Keywords: Side-channel Analysis · Invariance · Equivariance · Neural Networks

F. -H. Liu (Ed.): CT-RSAC 2026, LNCS 16496, pp. 198–228, 2026.
https://doi.org/10.1007/978-3-032-22931-1_8

1 Introduction

Side-channel analysis (SCA) has received significant attention from the research community in the last three decades. In such attacks, the relationship between secret-dependent computations and (physical) leakages (e.g., timing and power consumption) from cryptographic implementations is exploited to extract secret information [Koc96,KJJ99]. Today, there are many variations of side-channel attacks, but a common distinction is between direct and profiling attacks. In direct attacks, one could require millions of traces from the device under attack to obtain secret information. Profiling attacks, while depending on a stronger threat model, can also result in significantly more powerful attack performance than direct attacks [CRR02]. Indeed, in profiling attacks, if the attacker builds a good profile (template or machine learning model), the attack may require only a single trace from the device under attack. More recently, the SCA community has devoted significant efforts to profiling attacks based on machine (deep) learning (see [MPP16,ZBHV20,PWP22]), as such attacks could deliver optimal attack performance[1] with only limited manual effort in mounting the attack. In deep learning-based SCA, the most common approach today is to use a convolutional neural network (CNN) to build a profiling model [PPM+23]. One of the main advantages of CNNs over other deep learning architectures (e.g., multilayer perceptrons) is their shift invariance, which allows them to (partially) defeat desynchronization countermeasures. As such, the notion of shift invariance is often mentioned in the DLSCA literature [HSAM22,HCM24,KWPP24]. Still, very little effort has been made to understand what this notion truly means in the context of SCA.

Clearly, using CNNs without further consideration of invariance (and equivariance) is insufficient. Numerous studies have shown that larger desynchronization levels are more difficult to overcome, and sufficiently large desynchronization levels can also prevent the attack [CDP17,PPM+23,HSAM22]. The main approach to address this issue is to use data augmentation techniques to induce robustness during training [CDP17], but this limits the invariance to what the levels of desynchronization the model has seen during training [KWPP24]. Another direction to resolve this issue is to consider more recent developments in deep learning, where transformer-based architectures, combined with data augmentation, can handle longer measurements and larger desynchronization [HSAM22,HCM24]. In this work, we aim to determine whether understanding the notions of invariance and equivariance with respect to SCA can help design adapted CNNs that are robust to such transformations.

We begin by establishing the relevant theoretical foundations of invariance and equivariance in the context of SCA. We note that while these aspects are known in the general literature, to our knowledge, they have not been discussed in detail in the DLSCA context. Afterward, we design a neural network architecture that is equivariant, and we demonstrate its robustness to various transformations. More precisely, we conduct an extensive experimental analysis across

[1] Optimal performance is breaking a target with a single attack trace.

five datasets and three neural network models, demonstrating that an equivariant convolutional neural network can outperform even a transformer network. Our main contributions are:

- We establish a DLSCA design approach by utilizing equivariant and invariant operations with respect to a predetermined set of transformations against which we want the models to be robust. Based on this approach, we propose a CNN that is equivariant to relevant transformations, which we denote by EquivNet.[2] More precisely, we propose a convolutional model that is robust against shift changes and resilient to signal temporal scale changes.
- We conduct experimental analysis on five datasets and three neural network models, and demonstrate that equivariant CNNs can outperform even recent transformer-based architectures on datasets ASCADv1, AES_RD, and ESHARD. We also tested the robustness of the models against desynchronization and time dilation transformations, showing how EquivNet was generally the best-performing model.
- By experimentally comparing EquivNet and other CNN-based models against traces of varying scales, we show that EquivNet's ability to extract multi-scale features leads to more effective attacks.
- To assess the robustness of models to changes in device clock-frequency, we create datasets Nucleo_96MHz and Nucleo_168MHz,[3] to be used by the SCA community. With those, we performed a transfer of learning experiment, showing how EquivNet could attack traces generated with a clock frequency different from the one involved in its training.

1.1 Related Work

Since the introduction of deep learning to SCA in 2016 [MPP16], a large number of works have investigated improving profiling methods [PPM+23]. One of the main advantages of using DL for SCA is that networks can be resilient to the effects of transformations in the trace triggered by hiding countermeasures. Such transformations can be in the amplitude domain, where Gaussian noise is added to the traces [KPH+19], and in the temporal domain, where traces are misaligned due to, e.g., clock-jitter or random delays [CDP17].

In DLSCA, dealing with desynchronized traces is a common scenario that motivates numerous investigations, see, e.g., [HSAM22, KWPP24]. This is related to the desynchronization of traces, which is a common consequence of side-channel countermeasures, such as random delay insertion and dummy operation insertion. A common approach to creating desynchronization-robust models involves using data augmentation techniques [LZW+21], which increases the computational cost of training. Cagli et al. [CDP17] first considered using data augmentation to mitigate the effects of clock jitter, indicating that convolutional networks can effectively handle some misalignment in the traces. With

[2] The EquivNet code can be found at https://shorturl.at/lxW7K.

[3] Nucleo datasets can be found at https://shorturl.at/iV1zH.

the introduction of the ASCAD database in 2018 [BPS+20], which included artificially desynchronized versions, the robustness of networks to these desynchronizations became a standard benchmark for evaluating novel model architectures and methodologies.

More recently, there has been interest in the DLSCA community in the consequences for the leakage when changing the clock frequency of a cryptographic device [LCCR22]. This happens when the same device is used with different clock frequencies, because of the design or the environment in which it operates (thermal throttling). This is a consequence of the direct relation between frequency, power consumption, and heat generated. Concurrently, efforts have been made searching for optimal time-scales of the kernels used in CNN-based SCA [ZBHV20, PA20] and how features learned at different time scales can be combined to create more efficient attacks [HZG+24]. Zhou and Standaert [ZS20] showed that deep learning does not fully annihilate the need for re-synchronization and introduced a ResNet architecture to address desynchronization. Wu and Picek [WP20] showed that autoencoders can be trained to remove the effects of desynchronization (and other hiding countermeasures) if an attacker can capture a "clean" set of traces without these effects. Finally, Krček et al. [KWPP24] explored the robustness of CNNs to shifts by testing how various levels of data augmentation affect the robustness of convolutional networks to shifts.

The effectiveness of a CNN-based SCA is significantly influenced by the size and number of trainable parameters of the kernels used. As shown by Zaid et al. [ZBHV20], using small filters resulted in models whose intermediate values were less affected by the noise and redundancy of the features in the traces. On the other hand, Paguada and Armendariz [PA20] showed how the use of dilated kernels with large receptive fields allowed the convolutional layers to reduce overfitting. This reduction is achieved by analyzing at the same time more global features, composed of the leakage of the intermediate AES values and the masking countermeasure. He et al. [HZG+24] demonstrated how using convolutional layers with kernels of different sizes simultaneously resulted in increased model efficiency.

More recently, transformer-based models [VSP+17] have received attention from the SCA community due to their ability to handle long-range dependencies. Jin et al. [JZHY20] introduced attention-based modules inside convolutional blocks. Hajra et al. [HSAM22] introduced transformer-based architectures that are invariant to shifts in traces. In subsequent work, Hajra et al. introduced the EstraNet model [HCM24], which significantly improves the computational efficiency of attention mechanisms in these networks. This network could be considered state-of-the-art in DLSCA for transformer architectures. The level of robustness to shifts for both convolutional and transformer models often depends on the level of shifts occurring in the training dataset. However, Hajra et al. [HSAM22] demonstrated that TransNet could overcome this dependency, successfully attacking traces with larger shifts than those used in the training dataset. They linked this behavior with the use of a global average pooling.

We will examine this aspect further in the context of group equivariant deep learning. In this area, works like [CW16,RBTH20,WW19] study deep learning models that are naturally robust to a selected group of transformations over the input.

2 Group Equivariant Deep Learning

Group equivariant deep learning is a branch of geometric deep learning [BBCV21] initiated by Cohen and Welling [CW16], that attempts to define convolutional models that are naturally robust to transformations such as translations, rotations, and reflections of images. This was achieved by using models composed of a sequence of equivariant layers, followed by an invariant pooling operation with respect to the transformations the model should take into account.

These transformations are defined as a group $(G, *)$, where G is a set and $*$ is its binary operation under which the elements of G are closed. The equivariance of a mapping $f : X \rightarrow Y$ is formalized using a group G and two G-sets[4] X and Y. A mapping f is said to be equivariant if and only if

$$f(g * x) = g' * f(x), \tag{1}$$

for all $x \in X$ and $g, g' \in G$ that fulfill $g = g'$. When conditions are met, the function is called G-equivariant. If g' is the identity, the function is G-invariant.

Observe that desynchronization can be seen as a translation element $H_\theta \in G$, acting over an input f as $H_\theta * f(x) = f(H_\theta^{-1} * x) = f(x - \theta)$. Therefore, architectures incorporating translation-equivariant components, like convolutional layers, followed by invariant elements have shown advantages at generating models with built-in invariance to translations [BB21,LCY14].

Cohen and Welling [CW16] further generalized the convolution operation by making it equivariant not only to translations but to any element $g \in G$, defining the group convolution. Its formula is shown in Eq. (2), where $g, h \in G$, ψ is the kernel, f is the input function, $\circ$ is the composition operation, $\tilde{*}$ is the group convolution operator, and $d\mu(h)$ is the Haar measure over the group G.

$$(f \tilde{*} \psi)(g) = \int d\mu(h)\ f(h)\psi(g^{-1} \circ h). \tag{2}$$

2.1 Temporal-Scale Equivariance

Temporal-scale or time dilation transformations are elements $T_\alpha \in G$ that act on a function f as $T_\alpha * f(x) = f(T_\alpha^{-1} * x) = f(\alpha^{-1} x)$, where $\alpha \in \mathbb{R}^+$ is a positive real value known as the time dilation factor. Changing the clock frequency of a cryptographic device results in the same operations being performed in a shorter

[4] A G-set is a mathematical object consisting of a set S and a group action of G on S.

or longer amount of time. Additionally, changing the sample rate of the oscilloscope used to obtain the traces also changes the time scale of the same signal. Thus, achieving time-scale consistency between profiling and target traces poses a significant challenge. If $f(x)$ is the trace generated, it is related to its version obtained after changing the clock's frequency by $f(x) \sim f(\alpha^{-1}x) = T_\alpha * f(x)$. This results in time dilations being theoretically equivalent to changing the clock's frequency. In this situation, a convolution is not enough to analyze traces that differ in the frequency used to generate them. Since the convolutions are not equivariant to time dilations [AW19], as shown in Eq. (3), a standard CNN model will require training and data augmentation to build the time dilation robustness required to attack traces without depending on the clock's frequency used to generate them.

$$(T_\alpha * f\tilde{*}\psi)(y) = \int dx \; T_\alpha * f(x)\psi(x-y) = \int dx \; f(\alpha^{-1}x)\psi(x-y) \quad (3)$$

next, substitution is applied: $\alpha x' = x$.

$$\alpha \int dx' f(x')\psi\left(\alpha x' - y\right) \neq (f\tilde{*}\psi)(\alpha^{-1}y) = T_\alpha * (f\tilde{*}\psi)(y).$$

Group equivariant deep learning defines another way to approach this problem, through the use of time-scale equivariant layers [RBTH20,WW19,SMS21]. These models use a sequence of time dilation equivariant layers followed by a time dilation invariant layer. This ensures built-in robustness against time dilation transformations of the input. Since changing the clock's frequency results in theoretically equivalent traces to those obtained after applying a time dilation transform, the equivariant model would have an advantage over the non-equivariant one.

Given that the input analyzed by the model will consist of 1-D temporal signals, two types of time dilation equivariant layers are needed: the Lifting and the Time-Scale group convolutions. Both of them have their origin in the group convolution defined in Sect. 2. The Lifting convolution (Λ) [RBTH20] is a mapping that takes a function as input and returns its convolved version. It is used as the first convolutional layer in the model and is defined as a time-scale equivariant layer. This layer takes as input a trace $f(x)$ and lifts it to a higher-dimensional vector space that includes the convolved $f(x)$ along with the time-dilated convolved versions of it. This results in an output with a time dimension and a time dilation dimension. It is defined as shown in Eq. (4).

$$\Lambda(f)(y,s) = \int dx f(x)\frac{1}{s}\psi\left(\frac{x-y}{s}\right). \quad (4)$$

In Eq. (4), s is the time dilation factor and $\frac{1}{s}$ has its origin in the Haar measure over the group of translations not being invariant to time dilations $T_s \in G$ with $s \in R^+$. Thus, $dx = d\mu(x) \neq d\mu(T_s * x) = d\mu(sx) = s\ d(x) = s\ d\mu(x)$. To compensate for the change in the measure, it needs to be multiplied by $\frac{1}{s}$. Notice that ψ represents the trainable kernels used in the layer.

The Lifting convolution is equivariant to time dilation transformations $T_\alpha \in G$ as shown in Eq. (5).

$$\Lambda(T_\alpha * f)(y,s) = \int dx f(\alpha^{-1}x)\frac{1}{s}\psi\left(\frac{x-y}{s}\right) \tag{5}$$

when: $x = \alpha x'$.

$$\int dx' f(x')\frac{1}{\alpha^{-1}s}\psi\left(\frac{x'-\alpha^{-1}y}{\alpha^{-1}s}\right) = T_\alpha * \Lambda(f)(y,s).$$

The Time-Scale group convolution (Ω) [RBTH20] is a mapping that takes a function as input and returns its convolved version. It differs from the Lifting convolution in that the input and output have both time dimension (x, y) and time dilation dimension (p, s). This contrasts with the Lifting convolution that takes as input an object with only a time dimension. In this domain time dilation transformation T_α acts over a function $f(x,p)$ as $T_\alpha * f(x,p) = f(T_\alpha^{-1} * x, T_\alpha^{-1} * p) = f(\alpha^{-1}x, \alpha^{-1}p)$, with $\alpha \in R^+$. The formula for Ω is given in Eq. (6).

$$\Omega(f)(y,s) = \int dxdp f(x,p)\frac{1}{s^2}\psi\left(\frac{x-y}{s}, \frac{p}{s}\right). \tag{6}$$

In Eq. (6), similarly to the case of Lifting convolution, $\frac{1}{s^2}$ has its origin in the Haar measure over the group of translations not being invariant under time dilations T_s. Then, $dxdp = d\mu(x,p) \neq d\mu(T_s * (x,p)) = d\mu(sx, sp) = d(sx)d(sp) = s^2\ dxdp = s^2\ d\mu(x,p)$. To compensate for the change in the measure, in this case, it needs to be multiplied by $\frac{1}{s^2}$. Notice also that ψ represents the trainable kernels. The Time-Scale group convolution is equivariant to time dilation transformations $T_\alpha \in G$ as shown in Eq. (7).

$$\Omega(T_\alpha * f)(y,s) = \int dxdp f(\alpha^{-1}x, \alpha^{-1}p)\frac{1}{s^2}\psi\left(\frac{x-y}{s}, \frac{p}{s}\right) \tag{7}$$

next, substitutions are applied: $x = \alpha x',\ p = \alpha p'$.

$$\int dx'dp' f(x',p')\frac{1}{(\alpha^{-1}s)^2}\psi\left(\frac{x'-\alpha^{-1}y}{\alpha^{-1}s}, \frac{p'}{\alpha^{-1}s}\right) = T_\alpha * \Omega(f)(y,s).$$

To be able to dilate with s, the kernels ψ used in the Lifting and Time-Scale group convolution, it is required that they are continuous. The Lifting convolution's kernel is defined as:

$$\psi(x) = \sum_k^{TK} w^k B(x - \tau^k). \tag{8}$$

The Time-Scale group convolution's kernel is defined as:

$$\psi(x,p) = \sum_h^{TSK}\sum_k^{TK} w^{h,k} B(x-\tau^k)\delta(p-\beta^h). \tag{9}$$

Equations (8) and (9) show how the kernel ψ is defined as the weighted sum of a group of bell-shaped functions approximated with B-splines of second order (B). In the case of the Time-Scale group convolution, the functions are also multiplied by Dirac delta functions (δ). w^k and $w^{h,k}$ are the weight matrices of the kernel. $\tau^k \in \mathbb{Z}$ is a vector representing the centers (in the temporal dimension) of the B-splines. $\beta^h \in \mathbb{Z}$ is a vector representing the centers (in the time dilation dimension) of the Dirac functions. $k, h \in \mathbb{Z}$ are the indices used in the sums, with cardinality equal to TK and TSK, respectively. TK and TSK are hyperparameters that define the number of trainable weights w used to obtain a feature map with the Lifting and the Time-Scale group convolution layers.

Given the continuous definitions of Lifting and Time-Scale group convolutions, it is necessary to discretize to allow their usage with computers. This can be done by using the approximation $\int dx f(x) \approx \sum_i \Delta x^i f^i$, where Δx^i and f^i are vectors given by $\Delta x^i = x^i - x^{i-1}$ and $f^i = f(x^i)$. Notice that x^i is an ordered succession of x values and $i \in \mathbb{N}$ is an index. In the case of the Lifting (Λ) and Time-Scale (Ω) group convolutions the time domain gets discretized as $x^i \in \mathbb{Z}$, resulting in $dx \approx \Delta x^i = 1$ and $y^j \in \mathbb{Z}$. The time scale dimension gets discretized using the powers of the scalar hyperparameter factor $S \in \mathbb{R}^+$, $p^m = S^m \in \mathbb{R}^+$. This results in $dp \approx \Delta p^m = S^m - S^{m-1} = (S-1)S^{m-1} \in \mathbb{R}^+$, $s = S^n \in \mathbb{R}^+$. Notice that in this case, $i, j, m, n \in \mathbb{N}$ are indices used in the vectors.

The discretized versions of the Lifting (Λ) and Time-Scale (Ω) group convolutions, are as follows:

$$\Lambda(f)^{j,n} = \sum_i f^i \frac{1}{S^n} \psi_n^{i-j}. \tag{10}$$

$$\Omega(f)^{j,n} = \sum_{i,m} f^{i,m} \frac{(S-1)S^{m-1}}{S^{2n}} \psi_n^{i-j,m-n}. \tag{11}$$

Notice that $f^i = f(x^i)$, $f^{i,m} = f(x^i, S^m)$, $\psi_n^{i-j} = \psi\left(\frac{x^i - y^j}{S^n}\right)$, and $\psi_n^{i-j,m-n} = \psi\left(\frac{x^i - y^j}{S^n}, \frac{S^m}{S^n}\right)$. When dealing with the time dilation elements s, p, it is necessary to define a finite domain for them. As the number of time dilation transformations is infinite, it is compulsory to define a finite number of them to be used in the computations. This, along with $s = S^n$, $p = S^m$, provokes the establishment of maximum and minimum values for n and m. To minimize aliasing when sampling the dilated kernels, the minimum values of n and m are set to 0. TSK defines the maximum of the time dilation dimension of the kernels, while the maximum value of n is denoted by n_scales.

The Lifting and Time Dilation group convolution uses time-dilated kernels with different time dilation factors. This use of kernels of different sizes in the same model should provoke benefits similar to the ones obtained in [HZG+24]. Apart from these two advantages, the Lifting and Time-Scale group convolution should have two extra benefits. First, in comparison to the model of He et al. [HZG+24], the combined use of feature maps obtained with kernels of different sizes is executed in each Time Dilation group equivariant convolution, instead of just before the feed-forward network. This should allow a richer analysis by the model. Second, Young's convolution inequality [Bog07], shown in Eq. (12), states that the L^1-norm[5] of the convolution is less than or equal to the product of the L^1-norm of the functions involved. Because of this, changing the unit norm of the kernel changes the maximum limit of the unit norm of the convolution. As shown in Eq. (13), modifying the kernel size results in changes to its unit norm. Consequently, using larger kernels can lead to larger values in their feature maps. These values could receive more importance from the model because of the size of the kernels used.

$$\int dy |(f \tilde{*} \psi)(y)| \leq \left(\int dx |f(x)| \right) \left(\int dx |\psi(x-y)| \right). \tag{12}$$

$$\int dx \; |\psi\left(\frac{x-y}{s}\right)| \xrightarrow{x=y+sx'} s \int dx' |\psi(x')|. \tag{13}$$

Contrarily, the unit norm of the kernels used in the Lifting and Time Dilation group convolutions is invariant to the change in their size, as shown in Eqs. (14) and (15).

$$\int dx \; |\frac{1}{s}\psi(\frac{x-y}{s})| \xrightarrow{x=y+\alpha x'} \int dx' |\psi(x')|. \tag{14}$$

$$\int dxdp \; |\frac{1}{s^2}\psi(\frac{x-y}{s}, \frac{p}{s})| \xrightarrow[p=sp']{x=y+sx'} \int dx'dp' |\psi(x', p')|. \tag{15}$$

3 The EquivNet Model

Next, we introduce the EquivNet Model, a classification model developed based on the principles of group equivariant deep learning. It consists of a sequence of four convolutional blocks (convolution + pooling layer) and three fully connected layers. The details can be found in Table 4 and the code for the EquivNet can be found at https://shorturl.at/lxW7K. The Lifting and Time-Scale group convolution layers used in the convolutional blocks are both equivariant to temporal translation $H_\theta \in G$, along with time dilations $T_\alpha \in G$, as shown in Eqs. (16) and (17). Notice that $\circ$ is the composition operator, and H_θ does not change the time-scale of the signal, leaving p invariant. Finally, the use of global average pooling as the invariant function, connecting the last convolutional block and the first fully connected layer, makes the EquivNet model theoretically robust to both temporal translation and time dilations.

[5] L^1-norm of function f is equal to $\int_{-\infty}^{\infty} dx|f(x)|$, being $|f(x)|$ the absolute value of function f, evaluated in x.

$$\Lambda((T_\alpha \circ H_\theta) * f)(y, s) = \int dx f\left(\frac{x-\theta}{\alpha}\right) \frac{1}{s} \psi\left(\frac{x-y}{s}\right) \tag{16}$$

then, substitution is applied: $x = \theta + \alpha x'$.

$$\int dx' f(x') \frac{1}{\alpha^{-1}s} \psi\left(\frac{x' - \alpha^{-1}(y-\theta))}{\alpha^{-1}s}\right) = (T_\alpha \circ H_\theta) * \Lambda(f)(y, s).$$

$$\Omega((T_\alpha \circ H_\theta) * f)(y, s) = \int dx dp f(\alpha^{-1}(x-\theta), \alpha^{-1}p) \frac{1}{s^2} \psi\left(\frac{x-y}{s}, \frac{p}{s}\right) \tag{17}$$

with the following substitutions applied: $x = \alpha x' + \theta, p = \alpha p'$.

$$\int dx' dp' f(x', p') \frac{1}{(\alpha^{-1}s)^2} \psi\left(\frac{x' - \alpha^{-1}(y-\theta)}{\alpha^{-1}s}, \frac{p'}{\alpha^{-1}s}\right) =$$
$$= (T_\alpha \circ H_\theta) * \Omega(f)(y, s).$$

While preprocessing can improve performance [HZG+24], our model requires the preprocessing layer to be equivariant to time dilations ($T_\alpha \in G$) and translations ($H_\theta \in G$). A non-equivariant step would break the symmetry of subsequent group convolutions, compromising the model's built-in robustness. We selected BatchNorm1D as it meets this requirement. It normalizes the input using a global mean ($\mu \in \mathbb{R}$) and standard deviation ($\sigma \in \mathbb{R}$) computed across the entire signal. Since these scalar statistics are invariant to T_α and H_θ, the BatchNorm1D operation itself is equivariant. In contrast, techniques like MinMaxScaler and StandardScaler are not equivariant. They compute position-dependent mean $\boldsymbol{\mu} \in \mathbb{R}^n$ and standard deviation $\boldsymbol{\sigma} \in \mathbb{R}^n$, which are not invariant to these time-based transformations.

Another difference EquivNet has from other CNNs used in DLSCA is the use of the GELU activation function [HG23] in the convolutional blocks. GELU is a nonlinear, infinitely differentiable function whose formula can be found in Eq. (18).

$$GELU(x) = \frac{x}{2}\left(1 + tanh\left(\sqrt{\frac{2}{\pi}}(x + 0.044715x^3)\right)\right). \tag{18}$$

Regarding the hyperparameters of the Lifting and Time-Scale group convolution, we set the default base of the time dilation factor S to 1.2. n_scales is set to 7 for all experiments in Sect. 5. Lastly, TSK is set to 3. The primary reason for selecting these values is the trade-off between the model's computational cost and its robustness against time dilation. Increasing S, TSK, TK, and n_scales results in a larger number of more expensive convolutions. Equivariance is achieved by using finite sets formed from dilated versions of each kernel, where S (dilation base) and n_scale (dimension size) define the window of α-time dilation transformations to which EquivNet is theoretically robust.

Since the convolution between a kernel and a signal remains equal as long as both are equally time-dilated, the maximum time dilation for which this holds in EquivNet is $S^{n\_scales-1}$. If the signal is dilated more than this, the convolutions will not yield results related to those of the non-dilated signal. Time compression behaves symmetrically, making the theoretical interval of robustness for a dilation factor α $S^{-(n\_scales-1)} \leq \alpha < S^{n\_scales-1}$.

Notice that this defines a theoretical boundary; the effective boundary is smaller in practice. This is since, in an extreme case, a signal and its $S^{n\_scales-1}$-dilated version create outputs that are only related by the smallest and largest kernels of the set. The remaining kernels yield unrelated results, introducing noise and reducing EquivNet's efficiency.

4 Nucleo Dataset

To investigate the knowledge transferability of a model against changes in the clock frequency of the SCA target device, we acquired Nucleo datasets. These datasets include Nucleo_96MHz.h5 and Nucleo_168MHz. The datasets were obtained from a Nucleo-F429RZI board with a Nucleo Cortex-M4, 256 KB of RAM, and 2 MB of flash memory. The device executes AES-128 without any countermeasure against side-channel attacks. We use a probe to measure the electromagnetic emissions emitted by the device, which were then sampled and saved, forming the traces with an Lecroy WaveRunner9404M oscilloscope with 1 GS/s of sample frequency. The equipment allowed us to obtain the traces for the clock's frequencies of 96 MHz and 168 MHz, resulting in Nucleo_96MHz.h5 and Nucleo_168MHz.h5, respectively. As discussed in Sect. 2.1, the operations that need to be done to execute AES are still the same. Consequently, the biggest effect of changing the clock's frequency is that the time needed to perform the algorithm varies. It is also important to note that even though, ideally, changing the frequency should provoke the time dilation of the reference traces, most electronic components used on the devices exhibit behavior changes with the frequency of the electric signal. This is the case of capacitors and inductors whose impedance depends on the frequency. This dependence causes that in real-world scenarios, the relation between traces obtained for different clock frequency values to differ in more than one time dilation transformation. The datasets include profiling traces obtained for different plaintexts and keys. The attack traces were obtained for a fixed key and different plaintexts. Nucleo_96MHz and Nucleo_168MHz include the raw traces measured, with 90 000 and 50 000 samples, respectively. Both datasets include 100 000 profiling traces and 50 000 attack traces. The Nucleo datasets are publicly available at Zenodo.[6]

We calculated the absolute value of the Pearson correlation coefficient $|r|$ of the samples in the profiling traces and the first byte in the intermediate value. The result is displayed in Fig. 1. In each graph of Fig. 1, a main peak with a correlation magnitude exceeding 0.3 can be seen. The samples of the peaks leak more information about the target byte than the rest of the trace. Notice also how the positions of the samples that leak the most information for each dataset are related. As we mentioned, the number of operations required to execute AES

[6] https://shorturl.at/iV1zH.

(N_{op}) remains the same across the datasets. Thus, knowing that the clock's frequencies are used to define the speed at which operations are performed, the positions with maximum leakage, 11 275 for Nucleo_168MHz and 19 295 for Nucleo_96MHz, are related by $N_{op} = 11275 \cdot 168 \approx 19295 \cdot 96$.

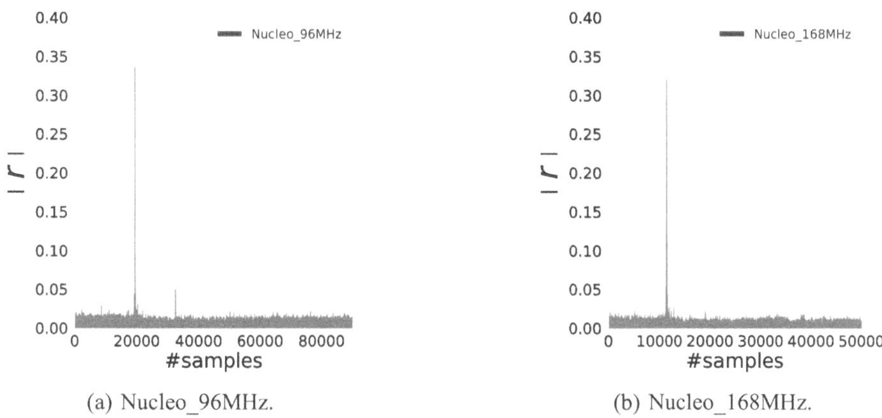

(a) Nucleo_96MHz.

(b) Nucleo_168MHz.

Fig. 1. Absolute value of the Pearson correlation coefficient between the traces and the first byte of the intermediate value, for datasets Nucleo_168MHz and Nucleo_96MHz.

5 Experimental Results

5.1 Experimental Settings and Methodology

The training setup consists of 100 epochs of training, using a batch size of 256 traces. The training dataset contains the entire profiling dataset. We employed the ADAM optimizer and the CrossEntropy loss function. Finally, the learning rate was managed by the OneCyleLR scheduler. It is configured with a maximum learning rate equal to 5E-3, and the warm-up process occupies 40% of the training process. The datasets used were AES_RD, ASCADr, ASCADf, ESHARD, with details provided in Appendix C, and Nucleo in Sect. 4.

The guessing entropy (GE) was used to evaluate the effectiveness achieved by the model trained for every epoch. This way, after training for 100 epochs, we can observe the evolution of GE with the training. We select the best version of each model, i.e., the one that obtained the lowest number of traces needed to reach GE equal to 0 ($N_{GE=0}$). If GE did not reach 0 for any epoch, then we select the one that reaches the lowest value of GE for the maximum number of attacking traces used. We repeat the training runs 5 times, obtaining from each run the best versions of the models. Using these models, we calculate the average guessing entropy of the model. This serves to reduce the dependence of the results on the initialization of the model. We compare our results with EffCNN from Zaid et al. [ZBHV20] and EstraNet from Hajra et al. [HCM24].

If possible, taking into account the dataset used, we employed the configuration given by the authors of the models. If not, we used a configuration from another compatible dataset. For EffCNN, we used the configuration given in [PA20] for ASCADr with ESHARD and Nucleo datasets. For EstraNet, we selected the configuration given for ASCADr, and we also utilized the training configuration specified by the authors.

5.2 Study of the Dilation Factor S

The EquivNet model is defined by a time dilation factor, S, which is used to generate dilated versions of the model's kernels. This parameter is expected to influence the model's effectiveness against time-dilated side-channel traces. To investigate this influence and justify our choice of $S = 1.2$ for all subsequent experiments, we trained a set of EquivNet models with varying S values on ASCADf and ASCADr datasets. During training, we saved a checkpoint of the model after each epoch. To identify the best performance for each value of S, we then evaluated every saved checkpoint by performing an attack with 1000 traces, artificially time-dilated by a factor α ranging from 0.5 to 1.5. To resample the traces, we have used the resample function from scipy.[7] The metric reported is the lowest guessing entropy (GE (1000)) value achieved across all epochs. To enhance the comparison between ASCADf and ASCADr, we divided every value by the maximum GE(1000) value found in each case, thereby normalizing the graph. The results of this analysis are presented in Fig. 2.

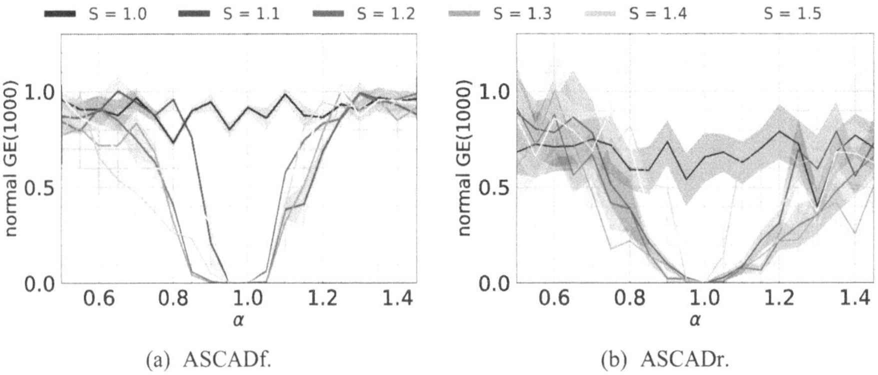

(a) ASCADf. (b) ASCADr.

Fig. 2. Evaluation of the minimum guessing entropy reached by EquivNet during the training in relation to the value S used in the architecture and the α factor for ASCADr and ASCADf traces.

Figure 2 reveals two main findings. First, the model without kernel dilation ($S = 1.0$) shows poor performance, yielding a guessing entropy of approximately

[7] https://docs.scipy.org/doc/scipy/reference/generated/scipy.signal.resample.html.

80 in ASCADf and 40 in ASCADr for all tested values of α. Second, models configured with $S > 1$ present cup shape performance curves with small differences, for instance, in the case of ASCADf with $\alpha < 1$, models with $S = 1.4$ and 1.5 exhibit the lowest values, whereas for all α values in ASCADr, the best results are achieved by $S = 1.2$ and 1.3. Notably, $S = 1.2$ and $S = 1.3$ consistently achieve low GE values for both ASCADf and ASCADr across the entire range of α. Thus, we selected $S = 1.2$ for our experiments, as it offers a similar level of robustness to time dilation as $S = 1.3$ but at a lower computational cost. This cost-saving is because a larger S value results in larger kernels.

5.3 Performance Evaluation

We train the models to attack the datasets AES_RD, ESHARD, ASCADf, and ASCADr. We provide the results in Fig. 3 and Table 6.

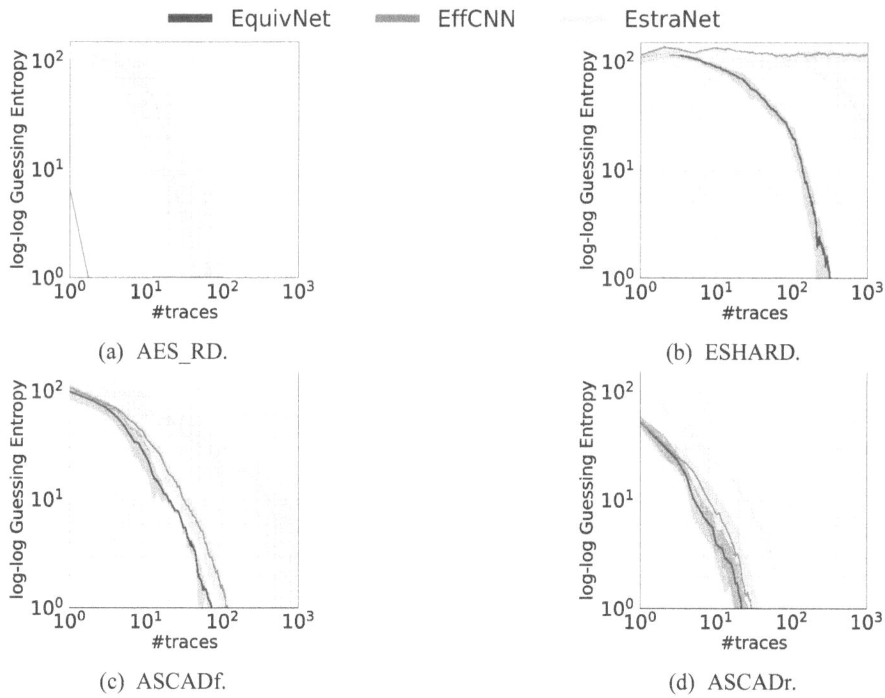

Fig. 3. Log-log representations of the average guessing entropy function obtained by each model attacking different datasets.

The results show that EquivNet achieved GE of 0 using only a single trace on the AES_RD dataset. As such, this results in EquivNet not appearing in the log-log plot of Fig. 3. For the ESHARD dataset, EquivNet was the only model among those evaluated to perform a successful attack. Furthermore, for the ASCADf and ASCADr datasets, EquivNet demonstrated the most rapidly decreasing GE curves when compared to EstraNet and EffCNN. To compare the models in terms of computational cost, we trained each model with the ASCADr dataset using a NVIDIA A100-SXM4-40GB and took the computational measures shown in Table 1. There we can see that EquivNet is more demanding to train than EstraNet or EffCNN as it required 64 min, whereas EstraNet and EffCNN required 15 min and 53 min, respectively. EquivNet is also the largest in terms of the number of parameters, but it requires less RAM during inference than EstraNet. Finally, the inference time required to process a batch of 256 traces shows similar results to the training times.

Table 1. Results of the computational costs of every tested model, obtained from training them with ASCADr.

	EquivNet	**EffCNN**	**EstraNet**
Number of parameters	864286	108828	349312
Ram used	3.36 MB	0.37 MB	9.83 MB
Training time	64 min	15 min	53 min
Inference time	54.50 ms	13.40 ms	45.44 ms

5.4 Model Evaluation with the Profiling Complexity

We are interested in studying the impact of training set size and training epochs on model performance. To evaluate it, we have trained EquivNet, EffCNN, and EstraNet using the synchronized ASCADr dataset with different values for the training epochs and the percentage of the dataset used for training. The results obtained are presented in Fig. 4.

Figure 4b shows that EstraNet's performance improves with larger training datasets. However, EquivNet and EffCNN still achieve lower $N_{GE=0}$ scores across all cases. Moreover, EstraNet failed to execute attacks when trained with 20% or lower of the profiling dataset used for training, whereas EquivNet and EffCNN still managed to attack. Notably, EquivNet obtained the lowest $N_{GE=0}$ for every case, even requiring an average $N_{GE=0}$ of 335 when trained on 10% of the profiling dataset. Even when trained on 5% of the profiling dataset, EquivNet achieved an average guessing entropy of 16.7 at 2000 traces, whereas EstraNet performed no better than random guessing. These findings support the hypothesis that EstraNet requires more training data than CNN-based models.

Similarly, Fig. 4a indicates that EstraNet's performance continually improves with more training epochs. In contrast, EquivNet and EffCNN continue to improve their results up to 200 and 300 training epochs, respectively. Both CNN-based models overfit, incrementing their average $N_{GE=0}$. While these results suggest that longer training could be beneficial, the corresponding two-to threefold

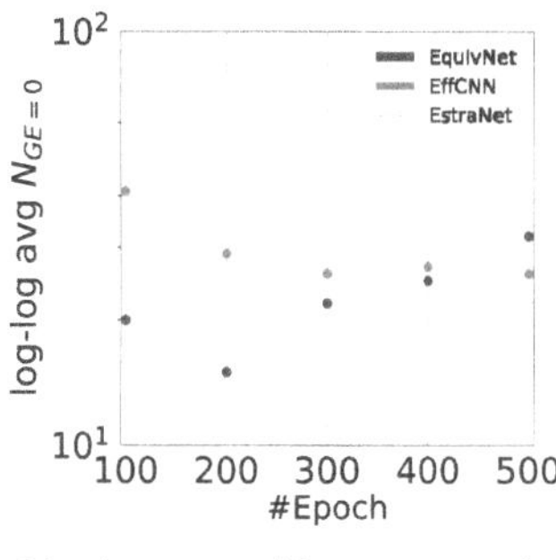

(a) Average $N_{GE=0}$ vs the number of training epochs.

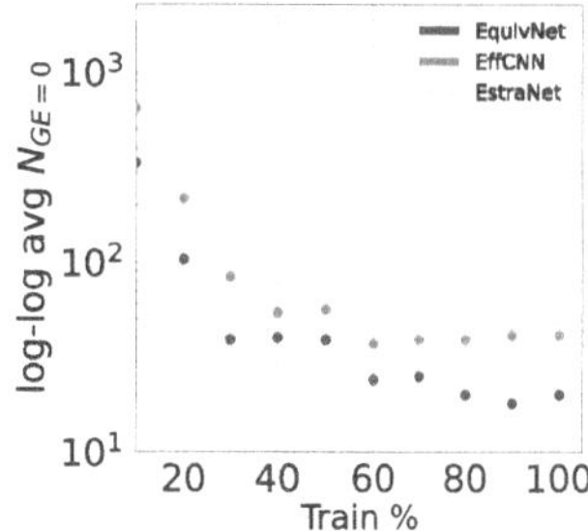

(b) Average $N_{GE=0}$ vs training dataset percentage.

Fig. 4. Average $N_{GE=0}$ reached by the models trained with ASCADr dataset for different training epochs and dataset sizes.

increase in training time, due to using 200 or 300 epochs, makes it computationally infeasible to run all our experiments.

5.5 Temporal Shift Robustness

EquivNet's architecture is defined using an equivariant-based methodology that should help create a built-in robustness of the model against desynchronization. To evaluate this robustness, we trained the models to attack ASCADr with desynchronization 50. Then, the trained models were evaluated with the same dataset, but with different values of desynchronization. These values are 50, 100, 200, and 400. To study the evolution of robustness with the addition of random circular shifting to the training, we gathered measurements obtained by models trained with $|\text{offset}| \leq 200$ and $|\text{offset}| \leq 400$. These two values were selected as half and the maximum offset that could appear in the dataset we would use for evaluation. We selected this dataset because of the availability of its raw traces, which permitted us to define the desynchronization of the traces. The results obtained by training without data augmentation can be found in Fig. 5 and Table 2.

We can see in Fig. 5 how EquivNet presents itself as the most robust model against desynchronization. Notice how EquivNet is considerably less affected by larger offsets than those used in its training compared to EffCNN. This is a consequence of using BatchNorm1D as the preprocessing technique, rather than the MinMaxScaler used in EffCNN. The use of global average pooling instead of the flatten layer also yields an edge in terms of creating a natural robustness to time translations of the input traces.

Compared to EstraNet, for ASCADr, both architectures present a natural robustness to desynchronization. If we compare the results of EquivNet and EstraNet from Table 2, EquivNet requires for every value of desynchronization a lower number of traces to attack. Moreover, if we calculate the increment in average $N_{GE=0}$ with each value of desynchronization, EquivNet presents smaller

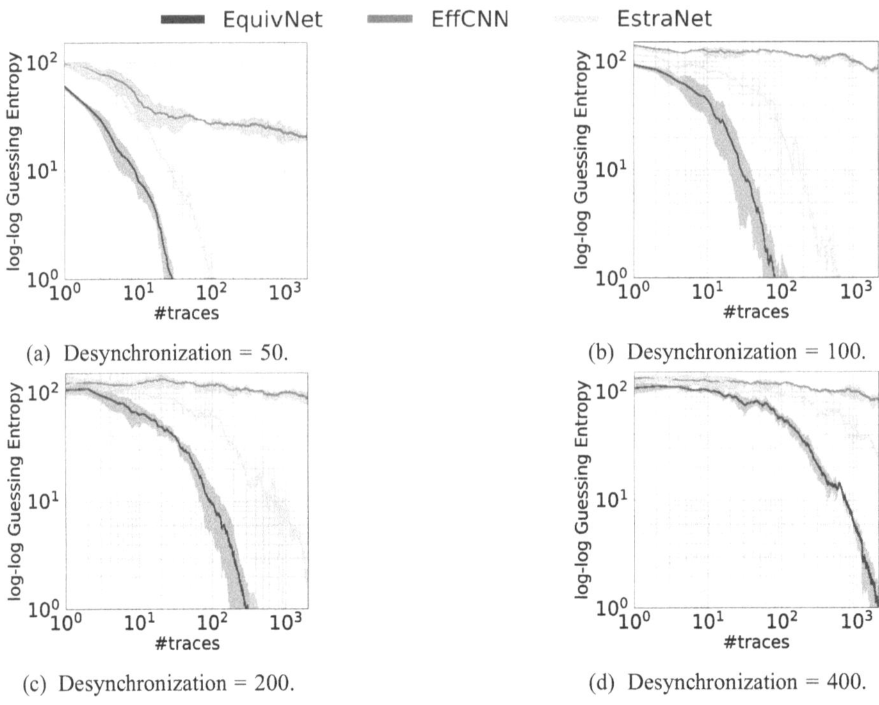

(a) Desynchronization = 50.

(b) Desynchronization = 100.

(c) Desynchronization = 200.

(d) Desynchronization = 400.

Fig. 5. Log-log representation of the average guessing entropy function obtained by each model at an attack over the desynchronized versions of ASCADr. In this case, training lacked data augmentation.

increments with the increase of the offset. The robustness of EstraNet against desynchronization could be the consequence of the attention mechanism and the Softmax-attention layer presented in the model. Attention mechanism is known for being permutation equivariant [HSAM22]. As the time translations can be seen as a composition of permutations, the attention mechanism is then equivariant to time translations. Softmax-attention calculates the attention of the input with a set of trainable queries, acting as the shift-invariant operation of EstraNet. The results of the models trained with data augmentation are shown in Figs. 9 and 10. The results are summarized in Table 2.

Examining the results obtained by the models trained with data augmentation, we see that EquivNet remains the most robust model among those evaluated. EquivNet achieves to attack with less than 2000 traces for every tested case, whereas EffCNN and EstraNet while managed to reduce their avg $N_{GE=0}$ for datasets with desynchronization 50, 100, they showed problems when dealing with bigger desynchronizations, requiring more than 1000 traces as EstraNet in the case of desynchronization 200 or directly being unable to attack with less than 2000 traces. It is also interesting to see how the models presented in general achieve better results when trained with data augmentation using offsets with

$|\text{offset}| \leq 200$ than with $|\text{offset}| \leq 400$. This could be due to an increase in the variability of the offsets presented in the dataset, which becomes too much of a problem for the models, given other hyperparameters that define the training, such as the number of epochs and the learning rate.

Table 2. Results of the guessing entropy value obtained with 2000 traces or the average number of traces to reach GE = 0 in bold, obtained by each model attacking ASCADr dataset, with desynchronization 50, 100, 200 and 400, and trained with NO/$|\text{offset}| \leq 200$/$|\text{offset}| \leq 400$ random circular shifting data augmentation.

Model	Desynchronization			
	50	100	200	400
EquivNet	**29**/**19**/**29**	**81**/**30**/**29**	**291**/**45**/**56**	**1929**/**275**/**180**
EffCNN	20.3/**72**/**206**	84.9/**121**/**740**	89.3/**921**/2.81	82.2/4.47/7.68
EstraNet	**99**/**112**/**628**	**497**/**154**/**687**	1.81/**230**/**1117**	26.2/0.16/2.53

5.6 Time Dilation Robustness

Following the analysis of time translation robustness, we now evaluate the models' robustness against time dilations. This property is a primary motivation for our proposed EquivNet model, which is based on time dilation-equivariant convolutions. To our knowledge, this is the first work in DLSCA to assess the performance of deep learning models on traces with varying time-scales. Therefore, we compare EquivNet against EstraNet and EffCNN trained with and without data augmentation. This comparison benchmarks the performance of a model with built-in invariance against a conventional approach with just data augmentation.

We begin by studying the models' built-in robustness. For this purpose, we reuse the models previously trained in Sect. 5.5 to attack the ASCADr dataset with desynchronization 50. However, the original EffCNN model cannot be used directly. Its architecture lacks a global average pooling (GAP) layer before the flatten layer, which means the input size of its first dense layer depends on the trace length. This dependency makes the model incompatible with variable-length inputs, a requirement for our time dilation experiment. To resolve this, we modified the EffCNN architecture by inserting a GAP layer immediately before the flatten layer.

The evaluation traces were transformed using dilation factors α defined as powers of 1.2 (i.e., $\alpha = 1.2^{\beta}$). This choice is motivated by the internal dilation factor $S = 1.2$ used in EquivNet. As EquivNet uses kernels dilated by factors of S^{β}, evaluating with corresponding α values allows assessing the upper limits of the model's effectiveness. The results for models trained without data augmentation are given in Fig. 6 and Table 3.

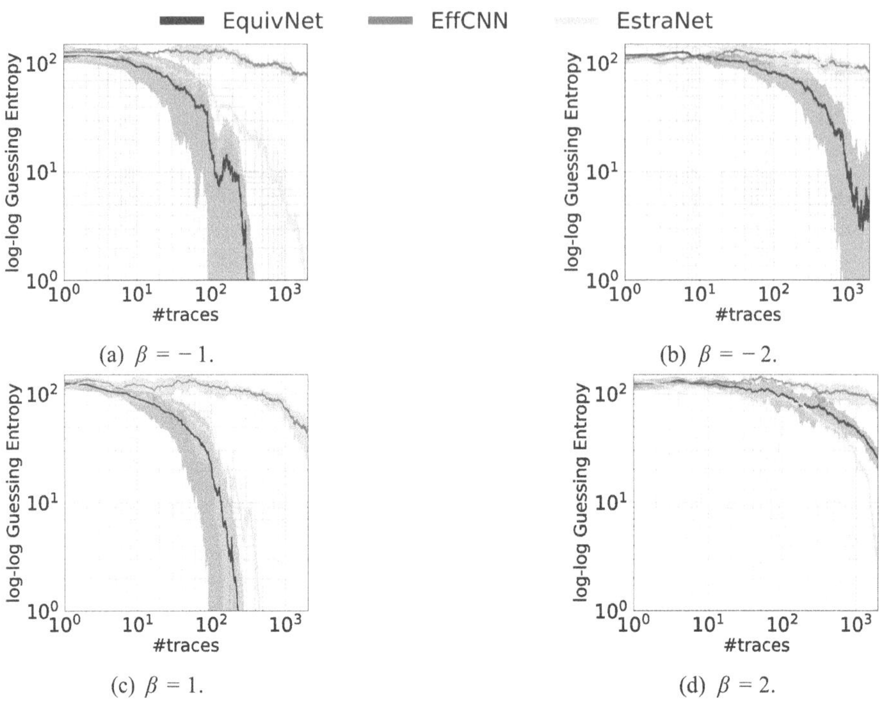

Fig. 6. Log-log representation of the average guessing entropy function obtained by each model at an attack over the time dilated versions of ASCADr with desynchronization 50.

Next, we retrained the models, but we also added data augmentation. Specifically, the original ASCADr training set was augmented with two additional copies, which were resampled with dilation factors of $\alpha = S^1$ and $\alpha = S^{-1}$ (where $S = 1.2$). This increase in available data comes at the cost of tripling the training time. The results for the models trained on this augmented dataset are presented in Fig. 11 and Table 3.

Finally, we retrained the models using more data augmentation. This time we used five copies of ASCADr generated by resampling the original dataset with a dilation factor of $1.2^{0,\pm1,\pm2}$. By doing this, every model is trained with traces having the same shape as the ones used in the evaluations. Notice also that this approach increases the training time fivefold compared to the baseline with no data augmentation. The results are shown in Fig. 12 and Table 3.

The results in Fig. 6, and Table 3 demonstrate that EffCNN fails to execute successful attacks in any tested scenarios, regardless of whether it was trained with or without data augmentation. A comparison of EquivNet and EstraNet reveals a clear trade-off between the amount of computation required for training and the quality of the attacks performed. Without data augmentation, EquivNet achieves a lower average $N_{GE=0}$ in all cases except for $\beta = 2$, where EstraNet

Table 3. Results of the guessing entropy value obtained with 2000 traces or the average number of traces to reach GE=0 in bold, obtained by each model attacking the ASCADr dataset time dilated with 1.2^β and trained with NO/$1.2^{0,\pm1}$/$1.2^{0,\pm1,\pm2}$ dilated copies-based data augmentation.

Model	$\beta = -2$	$\beta = -1$	$\beta = 1$	$\beta = 2$
EquivNet	3.52/1.34/**540**	**312**/**99**/**99**	**230**/**71**/**43**	24.7/**1015**/**677**
EffCNN	83.8/80/87.87	76.9/37.1/36	44.2/8.16/78.79	80.6/86.6/71.68
EstraNet	65.4/17.7/**143**	**1810**/**99**/**137**	**455**/**117**/**137**	3.03/**362**/**146**

performs better. When using data augmentation $1.2^{0,\pm1}$, we observe the same pattern as before, with the addition of a general improvement in both models, making them perform more similarly. Lastly, with $1.2^{0,\pm1,\pm2}$ data augmentation, we observe that EquivNet remains the superior model for $\beta = \pm1$, while EstraNet now achieves a better result for $\beta = -2$.

This suggests that, for EstraNet, combining attention mechanisms with small (size 3) convolutional kernels can yield a model more robust to time dilations than EffCNN, provided it is trained on an augmented dataset. With sufficient data augmentation, its components enable it to achieve attacks of similar quality. Notably, EstraNet appears more resilient than EquivNet when dealing with a time dilation of 1.2^{-2}. We suggest that this is mainly due to its attention block, the primary difference from the CNN-based models. In contrast, the EquivNet model is inherently robust to this type of input transformation due to its equivariant design, requiring no attention layers. While this robustness is a built-in feature, it is further enhanced by data augmentation.

5.7 Transfer Learning and Different Clock Frequencies

The clock frequency of cryptographic devices is commonly manipulated for reasons such as reducing power consumption, mitigating side-channel attacks via clock jitter, or managing heat through thermal throttling. As previously discussed, altering the clock frequency theoretically results in time-dilated power traces, since the sequence of cryptographic operations remains identical while the time to execute them changes.

Given that EquivNet has demonstrated robustness to time dilations, we now investigate its transfer learning capabilities. Specifically, we study the ability of a model trained on traces from a device operating at one clock frequency to successfully attack traces from the same device operating at another frequency. To this end, we use two datasets, Nucleo_96MHz and Nucleo_168MHz. The theoretical time dilation factor, α, relating these two datasets can be calculated from their respective clock frequencies: $\alpha = 168/96 = 1.75$. Therefore, to attack the Nucleo_168MHz dataset using a model trained only on Nucleo_96MHz traces, a good dilation factor for the EquivNet model would be $S = 1.75$. However, the large computational cost associated with this value makes us select $S = \sqrt{1.75} \approx 1.3$. This choice is motivated by the fact that the second-level dilated kernels in EquivNet (i.e., those dilated by S^2) will then match the theoretical dilation factor between the datasets. Moreover, we aim to showcase whether our neural network can still perform well even if the dilation factor used is not exactly the same as the one obtained through the theoretical calculations.

We adopt the OPOI scenario [PWP22] for this experiment. The models are trained on the maximum-correlation window [18000, 20625) from the Nucleo_96MHz dataset, targeting the first byte of an intermediate value as the leakage source. Following the same protocol as in Sect. 5.6, we train EquivNet (with $S = 1.3$), EstraNet, and EffCNN, both with and without data augmentation (which also uses $S = 1.3$). After training, we use the model checkpoint from each epoch to attack the [11000, 12500) window of the Nucleo_168MHz dataset. The results are presented in Fig. 7 and Table 7.

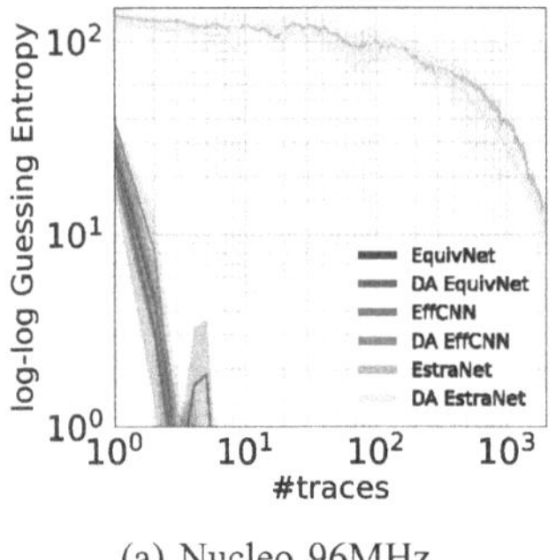

(a) Nucleo 96MHz.

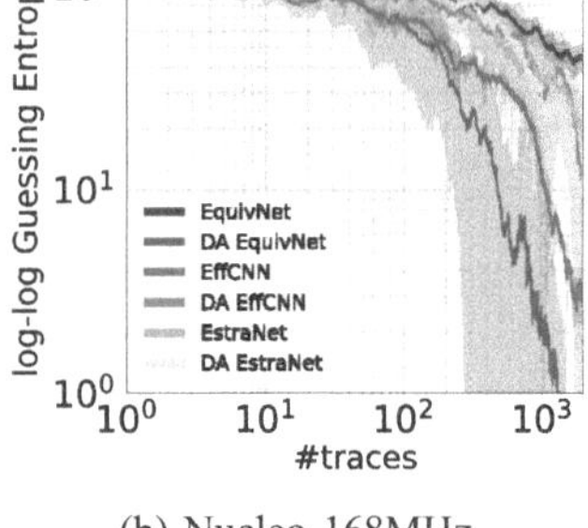

(b) Nucleo 168MHz.

Fig. 7. Log-log representation of the guessing entropy function obtained by each model at an attack over the datasets Nucleo_96MHz and Nucleo_168MHz Sect. 4, having been trained with just Nucleo_96MHz.

5.8 Limitations

While our experiments clearly show the advantages of equivariant CNNs, there are also some limitations. One consideration is that, in our experiments, we use a single hyperparameter and training setup derived from [ZBHV20]. In the original works, both EstraNet and the EffCNN are adapted to specific targets, allowing for performance improvements. As these do not provide a specifically adapted model for some (EffCNN) or all (EstraNet) scenarios we test, the obtained performance is not representative of what could be possible for these architectures. Tuning the models to each target should result in further performance improvements. However, we aimed for consistent training setups across experiments, rather than specific improvements, to showcase 'average' performance when applying the method to a new target.

6 Conclusions and Future Work

In this work, we propose EquivNet, a model based on group equivariant neural networks. More precisely, we propose a model with built-in robustness to transformations such as time translations and time dilations, As such, the EquivNet model can identify patterns in feature maps generated using kernels of varying sizes. EquivNet has been demonstrated to be a state-of-the-art model for executing attacks over the datasets AES_RD, ASCADv1, and ESHARD. Notably, in the case of ESHARD, EquivNet had an edge over the rest as it was the only model that successfully attacked. Of the models tested, EquivNet proved most effective at handling desynchronized traces with offsets exceeding those in the training data. This robustness was further increased by random circular shifting data augmentation, an effect that was more pronounced than in EffCNN and EstraNet. EquivNet also showed to be naturally robust against time dilation transformations. Furthermore, the experiments also demonstrated that this robustness can be further enhanced by utilizing data augmentation. By using data augmentation, it was also proven that a trade-off exists between the computational cost of training and the quality of the attacks performed. This is primarily illustrated by the contrasting behaviors of EstraNet and EquivNet. EstraNet achieved better results for time-dilated traces with factors $1.2^{\pm 2}$ by using augmented datasets, which increased training time up to fivefold. In contrast, EquivNet's inherent robustness allowed it to perform best on dilations of $1.2^{\pm 1}$, regardless of whether data augmentation was used. Moreover, EquivNet showed the capability of being trained with traces obtained from a device with one clock frequency and performing a successful attack over traces obtained from the same device but with a different clock frequency.

For future work, one direction could be related to mixing attention layers with the time dilation equivariant convolutional layers. This is based on the attention layer being permutation equivariant, which makes it compatible with the temporal translation equivariant layers. Results in Sect. 5.6 show how EstraNet could take more advantage of the data augmentation used in its training than EquivNet. Being the attention block of EstraNet, one of the main differences between the three models tested, its addition to EquivNet's architecture could lead to similar capabilities in terms of improving with augmented datasets. Since EquivNet does not have an attention layer, adding it could lead to better results, especially with the use of more data augmentation.

Acknowledgement. This work was supported by the Provincial Council of Bizkaia through the CyberAI2Grid Project (2019/0097).

A EquivNet Architecture

In Table 4, *c_out* denotes the number of output feature maps for convolutional layers or the output dimensionality for dense layers. *ks* specifies the temporal size of the pooling kernel used on the average pooling, applied over the time dimension, and *pred* represents the number of classes used to classify. *pred* depends on the leakage model used: If it is the Identity of the byte selected, then $pred = 256$. On the other hand, if the leakage model is the Hamming Weight of the same byte, then $pred = 9$. Finally, TK and TSK represent the sizes of the non-time-dilated kernels over the time and time dilation dimensions, respectively.

Table 4. EquivNet model architecture.

Position	Layer	Hyperparameters
0°	BatchNorm1D	
1°	Lifting Convolution	$c\_out = 32$, $TK = 13$
2°	BatchNorm2D	
3°	Activation Function	GELU
4°	Average Pooling	$ks = 2$
5°	Time-Scale Group Convolution	$c\_out = 64$, $TK = 15$, $TSK = 3$
6°	BatchNorm2D	
7°	Activation Function	GELU
8°	Average Pooling	$ks = 25$
9°	Time-Scale Group Convolution	$c\_out = 128$, $TK = 13$, $TSK = 3$
10°	BatchNorm2D	
11°	Activation Function	GELU
12°	Average Pooling	$ks = 2$
13°	Time-Scale Group Convolution	$c\_out = 128$, $TK = 9$, $TSK = 3$
14°	BatchNorm2D	
15°	Activation Function	GELU
16°	Global Average Pooling	
17°	Dense Layer	$c\_out = 20$, SELU
18°	Dense Layer	$c\_out = 20$, SELU
19°	Dense Layer	$c\_out = 20$, SELU
20°	Prediction Layer	$c\_out = pred$

B Ablation Study of EquivNet Features

To study the effects of our design choices on EquivNet's attack efficiency, we selected the synchronized ASCADv1r and trained a set of modified EquivNet models to evaluate how each modification affects the best-guessing entropy reached by the model. These modifications are:

SELU All activation functions were replaced with SELU.
ReLU All activation functions were replaced with ReLU.
No Batch0 The first BatchNorm1D layer of the model was removed.

2GroupConv The third Group Convolution layer was removed from EquivNet.

The best guessing entropy found by each of these modified models is compared with the best-guessing entropy found by the base EquivNet, referred to as Default. The comparisons are shown in Fig. 8 and Table 5.

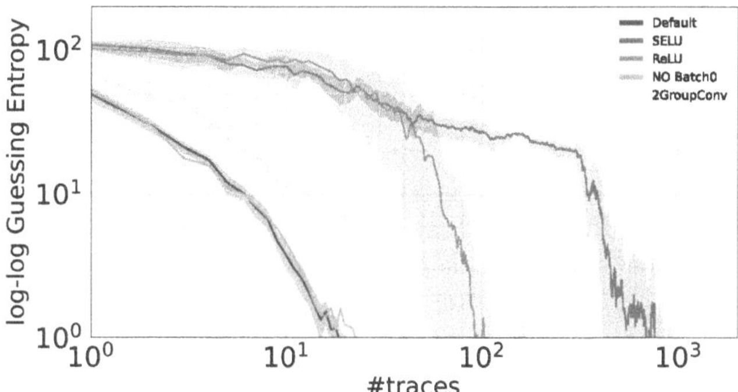

Fig. 8. Log-log representation of the average guessing entropy function obtained by each version of EquivNet for an attack on the ASCADr dataset.

Table 5. Average number of traces needed to reach $GE = 0$ for attacks on the ASCADr dataset using different versions of EquivNet.

Case	avg $N_{GE=0}$
Default	19
SELU	685
ReLU	93
NO Batch0	23
2GroupConv	31

The study in Fig. 8 reveals that the choice of activation function is the most critical design decision. Specifically the default model using GELU achieves an average $N_{GE=0} = 19$, whereas models using SELU and ReLU obtain $N_{GE=0} = 685$ and $N_{GE=0} = 93$, respectively. In contrast, the impact of the initial BatchNorm1D layer is negligible, as removing it from the model just increases $N_{GE=0}$ in 4. Finally, removing the last Group Convolution results, incrementing the average $N_{GE=0}$ to 31. This demonstrates the positive impact this layer has on the model's effectiveness, but at the same time, its addition is not compulsory for the model to function properly.

C Description of the Datasets

ASCADv1. ASCAD datasets represent the most common target for evaluating the performance of DLSCA. The first edition of the dataset (ASCADv1) contains two versions: one with a fixed key for the profiling set and the other with random keys for the profiling set. We denote the former as ASCADf and the latter as ASCADr. The ASCADf dataset[8] contains measurements from an 8-bit AVR microcontroller. The AES-128 implementation is protected with first-order Boolean masking, except for the first two bytes, which are left unprotected for testing purposes. The acquisition window covers only the first round of AES, and each trace consists of 100 000 sample points. The dataset contains 60 000 traces overall, which are split into 50 000 for the profiling phase and 10 000 for the attack. All encryption operations in both the profiling and attack groups are performed using the same fixed key. Following the recommendations from the datasets' authors, we consider the preselected interval of 700 features for our experiments. Note that this is the OPOI cases as discussed in [PWP22].

The ASCADr dataset[9] has a similar setup to ASCADf concerning the measurements source. The main difference is that the traces in the ASCADr profiling group use random keys to perform the encryption instead of a fixed key. The traces are also longer as they consist of 250 000 samples. In total, there are 200 000 traces for the profiling phase and 100 000 for the attack phase. The encryption for the attack group is still performed using a fixed key. We again work with a preselected window of features, which for this dataset contains 1 400 features. For both ASCAD datasets, we consider the Identity leakage model, and we attack the third key byte, as this is the first masked key byte.

ESHARD. The ESHARD dataset[10] contains EM emanations of a first-order boolean masked AES-128 implementation implemented on an STM32F4 microcontroller (Cortex-M4) and was introduced by Vasselle et al. [VTM23]. The datasets includes 100 000 traces with a fixed key, where we take 90 000 traces as the profiling set and 10 000 traces as the attack set. Each trace contains a window of 1 400 samples per trace, consisting of the loading of the mask and the 16 masked S-box operations. Note that we consider the non-shuffled version of the traces. In the case of attacking the ESHARD dataset, the leakage model selected is the Hamming weight of the first byte of the intermediate value, similarly to [WRAp+24].

AES_RD. The AES_RD dataset[11] is a protected software implementation of AES-128 on an 8-bit Atmel AVR microcontroller. The protection is a random

[8] https://github.com/ANSSI-FR/ASCAD/tree/master/ATMEGA_AES_v1/ATM_AES_v1_fixed_key.

[9] https://github.com/ANSSI-FR/ASCAD/tree/master/ATMEGA_AES_v1/ATM_AES_v1_variable_key.

[10] https://gitlab.com/eshard/nucleo_sw_aes_masked_shuffled/-/blob/main/Nucleo_AES_masked_non_shuffled.ets.

[11] https://github.com/ikizhvatov/randomdelays-traces.

delay countermeasure as described by Coron and Kizhvatov [CK09]. This countermeasure causes the misalignment of important features, making the attack more difficult to conduct. We attack the first AES key byte, targeting the first S-box operation. The dataset consists of 50 000 traces of 3 500 features each. The leakage model selected is the value of the first byte of the intermediate value, as in other works, see, e.g., [ZBHV20].

D Additional Results

Table 6. Results of the guessing entropy value obtained with 1000 traces or the average number of traces to reach GE = 0 in bold, obtained by each model attacking different datasets.

Model	AES_RD	ESHARD	ASCADf	ASCADr
EquivNet	**1**	**319**	**72**	**22**
EffCNN	**2**	114	**116**	**29**
EstraNet	**45**	26.8	2.51	**78**

Table 7. Results of the guessing entropy value obtained with 2000 traces and the average number of traces needed to reach GE=0 for the attacks over Nucleo_96MHz and ucleo_168MHz.

Case	Model	GE (2000)	avg $N_{GE=0}$
Nucleo_96MHz	EquivNet	0	3
	EffCNN	0	3
	EstraNet	12.4	None
	DA EquivNet	0	4
	DA EffCNN	0	3
	DA EstraNet	13.7	None
Nucleo_168MHz	EquivNet	42.7	None
	EffCNN	2.69	None
	EstraNet	17.7	None
	DA EquivNet	0	1288
	DA EffCNN	17.7	None
	DA EstraNet	12.9	None

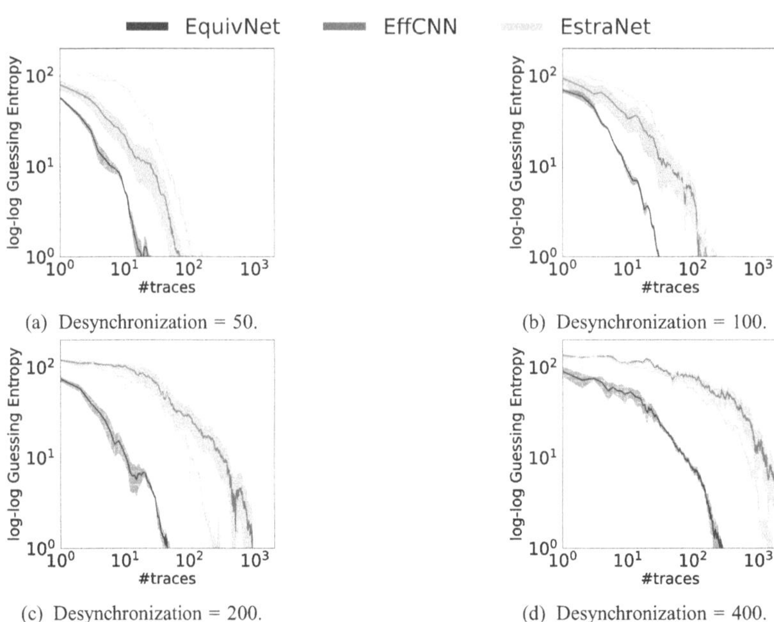

(a) Desynchronization = 50.
(b) Desynchronization = 100.
(c) Desynchronization = 200.
(d) Desynchronization = 400.

Fig. 9. Log-log representation of the average guessing entropy function obtained by each model at an attack over the desynchronized versions of ASCADr. The models were trained with random circular shifting data augmentation, using offsets with $|\text{offset}| \leq 200$.

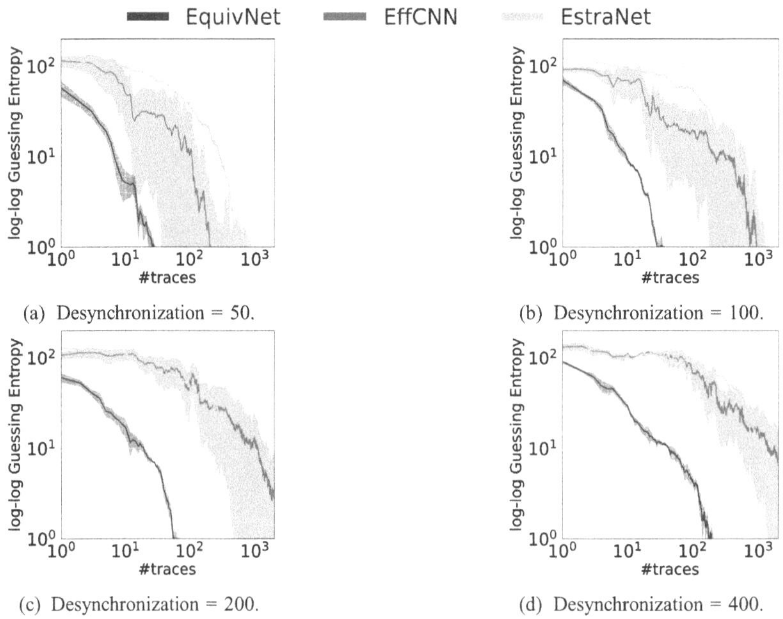

(a) Desynchronization = 50.
(b) Desynchronization = 100.
(c) Desynchronization = 200.
(d) Desynchronization = 400.

Fig. 10. Log-log representation of the average guessing entropy function obtained by each model at an attack over the desynchronized versions of ASCADr. The models were trained with random circular shifting data augmentation, using offsets with $|\text{offset}| \leq 400$.

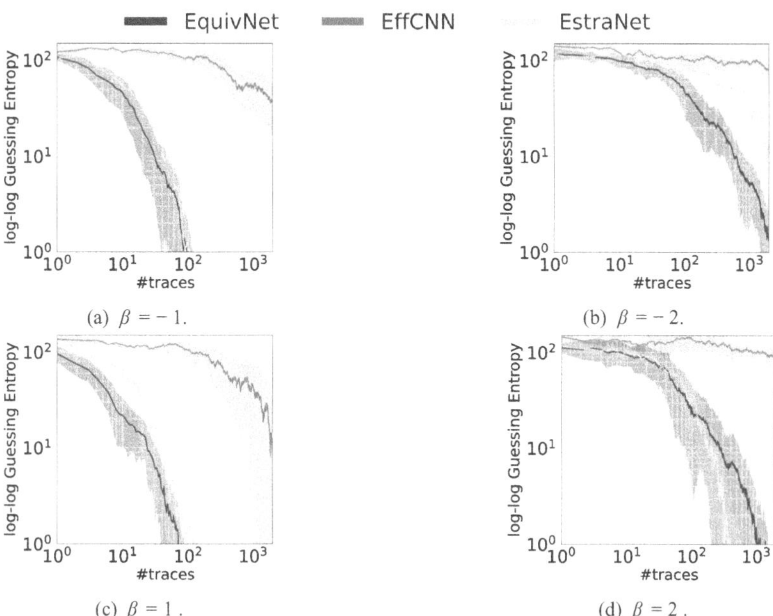

Fig. 11. Log-log representation of the average guessing entropy function obtained by each model at an attack over the time dilated versions of ASCADr with desynchronization 50. The models were trained with data augmentation using $\alpha = 1.2^{0,\pm 1}$.

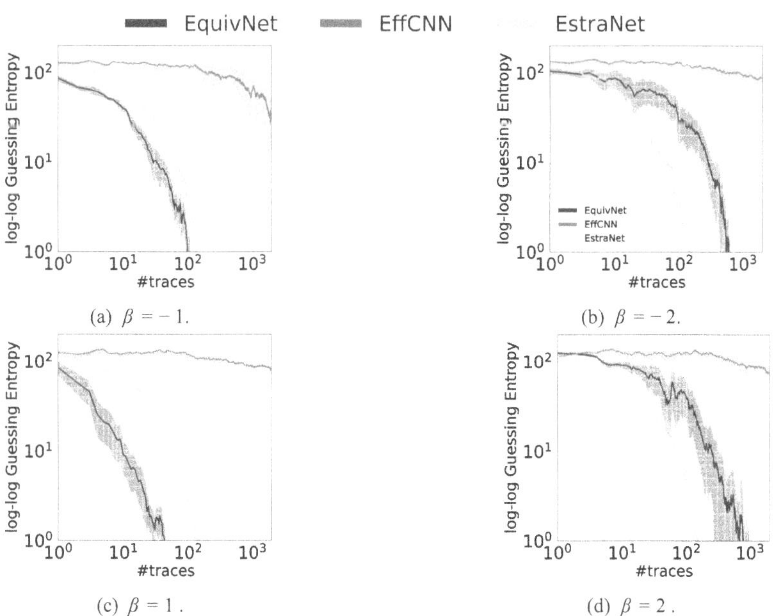

Fig. 12. Log-log representation of the average guessing entropy function obtained by each model at an attack over the time dilated versions of ASCADr with desynchronization 50. The models were trained with data augmentation using $\alpha = 1.2^{0,\pm 1,\pm 2}$.

References

[AW19] Azulay, A., Weiss, Y.: Why do deep convolutional networks generalize so poorly to small image transformations? J. Mach. Learn. Res. **20**, 184:1–184:25 (2019)

[BB21] Biscione, V., Bowers, J.S.: Convolutional neural networks are not invariant to translation, but they can learn to be. J. Mach. Learn. Res. **22**, 229:1–229:28 (2021)

[BBCV21] Bronstein, M.M., Bruna, J., Cohen, T., Velickovic, P.: Geometric deep learning: grids, groups, graphs, geodesics, and gauges. CoRR, abs/2104.13478 (2021)

[Bog07] Bogachev, V.I.: Measure Theory I. Springer, Berlin (2007)

[BPS+20] Benadjila, R., Prouff, E., Strullu, R., Cagli, E., Dumas, C.: Deep learning for side-channel analysis and introduction to ASCAD database. J. Cryptogr. Eng. **10**(2), 163–188 (2020)

[CDP17] Cagli, E., Dumas, C., Prouff, E.: Convolutional neural networks with data augmentation against jitter-based countermeasures. In: Fischer, W., Homma, N. (eds.) CHES 2017. LNCS, vol. 10529, pp. 45–68. Springer, Cham (2017). https://doi.org/10.1007/978-3-319-66787-4_3

[CK09] Coron, J.-S., Kizhvatov, I.: An efficient method for random delay generation in embedded software. In: Clavier, C., Gaj, K. (eds.) CHES 2009. LNCS, vol. 5747, pp. 156–170. Springer, Heidelberg (2009). https://doi.org/10.1007/978-3-642-04138-9_12

[CRR02] Chari, S., Rao, J.R., Rohatgi, P.: Template attacks. In: Kaliski, B.S., Koç, K., Paar, C. (eds.) CHES 2002. LNCS, vol. 2523, pp. 13–28. Springer, Heidelberg (2003). https://doi.org/10.1007/3-540-36400-5_3

[CW16] Cohen, T., Welling, M.: Group equivariant convolutional networks. In: Balcan, M.-F., Weinberger, K.Q. (eds.) Proceedings of the 33nd International Conference on Machine Learning, ICML 2016, New York City, NY, USA, 19–24 June 2016. JMLR Workshop and Conference Proceedings, vol. 48, pp. 2990–2999. JMLR.org (2016)

[HCM24] Hajra, S., Chowdhury, S., Mukhopadhyay, D.: Estranet: an efficient shift-invariant transformer network for side-channel analysis. IACR Trans. Cryptogr. Hardw. Embed. Syst. **2024**(1), 336–374 (2024)

[HG23] Hendrycks, D., Gimpel, K.: Gaussian error linear units (GELUs) (2023)

[HSAM22] Hajra, S., Saha, S., Alam, M., Mukhopadhyay, D.: Transnet: shift invariant transformer network for side channel analysis. In: Batina, L., Daemen, J. (eds.) Progress in Cryptology - AFRICACRYPT 2022. LNCS, vol. 13503, pp. 371–396. Springer, Cham (2022)

[HZG+24] He, P., Zhang, Y., Gan, H., Ma, J., Zhang, H.: Side-channel attacks based on attention mechanism and multi-scale convolutional neural network. Comput. Electr. Eng. **119**, 109515 (2024)

[JZHY20] Jin, M., Zheng, M., Hu, H., Yu, N.: An enhanced convolutional neural network in side-channel attacks and its visualization. CoRR, abs/2009.08898 (2020)

[KJJ99] Kocher, P., Jaffe, J., Jun, B.: Differential power analysis. In: Wiener, M. (ed.) CRYPTO 1999. LNCS, vol. 1666, pp. 388–397. Springer, Heidelberg (1999). https://doi.org/10.1007/3-540-48405-1_25

[Koc96] Kocher, P.C.: Timing attacks on implementations of Diffie-Hellman, RSA, DSS, and other systems. In: Koblitz, N. (ed.) CRYPTO 1996. LNCS, vol. 1109, pp. 104–113. Springer, Heidelberg (1996). https://doi.org/10.1007/3-540-68697-5_9

[KPH+19] Kim, J., Picek, S., Heuser, A., Bhasin, S., Hanjalic, A.: Make some noise. unleashing the power of convolutional neural networks for profiled side-channel analysis. IACR Trans. Cryptogr. Hardw. Embed. Syst. **2019**(3), 148–179 (2019)

[KWPP24] Krček, M., Wu, L., Perin, G., Picek, S.: Shift-invariance robustness of convolutional neural networks in side-channel analysis. Mathematics **12**(20) (2024)

[LCCR22] Liu, C., Chakraborty, A., Chawla, N., Roggel, N.: Frequency throttling side-channel attack. In: Yin, H., Stavrou, A., Cremers, C., Shi, E. (eds.) Proceedings of the 2022 ACM SIGSAC Conference on Computer and Communications Security, CCS 2022, Los Angeles, CA, USA, 7–11 November 2022, pp. 1977–1991. ACM (2022)

[LCY14] Lin, M., Chen, Q., Yan, S.: Network in network. In: Bengio, Y., LeCun, Y. (eds.) 2nd International Conference on Learning Representations, ICLR 2014, Banff, AB, Canada, 14–16 April 2014, Conference Track Proceedings (2014)

[LZW+21] Luo, Z., Zheng, M., Wang, P., Jin, M., Zhang, J., Hu, H.: Towards strengthening deep learning-based side channel attacks with mixup. In: 20th IEEE International Conference on Trust, Security and Privacy in Computing and Communications, TrustCom 2021, Shenyang, China, 20–22 October 2021, pp. 791–801. IEEE (2021)

[MPP16] Maghrebi, H., Portigliatti, T., Prouff, E.: Breaking cryptographic implementations using deep learning techniques. In: Carlet, C., Hasan, M.A., Saraswat, V. (eds.) SPACE 2016. LNCS, vol. 10076, pp. 3–26. Springer, Cham (2016). https://doi.org/10.1007/978-3-319-49445-6_1

[PA20] Paguada, S., Armendariz, I.: The forgotten hyperparameter: introducing dilated convolution for boosting CNN-based side-channel attacks. In: Zhou, J., et al. (eds.) ACNS 2020. LNCS, vol. 12418, pp. 217–236. Springer, Cham (2020). https://doi.org/10.1007/978-3-030-61638-0_13

[PPM+23] Picek, S., Perin, G., Mariot, L., Wu, L., Batina, L.: SoK: deep learning-based physical side-channel analysis. ACM Comput. Surv. **55**(11), 227:1–227:35 (2023)

[PWP22] Perin, G., Lichao, W., Picek, S.: Exploring feature selection scenarios for deep learning-based side-channel analysis. IACR Trans. Cryptogr. Hardw. Embed. Syst. **2022**(4), 828–861 (2022)

[RBTH20] Romero, D.W., Bekkers, E.J., Tomczak, J.M., Hoogendoorn, M.: Wavelet networks: scale equivariant learning from raw waveforms. CoRR, abs/2006.05259 (2020)

[SMS21] Sosnovik, I., Moskalev, A., Smeulders, A.W.M.: How to transform kernels for scale-convolutions. In: IEEE/CVF International Conference on Computer Vision Workshops, ICCVW 2021, Montreal, QC, Canada, 11–17 October 2021, pp. 1092–1097. IEEE (2021)

[VSP+17] Vaswani, A., et al.: Attention is all you need. In: Guyon, I., et al. (eds.) Advances in Neural Information Processing Systems 30: Annual Conference on Neural Information Processing Systems 2017, 4–9 December 2017, Long Beach, CA, USA, pp. 5998–6008 (2017)

[VTM23] Vasselle, A., Thiebeauld, H., Maurine, P.: Spatial dependency analysis to extract information from side-channel mixtures: extended version. J. Cryptogr. Eng. **13**(4), 409–425 (2023)

[WP20] Lichao, W., Picek, S.: Remove some noise: on pre-processing of side-channel measurements with autoencoders. IACR Trans. Cryptogr. Hardw. Embed. Syst. **2020**(4), 389–415 (2020)

[WRAp+24] Wu, L., Rezaeezade, A., Ali-pour, A., Perin, G., Picek, S.: Leakage model-flexible deep learning-based side-channel analysis. IACR Commun. Cryptol. **1**(3) (2024)

[WW19] Worrall, D.E., Welling, M.: Deep scale-spaces: equivariance over scale. In: Wallach, H.M., Larochelle, H., Beygelzimer, A., d'Alché-Buc, F., Fox, E.B., Garnett, R. (eds.) Advances in Neural Information Processing Systems 32: Annual Conference on Neural Information Processing Systems 2019, NeurIPS 2019, 8–14 December 2019, Vancouver, BC, Canada, pp. 7364–7376 (2019)

[ZBHV20] Zaid, G., Bossuet, L., Habrard, A., Venelli, A.: Methodology for efficient CNN architectures in profiling attacks. IACR Trans. Cryptogr. Hardw. Embed. Syst. **2020**(1), 1–36 (2020)

[ZS20] Zhou, Y., Standaert, F.-X.: Deep learning mitigates but does not annihilate the need of aligned traces and a generalized resnet model for side-channel attacks. J. Cryptogr. Eng. **10**(1), 85–95 (2020)

RSA and Group Signatures

HHGS: Forward-Secure Dynamic Group Signatures from Symmetric Primitives

Xuelian Cao[1], Zheng Yang[2], Daniel Reijsbergen[3], Jianting Ning[4,5](✉), Junming Ke[6], Zhiqiang Ma[7], and Jianying Zhou[3]

[1] Tsinghua University, Beijing, China
xl-cao@mail.tsinghua.edu.cn
[2] Southwest University, Chongqing, China
youngzheng@swu.edu.cn
[3] Singapore University of Technology and Design, Singapore, Singapore
{daniel_reijsbergen,jianying_zhou}@sutd.edu.sg
[4] Wuhan University, Wuhan, China
jtning88@gmail.com
[5] City University of Macau, Macau, China
jtning88@gmail.com
[6] Hangzhou Research Institute of AI and Holographic Technology, Hangzhou, China
junmingke@zjuqx.com
[7] Fujian Normal University, Fuzhou, China
zhiqiang.ma97@gmail.com

Abstract. Group signatures allow a group member to sign messages on behalf of the group while preserving the signer's anonymity, making them invaluable for privacy-sensitive applications. As quantum computing advances, post-quantum security in group signatures becomes essential. Symmetric primitives (SP) offer a promising pathway due to their simplicity, efficiency, and well-understood security foundations. In this paper, we introduce the first *forward-secure dynamic group signature* (FSDGS) framework relying solely on SP. We begin with *hierarchical hypertree group signatures* (HHGS), a basic scheme that securely organizes keys of one-time signatures (OTS) in a hypertree using puncturable pseudorandom functions to enable on-demand key generation and forward security, dynamic enrollment, and which provides resilience against attacks that exploit registration patterns by obfuscating the assignment and usage of keys. We then extend this foundation to HHGS$^+$, which orchestrates multiple HHGS instances in a generic way, significantly extending the total signing capacity to $O(2^{60})$, which outperforms HHGS's closest competitors while keeping signatures below 8 kilobytes. We prove the security of both schemes in the standard model. Our results outline a practical SP-driven pathway toward post-quantum-secure group signatures suitable for resource-constrained client devices.

Keywords: Group signatures · Forward security · Post-quantum security · Symmetric primitives · Standard model

F. -H. Liu (Ed.): CT-RSAC 2026, LNCS 16496, pp. 231–261, 2026.
https://doi.org/10.1007/978-3-032-22931-1_9

1 Introduction

Group signatures (GS) serve as an essential component in privacy-preserving applications such as anonymous credentials [10], trusted computing via direct anonymous attestation [15], enhanced privacy identification [26], digital rights management [36], and biometric authentication [16]. GS allow a group member to sign messages on behalf of the group while preserving anonymity, ensuring that a verifier can confirm the signature originates from a legitimate group member without uncovering the signer's identity. This powerful feature makes GS a fundamental cryptographic primitive for modern security architectures.

As quantum computing threatens the foundations of classical public-key cryptographic systems, the development of post-quantum secure group signatures has become imperative. Various post-quantum constructions have been proposed, leveraging lattice [9,44], code [39], isogeny [9], multivariate [40,43], and symmetric primitives (SP) [2,11,18,21,45]. Each approach has its strengths and limitations. For instance, lattice-based schemes offer resistance against quantum attacks and asymptotic efficiency, but the resulting group signatures still have a signature size of several hundred kilobytes [38]. In contrast, symmetric primitives offer simplicity and efficiency and, because the best known quantum attacks (e.g. [14,28]) against them are generic and predictably bounded.

Related Work. There are two primary ways for constructing GS schemes from SP. The first approach lies in the generic GS framework by Bellare et al. [4] based on non-interactive zero-knowledge (NIZK) proofs. The core design of the state-of-the-art NIZK-and-SP based GS [11,21] leverages the "MPC-in-the-Head" technique of Ishai et al. [33] being SP-compatible for achieving post-quantum security. However, the introduction of NIZK in [11,21] results in large signature sizes, with group signatures in [11,21] reaching sizes in the order of megabytes. Moreover, the NIZK-based GS schemes [11,21] are only proven secure in the random oracle model because of the use of Fiat-Shamir-like transformations [23]. However, most commonly-deployed hash functions deviate significantly from the ideal properties assumed in the random oracle model. This gap between the theoretical model and practical implementations can lead to invalid security guarantees [19,22]. Accordingly, although these NIZK-based GS schemes can provide full dynamic security properties [13] (such as full anonymity), they cannot achieve forward security because of the static signing keys of participants. Forward security is a fundamental requirement for group signatures, first formalized by Song [42], ensuring that compromise of a (current) signing key does not permit the forgery of valid group signatures for any earlier time period. NIZK-based GS schemes often require substantial computations on the client device (where the group credential is stored) to produce the zero-knowledge proofs. This high cost in both bandwidth and local processing can be particularly prohibitive for resource-constrained devices (e.g., smart cards or IoT devices whose computational and storage resources are limited).

The alternative approach explored in our paper leverages one-time signatures (OTS) [2,18,45] in combination with symmetric primitive-based authentication mechanisms, such as Merkle trees, to generate group authentication credentials for members' OTS keys. However, compared to NIZK-based schemes, OTS-based group signature schemes may offer weaker security (or fewer functionalities) and have smaller signing capacities. The G-Merkle scheme [2] supports only static group management, as it relies on a single Merkle tree and a pseudorandom permutation (PRP) scheme with fixed inputs. The enhanced GM^{MT} [45] employs a hypertree structure of multiple sub-trees to enable dynamic group management (**DGMA**), yet it guarantees anonymity only within a single sub-tree [45, $4.2]. That is, GM^{MT} cannot achieve anonymity across the entire group management lifecycle because an adversary can mount the OTS keys of two challenged parties in different sibling sub-trees rather than the same sub-tree (referred to as a *sibling attack*, see also in Sect. 4). Consequently, any signatures from sub-trees created before a member is joined is necessarily attributed to the older member. Additionally, G-Merkle and GM^{MT} offer limited signing capacities of $O(2^{20})$ and $O(2^{26})$, respectively. Another work following G-Merkle, called dynamic G-Merkle (DGM) [18], allows new users to join the group at any time and distributes members' OTS keys across different sub-trees. After each sub-tree is generated, its root r_{SMT} is transformed into an independent fallback key F_k via the symmetric encryption SE, i.e., $F_k := \text{SE.Dec}(F_n, r_{SMT})$ with an encryption key F_n. However, DGM requires the group manager to store all fallback keys and remain online to handle verifier queries concerning the validity of the corresponding fallback keys F_k in signatures. Consequently, it fails to provide members with *self-authenticable* group credentials (**SAGC**), which would allow them to independently validate and generate signatures without relying on the group manager for real-time support. In the latter, DGMT [25] extends DGM to enable SAGC, i.e., allowing non-interactive verification of signatures, by prepublishing fallback keys. However, this design introduces a centralization threat like G-Merkle: the manager, possessing all signing keys of members, could potentially forge signatures or suffer single-point failures, thus limiting applicability in settings requiring decentralized trust and user-controlled keys (**UCK**). Moreover, to the best of our knowledge, none of the existing OTS-based GS schemes can achieve forward security.

Motivations. To address the shortcomings of existing schemes, we focus on the fundamental research problem of how to design a forward-secure dynamic group signature (FSDGS) scheme using symmetric primitives that achieves the following properties: i) forward security, ii) DGMA, iii) SAGC, iv) UCK, v) small signature size, and vi) provable security in the standard model. We will follow the line of OTS-based approach, since it is friendly to resource-constrained devices requiring few OTS signing operations, rather than expensive NIZK operations. Although group credentials (such as Merkle proofs) in OTS-based schemes [2, 18, 45] might be large, they can be stored on any honest auxiliary device, rather than the device for storing the secret keys in NIZK-based GS schemes. That is, our design will target such a *resource constrained-auxiliary collaboration* (RCAC) scenario, including smart cards with mobile devices, drones with ground stations, and IoT devices with smart gateways. Meanwhile, our aim is to improve the signing capacity with both SAGC and UCK, and design techniques to avoid sibling attacks (unlike during dynamic group management).

Our Contributions and Techniques. This work presents the first SP-based FSDGS framework, addressing the motivated research problem. First, we propose HHGS, an innovative FSDGS scheme that leverages a hierarchical OTS-key management structure to enable efficient DGMA. HHGS is the first secure OTS-based GS to achieve DGMA, SAGC and UCK, alongside the resilience against sibling attacks (a security gap in existing schemes). By leveraging puncturable pseudorandom functions (PPRF), HHGS ensures forward security and significantly expands signing capacity to $O(2^{40})$, surpassing previous OTS-based GS schemes with SAGC and UCK by over 2^{14} times under similar join-time efficiency.[1] Second, we extend this design with HHGS^+, a scalable enhancement that integrates modular HHGS instances to significantly improve signing capabilities and accommodate larger group sizes. Consequently, the total signing capacity of HHGS^+ reaches $O(2^{60})$, accommodating most practical applications, while both schemes can maintain signature sizes under 8 kilobytes. Lastly, we rigorously prove the security of these schemes in the standard model, ensuring that they meet anonymity and traceability.

The core of our design lies in HHGS, which organizes OTS keys of a group manager (GM) and group members into an OTS hypertree (as in [7,31]) to support dynamic group management. The group credential of each member's OTS key is a signature from the hypertree indexed by a unique leaf. The key innovation of HHGS is a tailored obfuscated leaf layer of sub-trees mounted to the hypertree, which consists of two sub-layers (mixed sub-layer and member sub-layer). This design bridges the gap between the determinism of each sub-tree and the dynamic OTS mounting requirements within the sub-tree. All OTS keys in the member sub-layer are from different members joined at any time, each of which is mounted (signed) by its parent, an OTS key, in the mixed sub-layer. The mixed sub-layer encompasses the OTS keys from both members and GM to obfuscate the joining time of these OTS keys. We make use of the fact that the OTS keys from members and GM are generated from the same distribution, so they can be indistinguishable when the owners are uncorrupted. Thus, deterministic sub-trees enable GM to handle dynamic and unpredictable joining requests from members. Our construction addresses sibling attacks by customizing a randomized leaf assignment mechanism. This mechanism employs a pseudorandom function (PRF) to ensure that signing keys are independently distributed across members, preventing adversaries from exploiting shared structural information in signatures to identify members. Since the outputs of existing random functions including PRF are not truly random, potential collisions may occur during the key assignment. To address this, we utilize puncturable pseudorandom functions (PPRFs) in our customized random selection methods to track assigned signing

[1] Theoretically, all state-of-the-art OTS-based GS schemes supporting SAGC and UCK can achieve signing capacities approaching $O(2^{60})$. However, due to differences in underlying design principles, their practical performance can vary significantly. We aim to compare them under similar (reported) performance conditions.

keys. By puncturing previously assigned keys, PPRFs effectively prevent key reuse and resolve collisions. Additionally, PPRFs enable GM to update its secret key after each joining operation, ensuring forward security for its generated signatures. For resource-constrained members, pseudorandom generators serve as a lightweight alternative for generating independent OTS keys and updating secret keys to achieve forward security.

Building on the foundation of HHGS, we introduce HHGS^+, an extension designed to efficiently accommodate large group sizes and dynamic workloads. HHGS^+ adopts a modular framework by initializing multiple HHGS instances and organizing them within a unified structure. Specifically, a short-range PRF is used to randomly assign an OTS key to a suitable HHGS instance, utilizing collisions among PRF values. A key challenge in HHGS^+ lies in randomizing the assignment of OTS keys across HHGS instances while avoiding biases caused by the non-uniform distribution of PRF values, which could lead to earlier full-instance scenarios. To address this, HHGS^+ integrates redundancy within each HHGS instance, countering potential biases and mitigating adversarial exploitation of uneven assignments. Through formal analysis, we establish a redundancy model that ensures secure and balanced key distribution while maintaining minimal overhead, enabling HHGS^+ to handle dynamic group operations with high scalability and robustness.

Comparison. Table 1 summarizes a comparison of our proposed schemes with some existing ones according to underlying construction mechanisms. The first compared category involves group signatures (i.e., G-Merkle [2] and $\mathrm{GM}^{\mathrm{MT}}$ [45]) which are composed of OTS signatures and self-authenticable group membership credentials (which exclude DGM [18]). G-Merkle, $\mathrm{GM}^{\mathrm{MT}}$ and DGMT differ from the group credential and the features of supporting dynamic group management (DGMT) and user-centric key (UCK) management. G-Merkle uses a single Merkle tree to create group credentials, so it does not provide DGMA. Additionally, both G-Merkle and DGMT does not support UCK, making them less secure and considerably easier to construct compared to other schemes. In contrast, the group credentials in $\mathrm{GM}^{\mathrm{MT}}$ are generated using $\mathrm{XMSS}^{\mathrm{T}}$ [30] equipped with a hypertree. While it supports DGMA, it fails to provide resilience against sibling attacks (SA) [45, §4.2]. SA applies only to DGMA-enabled GS schemes.

Table 1. Comparison among SP-based Group Signature Schemes.

Schemes	Sig. Technique	Credential Structure	UCK Support	Group Management	Standard Model	Forward Security	SA Resilience	Group Size	Each Mem. Sig. Capacity	Sig. Size
G-Merkle [2]	OTS	Merkle tree	×	Static	√	×	-	2^6	2^{14}	1.9
$\mathrm{GM}^{\mathrm{MT}}$ [45]	OTS	Hypertree	√	Dynamic	√	×	×	2^{16}	2^{10}	3.3
DGMT [25]	OTS	Hypertree	×	Dynamic	√	×	√	2^7	$2^{26.76}$	5.344
BEB [11]	NIZK	Merkle tree	√	Static	×	×	-	2^{40}	unlimit	6650
SPHINX [21]	NIZK	Hypertree	√	Dynamic	×	×	√	2^{60}	unlimit	2000
HHGS	OTS	Hypertree	√	Dynamic	√	√	√	2^{20}	2^{20}	6.41
HHGS^+	OTS	Hypertree	√	Dynamic	√	√	√	2^{30}	2^{30}	7.04

In the second category, a group signature comprises of a SP-based NIZK proof of the knowledge of a group membership credential, such as BEB [11] and SPHINX [21]. The credential in BEB [11], is a signature of GM based on a single Merkle tree, so it only provides static group management. SPHINX [21] is a fully dynamic group signature with a hash-based signature, called F-SPHINCS+, and optimized for efficient NIZK proofs. Unlike previous works, it supports large group sizes (up to 2^{60}).

It is important to note that the comparison between OTS-based group signatures and NIZK-based schemes involves different design goals and security guarantees. In particular, NIZK-based schemes such as BEB and SPHINX can achieve strong anonymity properties, for example full anonymity that holds even against adversaries that obtain all users' secret keys, and they typically provide more compact user-side secret keys. This comes at the cost of larger signature sizes and higher computational overhead for signing and verification. In contrast, our OTS-based constructions are tailored to RCAC scenarios with forward security for resource-constrained devices. They avoid executing computationally intensive NIZK protocols on the client side, at the expense of larger credentials and relatively weaker anonymity guarantees under full key exposure.

Moreover, all compared schemes cannot provide forward security. Unlike NIZK-based GS schemes, our schemes are more suitable for RCAC scenarios involving resource-constrained devices, as they do not require running NIZK operations on devices that store the secret key. Instead, our schemes only need to execute one PRG operation, one OTS key generation, and two OTS signing operations on the client device (e.g., smart card). Although the group credentials are not small, they can be stored on an auxiliary storage device (e.g., mobile phone), and the leakage of group credentials does not compromise traceability. To further reduce storage costs, the client can register OTS keys on-demand, rather than registering all of them at once. Our schemes make a trade-off between group size and signature capacity. The total OTS keys' amount of our scheme is $O(2^{60})$, and it can *adaptively adjust the ratio of members to their OTS keys.* For simplicity, we consider an equal split (as an example), which can meet the requirements of most practical applications.

We also provide a rough comparison of the signature sizes (based on results from the relevant literature) across different schemes, considering the corresponding group sizes. While the signatures in our schemes are slightly larger than those of G-Merkle, $\mathrm{GM}^{\mathrm{MT}}$, and DGMT, this increase stems from our simultaneous support for dynamic group management, forward security, user-controlled key management, and sibling attack resilience. However, they are significantly smaller than those of the NIZK-based schemes.

2 Preliminaries

Notation. We let κ be the security parameter and $\emptyset$ be an empty string. The set of integers between 1 and n is represented by $[n] = \{1, \ldots, n\} \subset \mathbb{N}$. We use $\|$ to denote the string concatenation operation, and # to represent an operation to calculate the size of an element. Moreover, we denote by $y \leftarrow \mathcal{A}(x)$ the execution of algorithm $\mathcal{A}$ on input x, resulting in output y. The notation $x \xleftarrow{\$} X$ represents the operation of sampling x uniformly at random from a set X.

In the following, we manly review the syntax of the main cryptographic building blocks of our upcoming constructions. The security definitions of them are presented in Appendix A. We assume the *parameters* generated by the setup algorithm of a primitive may be implicitly used by its other algorithms.

Digital Signature. A digital signature scheme $\mathsf{SIG} = (\mathsf{Setup}, \mathsf{KGen}, \mathsf{Sign}, \mathsf{Verify})$ involves four algorithms. $\mathsf{Setup}(1^\kappa)$ initializes parameters pms_{SIG}, defining the randomness space $\mathcal{RS}_{\mathsf{SIG}}$, secret key $\mathcal{SK}_{\mathsf{SIG}}$, public key space $\mathcal{PK}_{\mathsf{SIG}}$, and signature space $\mathcal{S}_{\mathsf{SIG}}$. $\mathsf{KGen}(rs)$ uses randomness $rs \in \mathcal{RS}_{\mathsf{SIG}}$ to produce a secret key $sk \in \mathcal{SK}_{\mathsf{SIG}}$ and its corresponding public key $pk \in \mathcal{PK}_{\mathsf{SIG}}$. $\mathsf{Sign}(sk, m)$ generates a signature $\sigma \in \mathcal{S}_{\mathsf{SIG}}$ for a message $m \in \mathcal{M}_{\mathsf{SIG}}$ using the secret key sk. $\mathsf{Verify}(pk, m, \sigma)$ checks if σ is a valid signature on m under pk, outputting 1 if valid and 0 otherwise. One-time signature (OTS) schemes, designed for securely signing a single message with a unique key pair, ensure authenticity and resistance to forgery, with security analyzed under adaptive chosen message attacks.

Merkle Tree. A Merkle tree scheme consists of four algorithms, $\mathsf{MT} = (\mathsf{Setup}$, Build, GetPrf, $\mathsf{Verify})$. $\mathsf{Setup}(1^\kappa)$ takes as input 1^κ and outputs the parameter pms_{MT} defining leaf space $\mathcal{L}_{\mathsf{M}}$ and proof space $\mathcal{PF}_{\mathsf{M}}$. $\mathsf{Build}(\{\mathrm{lf}_i\}_{i \in [N]})$ constructs a Merkle tree instance Tr based on these leaves in $\mathcal{L}_{\mathsf{M}}$, and outputs the initial state $\mathsf{st}_{\mathrm{BDS}}$ for the tree traversal algorithm described in [17] (commonly referred to as the BDS algorithm). Moreover, we let $\mathsf{st}_{\mathrm{BDS}}^{\mathrm{lf}_i} \subseteq \mathsf{st}_{\mathrm{BDS}}$ denote the BDS state for a specific leaf lf_i. $\mathsf{GetPrf}(\mathsf{st}_{\mathrm{BDS}}, \mathrm{lf}_i)$ takes as input the state $\mathsf{st}_{\mathrm{BDS}}$ and a leaf lf_i, and out outputs a Merkle proof $\mathrm{pf}_{\mathrm{lf}_i} \in \mathcal{PF}_{\mathsf{M}}$ that attests to the inclusion of lf_i in the tree, along with the updated BDS state $\mathsf{st}_{\mathrm{BDS}}$. $\mathsf{Verify}(\mathrm{Tr.Rt}, \mathrm{lf}_i, \mathrm{pf}_{\mathrm{lf}_i})$ takes as input the root Tr.Rt, a leaf node lf_i, and the corresponding proof $\mathrm{pf}_{\mathrm{lf}_i}$, and returns 1 returning 1 if the proof validates lf_i's inclusion in Tr.Rt, and 0 otherwise. The Merkle proofs of a secure MT scheme should satisfy unforgeability.

Authenticated Encryption. An authenticated encryption (AE) scheme consists of four algorithms $\mathsf{AE} = (\mathsf{Setup}, \mathsf{KGen}, \mathsf{Enc}, \mathsf{Dec})$. $\mathsf{Setup}(1^\kappa)$ initializes the scheme with security parameter κ, outputting public parameters pms_{AE} that define the key space $\mathcal{K}_{\mathsf{AE}}$, plaintext space $\mathcal{M}_{\mathsf{AE}}$, and ciphertext space $\mathcal{C}_{\mathsf{AE}}$. $\mathsf{KGen}(rk)$ generates a symmetric key $k \in \mathcal{K}_{\mathsf{AE}}$ using randomness $rk \in \mathcal{RK}_{\mathsf{AE}}$. $\mathsf{Enc}(k, m)$ encrypts a message $m \in \mathcal{M}_{\mathsf{AE}}$ with key k, producing ciphertext $c \in \mathcal{C}_{\mathsf{AE}}$. $\mathsf{Dec}(k, c)$ decrypts $(k, c) \in \mathcal{K}_{\mathsf{AE}} \times \mathcal{C}_{\mathsf{AE}}$, outputting plaintext m or failure symbol $\perp$. For security of AE, we consider the security properties regarding indistinguishability under adaptive chosen-ciphertext attacks, and the integrity of ciphertext.

Pseudorandom Generators. A pseudorandom generator consists of three algorithms $\mathsf{PRG} = (\mathsf{Setup}, \mathsf{SGen}, \mathsf{Eval})$. $\mathsf{Setup}(1^\kappa)$ initializes the scheme with security parameter κ, producing parameters pms_{PRG} that define the input space $\mathcal{S}_{\mathsf{PRG}}$ and range space $\mathcal{R}_{\mathsf{PRG}}$. $\mathsf{SGen}(pms_{\mathsf{PRG}})$ uses these parameters to output a random seed $s \xleftarrow{\$} \mathcal{S}_{\mathsf{PRG}}$, while the randomness generation algorithm $\mathsf{Eval}(s)$ takes a seed

$s \in \mathcal{S}_{\mathsf{PRG}}$ and outputs a pseudorandom value $r \in \mathcal{R}_{\mathsf{PRG}}$. The output of PRG must be indistinguishable from a truly random value. For a specific PRG scheme G, we may use the shorthand notation $\mathsf{G}(s)$ to represent $\mathsf{G.Eval}(s)$.

(Puncturable) Pseudo-random Functions. We define a pseudorandom function (PRF) family with three algorithms $\mathsf{PRF} = (\mathsf{Setup}, \mathsf{KGen}, \mathsf{Eval})$. $\mathsf{Setup}(1^\kappa)$ initializes the scheme with security parameter κ, producing parameters pms_{PRF} that define the key space $\mathcal{K}_{\mathsf{PRF}}$, message space $\mathcal{M}_{\mathsf{PRF}}$, and range space $\mathcal{R}_{\mathsf{PRF}}$. $\mathsf{KGen}(pms_{\mathsf{PRF}})$ generates a random secret key $k \xleftarrow{\$} \mathcal{K}_{\mathsf{PRF}}$. $\mathsf{Eval}(k, x)$ computes the evaluation result $r \in \mathcal{R}_{\mathsf{PRF}}$ for a message $x \in \mathcal{M}_{\mathsf{PRF}}$ using the secret key k.

A puncturable pseudorandom function (PPRF) family is defined by four algorithms, $\mathsf{PPRF} = (\mathsf{Setup}, \mathsf{KGen}, \mathsf{Eval}, \mathsf{Punc})$, with the same spaces as PRF for simplicity. The syntax of the first two algorithms mirrors that of PRF. The puncturing algorithm $\mathsf{Punc}(k, x)$ takes as input a key $k \in \mathcal{K}_{\mathsf{PRF}}$ and a message $x \in \mathcal{M}_{\mathsf{PRF}}$, and outputs a punctured key in $\mathcal{K}_{\mathsf{PRF}}$. For a specific (P)PRF function F, we may use the shorthand notation $\mathsf{F}(k, x)$ to represent $\mathsf{F.Eval}(k, x)$.

Collision-Resistant Hash Functions. We define a collision-resistant (CR) hash function $\mathsf{CRH} = (\mathsf{Setup}, \mathsf{Eval})$ as a keyed hash function with two algorithms. $\mathsf{Setup}(1^\kappa)$ initializes the scheme with security parameter κ, producing parameters pms_{CRH} and a random key $hk \xleftarrow{\$} \mathcal{K}_{\mathsf{CRH}}$, where pms_{CRH} defines the key space $\mathcal{K}_{\mathsf{CRH}}$, message space $\mathcal{M}_{\mathsf{CRH}}$, and hash value space $\mathcal{Y}_{\mathsf{CRH}}$. $\mathsf{Eval}(hk, m)$ computes a hash value $y \in \mathcal{Y}_{\mathsf{CRH}}$ for a message $m \in \mathcal{M}_{\mathsf{CRH}}$ using key hk. For a given CRH scheme H, we use $\mathsf{H}(m)$ as shorthand for $\mathsf{H.Eval}(hk, m)$ when the hash key hk is clear from the context.

3 Security Model of FSDGS

Syntax. A FSDGS scheme involves a group manager (GM), verifiers, and group members. The GM is a trusted third party responsible for system initialization and group member management. Each group member has a unique identity ID and can anonymously create a group signature. Verifier, who might be an outsider or a member of the group, can verify the validity of a group signature. We define the syntax of FSDGS via the following algorithms $\Sigma = (\mathsf{GMInit}, \mathsf{MInit}, \mathsf{MRegGen}, \mathsf{Join}, \mathsf{Sign}, \mathsf{Verify}, \mathsf{Open}, \mathsf{Revoke})$:

- $(\mathsf{Pms}, \mathsf{gpk}, \mathsf{sk}_{\mathsf{GM}}, \mathsf{st}_{\mathsf{GM}}, \mathrm{RL}) \leftarrow \mathsf{GMInit}(1^\kappa, \mathsf{SP})$: The GM initialization algorithm takes as input the security parameter 1^κ and a setup parameter SP required by a specific scheme. This algorithm outputs a system parameter Pms, a group public and private key pair $(\mathsf{gpk}, \mathsf{sk}_{\mathsf{GM}})$, the group management state $\mathsf{st}_{\mathsf{GM}}$ of the group manager GM, and a revocation list RL.
- $(sk_{\mathsf{ID}}, \mathsf{st}_{\mathsf{ID}}) \leftarrow \mathsf{MInit}(\mathsf{ID})$: A group member ID runs the member initialization algorithm to generate its secret key sk_{ID} and the initial state $\mathsf{st}_{\mathsf{ID}}$.
- $\mathrm{RF}_{\mathsf{ID}} \leftarrow \mathsf{MRegGen}(sk_{\mathsf{ID}})$: A group member ID uses its secret key sk_{ID} to generate the registration file $\mathrm{RF}_{\mathsf{ID}} \in \mathcal{RF}$ from the corresponding space $\mathcal{RF}$.

- $(\mathsf{Vt}, \mathrm{RR}_{\mathsf{ID}}) \leftarrow \mathsf{Join}(\mathsf{sk}_{\mathsf{GM}}, \mathsf{st}_{\mathsf{GM}}, \mathsf{ID}, \mathrm{RF}_{\mathsf{ID}})$: The join protocol is an interactive procedure between the group manager and a member ID seeking to join the group with its registration file $\mathrm{RF}_{\mathsf{ID}}$. The group manager GM utilizes the group secret key $\mathsf{sk}_{\mathsf{GM}}$ and its local state $\mathsf{st}_{\mathsf{GM}}$. Upon completion of the protocol, GM updates the group secret key $\mathsf{sk}_{\mathsf{GM}}$ and its management state $\mathsf{st}_{\mathsf{GM}}$, respectively. ID will update its state $\mathsf{st}_{\mathsf{ID}}$ using the registration result $\mathrm{RR}_{\mathsf{ID}}$ obtained from GM. Furthermore, the transcript of the protocol's execution is recorded in the variable Vt which may be $\perp$ indicating any join failure. A group member ID can register different registration files many times.
- $(sk'_{\mathsf{ID}}, \mathsf{st}'_{\mathsf{ID}}, \sigma) \leftarrow \mathsf{Sign}(sk_{\mathsf{ID}}, \mathsf{st}_{\mathsf{ID}}, m)$: The signing algorithm takes as input the secret key sk_{ID} of ID, along with its state $\mathsf{st}_{\mathsf{ID}}$, and a message $m \in \mathcal{M}$. The algorithm generates a group signature σ on the message m and also outputs an updated secret key sk'_{ID} and state $\mathsf{st}'_{\mathsf{ID}}$, for ID.
- $\{0,1\} \leftarrow \mathsf{Verify}(\mathsf{gpk}, m, \sigma, \mathrm{RL})$: The signature verification algorithm takes as input the group public key gpk, a message m, a group signature σ on m, and a public revocation list RL. It outputs 1 if the signature is valid, and 0 otherwise.
- $\mathsf{ID} \leftarrow \mathsf{Open}(\mathsf{gpk}, \mathsf{sk}_{\mathsf{GM}}, m, \sigma)$: The opening algorithm takes as input the group public key gpk, the group secret key $\mathsf{sk}_{\mathsf{GM}}$, a message m, and a group signature σ for m to return an identity ID or the symbol $\perp$ to indicate failure.
- $\mathrm{RL}' \leftarrow \mathsf{Revoke}(\mathsf{gpk}, \mathsf{sk}_{\mathsf{GM}}, \mathrm{RL}, \mathsf{ID}, \mathrm{RSS})$: The revocation algorithm takes as input the group public key gpk, the group secret key $\mathsf{sk}_{\mathsf{GM}}$, the revocation list RL, the revoking identity ID, and a set of group signatures RSS to be revoked. This algorithm updates the revocation list RL to RL'.

Correctness. A correct FSDGS scheme should ensure that all honest members' unrevoked signatures on any messages should pass the verification algorithm, i.e., $\Pr[\mathsf{Exp}_{\mathcal{A},\Sigma}^{\mathsf{Correct}}(\kappa, q_s, \mathsf{SP}) \Rightarrow 1] = 1$, where is $\mathsf{Exp}_{\mathcal{A},\Sigma}^{\mathsf{Correct}}(\kappa, q_s, \mathsf{SP})$ the correctness ($\mathsf{Correct}$) experiment defined in Fig. 1 for exp $=$ $\mathsf{Correct}$.

Security Definition. The security properties that we consider in this work, are adapted from [4,5,13,21,37], including two critical properties: forward-secure traceability (Trace) and anonymity (Anony) with forward privacy, in a dynamic group management setting. For the security definition, we formalize these properties through the security experiments defined in Fig. 1. These experiments are indexed by the variable exp $\in \{\mathsf{Trace}, \mathsf{Anony}\}$, respectively. Moreover, we let $\mathsf{GetCT}()$ be a generic timestamp function that outputs the current system time, e.g., by counting the steps executed by the Turing Machine.

Informally speaking, forward-Secure traceability requires that even an adversary, capable of corrupting the tracing manager and potentially some or all group members (via $\mathsf{Corrupt}$ queries), cannot produce a valid signature under two conditions (**Trace-Cons**): i) The signature cannot be opened to a non-corrupted group member, ensuring that honest users remain protected; ii) The signature cannot be traced to a corrupted member if it was created in a time period before the adversary accessed that the secret key of a member or the group manager. These properties strengthen the standard traceability requirement, as established in [4,5], to include forward-security, ensuring that prior signatures remain secure even after either a member or group manager is compromised. Anonymity with forward privacy ensures that a PPT adversary cannot distinguish (**Anony-Cons**) which of two honest group members signed a challenged message, provided that GM remains uncorrupted, the signatures stay unopened, and the signers were uncorrupted when they generated their signatures. This holds even when the adversary selects the members (adding honest and malicious ones via AddHM and AddMM queries, respectively), the signing message of honest members (using HMSign queries), and the time period. Meanwhile, an adversary may exploit the dynamics of the group management (e.g., registering malicious members, revoking members, opening identities of signatures) trying to gain extra advantage for breaking these two properties.

Definition 1 (FSDGS Security). *We say that a correct FSDGS scheme Σ is secure if the advantages, $\mathsf{Adv}^{\mathsf{Trace}}_{\mathcal{A},\Sigma}(\kappa, q_s, \mathsf{SP})$ and $\mathsf{Adv}^{\mathsf{Anony}}_{\mathcal{A},\Sigma,\frac{1}{2}}(\kappa, q_s, \mathsf{SP})$ (as defined in Appendix A), of any PPT adversaries are negligible in the corresponding security experiments.*

$\underline{\mathsf{Exp}^{\mathsf{exp}}_{\mathcal{A},\Sigma}(\kappa, q_s, \mathsf{SP}):}$
$b \xleftarrow{\$} \{0,1\};\ T_p := \infty$ ▷ Anonymity test bit and time
$t_s := 0$ ▷ Number of asked signing queries
$T_c^{\mathsf{GM}} := \infty$ ▷ Corrupt time of GM
$\mathsf{L}_{\mathrm{C}} := \mathsf{L}_{\mathrm{HM}} := \emptyset$ ▷ Lists of corrupted and honest IDs
$\mathsf{L}_{\mathrm{Op}} := \mathsf{L}_{S} := \emptyset$ ▷ Lists of opened and queried signatures
$\mathsf{L}_{\mathrm{R}} := \emptyset$ ▷ Lists of revoked IDs and signatures
$(\mathsf{Pms}, \mathsf{gpk}, \mathsf{sk}_{\mathsf{GM}}, \mathsf{st}_{\mathsf{GM}}, \mathrm{RL}) \leftarrow \mathsf{GMInit}(1^\kappa, \mathsf{SP})$
$(b^*, m^*, \sigma^*) \leftarrow \mathcal{A}^{\mathcal{O}_{\mathsf{FSDGS}}(\cdot), \mathcal{O}_{\mathsf{PriTest}}(\cdot,\cdot,\cdot)}(\mathsf{Pms}, \mathsf{gpk})$
$T^* := \mathsf{GetCT}()$
  $vr^* \leftarrow \mathsf{Verify}(\mathsf{gpk}, m^*, \sigma^*, \mathrm{RL})$
  $\mathsf{ID}^* \leftarrow \Sigma.\mathsf{Open}(\mathsf{gpk}, \mathsf{sk}_{\mathsf{GM}}, m^*, \sigma^*)$
IF $\mathsf{exp} = \mathsf{Correct}$
  IF $(\mathsf{ID}^* \notin \mathsf{L}_{\mathrm{HM}}) \vee (\mathsf{ID}^* \in \mathsf{L}_{\mathrm{R}}) \vee (\sigma^* \in \mathsf{L}_{\mathrm{R}})$, OUTPUT 1
  OUTPUT $((vr^* = 1) \wedge ((\mathsf{ID}^*, m^*, \sigma^*) \in \mathsf{L}_S))$
IF $\mathsf{exp} = \mathsf{Trace}$ ▷ **Trace-Cons**
  IF $(\mathsf{ID}^* \notin \mathsf{L}_{\mathrm{HM}}) \vee ((\mathsf{ID}^* \in \mathsf{L}_{\mathrm{HM}}) \wedge (T_c^{\mathsf{ID}^*} > T^*))$, $idc := 1$
  IF $T_c^{\mathsf{GM}} > T^*$, $gmc := 1$
  OUTPUT $(vr^* = 1) \wedge idc \wedge gmc$
IF $\mathsf{exp} = \mathsf{Anony}$ ▷ **Anony-Cons**
  IF $((\mathsf{ID}_0^*, \mathsf{ID}_1^*) \notin \mathsf{L}_{\mathrm{HM}}) \vee (T_p \geq T_c^{\mathsf{ID}_0^*}) \vee (T_p \geq T_c^{\mathsf{ID}_1^*})$
    $\vee\ (\mathsf{GM} \in \mathsf{L}_{\mathrm{C}}) \vee (\hat{\sigma}_0 \in \mathsf{L}_{\mathrm{Op}}) \vee (\hat{\sigma}_1 \in \mathsf{L}_{\mathrm{Op}})$, OUTPUT $\perp$
  OUTPUT $b^* = b$

$\underline{\mathcal{O}_{\mathsf{PriTest}}(\mathsf{ID}_0^*, \mathsf{ID}_1^*, m):}$
IF $(\mathsf{exp} \neq \mathsf{Anony}) \wedge ((\mathsf{ID}_0^*, \mathsf{ID}_1^*) \notin \mathsf{L}_{\mathrm{HM}})$, OUTPUT $\perp$
$T_p := \mathsf{GetCT}()$
$(sk'_{\mathsf{ID}_0^*}, \mathsf{st}'_{\mathsf{ID}_0^*}, \hat{\sigma_0}) \leftarrow \mathsf{Sign}(sk_{\mathsf{ID}_0^*}, \mathsf{st}_{\mathsf{ID}_0^*}, m)$
$(sk'_{\mathsf{ID}_1^*}, \mathsf{st}'_{\mathsf{ID}_1^*}, \hat{\sigma_1}) \leftarrow \mathsf{Sign}(sk_{\mathsf{ID}_1^*}, \mathsf{st}_{\mathsf{ID}_1^*}, m)$
OUTPUT $\hat{\sigma_b}$

$\underline{\mathcal{O}_{\mathsf{FSDGS}}(Query):}$
$T_\delta := \mathsf{GetCT}()$
IF $Query = \mathsf{AddHM}(\mathsf{ID})$:
  IF $\mathsf{ID} \in \mathsf{L}_{\mathrm{C}} \cup \perp$, OUTPUT $\perp$
  IF $\mathsf{ID} \notin \mathsf{L}_{\mathrm{HM}}$, $(sk_{\mathsf{ID}}, \mathsf{st}_{\mathsf{ID}}) \leftarrow \mathsf{MInit}(\mathsf{ID})$
  $T_c^{\mathsf{ID}} := \infty;\ \mathrm{RF}_{\mathsf{ID}} \leftarrow \mathsf{MRegGen}(sk_{\mathsf{ID}})$
  $(\mathsf{Vt}, \mathrm{RR}_{\mathsf{ID}}) \leftarrow \mathsf{Join}(\mathsf{sk}_{\mathsf{GM}}, \mathsf{st}_{\mathsf{GM}}, \mathsf{ID}, \mathrm{RF}_{\mathsf{ID}})$
  OUTPUT $\mathsf{Vt} \neq \perp$
IF $Query = \mathsf{AddMM}(\mathsf{ID}, \mathrm{RF}_{\mathsf{ID}})$
  IF $\mathsf{ID} \in \mathsf{L}_{\mathrm{HM}} \cup \perp$, OUTPUT $\perp$
  $T_c^{\mathsf{ID}} := T_\delta;\ \mathsf{L}_{\mathrm{C}} := \mathsf{L}_{\mathrm{C}} \cup (\mathsf{ID}, T_c^{\mathsf{ID}}) \rightarrow \mathsf{L}_{\mathrm{C}}$
  OUTPUT $\mathsf{Join}(\mathsf{sk}_{\mathsf{GM}}, \mathsf{st}_{\mathsf{GM}}, \mathsf{ID}, \mathrm{RF}_{\mathsf{ID}})$
IF $Query = \mathsf{HMSign}(\mathsf{ID}, m)$
  IF $(\mathsf{ID} \notin \mathsf{L}_{\mathrm{HM}}) \vee (t_s \geq q_s)$, OUTPUT $\perp$
  $(sk'_{\mathsf{ID}}, \mathsf{st}'_{\mathsf{ID}}, \sigma) \leftarrow \Sigma.\mathsf{Sign}(sk_{\mathsf{ID}}, \mathsf{st}_{\mathsf{ID}}, m)$
  $\mathsf{L}_S := \mathsf{L}_S \cup (\mathsf{ID}, m, \sigma);\ t_s := t_s + 1$
  OUTPUT σ
IF $Query = \mathsf{Corrupt}(P)$
  IF $(P \in \mathsf{L}_{\mathrm{C}}) \vee (P \notin \mathsf{L}_{\mathrm{HM}} \cup \mathsf{GM})$, OUTPUT $\perp$
  $T_c^P := T_\delta;\ \mathsf{L}_{\mathrm{C}} := \mathsf{L}_{\mathrm{C}} \cup (P, T_c^P)$
  OUTPUT sk_P
IF $Query = \mathsf{OpenID}(m, \sigma)$
  $\mathsf{L}_{\mathrm{Op}} := \mathsf{L}_{\mathrm{Op}} \cup \sigma$
  OUTPUT $\Sigma.\mathsf{Open}(\mathsf{gpk}, \mathsf{sk}_{\mathsf{GM}}, m, \sigma)$
IF $Query = \mathsf{Revoke}(\mathsf{ID}, \mathrm{RSS})$
  $\mathsf{L}_{\mathrm{R}} := \mathsf{L}_{\mathrm{R}} \cup (\mathsf{ID}, \mathrm{RSS})$
  OUTPUT $\mathsf{Revoke}(\mathsf{gpk}, \mathsf{sk}_{\mathsf{GM}}, \mathrm{RL}, \mathsf{ID}, \mathrm{RSS})$

Fig. 1. Security Experiments for Forward Secure Dynamic Group Signature.

4 Our FSDGS Constructions

In this section, we introduce two novel FSDGS schemes based on OTS. The first scheme is built upon an OTS hypertree, while the second securely leverages the first as a building block to further extend the signing capability.

4.1 An Efficient Solution HHGS with Hypertree

Construction Overview. The goals of HHGS include: post-quantum security (G1), efficient dynamic group management (G2), forward security (G3), and provable security in standard model (G4).

Technical Challenges. One approach for achieving the above goals is to follow the research line of OTS-based group signatures. A member requests to join a group with its OTS public key and the group manager GM adds the member to the group by signing that member's key using GM's OTS secret key. The member can anonymously sign a message using the OTS secret key corresponding to the public key certified with signatures from GM. A dynamic group with a large size demands a large number of OTS key pairs of GM. Updating the group public key whenever the group changes might pose an inconvenience for existing members. A natural way for achieving G2 is to use a Merkle tree to manage GM's OTS key pairs, where each leaf corresponds to a key pair of GM. Note that the authentication paths of the signatures generated by GM would share nodes in the tree. An adversary can launch a **sibling attack** by exploiting the shared information to infer the identity of the member who generates the group signature and thus break the anonymity. This naturally leads to the question of achieving resilience against sibling attacks in a dynamic group with a large group size. To answer this question, we need to ensure that the OTS key pairs of GM are randomly assigned to members to be joined. A straightforward randomization approach using pseudorandom permutations is impractical since the member can dynamically join the group with unpredictable keys and handling permutations over a large set becomes computationally infeasible. Hence, realizing random selection of a large number of GM's OTS key pairs remains a challenge.

To meet the requirements of G2 and G3, we cannot simply adopt the stateless hypertree used in previous signature schemes, such as those in the SPHINCS+ family [7,31], where secret keys remain static throughout the scheme's lifetime and can derive all keys within the hypertree. However, incorporating dynamic group management (G2) or key-evolving techniques for achieving PFS (G3) inevitably introduces dynamic states for managing the group structure or evolving keys, thereby violating their stateless nature. For instance, the FORS+C layer of SPHINCS+C [31] involves more than 2^{77} leaves, which may require extensive state management. Thus, we need to seek an optimized stateful hypertree structure suitable for G2 and G3 from scratch. Meanwhile, we should avoid the repeated selection of the same key pair in the random selection process. In addition, all construction details should satisfy G4, which makes it harder to build, especially when considering adversaries who can adaptively register both honest and malicious members and compromise honest members.

Construction Ideas. Our construction starts from organizing OTS key pairs to align with all the aforementioned design goals, following the approach of stateful signature schemes like XMSS-T [32], which offer a more efficient signature structure compared to stateless alternatives such as SPHINCS+C [31]. Our main idea is to adopt a hypertree structure which consists of a GM's OTS hypertree and multiple mixed OTS mount sub-trees (MMT) with obfuscated OTS layers. The leaves of the trees in the hypertree are used to sign the root of the trees or the sub-trees below. This structure allows GM to generate one tree (sub-tree) on each layer on demand, significantly reducing signature sizes and computational overhead compared to a single large tree. To further optimize GM's computational cost and members' storage requirements, the leaves computed during constructing MMT not only derive from OTS key pairs of GM but also from members' OTS key pairs. This design results in a mixed sub-layer in MMT. However, a security issue arises if the members' OTS secret keys corresponding to their OTS public keys in the mixed sub-layer are used to sign messages directly. In this case, the group signatures generated from these two types of leaves differ in form and can reflect a certain chronological order. An adversary can infer the identity of the member who generates the challenge group signature according the joining order of members. Thus, all keys in the above mixed sub-layer are used to sign the OTS public keys (in the bottom member sub-layer) from members, which will be used to sign messages. To realize the indistinguishability of the group signatures, we bind the OTS public keys of GM and members with fake Identity-OPK ciphertexts (IOCs) and members' IOCs, respectively. The hashes generated from these OTS public keys and ciphertexts serve as the real leaves of MMT.

To realize G3, we use PPRFs to generate OTS key pairs for GM. Within each layer of the hypertree structure, all OTS key pairs of GM are derived using a PPRF specific to that layer. GM maintains the punctured key and state for each PPRF to track which indices and corresponding key pairs have already been used. A used index will be punctured to prevent the reuse of assigned key pairs, thereby ensuring forward security. After each puncturing operation, the BDS state of each tree is updated accordingly, enabling on-demand Merkle proof generation for the remaining available OTS key pairs. Simultaneously, each member uses a pseudorandom generator to generate its OTS key pairs, ensuring the forward security of the signatures (Fig. 2).

A critical component of our design is to assign OTS key pairs in the mixed sub-layer to members dynamically. To achieve resilience against sibling attacks, the assignment must be random and independent. Random functions can be used to realize the random selection of OTS key pairs, i.e., determine the index of a leaf in the mixed sub-layer randomly. However, the outputs of existing random functions (like keyed hash functions) are not uniformly random, potentially leading to collisions in indices chosen by GM. There are two main challenges for resolving collisions: how to know which index corresponding to a OTS key pair has been used yet (Q1)? and how to randomly choose an unused key pair from the remaining available key pairs (Q2)? For Q1, PPRFs can be used to trace allocated indices, thereby supporting the subsequent random selection

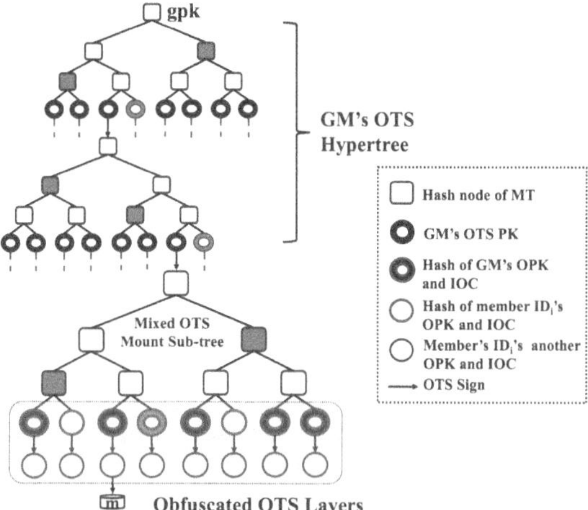

Fig. 2. A visualization of HHGS with a compact structure. The elements highlighted in blue are included in the group credential used for signing m. (Color figure online)

approaches. To answer Q2, we explore two approaches: recomputation and random range. Recomputation iteratively modifies the input of the random function (e.g., appending a counter) and repeats the calculation to generate a new index until an unused index is found. This approach becomes computationally expensive as the number of available indices diminishes. Alternatively, random range allows direct sampling from unused indices tracked by the PPRFs, significantly reducing the overhead associated with collision resolution.

Construction Preliminaries. To facilitate the description of our construction, we first review the hypertree structure [7,31] and define functions for obtaining/verifying the authentication credential of a message based on the hypertree.

Hypertree. A hypertree (i.e., a tree of trees) of total height $h \in \mathbb{N}$ consists of d layers of trees, each having height $h' = \frac{h}{d}$. On layer $i \in [d]$, the hypertree has $TN_i = 2^{(d-i)h'}$ trees. Let HI_i denote the index of a OTS key pair at the i-th layer. The OTS key pair $(osk^{\mathsf{HI}_1}, opk^{\mathsf{HI}_1})$ belonging to a tree at the bottom layer (i.e., layer 1), which is to be used to sign a message m. We denote HI_i as the first $(d+1-i) \times h'$ bits of HI_1 for $i \in [d]$. On layer $1 < i \leq d$, the OTS key pair $(osk^{\mathsf{HI}_i}, opk^{\mathsf{HI}_i})$ with the index HI_i is used to sign the root of the tree which has the OTS public key $osk^{\mathsf{HI}_{i-1}}$ as a leaf node. For a message m, its authentication credential $\mathsf{Auth}[m] = \{(opk^{\mathsf{HI}_i}, \mathrm{pf}_{\mathrm{lf}}^{\mathsf{HI}_i}, \sigma^{\mathsf{HI}_i})\}_{i \in [d]}$ can be generated (verified) by running the following $\mathsf{GetAuth}$ ($\mathsf{AuthVrfy}$) algorithm. The i-th tuple in $\mathsf{Auth}[m]$ contains the OTS public key opk^{HI_i} for verifying σ^{HI_i}, the Merkle proof $\mathrm{pf}_{\mathrm{lf}}^{\mathsf{HI}_i}$ for authenticating opk^{HI_i}, and the signature σ^{HI_i} on the message m ($i = 1$) or on the root of a below tree including $opk^{\mathsf{HI}_{i-1}}$ ($i > 1$).

–$\mathsf{GetAuth}(sk, m, \mathsf{HI}_1)$. Given a secret key sk, a message m, and an index HI_1, this algorithm outputs the authentication credential $\mathsf{Auth}[m]$ for m. For layers 1 to

d, this algorithm repeatedly uses sk to generate the tree at the i-th layer which include the OTS key pair $(osk^{\mathsf{HI}_i}, opk^{\mathsf{HI}_i})$ and computes the Merkle proof $\mathrm{pf}_{\mathrm{lf}}^{\mathsf{HI}_i}$ for the leaf lf associated with opk^{HI_i}. Meanwhile, the root of the tree generated at the end of the previous iteration is signed by the OTS secret key computed in the next iteration. The signature σ^{HI_1} on m is signed by osk^{HI_1}. Finally, this algorithm outputs $\mathsf{Auth}[m] := \{(opk^{\mathsf{HI}_i}, \mathrm{pf}_{\mathrm{lf}}^{\mathsf{HI}_i}, \sigma^{\mathsf{HI}_i})\}_{i\in[d]}$.

-$\mathsf{AuthVrfy}(pk, m, \mathsf{Auth}[m])$. Given a public key pk, a message m, and an authentication credential $\mathsf{Auth}[m]$, this algorithm checks the validity of $\mathsf{Auth}[m]$. For layers 1 to d, this algorithm gets repeated to check whether the leaf lf derived from opk^{HI_i} belongs to the tree on that layer and whether σ^{HI_i} is a valid signature on the message m $(i = 1)$ or the root Rt_i $(i > 1)$. During the verification, the root of each tree is computed with the corresponding leaf and Merkle proof in $\mathsf{Auth}[m]$ by following the root-computation algorithm in [6]. In the final repetition, the generated Rt_d for the root of the top-most tree on layer d is compared to pk. Finally, this algorithm outputs 1 if $\mathrm{Rt}_d = pk$ and 0 otherwise.

Detailed Algorithms of HHGS. We define the algorithms of HHGS as follows:

- $\mathsf{GMInit}(1^\kappa, \mathsf{SP})$: Given the security parameter 1^κ and a setup parameter $\mathsf{SP} = (h, d)$, the group manager GM initializes a set of PPRF schemes as $\{pms_{\mathsf{F}_p^i} := \mathsf{F}_p^i.\mathsf{Setup}(1^\kappa)\}_{0\le i\le d}$, a OTS scheme S as $pms_{\mathsf{S}} := \mathsf{S}.\mathsf{Setup}(1^\kappa)$, a MT scheme M as $pms_{\mathsf{M}} := \mathsf{M}.\mathsf{Setup}(1^\kappa)$, a AE scheme E as $pms_{\mathsf{E}} := \mathsf{E}.\mathsf{Setup}(1^\kappa)$, a PRG scheme G as $pms_{\mathsf{G}} := \mathsf{G}.\mathsf{Setup}(1^\kappa)$, a CRH scheme H as $(hk, pms_{\mathsf{H}}) := \mathsf{H}.\mathsf{Setup}(1^\kappa)$, the PRF schemes F_1 and F_2 as $pms_{\mathsf{F}_i} := \mathsf{F}_i.\mathsf{Setup}(1^\kappa)$ for $i \in [2]$. We assume that the spaces of each building block are compatible with those of other building blocks when their algorithms interact or invoke each other. The system parameter is set as $\mathsf{Pms} := (\{pms_{\mathsf{F}_p^i}\}_{0\le i\le d}, pms_{\mathsf{S}}, pms_{\mathsf{M}}, pms_{\mathsf{E}}, pms_{\mathsf{G}}, pms_{\mathsf{H}}, pms_{\mathsf{F}_1}, pms_{\mathsf{F}_2}, hk)$.

For $0 \le i \le d$, GM computes a random secret key $k_p^i := \mathsf{F}_p^i.\mathsf{KGen}(pms_{\mathsf{F}_p^i})$ to generate OTS key pairs. The i-th layer for $1 \le i \le d$ is a hypertree structure, and the 0-th layer is used to mount the members' OTS keys (which will be defined later). GM also generates a random secret key $k_{\mathsf{GM}} := \mathsf{F}_1.\mathsf{KGen}(pms_{\mathsf{F}_1})$ for F_1. The group secret key $\mathsf{sk}_{\mathsf{GM}}$ consists of the random secret keys of PPRFs and F_1, i.e., $\mathsf{sk}_{\mathsf{GM}} := (\{k_p^i\}_{0\le i\le d}, k_{\mathsf{GM}})$. Then, GM computes the group public key gpk through the following steps:

- Compute the randomnesses $\{rs_{\mathsf{GM}}^{d,1,v}\}_{v\in[2^{h'}]}$ to be used in the generation of leaves $\{\mathrm{lf}_{d,1,v}\}_{v\in[2^{h'}]}$, where each randomness value is defined as $rs_{\mathsf{GM}}^{d,1,v} := \mathsf{F}_p^d(k_p^d, v)$, with v representing a h'-bit index of the leaf $\mathrm{lf}_{d,1,v}$ in the top-most tree of the hypertree structure.
- Compute the OTS key pairs $\{(osk_{\mathsf{GM}}^{d,1,v}, opk_{\mathsf{GM}}^{d,1,v}) := \mathsf{S}.\mathsf{KGen}(rs_{\mathsf{GM}}^{d,1,v})\}_{v\in[2^{h'}]}$ and the leaves $\{\mathrm{lf}_{d,1,v} := opk_{\mathsf{GM}}^{d,1,v}\}_{v\in[2^{h'}]}$.
- Generate the group public key $\mathsf{gpk} := \mathrm{Tr}_{d,1}.\mathrm{Rt}$, where top-most tree $\mathrm{Tr}_{d,1}$ is built via the tree-building algorithm $(\mathrm{Tr}_{d,1}, \mathsf{st}_{\mathrm{BDS}}^{d,1}) := \mathsf{M}.\mathsf{Build}(\{\mathrm{lf}_{d,1,v}\}_{v\in[2^{h'}]})$.

Meanwhile, GM initializes the group management state $\mathsf{st}_{\mathsf{GM}}$ to store a registered identity list RegIDL := $\emptyset$ recording the identities of registered group members and a revocation list RL := $\emptyset$.

- $\mathsf{MInit}(\mathsf{ID})$: The member ID computes a secret seed $sd_{\mathsf{ID}} := \mathsf{G.SGen}(pms_{\mathsf{G}})$ and defines its secret key as $sk_{\mathsf{GM}} := sd_{\mathsf{ID}}$. Meanwhile, ID initializes $\mathsf{st}_{\mathsf{ID}} := \emptyset$.
- $\mathsf{MRegGen}(sk_{\mathsf{ID}})$: ID runs this algorithm to generate $\ell_r \in \mathbb{N}$ OTS public keys to be registered. The member first gets the current secret seed sd_{ID} from its secret key sk_{GM}. For $v \in [\ell_r]$, ID sets the PRG seed as $sd^0_{\mathsf{ID}} := sd_{\mathsf{ID}}$ and generates the v-th OTS key pair $(osk^v_{\mathsf{ID}}, opk^v_{\mathsf{ID}}) := \mathsf{S.KGen}(rs^{v,1}_{\mathsf{ID}})$, where $(rs^{v,1}_{\mathsf{ID}}, rs^{v,2}_{\mathsf{ID}}) := \mathsf{G}(rs^v_{\mathsf{ID}})$ and $(sd^v_{\mathsf{ID}}, rs^v_{\mathsf{ID}}) := \mathsf{G}(sd^{v-1}_{\mathsf{ID}})$. Finally, the registration file is set as $\mathrm{RF}_{\mathsf{ID}} := \{opk^v_{\mathsf{ID}}\}_{v\in[\ell_r]}$, and the secret key is updated to $sk_{\mathsf{ID}} := sd^{\ell_r}_{\mathsf{ID}}$.
- $\mathsf{Join}(\mathsf{sk}_{\mathsf{GM}}, \mathsf{st}_{\mathsf{GM}}, \mathsf{ID}, \mathrm{RF}_{\mathsf{ID}})$: For each $opk_{\mathsf{ID}} \in \mathrm{RF}_{\mathsf{ID}}$, GM randomly selects an unused *mount index* MI := $\mathsf{RandSelect}(\mathsf{sk}_{\mathsf{GM}}, \mathsf{ID}, opk_{\mathsf{ID}})$ that is to mount opk_{ID} (at the layer 0 below the hybertree), where the concrete steps of the random selection function RandSelect is defined later. We further decompose MI into two sub-indices as MI = sTI||sMI, where sTI := MI(h) comprises the first h bits of MI, indexing a MMT. The remaining $|\mathrm{MI}|-h$ bits specify the leaf index, sMI, within the corresponding MMT. Then, GM adds the tuple $(\mathsf{ID}, opk^{\mathrm{MI}}_{\mathsf{ID}}, \mathrm{MI})$ to a registration cache file $\mathsf{RFCa}^{\mathsf{sTI}}_{\mathsf{MMT}}$ for the sub-tree MMT[sTI] with the index sTI. Note that sTI is also the index of the leaf in the hypertree that is used to sign the root of MMT[sTI].

GM checks whether MMT[sTI] has been created by computing $\mathsf{F}^1_p(k^1_p, \mathsf{sTI})$. It then generates authentication credentials for the member's OTS keys in $\mathsf{RFCa}^{\mathsf{sTI}}_{\mathsf{MMT}}$ based on one of the following two cases for constructing the obfuscated OTS layer in MMT.

- **Case** 1 ($\mathsf{F}^1_p(k^1_p, \mathsf{sTI}) \neq \perp$) for MMT initialization: GM needs to build MMT[sTI] using member's keys in $\mathsf{RFCa}^{\mathsf{sTI}}_{\mathsf{MMT}}$ and the supplementary OTS keys generated by itself (for future usage). Let L_{mI} be a list storing the indices of members in $\mathsf{RFCa}^{\mathsf{sTI}}_{\mathsf{MMT}}$ and $\overline{\mathsf{L}}_{\mathrm{mI}}$ be the complement of L_{mI} such that $\mathsf{L}_{\mathrm{mI}} \cup \overline{\mathsf{L}}_{\mathrm{mI}}$ covers all indices of leaves in MMT[sTI]. GM prepares the leaves of MMT[sTI] based on L_{mI} and $\overline{\mathsf{L}}_{\mathrm{mI}}$ respectively as follows.
  - For each index sMI $\in \mathsf{L}_{\mathrm{mI}}$, GM generates an Identity-OPK ciphertext (IOC) $c^1_{\mathrm{MI}} := \mathsf{E.Enc}(ke^1_{\mathrm{MI}}, \mathsf{ID}; re^1_{\mathrm{MI}})$, where $ke^1_{\mathrm{MI}} := \mathsf{F}_1(k_{\mathsf{GM}}, \text{"K-Mix"} || \mathrm{MI})$ and $re^1_{\mathrm{MI}} := \mathsf{F}_1(k_{\mathsf{GM}}, \text{"R-Mix"}||\mathrm{MI})$. It computes a leaf $\mathrm{lf}_{\mathrm{sMI}} := \mathsf{H}(opk^{\mathrm{MI}}_{\mathsf{ID}}||c^1_{\mathrm{MI}})$ in MMT[sTI]. It sets $c^2_{\mathrm{MI}} := \emptyset$, $opk^{\mathrm{MI}}_{\mathsf{GM}} := \emptyset$ and $\sigma^{\mathrm{sMI}}_{\mathsf{GM}} := \emptyset$. These values should be completed by the member during signing a message. Additionally, GM also punctures MI as $k^{0'}_p := \mathsf{F}^0_p.\mathsf{Punc}(k^0_p, \mathrm{MI})$ at level 0 (in a MMT).
  - For each index sMI$' \in \overline{\mathsf{L}}_{\mathrm{mI}}$, GM sets MI$'$:= sTI||sMI$'$ and computes the key pair $(osk^{\mathrm{MI}'}_{\mathsf{GM}}, opk^{\mathrm{MI}'}_{\mathsf{GM}}) := \mathsf{S.KGen}(rs^{\mathrm{MI}'}_{\mathsf{GM}})$, where $rs^{\mathrm{MI}'}_{\mathsf{GM}} := \mathsf{F}^0_p(k^0_p, \mathrm{MI}')$. It computes the encryption key $ke^1_{\mathrm{MI}'} := \mathsf{F}_1(k_{\mathsf{GM}}, \text{"K-Mix"}||\mathrm{MI}')$ and randomness $re^1_{\mathrm{MI}'} := \mathsf{F}_1(k_{\mathsf{GM}}, \text{"R-Mix"}||\mathrm{MI}')$ to generate a fake IOC (encrypting GM) for $opk^{\mathrm{MI}'}_{\mathsf{GM}}$, as $c^1_{\mathrm{MI}} := \mathsf{E.Enc}(ke^1_{\mathrm{MI}'}, \mathsf{GM}; re^1_{\mathrm{MI}'})$.

Then, GM runs $(\mathsf{MMT}[\mathsf{sTI}], \mathsf{st}_{\mathrm{BDS}}^{\mathsf{MMT}[\mathsf{sTI}]}) := \mathsf{M.Build}(\{\mathrm{lf}_v\}_{v\in[2^{|\mathrm{sMI}|}]})$ to build the sub-tree $\mathsf{MMT}[\mathsf{sTI}]$, and obtains $\mathsf{Auth}[\mathsf{MMT}[\mathsf{sTI}].\mathrm{Rt}] := \mathsf{GetAuth}(\{k_p^i\}_{i\in[d]}, \mathsf{MMT}[\mathsf{sTI}].\mathrm{Rt}, \mathsf{sTI})$. Next, it derives the Merkle proof of each $\mathrm{lf}_{\mathrm{sMI}}$ associated with ID's OTS key as $\mathrm{pf}_{\mathrm{lf}_{\mathrm{sMI}}} := \mathsf{M.GetPrf}(\mathsf{st}_{\mathrm{BDS}}^{\mathsf{MMT}[\mathsf{sTI}]}, \mathrm{lf}_{\mathrm{sMI}})$. To achieve forward security, GM punctures the used leaves on the hypertree as $k_p^{i\prime} := \mathsf{F}_p^i.\mathsf{Punc}(k_p^i, \mathrm{MI}(w))$ for the PPRF F_p^i associated with the tree on the i-th layer, where $1 \le i \le d$ and $\mathrm{MI}(w)$ denotes the first $w = \frac{(d+1-i)h}{d}$ bits of MI. In order to compute the Merkle proofs of the GM's OTS keys indexed by any $\mathrm{sMI}' \in \mathsf{L}_{\mathrm{mI}}$ in the future, GM stores the corresponding state $\mathsf{st}_{\mathrm{BDS}}^{\mathrm{lf}_{\mathrm{sMI}'}}$ and $\mathsf{Auth}[\mathsf{MMT}[\mathsf{sTI}].\mathrm{Rt}]$ into $\mathsf{st}_{\mathsf{GM}}$.

- **Case** 2 $(\mathsf{F}_p^1(k_p^1, \mathsf{sTI}) = \bot)$ for MMT usage: In this scenario, each $opk_{\mathsf{ID}}^{\mathrm{MI}}$ in $\mathsf{RFCa}_{\mathsf{MMT}}^{\mathsf{sTI}}$ must reside within the member OTS sub-layer and should therefore be authenticated using GM's OTS key in the mixed sub-layer. GM generates the keys $(osk_{\mathsf{GM}}^{\mathrm{MI}}, opk_{\mathsf{GM}}^{\mathrm{MI}}) := \mathsf{S.KGen}(rs_{\mathsf{GM}}^{\mathrm{MI}})$, where $rs_{\mathsf{GM}}^{\mathrm{MI}} := \mathsf{F}_p^0(k_p^0, \mathrm{MI})$ and the IOC c_{MI}^1 for $opk_{\mathsf{GM}}^{\mathrm{MI}}$ as in Case 1. Then, GM computes the leaf $\mathrm{lf}_{\mathrm{sMI}} := \mathsf{H}(opk_{\mathsf{GM}}^{\mathrm{MI}} || c_{\mathrm{MI}}^1)$ and gets its Merkle proof $\mathrm{pf}_{\mathrm{lf}_{\mathrm{sMI}}} := \mathsf{M.GetPrf}(\mathsf{st}_{\mathrm{BDS}}^{\mathrm{lf}_{\mathrm{sMI}}}, \mathrm{lf}_{\mathrm{sMI}})$, where $\mathsf{st}_{\mathrm{BDS}}^{\mathrm{lf}_{\mathrm{sMI}}} \in \mathsf{st}_{\mathsf{GM}}$. It also retrieves $\mathsf{Auth}[\mathsf{MMT}[\mathsf{sTI}].\mathrm{Rt}]$ from $\mathsf{st}_{\mathsf{GM}}$, and generates an IOC $c_{\mathrm{MI}}^2 := \mathsf{E.Enc}(ke_{\mathrm{MI}}^2, \mathsf{ID}; re_{\mathrm{MI}}^2)$ with $ke_{\mathrm{MI}}^2 := \mathsf{F}_1(k_{\mathsf{GM}}, \text{“K-Mem”}||\mathrm{MI})$ and $re_{\mathrm{MI}}^2 := \mathsf{F}_1(k_{\mathsf{GM}}, \text{“R-Mem”}||\mathrm{MI})$. Lastly, GM creates the signature $\sigma_{\mathsf{GM}}^{\mathrm{sMI}} := \mathsf{S.Sign}(osk_{\mathsf{GM}}^{\mathrm{sMI}}, opk_{\mathsf{ID}}^{\mathrm{MI}} || c_{\mathrm{MI}}^2)$ over $opk_{\mathsf{ID}}^{\mathrm{MI}}$. GM removes $\mathsf{st}_{\mathrm{BDS}}^{\mathrm{lf}_{\mathrm{sMI}}}$ and punctures MI as $k_p^{0\prime} := \mathsf{F}_p^0.\mathsf{Punc}(k_p^0, \mathrm{MI})$.

The authentication credential for each $opk_{\mathsf{ID}}^{\mathrm{MI}} \in \mathsf{RFCa}_{\mathsf{MMT}}^{\mathsf{sTI}}$ is set as $\mathsf{Auth}[opk_{\mathsf{ID}}^{\mathrm{MI}}] := (opk_{\mathsf{GM}}^{\mathrm{MI}}, c_{\mathrm{MI}}^1, c_{\mathrm{MI}}^2, \mathrm{pf}_{\mathrm{lf}_{\mathrm{sMI}}}, \sigma_{\mathsf{GM}}^{\mathrm{sMI}}, \mathsf{MMT}[\mathsf{sTI}].\mathrm{Rt}, \mathsf{Auth}[\mathsf{MMT}[\mathsf{sTI}].\mathrm{Rt}])$. GM iterates through all OTS keys in $\mathrm{RF}_{\mathsf{ID}}$, processing each as described. It then appends every $\mathsf{Auth}[opk_{\mathsf{ID}}^{\mathrm{MI}}]$ to the registration result $\mathrm{RR}_{\mathsf{ID}}$ and returns it to ID, which updates its state $\mathsf{st}_{\mathsf{ID}}$ accordingly.[2] During the execution of this protocol, the sent registration file and the received registration result of ID are recorded in the transcript Vt. Meanwhile, GM adds ID to the registered identity list RegIDL if ID has not previously submitted a join request.

We assume that the join sessions for processing different registration requests from members share the state $\mathsf{st}_{\mathsf{GM}}$. These sessions can be collectively handled by GM through a unified join-hyper routine, reducing the GM's computational and storage costs.

- $\mathsf{Sign}(sk_{\mathsf{ID}}, \mathsf{st}_{\mathsf{ID}}, m)$: A member ID computes the next secret seed and the current key generation randomness as $(sd_{\mathsf{ID}}^v, rs_{\mathsf{ID}}^v) := \mathsf{G}(sd_{\mathsf{ID}}^{v-1})$ and $(rs_{\mathsf{ID}}^{v,1}, rs_{\mathsf{ID}}^{v,2}) := \mathsf{G}(rs_{\mathsf{ID}}^v)$, respectively. Using the randomness $rs_{\mathsf{ID}}^{v,1}$, ID generates a OTS key pair $(osk_{\mathsf{ID}}, opk_{\mathsf{ID}}) := \mathsf{S.KGen}(rs_{\mathsf{ID}}^{v,1})$. Next, ID must determine the sub-layer (either the mixed sub-layer or the member sub-layer) where the OTS public key opk_{ID} resides within the obfuscated layer. To accomplish this, ID retrieves the first (i.e., most recent) authentication credential

[2] GM may optionally returns ke_{MI}^1 and ke_{MI}^2 to enable the member to check the corresponding ciphertext.

$\mathsf{Auth}[opk_{\mathsf{ID}}]$ from $\mathsf{st}_{\mathsf{ID}}$. If $\sigma_{\mathsf{GM}}^{\mathrm{sMI}} \in \mathsf{Auth}[opk_{\mathsf{ID}}]$ is non-empty, this indicates that opk_{ID} belongs to the member sub-layer, and osk_{ID} can be directly used to sign the message m, producing the signature $\sigma_{\mathsf{ID}} := \mathsf{S.Sign}(osk_{\mathsf{ID}}, m)$. Eventually, ID constructs the group signature as $\sigma := (opk_{\mathsf{ID}}, \mathsf{Auth}[opk_{\mathsf{ID}}], \sigma_{\mathsf{ID}})$.

For $\sigma_{\mathsf{GM}}^{\mathrm{sMI}} = \emptyset$, opk_{ID} must reside in the mixed sub-layer. In this case, ID generates an additional key pair $(osk_{\mathsf{ID}}^{'}, opk_{\mathsf{ID}}^{'}) := \mathsf{S.KGen}(rs_{\mathsf{ID}}^{v,2})$ for signing the message, i.e., $\sigma_{\mathsf{ID}} := \mathsf{S.Sign}(osk_{\mathsf{ID}}^{'}, m)$. Additionally, ID randomly generates an IOC c_{ID}' for $opk_{\mathsf{ID}}^{'}$ as in the Join protocol but uses the random key $ke' \xleftarrow{\$} \mathcal{K}_{\mathsf{AE}}$ and the randomness $re' \xleftarrow{\$} \mathcal{ER}_{\mathsf{AE}}$. Next, ID produces the signature $\sigma_{\mathsf{ID}}' := \mathsf{S.Sign}(osk_{\mathsf{ID}}, opk_{\mathsf{ID}}^{'} || c_{\mathsf{ID}}')$ and completes the values regarding $(opk_{\mathsf{GM}}^{\mathrm{MI}}, \sigma_{\mathsf{GM}}^{\mathrm{sMI}}, c_{\mathrm{MI}}^{2})$ in the authentication credential $\mathsf{Auth}[opk_{\mathsf{ID}}]$ by incorporating opk_{ID}, σ_{ID}', and c_{ID}'. The group signature is then defined as $\sigma := (opk_{\mathsf{ID}}^{'}, \mathsf{Auth}[opk_{\mathsf{ID}}], \sigma_{\mathsf{ID}})$.

Finally, ID updates it secret key with the new secret seed, i.e., $sk_{\mathsf{ID}}' := sd_{\mathsf{ID}}^{v}$, and gets an updated state $\mathsf{st}_{\mathsf{ID}}' := \mathsf{st}_{\mathsf{ID}} \setminus (opk_{\mathsf{ID}}, \mathsf{Auth}[opk_{\mathsf{ID}}])$.

- $\mathsf{Verify}(\mathsf{gpk}, m, \sigma, \mathrm{RL})$: The verifier parses $\sigma = (opk_{\mathsf{ID}}^{'}, \mathsf{Auth}[opk_{\mathsf{ID}}], \sigma_{\mathsf{ID}})$ and $\mathsf{Auth}[opk_{\mathsf{ID}}] = (opk_{\mathsf{GM}}^{\mathrm{MI}}, c_{\mathrm{MI}}^{1}, c_{\mathrm{MI}}^{2}, \mathrm{pf}_{\mathrm{lf}_{\mathrm{sMI}}}, \sigma_{\mathsf{GM}}^{\mathrm{sMI}}, \mathsf{MMT}[\mathsf{sTI}].\mathrm{Rt}, \mathsf{Auth}[\mathsf{MMT}[\mathsf{sTI}].\mathrm{Rt}])$. This algorithm outputs 0 if one of the following conditions is met: i) $c_{\mathrm{MI}}^{1} \in \mathrm{RL}$; ii) $\mathsf{AuthVrfy}(\mathsf{gpk}, \mathsf{MMT}[\mathsf{sTI}].\mathrm{Rt}, \mathsf{Auth}[\mathsf{MMT}[\mathsf{sTI}].\mathrm{Rt}]) = 0$; iii) $\mathsf{M.Verify}(\mathsf{MMT}[\mathsf{sTI}].\mathrm{Rt}, \mathrm{lf}_{\mathrm{sMI}}, \mathrm{pf}_{\mathrm{lf}_{\mathrm{sMI}}}) = 0$, where $\mathrm{lf}_{\mathrm{sMI}} = \mathsf{H}(opk_{\mathsf{GM}}^{\mathrm{MI}} || c_{\mathrm{MI}}^{1})$; iv) $\mathsf{S.Verify}(opk_{\mathsf{GM}}^{\mathrm{MI}}, opk_{\mathsf{ID}}^{'} || c_{\mathrm{MI}}^{2}, \sigma_{\mathsf{GM}}^{\mathrm{sMI}}) = 0$; v) $\mathsf{S.Verify}(opk_{\mathsf{ID}}^{'}, m, \sigma_{\mathsf{ID}}) = 0$. Otherwise, the verifier outputs 1.
- $\mathsf{Open}(\mathsf{gpk}, \mathsf{sk}_{\mathsf{GM}}, m, \sigma)$: The algorithm outputs 0 if the group signature is not valid, i.e., $\mathsf{Verify}(\mathsf{gpk}, m, \sigma, T, \emptyset) = 0$. GM gets the index MI from σ according to its the authentication credential. Next, it computes keys randomness $(ke_{\mathrm{MI}}^{1}, re_{\mathrm{MI}}^{1})$ and $(ke_{\mathrm{MI}}^{2}, re_{\mathrm{MI}}^{2})$ as in Join protocol based on k_{GM}. GM decrypts $\hat{\mathsf{ID}}_1 := \mathsf{E.Dec}(ke_{\mathrm{MI}}^{1}, c_{\mathrm{MI}}^{1}; re_{\mathrm{MI}}^{1})$ and $\hat{\mathsf{ID}}_2 := \mathsf{E.Dec}(ke_{\mathrm{MI}}^{2}, c_{\mathrm{MI}}^{2}; re_{\mathrm{MI}}^{2})$. If $\hat{\mathsf{ID}}_1 = \mathsf{GM}$ then return $\hat{\mathsf{ID}}_2$; otherwise $\hat{\mathsf{ID}}_1$ is returned.
- $\mathsf{Revoke}(\mathsf{gpk}, \mathsf{sk}_{\mathsf{GM}}, \mathrm{RL}, \mathsf{ID}, \mathrm{RSS})$: For each tuple $(\sigma, m) \in \mathrm{RSS}$, GM returns 0 if $\mathsf{Verify}(\mathsf{gpk}, m, \sigma, \mathrm{RL}) = 0$ or $\mathsf{Open}(\mathsf{gpk}, \mathsf{sk}_{\mathsf{GM}}, m, \sigma) \neq \mathsf{ID}$. Otherwise, GM gets c_{MI}^{1} from each $\sigma \in \mathrm{RSS}$ and puts it into RL.

Instantiations of $\mathsf{RandSelect}(\mathsf{sk}_{\mathsf{GM}}, \mathsf{ID}, opk_{\mathsf{ID}})$**.** One method for random index selection applies a pseudorandom permutation to shuffle all leaf indices in a HHGS instance [2]. However, this becomes impractical for trees with over 2^{20} leaves due to the scaling costs of permutation [2, \$4.2].

Alternatively, we propose using a short-range PRF scheme, F_2, with range $\{0,1\}^{\ell_I}$ to generate indices for OTS mounting. The first approach mimics random sampling without replacement, while the second directly selects from remaining available indices. In the first approach, collisions may occur due to the birthday paradox. To address this, the F_2 process can be repeated with different inputs to avoid collisions (referred to as **AP1**). However, as the number of available indices, denoted by ϕ, decreases, the likelihood of collisions increases. When this happens, we can leverage the PPRF keys, which encode the available keys, to directly select an index from the remaining indices (referred to as **AP2**), provided the number of remaining indices is not excessively large (e.g., $\leq 2^{20}$). We define ξ as the threshold for the number of available indices, marking the point at which we switch from the initial random selection method to the latter approach. To support this second selection method, we introduce an additional algorithm for PPRF, denoted as $\mathsf{GetMsg}(k, i)$. This algorithm enables the retrieval of the i-th unpunctured message. Specifically, $\mathsf{GetMsg}(k, i)$ takes as input the current key $k \in \mathcal{K}_{\mathsf{PRF}}$ and returns the i-th accessible message x_i from the remaining computable message set. The realization of this algorithm is detailed in Appendix B.

Specifically, GM generates a random selection key, $k_s := \mathsf{F}_1(k_{\mathsf{GM}}, \text{“}RandSel\text{”})$, and computes the index KI as follows:

- **AP1**. If $\phi < \xi$, compute $\mathsf{KI} := \mathsf{F}_2(k_s, \mathsf{ID}||opk_{\mathsf{ID}}||ctr)$ using an incremental counter ctr (initialized to 0) and repeat this process until $\mathsf{F}_p^0.\mathsf{Eval}(k_p^0, \mathsf{KI}) \neq \perp$. Thereafter, $\phi := \phi - 1$.
- **AP2**. Otherwise, compute $tmp := \mathsf{F}_2(k_s, \mathsf{ID}||opk_{\mathsf{ID}})$, then set $tmp := tmp \bmod \phi$, and derive $\mathsf{KI} := \mathsf{F}_p^0.\mathsf{GetMsg}(k_p^0, tmp)$.

The complexity of the above instantiation of RandSelect is determined by the signing $Y = 2^{\tilde{h}}$ of HHGS, where $\tilde{h} = h + \frac{h}{d}$ is the total height of the hypertree structure. The computational cost of **AP1** is determined by the number n_r of PRF recomputations for selecting an unused index. Let ϕ denote the remaining indices that can be chosen. The probability of selecting an occupied index is about $1 - \frac{\phi}{Y}$, while considering PRF as a random function. The number of PRF recomputations follows a geometric distribution with success probability $p = \frac{\phi}{Y}$. The expected value of n_r is $\mathbb{E}[n_r] = \frac{Y}{\phi}$, which can be used as the threshold for switching between AP1 and AP2. As ϕ decreases, $\mathbb{E}[n_r]$ grows inversely proportional to ϕ. The total computational cost of **AP1** scales with the reduction in the number of remaining indices, ϕ. In contrast, the cost of **AP2** is directly proportional to ϕ, as determined by the cost of GetMsg (analyzed in Appendix B). Consequently, as ϕ decreases, the overhead of **AP2** also reduces.

In a nutshell, the signing capacity, Y, of HHGS is inherently limited. For instance, when $\mathbb{E}[n_r] = \phi = O(2^{20})$, Y is in $O(2^{40})$.

Correctness. According to the correctness experiment $\mathsf{Exp}_{\mathcal{A},\mathsf{HHGS}}^{\mathsf{Correct}}$, the correctness of HHGS encompasses two key aspects: (i) the adversary can register honest parties under chosen identities, and all signatures generated by honest parties must pass verification; and (ii) signatures produced by honest parties must be accurately opened (traced) to their legitimate owners.

The registration process in HHGS primarily involves locating a mount point on the mixed OTS mount sub-tree (MoMSt). Since each OTS is uniquely associated with a leaf node, successful registration is guaranteed as long as there are available vacancies in the tree structure. The validity of an honest party's signature during verification is inherently ensured by the correctness of OTS and MT. Moreover, the oracle queries in the correctness game are simulated using secret keys (including sub-secret keys of the building blocks, such as AE, PPRF, and PRF) generated by the challenger. The correctness of these building blocks ensures that all queries and protocol executions involving them are processed correctly in accordance with the protocol's specifications.

Security Analysis. The security of HHGS is demonstrated through the following theorems with detailed proofs in the full version of this paper [20].

Theorem 1. *Assume that the* OTS *scheme* S, *the* PPRF *functions* $\{\mathsf{F}_p^i\}_{0\leq i\leq d}$, *the* PRF *functions* F_1 *and* F_2, *the* MT *scheme* M, *the* AE *scheme* E, *the* PRG *scheme* G, *and the hash function* H *are secure as defined in Appendix A, then* HHGS *satisfies traceability.*

The proof employs a sequence of game transformations, starting with the Trace experiment, to incrementally restrict the adversary's ability to forge signatures under HHGS. Starting from the original Trace experiment, the challenger incrementally modifies the game by introducing abort conditions to enable the reduction of security to the hardness of underlying cryptographic primitives.

Theorem 2. *Under the same assumptions as Theorem 1,* HHGS *achieves anonymity.*

The core idea involves progressively replacing PRF values, random selection keys, encryption keys, and randomness with random values, leveraging the security of the underlying primitives such as PRF and PRG. Consequently, the OTS keys and ciphertexts associated with the $\mathcal{O}_{\mathsf{PriTest}}(\mathsf{ID}_0^*, \mathsf{ID}_1^*, m)$ query for the challenged members and GM are shown to follow identical distributions, preventing the adversary from distinguishing between them. Finally, the mount indices of the target OTS keys are selected randomly, limiting the adversary's success to a random guess due to the independence of the selection process.

The security of HHGS also ensures its resilience to sibling attacks. The key insight lies in the randomness of the selection process for the leaves at level 0 of the hypertree structure, which prevents the attacker from distinguishing between the positions of the two candidate challenge signatures on the tree. Although the attacker knows the results of the other $2^{\tilde{h}} - 2$ selections, the two remaining unknown selections concerning the challenged identities' OTS keys are drawn randomly and without replacement. Since the selection process is independent and unbiased in the final game, the distribution of these two unknown selections appears identical from the attacker's perspective.

4.2 Signing Capability Extension

This section focuses on improving the signing capability of HHGS. A group signature with a large signing capacity is vital for applications with numerous users or frequent signing demands, such as privacy-preserving IoT networks in smart cities or industrial IoT systems. A naive solution to support larger groups and signing capabilities is to increase the parameters of HHGS. However, this is not efficient due to the complexity of the RandSelect algorithm analyzed in the previous section. Alternatively, using multiple independent PPRF keys could address this inefficiency, but it introduces the challenge of privately determining which member's OTS key should be associated with which PPRF key. This requires a method to securely partition members' OTS keys into subgroups.

Construction Overview. We address this challenge with HHGS^+, an improved FSDGS scheme that generically builds on HHGS. Specifically, HHGS^+ initializes $W \in \mathbb{N}$ copies of HHGS and employs the MT scheme M to construct a tree, where the leaves are the group public keys $\{\mathsf{gpk}_i\}_{i\in[W]}$ generated by the HHGS instances. To ensure efficiency, we use a single Merkle tree over a hypertree structure. This design minimizes additional tree layers, avoiding the need to store more PPRF keys. Moreover, using multiple independent HHGS instances could enable parallelization of group management.

To securely group members' OTS keys, we randomly associate each OTS key with a specific HHGS instance using a short-range PRF function, which takes as input a OTS key and its owner's identity. Due to the short range of the PRF, different OTS keys may yield the same PRF value (referred to as OTS collision), enabling the grouping feature. However, as OTS collisions are not uniformly distributed among PRF values, the volume of each HHGS instance poses a challenge. That is, the non-uniform distribution of OTS collisions creates challenges in *balancing the load across* HHGS *instances and ensuring the security.*[3] In an insecure scenario, referred to as the **Full-instance Attack (FIA)**, if a HHGS instance becomes full early in the process (e.g., while registering ID_0^*), it will not be selected in subsequent steps (e.g., during the registration of ID_1^*), potentially creating a bias in the remaining selections. This temporal dependency in the selection process allows an attacker to exploit the evolving probabilities as trees fill, compromising the randomness and enabling prediction of future instance choices. To counter this, each HHGS instance should contain sufficient redundancy (see Lemma 1) to accommodate the non-uniform distribution of PRF values, ensuring they can handle varying numbers of OTS keys securely.

Detailed Algorithms. We define the algorithms of HHGS^+ as follows:

- $\mathsf{GMInit}(1^\kappa, \mathsf{SP})$: For $i \in [W]$, GM creates $W \in \mathbb{N}$ HHGS instances as $(\mathsf{Pms}_i, \mathsf{gpk}_i,$ $\mathsf{sk}_{\mathsf{GM}}^i, \mathsf{st}_{\mathsf{GM}}^i, \mathrm{RL}_i) := \mathsf{HHGS.GMInit}(1^\kappa, \mathsf{SP})$. Subsequently, it builds the Merkle tree instance as $(\mathrm{Tr}', \mathsf{st}'_{\mathrm{BDS}}) := \mathsf{M.Build}(\{\mathsf{gpk}_i\}_{i\in[W]})$. GM sets $\mathsf{gpk} := \mathrm{Tr}'.\mathrm{Rt}$, $\mathsf{sk}_{\mathsf{GM}} := \{\mathsf{sk}_{\mathsf{GM}}^i\}_{i\in[W]}$, $\mathsf{Pms} := \{\mathsf{Pms}_i\}_{i\in[W]}$, $\mathsf{st}_{\mathsf{GM}} := \{\mathsf{st}_{\mathsf{GM}}^i\}_{i\in[W]}$, and $\mathrm{RL} := \{\mathrm{RL}_i\}_{i\in[W]}$. We will use the building blocks initiated in HHGS instances such as the PRG scheme G, the PRF schemes F_1 and F_2, and the MT scheme M. Additionally, GM samples a random PRF key for $k_{\mathsf{GM}} := \mathsf{F}_1.\mathsf{KGen}(pms_{\mathsf{PRF}})$. To save space, GM replaces with $k_{\mathsf{GM}}^i := \mathsf{F}_1(k_{\mathsf{GM}}, \text{“}i||SubInstance\text{”})$, so that it can be recovered from k_{GM}.

[3] Note that, the RandSelect function selects nodes randomly from all available nodes (independent of MMTs), while the approach here introduces a structured process, selecting HHGS instances first, creating dependencies in the selection sequence.

- The algorithms MInit and $\mathsf{MRegGen}$ in HHGS^+ are identical to those in HHGS.
- $\mathsf{Join}(\mathsf{sk}_{\mathsf{GM}}, \mathsf{st}_{\mathsf{GM}}, \mathsf{ID}, \mathrm{RF}_{\mathsf{ID}})$: Although GM can utilize a hyper-join routine to process join requests of members in batches, as implemented in HHGS, we focus here solely on ID for simplicity, to convey the main idea. Let $\mathsf{LR}_{\mathsf{ID}}$ denote the list recording the indices of HHGS instances involved, and $\mathrm{RF}^i_{\mathsf{ID}}$ represent the registration file used in the i-th HHGS instance.

For each opk^j_{ID} in $\mathrm{RF}_{\mathsf{ID}}$ (where $j \in [\#\mathrm{RF}_{\mathsf{ID}}]$), GM randomly assigns it to a HHGS instance and fills $\mathrm{RF}^i_{\mathsf{ID}}$ and $\mathsf{LR}_{\mathsf{ID}}$ accordingly. Specifically, it computes the random selection key $k_j := \mathsf{F}_1(k_{\mathsf{GM}}, \mathsf{ID}||opk^j_{\mathsf{ID}})$ and determines the HHGS instance index as $\mathsf{il} := \mathsf{F}_2(k_j, \mathsf{ID}||opk^j_{\mathsf{ID}})$. Next, GM inserts opk^j_{ID} into $\mathsf{RFCa}^{\mathsf{il}}_{\mathsf{ID}}$ and adds il to $\mathsf{LR}_{\mathsf{ID}}$ if $\mathsf{il} \notin \mathsf{LR}_{\mathsf{ID}}$.

For $i \in \mathsf{LR}_{\mathsf{ID}}$, GM executes $(\mathsf{Vt}_i, \mathrm{RR}^i_{\mathsf{ID}}) \leftarrow \mathsf{Join}(\mathsf{sk}^i_{\mathsf{GM}}, \mathsf{st}^i_{\mathsf{GM}}, \mathsf{ID}, \mathrm{RF}^i_{\mathsf{ID}}, T_\delta)$ with ID, where $\mathrm{RR}^i_{\mathsf{ID}} = (k_{\mathsf{ID}}, \{\mathsf{Auth}[opk^{i,j}_{\mathsf{ID}}]\}_{j \in [\#\mathrm{RF}^i_{\mathsf{ID}}]})$ is the authentication credentials generated for $opk^{i,j}_{\mathsf{ID}}$, and $opk^{i,j}_{\mathsf{ID}}$ is the j-th OTS key in the registration file $\mathrm{RF}^i_{\mathsf{ID}}$ for the ID in the i-th HHGS instance. The overall transcript of the protocol is the union of the sub-transcripts from each join session, i.e., $\mathsf{Vt} = \bigcup_{i \in \mathsf{LR}_{\mathsf{ID}}} \mathsf{Vt}_i$. Meanwhile, GM appends each authentication credential in $\mathrm{RR}^i_{\mathsf{ID}}$ with the corresponding index i to yield a modified registration result set $\{\hat{\mathrm{RR}}^i_{\mathsf{ID}}\}_{i \in \mathsf{LR}_{\mathsf{ID}}} = \{(i, \mathsf{Auth}[opk^{i,j}_{\mathsf{ID}}])\}_{i \in \mathsf{LR}_{\mathsf{ID}}, j \in [\#\mathrm{RF}^i_{\mathsf{ID}}]}$.

GM builds the states $\hat{\mathsf{st}}_{\mathsf{ID}} = \{\hat{\mathrm{RR}}^i_{\mathsf{ID}}\}_{i \in \mathsf{LR}_{\mathsf{ID}}}$ and $\mathsf{st}^{\mathrm{pf}}_{\mathsf{ID}} := \{\mathsf{gpk}_i, \mathrm{pf}_{\mathsf{gpk}_i}\}_{i \in \mathsf{LR}_{\mathsf{ID}}}$ for ID. Finally, it defines $\mathrm{RR}_{\mathsf{ID}} = (k_{\mathsf{ID}}, \mathsf{st}^{\mathrm{pf}}_{\mathsf{ID}}, \hat{\mathsf{st}}_{\mathsf{ID}})$, which is returned to ID. Upon receiving $\mathrm{RR}_{\mathsf{ID}}$, ID updates its states $\mathsf{st} := \mathsf{st} \cup (\mathsf{st}^{\mathrm{pf}}_{\mathsf{ID}}, \hat{\mathsf{st}}_{\mathsf{ID}})$ and secret key $sk_{\mathsf{ID}} := sk_{\mathsf{ID}} \cup k_{\mathsf{ID}}$. If necessary, the member may delete duplicate states and secret keys to save storage.

- $\mathsf{Sign}(sk_{\mathsf{ID}}, \mathsf{st}_{\mathsf{ID}}, m)$: ID first pops up the first tuple $(i, \mathsf{Auth}[opk^j_{\mathsf{ID}}])$ from $\hat{\mathsf{st}}_{\mathsf{ID}}$, where opk^j_{ID} is the OTS public key opk^j_{ID} (to be generated within $\mathsf{HHGS.Sign}$ later) for verifying the signature about to generate. It then retrieves $(\mathsf{gpk}_i, \mathrm{pf}_{\mathsf{gpk}_i})$ from $\mathsf{st}^{\mathrm{pf}}_{\mathsf{ID}}$ based on i. To proceed with the HHGS instance, ID constructs a sub-state $\mathsf{st}^i_{\mathsf{ID}} := \mathsf{Auth}[opk^j_{\mathsf{ID}}]$. For singing the message m, ID executes $(sk'_{\mathsf{ID}}, \sigma^i_{\mathsf{ID}}) := \mathsf{HHGS.Sign}(sk_{\mathsf{ID}}, \mathsf{st}_{\mathsf{ID}}, T_\delta, m)$ and composes the final signature as $\sigma_{\mathsf{ID}} := (\sigma^i_{\mathsf{ID}}, \mathsf{gpk}_i, \mathrm{pf}_{\mathsf{gpk}_i})$. Lastly, the tuple $(i, \mathsf{Auth}[opk^j_{\mathsf{ID}}])$ is removed from $\mathsf{st}_{\mathsf{ID}}$.
- $\mathsf{Verify}(\mathsf{gpk}, m, \sigma_{\mathsf{ID}}, \mathrm{RL})$: The verifier parses $\sigma_{\mathsf{ID}} = (\sigma^i_{\mathsf{ID}}, \mathsf{gpk}_i, \mathrm{pf}_{\mathsf{gpk}_i})$, and it performs two verification steps: i) $mtV := \mathsf{M.Verify}(\mathsf{gpk}, \mathrm{lf}_{\mathsf{gpk}_i}, \mathrm{pf}_{\mathsf{gpk}_i})$, where $(\mathsf{gpk}_i, \mathrm{pf}_{\mathsf{gpk}_i}) \in \sigma_{\mathsf{ID}}$; ii) $dsV := \mathsf{HHGS.Verify}(\mathsf{gpk}_i, m, \sigma^i_{\mathsf{ID}}, \mathrm{RL}_i)$. The index i can be inferred analogously from σ_{ID}. If $mtV = dsV = 1$, the algorithm outputs 1; otherwise it outputs 0.
- $\mathsf{Open}(\mathsf{gpk}, \mathsf{sk}_{\mathsf{GM}}, m, \sigma_{\mathsf{ID}})$: If $\mathsf{M.Verify}(\mathsf{gpk}, \mathsf{gpk}_i, \mathrm{pf}_{\mathsf{gpk}_i}) = 1$, it outputs the execution result $\mathsf{HHGS.Open}(\mathsf{gpk}_i, \mathsf{sk}^i_{\mathsf{GM}}, m,$
$\sigma^i_{\mathsf{ID}})$, where $(\mathsf{gpk}_i, \mathrm{pf}_{\mathsf{gpk}_i}, \sigma^i_{\mathsf{ID}}) \in \sigma_{\mathsf{ID}}$.

- $\mathsf{Revoke}(\mathsf{gpk}, \mathsf{sk}_{\mathsf{GM}}, \mathrm{RL}, \mathsf{ID}, \mathrm{RSS})$: For each signature $\sigma \in \mathrm{RSS}$, GM gets the index i of the HHGS instance according to the Merkle proofs in σ, and runs $\mathrm{RL}'_i := \mathsf{HHGS.Revoke}(\mathsf{gpk}_i, \mathsf{sk}^i_{\mathsf{GM}}, \mathrm{RL}_i, \mathsf{ID}, \sigma)$. After this, the revocation list is updated to $\mathrm{RL}' := \{\mathrm{RL}'_i\}$.

Security Analysis. The correctness of HHGS^+ is inherently ensured by the correctness of HHGS, MT, and PRF. Therefore, the analysis is omitted for simplicity. The security of HHGS^+ is essentially implied by that of HHGS, along with the security of PRF and M. Here, we mainly present the key security results through the following theorems and outline their proof strategies. We analyze the redundancy in HHGS to resist the FIA, as formally established by Lemma 1, thereby laying the security foundation for HHGS^+.

Lemma 1 (Resilience of FIA). *Suppose each* HHGS *instance has a maximum capacity of Y leaves, and is expected to register at least Z OTS keys. Given $B = W \cdot Z$ total OTS keys from members, and F_2 is a secure* PRF *whose output distribution has a statistical distance of at most ϵ_{F_2} from the uniform distribution. Then, the probability that no* HHGS *instance exceeds its capacity is bounded by a negligible probability $\epsilon_{\mathsf{FIA}} = \epsilon_{\mathsf{FIA}}(\kappa)$, provided that Y satisfies the condition $Y \geq Z + \sqrt{2Z \ln((1 + O(\epsilon_{\mathsf{F}_2}))/\epsilon_{\mathsf{FIA}})}$.*

Proof. The scenario resembles the Coupon Collector's Problem [8], where we aim to collect Z values in each of W instances, and we wish to ensure that no instance exceeds its capacity. The number of OTS keys involved in each instance can be approximated using a binomial distribution. Let X_j denote the number of values assigned to the j-th instance. We aim to find the value of Y such that the probability of any instance exceeding its capacity is negligible. Formally, we want the event $A_j = \{X_j \geq Y\}$ (i.e., the j-th HHGS instance is full) to satisfy $\Pr(A_j) \leq \epsilon_{\mathsf{FIA}}$. The expected number of OTS keys assigned to any HHGS instance is about $\mathbb{E}[X_j] \approx \frac{B}{W} = Z$. Meanwhile, the statistical distance ϵ_{F_2} between the output of F_2 and a uniform distribution introduces a slight deviation from perfect uniformity. This deviation affects the variance, thereby introducing a correction term in the overflow probability bound. Using the Chernoff bound [8], for large Z, the probability of the event A_j is given by $\Pr(X_j \geq Y) \leq \exp\left(-\frac{(Y-Z)^2}{2Z}\right)(1 + O(\epsilon_{\mathsf{F}_2}))$, where exp refers to the exponential function. To ensure that this probability is negligible, we require $\exp\left(-\frac{(Y-Z)^2}{2Z}\right)(1 + O(\epsilon_{\mathsf{F}_2})) \leq \epsilon_{\mathsf{FIA}}$. Taking the natural logarithm of both sides $-\frac{(Y-Z)^2}{2Z} \geq \ln((1 + \epsilon_{\mathsf{F}_2})/\epsilon_{\mathsf{FIA}})$. Solving for Y, we have $Y \geq Z + \sqrt{2Z \ln((1 + O(\epsilon_{\mathsf{F}_2}))/\epsilon_{\mathsf{FIA}})}$. This complete the proof.

For our target $Z \in O(2^{40})$, Y can be configured around $2^{40} + 2^{20.5}$, ensuring a negligible overflow probability of $\epsilon_{\mathsf{FIA}} \leq 2^{-128}$.

Theorem 3. *Assume that* HHGS *provides traceability and the* MT *scheme* M *is secure, then* HHGS^+ *satisfies traceability.*

The proof of Theorem 3 closely follows that of Theorem 1, with the primary distinction being the need for an additional game to reduce the security of HHGS^+ to that of MT.

Table 2. Performance. Runtime in milliseconds (ms) and size in kilobytes (KB).

κ	HHGS						HHGS^+					
	Signing Capacity (d)	Setup	Join	Sign	Verify	Sig. Size	Signing Capacity (d)	Setup	Join	Sign	Verify	Sig. Size
128	$2^{39}(12)$	1.53	301.68	2.3	1.08	7.95	$2^{59}(12)$	16×10^5	303.73	2.3	1.09	8.58
	$2^{40}(9)$	3.14	318.89	2.3	0.82	6.41	$2^{60}(9)$	33×10^5	323.07	2.3	0.83	7.04
	$2^{40}(19)$	0.74	294.59	2.3	1.64	11.58	$2^{60}(19)$	7.7×10^5	295.29	2.3	1.65	12.21
256	$2^{39}(12)$	7.29	654.62	12.87	5.86	20.25	$2^{59}(12)$	76×10^5	676.22	12.87	5.87	20.88
	$2^{40}(9)$	14.68	713.46	12.87	4.40	16.24	$2^{60}(9)$	153×10^5	730.85	12.87	4.41	16.87
	$2^{40}(19)$	3.62	632.91	12.87	8.77	29.72	$2^{60}(19)$	38×10^5	637.34	12.87	8.78	30.35

Theorem 4. *Assume that* HHGS *provides anonymity and the* PRF *families* $(\mathsf{F}_1, \mathsf{F}_2)$ *are secure, then* HHGS^+ *satisfies anonymity.*

To prove this theorem, it suffices to demonstrate that random selection among HHGS instances does not leak identity-related information, since OTS keys within each HHGS instance are indistinguishable due to its security. It is straightforward to observe that if no HHGS instance becomes fully occupied during the lifetime of HHGS^+ (i.e., the resilience against FIA attacks), then OTS keys are randomly assigned to W independent HHGS instances with nearly identical probability (with negligible differences due to the security of F). Using Lemma 1, we show that by properly configuring the size of each HHGS instance, the probability of a successful FIA attack is negligible.

5 Evaluation

In this section, we evaluate the performance of our proposed FSDGS schemes.

In the performance analysis, we instantiate the OTS scheme using the state-of-the-art OTS scheme WOTS+C [31,41], and use AES-GCM-SIV [29] for the authenticated encryption E.[4] For the PRG, we use counter-mode AES [3]. The hash functions in our schemes are implemented using the SHA-3 family [24]. The PPRF is implemented with the GGM construction [12]. Meanwhile, we consider 128-bit security against classical attacks and (roughly) double the security parameter to ensure post-quantum security.

For the parameters of WOTS+C, we aim to strike a trade-off between signature size and computational cost by selecting a relatively small number of 2^5 of

[4] Although the newer signature scheme [34] provides shorter signatures and more efficient verification, this work adopts WOTS+C for its superior signing efficiency, making it better suited to computation-constrained signers nor powerful verifier.

signature chains, with a Winternitz parameter of 2^4 for the length of each chain, and a 9-bit checksum size. The signature size of HHGS is primarily determined by the signing capacity ($Y = 2^{\tilde{h}}$), selected as either 2^{39} or 2^{40} to accommodate the corresponding group size. The cost of authenticating one OTS in the Join protocol, involve at most $d+1$ OTS signing operations and the cost of RandSelect (about $O(2^{20})$ F_2 operations in the worst case). Let B (e.g., $B \in O(2^{15})$) denote the maximum number of OTS keys a member retains. Consequently, the credentials stored in the member's cache have a size of $O(B \cdot h)$. Members can adjust B based on the storage capacity of their auxiliary storage devices. We consider a practical scenario where, for the first join request, a member must submit at least B OTS keys, and the GM processes join requests from U members in a batch. For simplicity, we assume $B \cdot U = \sqrt{Y}$. Thus, the storage cost of the GM's state, dominated by the PPRF keys, is of magnitude $O(\sqrt{Y})$. The signing process on the member's device is efficient, with the worst-case computational cost dominated by two WOTS+C key generation and signing operations.

We benchmark the performance of the algorithms in our proposed schemes using a Raspberry Pi 3 to simulate the client's signing operation, and a PC with an Intel(R) Core(TM) i5-13500H, 2.60 GHz, and 16 GB RAM, which serves as the verifier and GM. Table 2 provides a summary of the performance of our schemes across key metrics, as in prior works [2,21,45].[5] For simplicity, we do not benchmark the full schemes. The performance of Open and Revoke can be inferred from that of Verify. Specifically, the cost of Open is primarily determined by a single Verify operation along with one encryption and one decryption. To revoke a single signature, the overhead of Revoke consists of the combined costs of one Verify and one Open operation. Additionally, the runtime of the join protocol is measured based on handling a single OTS key in the worst-case scenario, dominated by $O(2^{20})$ F_2 operations. The height of the upper layer Merkle tree of HHGS$^+$ is $W = 2^{20}$ in our benchmark. As a result, the setup time (about a few minutes) for HHGS$^+$ is W times that of HHGS.

Acknowledgment. This work was supported by the Natural Science Foundation of China under Grant No. 12441101 and Grant No. 62372386, the National Cryptography Science Foundation of China under Grant No. 2025NCSF02055, and by the National Key Research and Development Program of China under Grant No. 2025YFE0220300.

A Security Notions of Building Blocks

In this section, we define the security notions of the building blocks used in our constructions.

Let $\mathsf{negl}(\kappa) : \mathbb{N} \rightarrow \mathbb{R}+$ denote a negligible function, defined such that for every polynomial $P(\kappa)$ there exists a $e_0 \in \mathbb{N}$ s.t. for all $e > e_0$, $\mathsf{negl}(e) \leq 1/P(e)$. We write $\mathcal{A}^{\mathcal{O}}$ to denote the an algorithm $\mathcal{A}$ with access to oracle $\mathcal{O}$ where $\mathcal{O}$ may represent multiple oracles, i.e., $\mathcal{O} = \{\mathcal{O}_1, \ldots, \mathcal{O}_n\}$. For security definitions,

[5] The source code of our implementation is available at https://github.com/WithoutNi/GS.

we use $\mathsf{Exp}^{\Psi}_{\mathcal{A},\Sigma}(1^\kappa, \rho) \Rightarrow 1$ to denote that the experiment Exp, when instantiated with security parameter κ, system parameters ρ, under an adversary $\mathcal{A}$ attacking the security property Ψ of the primitive Σ, returns 1 (indicating success). The parameters ρ, $\mathcal{A}$, and Ψ may be omitted when clear from context. We define the advantage of $\mathcal{A}$ in this experiment as

$$\mathsf{Adv}^{\Psi}_{\mathcal{A},\Sigma,\lambda} := \left|\Pr[\mathsf{Exp}^{\Psi}_{\mathcal{A},\Sigma}(1^\kappa, \rho) \Rightarrow 1] - \lambda\right|,$$

where λ may be omitted if $\lambda = 0$.

Digital Signature. We say that a SIG scheme S is correct if for all $m \in \mathcal{M}_{\mathsf{SIG}}$ it holds that

$$\Pr\left[\mathsf{S.Verify}(pk, m, \sigma) = 1 \,\middle|\, \begin{array}{c} pms_{\mathsf{SIG}} \leftarrow \mathsf{S.Setup}(1^\kappa);\ rs \stackrel{\$}{\leftarrow} \mathcal{RS}_{\mathsf{SIG}};\ (sk, pk) \leftarrow \mathsf{S.KGen}(rs) \\ \sigma \leftarrow \mathsf{S.Sign}(sk, m) \end{array}\right] = 1.$$

To capture existential unforgeability under adaptive chosen message attacks (EUF-CMA), we define a security experiment $\mathsf{Exp}^{\mathsf{EUF\text{-}CMA}}_{\mathcal{A},\mathsf{S}}(\kappa, q)$ as below:

$\underline{\mathsf{Exp}^{\mathsf{EUF\text{-}CMA}}_{\mathcal{A},\mathsf{S}}(\kappa, q):}$
$pms_{\mathsf{SIG}} \leftarrow \mathsf{S.Setup}(1^\kappa);\ rs \stackrel{\$}{\leftarrow} \mathcal{RS}_{\mathsf{SIG}};\ (sk, pk) \leftarrow \mathsf{S.KGen}(rs)$
$ct := 0;\ \mathsf{L}_S := \emptyset$
$(m^*, \sigma^*) \leftarrow \mathcal{A}^{\mathsf{HMSign}(\cdot)}(\kappa, pms_{\mathsf{SIG}}, pk);$
$\mathsf{OUTPUT}\ ((m^*, \sigma^*) \notin \mathsf{L}_S) \wedge (\mathsf{S.Verify}(pk, m^*, \sigma^*) = 1)$

$\underline{\mathsf{HMSign}(m):}$
$\mathsf{IF}\ ct \geq q,\ \mathsf{OUTPUT}\ \perp$
$ct := ct + 1;\ \sigma \leftarrow \mathsf{S.Sign}(sk, m)$
$\mathsf{APPEND}\ (m, \sigma) \rightarrow \mathsf{L}_S$
$\mathsf{OUTPUT}\ \sigma$

Definition 2 (EUF-CMA **for** SIG). *We say that* S *is an EUF-CMA secure* SIG *scheme if for any PPT $\mathcal{A}$, the advantage* $\mathsf{Adv}^{\mathsf{EUF\text{-}CMA}}_{\mathcal{A},\mathsf{S}}(\kappa, q)$ *of $\mathcal{A}$ in* $\mathsf{Exp}^{\mathsf{EUF\text{-}CMA}}_{\mathcal{A},\mathsf{S}}(\kappa, q)$ *is negligible. An EUF-CMA secure* SIG *scheme* S *with $q = 1$ is referred to as a one-time signature (OTS) scheme.*

Merkle Tree. We say that a MT scheme M is correct if for a polynomial number N defined by κ, any $\{\mathsf{lf}_i\}_{i\subset[N]}$ (s.t. $\mathsf{lf}_i \in \mathcal{L}_{\mathsf{M}}$) and $\mathrm{lf}_j \in \{\mathrm{lf}_i\}_{i\in[N]}$, it holds that

$$\Pr\left[\mathsf{M.Verify}(\mathrm{Tr.Rt}, \mathrm{lf}_j, \mathrm{pf}_{\mathrm{lf}_j}) = 1 \,\middle|\, \begin{array}{c} pms_{\mathsf{MT}} \leftarrow \mathsf{M.Setup}(1^\kappa);\ (\mathrm{Tr}, \mathsf{st}_{\mathrm{BDS}}) \leftarrow \mathsf{M.Build}(\{\mathrm{lf}_i\}_{i\in[N]}) \\ \mathrm{pf}_{\mathrm{lf}_j} \leftarrow \mathsf{M.GetPrf}(\mathsf{st}_{\mathrm{BDS}}, \mathrm{lf}_j) \end{array}\right] = 1.$$

We define a security experiment $\mathsf{Exp}^{\mathsf{UF}}_{\mathcal{A},\mathsf{M}}(\kappa)$ regarding unforgeability (UF) for a MT scheme M as below:

$\underline{\mathsf{Exp}^{\mathsf{UF}}_{\mathcal{A},\mathsf{M}}(\kappa):}$
$pms_{\mathsf{MT}} \leftarrow \mathsf{M.Setup}(1^\kappa)\ ;\ (st, \{\mathrm{lf}_i\}_{i\in[N]}) \leftarrow \mathcal{A}_1(\kappa, pms_{\mathsf{MT}})$
$(\mathrm{Tr}, \mathsf{st}_{\mathrm{BDS}}) \leftarrow \mathsf{M.Build}(\{\mathrm{lf}_i\}_{i\in[N]});\ (\mathrm{lf}^*, \mathrm{pf}^*) \leftarrow \mathcal{A}_2(st, \mathrm{Tr})$
$\mathsf{OUTPUT}\ (\mathsf{M.Verify}(\mathrm{Tr.Rt}, \mathrm{lf}^*, \mathrm{pf}^*) = 1) \wedge (\mathrm{lf}^* \notin \{\mathrm{lf}_i\}_{i\in[N]})$

Definition 3 (Unforgeability of MT**).** *We say that* M *is a secure* MT *scheme if the advantage* $\mathsf{Adv}^{\mathsf{UF}}_{\mathcal{A},\mathsf{M}}(\kappa)$ *of any PPT adversary* $\mathcal{A} = (\mathcal{A}_1, \mathcal{A}_2)$ *in* $\mathsf{Exp}^{\mathsf{UF}}_{\mathcal{A},\mathsf{M}}(\kappa)$ *is negligible.*

Authenticated Encryption. An AE scheme E is said to be correct if for any $m \in \mathcal{M}_{\mathsf{AE}}$ it holds that

$$\Pr\left[\mathsf{E.Dec}(k, c) = m \,\middle|\, \begin{array}{r} pms_{\mathsf{AE}} \xleftarrow{\$} \mathsf{E.Setup}(1^\kappa);\ rk \xleftarrow{\$} \mathcal{RK}_{\mathsf{AE}};\ k \leftarrow \mathsf{E.KGen}(rk) \\ re \xleftarrow{\$} \mathcal{ER}_{\mathsf{AE}};\ c \leftarrow \mathsf{E.Enc}(k, m; re) \end{array}\right] = 1.$$

In the following, we first define the experiment for the security property regarding indistinguishability under adaptive chosen-ciphertext attacks (IND-CCA).

$\underline{\mathsf{Exp}^{\mathsf{IND\text{-}CCA}}_{\mathcal{A},\mathsf{E}}(\kappa):}$
$pms_{\mathsf{AE}} \xleftarrow{\$} \mathsf{E.Setup}(1^\kappa);\ b \xleftarrow{\$} \{0,1\};\ rk \xleftarrow{\$} \mathcal{RK}_{\mathsf{AE}};\ k \leftarrow \mathsf{E.KGen}(rk)$
$(m_0, m_1, st) \leftarrow \mathcal{A}_1^{\mathcal{O}_{\mathsf{Dec}}(\cdot)}(\kappa, pms_{\mathsf{AE}});\ re^* \xleftarrow{\$} \mathcal{ER}_{\mathsf{AE}};\ c^* \leftarrow \mathsf{E.Enc}(k, m_b; re^*)$
$b' \leftarrow \mathcal{A}_2^{\mathcal{O}_{\mathsf{Dec}}(\cdot)}(c^*, m_0, m_1, st);$
$\mathsf{OUTPUT}\ b = b'$

$\underline{\mathcal{O}_{\mathsf{Dec}}(c):}$
If $c = c^*$, $\mathsf{OUTPUT}\ \bot$
$m \leftarrow \mathsf{E.Dec}(k, c)$
$\mathsf{OUTPUT}\ m$

Definition 4 (IND-CCA **for AE**). *We say that* E *is an* IND-CCA*-secure AE scheme if the advantage* $\mathsf{Adv}^{\mathsf{IND\text{-}CCA}}_{\mathcal{A},\mathsf{E},\frac{1}{2}}(\kappa)$ *of all PPT adversaries* $\mathcal{A} = (\mathcal{A}_1, \mathcal{A}_2)$ *in* $\mathsf{Exp}^{\mathsf{IND\text{-}CCA}}_{\mathcal{A},\mathsf{E}}(\kappa)$ *is negligible.*

Also, we need the AE to provide integrity CT-INT of ciphertext against adaptive-chosen message attacks, which is formalized by the following experiment.

$\underline{\mathsf{Exp}^{\mathsf{CT\text{-}INT}}_{\mathcal{A},\mathsf{E}}(\kappa):}$
$pms_{\mathsf{AE}} \xleftarrow{\$} \mathsf{E.Setup}(1^\kappa);\ \mathsf{L}_{\mathsf{AE}} := \emptyset;\ rk \xleftarrow{\$} \mathcal{RK}_{\mathsf{AE}};\ k \xleftarrow{\$} \mathsf{E.KGen}(rk)$
$c^* \leftarrow \mathcal{A}^{\mathcal{O}_{\mathsf{Enc}}(\cdot)}(\kappa, pms_{\mathsf{AE}});\ m^* \leftarrow \mathsf{Dec}(k, c^*);$
$\mathsf{OUTPUT}\ c^* \notin \mathsf{L}_{\mathsf{AE}} \wedge m^* \neq \bot$

$\mathcal{O}_{\mathsf{Enc}}(m):$
$re \xleftarrow{\$} \mathcal{ER}_{\mathsf{AE}}$
$c \leftarrow \mathsf{E.Enc}(k, m; re)$
$\mathsf{APPEND}\ c \rightarrow \mathsf{L}_{\mathsf{AE}}$
Return c

Definition 5 (CT-INT **for AE**). *We say that* E *is a* CT-INT*-secure AE if the advantage* $\mathsf{Adv}^{\mathsf{CT\text{-}INT}}_{\mathcal{A},\mathsf{E}}(\kappa)$ *of all PPT adversaries* $\mathcal{A}$ *in* $\mathsf{Exp}^{\mathsf{CT\text{-}INT}}_{\mathcal{A},\mathsf{E}}(\kappa)$ *is negligible.*

Pseudorandom Generators. We define the following security experiment $\mathsf{Exp}^{\mathsf{IND}}_{\mathcal{A},\mathsf{G}}(\kappa)$ to formalize the security of a PRG scheme G based on indistinguishability (IND):

$\underline{\mathsf{Exp}^{\mathsf{IND}}_{\mathcal{A},\mathsf{G}}(\kappa):}$
$b \xleftarrow{\$} \{0,1\};\ pms_{\mathsf{PRG}} \leftarrow \mathsf{G.Setup}(1^\kappa);\ s \xleftarrow{\$} \mathsf{G.SGen}(pms_{\mathsf{PRG}});\ r_0 \xleftarrow{\$} \mathcal{R}_{\mathsf{PRG}};\ r_1 \leftarrow \mathsf{G.Eval}(s)$
$b^* \leftarrow \mathcal{A}(\kappa, pms_{\mathsf{PRG}}, r_b);$
$\mathsf{OUTPUT}\ b = b^*$

Definition 6 (IND for PRG). *We say that* G *is a secure* PRG *scheme if for any probabilistic polynomial time (PPT) adversary* $\mathcal{A}$, *it holds that the advantage* $\mathsf{Adv}^{\mathsf{IND}}_{\mathcal{A},\mathsf{G},\frac{1}{2}}(\kappa)$ *of* $\mathcal{A}$ *in* $\mathsf{Exp}^{\mathsf{IND}}_{\mathcal{A},\mathsf{G}}(\kappa)$ *is negligible.*

(Puncturable) Pseudo-random Functions. We say that a PPRF scheme F is correct if for every subset $\mathcal{S} = \{x_1, \ldots, x_q\} \subseteq \mathcal{M}_{\mathsf{PRF}}$ and any $x \in \mathcal{M}_{\mathsf{PRF}} \setminus \mathcal{S}$ it holds that

$$\Pr\left[\mathsf{F.Eval}(k_0, x) = \mathsf{F.Eval}(k_t, x) \,\middle|\, \begin{array}{c} pms_{\mathsf{PRF}} \leftarrow \mathsf{F.Setup}(1^\kappa);\ k \xleftarrow{\$} \mathsf{F.KGen}(pms_{\mathsf{PRF}}) \\ \text{for } i \in [q] : k_i \leftarrow \mathsf{F.Punc}(k_{i-1}, x_i) \end{array}\right] = 1.$$

We define a security experiment $\mathsf{Exp}^{\mathsf{IND\text{-}CMA}}_{\mathcal{A},\mathsf{F}}(\kappa, q_f)$ for (P)PRF below. The boxed lines are exclusively used in the security experiment for PPRF.

$\underline{\mathsf{Exp}^{\mathsf{IND\text{-}CMA}}_{\mathcal{A},\mathsf{F}}(\kappa, q_f):}$
$b \xleftarrow{\$} \{0,1\};\ ct := 0;\ pms_{\mathsf{PRF}} \leftarrow \mathsf{F.Setup}(1^\kappa);\ k \xleftarrow{\$} \mathsf{F.KGen}(pms_{\mathsf{PRF}})$
$(x^*, st) \leftarrow \mathcal{A}_1^{\mathcal{O}_{\mathsf{PRF}}(\cdot)}(\kappa, pms_{\mathsf{PRF}});\ r_0 \xleftarrow{\$} \mathcal{R}_{\mathsf{PRF}};\ r_1 \leftarrow \mathsf{F.Eval}(k, x^*)$
IF $x^* \in \mathsf{L}_{\mathsf{PRF}}$, OUTPUT $\perp$
$\boxed{k \leftarrow \mathsf{F.Punc}(k, x^*)};\ b' \leftarrow \mathcal{A}_2^{\mathcal{O}_{\mathsf{PRF}}(\cdot)}(st, r_b, \boxed{k})$
OUTPUT $(b' = b)$

$\underline{\mathcal{O}_{\mathsf{PRF}}(x):}$
IF $ct \geq q_f$, OUTPUT $\perp$
APPEND $x \rightarrow \mathsf{L}_{\mathsf{PRF}}$
$r \leftarrow \mathsf{F.Eval}(k, x)$
$\boxed{k \leftarrow \mathsf{F.Punc}(k, x)}$
OUTPUT r

Definition 7 (IND-CMA for **(P)PRF**). *We say that* F *is a secure (P)PRF scheme if, in the experiment* $\mathsf{Exp}^{\mathsf{IND\text{-}CMA}}_{\mathcal{A},\mathsf{F}}(\kappa, q_f)$, *the advantage* $\mathsf{Adv}^{\mathsf{IND\text{-}CMA}}_{\mathcal{A},\mathsf{F},\frac{1}{2}}(\kappa, q_f)$ *of any PPT adversary* $\mathcal{A} = (\mathcal{A}_1, \mathcal{A}_2)$ *is negligible.*

In addition, we define the statistical distance (SD) of F (with a random key $k \xleftarrow{\$} \mathcal{K}_{\mathsf{PRF}}$) to a uniform random function $\mathsf{U} : \mathcal{M}_{\mathsf{PRF}} \rightarrow \mathcal{R}_{\mathsf{PRF}}$, as $\Delta(\mathsf{F}, \mathsf{U}) = \frac{1}{2}\sum_{x \in \mathcal{M}_{\mathsf{PRF}}} \left|\Pr[\mathcal{F}(k, x) = y] \quad \Pr[\mathsf{U}(x) = y]\right|$.

Collision-Resistant Hash Functions. We define the security experiment $\mathsf{Exp}^{\mathsf{CR}}_{\mathcal{A},\mathsf{H}}(\kappa)$ for a CRH scheme H as follows.

$\underline{\mathsf{Exp}^{\mathsf{CR}}_{\mathcal{A},\mathsf{H}}(\kappa):}$
$(hk, pms_{\mathsf{CRH}}) \leftarrow \mathsf{H.Setup}(1^\kappa);\ (m_0, m_1) \leftarrow \mathcal{A}(\kappa, pms_{\mathsf{CRH}}, hk)$
OUTPUT $(m_0 \neq m_1) \wedge (\mathsf{H.Eval}(hk, m_0) = \mathsf{H.Eval}(hk, m_1))$

Definition 8. *We say* H *is secure if no PPT adversary has non-negligible advantage* $\mathsf{Adv}^{\mathsf{CR}}_{\mathcal{A},\mathsf{H}}(\kappa)$ *in* $\mathsf{Exp}^{\mathsf{CR}}_{\mathcal{A},\mathsf{H}}(\kappa)$.

B Tree-Based PPRF

In this section, we briefly revisit the key concept of tree-based PPRFs [1,12,35], built from the well-known one-way function based PRF construction, proposed by Goldreich, Goldwasser, and Micali (GGM) [27].

The GGM construction leverages on a pseudorandom generator (PRG) $\mathsf{G} : \{0,1\}^\ell \to \{0,1\}^{2\ell}$. The output string is then split into two equal parts, denoted as $\mathsf{G}_0(k)$ and $\mathsf{G}_1(k)$, representing the first and second halves, respectively. To define the PRF $\mathsf{F} : \{0,1\}^\ell \times \{0,1\}^n \to \{0,1\}^\ell$, the GGM construction organizes its domain as a binary tree. The PRF key k, generated by $\mathsf{F.Setup}(1^\kappa)$, serves as the root seed. Each leaf corresponds to a unique PRF output, while edges and internal nodes facilitate computation. Edges are labeled 0 or 1, indicating connections to left or right children, respectively, and each node is identified by the binary string of edge labels along the path from the root. For a message $x = x_1 x_2 \cdots x_n \in \{0,1\}^n$, the PRF value is computed by traversing the tree from the root to the leaf specified by x. Starting with the root seed k, the PRG G is iteratively applied along the path dictated by the bits of x. At each step, G_{x_i} (either G_0 or G_1) is applied to the current intermediate value. This process yields the final output:

$$\mathsf{F.Eval}(k, x) = \mathsf{G}_{x_n} \circ \mathsf{G}_{x_{n-1}} \circ \cdots \circ \mathsf{G}_{x_1}(k) \in \{0,1\}^\ell.$$

The hierarchical structure of this tree-based construction ensures pseudo-randomness and allows for efficient operations. Moreover, its flexibility enables the introduction of puncturing mechanisms. To puncture at $x = x_1 x_2 \ldots x_n$, realizing $\mathsf{PPRF.Punc}(k, x)$, the initial root key k is replaced with intermediate node evaluations for prefixes $\overline{x_1}, x_1\overline{x_2}, x_1 x_2 \overline{x_3}, \ldots, x_1 x_2 \ldots \overline{x_n}$. That is, these values are taken as the new key k' output by $\mathsf{F.Punc}$ algorithm, allowing recomputation of the PRF for all inputs except x.

For implement the $\mathsf{RandSelect}$ function in our FSDGS constructions, we need and additional algorithm of PPRF, i.e., $\mathsf{GetMsg}(k, i)$ to enable the retrieval of the i-th unpunctured message. To implement the $\mathsf{F.GetMsg}(k', i)$ algorithm based on the GGM construction, we devise the following steps:

1. Initialize currentPrefix $= \emptyset$.
2. For each level $j = 1$ to n:
   - Compute the number ν of accessible leaves in the left subtree:
     - Count the number μ of punctured message according to the prefixes with currentPrefix$||0$;
     - Compute $\nu := 2^{n-j} - \mu$.
   - If $i \leq \nu$, append $0 \to$ currentPrefix. Otherwise, append $1 \to$ currentPrefix and sets $i := i - \nu$.
3. Return currentPrefix as the binary representation of the i-th accessible input message.

The complexity of F.GetMsg primarily depends on the depth of the binary tree, which is determined by the bit-length n of the key, and the number of stored intermediate evaluations, ϕ, corresponding to the punctured points. The algorithm retrieves the i-th accessible input message by iterating through the nodes in the path from the root to the leaf representing the i-th unpunctured message. For each level in the tree, the algorithm verifies whether the current node or path is part of the stored intermediate evaluations. This lookup is $O(m)$ for each level since we may need to search among ϕ intermediate evaluations. Since there are n levels in the tree, the overall complexity of the algorithm is $O(n \cdot \phi)$. This complexity reflects the worst-case scenario where all ϕ punctured points must be checked at each level.

References

1. Aviram, N., Gellert, K., Jager, T.: Session resumption protocols and efficient forward security for TLS 1.3 0-RTT. J. Cryptol. **34**(3), 20 (2021)
2. Bansarkhani, R.E., Misoczki, R.: G-merkle: a hash-based group signature scheme from standard assumptions. In: PQCrypto, pp. 441–463. Springer (2018)
3. Barker, E.B., Kelsey, J.M.: Recommendation for random number generation using deterministic random bit generators (revised). US Department of Commerce, Technology Administration, NIST (2007)
4. Bellare, M., Micciancio, D., Warinschi, B.: Foundations of group signatures: formal definitions, simplified requirements, and a construction based on general assumptions. In: EUROCRYPT, pp. 614–629. Springer (2003)
5. Bellare, M., Shi, H., Zhang, C.: Foundations of group signatures: the case of dynamic groups. In: CT-RSA, pp. 136–153. Springer (2005)
6. Bernstein, D.J., et al.: SPHINCS: practical stateless hash-based signatures. In: EUROCRYPT, pp. 368–397. Springer (2015)
7. Bernstein, D.J., Hülsing, A., Kölbl, S., Niederhagen, R., Rijneveld, J., Schwabe, P.: The sphincs$^+$ signature framework. In: CCS, pp. 2129–2146. ACM (2019)
8. Bertsekas, D., Tsitsiklis, J.N.: Introduction to Probability, vol. 1. Athena Scientific (2008)
9. Beullens, W., Dobson, S., Katsumata, S., Lai, Y., Pintore, F.: Group signatures and more from isogenies and lattices: generic, simple, and efficient. In: EUROCRYPT, pp. 95–126. Springer (2022)
10. Bobolz, J., Diaz, J., Kohlweiss, M.: Foundations of anonymous signatures: formal definitions, simplified requirements, and a construction based on general assumptions. In: Financial Crypto, pp. 121–139. Springer (2024)
11. Boneh, D., Eskandarian, S., Fisch, B.: Post-quantum EPID signatures from symmetric primitives. In: CT-RSA, pp. 251–271. Springer (2019)
12. Boneh, D., Waters, B.: Constrained pseudorandom functions and their applications. In: ASIACRYPT, pp. 280–300. Springer (2013)
13. Bootle, J., Cerulli, A., Chaidos, P., Ghadafi, E., Groth, J.: Foundations of fully dynamic group signatures. J. Cryptol. **33**(4), 1822–1870 (2020)
14. Brassard, G., Høyer, P., Tapp, A.: Quantum cryptanalysis of hash and claw-free functions. In: LATIN. LNCS, pp. 163–169. Springer (1998)
15. Brickell, E.F., Camenisch, J., Chen, L.: Direct anonymous attestation. In: CCS, pp. 132–145. ACM (2004)

16. Bringer, J., Chabanne, H., Pointcheval, D., Zimmer, S.: An application of the boneh and shacham group signature scheme to biometric authentication. In: IWSEC, pp. 219–230. Springer (2008)
17. Buchmann, J., Dahmen, E., Schneider, M.: Merkle tree traversal revisited. In: PQCrypto, pp. 63–78. Springer (2008)
18. Buser, M., Liu, J.K., Steinfeld, R., Sakzad, A., Sun, S.: DGM: a dynamic and revocable group merkle signature. In: ESORICS, pp. 194–214. Springer (2019)
19. Canetti, R., Goldreich, O., Halevi, S.: The random oracle methodology, revisited. J. ACM **51**(4), 557–594 (2004)
20. Cao, X., et al.: HHGS: forward-secure dynamic group signatures from symmetric primitives. Cryptology ePrint Archive, Paper 2025/2270 (2025). https://eprint.iacr.org/2025/2270
21. Chen, L., Dong, C., Newton, C.J.P., Wang, Y.: Sphinx-in-the-head: group signatures from symmetric primitives. ACM Trans. Priv. Secur. **27**(1), 11:1–11:35 (2024)
22. Cheval, V., Cremers, C., Dax, A., Hirschi, L., Jacomme, C., Kremer, S.: Hash gone bad: automated discovery of protocol attacks that exploit hash function weaknesses. In: USENIX Security Symposium, pp. 5899–5916. USENIX Association (2023)
23. Dagdelen, Ö., Fischlin, M., Gagliardoni, T.: The Fiat-Shamir transformation in a quantum world. In: ASIACRYPT, pp. 62–81. Springer (2013)
24. Dworkin, M.J.: Sha-3 standard: permutation-based hash and extendable-output functions (2015)
25. Fadavi, M., Karati, S., Erfanian, A., Safavi-Naini, R.: DGMT: a fully dynamic group signature from symmetric-key primitives. Cryptography **9**(1), 12 (2025)
26. Faonio, A., Fiore, D., Nizzardo, L., Soriente, C.: Subversion-resilient enhanced privacy ID. In: CT-RSA, pp. 562–588. Springer (2022)
27. Goldreich, O., Goldwasser, S., Micali, S.: How to construct random functions. J. ACM **33**(4), 792–807 (1986)
28. Grover, L.K.: A fast quantum mechanical algorithm for database search. In: STOC, pp. 212–219. ACM (1996)
29. Gueron, S.: AES-GCM-SIV implementations (128 and 256 bit) (2018). https://github.com/Shay-Gueron/AES-GCM-SIV
30. Hülsing, A., Butin, D., Gazdag, S., Rijneveld, J., Mohaisen, A.: XMSS: extended merkle signature scheme. RFC **8391**, 1–74 (2018)
31. Hülsing, A., Kudinov, M.A., Ronen, E., Yogev, E.: SPHINCS+C: compressing SPHINCS+ with (almost) no cost. In: SP, pp. 1435–1453. IEEE (2023)
32. Hülsing, A., Rijneveld, J., Song, F.: Mitigating multi-target attacks in hash-based signatures. In: PKC. LNCS, pp. 387–416. Springer (2016)
33. Ishai, Y., Kushilevitz, E., Ostrovsky, R., Sahai, A.: Zero-knowledge proofs from secure multiparty computation. SIAM J. Comput. **39**(3), 1121–1152 (2009)
34. Khovratovich, D., Kudinov, M., Wagner, B.: At the top of the hypercube - better size-time tradeoffs for hash-based signatures. In: Tauman Kalai, Y., Kamara, S.F. (eds.) CRYPTO 2025, pp. 93–123. Springer (2025)
35. Kiayias, A., Papadopoulos, S., Triandopoulos, N., Zacharias, T.: Delegatable pseudorandom functions and applications. In: CCS, pp. 669–684. ACM (2013)
36. Kiayias, A., Yung, M.: Extracting group signatures from traitor tracing schemes. In: EUROCRYPT, pp. 630–648. Springer (2003)
37. Ling, S., Nguyen, K., Wang, H., Xu, Y.: Forward-secure group signatures from lattices. In: PQCrypto, pp. 44–64. Springer (2019)

38. Lyubashevsky, V., Nguyen, N.K., Plançon, M., Seiler, G.: Shorter lattice-based group signatures via "almost free" encryption and other optimizations. In: ASIACRYPT, pp. 218–248. Springer (2021)
39. Nguyen, K., Tang, H., Wang, H., Zeng, N.: New code-based privacy-preserving cryptographic constructions. In: ASIACRYPT, pp. 25–55. Springer (2019)
40. Omar, S., Padhye, S.: Multivariate linkable group signature scheme. In: Proceedings of the International Conference on Computing and Communication Systems, pp. 623–632. Springer, Singapore (2021)
41. Ronen, E.: Software for the SPHINCS+C scheme (2022). https://github.com/eyalr0/sphincsplusc
42. Song, D.X.: Practical forward secure group signature schemes. In: CCS, pp. 225–234. ACM (2001)
43. Yang, G., Tang, S., Yang, L.: A novel group signature scheme based on MPKC. In: ISPEC, pp. 181–195. Springer (2011)
44. Yang, R., Au, M.H., Zhang, Z., Xu, Q., Yu, Z., Whyte, W.: Efficient lattice-based zero-knowledge arguments with standard soundness: construction and applications. In: CRYPTO, pp. 147–175. Springer (2019)
45. Yehia, M., AlTawy, R., Gulliver, T.A.: $\mathrm{Gm}^{\mathrm{mt}}$: a revocable group merkle multi-tree signature scheme. In: CANS, pp. 136–157. Springer (2021)

Efficient $e = 3$ Threshold RSA via Integer Coordinates for Intel SGX

Sam Ng(✉) and Jason Lau

Vision City, Hong Kong
samngms@gmail.com, jason@zeroclicks.ai

Abstract. Threshold RSA signatures face a fundamental obstacle: reconstructing the private exponent from Shamir shares requires Lagrange coefficients whose computation involves modular division by values tied to $\phi(N)$, which must remain hidden. This obstacle is particularly acute for critical deployments such as Intel SGX code signing, which mandates $e = 3$. Existing $e = 3$-compatible approaches incur substantial overhead, increased share sizes, or sacrifice security properties such as perfect secrecy. This work introduces the integer coordinate framework, achieving $e = 3$ support with EUF-CMA security under the standard RSA assumption alone. By carefully selecting interpolation coordinates that yield integer-valued Lagrange coefficients, we eliminate all modular inversions modulo $\phi(N)$, requiring only standard integer arithmetic and modular exponentiation. The framework achieves $O(\kappa)$-bit share sizes, perfect secrecy, and computational efficiency previously unattained for $e = 3$-compatible schemes.

Although we currently lack an efficient general algorithm for constructing coordinate sets for arbitrary (t, n)—a challenging open problem for future work—the coordinate families found via heuristic search achieve coverage for $2 \leq t \leq n \leq 9$ and selected $n = 10$ configurations, sufficient for small boardroom-size deployments. The resulting online protocol is extremely simple and immediately enables practical $e = 3$ threshold RSA for Intel SGX and similar applications.

1 Introduction

1.1 Motivation and Background

Threshold cryptography [5,8] enables cryptographic operations to be performed collaboratively by multiple parties without requiring any single entity to possess complete secret key material. This distribution of trust is fundamental to securing critical infrastructure where single points of failure are unacceptable. Threshold RSA signatures [17] are particularly significant given RSA's pervasive deployment in code signing systems, certificate authorities, and hardware security modules.

Intel SGX enforces a hard requirement that enclave signing keys use public exponent $e = 3$ and will reject signatures using the industry-standard exponent $e = 65537$ [4]. While threshold RSA schemes such as Shoup [20] support

F. -H. Liu (Ed.): CT-RSAC 2026, LNCS 16496, pp. 262–287, 2026.
https://doi.org/10.1007/978-3-032-22931-1_10

arbitrary exponents efficiently, they cannot be applied to SGX code signing due to this fixed-exponent constraint. This paper's integer coordinate framework directly addresses the SGX-mandated $e = 3$ requirement, enabling secure threshold signing infrastructure for enclave code.

The application of Shamir Secret Sharing [19] to RSA private exponents encounters a fundamental mathematical obstacle. Standard Lagrange interpolation requires computing coefficients of the form $\lambda_i = \prod_{j \in S, j \neq i} \frac{x_j}{x_j - x_i} \pmod{\phi(N)}$, where S denotes the set of participating parties and $\phi(N)$ is the Euler totient function[1] of the RSA modulus N. Security of RSA fundamentally depends on $\phi(N)$ remaining computationally infeasible to compute, creating an inherent tension: threshold reconstruction appears to require arithmetic operations using a value whose secrecy is essential.

1.2 Integer Coordinate Approach: Mathematical Foundation

This work establishes a fundamentally different mathematical framework based on the following observation: for appropriately chosen interpolation coordinates $\{x_1, \ldots, x_n\} \subset \mathbb{Z}$, the Lagrange coefficients $\lambda_i(S) = \prod_{j \in S, j \neq i} \frac{x_j}{x_j - x_i}$ evaluated over $\mathbb{Z}$ (without any modular reduction) are integers for all relevant subsets S. This integrality property eliminates all modular arithmetic modulo $\phi(N)$ from the online signing protocol, yielding a reconstruction procedure requiring only integer operations and standard modular exponentiation modulo N.

Theoretical Significance. The existence of such integer coordinate families constitutes a non-trivial mathematical property. For a (t, n) threshold scheme, integrality must hold for all $\binom{n}{t}$ possible signing coalitions simultaneously, imposing a complex system of divisibility constraints on the coordinate selection. Understanding when such families exist, characterizing their minimal growth rates, and developing efficient construction algorithms represent fundamental questions at the intersection of combinatorics, number theory, and cryptographic protocol design.

1.3 Contributions

This work makes the following contributions to the theory and practice of threshold RSA:

1. **Most Efficient EUF-CMA Secure Threshold RSA for $e = 3$:** Among schemes supporting $e = 3$, this work provides the first scheme to achieve EUF-CMA security (unforgeability) against malicious adversaries under the standard RSA assumption alone, with standard $O(\kappa)$-bit share sizes and perfect secrecy. The framework achieves universal parameter compatibility for

[1] More precisely, Carmichael's totient function $\lambda(N)$ [18] suffices. For expository clarity, $\phi(N)$ is employed throughout this work; the mathematical framework applies identically to $\lambda(N)$.

discovered coordinate families—supporting $e = 3$ for all threshold configurations with $n \leq 9$ without restrictions on t (unlike prior approaches requiring $n > 2t$)—without requiring additional cryptographic primitives. Comprehensive comparison (Table 1) demonstrates substantial advantages over existing $e = 3$-compatible approaches.

2. **Integer Coordinate Framework with Proven Unforgeability:** Formal establishment of the integer coordinate paradigm for threshold RSA, including complete correctness proofs and EUF-CMA security analysis against static malicious adversaries under the standard RSA assumption (Theorem 1). The framework provides a clean separation between unforgeability (proven) and robustness (practical extension discussed in Appendix A).
3. **Complete Coordinate Characterization for $n \leq 9$ and Structural Phenomena:** Construction of integer coordinate families providing universal coverage for (t, n) configurations with $2 \leq t \leq n \leq 9$, along with selected high-threshold configurations for $n = 10$ (Sect. 4). This demonstrates immediate applicability to small-to-moderate group sizes common in practical threshold deployments. Empirical identification and characterization of mathematical patterns governing coordinate existence, including lifting properties, multiplicative scaling, and smoothness requirements.
4. **Practical Validation and Comparative Analysis:** Detailed evaluation of existing $e = 3$-compatible threshold RSA schemes across multiple dimensions: share size, computational cost, security model, perfect secrecy, and hardware suitability. The integer coordinate approach proves ideal for hardware-constrained environments (HSMs, secure enclaves) through elimination of polynomial arithmetic and complex interactive protocols. Implementation and performance analysis demonstrating practical feasibility, including successful deployment on resource-constrained Ledger hardware wallets (Sect. 6).

1.4 Scope and Limitations

This work addresses the threshold signature reconstruction problem under the following model:

- **Trusted Dealer Model:** A trusted dealer generates RSA keys and distributes shares via secure channels
- **Adversary Model:** Static, malicious (active) adversaries corrupting up to $t - 1$ parties. The core security analysis (Theorem 1) establishes EUF-CMA security (unforgeability) under the standard RSA assumption alone. This is the primary contribution and stands as a complete result.
- **Robustness (Optional Extension):** An optional DLEQ-based verification mechanism is presented in Appendix A for practical deployments requiring robustness against denial-of-service attacks. Formal security analysis of this extension to adaptive adversaries requires careful treatment of witness dependencies and is left as future work.
- **Coordinate Families:** Coordinate families are provided for (t, n) configurations with $n \leq 9$, along with selected configurations for $n = 10$. *We*

currently do not have an efficient general algorithm for constructing integer coordinate sets for arbitrary threshold sizes beyond $n = 10$. All coordinate families reported in this work were discovered through ultimately heuristic computational search with some minor optimizations (Sect. 4). Development of efficient constructive algorithms for larger thresholds represents an important open problem.
- **Out of Scope:** Distributed Key Generation (DKG) [11,16] and proactive refresh [13]

The integer coordinate framework's public coordinate structure naturally supports optional extensions for verification and robustness. The DLEQ-based approach (Appendix A) has been successfully deployed in practice and provides pragmatic security, though formal proofs under all attack models remain open. Further extensions such as DKG and proactive refresh are compatible with the framework and constitute future work.

1.5 Organization

The remainder of this paper is organized as follows. Section 2 analyzes prior threshold RSA approaches and their limitations. Section 3 establishes notation, formal definitions, and the security model. Section 4 presents the main construction, including formal algorithms, correctness proofs, and the coordinate search methodology. Section 5 provides comprehensive security analysis establishing the unforgeability result. Section 6 reports implementation results and performance characteristics. Section 7 concludes with discussion of open problems and future directions. Appendix A presents an optional DLEQ-based robustness extension for deployments requiring verification of partial signatures, including detailed algorithms (Algorithm 3–6) and security discussion.

2 Related Work

Threshold RSA signature research has developed along three primary directions: denominator elimination techniques, polynomial ring-based share representation, and parameter restriction approaches. This section analyzes these approaches and their fundamental limitations, particularly regarding support for small public exponents.

2.1 Denominator Elimination Approaches

Shoup's Fundamental Construction. The foundational work of Shoup [20] established the denominator elimination paradigm through multiplicative clearing. The scheme computes modified Lagrange coefficients $\Delta \cdot \lambda_i$ where $\Delta = n!$, ensuring integrality through the divisibility property: for any subset S of size t and any $i \in S$, the denominator $\prod_{j \in S \setminus \{i\}} (x_j - x_i)$ divides Δ when standard coordinates $x_i = i$ are employed.

The critical constraint is $\gcd(e, 4\Delta^2) = 1$. For $e = 3$, this requires $3 \nmid 4\Delta^2$, equivalently $3 \nmid \Delta = n!$. Since $3 \mid n!$ for all $n \geq 3$, the scheme excludes $e = 3$ with $n > 2$ participants. This algebraic incompatibility renders Shoup's approach unsuitable for applications mandating $e = 3$ [14,20].

Refined Denominator Analysis. Subsequent work has refined the denominator elimination technique. Damgård and Dupont [6] observe that the least common multiple of all possible denominators is strictly smaller than $n!$ for many coordinate choices, permitting a reduced clearing factor Δ'. However, the fundamental constraint $\gcd(e, 4(\Delta')^2) = 1$ persists, maintaining restrictions on small exponents: when e is small relative to n, the coprimality condition remains difficult to satisfy.

Damgård and Koprowski [7] extend denominator elimination to generalized secret sharing structures and develop techniques for trustless setup via distributed key generation. Their protocol maintains the core algebraic framework and inherits similar exponent restrictions. The polynomial structure analysis required to ensure simultaneous denominator elimination and RSA parameter validity introduces additional complexity without fundamentally resolving the small-exponent limitation.

2.2 Polynomial Ring-Based Share Representation

Cyclotomic Polynomial Framework. Frankel and Desmedt [10] introduce a fundamentally different algebraic structure by embedding shares in polynomial rings $\mathbb{Z}_{\phi(N)}[X]/(\Phi_r(X))$, where $\Phi_r(X)$ denotes the r-th cyclotomic polynomial [21]. Share values are polynomials of degree $O(\max(t, n))$ rather than field elements. The cyclotomic structure permits precomputation of all required inversions during share generation, eliminating online modular arithmetic modulo $\phi(N)$.

This approach successfully avoids exponent restrictions: $e = 3$ is fully compatible with the framework. However, the representation incurs substantial overhead. Share size grows linearly with the polynomial degree, and reconstruction requires polynomial arithmetic in the quotient ring rather than simple field operations. For a (t, n) threshold scheme, each share comprises $\Theta(n)$ field elements, and combining operations require $O(n^2)$ multiplications in $\mathbb{Z}_{\phi(N)}$. This complexity increase renders the approach less attractive for resource-constrained deployments despite its theoretical elegance.

2.3 Collaborative Inversion Framework: Catalano et al.

Catalano et al. [2] introduce a fundamentally distinct approach that circumvents the modular inversion problem through collaborative computation over a publicly shared auxiliary modulus, entirely independent of $\phi(N)$. The protocol has participating parties jointly compute modular inverses through multiple rounds of interaction, enabling compatibility with arbitrary public exponents including $e = 3$ without the algebraic constraints of denominator elimination. However, the approach imposes the structural restriction $n > 2t$ on threshold configurations, excluding high-threshold scenarios such as $(n-1)$-of-n or n-of-n deployments. The joint inversion protocol requires $O(n^2)$ message complexity across multiple interaction rounds, increasing both latency and implementation complexity compared to non-interactive approaches.

2.4 Extended-Modulus Approaches

Xu and Chen [22] develop an alternative extended-modulus approach that achieves $e = 3$ compatibility by performing Shamir secret sharing over an auxiliary modulus r (chosen such that $e \nmid r$ and $\gcd(r, \phi(N)) = 1$) rather than over $\mathbb{Z}_{\phi(N)}$. The scheme computes shares as $d_i = f(i) \bmod r$ where $f(X)$ is a degree-$(t-1)$ polynomial with $f(0) = d \bmod r$. During reconstruction, parties compute partial results $y_i = m^{d_i} \bmod N$, and an additional exponentiation with precomputed auxiliary parameter k yields the final signature $m^d \bmod N$. This approach supports arbitrary thresholds including $(n-1)$-of-n configurations.

Potential Security Concern: The Xu-Chen scheme may have a potential information leakage concern related to the perfect secrecy property of Shamir secret sharing. In standard Shamir secret sharing over $\mathbb{Z}_{\phi(N)}$, any $t-1$ shares reveal zero information about the secret d or about any other party's share. However, working over $\mathbb{Z}_r$ instead of the natural domain $\mathbb{Z}_{\phi(N)}$ may create additional algebraic structure that could potentially be exploited:

- Consider a $(3, 3)$-threshold configuration with evaluation points $x_1 = 1, x_2 = 2, x_3 = 3$, where party 3 is the sole honest participant while parties 1 and 2 are corrupted.
- During secret reconstruction, the Lagrange coefficient for party 3 is $\lambda_3 = \frac{2}{2-3} \cdot \frac{1}{1-3} = 1$, implying that $y_3 = d - (\lambda_1 y_1 + \lambda_2 y_2) \pmod{r}$.
- The corrupted coalition can compute $\lambda_1 y_1 + \lambda_2 y_2 \pmod{r}$. If, for example, the value equals approximately $\frac{3r}{2}$ before reduction modulo r, yielding a value near $\frac{r}{2}$ after reduction, then observing certain values in the reconstruction protocol could potentially reveal whether a modular wrap-around occurred.
- Under specific parameter choices and coalition structures, this observation could potentially leak information about the most significant bit of the honest party's share y_3.

While a rigorous analysis with formal probability bounds and concrete simulations would be needed to establish the practical severity of this concern, the structural difference of working over $\mathbb{Z}_r$ rather than $\mathbb{Z}_{\phi(N)}$ warrants careful consideration. The scheme maintains unforgeability (malicious parties cannot forge signatures), but whether it fully preserves the information-theoretic privacy guarantees of threshold cryptography—where $t-1$ parties should learn nothing about honest parties' shares beyond what valid signatures reveal—requires further investigation.

2.5 Application-Specific Workarounds

Joye and Michalevsky [14] address the specific challenge of RSA signatures with $e = 3$ in Hardware Security Modules (HSMs) through signature conversion. The technique generates signatures under an exponent compatible with existing threshold schemes (typically $e = 65537$) and applies an algebraic transformation yielding signatures verifiable under $e = 3$. This approach resolves the immediate compatibility issue for single-signer HSM deployments but does not extend to threshold scenarios, as the conversion itself is not distributible among multiple parties. The method underscores the practical significance of $e = 3$ support in deployed cryptographic systems.

2.6 Comparative Analysis

Table 1 summarizes the key characteristics of the threshold RSA approaches discussed in the preceding subsections.

Table 1. Comprehensive comparison of threshold RSA schemes. Notation: κ = security parameter (RSA modulus bit-length), n = total parties, t = threshold, $\Delta = n!$.

Scheme	$e = 3$ Support	Share Size (bits)	Online Ops (per party)	Secrecy
Shoup [20]	No ($e \nmid 4\Delta^2$)	$O(\kappa)$	1 exp.	Yes
Damgård-Dupont [6]	No ($e \nmid 4(\Delta')^2$)	$O(\kappa)$	1 exp.	Yes
Frankel-Desmedt [10]	**Yes**	$O(n\kappa)$ (polynomial)	$O(n^2)$ poly. ops	Yes
Catalano et al. [2]	**Yes** ($n > 2t$)	$O(\kappa)$	$O(n^2)$ msgs. interactive	Yes
Xu-Chen [22]	**Yes**	$O(\kappa)$	1 exp. + 2 comb. exp.	Concern (potential)
Joye-Michalevsky [14]	**Yes** (conversion)	N/A (single-party)	N/A (non-threshold)	N/A
Integer Coordinates (This work)	**Yes (universal)**	**$O(\kappa)$ (standard)**	**1 exp.**	**Yes**

3 Preliminaries

3.1 Notation

The following notation is employed throughout:

- $\kappa \in \mathbb{N}$ denotes the security parameter
- $N = pq$ where p, q are distinct primes of bit-length $\Theta(\kappa)$; N is the RSA modulus

- $\phi(N) = (p-1)(q-1)$ denotes the Euler totient function
- $e \in \mathbb{Z}^+$ denotes the public exponent satisfying $\gcd(e, \phi(N)) = 1$
- $d \in \mathbb{Z}_{\phi(N)}$ denotes the private exponent satisfying $ed \equiv 1 \pmod{\phi(N)}$
- $t, n \in \mathbb{N}$ with $2 \leq t \leq n$ denote threshold and total party count respectively
- $[n] := \{1, 2, \ldots, n\}$ denotes the party index set
- $\mathcal{P} = \{P_1, \ldots, P_n\}$ denotes the party set
- $S \subseteq [n]$ with $|S| = t$ denotes a signing coalition
- $\mathcal{X} = \{x_1, \ldots, x_n\} \subset \mathbb{Z}$ denotes the coordinate family with $x_i \neq x_j$ for $i \neq j$
- $f(X) = \sum_{j=0}^{t-1} a_j X^j \in \mathbb{Z}_{\phi(N)}[X]$ denotes the secret sharing polynomial with $a_0 = d$
- $y_i = f(x_i) \bmod \phi(N) \in \mathbb{Z}_{\phi(N)}$ denotes the share of party P_i
- $\lambda_{i,S} = \prod_{j \in S \setminus \{i\}} \frac{x_j}{x_j - x_i}$ denotes the Lagrange coefficient for party i under coalition S; subscript S is omitted when clear from context
- $m \in \mathbb{Z}_N$ denotes a message representative (after encoding via PSS [15] or similar)
- $\sigma \in \mathbb{Z}_N$ denotes a complete RSA signature
- $\sigma_i \in \mathbb{Z}_N$ denotes a partial signature from party P_i
- $\binom{n}{k} = \frac{n!}{k!(n-k)!}$ denotes the binomial coefficient

3.2 Standard Definitions

Definition 1 (RSA Problem). *Let* $\mathsf{RSAGen}(1^\kappa)$ *denote an algorithm that outputs* (N, e, d) *where* $N = pq$ *is a product of two* κ*-bit primes,* e *is chosen with* $\gcd(e, \phi(N)) = 1$*, and* $d = e^{-1} \bmod \phi(N)$*. The RSA problem is: given* (N, e) *and* $y = x^e \bmod N$ *for uniformly random* $x \in \mathbb{Z}_N^*$*, compute* x*. The RSA assumption states that for all probabilistic polynomial-time (PPT) algorithms* $\mathcal{A}$*,*

$$\Pr\left[(N, e, d) \leftarrow \mathsf{RSAGen}(1^\kappa), x \xleftarrow{\$} \mathbb{Z}_N^*, y \leftarrow x^e \bmod N : \mathcal{A}(N, e, y) = x\right] = \mathsf{negl}(\kappa).$$

Definition 2 (Threshold RSA Signature Scheme). *A* (t, n)*-threshold RSA signature scheme is a tuple of PPT algorithms* $(\mathsf{KeyGen}, \mathsf{Share}, \mathsf{PartialSign}, \mathsf{Combine})$*:*

- $\mathsf{KeyGen}(1^\kappa, e) \to (N, e, d)$*: generates RSA parameters with specified public exponent* e
- $\mathsf{Share}(d, \phi(N), t, n, \mathcal{X}) \to (y_1, \ldots, y_n)$*: creates shares using coordinate family* $\mathcal{X} = \{x_1, \ldots, x_n\}$
- $\mathsf{PartialSign}(i, y_i, m, S, \mathcal{X}) \to \sigma_i$*: party* P_i *generates partial signature for coalition* $S \ni i$
- $\mathsf{Combine}(\{\sigma_i\}_{i \in S}, m, N) \to \sigma$*: reconstructs complete signature from partial signatures*

Correctness requires that for all $(N, e, d) \leftarrow \mathsf{KeyGen}(1^\kappa, e)$*, all* $(y_1, \ldots, y_n) \leftarrow \mathsf{Share}(d, \phi(N), t, n, \mathcal{X})$*, all* $S \subseteq [n]$ *with* $|S| = t$*, and all* $m \in \mathbb{Z}_N^*$*,*

$$\mathsf{Combine}\big(\{\mathsf{PartialSign}(i, y_i, m, S, \mathcal{X})\}_{i \in S}, m, N\big) = m^d \bmod N.$$

Definition 3 (Shamir Secret Sharing and Lagrange Interpolation). *For a degree-$(t-1)$ polynomial $f(X) = \sum_{j=0}^{t-1} a_j X^j$ over a ring R, given evaluations $\{f(x_i)\}_{i \in S}$ at distinct points $\{x_i\}_{i \in S}$ where $|S| = t$, the constant term is recovered via Lagrange interpolation:*

$$f(0) = \sum_{i \in S} f(x_i) \cdot \lambda_{i,S}, \quad \text{where} \quad \lambda_{i,S} = \prod_{j \in S \setminus \{i\}} \frac{x_j}{x_j - x_i}.$$

In threshold RSA, f is defined over $\mathbb{Z}_{\phi(N)}$ with $f(0) = d$. Standard application requires computing $\lambda_{i,S} \bmod \phi(N)$, necessitating knowledge of $\phi(N)$.

Definition 4 (Integer Coordinate Family). *A coordinate family $\mathcal{X} = \{x_1, \ldots, x_n\} \subset \mathbb{Z}$ with distinct elements is* (t, n)-integer *if for all subsets $S \subseteq [n]$ with $|S| = t$ and all $i \in S$, the Lagrange coefficient*

$$\lambda_{i,S} = \prod_{j \in S \setminus \{i\}} \frac{x_j}{x_j - x_i}$$

is an integer when evaluated over $\mathbb{Z}$ (i.e., $\lambda_{i,S} \in \mathbb{Z}$).

The significance of Definition 4 is that when $\mathcal{X}$ is (t, n)-integer, signature reconstruction requires only integer arithmetic and modular exponentiation modulo N, with no dependence on $\phi(N)$. This constitutes the foundational insight of the integer coordinate framework.

Example 1 ($(2,3)$*-Integer Coordinate Family).* Consider the coordinate family $\mathcal{X} = \{3, 4, 6\}$. For each possible 2-element signing coalition $S \subseteq \{1, 2, 3\}$, the Lagrange coefficients are:

$$\begin{aligned}
S = \{1,2\}: &\quad \lambda_1 = \frac{4}{4-3} = 4, \quad \lambda_2 = \frac{3}{3-4} = -3 \\
S = \{2,3\}: &\quad \lambda_2 = \frac{6}{6-4} = 3, \quad \lambda_3 = \frac{4}{4-6} = -2 \\
S = \{1,3\}: &\quad \lambda_1 = \frac{6}{6-3} = 2, \quad \lambda_3 = \frac{3}{3-6} = -1
\end{aligned}$$

All coefficients are integers, verifying that $\mathcal{X}$ is $(2, 3)$-integer. Note that coordinate families are closed under negation: $\{-3, -4, -6\}$ is also $(2, 3)$-integer, and more generally under uniform scaling by any nonzero integer.

4 Integer Coordinate Threshold RSA Construction

This section presents the complete threshold RSA signature scheme based on integer coordinate families, establishing the core unforgeability result (Theorem 1). The construction assumes a trusted dealer model for key generation and share distribution. An optional robustness extension via DLEQ-based verification is presented separately in Appendix A.

Protocol Description. The scheme is compatible with standard RSA message encoding (PSS [15], PKCS#1, etc.) and requires only that encoded messages m satisfy $\gcd(m, N) = 1$, which holds with overwhelming probability for properly encoded messages.

The integer coordinate threshold RSA signature scheme consists of two primary algorithms presented below. Algorithm 1 describes the key generation and share distribution procedure executed by the trusted dealer, which generates RSA keys, creates Shamir secret shares using the integer coordinate family $\mathcal{X}$, and securely distributes shares to parties. Algorithm 2 specifies the distributed signing protocol, where a coalition of t parties collaboratively generates an RSA signature by computing partial signatures using their shares and the integer Lagrange coefficients, then combining these partial signatures to reconstruct the complete signature—all without any party requiring knowledge of $\phi(N)$.

Algorithm 1. $\mathsf{KeyGen}(1^\kappa, e, t, n, \mathcal{X})$ – Key Generation and Share Distribution

1: **Input:** Security parameter κ, public exponent e, threshold parameters (t, n), (t, n)-integer coordinate family $\mathcal{X} = \{x_1, \ldots, x_n\}$
2: **RSA Key Generation:**
3: Generate random κ-bit primes p, q
4: Compute $N \leftarrow p \cdot q$ and $\phi(N) \leftarrow (p-1)(q-1)$
5: Verify $\gcd(e, \phi(N)) = 1$; if not, regenerate primes
6: Compute $d \leftarrow e^{-1} \bmod \phi(N)$
7: **Secret Sharing:**
8: Sample $a_1, a_2, \ldots, a_{t-1} \xleftarrow{\$} \mathbb{Z}_{\phi(N)}$ uniformly at random
9: Define polynomial $f(X) \leftarrow d + \sum_{j=1}^{t-1} a_j X^j \in \mathbb{Z}_{\phi(N)}[X]$
10: For $i = 1, \ldots, n$: compute $y_i \leftarrow f(x_i) \bmod \phi(N)$
11: **Distribution:**
12: **for** $i = 1$ to n **do**
13: Securely transmit (x_i, y_i) to party P_i via authenticated private channel
14: **end for**
15: Publish public parameters $(N, e, \mathcal{X})$
16: **Secure Erasure:** Destroy $p, q, \phi(N), d, \{a_j\}_{j=1}^{t-1}$
17: **Output:** Public key $(N, e, \mathcal{X})$; private shares $\{(x_i, y_i)\}_{i=1}^{n}$ distributed to parties

Following the key generation and share distribution in Algorithm 1, the distributed signing protocol (Algorithm 2) enables any coalition S of t parties to collaboratively generate RSA signatures. The key feature of this protocol is that all Lagrange coefficients λ_i are computed as integers over $\mathbb{Z}$ (by virtue of the integer coordinate property of $\mathcal{X}$), eliminating the need for any party to know or compute with $\phi(N)$. Each party computes their partial signature through a single modular exponentiation, and the combiner reconstructs the complete signature by multiplying these partial signatures modulo N.

Key Observations. Algorithm 2 requires no knowledge of $\phi(N)$ for any party. All Lagrange coefficients λ_i are computed as integers over $\mathbb{Z}$ by Definition 4, and

Algorithm 2. ThresholdSign$(m, S, \{(x_i, y_i)\}_{i \in S}, N, e, \mathcal{X})$ – Distributed Signature Generation with Malicious Security

1: **Input:** Message representative $m \in \mathbb{Z}_N^*$, signing coalition $S \subseteq [n]$ with $|S| = t$, shares $\{(x_i, y_i)\}_{i \in S}$, public key $(N, e, \mathcal{X})$
2: **Partial Signature Generation (executed by each P_i for $i \in S$):**
3: Compute integer Lagrange coefficient:

$$\lambda_i \leftarrow \prod_{j \in S \setminus \{i\}} \frac{x_j}{x_j - x_i} \in \mathbb{Z}$$

4: Compute exponent: $w_i \leftarrow \lambda_i \cdot y_i \in \mathbb{Z}$
5: **if** $\lambda_i > 0$ **then**
6: $\sigma_i \leftarrow m^{w_i} \bmod N$
7: **else** ▷ Handle negative coefficient
8: Compute $m^{-1} \bmod N$ via extended Euclidean algorithm
9: $\sigma_i \leftarrow (m^{-1})^{-w_i} \bmod N$
10: **end if**
11: Broadcast σ_i to all parties in S
12:
13: **Signature Combination:**
14: Compute complete signature: $\sigma \leftarrow \prod_{i \in S'} \sigma_i \bmod N$
15: **Output:** RSA signature $\sigma \in \mathbb{Z}_N$

exponentiation is performed modulo N only. Negative coefficients (which may arise depending on coordinate ordering) are handled via modular inversion of the message, which is efficiently computable since $\gcd(m, N) = 1$ holds unless m contains a factor of N which is with negligible probability.

Handling Negative Coefficients. When $\lambda_i < 0$, the partial signature computation uses the identity $m^{\lambda_i \cdot y_i} \equiv (m^{-1})^{-\lambda_i \cdot y_i} \pmod N$ as shown in Algorithm 2. The modular inverse $m^{-1} \bmod N$ is efficiently computable via the extended Euclidean algorithm. For properly encoded messages (RSA-PSS [15], PKCS#1), $\gcd(m, N) = 1$ holds except with negligible probability $O(2^{-\kappa})$.

Signature Reconstruction Correctness. The complete signature is reconstructed as

$$\sigma \equiv \prod_{i \in S} \sigma_i \equiv \prod_{i \in S} m^{\lambda_i \cdot y_i} \equiv m^{\sum_{i \in S} \lambda_i \cdot y_i} \pmod N.$$

By Lagrange interpolation over $\mathbb{Z}_{\phi(N)}$, $\sum_{i \in S} \lambda_i \cdot y_i \equiv d \pmod{\phi(N)}$, ensuring $\sigma \equiv m^d \pmod N$ by Euler's theorem.

4.1 Integer Coordinate Construction: The Search Problem

Problem Formalization

Problem 1 (Problem 1 (Coordinate Construction)). Given threshold parameters (t, n) with $2 \leq t \leq n$, determine:

1. **(Existence)** Do there exist (t, n)-integer coordinate families?
2. **(Construction)** If so, provide an efficient algorithm that outputs such a family $\mathcal{X} = \{x_1, \ldots, x_n\} \subset \mathbb{Z}$.
3. **(Bounds)** Characterize the minimal achievable coordinate magnitudes: what is $\min_{\mathcal{X}} \max_{i\in[n]} |x_i|$ over all (t, n)-integer families?

Divisibility Characterization. A family $\mathcal{X} = \{x_1, \ldots, x_n\}$ is (t, n)-integer if and only if for all $S \subseteq [n]$ with $|S| = t$ and all $i \in S$,

$$\prod_{j\in S\setminus\{i\}} (x_j - x_i) \,\Big|\, \prod_{j\in S\setminus\{i\}} x_j, \tag{1}$$

where $a \mid b$ denotes "a divides b". This formulation as a divisibility constraint is algorithmically convenient for verification but provides limited insight into constructive existence.

Computational Search Methodology. At present, no efficient general algorithm for Problem 1 is known. The coordinate families presented in this work (Table 2) were obtained via heuristic computational search employing the following strategies:

Hierarchical Construction.

1. **Base Case ($t = 2$):** A pair $\{a, b\}$ is $(2, 2)$-integer if and only if $(b - a) \mid a$ and $(a - b) \mid b$, equivalently $\frac{b}{b-a}, \frac{a}{a-b} \in \mathbb{Z}$. Enumerate small pairs satisfying this condition.
2. **Incremental Extension:** Extend the solution sets by ensuring every pair within a candidate set satisfies the $(t+1, n)$-integer condition. For example, if $\{a, b\}$, $\{b, c\}$, and $\{a, c\}$ are each valid $(2, 2)$-integer pairs, then $\{a, b, c\}$ forms a valid $(2, 3)$-integer set because every 2-subset among $\{a, b, c\}$ satisfies the integrality condition.
3. **Direct Search for $t \geq 3$:** For higher thresholds, direct enumeration begins with (t, t)-integer seeds (complete t-element families) and extends incrementally. This avoids dependence on $(2, n)$ families, as lifting (see below) from $t = 2$ to $t \geq 3$ does not hold universally.

Lifting Phenomenon. Empirically, certain (t, n)-integer families satisfy the (t', n)-integer property for $t' > t$. For instance, the $(2, 9)$-integer family presented in Table 2 is verified to be $(t, 9)$-integer for all $t \in \{2, \ldots, 9\}$. This phenomenon suggests structural properties warranting theoretical investigation, but no general characterization of liftable families is currently known.

Multiplicative Scaling and Smoothness. Coordinates with highly composite (smooth) structures exhibit higher success rates in satisfying divisibility constraints (1). The $(2, 9)$-integer family was constructed by scaling a $(2, 8)$-integer family's largest coordinate by

$$D = 2^{10} \cdot 3^5 \cdot 5^5 \cdot 7 \cdot 11^4 \cdot 13 \cdot 17 \cdot 19 \cdot 29 \cdot 31 \cdot 37 \cdot 41 \cdot 43,$$

yielding the base coordinate $552720 \cdot D = 1084650485486773823256038400000\mathrm{0}$ in Table 2. This multiplicative augmentation technique—incorporating abundant prime factors to facilitate divisibility—proved effective but lacks theoretical justification or optimality guarantees. The specific exponents (e.g., 2^{10} rather than 2^{20}) were determined empirically through heuristic search and do not possess any special theoretical significance. We observe that successful coordinate families typically incorporate many small prime factors, though the precise values employed here represent heuristic choices rather than theoretically optimal parameters. Following initial discovery, a reduction step is applied to eliminate common factors among the coordinates.

Complexity Analysis and Current Limitations. The computational cost of searching for (t, n)-integer families with coordinates bounded by B exhibits the following time complexity:

Exhaustive search over candidate coordinate families scales as $O(B^n)$, where each candidate requires verification of $\binom{n}{t}$ divisibility constraints (1). Each constraint verification involves computing products of up to t terms, requiring $O(t^2 \ln B)$ arithmetic operations. This yields an overall complexity of

$$O\left(B^n \cdot \binom{n}{t} \cdot t^2 \ln B\right).$$

This exponential scaling in the coordinate bound renders brute-force search infeasible for large B or large n. The coordinate families in Table 2 were obtained through heuristic search strategies that exploit divisibility structure and smooth number properties, as described in the preceding subsection.

Existence and Computational Status. The current state of Problem 1 is:

- **Established Results:** Universal (t, n)-integer families for all (t, n) with $2 \leq t \leq n \leq 9$, plus selected high-threshold configurations for $n = 10$ (Table 2).
- **Computational Barrier:** Current heuristic methods are effective for $n \leq 9$ but do not scale to $n \gtrsim 12$ without theoretical breakthroughs. Coordinate magnitude growth (Table 2) suggests potential inherent complexity.

Table 2 summarizes established coordinate families, providing universal coverage for $n \leq 9$ and exemplary high-threshold configurations for $n = 10$.

5 Security Analysis

This section establishes the EUF-CMA security (existential unforgeability under chosen-message attacks) of the integer coordinate threshold RSA scheme under the standard RSA assumption. The analysis considers a static, malicious (active) adversary corrupting up to $t-1$ parties. We prove that the adversary cannot forge signatures, even with full control over corrupted parties' behavior. Note that the proof establishes unforgeability but not robustness: malicious parties may cause signing operations to fail (denial-of-service). Robustness can be achieved through optional verification mechanisms such as the DLEQ-based extension presented in Appendix A.

Table 2. Discovered coordinate sets for various threshold configurations

$(t, 9)$ with $2 \leq t \leq 9$	108465048548677382325603840000000, 108465048548677382325603837732 00, 108465048548677382325603835688 00, 108465048548677382325603835662 45, 108465048548677382325603835524 48, 108465048548677382325603835432 50, 108465048548677382325603835366 80, 108465048548677382325603835104 00, 108465048548677382325603834972 60
$(t, 8)$ with $2 \leq t \leq 8$	552720, 552825, 552960, 553000, 553014, 553140, 553280, 554400
$(6, 8)$	210, 215, 216, 217, 220, 222, 224, 225
$(7, 9)$	210, 216, 219, 220, 224, 225, 231, 234, 240
$(8, 10)$	210, 216, 220, 224, 225, 228, 230, 231, 234, 240
$(9, 10)$	39, 40, 42, 45, 46, 48, 49, 52, 54, 55
$(10, 10)$	1, 2, 3, 4, 5, 6, 7, 8, 9, 10

5.1 Security Model

Definition 5 (Security Model Parameters). *The threshold signature scheme operates under the following trust and adversary model:*

- ***Setup:*** *A trusted dealer executes* KeyGen *and distributes shares via authenticated private channels. After distribution, the dealer is assumed to securely erase all secret material.*
- ***Adversary Type:*** *Static, malicious (active) adversary* $\mathcal{A}$.
  - Static corruption: $\mathcal{A}$ *selects the corruption set* $\mathcal{C} \subseteq [n]$ *with* $|\mathcal{C}| \leq t-1$ *before protocol execution begins*
  - Malicious behavior: *Corrupted parties may deviate arbitrarily from the protocol specification, including:*
    - *Submitting invalid or incorrectly computed partial signatures*
    - *Refusing to participate in signing rounds*
    - *Attempting to learn information about honest parties' shares through malformed messages*
    - *Coordinating arbitrary attacks across corrupted parties*

- ***Communication Model:*** *After initial share distribution, all signing operations occur over public authenticated channels. Adversary $\mathcal{A}$ observes all protocol messages and controls corrupted parties' behavior.*
- ***Security Goal:*** Existential unforgeability under chosen-message attacks (EUF-CMA) *[12]: $\mathcal{A}$ cannot produce a valid signature on a message not previously signed, even with adaptive access to the signing oracle and control over up to $t-1$ corrupted parties. Note that malicious parties may cause signing operations to fail by submitting invalid partial signatures (denial-of-service), but this does not enable forgery.*

5.2 EUF-CMA Security Game

Definition 6 (EUF-CMA Game for Threshold Signatures). *For security parameter κ, threshold parameters (t, n), and adversary $\mathcal{A}$, the EUF-CMA game $\mathsf{Game}_{\mathcal{A}}^{\mathsf{EUF-CMA}}(\kappa, t, n)$ proceeds as follows:*

1. ***Setup:*** *The challenger runs $(N, e, d) \leftarrow \mathsf{KeyGen}(1^\kappa, e)$ and $(y_1, \ldots, y_n) \leftarrow \mathsf{Share}(d, \phi(N), t, n, \mathcal{X})$ for a (t, n)-integer family $\mathcal{X}$. The public key $(N, e, \mathcal{X})$ is given to $\mathcal{A}$.*
2. ***Static Corruption:*** *Adversary $\mathcal{A}$ selects corruption set $\mathcal{C} \subseteq [n]$ with $|\mathcal{C}| \leq t-1$. The challenger provides $\{(x_i, y_i)\}_{i \in \mathcal{C}}$ to $\mathcal{A}$.*
3. ***Signing Queries:*** *Adversary $\mathcal{A}$ makes adaptive signature queries. For query $m_j \in \mathbb{Z}_N^*$:*
   - *The challenger selects signing coalition $S_j \subseteq [n]$ with $|S_j| = t$*
   - *For each $i \in S_j$, the challenger computes partial signature $\sigma_{i,j} \leftarrow \mathsf{PartialSign}(i, y_i, m_j, S_j, \mathcal{X})$*
   - *The challenger provides $\{\sigma_{i,j}\}_{i \in S_j}$ to $\mathcal{A}$ and computes $\sigma_j \leftarrow \mathsf{Combine}(\{\sigma_{i,j}\}_{i \in S_j}, m_j, N)$*

   Let $\mathcal{Q} = \{m_1, m_2, \ldots, m_q\}$ denote the set of queried messages.
4. ***Forgery:*** *Adversary $\mathcal{A}$ outputs (m^*, σ^*).*

Adversary $\mathcal{A}$ wins *the game if:*

- $(\sigma^*)^e \equiv m^* \pmod{N}$ *(validity)*
- $m^* \notin \mathcal{Q}$ *(non-trivial forgery)*

The advantage of $\mathcal{A}$ is defined as

$$\mathsf{Adv}_{\mathcal{A}}^{\mathsf{EUF-CMA}}(\kappa, t, n) := \Pr[\mathcal{A} \text{ wins } \mathsf{Game}_{\mathcal{A}}^{\mathsf{EUF-CMA}}(\kappa, t, n)].$$

The threshold signature scheme is EUF-CMA secure *if for all probabilistic polynomial-time (PPT) adversaries $\mathcal{A}$, $\mathsf{Adv}_{\mathcal{A}}^{\mathsf{EUF-CMA}}(\kappa, t, n) = \mathsf{negl}(\kappa)$.*

5.3 Main Security Theorem

Theorem 1 (EUF-CMA Security Against Malicious Adversaries). *Let $\mathcal{X}$ be a (t, n)-integer coordinate family. Under the RSA assumption, the threshold signature scheme (Algorithms 1, 2) is EUF-CMA secure (Definition 6) against static, malicious adversaries corrupting up to $t - 1$ parties.*

More precisely, for any PPT adversary $\mathcal{A}$ attacking the threshold signature scheme with arbitrary malicious behavior, there exists a PPT algorithm $\mathcal{B}$ solving the RSA problem such that

$$\mathsf{Adv}_{\mathcal{A}}^{\mathsf{EUF-CMA}}(\kappa, t, n) \leq \mathsf{Adv}_{\mathcal{B}}^{\mathsf{RSA}}(\kappa) + \mathsf{negl}(\kappa),$$

where the running time of $\mathcal{B}$ is polynomial in that of $\mathcal{A}$ and κ.

Scope of Security Result. This theorem establishes unforgeability: adversaries cannot produce valid signatures on messages they haven't queried, even with control over $t-1$ parties. The result requires only the standard RSA assumption with no additional cryptographic primitives.

Proof High-Level Strategy. The simulator $\mathcal{S}$ receives an RSA challenge (N, e, y) where $y = x^e \bmod N$ for unknown $x \in \mathbb{Z}_N^*$, and must compute x. Simulator $\mathcal{S}$ simulates the threshold signature game for $\mathcal{A}$ by:

1. Programming the public key to embed the challenge
2. Simulating corrupted party shares as random field elements
3. Answering signing queries using the RSA signing oracle, while handling malicious partial signatures from corrupted parties
4. Extracting an RSA solution from $\mathcal{A}$'s forgery

Let $\mathcal{C} \subseteq [n]$ denote the corruption set selected by $\mathcal{A}$ with $|\mathcal{C}| \leq t - 1$, and let $\mathcal{H} = [n] \setminus \mathcal{C}$ denote honest parties with $|\mathcal{H}| \geq n - t + 1 \geq 1$.

Simulation Construction. **1. Setup Phase:** Simulator $\mathcal{S}$ receives RSA challenge (N, e, y).

- Publish public key $(N, e, \mathcal{X})$ to $\mathcal{A}$
- Adversary $\mathcal{A}$ selects corruption set $\mathcal{C}$
- For each $i \in \mathcal{C}$: sample $y_i \xleftarrow{\$} \mathbb{Z}_{\phi(N)}$ uniformly at random and provide (x_i, y_i) to $\mathcal{A}$

Note that $\mathcal{S}$ does not know the actual private exponent d or honest parties' shares.

2. Signing Query Simulation: For signing query m_j from $\mathcal{A}$:

- The challenger selects signing coalition $S_j \subseteq [n]$ with $|S_j| = t$
- Obtain reference signature: query RSA signing oracle on m_j to receive $\sigma_j = m_j^d \bmod N$

- **Handle Malicious Partial Signatures:** The adversary $\mathcal{A}$ controls corrupted parties and may cause them to submit arbitrary values as partial signatures
- Simulate honest partial signatures:
  - Expected corrupted contribution (if honest): $\sigma_{\mathcal{C}}^{\text{honest}} \leftarrow \prod_{i \in S_j \cap \mathcal{C}} m_j^{\lambda_i \cdot y_i} \bmod N$ using simulated shares
  - Actual corrupted contribution: $\sigma_{\mathcal{C}}^{\text{actual}} \leftarrow$ the product of actual partial signatures submitted by corrupted parties (potentially malicious)
  - Compute required honest contribution: $\sigma_{\mathcal{H}} \leftarrow \sigma_j \cdot (\sigma_{\mathcal{C}}^{\text{honest}})^{-1} \bmod N$
  - Distribute $\sigma_{\mathcal{H}}$ among honest parties in $S_j \cap \mathcal{H}$:
    * If $|S_j \cap \mathcal{H}| = 1$: set $\sigma_{i,j} \leftarrow \sigma_{\mathcal{H}}$ for the unique $i \in S_j \cap \mathcal{H}$
    * If $|S_j \cap \mathcal{H}| \geq 2$: fix $k \in S_j \cap \mathcal{H}$, sample $\sigma_{i,j} \xleftarrow{\$} \mathbb{Z}_N^*$ for $i \in (S_j \cap \mathcal{H}) \setminus \{k\}$, set $\sigma_{k,j} \leftarrow \sigma_{\mathcal{H}} \cdot \left(\prod_{i \in (S_j \cap \mathcal{H}) \setminus \{k\}} \sigma_{i,j}\right)^{-1} \bmod N$
- Provide honest partial signatures $\{\sigma_{i,j}\}_{i \in S_j \cap \mathcal{H}}$ to $\mathcal{A}$; adversary controls corrupted parties' outputs

Indistinguishability Analysis. The simulated view must be indistinguishable from the real protocol execution. Consider:

- **Corrupted Shares Distribution:** In the real protocol, shares $\{y_i\}_{i \in \mathcal{C}}$ are evaluations $y_i = f(x_i) \bmod \phi(N)$ of a random degree-$(t-1)$ polynomial f with $f(0) = d$. By Shamir secret sharing properties, these $|\mathcal{C}| \leq t-1$ evaluations are uniformly distributed in $\mathbb{Z}_{\phi(N)}^{|\mathcal{C}|}$ independent of d. The simulated shares (uniformly random in $\mathbb{Z}_{\phi(N)}$) match this distribution exactly.
- **Partial Signatures Distribution:** For signing coalition S_j:
  - **Corrupted partial signatures:** In both real and simulated executions, malicious parties controlled by $\mathcal{A}$ can output arbitrary values. The simulation allows $\mathcal{A}$ full control over corrupted parties' outputs, matching the real execution.
  - **Honest partial signatures:** In the real protocol, these satisfy $\prod_{i \in S_j \cap \mathcal{H}} \sigma_{i,j} = \sigma_{\mathcal{H}} \pmod N$ where $\sigma_{\mathcal{H}}$ is the honest parties' contribution to the complete signature $\sigma_j = m_j^d$. The simulation enforces this same constraint.
  - When $|S_j \cap \mathcal{H}| \geq 2$, individual honest partial signatures are randomized subject only to the product constraint. This matches the information-theoretic view of $\mathcal{A}$: since $\mathcal{A}$ controls fewer than t parties, it cannot learn individual shares of honest parties, only their combined contribution.

Formal Claim: The simulated view is statistically indistinguishable from the real protocol view: for any distinguisher $\mathcal{D}$,

$$|\Pr[\mathcal{D}(\text{RealView}) = 1] - \Pr[\mathcal{D}(\text{SimView}) = 1]| = \mathsf{negl}(\kappa).$$

Forgery Extraction. Suppose $\mathcal{A}$ outputs forgery (m^*, σ^*) with $m^* \notin \mathcal{Q}$ and $(\sigma^*)^e \equiv m^* \pmod{N}$. Then $\sigma^* \equiv (m^*)^d \pmod{N}$ is a valid RSA signature on a message not queried to the oracle. The simulator outputs σ^* as the solution to the RSA problem, successfully breaking the RSA assumption.

Probability Analysis. If $\mathcal{A}$ succeeds with probability ϵ in the EUF-CMA game, and the simulation is statistically indistinguishable (deviation $\mathsf{negl}(\kappa)$), then $\mathcal{S}$ succeeds in solving the RSA problem with probability $\epsilon - \mathsf{negl}(\kappa)$. By contrapositive, if RSA is secure (no PPT adversary succeeds with non-negligible probability), then ϵ must be negligible.

This completes the reduction, establishing EUF-CMA security:

$$\mathsf{Adv}_{\mathcal{A}}^{\mathsf{EUF-CMA}}(\kappa, t, n) \leq \mathsf{Adv}_{\mathcal{B}}^{\mathsf{RSA}}(\kappa) + \mathsf{negl}(\kappa).$$

6 Implementation and Evaluation

This section validates two key practical claims: (1) that large coordinate values do not create computational bottlenecks, and (2) that the algorithm's simplicity enables deployment on resource-constrained hardware security modules.

6.1 Performance Evaluation and Comparison

We validate that large coordinate values do not create performance bottlenecks through a Python prototype implementation using `gmpy2` [1] on an Apple M1 Max processor with 3072-bit RSA and $e = 3$. Table 3 compares standard RSA against threshold configurations $(3, 5)$, $(5, 9)$, and $(9, 9)$ over 100 iterations using coordinate set $(2, 9)$.

Table 3. Performance comparison: Standard RSA vs. Threshold RSA with integer coordinates (3072-bit modulus, $e = 3$, 100 iterations, Apple M1 Max)

Configuration	Avg. Total Time	Per-Party Time	Per-Party Overhead
Standard RSA	6.18 ms	6.18 ms	N/A
Threshold (3-of-5)	19.56 ms	6.50 ms	5%
Threshold (5-of-9)	33.86 ms	6.75 ms	9%
Threshold (9-of-9)	66.96 ms	7.45 ms	20%

Key Finding. The time for combining the partial signatures is negligible compared to the per-party signing time. Per-party signing time remains 6.5–7.5 ms across all configurations, representing 5–20% overhead compared to standard RSA (6.2 ms). This overhead is acceptable and not a deployment blocker—each party performs a single modular exponentiation followed by integer arithmetic for Lagrange coefficients. Even for $(9, 9)$ configurations using 32-digit coordinate values (Table 2), coefficient computation remains dominated by the core exponentiation operation. Total signing time scales linearly with threshold t due to sequential execution in the test harness; in parallel deployments where parties compute simultaneously, effective latency is $\approx$ 6.5–7.5 ms.

6.2 Validation: Implementability on Resource-Constrained Hardware

The critical validation is demonstrating that the integer coordinate framework *can be implemented* on severely resource-constrained hardware. Many existing threshold RSA schemes—polynomial arithmetic frameworks [10], interactive multi-round protocols [2], zero-knowledge proof systems—are impractical for HSMs, secure enclaves, and hardware wallets. If the framework cannot execute within such constraints, it cannot serve its intended purpose of enabling threshold RSA for Intel SGX code signing.

Ledger Implementation. The threshold signing infrastructure is implemented on Ledger Stax devices to generate valid RSA–$e = 3$ signatures for SGX enclave code signing. Each Ledger holds one secret share and runs Algorithm 2 (lines 2–7) within its secure element to produce a partial signature with exponent $e = 3$. These partial signatures are combined off-device into a single RSA signature that satisfies SGX's hard-coded $e = 3$ check. Ledger hardware wallets represent an extreme environment: approximately 4KB RAM, no floating-point unit, limited flash storage, and restricted C development. The implementation uses hierarchical key management where each device derives an RSA key pair from its hardware-backed seed (via BIP-39/BIP-32) as a key-wrapping key (KWK) for protecting the threshold share y_i. The signing protocol executes entirely within the secure element: decrypt share y_i using the KWK, retrieve pre-computed Lagrange coefficient λ_i (using the $(2, 8)$-integer coordinate set with all values fitting in 32-bit integers), and generate partial signature $\sigma_i = m^{\lambda_i \cdot y_i} \bmod N$ through modular exponentiation. The entire signing logic occupies approximately 1,000 lines of C code using the Ledger SDK's `cx_math` library, demonstrating that the framework is *fundamentally compatible* with commodity secure hardware constraints—making it viable for Intel SGX enclaves, HSMs, and similar environments requiring threshold RSA with $e = 3$. End-to-end latency (host-to-Ledger communication plus on-device signing) is approximately 1.3 s per device, which is acceptable for hardware wallet deployments where user approval is required before each signature operation.

7 Conclusion

This work establishes the integer coordinate framework for threshold RSA signatures, addressing the fundamental tension between Shamir secret sharing reconstruction (which requires Lagrange coefficient computation modulo $\phi(N)$) and

RSA security (which requires $\phi(N)$ to remain secret). The approach is based on the mathematical observation that appropriately selected interpolation coordinates yield integer-valued Lagrange coefficients, eliminating all modular arithmetic modulo $\phi(N)$ from the online signing protocol.

7.1 Fundamental Open Problem

The central limitation is the absence of efficient constructive algorithms for Problem 1. All coordinate families presented result from heuristic computational search. The following questions remain open:

1. **Universal Existence:** Do (t, n)-integer families exist for all (t, n)? If not, characterize parameter regimes admitting solutions.
2. **Constructive Algorithms:** Develop polynomial-time algorithms (in n, t, and output size) for coordinate generation, or establish complexity-theoretic barriers.
3. **Size Bounds:** Characterize the asymptotic growth of $\min_{\mathcal{X}} \max_i |x_i|$ as a function of (t, n). Current empirical data (Table 2) shows exponential growth from $n = 8$ to $n = 9$; determine whether this is fundamental or an artifact of search heuristics.
4. **Algebraic Structure:** Connect integer coordinate families to established mathematical frameworks (combinatorial designs, lattice theory, Diophantine equations) to enable theoretical characterization.

Resolution of these questions will determine whether the integer coordinate framework scales to large n (with efficiently computable small coordinates) or is inherently limited to small-to-moderate group sizes.

7.2 Concluding Remarks

The integer coordinate framework provides the most efficient known approach to threshold RSA with $e = 3$ support and proven unforgeability for small-to-moderate group sizes. Among existing $e = 3$-compatible schemes, the integer coordinate method uniquely achieves the combination of: (1) EUF-CMA security (unforgeability) against malicious adversaries under the standard RSA assumption alone (Theorem 1), (2) standard $O(\kappa)$-bit share sizes, and (3) perfect secrecy preservation of Shamir secret sharing. For deployments requiring robustness against denial-of-service, an optional DLEQ-based verification extension (Appendix A) provides practical security with approximately $2\times$ overhead, though formal analysis under adaptive adversaries remains future work.

The integer coordinate framework demonstrates that fundamental cryptographic challenges—here, the tension between secret sharing reconstruction and RSA security—can be resolved through careful mathematical structure rather than additional cryptographic assumptions. By eliminating modular arithmetic modulo $\phi(N)$ via integer-valued Lagrange coefficients, the approach achieves proven unforgeability, perfect secrecy, and practical efficiency simultaneously.

The successful Ledger deployment validates that this theoretical elegance translates to real-world feasibility in severely constrained environments.

For the practically important regime of small-to-moderate group sizes ($n \leq 9$), the integer coordinate framework provides immediate, deployment-ready threshold RSA with $e = 3$ support—addressing a long-standing limitation in cryptographic infrastructure ranging from Intel SGX enclaves to hardware security modules. Resolution of the coordinate construction problem (Sect. 7.2) represents the path to broader applicability, though current results already serve a significant deployment space. The clean separation between unforgeability (proven) and robustness (practical extension) reflects mature cryptographic engineering: providing strong theoretical foundations while acknowledging practical requirements and open problems honestly.

A Optional DLEQ-Based Robustness Extension

This appendix presents an optional extension to the threshold RSA scheme that provides robustness against denial-of-service attacks through verification of partial signatures. The extension employs Discrete Logarithm Equivalence (DLEQ) proofs to enable parties to detect and identify malicious behavior during signature generation.

Optional DLEQ-Based Robustness Extension. For practical deployments requiring robustness against denial-of-service, we develop non-interactive partial signature verification using DLEQ proofs with computational overhead of approximately $2\times$ compared to the base scheme—substantially lower than traditional robust threshold schemes. This extension is presented as an optional enhancement; the core unforgeability result (Theorem 1) stands independently.

Relationship to Main Result. The core contribution of this work is the unforgeability result (Theorem 1) for the base integer coordinate scheme, which requires no additional cryptographic assumptions beyond RSA. The DLEQ-based verification mechanism presented in this appendix is an *optional enhancement* for deployments requiring robustness properties. While this extension has been successfully deployed in practice (Sect. 6) and follows standard DLEQ proof techniques, formal security analysis under adaptive malicious adversaries requires careful treatment of witness dependencies. The simulation challenge arises because witness values $w_i = m_0^{y_i}$ commit to shares before the adversary's strategy is known, creating extraction problems in security proofs. We present the mechanism with an honest assessment of its practical value and theoretical limitations.

Protocol Approach. The verification mechanism employs witness-based Non-Interactive Discrete Logarithm Equivalence (DLEQ) proofs [3,9], which allow each party to prove that their partial signature was correctly computed from their share without revealing the share itself.

A.1 Protocol Specification

This section provides the complete algorithmic specification of the DLEQ-based verification protocol, including witness generation, proof construction, verification algorithms, and the modified signing protocol.

Protocol Overview. The witness-based DLEQ approach enables verification of partial signatures by proving that the same secret share was used in both a public witness value and the partial signature for a given message. The protocol consists of three phases:

1. **Witness Generation:** Each party publishes a commitment to their share
2. **Proof Generation:** During signing, each party generates a DLEQ proof alongside their partial signature
3. **Verification:** Any party can verify the proof to ensure correctness of the partial signature

A.2 Witness Generation Protocol

After the trusted dealer distributes shares in Algorithm 1, each party generates a witness value.

Algorithm 3. $\mathsf{WitnessGen}(i, y_i, m_0, N)$ – Witness Value Generation

---

1: **Input:** Party index i, share $y_i \in \mathbb{Z}_{\phi(N)}$, witness message $m_0 \in \mathbb{Z}_N^*$, modulus N
2: **Witness Message Selection:** If not already specified, set $m_0 \leftarrow H(\text{"threshold-rsa-witness"} \| N)$ where H is a cryptographic hash function mapping to $\mathbb{Z}_N^*$
3: **Witness Computation:** Compute $w_i \leftarrow m_0^{y_i} \bmod N$
4: **Publication:** Broadcast w_i to all parties via authenticated channel
5: **Output:** Witness value $w_i \in \mathbb{Z}_N$

Security Note. The witness value $w_i = m_0^{y_i} \bmod N$ does not reveal the share y_i under the RSA assumption (computing discrete logarithms modulo N without knowing the factorization is equivalent to breaking RSA). However, it serves as a public commitment that can be used to verify future partial signatures.

A.3 DLEQ Proof Construction

The DLEQ proof, Algorithm 4, demonstrates that $\log_{m_0}(w_i^{\lambda_i}) = \log_m(\sigma_i)$, i.e., that both values have the same discrete logarithm (namely, $\lambda_i \cdot y_i$) with respect to different bases.

Algorithm 4. DLEQProve$(y_i, \lambda_i, m_0, w_i, m, \sigma_i, N)$ – DLEQ Proof Generation

1: **Input:** Share y_i, Lagrange coefficient λ_i, witness message m_0, witness w_i, message m, partial signature σ_i, modulus N
2: **Common Parameters:** Bases $(g_1, h_1) = (m_0, w_i^{\lambda_i})$ and $(g_2, h_2) = (m, \sigma_i)$
3: **Shared Secret:** $s = \lambda_i \cdot y_i$ (such that $h_1 \equiv g_1^s \pmod{N}$ and $h_2 \equiv g_2^s \pmod{N}$)
4:
5: **Commitment Phase:**
6: Sample random $r \xleftarrow{\$} \mathbb{Z}_{\phi(N)}$
7: Compute commitments:
8: $a_1 \leftarrow m_0^r \bmod N$
9: $a_2 \leftarrow m^r \bmod N$
10:
11: **Challenge Phase (Fiat-Shamir):**
12: Compute challenge: $c \leftarrow H(m_0 \| w_i^{\lambda_i} \| m \| \sigma_i \| a_1 \| a_2 \| N)$
13: where H is a cryptographic hash function mapping to $\mathbb{Z}_{2^\kappa}$ (for security parameter κ)
14:
15: **Response Phase:**
16: Compute response: $z \leftarrow r + c \cdot s$ (computed over $\mathbb{Z}$, no modular reduction)
17:
18: **Output:** Proof $\pi = (c, z)$

Non-interactive Conversion. The Fiat-Shamir heuristic [9] converts the interactive Chaum-Pedersen protocol into a non-interactive proof by deriving the challenge c from a hash of the protocol transcript. This eliminates interaction at the cost of requiring the random oracle model.

A.4 DLEQ Proof Verification

Refer to Algorithm 5 for the DLEQ proof verification algorithm.

A.5 Modified Signing Protocol with DLEQ

The threshold signing protocol Algorithm 2 is modified to Algorithm 6 to include DLEQ proof generation and verification:

Algorithm 5. $\mathsf{DLEQVerify}(\pi, m_0, w_i, \lambda_i, m, \sigma_i, N)$ – DLEQ Proof Verification

1: **Input:** Proof $\pi = (c, z)$, witness message m_0, witness w_i, Lagrange coefficient λ_i, message m, partial signature σ_i, modulus N
2: **Common Parameters:** Bases $(g_1, h_1) = (m_0, w_i^{\lambda_i})$ and $(g_2, h_2) = (m, \sigma_i)$
3:
4: **Recompute Commitments:**
5: $a_1' \leftarrow m_0^z \cdot (w_i^{\lambda_i})^{-c} \bmod N$
6: $a_2' \leftarrow m^z \cdot \sigma_i^{-c} \bmod N$
7:
8: **Recompute Challenge:**
9: $c' \leftarrow H(m_0 \| w_i^{\lambda_i} \| m \| \sigma_i \| a_1' \| a_2' \| N)$
10:
11: **Verification Check:**
12: **if** $c' = c$ **then**
13: **Output:** 1 (accept)
14: **else**
15: **Output:** 0 (reject)
16: **end if**

Algorithm 6. $\mathsf{ThresholdSignDLEQ}(m, S, \{(x_i, y_i, w_i)\}_{i \in S}, N, e, \mathcal{X}, m_0)$ – Signing with DLEQ Verification

1: **Input:** Message m, coalition S with $|S| = t$, shares and witnesses $\{(x_i, y_i, w_i)\}_{i \in S}$, public key $(N, e, \mathcal{X})$, witness message m_0
2:
3: **Partial Signature Generation (each party P_i for $i \in S$):**
4: Compute $\lambda_i \leftarrow \prod_{j \in S \setminus \{i\}} \frac{x_j}{x_j - x_i}$
5: Compute $\sigma_i \leftarrow m^{\lambda_i \cdot y_i} \bmod N$ (handling negative λ_i as in Algorithm 2)
6: Generate DLEQ proof: $\pi_i \leftarrow \mathsf{DLEQProve}(y_i, \lambda_i, m_0, w_i, m, \sigma_i, N)$
7: Broadcast (σ_i, π_i)
8:
9: **Verification and Combination (combiner or any party):**
10: Initialize valid set $S' \leftarrow \emptyset$
11: **for** each $i \in S$ **do**
12: Compute $\lambda_i \leftarrow \prod_{j \in S \setminus \{i\}} \frac{x_j}{x_j - x_i}$
13: **if** $\mathsf{DLEQVerify}(\pi_i, m_0, w_i, \lambda_i, m, \sigma_i, N) = 1$ **then**
14: $S' \leftarrow S' \cup \{i\}$
15: **else**
16: Report: "Party i provided invalid DLEQ proof"
17: **end if**
18: **end for**
19: **if** $|S'| < t$ **then**
20: **abort** with "Insufficient valid partial signatures"
21: **end if**
22: Compute complete signature: $\sigma \leftarrow \prod_{i \in S'} \sigma_i \bmod N$
23: **Output:** σ

References

1. Gmpy2: Multiple-precision arithmetic for python. Python Package Index (2021)
2. Catalano, D., Gennaro, R., Halevi, S.: Computing inverses over a shared secret modulus. In: Preneel, B. (ed.) EUROCRYPT 2000. LNCS, vol. 1807, pp. 190–206. Springer, Heidelberg (2000). https://doi.org/10.1007/3-540-45539-6_14
3. Chaum, D., Pedersen, T.P.: Wallet databases with observers. In: Brickell, E.F. (ed.) Advances in Cryptology — CRYPTO 1992, pp. 89–105. Springer, Heidelberg (1993)
4. Intel Corporation. Intel software guard extensions programming reference. Intel Developer Documentation (2016)
5. Cramer, R., Damgrd, I.B., Nielsen, J.B.: Secure Multiparty Computation and Secret Sharing, 1st edn. Cambridge University Press, USA (2015)
6. Damgård, I., Dupont, K.: Efficient threshold RSA signatures with general moduli and no extra assumptions. In: Vaudenay, S. (ed.) PKC 2005. LNCS, vol. 3386, pp. 346–361. Springer, Heidelberg (2005). https://doi.org/10.1007/978-3-540-30580-4_24
7. Damgård, I.B., Koprowski, M.: Practical threshold RSA signatures without a trusted dealer. BRICS Rep. Ser. **7**(30) (2000)
8. Desmedt, Y., Frankel, Y.: Threshold cryptosystems. In: Advances in Cryptology—CRYPTO'89 Proceedings, pp. 307–315. Springer (1989)
9. Fiat, A., Shamir, A.: How to prove yourself: Practical solutions to identification and signature problems. In: Conference on the Theory and Application of Cryptographic Techniques, pp. 186–194. Springer (1986)
10. Frankel, Y., Desmedt, Y.: Parallel reliable threshold multisignature. Department of Electrical Engineering and Computer Science, University of Wisconsin-Milwaukee, Technical Report TR-92-04-02 (1992)
11. Gennaro, R., Jarecki, S., Krawczyk, H., Rabin, T.: Robust threshold DSS signatures. In: International Conference on the Theory and Applications of Cryptographic Techniques, pp. 354–371. Springer (1996)
12. Goldwasser, S., Micali, S., Rivest, R.L.: A digital signature scheme secure against adaptive chosen-message attacks. SIAM J. Comput. **17**(2), 281–308 (1988)
13. Herzberg, A., Jarecki, S., Krawczyk, H., Yung, M.: Proactive secret sharing or: how to cope with perpetual leakage, pp. 339–352 (1995)
14. Joye, M., Michalevsky, Y.: RSA signatures under hardware restrictions. In: Proceedings of the 2018 Workshop on Attacks and Solutions in Hardware Security, ASHES 2018, pp. 51–54. Association for Computing Machinery, New York, NY, USA (2018)
15. Moriarty, K., Kaliski, B., Jonsson, J., Rusch, A.: PKCS #1: RSA cryptography specifications version 2.2. RFC 8017 (2016)
16. Pedersen, T.P.: Non-interactive and information-theoretic secure verifiable secret sharing. In: Annual International Cryptology Conference, pp. 129–140. Springer (1991)
17. Rivest, R.L., Shamir, A., Adleman, L.: A method for obtaining digital signatures and public-key cryptosystems. Commun. ACM **21**(2), 120–126 (1978)
18. Rivest, R., Silverman, R.: Are 'strong' primes needed for RSA. Cryptology ePrint Archive, Paper 2001/007 (2001)
19. Shamir, A.: How to share a secret. Commun. ACM **22**(11), 612–613 (1979)

20. Shoup, V.: Practical threshold signatures. In: Preneel, B. (ed.) EUROCRYPT 2000. LNCS, vol. 1807, pp. 207–220. Springer, Heidelberg (2000). https://doi.org/10.1007/3-540-45539-6_15
21. Washington, L.C.: Introduction to Cyclotomic Fields, vol. 83. Springer (1997)
22. Qiu-Liang, X., Chen, T.-S.: An efficient threshold RSA digital signature scheme. Appl. Math. Comput. **166**(1), 25–34 (2005)

Hash and Zero-Knowledge

Improved Collision Attacks on 4-Round SHA3-384

Longzheng Cui[1,2,3], Kai Hu[1,2,3,4], Jiamin Cui[1,2,3(✉)], and Meiqin Wang[1,2,3]

[1] School of Cyber Science and Technology, Shandong University, Qingdao 266237, Shandong, China
cuilongzheng@mail.sdu.edu.cn, {kai.hu,cuijiamin,mqwang}@sdu.edu.cn
[2] Quancheng Laboratory, Jinan 250103, China
[3] Key Laboratory of Cryptologic Technology and Information Security, Ministry of Education, Shandong University, Qingdao 266237, Shandong, China
[4] Suzhou Research Institute, Shandong University, Suzhou 215123, China

Abstract. The Keccak hash function was selected as the winner of the SHA-3 competition, and officially published as the SHA-3 standard in 2015. As a fundamental cryptographic primitive, the Keccak hash function has undergone intense and widespread cryptanalysis since its introduction.

In this paper, we advance this line of research by presenting an improved collision attack on 4-round SHA3-384. Our framework builds upon the three-stage framework for collision attacks proposed by Huang et al. at FSE 2022. We observe that the deduce-and-sieve algorithm in the SAT-based connecting stage dominates the overall time complexity. To optimize this stage, we propose a new method to derive additional constraints on the chaining values during the block generation stage by extracting extra conditions from invalid input/output difference pairs. This reduces the number of message pairs entering the deduce-and-sieve algorithm by a factor of $2^{3.29}$. Furthermore, we optimize the SAT model itself, which decreases the runtime of SAT-based search by a factor of $2^{4.22}$. These combined improvements lower the time complexity of a 4-round SHA3-384 collision attack from $2^{59.64}$ to $2^{56.11}$. This corresponds to a practical runtime reduction from 7.3 years to 0.63 years.

Keywords: SHA-3 · collision attack · SAT-based automatic search

1 Introduction

As MD4 [13], MD5 [14], SHA-0 [2], and SHA-1 [8] were successfully broken, the National Institute of Standards and Technology of the U.S.(NIST) published the Secure Hash Algorithm-3 (SHA-3) competition in 2007 to select a new hash standard. The Keccak hash function, designed by Guido Bertoni, Joan Daemen, Michaël Peeters, and Gilles Van Assche [3], was selected as the winner of the SHA-3 competition, and officially published as the SHA-3 standard in 2015 [7].

F. -H. Liu (Ed.): CT-RSAC 2026, LNCS 16496, pp. 291–309, 2026.
https://doi.org/10.1007/978-3-032-22931-1_11

The SHA-3 family consists of four hash functions with fixed digest lengths $d \in \{224, 256, 384, 512\}$, namely SHA3-224, SHA3-256, SHA3-384, and SHA3-512. It also contains two extendable-output functions (XOFs) called SHAKE128 and SHAKE256, which can produce digests of arbitrary length.

Keccak adopts a sponge construction, which takes a variable-length message as input. The process begins with the absorbing phase, where a message is padded and divided into r-bit blocks. These blocks are sequentially XORed into a b-bit internal state, followed by a 24-round permutation applying to the state after each block is absorbed. $c = b - r$ is called the capacity. In the squeezing phase, it produces the digests. Since its introduction in 2008, Keccak has become a crucial cryptographic primitive, receiving extensive security analysis including preimage and collision attacks.

Related Works. A collision attack is to find two messages that produce the same digests. In 2012, Dinur et al. developed a framework for finding collisions. Based on the framework, they proposed practical collision attacks against 4-round Keccak-224/256 [5]. This $(r_1 + r_2)$-round attack consists of two stages: a r_1-round connecting stage and a r_2-round collision searching stage. Let ΔS_I and ΔS_O denote the input difference and the output difference of a r_2-round differential characteristic, where the first d bits of ΔS_O are zero. The r_1-round connecting stage generates message pairs (M, M') such that $f_{r_1}(\bar{M}||0^c) + f_{r_1}(\bar{M'}||0^c) = \Delta S_I$, where f_i denotes permutation of i rounds. In the collision searching phase, a colliding pair satisfying the r_2-round differential trail is obtained by enumerating the valid message pairs (M, M') derived in the connecting stage.

To accelerate the connecting stage, Dinur et al. proposed the target difference algorithm to find the message pairs in the 1-round connector in the same work. At EUROCRYPT 2017, Qiao et al. developed an algebraic and differential hybrid method for the connecting stage [12]. The core idea is to convert the problem of finding valid message pairs into solving a linear equation systems by linearizing the S-boxes in the connecting stage. The connectors can be extended up to 2 rounds and they successfully proposed practical collisions attacks on 5-round SHAKE-128. Subsequent studies [10,15] further advanced this line of research by non-full S-box linearization techniques. The connectors can be extended up to 3 rounds, resulting in practical collision attacks on 5-round SHA3-224 and SHA3-256. However, the main drawback of the algebraic and differential hybrid methods [10,12,15] is the quick reduction of degree of freedom caused by linearization. In [11], Huang et al. introduced a three-stage attack framework, consisting of a message generation stage, a SAT-based connecting stage, and a collision search stage. This framework targets 2-block message pairs instead of single block messages. By employing a SAT-based search and using a deduce-and-sieve algorithm to filter valid message pairs, they gained additional degrees of freedom and proposed a collision attack on SHA3-384 with a complexity of $2^{59.64}$. Another line of works focuses on internal difference. At EUROCRYPT 2023 [19], Zhang et al. proposed the conditional internal differentials, presenting the first collision attack on 4/5- round SHAKE256 and the best collision attack on 4-round SHA3-512. At CRYPTO 2024 [20], they further developed a new target internal difference algorithm by probabilistic linearization, leading to the best collision attacks on four round-reduced variants of the SHA-3 instances.

Our Contribution. In this work, we enhance the three-stage framework for SHA3-384 collision attacks proposed by Huang et al. [11]. We observe that in the SAT-based connecting stage, the calling of the deduce-and-sieve algorithm for each potential message pair derived in the message generation stage constitutes a major portion of the overall time complexity. To mitigate this, we develop a method to derive additional constraints on the chaining values during the block generation stage by identifying and utilizing invalid input/output difference pairs. This approach increases the number of derived conditions from 39 to 49, resulting in a reduction of message pairs passing the filtering process by a factor of $2^{3.29}$. Furthermore, we optimize the SAT model by employing a new modeling technique. This approach decreases the number of variables and CNF clauses from 8696 and 45888 to 6934 and 39984, respectively, which yields a significant runtime reduction of SAT-based search by a factor of $2^{4.22}$. For 4-round SHA3-384, the time complexity reduces from $2^{59.64}$ to $2^{56.11}$, which corresponds to a practical reduction in runtime from 7.3 years to 0.63 years. Our results are summarized in Table 1.

Table 1. Attack Results on SHA3-384

Target	Rounds	Complexity	Reference
SHA3-384	3	Practical	[6]
	4	2^{147}	[6]
	4	2^{76}	[19]
	4	$2^{59.64}$	[11]
	4	$2^{56.11}$	Ours
	5	$2^{170.73}$	[20]

Organization. The rest of the paper is organized as follows. In Sect. 2, we introduce some background knowledge needed in the paper. In Sect. 3, we show how to derive more conditions for the chaining values. In Sect. 4, we propose a new SAT model for the connectivity problem. We propose our improved framework for collision attacks against SHA3-384 in Sect. 5. Finally, we give the conclusion of our work in Sect. 6.

2 Preliminaries

2.1 Sponge Construction

The Keccak hash function applies the sponge construction, as depicted in Fig. 1. The sponge construction works on a b-bit internal state, which is divided into two parts: an r-bit outer part (r is called the rate), and an c-bit inner part (c is called the capacity). A message M is first padded by appending a bit string of $10*1$, where $0*$ represents the minimum number of 0 bits that make the length of the padding message $\bar{M} = M||10*1$ is a multiple of r. The b-bit internal state is initialized with all 0. In the absorbing phase, $\bar{M}$ is split into r-bit blocks. Each r-bit block $\bar{M}_i$ is XORed into the first r-bit of the current internal state, and followed by the application of the underlying permutation f. In the squeezing phase, it produces the d-bit digest.

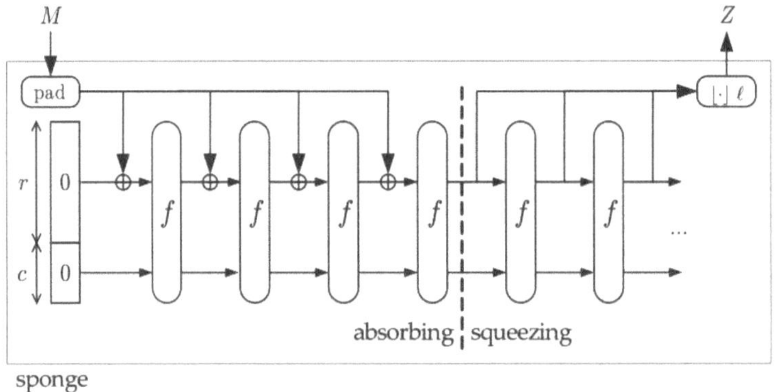

Fig. 1. Sponge construction [7]

2.2 Description of SHA-3

The underlying permutation of Keccak hash function operates on a 1600-bit state A. Each bit of the state can be represented as $A[i]$ for $0 \leq i < 1600$. Alternatively, the state can be organized as a three-dimensional array of bits denoted by $A[5][5][64]$. As illustrated in Fig. 2, $A[*][y][z]$, $A[x][*][z]$ and $A[x][y][*]$ represent a row, a column, and a lane, respectively, where $0 \leq x, y < 5$ and $0 \leq z < 64$. $A[*][*][z]$, $A[*][y][*]$ and $A[x][*][*]$ represent a slice, a plane, and a sheet, respectively. The bit located at position (x, y, z) is denoted by $A[x][y][z]$ and can be mapped to the i-th bit $A[i]$ in the one-dimensional representation, where $i = 64(x + 5y) + z$. Conversely, we can use $A[i]$ to represent the bit $A[\psi_0(i)][\psi_1(i)][\psi_2(i)]$, where $\psi_0(i) = \lfloor i/320 \rfloor$, $\psi_1(i) = \lfloor i/64 \rfloor \mod 5$ and $\psi_2(i) = i \mod 64$. The column index of one bit is represented by $\phi_0(i) = 64\psi_1(i) + \psi_2(i)$.

The Keccak permutation has 24 rounds. Each round consists of five operations θ, ρ, π, χ, ι.

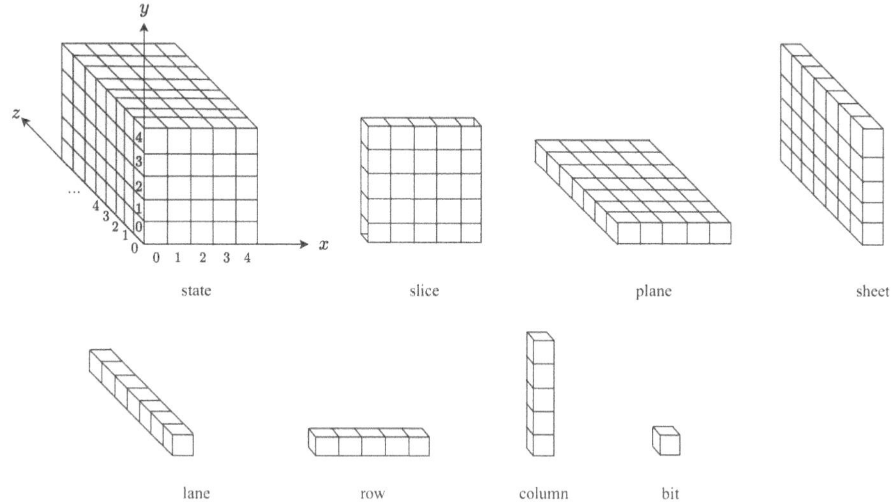

Fig. 2. Keccak state

θ: $A[x][y][z] \leftarrow A[x][y][z] + \sum_{y'=0}^{4} A[x-1][y'][z] + \sum_{y'=0}^{4} A[x+1][y'][z-1]$.
ρ: $A[x][y][z] \leftarrow A[x][y][z+T(x,y)]$ where $T(x,y)$ is a predefined constant.
π: $A[x][y][z] \leftarrow A[x'][y'][z]$, where $\begin{pmatrix} x \\ y \end{pmatrix} = \begin{pmatrix} 0 & 1 \\ 2 & 3 \end{pmatrix} \cdot \begin{pmatrix} x' \\ y' \end{pmatrix}$.
χ: $A[x][y][z] \leftarrow A[x][y][z] + (A[x+1][y][z]+1) \cdot A[x+2][y][z]$.
ι: $A \leftarrow A + RC[r]$, where $RC[r]$ is round constant of r-th round.

χ is the only nonlinear function. We denote the composition of linear function $\pi \circ \rho \circ \theta$ by L and $\pi \circ \rho$ by σ. $\phi_1(i)$ and $\phi_2(i)$ denote the two columns of bits that are added to $A[i]$ during the θ operation, where $\phi_1(i) = 64((\psi_0(i)-1) \mod 5) + \psi_2(i)$ and $\phi_2(i) = 64((\psi_0(i)+1) \mod 5) + ((\psi_2(i)-1) \mod 5)$.

There are four instances Keccak-d of the Keccak sponge function, where $b = 1600$, $c = 2d$, $d \in \{224, 256, 384, 512\}$. The SHA-3 standard adopts 4 instances of Keccak-d, denoted by SHA3-d. The only difference lies in the padding rules. Specifically, the message M is padded by $0110 * 1$ in SHA3-d. In this paper, we focus on the instance SHA3-384.

2.3 Previous Collision Attacks on SHA3-384

The main drawback of the algebraic and differential hybrid method proposed by Guo et al. [9] is the quick reduction of degree of freedom caused by linearization. When the rate r decreases, the available degrees of freedom become even more limited, eventually making the linearization infeasible. As a result, the method of Guo et al. could not be directly applied to 4-round SHA3-384. To mitigate this problem, Huang et al. introduced a 3-stage attack framework in [11] and proposed a collision attack on SHA3-384 with a complexity of $2^{59.64}$. The attack framework consists of a block generation stage, a 1-round SAT-based connecting stage, and a 3-round collision search stage. In the following, we will briefly introduce this attack framework. In particular, this framework targets 2-block message pairs (M_1, M_1') and (M_2, M_2'), namely prefix pairs and suffix pairs, rather than single block messages. The input difference of the i-th round in the second block is denoted by α_i and the difference of χ in the i-th round is denoted by β_i, $0 \leq i \leq 3$ as shown below:

$$\alpha_0 \xrightarrow{L} \beta_0 \xrightarrow{\chi} \alpha_1 \rightarrow \cdots \rightarrow \beta_3 \xrightarrow{\chi} \alpha_4.$$

α_4 denote the output difference. The 3-round differential characteristic $\alpha_1 \rightarrow \alpha_4$ of probability 2^{-42} used in [11] is given in Table 6.

Block Generation Stage. Due to the padding rules of SHA-3, the last $c + 4$ bits of the input state of the second block are known when choosing a given (M_1, M_1'), referred to as *chaining values.* However, the chaining values exhibit some inherent relations as the output difference of nonlinear layer α_1 is already known according to Observation 1. We then leverage the information of the input difference to derive constraints on the corresponding chaining values and generate valid message pairs (M_1, M_1').

Observation 1. *[11] For each S-box, when the output difference δ_{out} is known and chosen from a specific set, we can obtain linear equations for input difference δ_{in} as shown in Table 2.*

Table 2. Conditions of δ_{in} for specific δ_{out} in χ

Conditions	Output Difference	Conditions	Output Difference
$\delta_{in}[0] = 1$	0×01	$\delta_{in}[1] + \delta_{in}[3] = 1$	0×03
$\delta_{in}[1] = 1$	0×02	$\delta_{in}[2] + \delta_{in}[4] = 1$	0×06
$\delta_{in}[2] = 1$	0×04	$\delta_{in}[3] + \delta_{in}[0] = 1$	$0 \times 0c$
$\delta_{in}[3] = 1$	0×08	$\delta_{in}[4] + \delta_{in}[1] = 1$	0×18
$\delta_{in}[4] = 1$	0×10	$\delta_{in}[0] + \delta_{in}[2] = 1$	0×11

If δ_{out} satisfies the form of $\{0 \times 01, 0 \times 02, 0 \times 04, 0 \times 08, 0 \times 10\}$ in Observation 1, 1 bit with value 1 of β_0 is obtained and record the bit index in S_1. If $\delta_{out} = 0$, then 5 bits of β_0 can be derived as 0 and record the indexes of 5 bit in S_0. Then derive linear constraints as follows.

1. Introduce $b = 1600$ variables for the α_0 to represent β_0, $\beta_0 = L(\alpha_0)$.
2. Starting from α_1, check the output difference of the S-boxes one by one. If $\delta_{out} = 0$, then 5 linear equations of α_0 can be derived. If δ_{out} satisfies the form in Observation 1, 1 linear equation for α_0 is obtained.

3. Applying Gaussian elimination on the linear equation system and retain the u linear equations that are only relevant to $\alpha_0[828], \cdots, \alpha_0[1599]$.
4. Randomly generate 2^n M_1 and 2^n M_1' of 832 bits and compute the corresponding 39-bit value string c_1 and c_1' derived using the linear conditions, respectively. Store the pair (M_1, c_1) and (M_1', c_1') into two hash tables H and H'.
5. Match entries from H and H' by comparing c_1 and c_1' under the u linear constraints to generate valid message pairs (M_1, M_1').

In the block generation stage, a threshold of $u \leq 50$ is set to keep the attack practical. In total, $u = 39$ conditions for chaining values are derived. Set $n = 45.92$, $2^n \cdot 2^{n-1} \cdot 2^{-u} = 2^{2n-40} = 2^{51.83}$ valid (M_1, M_1') pairs are generated, and the time complexity is $T_1 = 2^{45.92}$.

SAT-Based Connecting Stage. Given a set of (M_1, M_1') and the input difference α_1, the connecting stage aims to solve the connectivity problem: to generate message pairs (M_2, M_2') such that

$$f_1(f_4(M_1||0) + (M_2||0)) + f_1(f_4(M_1'||0) + (M_2'||0)) = \alpha_1.$$

This problem can be formulated as a satisfiability (SAT) problem.

To improve the overall efficiency of the SAT search, it is crucial to efficiently filter out invalid message pairs (M_1, M_1') beforehand. To this end, Huang et al. proposed a so-called deduce-and-sieve algorithm, which incrementally deduces new constraints and eliminates inconsistent pairs before entering the SAT-solving phase. The deduce-and-sieve algorithm consists of 2 phases: the difference phase and the value phase. In the difference phase, for a given pair (M_1, M_1'), the difference of the corresponding chaining value can be obtained, enabling the deduction of more additional linear conditions for α_0 and β_0. In the value phase, the corresponding actual chaining values are further examined to impose stronger consistency checks, thereby filtering out more invalid pairs and significantly reducing the search space. The remaining message pairs (M_1, M_1') are used to construct the final SAT instances. In each iteration, the one-round differential conditions are encoded as conjunctive normal form (CNF) clauses, involving $2(r-4)$ variables to represent (M_2, M_2'). These SAT instances are then solved using an off-the-shelf SAT solver. The resulting solutions (M_2, M_2') serve as seed pairs $(\hat{M_2}, \hat{M_2'})$ for the subsequent collision search stage.

In the SAT-based connecting stage, the time complexity of each iteration of the deduce-and-sieve algorithm and SAT instances is evaluated based on actual runtime measurements, corresponding to approximately $2^{7.25}$ and $2^{25.55}$ SHA3-384 operations, respectively. The complexity of the deduce-and-sieve algorithm is evaluated as $T_{21} = 2^{2n-40} \times 2^{7.25} = 2^{2n-32.75} = 2^{59.1}$. The filter rate of the deduce-and-sieve algorithm is $2^{-19.42}$. Thus, around $2^{2n-59.42}$ valid (M_1, M_1') pairs are retained. The complexity of the SAT-based search is evaluated as $T_{22} = 2^{2n-59.42} \times 2^{25.55} = 2^{2n-33.87} = 2^{57.96}$. So the overall complexity of the SAT-based connecting stage is $T_2 = T_{21} + T_{22} = 2^{59.1} + 2^{57.96} \approx 2^{59.64}$.

Collision Search Stage. For each (M_1, M_1'), we find a colliding pair following the 3-round differential trail in Table 6 from the subspace of the messages that matching $\Delta M_2 = \hat{M}_2 + \hat{M}_2'$. When the input and output differences of χ operation are fixed, we obtain an affine subspace following the differential trail. In the collision search stage, as the solution space is sufficiently large according to the experiment, the time complexity is $T_3 = 2^{42}$.

2.4 SAT and SAT Solvers

In computer science, the Boolean Satisfiability Problem (SAT) is the problem of determining if there exists an interpretation that satisfies a given Boolean formula. As automatic tools play a more and more important role in the design and cryptanalysis of symmetric ciphers [1,16–18], we transform the connectivity problem into SAT problems and search for the solutions using modern solvers. We construct our model using Conjunctive Normal Form (CNF) clauses, which are expressed as conjunction($\wedge$) of disjunction($\vee$) of Boolean literals. There are many public available solvers to solve SAT problem, among which we take Kissat [4] as our solvers in this paper for its excellent performance.

3 Deriving More Conditions for Block Generation Stage

From the complexity analysis of the three-stage collision attack framework, it is clear that the SAT-based connecting stage dominates the overall attack complexity, with the deduce-and-sieve algorithm being the main contributor. In this section, we show how additional conditions on the chaining values can be derived during the block generation stage. By increasing the number of such conditions we raise the filter rate of the block generation stage, which in turn reduces the number of iterations required in the deduce-and-sieve algorithm.

Since the output difference α_1 is already determined, we introduce the *Truncated Difference Transition Table* (TDTT) to gain a deeper understanding for the properties of the input differences of the χ operation.

Definition 1. *[11] For a pair of truncated input difference Δ_{in}^T and an output difference Δ_{out},*

$$TDTT(\Delta_{in}^T, \Delta_{out}) = \begin{cases} \Delta_{in}^T, & \textit{when no bits of } \Delta_{in}^T \textit{ can be deduced} \\ \Delta_{in}^{T\prime}, & \textit{when new bits are deduced from difference pair} \\ null, & \textit{when } \Delta_{in}^T \rightarrow \Delta_{out} \textit{ is not a valid transaction} \end{cases}$$

In TDTT, $\Delta_{\rm in}^T$ is a 10-bit vector of the form $\delta_{\rm in} \,||\, T$ where $\delta_{\rm in}$ is 5-bit input difference of an S-box. When u bits of $\delta_{\rm in}$ is known where $u < 5$, $\delta_{\rm in}$ is called truncated difference. Truncated pattern T is a 5-bit vector, where 0 denotes unknown bit and 1 denotes known bit in corresponding position of $\delta_{\rm in}$. $\Delta_{\rm in}^{T\prime}$ is new truncated input difference with more known bits than $\Delta_{\rm in}^T$. Given a truncated difference pair

$(\Delta_{in}^T, \Delta_{out})$, new bits can be deduced by traversing all the input differences that conform to the truncated pattern T and extracting their common bits.

In [11], Observation 1 was utilized to derive constraints on the input difference. Specifically, when the output difference satisfies certain conditions, one linear relation on the input difference can be deduced. To obtain more constraints, we remove the restriction on the output difference and further take into account not only the valid input differences corresponding to a given output difference, but also the invalid input/output difference pairs. In the following, we give the definition of *check bits*.

Definition 2 (Check Bits). *Given an output difference δ_{out} and a truncated pattern T of input differences for an S-box, define the set*

$$S_{discard} = \{\, \delta_{in} \mid \mathrm{TDTT}[\delta_{in} \,||\, T][\delta_{out}] = \varnothing \,\}.$$

Check bits are defined as the bit positions that are not exhaustively enumerated among all possible $\delta_{in} \in S_{discard}$. The values of these check bits that render the difference transition invalid are defined as discard values.

The set S_{discard} contains all the input difference δ_{in} that satisfy the truncated pattern T, but fail to propagate to the output difference δ_{out}. The discard value of a check bit at position (x, y, z) is denoted by $dv(x, y, z)$, or equivalently by $dv(i)$ for the corresponding index i in the 1600-bit representation.

Example 1. When $(y, z) = (0, 42)$, $\delta_{out} = [1, 1, 0, 0, 0]$ and truncated pattern is $[0, 0, 1, 1, 1]$, the input differences $[0, 0, 1, 0, 0]$ and $[0, 0, 1, 1, 0]$ are impossible. Only three bits with $x = 2$, $x = 3$ and $x = 4$ are known. Bit with $x = 3$ is exhaustively enumerated. Accordingly, we identify $(2, 0, 40)$ and $(4, 0, 40)$ as check bits.

Constraints on Check Bits. Suppose $s_i = \sigma^{-1}(i)$, a check bit i contributing to the information of chaining values must satisfy the following two properties:

1. $s_i \geq 828$,
2. There exist at least one s_j in the same column as s_i such that $s_j \geq 828$ and $\sigma(s_j)$ in S_0 or S_1.

When check bits satisfy the two properties above, the corresponding S-box position which is denoted by two coordinates (x, y) is called discard position, and there is equation: $\alpha_0[s_i] + \alpha_0[s_j] = \beta_0[i] + 0/1$ according to CP-kernel equation.

Definition 3 (CP-Kernel Equation). *For each $0 \leq i, j < 1600$ and $\phi_0(i) = \phi_0(j)$, we have $A[i] \oplus A[j] = B[\sigma(i)] \oplus B[\sigma(j)]$, where A and B are the input and output states of L.*

In Example 1, if we want a valid difference transition, $\beta_0[(2, 0, 40)] \neq 0$ or $\beta_0[(4, 0, 40)] \neq 0$ must hold, so we have $\alpha_0[830] \neq \alpha_0[1150]$ or $\alpha_0[923] \neq \alpha_0[1563]$. We also give the Algorithm 1 to derive new conditions.

Table 3. New conditions derived using Algorithm 1

No.	Conditions	Discard position	Probability
1	$\alpha_0[830] = \alpha_0[1150]$ or $\alpha_0[923] \neq \alpha_0[1563]$	$(0, 41)$	3/4
2	$\alpha_0[829] \neq \alpha_0[1149]$ or $\alpha_0[1491] \neq \alpha_0[1171]$	$(0, 40)$	3/4
3	$\alpha_0[831] = \alpha_0[1151]$ or $\alpha_0[924] \neq \alpha_0[1564]$	$(0, 42)$	3/4
4	$\alpha_0[847] \neq \alpha_0[1487]$ or $\alpha_0[923] \neq \alpha_0[1563]$	$(2, 40)$	3/4
5	$\alpha_0[850] = \alpha_0[1490]$ or $\alpha_0[931] \neq \alpha_0[1251]$ or $\alpha_0[985] = \alpha_0[1305]$	$(2, 43)$	7/8
6	$\alpha_0[850] \neq \alpha_0[1490]$ or $\alpha_0[931] \neq \alpha_0[1251]$ or $\alpha_0[985] \neq \alpha_0[1305]$	$(2, 43)$	7/8
7	$\alpha_0[851] = \alpha_0[1491]$ or $\alpha_0[986] \neq \alpha_0[1306]$	$(2, 44)$	3/4
8	$\alpha_0[933] \neq \alpha_0[1253]$ or $\alpha_0[987] \neq \alpha_0[11307]$	$(2, 45)$	3/4
9	$\alpha_0[853] = \alpha_0[1493]$ or $\alpha_0[1254] \neq \alpha_0[1574]$ or $\alpha_0[988] \neq \alpha_0[1308]$	$(2, 46)$	7/8
10	$\alpha_0[854] = \alpha_0[1494]$ or $\alpha_0[1575] \neq \alpha_0[1255]$ or $\alpha_0[989] \neq \alpha_0[1309]$	$(2, 47)$	7/8

Algorithm 1: Derive-new-conditions

Input: α_1, TDTT, S_0, S_1
Output: new conditions set S_3, discard positions set $P_{discard}$

1 α_0^S, β_0^S =Derive-known-bit-position(S_0,S_1)
2 $P_{discard} = \emptyset$, $S_3 = \emptyset$
3 **for** *each S-box with position* (y, z) **do**
4 Check TDTT to get discard input difference $S_{discard}$
5 Calculate check bits of $S_{discard}$,discard condition= $\emptyset$,$flag = -1$
6 **for** *each bit i in check bits* **do**
7   **if** $s_i = \sigma^{-1}(i) \geq 828$ **then**
8   **for** *each bit* s_j *in the same column of bits* s_i **do**
9   **if** $s_j \geq 828$ *and* $\sigma(s_j) \in S_0$ *or* S_1 **then**
10      $flag = s_j$
11   **end**
12   **end**
13   **if** *flag* ≥ 0 **then**
14   Add a sub-condition $\alpha_0[s_i] \neq \alpha_0[s_j]$ when $c + dv(i) = 0$ and $\alpha_0[s_i] = \alpha_0[s_j]$ when $c + dv(i) = 1$ to discard condition where $c = 0$ when $\sigma(s_j) \in S_0$ and $c = 1$ when $\sigma(s_j) \in S_1$
15   **end**
16   **end**
17 **end**
18 **if** *flag*$\geq$ 0 **then**
19   **for** *each sub-condition* $\in$ *discard condition* **do**
20   Connect every sub-condition with or to form a final condition
21   **end**
22   Add final condition to S_3
23   Add position (y, z) to $P_{discard}$
24 **end**
25 **end**

By checking the TDTT of the S-box and the two constraints on check bits in Algorithm 1, we get all the discard positions:

$$(y, z) \in \{(0, 40), (0, 41), (0, 42), (2, 40), (2, 43), (2, 44), (2, 45), (2, 46), (2, 47)\},$$

We list all the conditions derived using Algorithm 1 in Table 3. All ten additional conditions are linearly independent of 39 original conditions in [11] based on our experiments. For a random message prefix pair (M_1, M_1') , we can estimate the probability satisfying these conditions. For example, for condition $\alpha[830] \neq \alpha[1150]$ or $\alpha[923] \neq \alpha[1563]$, the probability is $1-(1/2)^2 = 3/4$. Conditions 5 and 6 can be combined into a single condition with probability of $3/4$. Considering all derived conditions, the overall probability that a random prefix pair satisfies them is $(3/4)^7 \times (7/8)^2 \approx 0.102 \approx 2^{-3.29}$.

4 Our New SAT Model for Connectivity Problem

In Huang's framework, the connectivity problem is modeled based on value transitions: the output difference is represented as the XOR of two output values, and the (M_2, M_2') is modeled as a set of variables. However, since we are only concerned with the difference between (M_2, M_2'), it is unnecessary to model their actual values directly. By focusing on the differential information, we can capture additional constraints that accelerate the SAT solving process and reduce redundant search.

We observe that the difference bits in positions $[828, 1599]$ are already known. If we can establish relationships between a bit in $[0, 827]$ and a bit in $[828, 1599]$, we can deduce the value of the bit in $[0, 827]$. In Algorithm 2, we focus on difference bits in these positions and derive 162 additional conditions.

Initially, we only add these additional difference assignments to Huang's SAT model. To encode each difference value assignment $\alpha_0[i] = c$, we add more clauses to model equation $A[i] + A'[i] = c$. However, this approach proved less effective than expected and even resulted in a significantly larger number of clauses. To address this, we explored an alternative modeling method that better leverages these conditions. Specifically, for the χ transformation, the output difference δ_{out} can be expressed as a function of the input difference δ_{in} and the 5-bit input value $x_1x_2x_3x_4x_5$ as follows:

$$\delta_{out}[i] = x_{i+1}\delta_{in}[i+2] + x_{i+2}\delta_{in}[i+1] + \delta_{in}[i] + \delta_{in}[i+1]\delta_{in}[i+2] + \delta_{in}[i+2],$$

where $\delta_{in}[i]$ and $\delta_{out}[i]$ are i-th bit of input and output difference. All the indexes are mod 5.

We assign both input values and input differences as variables for positions in $[0, 827]$ that cannot be determined by the 162 additional conditions. These variables then propagate through the linear transformation as in the original model. In the nonlinear layer, we model the χ transition rules using the 9 clauses listed in Table 4. For the output difference, we only need to include clauses enforcing equality with α_1. The complete SAT model generation procedure is

Algorithm 2: Derive-new-difference-bits

Input: S_0, S_1
Output: New difference bits result set S_d

```
1  for each integer i ∈ [0, 828) do
2      for each integer j ∈ [828, 1600) do
3          if σ(i),σ(j) in same column, (σ(i), σ(j) ∈ S0 or S1 then
4              Compute α0[i] = α0[j]
5              Add α0[i] to Sd
6          end
7          else
8              if σ(i), σ(j) in same
                 column,(σ(i) ∈ S0, σ(j) ∈ S1 or σ(i) ∈ S1, σ(j) ∈ S0) then
9                  Compute α0[i] = α0[j] + 1
10                 Add α0[i] to Sd
11             end
12         end
13     end
14 end
15 return Sd
```

Table 4. Clauses of χ

No.	Clause
1	$(x[i+1] \vee \neg x[i+2] \vee \neg \delta_{in}[i+2] \vee \delta_{out}[i])$
2	$(\neg x[i+2] \vee \neg \delta_{in}[i+1] \vee \delta_{in}[i+2] \vee \delta_{out}[i])$
3	$(x[i+1] \vee \delta_{in}[i+1] \vee \neg \delta_{in}[i+2]\delta_{out}[i])$
4	$(\neg x[i+1] \vee x[i+2] \vee \neg \delta_{in}[i+1] \vee \neg \delta_{in}[i+2] \vee \delta_{out}[i])$
5	$(\delta_{in}[i+1] \vee \delta_{in}[i+2] \vee \neg \delta_{out}[i])$
6	$(x[i+2] \vee \delta_{in}[i+2] \vee \neg \delta_{out}[i])$
7	$(\neg x[i+1] \vee \delta_{in}[i+1] \vee \neg \delta_{out}[i])$
8	$(x[i+1] \vee x[i+2] \vee \neg \delta_{in}[i+1] \vee \neg \delta_{out}[i])$
9	$(\neg x[i+1] \vee \neg x[i+2] \vee \neg \delta_{in}[i+2] \vee \neg \delta_{out}[i])$

summarized in Algorithm 7. Notably, the solvability of the connectivity problem holds if and only if the result of the SAT model is satisfiable, and vice versa.

Our new SAT model based on difference transition rules on χ function has fewer variables and clauses than before. The reason is that 3200 variables are needed to express output value of χ in Huang's model, and we just need 1600 variables to denote output difference without value. And for XOR operation, we traverse all possible values of the input and output variables and then exclude the impossible variable assignments. Because we express output difference after one round is equal to α_1 directly, whereas previous model has to express output difference through XOR of two values, the total number of clauses is still 1800 less than before, even though we need 3 additional clauses for each bit when performing nonlinear operations. Moreover, by reducing 162 differential variables through additional conditions, we can further reduce the number of constraints for linear transformations. We list model scales of the three in the Table 5.

Table 5. Comparison of different SAT models

Model	Number of variables	Number of clauses	Running time
[11]	8696	45888	3.93 s
Only difference	7096	41088	0.23 s
Difference with variables reduced	6934	39984	0.21 s

Algorithm 3: Non-linear-Model

Input: B, β_0, $Clause$, var_{cnt}
Output: $Clause$ of χ, var_{cnt}

1 **for** *each* $i \in [0, 1600)$ **do**
2 $C[i] = var_{cnt}$, $var_{cnt}+ = 1$
3 Compute three coordinates x, y, z of i.
4 Compute bit index j and k of $(x+1, y, z)$ and $(x+2, y, z)$ respectively.
5 Add 9 clauses of $C[i], B[j], B[k], \beta_0[j], \beta_0[k]$ according to Table 4 to Clause
6 **end**
7 **return** *Clause*

Algorithm 4: Linear-Model

Input: A, α_0, $Clause$, var_{cnt}
Output: $Clause$ of L, B, β_0, var_{cnt}

1 **for** *each* $i \in [0, 1600)$ **do**
2 $B[i] = var_{cnt}$, $var_{cnt}+ = 1$, $\beta_0[i] = var_{cnt}$, $var_{cnt}+ = 1$
3 **end**
4 **for** *each* $i \in [0, 320)$ **do**
5 $\Sigma[i] = var_{cnt}$, $var_{cnt}+ = 1$, $\Sigma'[i] = var_{cnt}$, $var_{cnt}+ = 1$ for Add clauses of $\Sigma[i] = A[i] + A[i+320] + A[i+640] + A[i+960] + A[i+1280]$ and $\Sigma'[i] = \alpha_0[i] + \alpha_0[i+320] + \alpha_0[i+640] + \alpha_0[i+960] + \alpha_0[i+1280]$ to Clause
6 **end**
7 **for** *each* $i \in [0, 320)$ **do**
8 Add clauses of $B[\sigma(i)] = A[i] + \Sigma[\phi_1(i)] + \Sigma[\phi_2(i)]$, $\beta_0[\sigma(i)] = \alpha_0[i] + \Sigma'[\phi_1(i)] + \Sigma'[\phi_2(i)]$ to Clause
9 **end**
10 **return** *Clause*, B, β_0, var_{cnt},

Algorithm 5: Generate-SAT-model

```
   Input: S_d, M_1, M'_1
   Output: Clause
1  A, A' = DS(M_1, M'_1),  Clause = ∅,  var_cnt = 1
2  for each i ∈ [0, 1600) do
3  |  α_0[i] = A[i] + A'[i]
4  end
5  for each i ∈ [0, 828) do
6  |  A[i] = var_cnt, var_cnt = var_cnt + 1
7  |  if i ∉ S_d then
8  |  |  α_0[i] = var_cnt, var_cnt+ = 1
9  |  end
10 |  else
11 |  |  Assign value to α_0[i] according to S_d
12 |  end
13 end
14 Clause, B, β_0, var_cnt=Linear-Model(A, α_0, Clause, var_cnt)
15 Clause=Non-linear-Model(B, β_0, Clause, var_cnt)
16 for each i ∈ [0, 1600) do
17 |  Add clauses of α_1 = C[i] + β_0[i] to Clause
18 end
19 return Clause
```

5 A New Framework for Collision Attacks on SHA3-384

In this section, we present our improved framework for collision attacks on SHA3-384. Our improved framework is illustrated in Fig. 3. We run our experiments on a single core of AMD EPYC 7302.

5.1 Block Generation Stage

In the block generation stage, the corresponding chaining values are required to satisfy two types of conditions: the 39 linear conditions derived in [11] and 10 additional conditions derived in Sect. 3. A set of message pairs (M_1, M'_1) are generated as described in Sect. 2.3 and apply the 10 additional conditions to filter (M_1, M'_1):

In the block generation stage, $2^n \cdot 2^{n-1} \cdot 2^{-39} \cdot 2^{-3.29} = 2^{2n-43.29}$ valid (M_1, M'_1) pairs are generated. For the 10 additional conditions, it takes only 2.27×10^{-8}s, which is equivalent to 0.28 SHA3-384 operations. It runs much faster than deduce-and-sieve which takes 1.22×2^{-5}s, so the complexity is negligible. The time complexity of this stage is $T'_1 = 2^n$. The memory and data complexity is also 2^n.

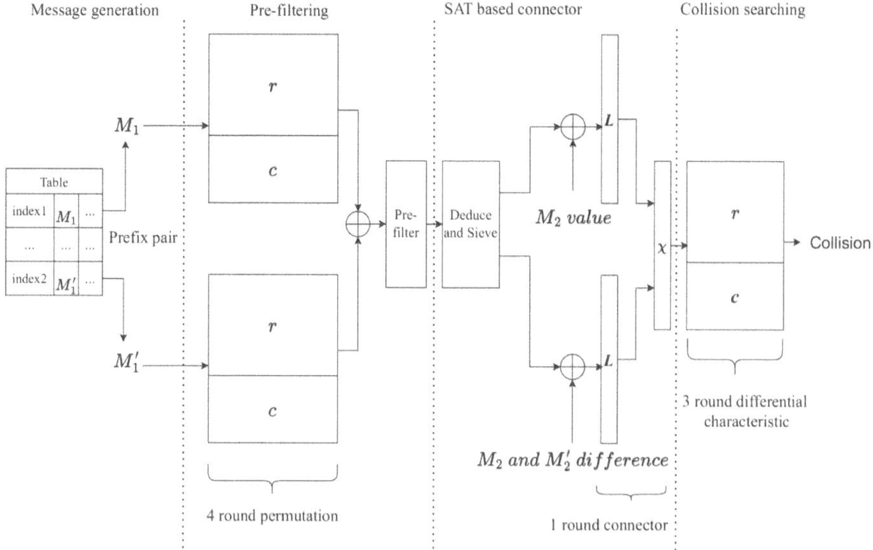

Fig. 3. Our new framework for collision attacks

5.2 SAT-Based Connecting Stage

For the $2^{2n-43.29}$ valid (M_1, M_1') pairs, we employ the deduce-and-sieve algorithm to deduce new constraints and eliminate inconsistent pairs before entering the SAT-solving phase. Since a single call to the deduce-and-sieve algorithm has a time complexity equivalent to $2^{7.25}$ SHA3-384 operations, the overall complexity of this algorithm is $T_{21}' = 2^{2n-43.29} \times 2^{7.25} = 2^{2n-36.04}$ with negligible memory complexity. Since the change of the block generation stage does not change the overall filtering rate, there are still $2^{2n-59.42}$ (M_1, M_1') pairs. Then we use our new SAT model proposed in Sect. 4 to model the connectivity problem for each (M_1, M_1'). From our experiments, new SAT model just takes 0.21 s per prefix pairs, which is 18.71 times faster than Huang's model. So the time complexity of one new SAT instances is evaluated as $(0.21/3.93) \times 2^{25.55} = 2^{21.32}$. The complexity of SAT-solving is $T_{22}' = 2^{2n-59.42} \times 2^{21.32} = 2^{2n-38.1}$.

5.3 Collision Search Stage

In the collision search stage, for each (M_1, M_1'), we obtain a seed pair $(\hat{M}_2, \hat{M}_2')$ from the SAT-based connecting stage. The absolute values of $(\hat{M}_2, \hat{M}_2')$ are irrelevant for the subsequent stages, only their difference $\Delta M_2 = \hat{M}_2 + \hat{M}_2'$ matters. Given ΔM_2, the corresponding input-difference β_0 can be fully determined. We then enumerate all the possible solutions of the given input and output difference to obtain a valid colliding pair. As the solution space is sufficiently large according to the experiment, the time complexity is $T_3 = 2^{42}$.

In all, to find a real collision, we set $n = 45.92$. Then $T_{21}' = 2^{55.8}$ and $T_{22}' = 2^{53.74}$. The time complexity of the SAT-based connecting phase is therefore $T_2' = T_{21}' + T_{22}' \approx 2^{56.11}$, which dominates the overall attack complexity.

6 Conclusion

In this paper, we build upon Huang's framework for two-block collision attacks on SHA3-384 and propose a method to derive additional conditions on the input difference of the second message block. By filtering first-block message pairs using these conditions before applying the deduce-and-sieve algorithm, the filter rate is improved by a factor of approximately $2^{3.29}$. To further accelerate the SAT solver, we introduce additional difference constraints between chaining values and free variables, and integrate them into a new SAT model based on the input values and differences of the χ function. This optimized SAT model runs 18.71 times faster than Huang's original model, reducing the overall time complexity to $2^{56.11}$. Extending these techniques to 5-round collision attacks on SHA3-384 is left for future work.

Acknowledgements. We are deeply indebted to the anonymous reviewers for their insightful comments, whose constructive suggestions have greatly improved the overall quality of this work. This work is supported by the National Key R&D Program of China (Grant No. 2024YFA1013000, 2023YFA1009500), the National Natural Science Foundation of China (Grant No. 62032014, U2336207), and the National Cryptologic Science Fund of China (Grant No. 2025NCSF01013). Kai Hu is supported by National Cryptologic Science Fund of China(2025NCSF02007), the National Natural Science Foundation of China (62402283), Shandong Provincial Natural Science Foundation(No.2025HWYQ-025), the Natural Science Foundation of Jiangsu Province (BK20240420), Program of TaiShan Scholars Special Fund for young scholars (Grant NO.tsqn202507063) and Program of Qilu Young Scholars of Shandong University.

A 3-Round Differential Characteristic

Table 6. The 3-round differential trail [11]

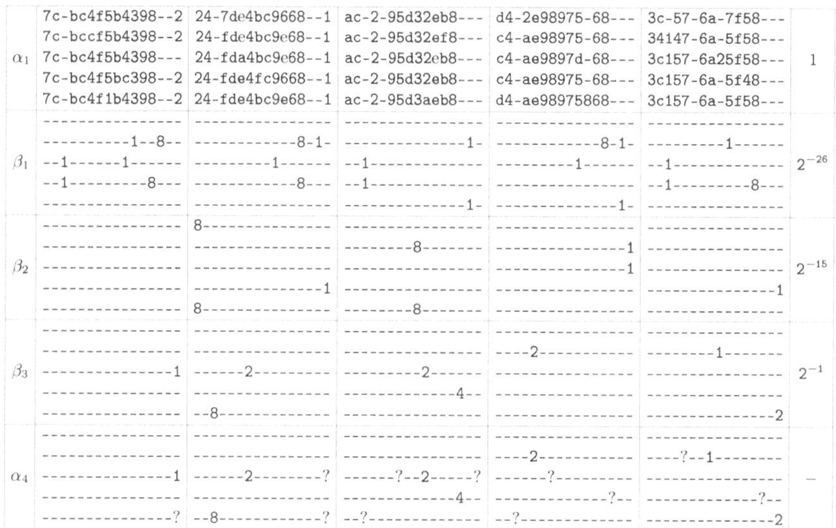

α_1	7c-bc4f5b4398--2 7c-bccf5b4398--2 7c-bc4f5b4398--- 7c-bc4f5bc398--2 7c-bc4f1b4398--2	24-7de4bc9668--1 24-fde4bc9e68--1 24-fda4bc9e68--1 24-fde4fc9668--1 24-fde4bc9e68--1	ac-2-95d32eb8--- ac-2-95d32ef8--- ac-2-95d32eb8--- ac-2-95d32eb8--- ac-2-95d3aeb8---	d4-2e98975-68--- c4-ae98975-68--- c4-ae9897d-68--- c4-ae98975-68--- d4-ae98975868---	3c-57-6a-7f58--- 34147-6a-5f58--- 3c157-6a25f58--- 3c157-6a-5f48--- 3c157-6a-5f58---	1
β_1	---------------- ----------1--8-- --1------1------ --1---------8--- ----------------	---------------- ------------8-1- ---------1------ ------------8--- ----------------	---------------- --------------1- --1------------- --1------------- --------------1-	---------------- ------------8-1- ---------1------ ---------------- --------------1-	---------------- ---------1------ --1------------- --1---------8--- ----------------	2^{-26}
β_2	---------------- ---------------- ---------------- ---------------- ----------------	8--------------- ---------------- ---------------- ---------------1 8---------------	---------------- --------8------- ---------------- ---------------- --------8-------	---------------- ---------------1 ---------------1 ---------------- ----------------	---------------- ---------------- ---------------- ---------------1 ----------------	2^{-15}
β_3	---------------- ---------------- ---------------1 ---------------- ----------------	---------------- ---------------- ------2--------- ---------------- --8-------------	---------------- ---------------- ---------2------ -------------4-- ----------------	---------------- ----2----------- ---------------- ---------------- ----------------	---------------- --------1------- ---------------- ---------------- ---------------2	2^{-1}
α_4	---------------- ---------------- ---------------1 ---------------- ---------------?	---------------- ---------------- ------2--------? ---------------- --8------------?	---------------- ---------------- ------?--2-----? -------------4-- --?-------------	---------------- ----2----------- ------?--------- -------------?-- --?-------------	---------------- ----?--1-------- ---------------- -------------?-- ---------------2	–

B Deducing Known Bit Positions

Algorithm 6: Update-Column

Input: α_0^S, β_0^S, i

Output: α_0^S, β_0^S

1 Compute the indices of the five bits in the i-th column as i_0, i_1, i_2, i_3, i_4
2 flag=0
3 **for** *each integer* $j \in [0, 5)$ **do**
4   **if** $\alpha_0^S[i_j] = 1$ *and* $\beta_0^S[\sigma(i_j)] = 1$ **then**
5   flag=1
6   **end**
7   **if** *flag=1* **then**
8   **for** *each integer* $j \in [0, 5)$ **do**
9   **if** $\alpha_0^S[i_j] = 1$ *and* $\beta_0^S[\sigma(i_j)] = 0$ **then**
10                 $\beta_0^S[\sigma(i_j)] = 1$
11   **end**
12   **else**
13   **if** $\alpha_0^S[i_j] = 0$ *and* $\beta_0^S[\sigma(i_j)] = 1$ **then**
14                     $\alpha_0^S[\sigma(i_j)] = 1$
15   **end**
16   **end**
17   **end**
18   **end**
19 **end**

Algorithm 7: Deduce-known-bit-position

```
   Input: S_0,S_1
   Output: α_0^S, β_0^S
 1 for each integer i ∈ [0,1600) do
 2 |   if i ≥ 828 then
 3 |   |   α_0^S[i] = 1
 4 |   end
 5 |   else
 6 |   |   α_0^S[i] = 0
 7 |   end
 8 |   if i ∈ S_0 then
 9 |   |   β_0^S[i] = 1
10 |   end
11 |   else
12 |   |   if i ∈ S_1 then
13 |   |   |   β_0^S[i] = 1
14 |   |   end
15 |   |   else
16 |   |   |   β_0^S[i] = 0
17 |   |   end
18 |   end
19 end
20 for each integer i ∈ [0,320) do
21 |   α_0^S, β_0^S=Update-Column(α_0^S, β_0^S, i)
22 end
```

References

1. Alamgir, N., Nejati, S., Bright, C.: Sha-256 collision attack with programmatic sat. arXiv preprint arXiv:2406.20072 (2024)
2. Barker, E., et al.: Secure hash standard (shs) (1993)
3. Bertoni, G., Daemen, J., Peeters, M., Van Assche, G.: Keccak sponge function family main document. Submission to NIST (Round 2) **3**(30), 320–337 (2009)
4. Biere, A., et al.: entering the SAT competition 2024. In: Heule, M., Iser, M., Järvisalo, M., Suda, M., (eds.), Proc. of SAT Competition 2024 – Solver, Benchmark and Proof Checker Descriptions, vol. B-2024-1 of Department of Computer Science Report Series B, pp. 8–10. University of Helsinki (2024)
5. Dinur, I., Dunkelman, O., Shamir, A.: New attacks on Keccak-224 and Keccak-256. In: Canteaut, A. (ed.) FSE 2012. LNCS, vol. 7549, pp. 442–461. Springer, Heidelberg (2012). https://doi.org/10.1007/978-3-642-34047-5_25
6. Dinur, I., Dunkelman, O., Shamir, A.: Collision attacks on up to 5 rounds of SHA-3 using generalized internal differentials. In: Moriai, S., (eds.), Fast Software Encryption - 20th International Workshop, FSE 2013, Singapore, 11-13 March (2013). Revised Selected Papers, vol. 8424 of Lecture Notes in Computer Science, pp. 219–240. Springer (2013)
7. Dworkin, M.J., et al.: Sha-3 standard: permutation-based hash and extendable-output functions (2015)

8. Gallagher, P., Director, A.: Secure hash standard (shs). FIPS PUB **180**, 183 (1995)
9. Guo, J., Liao, G., Liu, G., Liu, M., Qiao, K., Song, L.: Practical collision attacks against round-reduced SHA-3. J. Cryptol. **33**(1), 228–270 (2020)
10. Guo, J., Liu, G., Song, L., Tu, Y.: Exploring SAT for cryptanalysis: (quantum) collision attacks against 6-round SHA-3. In: Agrawal, S., Lin, D., (eds.), Advances in Cryptology - ASIACRYPT 2022 - 28th International Conference on the Theory and Application of Cryptology and Information Security, Taipei, Taiwan, 5-9 December (2022), Proceedings, Part III, vol. 13793 of Lecture Notes in Computer Science, pp. 645–674. Springer (2022)
11. Huang, S., Agmon Ben-Yehuda, O., Dunkelman, O., Maximov, A.: Finding collisions against 4-round sha-3-384 in practical time. In: IACR Transactions on Symmetric Cryptology, pp. 239–270 (2022)
12. Qiao, K., Song, L., Liu, M., Guo, J.: New collision attacks on round-reduced Keccak. In: Coron, J.-S., Nielsen, J.B. (eds.) EUROCRYPT 2017. LNCS, vol. 10212, pp. 216–243. Springer, Cham (2017). https://doi.org/10.1007/978-3-319-56617-7_8
13. Rivest, R.L.: The MD4 message digest algorithm. In: Menezes, A., Vanstone, S.A., (eds.), Advances in Cryptology - CRYPTO '90, 10th Annual International Cryptology Conference, Santa Barbara, California, USA, 11-15 August 1990, Proceedings, vol. 537 of Lecture Notes in Computer Science, pp. 303–311. Springer (1990)
14. Rivest, R.L.: The MD5 message-digest algorithm. RFC **1321**, 1–21 (1992)
15. Song, L., Liao, G., Guo, J.: Non-full Sbox linearization: applications to collision attacks on round-reduced Keccak. In: Katz, J., Shacham, H. (eds.) CRYPTO 2017. LNCS, vol. 10402, pp. 428–451. Springer, Cham (2017). https://doi.org/10.1007/978-3-319-63715-0_15
16. Soos, M., Nohl, K., Castelluccia, C.: Extending sat solvers to cryptographic problems. In: International Conference on Theory and Applications of Satisfiability Testing, pp. 244–257. Springer (2009)
17. Sun, L., Wang, M.: Sok: modeling for large s-boxes oriented to differential probabilities and linear correlations. IACR Trans. Symmetric Cryptol. (1), 111–151 (2023)
18. Sun, L., Wang, W., Wang, M.: Automatic search of bit-based division property for ARX ciphers and word-based division property. In: Takagi, T., Peyrin, T. (eds.) ASIACRYPT 2017. LNCS, vol. 10624, pp. 128–157. Springer, Cham (2017). https://doi.org/10.1007/978-3-319-70694-8_5
19. Zhang, Z., Hou, C., Liu, M.: Collision attacks on round-reduced SHA-3 using conditional internal differentials. In: Hazay, C., Stam, M., (eds.), Advances in Cryptology - EUROCRYPT 2023 - 42nd Annual International Conference on the Theory and Applications of Cryptographic Techniques, Lyon, France, 23-27 April (2023), Proceedings, Part IV, vol. 14007 of Lecture Notes in Computer Science, pp. 220–251. Springer (2023)
20. Zhang, Z., Hou, C., Liu, M.: Probabilistic linearization: internal differential collisions in up to 6 rounds of sha-3. In: Annual International Cryptology Conference, pp. 241–272. Springer (2024)

Tunable Zero-Knowledge Proof of Inference in Machine Learning via Protocols over $\mathbb{Z}_{2^k}$

Yi Kuang, Fuchun Lin(✉), and Chaoping Xing(✉)

Shanghai Jiao Tong University, Shanghai 200240, China
{schemer,fuchunlin,xingcp}@sjtu.com

Abstract. Previously implemented zero-knowledge proof of inference (zk-PoI) frameworks all have both their discretization ring and proof soundness tight up to a fixed-size finite field, and the benchmarked efficiency depends, to a large extent, on the existence of some specific prime number (Mersenne $2^{61}-1$, Goldilocks $2^{64}-2^{32}+1$). Implementing these frameworks outside that particular parameter range incurs significant slowdown and requires a total re-write of the low-level codes. To eliminate this sore spot, we put forward a tunable zk-PoI framework that allows customized independent fine-tuning of the desired size of the discretization ring and soundness without interfering with each other, and without altering the low-level design logic. Moreover, the efficiency degrades gracefully as the desired ring size or security level increases without abrupt jumps.

We implement the tunable zk-PoI framework using ZK protocols over $\mathbb{Z}_{2^k}$. In particular, we integrate, into the modified framework, the recent successful line of works building generic ZKP and efficient conversions over $\mathbb{Z}_{2^k}$ in the VOLE-based ZK protocol paradigm, which features fast proof generation and optimal memory footprint. We also provide $\mathbb{Z}_{2^k}$ variant of the other required sub-protocols in the zk-PoI framework not discussed in the mentioned line of works and propose new optimizations. Our implementation shows that working over $\mathbb{Z}_{2^k}$ not only enables fine-tuning of parameters, but also simplifies the design of verification circuits, which translates into efficiency gain. We compare the performance of our protocols against Mystique, in the same hardware/software environment and at its best performing parameter range. The experimental results show an up to 3.9 times improvement in time and 1.5 in communication over Mystique.

Optimizations of verification algorithms for linear layer computation in machine learning have played an important role in the previously implemented zk-PoI frameworks. We take on the challenge of enabling similar optimizations in the tunable zk-PoI framework by studying the $\mathbb{Z}_{2^k}$ equivalent of these algorithms. In particular, we tackled the challenging problem of extending the Freivald's sublinear-time algorithm for verifying matrix multiplication to work over $\mathbb{Z}_{2^k}$.

F. -H. Liu (Ed.): CT-RSAC 2026, LNCS 16496, pp. 310–337, 2026.
https://doi.org/10.1007/978-3-032-22931-1_12

1 Introduction

As more and more powerful machine learning models are trained to accomplish many difficult tasks that once were believed to be impossible for machines, their predecessors are becoming unglamorous and low in commercial value. It is common practice in the business world to open source older versions of these models to general public for free usage and focus on merchandising the most up-to-date cutting-edge models. This pattern in business world dictates that cryptography techniques developed for machine learning must have good scalability and enough flexibility so that once a newer model (usually with more sophisticated structure and larger parameters) replaces its predecessor, the same cryptography techniques are readily adapted to guarantee a timely merchandisation. Motivated by the high profit promised by the market, AI companies invest huge amount of money into securing sensitive data and state-of-the-art hardware for training competitive models. The companies then offer verifiable paid inference services without revealing the trained model parameters, using specially designed zero-knowledge proof (ZKP). The buyers can verify that they get their money's worth and the AI companies get to keep their models secret for running the business.

The research on zero-knowledge proof of inference (zk-PoI) answers to this need [9,11,14,17,21,23,26,28,29,31]. The pioneer work [31] restricts to a decision tree structure and initiated the study of zk-PoI as a triple of algorithms (Commit, Prove, Verify) after the generation of public parameters. Following up works vCNN [14], pvCNN [29] and ZEN [9] studied convolutional neural networks (CNN) and focused on finding specific zero-knowledge succinct non-interactive argument of knowledge (zk-SNARK) friendly representations of machine learning tasks: quadratic arithmetic program (QAP), polynomial QAP and rank-1 constraint system (R1CS) friendly optimizations, respectively. In zkCNN [17], a task-specific sum-check protocol that proves convolution with running time significantly lower than the computation itself was discovered, which together with the similarly efficient sum-check protocol for matrix multiplication in [25] have become key drivers in the creation of specialized ZKPs for deep learning. Very recently, these sum-check based techniques were combined with table-look-up techniques to yield zk-PoI with fast proof generation and succinct proofs, which are specialized to large language models (LLM) [21,23] (some of these are practical for rather large models in terms of proof generation time and proof size, see Sect. 1.3 for further discussion).

However, all the above mentioned works rely on zk-SNARK type of approach to ZKP. The development of zk-SNARK was motivated by its applications in block-chain, where the verifier is computationally very weak and the need to cater for a weak verifier imposes huge burden on the proof generation, resulting in unavoidable large memory consumption. The zk-PoI framework Mystique [28] departed from the approach of relying on zk-SNARK type of techniques and introduced VOLE-based ZKP into zk-PoI, where VOLE stands for vector oblivious linear function evaluation. VOLE-based ZKP (see [30] and references therein) is famous for its light prover (linear time with small hidden constant in general and sublinear for special computation such as matrix multiplication;

optimal memory footprint), although the proof is in general not succinct, which is not an issue if the only concern here is zero-knowledge property and the verifier is not as weak as in block chain application. Another drawback in the Mystique framework is that their backend zero-knowledge protocol is implemented with a pseudo-random correlation generator (PCG) based VOLE, which renders it a designated verifier proof under Fiat Shamir. On the positive side, Mystique initiated several measures for enhancing inference accuracy including a floating point number aided trick: almost the entire computation of inference, except for simple addition and multiplication, happens in floating-point world and intermediate values are only converted into fixed-point numbers for authentication. In particular, complicated functions such as exponentiation is computed as floating-point numbers and then mapping the output back to fixed-point for authentication. Such a trick can be very useful when the scale of the fixed point number is set lower than the computation task demands. More recently, [11] replaced the computation of these complicated functions in Mystique with elaborate table-look-up technique and claimed significant improvements in proof generation time over Mystique. But the optimal memory footprint of Mystique is not preserved due to the excessive use of table-look-up techniques (see Sect. 1.3 for further discussion). In this work, we want to focus on zk-PoT frameworks with optimal memory footprint.

On the other hand, from the practitioners' point of view, there are specific application scenarios that involve situations where one needs to perform calculations on very large numbers and require extremely fine fractional precision at the same time with fixed point numbers. One critical example is the high-precision financial computing. While 64-bit is perfect for most financial calculations, the most demanding institutions require more, for instance, calculating interest on the national debt (the U.S. National debt is 34 trillion). A 64-bit fixed-point number scaled to micro-cents ($1/1,000,000$ of a cent) might struggle to represent the whole dollar amount and the tiny fractions of interest accumulating every nanosecond. A 128-bit number provides a colossal "headroom" for both the massive principal and the infinitesimally compounded interest. Cryptocurrency and blockchain is another such example. Many cryptocurrencies have a high value and a fixed, fine-grained divisibility (e.g., Bitcoin is divisible to 8 decimal places, or 1 Satoshi). Large-scale accounting for an exchange or a fund dealing with millions of BTC requires 128-bit arithmetic to avoid overflow and maintain exact precision. There are also scientific and mathematical computing, such as high-energy physics and quantum mechanics. 128-bit fixed-point can be a building block in these implementations. We note that the models used for benchmarking in the zk-PoI literature are open-source general purpose models. It is not clear how well the existing zk-PoI protocols fare with the special purpose models that deal with the application scenario listed above. This brings out an important aspect of practicality not discussed in previous studies: how do we make sure that a zk-PoI framework developed and tested on open-source general purpose models is useful for high commercial value special-task models? We argue that a zk-PoI framework of practical importance should at least support customised fine-tuning of parameters to cater for the specific application setting. Moreover, one can further request that the modification be simple (preferably a process without involving cryptographers or experienced programmers) and its efficiency overhead due to the modification be minimum. Mystique uses the prime number field modulo the Mersenne prime $p = 2^{61} - 1$ and encode fixed-point numbers into a 30-bit range (with precision parameter 16). Arithmetic modulo p is especially efficient because

$$2^i \equiv 2^{(i \mod 61)} \mod p \quad (1)$$

and the modulo operation becomes grouping the binary representation 61 bits in one block and summing up the resulting numbers (each number in one block is at most p) across blocks. The issue with relying on the particular Mersenne prime $p = 2^{61} - 1$) is that the accommodatable bit length for the fixed-point numbers is limited. If longer bit length for higher precision is required, the only solutions are either to switch to an ordinary prime number or to use the next Mersenne prime that is much bigger than the desired size (due to the increasing sparsity of the Mersenne primes as the size grows). The former solution demands a complete re-write of the low-level codes and the new codes would become much slower due to the lack of efficient computation as in (1). The later solution requires less modification. But in extreme cases, can lead to significant slowdown and communication overhead.

1.1 Our Contributions

- we put forward a tunable zk-PoI framework that allows customized independent fine-tuning of the desired discretization ring size and soundness without interfering with each other, and without altering the low-level design logic. Moreover, the efficiency degrades gracefully as the desired discretization ring size or security level increases without abrupt jumps.
- We implement the tunable zk-PoI framework using ZK protocols over $\mathbb{Z}_{2^k}$. In particular, we integrate, into the modified framework, the recent successful line of works building generic ZK protocols and efficient conversions over $\mathbb{Z}_{2^k}$ in the VOLE-based ZK proof paradigm, which features fast proof generation and optimal memory footprint. We also provide $\mathbb{Z}_{2^k}$ variant of the other required sub-protocols in the zk-PoI framework not discussed in the mentioned line of works. We compare the performance of our protocol proposed for the modified zk-IoP framework against Mystique (we note that although its look-up-table modification [11] is faster, Mystique remains the best in the low memory consumption regime), in the same hardware/software environment and at the best performing parameter range of Mystique. The experimental results show that the new protocol not only facilitates independent customized fine-tuning of precision and soundness parameters, but also its use of $\mathbb{Z}_{2^k}$ to encode real numbers with fixed precision simplifies the circuit design and leads to new efficiency gains (up to 3.9 times in time and 1.5 in communication, see Table 4).

- We take on the challenge of enabling optimizations of VOLE-based ZKP over $\mathbb{Z}_{2^k}$ for specific tasks in linear layers of neural network, by exploring $\mathbb{Z}_{2^k}$ equivalent of faster proving than computation ZKP [17,25,28]. In particular, we tackled the challenging problem of extending the Freivald's sublinear-time algorithm for verifying matrix multiplication to work over $\mathbb{Z}_{2^k}$. The optimization alone yields about 2 times saving in time and more than 2 in communication (Table 1 v.s. Table 4).

1.2 Technical Overviews

A better finite ring than Mersenne prime number field in terms of efficient modulo operation is $\mathbb{Z}_{2^k}$. The arithmetic modulo 2^k

$$2^i \equiv \begin{cases} 2^i \mod 2^k & i < k \\ 0 \mod 2^k & i \geq k \end{cases} \tag{2}$$

becomes keeping the first k lower bits (dropping the rest). But unfortunately, the ring $\mathbb{Z}_{2^k}$ has very limited algebraic properties to support cryptographical constructions. There were studies, first in secure multi-party computation (MPC) literature initiated in SPDZ2k [5] and then extended to VOLE-based ZKP [3] and beyond [15], showing a weaker form of Schwartz-Zippel lemma. There were also works, first in MPC literature [8] and then extended to VOLE-based ZKP [16] and beyond [6], considering a degree-d Galois extension of $\mathbb{Z}_{2^k}$, which has a form of Schwartz-Zippel lemma similar to the finite field $\mathbb{F}_{2^d}$ and supports polynomial interpolation. There are breakthrough results on constructing SNARK over $\mathbb{Z}_{2^k}$ [13]. But this approach should pair with the use of a reversed multiplication friendly embedding (RMFE) to amortize the cost of working over a degree d extension. The arithmetic over the degree-d Galois extension involves multiplication and division of polynomials over $\mathbb{Z}_{2^k}$, incurring significant computational overhead. These complications render the second approach implementation-wise less appealing.

We conducted a thorough testing of these different schemes with particular emphasis on their potential of facilitating tunable zk-PoI and identified the QuarkSilver proposed in Moz$\mathbb{Z}_{2^k}$arella [3] as the best candidate for the base ZKP for proving arithmetic computation in linear layers. Note that Mystique [28] uses the QuickSilver [30] (the finite field counterpart of QuarkSilver) as its base ZKP, which makes it the perfect baseline zk-PoI for comparison. We adopt the same *mixed circuit* framework for machine learning as adopted in Mystique [28] and extended several finite field-based building blocks to work over $\mathbb{Z}_{2^k}$, which maximize the benefit originated from replacing (1) with (2), which is the fundamental source of efficiency gain. We also propose new optimizations at applications level that contribute to 7.5x, 12.9x, and 6.4x) over Mystique for trunc, batch normalization, and layer normalization, respectively. These optimizations include i) removing certain vacuous conversions between floating-point and fixed-point numbers; ii) directly extracting sign-bit; iii) optimizing selection operation.

Mystique [28] generalized the Freivalds algorithm to a ZK protocol for $n \times n$ matrix multiplication over a finite field $\mathbb{F}_p$ (for any prime $p \geq 2$ using VOLE-based ZK protocols. Naively replacing the finite field $\mathbb{F}_p$ with the ring $\mathbb{Z}_{2^k}$ leads to the same issue of insufficient algebraic structures. The challenge of applying the SPDZ2k [5] technique here is the involvement of multiple layers of linear combination of random variables, as is typical in matrix multiplication. We then use the security game tailored exactly for this setting for bounding adversary's success probability recently proposed in [15], where the setting is MPC and the design goal is a distributed product proof that upgrades a semi-honestly secure MPC protocol to a maliciously secure MPC protocol. Distributed product proofs reduce the correct computation of all the multiplication gates to proving a long inner product relation, which is further reduced recursively to a shorter inner product relation till its logical end a multiplication relation, and the fact that some matrix multiplication related techniques can be distilled from such protocols is highly non-trivial. In more technical details, the way [15] used the game in their analysis of soundness is reducing an inner product proof to a matrix multiplication proof (as an intermediate step for reducing an inner product proof to a shorter inner product proof), which is the opposite of Freivalds idea. It was not at all clear whether it could be modified to bound the soundness error the other way around.

1.3 Related Works

The recent improvement on Mystique through table-look-up techniques [11] achieves faster protocols but incurs much bigger memory. Besides, their protocols use the fixed-point based mathematical function evaluation and it was highlighted as an open question as to how to combine the floating-point technique with table-look-up. The framework is lack of floating point aided accuracy enhancing component and has limitations for accuracy sensitive application scenarios. More importantly, same as all existing zk-PoI frameworks, it is not tunable. Concurrent to the table-look-up modification [11] of Mystique, specialized zk-PoI's for large language model (LLM) called zkLLM [23] and zkGPT [21] were proposed. The zkLLM also relies on table-look-up techniques for efficiently proving the non-arithmetic functions while, on the other hand, it uses the zk-SNARK type of ZKP instead of the VOLE-based ZKP for achieving a smaller proof size. Since the zk-SNARK type of ZKP already requires larger memory consumption, combining with table-look-up techniques does not change the overall profiling. The main focus of zkLLM is to initiate the study of zk-PoI for LLM with practical size of parameters through exploiting excessive parallelization using CUDA and GPU acceleration. The recorded performance is proof generation in less than 15 minutes for LLMs with up to 13 billion parameters while keeping the proof size below 200 kB and the memory consumption under 23.1 GB. Followup work zkGPT [21] proposed several LLM-specific speedups for zk-SNARK type of ZKP (matrix multiplication) and the table-look-up techniques (non-arithmetic functions), which reduces proof generation to less than 25 seconds for GPT-2 while significantly increases memory consumption (evaluation done on hardware with 200 GB memory).

Another point of reference is the recently initiated study of zero-knowledge proof of training (zk-PoT) [1,10], where the computation tasks to be proved involves multiple iterations and each iteration can be even 100× more expensive than an inference. The state-of-the-art [1] in this paradigm combined the sum-check based efficient proof for matrix multiplication [25] and convolution [17] with the *recursive proof composition* techniques to achieve a proof size of 1.63 MB and a prover run time of 15 minutes per iteration for VGG-11 with 10 million parameters.

It is informative to compare the scalability of the state-of-the-art zk-PoI protocols with that of private inference (PI) (c.f. COINN [12], GForce [19], CryptGPU [24], BumbleBee [18], NEXUS [32]), where both the privacy of the trained model and the privacy of the user data sample must be protected at the same time. According to the recent update [7] proposing polynomial approximation of the ReLU and co-designing with a polynomial evaluation friendly MPC protocol, close to plaintext accuracy on models as deep as ResNet-110 and as large as a ResNet-50 on ImageNet (23 million parameters) can be achieved. ChatGPT-4 is estimated to have roughly 1.8 trillion parameters. The achievable size of parameters is far from the practical models and unlike the zk-PoI, the parties executing the PI protocol are assumed to be semi-honest, which means that they are assumed to exactly follow the protocol specification and never deviate from their expected execution.

2 Preliminaries

In cryptographic applications, real numbers must be encoded into a format compatible with integer-based cryptographic primitives. To address this, *fixed-point representation* is employed for encoding real numbers as integers. This approach involves allocating a fixed number of bits for the integer and fractional parts of the number. The total number of bits n is divided into n_I integer bits and n_f fractional bits, such that $n = n_I + n_f$, where the precision of the representation is determined by n_f. Specifically, a fixed-point number is represented as an integer I, such that:

$$x = I \cdot 2^{-n_f}.$$

To handle signed fixed-point numbers efficiently, *two's complement encoding* is employed. Two's complement is a standard method for encoding signed integers in binary form, where the most significant bit (MSB) serves as the sign bit: 0 for positive numbers and 1 for negative numbers. Two's complement encoding ensures that arithmetic operations such as addition and subtraction can be performed uniformly on both positive and negative numbers.

In this work, a real number x is encoded into $\mathbb{Z}_{2^k}$ with n_f-bit precision as follows: if $x \geq 0$, it is encoded as $I = \lfloor x \cdot 2^{n_f} \rfloor$; if $x < 0$, it is encoded as $I = 2^{k-1} + \lfloor x \cdot 2^{n_f} \rfloor$. This encoding scheme leverages the properties of two's complement and the structure of $\mathbb{Z}_{2^k}$, ensuring that both positive and negative numbers are represented consistently and efficiently.

In VOLE-based zero-knowledge proofs (ZKP), VOLE is used to commit to the prover's private inputs or intermediate values in the circuit. Specifically, each output of VOLE acts as an information-theoretic message authentication code (IT-MAC) [4,20] for some value x, represented as $M[x] = x \cdot \Delta_A + K[x]$, here the subscript $_A$ indicates that the committed value is arithmetic, as opposed to Boolean (indicated using subscript $_B$) . A value x committed using VOLE is referred to as an authenticated value. In this work, an authenticated value is denoted as $[x]_{2^k}$, where the subscript $_{2^k}$ indicates the modulus 2^k of the underlying algebraic structure.

When working over $\mathbb{Z}_{2^k}$, half of the elements in $\mathbb{Z}_{2^k}$ are zero-divisors, enabling a malicious prover to cheat as follows. The prover can set $x' = x + 2^{k-1}$, and if Δ_A is even, the prover can replace the authenticated value without being detected. Moz$\mathbb{Z}_{2^k}$arella [3] addresses this problem by performing authentication over a larger ring $\mathbb{Z}_{2^{k+s}}$, $s := \rho + \log \rho + 3$ for ρ-bit soundness, where an efficient protocol for generating this type of random VOLE was proposed.

In addition to authenticating values, VOLE-based ZKP proves multiplication using authenticated values by verifying that Δ_A is a root of some quadratic equation:

$$a\Delta_A^2 + b\Delta_A + c = 0 \bmod 2^k.$$

If $b = c = 0$ and $a = 2^{k-2}$, any even choice of Δ_A will vacuously satisfy the equation leading to soundness loss. Moz$\mathbb{Z}_{2^k}$arella [3] addresses this problem by performing authentication and computation over a larger ring. They propose a ZKP system named QuarkSilver and prove [3, Corollary 10] that, for a statistical security parameter $\rho \geq 7$, by setting $s := \rho + \log \rho + 3$ and $\ell := k + 2s$, choosing $\Delta_A \in \mathbb{Z}_{2^s}$, and performing operations over $\mathbb{Z}_{2^\ell}$, the success probability of a malicious prover is bounded by $2^{-\rho}$. We adopt their QuarkSilver $\Pi_{QS}^{2^k}$ as one of our base protocols for proving arithmetic operations.

For Boolean circuits, we use another VOLE-based ZKP system called Quick-Silver $\Pi_{ZK}^{p,r}$ [30], which works over any field $\mathbb{F}_p$. A single bit $b \in \{0,1\}$ is authenticated as:

$$M[b] = b \cdot \Delta_B + K[b],$$

where $M[b], K[b], \Delta_B \in \mathbb{F}_{2^\kappa}$. To authenticate bits of a value $x \in \mathbb{Z}_{2^k}$, we first decompose it into bits $x[0], \ldots, x[k-1] \in \{0,1\}$ such that $x = \sum_{i=0}^{k-1} x[i] \cdot 2^i$, and then authenticate each bit individually.

We denote authenticated bits of the value as $[x]_B = \{[x[0]]_2, \ldots, [x[k-1]]_2\}$, authenticated value as $[x]_A = [x]_{2^k}$ and refer to the two VOLE-based ZKP systems as $\Pi_{QS}^{2^k}$ and Π_{QS}^{2}, respectively. We explicitly specify the functionality for arithmetic circuit in Appendix A.1 and omit the Boolean circuit version.

We formerly define an (ℓ, ρ, λ)-zk-PoI in the Appendix A.2, which will be the main object of this work. The advantage of this modified notion of zk-PoI over conventional ones lies in that it made explicit the involvement of the discretization in the zk-PoI and facilitates a handle for fine-tuning of the discretization (through altering the bit-length ℓ) before each deployment to reach a desired accuracy loss[1]. One can imagine that before a new service is officially put on the market, several rounds of internal test-runs are conducted to find a sweet spot balancing the inference accuracy and the user experience (for instance proof generation time and verification cost).

3 Instantiating (ℓ, ρ, λ)-zk-PoI Protocols Using ZK Protocols over $\mathbb{Z}_{2^k}$

In this section, we provide details on how to instantiate the proposed framework over $\mathbb{Z}_{2^k}$.

3.1 Framework Overview

The architecture of our framework, as shown in Fig. 1, can be summarized into four layers. The bottom layer corresponds to the two base ZKP systems, which are designed to handle arithmetic and Boolean operations, respectively, reflecting the *mixed circuit* approach to efficient proving for machine learning tasks. The second layer is the conversion layer, which includes arithmetic-Boolean conversion and fixed-floating conversion. The third layer consists of the building blocks for machine learning, and the top layer is the application layer.

3.2 Conversions of Authenticated Values

Arithmetic-Boolean Conversion. Working over mixed circuits, conversions between arithmetic and Boolean circuits are essential. In the ZK setting, such conversions are equivalent to transforming between two types of authentication for the same value. To address this, Mystique introduces *zk-edaBits* [28], a randomized value authenticated over both arithmetic and Boolean circuits, enabling efficient conversions between the two representations. Appenzeller adopts an alternative approach by directly proving the consistency of two types of already authenticated values [2]. The original zk-edaBits was proposed for $\mathbb{F}_2$, but we adapt it for $\mathbb{Z}_{2^k}$, as detailed in Algorithm 1. With pre-generated zk-edaBits, we achieve efficient conversions between the two types of authenticated values. The conversion protocols are demonstrated in Algorithms 2 and 3. It's worth noting that, due to the use of $\mathbb{Z}_{2^k}$, in all three protocols, the addition circuit for authenticated bits automatically implements modular addition modulo 2^k, so no separate modulo reduction is needed.

[1] We note that ZEN [9] contains a quantization scheme that considers encoding (called stranded encoding) several copies of low precision integers into one finite field element, which in effect decouples the quantization precision from the proof soundness parameter (logarithmic of the field size). But this stranded encoding only works when quantization precision is much lower than soundness parameter.

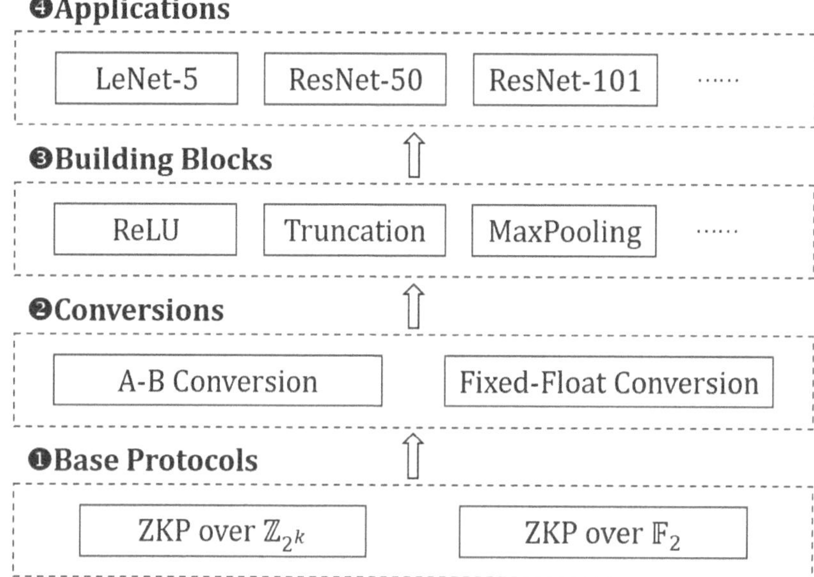

Fig. 1. Overview of our zk-PoI framework

Algorithm 1. Protocol $\Pi^{\mathbb{Z}_{2^k}}_{\text{zk-edaBits}}$

Assume parties have run `init` for both base ZKP protocols, and the verifier has obtained two global keys.

INPUTS: N: The number of random zk-edaBits to be generated; B, C: Parameters for the cut-and-choose procedure.

PROTOCOL EXECUTION: Prover $\mathcal{P}$ and verifier $\mathcal{V}$ generate n random zk-edaBits as follows:

Step One. Generate $nb + c$ random zk-edaBits:

1. Generate $nb + c$ random authenticated values $[r_i]_A$ for $i \in [1, nb + c]$ by invoking $\Pi^{2^k}_{QS}$. $\mathcal{P}$ decomposes r_i into $\{r_i[0], \ldots, r_i[\ell - 1]\}$ such that $r_i = \sum_{j=0}^{\ell-1} r_i[j] \cdot 2^j \bmod \mathbb{Z}_{2^\ell}$.
2. For $i \in [1, nb + c]$, generate $[r_i]_B$ by invoking Π^2_{QS}.

Step Two. Verify the correctness of the generated zk-edaBits and output n valid ones:

1. Place the first n zk-edaBits into n individual buckets.
2. $\mathcal{V}$ generates a random permutation π and sends it to $\mathcal{P}$. Shuffle the remaining $(n - 1)b + c$ zk-edaBits.
3. Open and verify the correctness of the last c zk-edaBits. If any are invalid, abort.
4. Divide the remaining $(n - 1)b$ zk-edaBits into n groups and assign each group to a bucket, ensuring each bucket contains exactly b zk-edaBits.
5. For each bucket, verify the first zk-edabit using the others in the bucket. Let $([r]_A, [r]_B)$ denote the first and $([s]_A, [s]_B)$ the rest:
   5.1. Locally compute $[t]_A = [r]_A + [s]_A$. Execute an addition circuit to obtain $[t]_B = \text{Adder}([r]_B, [s]_B)$ by invoking Π^2_{QS}.
   5.2. Open and check if $t = \sum_{j=0}^{\ell-1} t[j] \cdot 2^j \bmod \mathbb{Z}_{2^\ell}$. If not, abort.
6. Output the first zk-edabit from each bucket if no abort occurs.

Fixed-Floating Conversion. For values represented in fixed-point form, most operations can be handled efficiently using arithmetic-Boolean conversion. However, the precision of fixed-point representation may not always suffice for certain computations, even when implemented in Boolean circuits. This limitation arises because fixed-point values are effectively represented as integers in Boolean circuits, which inherently restricts their precision.

Algorithm 2. Protocol $\Pi^{\mathbb{Z}_{2^k}}_{\text{A2B}}$

Assume parties have run $\Pi^{\mathbb{Z}_{2^k}}_{\text{zk-edaBits}}$ and obtained a batch of zk-edaBits.
INPUTS: Parties hold an authenticated value $[x]_A$.
PROTOCOL EXECUTION: Prover $\mathcal{P}$ and verifier $\mathcal{V}$ convert $[x]_A$ to $[x]_B$ as follows:

1. Select an unused zk-edabit $([r]_A, [r]_B)$.
2. Locally compute $[t]_A = [x]_A + [r]_A$ and open it to obtain t.
3. Decompose t into $\{t[0], \ldots, t[\ell-1]\}$ such that $t = \sum_{j=0}^{\ell-1} t[j] \cdot 2^j \bmod \mathbb{Z}_{2^\ell}$.
4. Execute an addition circuit to compute $[x]_B = \text{Adder}([r]_B, t[0], \ldots, t[\ell-1])$ by invoking Π^2_{QS}.

Algorithm 3. Protocol $\Pi^{\mathbb{Z}_{2^k}}_{\text{B2A}}$

Assume parties have run $\Pi^{\mathbb{Z}_{2^k}}_{\text{zk-edaBits}}$ and obtained a batch of zk-edaBits.
INPUTS: Parties hold an authenticated value $[x]_2$.
PROTOCOL EXECUTION: Prover $\mathcal{P}$ and verifier $\mathcal{V}$ convert $[x]_B$ to $[x]_A$ as follows:

1. Select an unused zk-edabit $([r]_A, [r]_B)$.
2. Execute an addition circuit to compute $[t]_B = \text{Adder}([r]_B, [x]_B)$ by invoking Π^2_{QS}.
3. Open $[t]_2$ to obtain bits $\{t[0], \ldots, t[\ell-1]\}$, and compose them to get $t = \sum_{j=0}^{\ell-1} t[j] \cdot 2^j \bmod \mathbb{Z}_{2^\ell}$.
4. Compute $[x]_A = t - [r]_A$.

A potential solution to this issue is to convert the authenticated bits from fixed-point representation to floating-point representation, enabling operations to be performed under Boolean circuits designed for floating-point arithmetic. In floating-point representation, the bits are divided into distinct components: for instance, the IEEE-754 single-precision standard uses 32 bits in total, with 1 bit for the sign, 8 bits for the exponent, and 23 bits for the mantissa. We leverage the single-precision floating-point Boolean circuits provided in EMP [27], which adhere to the IEEE-754 standard. Using $[x]_F$ to denote the authenticated bits of a floating-point value, the detailed conversion protocols are outlined in Algorithm 4 and Algorithm 5, respectively.

3.3 Building Blocks for Machine Learning

With the two base ZKP protocols in the bottom layer of our framework and the two conversion mechanisms built on top of them, we can now build building blocks for machine learning inference applications. Arithmetic operations, such as linear layers in neural networks, can be directly handled using authenticated values $[x]_A$ operating on arithmetic circuits. For more complex non-arithmetic operations we can leverage authenticated bits in either fixed-point or floating-point representation. The former offers higher efficiency, while the latter provides greater precision. In this section, we focus on how to implement building blocks for non-arithmetic operations, as these pose unique challenges and opportunities for optimization.

Algorithm 4. Protocol $\Pi^{\mathbb{Z}_{2^k}}_{\text{Fx2Fp}}$ (Conversion from Fixed-Point to Floating-Point)

INPUTS: Authenticated bits of a fixed-point value $[x]_B$ with precision n_f.
PROTOCOL EXECUTION: Parties convert authenticated bits to a floating-point representation $[x]_F$ as follows:

1. Compute the absolute value of x: $[|x|]_B = \text{Abs}([x]_B)$.
2. Determine the index of first non-zero bit of $|x|$: $[\text{FOI}]_B = k - 1 - \text{LeadingZeros}([|x|]_B)$.
3. Compute the shift offset: $[\text{sft}]_B = \text{If}([\text{FOI}]_B \geq 23, [\text{FOI}]_B - 23, 23 - [\text{FOI}]_B)$.
4. Shift the value to align the MSB with the mantissa: $[x_{\text{sft}}]_B = \text{If}([\text{FOI}]_B \geq 23, [|x|]_B \gg [\text{sft}]_B, [|x|]_B \ll [\text{sft}]_B)$.
5. Compute the exponent: $[\text{exp}]_B = [\text{FOI}]_B + 127 - n_f$.
6. Construct the floating-point representation: $[x]_F = \text{Concat}([x]_B.\text{MSB}, [\text{exp}]_B, [x_{\text{sft}}]_B)$.

Algorithm 5. Protocol $\Pi^{\mathbb{Z}_{2^k}}_{\text{Fp2Fx}}$ (Conversion from Floating-Point to Fixed-Point)

INPUTS: Authenticated bits of a floating-point representation $[x]_F$.
PROTOCOL EXECUTION: Parties convert authenticated bits to fixed-point representation $[x]_B$ with precision n_f as follows:

1. Extract the sign, exponent, and mantissa from $[x]_F$: $[\text{sign}]_2, [\text{exp}]_B, [\text{mts}]_B = \text{Decompose}([x]_F)$.
2. Reconstruct the mantissa with the implicit leading 1: $[\text{mts}]_B = [\text{mts}]_B \mid (1 \ll 23)$.
3. Compute the actual exponent: $[\text{exp}_{\text{act}}]_B = [\text{exp}]_B - 127$.
4. Compute the shift offset: $[\text{sft}]_B = [\text{exp}_{\text{act}}]_B - 23 + n_f$.
5. Shift the mantissa to align with the fixed-point representation: $[x_{\text{sft}}]_B = \text{If}([\text{sft}]_B \geq 0, [\text{mts}]_B \ll [\text{sft}]_B, [\text{mts}]_B \gg -[\text{sft}]_B)$.
6. Handle underflow: $[x_{\text{sft}}]_B = \text{If}([\text{sft}]_B \leq -k, 0, [x_{\text{sft}}]_B)$.
7. Apply the sign: $[x]_B = \text{If}([\text{sign}]_2, -[x_{\text{sft}}]_B, [x_{\text{sft}}]_B)$.

A general approach to handling non-arithmetic operations with high precision involves the following steps: (1) use $\Pi_{\mathrm{A2B}}^{\mathbb{Z}_{2^k}}$ to transform authenticated values into authenticated bits in fixed-point representation; (2) use $\Pi_{\mathrm{Fx2Fp}}^{\mathbb{Z}_{2^k}}$ to transform the authenticated bits into floating-point representation; (3) perform the operation using floating-point circuits; (4) use $\Pi_{\mathrm{Fp2Fx}}^{\mathbb{Z}_{2^k}}$ to transform the result back into fixed-point representation; and (5) finally, convert the fixed-point authenticated bits back into authenticated values using $\Pi_{\mathrm{B2A}}^{\mathbb{Z}_{2^k}}$. Mystique employ this strategy for almost all non-arithmetic operations. We construct our building blocks mainly following this paradigm but with some optimizations. Due to space constraints, we present only the most representative building blocks in this work.

Avoiding Vacuous Floating-Point Conversion. Through analysis, we identified that certain operations can be performed directly in fixed-point representation without precision loss, eliminating the need for conversion to floating-point representation.

Algorithm 6. Protocol $\Pi_{\mathrm{Trunc}}^{\mathbb{Z}_{2^k}}$

INPUTS: An authenticated fixed-point value $[x]_A$ with precision n_f.
PROTOCOL EXECUTION: Parties compute authenticated truncated value $[y]_A$ as follows:

1. Convert $[x]_A$ to its Boolean representation $[x]_B$ using $\Pi_{\mathrm{A2B}}^{\mathbb{Z}_{2^k}}$.
2. Perform an arithmetic right shift on $[x]_B$:
   2.1. $[x_{\mathrm{sft}}]_B = [x]_B \gg n_f$.
   2.2. $[y]_B = \mathrm{Resize}([x_{\mathrm{sft}}]_B, \mathrm{Size}())$
3. Convert the truncated Boolean representation $[y]_B$ back to a fixed-point value $[y]_A$ using $\Pi_{\mathrm{B2A}}^{\mathbb{Z}_{2^k}}$.

Truncation is a critical operation in fixed-point arithmetic. After multiplication, the fixed-point precision doubles, and truncation is required to maintain consistent precision and avoid overflow. By definition, truncation discards the least significant n_f bits while preserving the higher-order bits, including the sign bit for signed numbers. This operation can be fully carried out in the fixed-point domain without any loss, as it simply involves an arithmetic right shift by n_f bits: the least significant n_f bits are dropped, and the sign bit is extended accordingly. The result preserves the intended fixed-point value exactly and can be implemented directly in Boolean circuits. The details of this process are outlined in Algorithm 6.

Additionally, for operations that inherently require floating-point precision, certain intermediate steps can still be executed in fixed-point representation to minimize overhead. For instance, in the **Softmax** function, given a vector

$\mathbf{x} = (x_1, \ldots, x_n)$, the output $\mathbf{y} = (y_1, \ldots, y_n)$ is computed as:

$$y_i = \frac{e^{x_i - x_{\max}}}{\sum_{j=1}^{n} e^{x_j - x_{\max}}}.$$

While e^x must be computed in floating-point representation for precision, the selection of the maximum value $x_{\max}$ can be performed in fixed-point representation. This is because the core operation of finding the maximum involves comparison, which incurs no precision loss. Furthermore, comparison using a Boolean circuit for fixed-point representation is simpler and more efficient than for floating-point representation.

Directly Extract Sign-Bit. Another optimization leverages the advantages of $\mathbb{Z}_{2^k}$. Many non-arithmetic operations require determining the sign of a value. For fields $\mathbb{F}_p$, extracting the sign relies on a comparison circuit. However, in $\mathbb{Z}_{2^k}$, we can directly extract the sign by taking the most significant bit (MSB), as fixed-point values are encoded using two's complement representation.

ReLU is a widely used activation function in neural networks, defined as $\text{ReLU}(x) = \max(0, x)$. The core operation of ReLU involves extracting the sign of the input value, which can be efficiently performed in $\mathbb{Z}_{2^k}$ by leveraging the MSB. The details of this process are outlined in Algorithm 7.

Algorithm 7. Protocol $\Pi_{\text{ReLU}}^{\mathbb{Z}_{2^k}}$

INPUTS: An authenticated fixed-point value $[x]_A$.
PROTOCOL EXECUTION: Parties compute authenticated value $[y]_A$ where $y = \text{ReLU}(x)$ as follows:

1. Convert $[x]_A$ to its Boolean representation $[x]_B$ using $\Pi_{\text{A2B}}^{\mathbb{Z}_{2^k}}$.
2. Compute the ReLU: $[y]_B = \text{If}([x]_B.\text{MSB}, 0, [x]_B)$.
3. Convert the resulting Boolean representation $[y]_B$ back to a fixed-point value $[y]_A$ using $\Pi_{\text{B2A}}^{\mathbb{Z}_{2^k}}$.

Optimizing Selection Operations. In addition to sign extraction, ReLU involves another operation: selection, which chooses one of two options based on a given bit. Selection is a common operation that appears in many building blocks. In some cases, the selection logic can become complex, leading to multiple selection operations. However, these operations can often be merged and optimized through pre-analysis.

Max is a widely used operation in machine learning applications, as seen in Softmax. The max function computes the element-wise maximum of two values x and y, defined as $\max(x, y)$. A direct approach to compute max involves: (1) if x and y have the same sign, select the larger value; (2) if x and y have different signs, select the positive value. In two's complement representation, selecting the positive value when the signs differ is equivalent to selecting the smaller value. This allows us to simplify the logic into a single selection operation using an free XOR gate. Specifically, we consider two bits: (1) whether x and y have the same sign, and (2) whether $x \geq y$. If both bits are true or both are false, we choose x; otherwise, we choose y.

By leveraging this observation and the properties of $\mathbb{Z}_{2^k}$, we significantly optimize the computation by reducing the number of comparison circuits and selection circuits to just one each. In contrast, Mystique [28] requires three comparison circuits (two of which are used to determine signs due to its $\mathbb{F}_p$ setting) and three selection circuits. The detailed steps for computing the max function are outlined in Algorithm 8.

Algorithm 8. Protocol $\Pi_{\text{Max}}^{\mathbb{Z}_{2^k}}$

INPUTS: Two authenticated fixed-point values $[x]_A$ and $[y]_A$.

PROTOCOL EXECUTION: Parties compute authenticated value $[z]_A$ where $z = \max(x, y)$.

1. Convert $[x]_A$ and $[y]_A$ to their Boolean representations $[x]_B$ and $[y]_B$ using $\Pi_{\text{A2B}}^{\mathbb{Z}_{2^k}}$.
2. Compute the max operation on $[x]_B$ and $[y]_B$:
   2.1. Compute $\text{sign}_{\text{xor}} = [x]_B.\text{MSB} \oplus [y]_B.\text{MSB}$.
   2.2. Compute $\text{cmp} = [x]_B \geq [y]_B$.
   2.3. Compute $[z]_B = \text{If}(\text{sign}_{\text{xor}} \oplus \text{cmp}, [y]_B, [x]_B)$
3. Convert the resulting Boolean representation $[z]_B$ back to a fixed-point value $[z]_A$ using $\Pi_{\text{B2A}}^{\mathbb{Z}_{2^k}}$.

4 Matrix Multiplication Protocols over $\mathbb{Z}_{2^k}$ with Faster Proving Than Computing

Compared to the Galois rings approach, the SPDZ2k [5] trick is much more efficient both in terms of computation and representing ring elements: it only requires working over the ring $\mathbb{Z}_{2^{k+s}}$ where s is roughly the statistical security parameter, which for $k > s$ is at most twice the size as $\mathbb{Z}_{2^k}$ and it allows fine-tuning of k and s independently (whereas the element size of a Galois ring offering the same level of statistical security would be ks), and furthermore computing over this ring is quite efficient as it is simple arithmetic modulo a power of two (instead of large-degree polynomials over these rings). Unfortunately, the SPDZ2k [5] trick is far less flexible and way less algebraically elegant than using Galois rings. It is only useful for enabling low-degree version of Schwartz-Zippel lemma [3,5] and it does not enable things like polynomial interpolation or higher degree Schwartz-Zippel. Unfortunately, these properties are essential in the design of all existing efficient protocols for proving the linear layer computation in machine learning that boost faster proving than computing the matrix product or convolution itself [17,25]. It remains an interesting open question whether one can extend these powerful sum-check protocols to work efficiently over the ring $\mathbb{Z}_{2^k}$. We now derive a $\mathbb{Z}_{2^k}$ version of the Freivalds matrix multiplication that has faster proving than computing the product.

4.1 Protocol Description

Mystique generalized the Freivald's algorithm to a ZK protocol for $n \times n$ matrix multiplication over a finite field $\mathbb{F}_p$ (for any prime $p \geq 2$ using VOLE-based ZK protocols. The protocol only needs to prove n private multiplications rather than n^3 using a naive algorithm. We further generalize this protocol to work for matrices over $\mathbb{Z}_{2^k}$.

The idea of Freivalds algorithm in Mystique [28] is that instead of verifying $\mathbf{A} \cdot \mathbf{B} = \mathbf{C}$, one verifies

$$\left(\mathbf{u}^\top \cdot \mathbf{A}\right) \cdot (\mathbf{B} \cdot \mathbf{v}) = \mathbf{u}^\top \cdot \mathbf{C} \cdot \mathbf{v}$$

for random vectors $\mathbf{u}, \mathbf{v}$ over a finite field. It is easy to see that soundness is preserved while the new relation for verification becomes an inner product relation, a much easier relation. Now suppose that we sample random vectors $\mathbf{u}, \mathbf{v}$ over $\mathbb{Z}_{2^k}$ and verify the inner product modulo 2^k. This does not seem to work the same way as with finite fields. Let us consider an extreme case of $n = 1$ and do a sanity check. The equality $uabv = ucv$ holds vacuously if $uv \equiv 0 \mod 2^k$, which happens with considerable probability, since, unlike finite fields, the ring $\mathbb{Z}_{2^k}$ contains many zero-divisors. Jumping ahead, using Lemma 1 and an argument concerning the tightness of the bound in [15], one can show that the soundness degrades to $\frac{1}{2}$. In order to preserve the soundness while working over this type of ring, we adapt the SPDZ2k [5] technique and conduct the reduction from matrix product verification to inner product verification over a larger ring $\mathbb{Z}_{2^{k+s}}$ instead, where s can be determined according to the desired soundness. In order to analyze the minimum size of s required in our reduction, we adapt a highly non-trivial soundness analysis proposed in [15], where a sophisticated security analysis game was proposed for analyzing an iterative reduction from an inner product verification to a shorter inner product verification.

After our reduction, the resulting inner product relation can be efficiently proved using the VOLE-based ZK protocol for low degree polynomials proposed in [30]. The idea is to have both the prover and the verifier substitute the secret values and their corresponding individual keys, respectively, into the verification relation and find out the difference as a univariate polynomial in the global key Δ. More precisely, recall that in a MAC relation, the prover holds the secret value x and its MAC $M[x]$ while the verifier holds a global key Δ and an individual key $K[x]$ satisfying $K[x] = x\Delta + M[x]$. Substituting the verifier's individual keys into the degre-d verification relation yields a degree-d univariate polynomial in Δ where secret values may appear in the coefficients of different degrees, which renders it difficult for comparing with substituting the prover's secret values into the same verification relation. A modification was proposed to align these secret values by having the verifier substitute the individual keys into the degre-d verification relation term-by-term and when the term has degree $i < d$, multiply Δ^{d-i}

so that the corresponding secret values always appear in the coefficient of Δ^d. Now if substituting the prover's secret values into the verification relation yields 0, then substituting the verifier's corresponding individual keys into the verifica-

Algorithm 9. Protocol $\Pi_{\text{MatMul}}^{\mathbb{Z}_{2^k}}$

INPUTS: A prover $\mathcal{P}$ and a verifier $\mathcal{V}$ have three authenticated matrices $[\mathbf{A}]_{2^k}$, $[\mathbf{B}]_{2^k}$ and $[\mathbf{C}]_{2^k}$, where $\mathbf{A} \in \mathbb{Z}_{2^k}^{m \times n}$, $\mathbf{B} \in \mathbb{Z}_{2^k}^{n \times r}$ and $\mathbf{C} \in \mathbb{Z}_{2^k}^{m \times r}$.
PROTOCOL EXECUTION: $\mathcal{P}$ proves in zero-knowledge that $\mathbf{A} \cdot \mathbf{B} = \mathbf{C}$ holds by interacting with $\mathcal{V}$ as follows:
Step One. Reduction from matrix multiplication to inner product.
1.1. $\mathcal{V}$ samples $\mathbf{u} \leftarrow \mathbb{Z}_{2^{k+s}}^m$, $\mathbf{v} \leftarrow \mathbb{Z}_{2^{k+s}}^r$, and then sends them to $\mathcal{P}$.
1.2. $\mathcal{P}$ and $\mathcal{V}$ locally compute authenticated vectors

$$[\mathbf{x}]^\top := \mathbf{u}^\top \cdot [\mathbf{A}], \ [\mathbf{y}] := [\mathbf{B}] \cdot \mathbf{v}$$

and authenticated value

$$[z] := \mathbf{u}^\top \cdot [\mathbf{C}] \cdot \mathbf{v},$$

where the secret values of $\mathcal{P}$ are computed modulo 2^{k+s}.

Step Two. VOLE-based ZK protocol for degree-2 polynomials.
Recall that $[\mathbf{x}]_{2^{k+s}}, [\mathbf{y}]_{2^{k+s}}, [z]_{2^{k+s}}$ denote that $\mathcal{P}$ holds secret values over $\mathbb{Z}_{2^{k+s}}$

$$\mathbf{x} = (x_1, \ldots, x_n), \mathbf{y} = (y_1, \ldots, y_n), z$$

and their MAC's over $\mathbb{Z}_{2^{k+s+2s'}}$, where $s' = \rho + \log \rho + 3$

$$M[\mathbf{x}] = (M[x_1], \ldots, M[x_n]), M[\mathbf{y}] = (M[y_1], \ldots, M[y_n]), M[z],$$

while $\mathcal{V}$ holds the global key $\Delta \leftarrow \mathbb{Z}_{2^{s'}}$ and individual keys

$$K[\mathbf{x}] = (K[x_1], \ldots, K[x_n]), K[\mathbf{y}] = (K[y_1], \ldots, K[y_n]), K[z],$$

satisfying

$$(K[\mathbf{x}]||K[\mathbf{y}]||K[z]) = (\mathbf{x}||\mathbf{y}||z)\, \Delta + (M[\mathbf{x}]||M[\mathbf{y}]||M[z]) \,.$$

2.1. $\mathcal{P}$ and $\mathcal{V}$ locally compute a VOLE correlation that accounts for the difference between verifying the inner product relation using secret values and using the corresponding individual keys. $\mathcal{V}$ retains the global key Δ and computes a new individual key

$$K = K[\mathbf{x}]^\top \cdot K[\mathbf{y}] + K[z]\Delta.$$

$\mathcal{P}$ computes

$$e = \sum_{i=1}^{n} M[x_i]M[y_i] \sum_{i=1}^{n} (M[x_i] - x_i)(M[y_i] - y_i) - (M[z] - z)$$

and sets $M[e] = \sum_{i=1}^{n} M[x_i]M[y_i]$.
2.2. $\mathcal{P}$ sends (Input, e) to $\mathcal{F}_{\text{authZK}}$ so that $\mathcal{P}$ and $\mathcal{V}$ have authenticated value $[e]$.
2.3. $\mathcal{P}$ and $\mathcal{V}$ locally compute the authenticated difference $[d]$ between the authenticated value $[e]$ and the authenticated error correction term computed in 2.2. $\mathcal{P}$ and $\mathcal{V}$ send (Output, $[d]$) to $\mathcal{F}_{\text{authZK}}$. If the check fails or a non-zero value is output to $\mathcal{V}$, $\mathcal{V}$ outputs false and aborts; otherwise, it outputs true.

tion relation with the above twist should yield a univariate polynomial $D(\Delta)$ in Δ of degree less than d, whose coefficients are consist of secret values and their MAC's, hence locally computable by the prover. If the prover has an efficient protocol to convince the verifier in zero-knowledge that the verifier's global key Δ, the new individual key K obtained by substituting the verifier's individual keys into the verification relation with the above twist, together with the prover's coefficients of $D(\Delta)$ (as a polynomial in Δ) satisfy the relation $D(\Delta) = K$, then the prover's secret values satisfy the verification relation with a soundness error that can be bounded using Schwartz-Zippel lemma. Adapting this technique to work over the ring $\mathbb{Z}_{2^{k+s}}$ for general polynomials suffers from efficiency loss due to the low quality of the Schwartz-Zippel lemma over such rings. Fortunately, the inner product relation is of degree two, same as verification of multiplication (Mult functionality) and we can recycle the Schwartz-Zippel lemma for degree two polynomial proved in [3]. The protocol is given in Algorithm 9.

4.2 Security Analysis

We will need the following security analysis game defined in [15].

$\mathcal{G}\mathrm{ame}(\mathbf{k}, \mathbf{s}, \mathbf{T})$. Consider an interactive game between an adversary $\mathcal{A}_g$ and a challenger $\mathcal{C}_g$. For all $x \in \mathbb{Z}_{2^{k+s}}$ and $x \neq 0$, we define $\mathrm{Po2}(x)$ to be the number of 2-factors in x, i.e., the largest integer u such that 2^u divides x, and $\mathrm{Po2}(x) := k+s$ if $x = 0$. Given the number of interactive rounds T, the game works as follows.

1. $\mathcal{A}_g$ and $\mathcal{C}_g$ initially have $E_0 = k - 1$.
2. In each round $i (1 \leq i \leq T)$, $\mathcal{A}_g$ and $\mathcal{C}_g$ repeat the following:
   (a) $\mathcal{A}_g$ chooses arbitrary $e_i, c_i \in \mathbb{Z}_{2^{k+s}}$ under the requirement that $\mathrm{Po2}(e_i) \leq E_{i-1}$, and sends the two values to $\mathcal{C}_g$.
   (b) $\mathcal{C}_g$ picks a uniformly random value $r_i \in \mathbb{Z}_{2^{k+s}}$ and responds r_i to $\mathcal{A}_g$.
   (c) $\mathcal{A}_g$ and $\mathcal{C}_g$ compute $E_i = \mathrm{Po2}(r_i \cdot e_i + c_i)$.
3. $\mathcal{A}_g$ wins if and only if in the last round T, $E_T = k + s$.

Lemma 1. *[15] Let k, s, T be positive integers. For any adversary $\mathcal{A}_g$, the probability that $\mathcal{A}_g$ wins $\mathcal{G}ame(k, s, T)$ is at most*

$$\sum_{j=0}^{T-1} \binom{s+j}{s} \cdot \frac{1}{2^{s+1+j}}.$$

In particular, when $s = \rho + T\left(\frac{1}{2} + \log\left(\frac{5}{2} + \frac{3\rho}{T}\right)\right)$ and assume that $T \leq \rho$ and $3T \leq s$, the winning probability of $\mathcal{A}_g$ is at most $2^{-\rho}$.

Theorem 1. *Assume that ρ is the security parameter. When $s = \rho + 1 + 2\log\left(\frac{5}{2} + \frac{3\rho}{2}\right)$, and $s' = \sigma + \log\sigma + 3$ then protocol $\Pi_{\mathrm{MatMul}}^{\mathbb{Z}_{2^k}}$ achieves soundness error $2^{-\rho}$.*

Proof. In the first part of the proof, we show the reduction from the malicious prover $\mathcal{A}$ in the protocol $\Pi_{\text{MatMul}}^{\mathbb{Z}_{2^k}}$ to $\mathcal{A}_g$ in $\mathcal{G}\text{ame}(k,s,T)$. Assume that $\mathbf{A} \cdot \mathbf{B} \neq \mathbf{C}$ in the protocol. Then at least for one of the entries (i^*, j^*), we have

$$(\mathbf{A} \cdot \mathbf{B})_{(i^*,j^*)} - \mathbf{C}_{(i^*,j^*)} \equiv \epsilon_{(i^*,j^*)} \mod 2^k$$

satisfying $\text{Po2}(\epsilon_{(i^*,j^*)}) \leq k - 1 = E_0$. Note that the additive error $\epsilon = \mathbf{x}^\top \cdot \mathbf{y} - z$ in 2.2 can be computed as $\epsilon = \sum_{j=1}^{r} v_j \left(\sum_{i=1}^{m} u_i \epsilon_{(i,j)}\right)$. Let us write $\epsilon_j = \sum_{i=1}^{m} u_i \epsilon_{(i,j)}$. Then we have $\epsilon = \sum_{j=1}^{r} v_j \epsilon_j$. Now observe that

$$\epsilon_{j^*} = \sum_{i=1}^{m} u_i \epsilon_{(i,j^*)} = u_{i^*} \epsilon_{(i^*,j^*)} + \sum_{i \neq j^*}^{m} u_i \epsilon_{(i,j^*)}.$$

We can let $\mathcal{A}_g$ pick $c_1 = \sum_{i \neq j^*}^{m} u_i \epsilon_{(i,j^*)}$ in the first round of the game $\mathcal{G}\text{ame}(k,s,T)$. Since u_{i^*} is uniform, we interpret it as the first challenge r_1 that $\mathcal{C}_g$ samples, that is $r_1 = u_{j^*}$. Then we have defined the first round of the game $\mathcal{G}\text{ame}(k,s,T)$, where the $e_1 = \epsilon_{(i^*,j^*)}$ does satisfy the condition $\text{Po2}(\epsilon_{(i^*,j^*)}) \leq k - 1 = E_0$. We then have $E_1 = \text{Po2}(r_1 e_1 + c_1) = \text{Po2}(\epsilon_{j^*})$ according to (2.c) step of the game. Next we invoke the equality

$$\epsilon = \sum_{j=1}^{r} v_j \epsilon_j = v_{j^*} \epsilon_{j^*} + \sum_{j \neq j^*}^{r} v_j \epsilon_j$$

and let $\mathcal{A}_g$ pick $c_2 = \sum_{j \neq j^*}^{r} v_j \epsilon_j$, $e_2 = \epsilon_{j^*}$, where $\text{Po2}(\epsilon_{j^*}) \leq E_1$ by the definition of E_1 a few lines ago. Similarly, the uniform v_{j^*} can be interpreted as the challenge r_2 that $\mathcal{C}_g$ samples, that is $r_2 = v_{j^*}$. Then we have defined the second round of the game $\mathcal{G}\text{ame}(k,s,T)$ and obtained $E_2 = \text{Po2}(r_2 e_2 + c_2) = \text{Po2}(\epsilon)$ according to (2.c) step of the game.

The second part of the proof follows trivially from the Schwartz-Zippel lemma for degree two polynomial proved in [3, Theorem 10, Corollary 13].

4.3 Complexity Analysis

Consider the multiplication of two $n \times n$ matrices A and B. Naively expressing the computation of the product of A and B as a circuit of $O(n^3)$ gates and applying the VOLE-based ZK protocol yields a protocol with $O(n^3)$ time proof generation and $O(n^3)$ communication. The Freivald's algorithm allows the prover to generate the proof in $O(n^2)$ time (two matrix-vector multiplications and computing the value e in step 2.1). The communication complexity is also reduced to $O(n^2)$ (sending the authenticated matrices A, B, C and the authenticated value e). Provided that there is no known $O(n^2)$-time algorithm that finds the product of matrices A and B, this protocol achieves faster proving than computing.

5 Experiments

In this section, we report the performance of our zk-PoI framework and compare it with Mystique. Our framework is implemented on top of the EMP-toolkit in

C++. The two base ZKP systems we use are QuickSilver (for Boolean circuits) and QuarkSilver (for arithmetic circuits). While QuickSilver is already implemented within the EMP-toolkit, QuarkSilver, originally implemented in Rust, was reimplemented by us in C++ to ensure compatibility with the EMP-toolkit. On top of these base protocols, we implemented the conversion protocols proposed in this work, followed by the building blocks and three neural network applications: Lenet-5, ResNet-50, and ResNet-101, which were also tested in Mystique for fair comparison.

Our implementation achieves computational security parameters $\lambda = 128$ and a static statistical security parameter $\sigma \approx 40$, consistent with prior works. To ensure a fair comparison with Mystique, we set $k = 64$ and fixed-point precision $n_f = 16$, simulating a similar experimental setup to Mystique's use of a 61-bit Mersenne prime $p = 2^{61} - 1$ with the same fixed-point precision (the low-level code is running over $\mathbb{Z}_{2^{192}}$ hence denoted Ours-192).

All experiments were conducted on a Supermicro SYS-7049GP-TRT server equipped with two Intel(R) Xeon(R) Gold 5220R CPUs (2.20 GHz, 24 cores per processor, hyper-threading) and 128 GB of RAM, using a single thread. We simulated different network environments by varying bandwidths, including 200Mbps, 500Mbps, and 1Gbps.

Table 1. Comparison of our basic protocols over $\mathbb{Z}_{2^{128}}$, $\mathbb{Z}_{2^{192}}$, $\mathbb{Z}_{2^{256}}$ covering a wide range of (ℓ, σ) satisfying $\ell + 2(\sigma + \log \sigma + 3) \leq c$, $c = 128, 192, 256$. Runtime is measured in seconds (s) under bandwidths 1Gbps, communication in megabytes (MB), and memory usage in gigabytes (GB).

	Runtime (s)			Comm. (MB)			Mem. (GB)		
	128	192	256	128	192	256	128	192	256
LeNet-5	25.33	34.83	36.38	59.96	79.96	93.34	5.37	7.05	7.56
ResNet-50	287.84	432.54	477.17	10016.28	12597.34	15108.72	6.37	8.38	9.03
ResNet-101	426.45	684.60	778.29	16112.39	20868.28	25525.47	6.51	8.62	9.37

5.1 Evidence of Tunability

We implement our basic protocols (without the optimization of Freivald's matrix multiplication) over $\mathbb{Z}_{2^{128}}$, $\mathbb{Z}_{2^{192}}$, $\mathbb{Z}_{2^{256}}$ covering a wide range of (ℓ, σ) satisfying $\ell + 2(\sigma + \log \sigma + 3) \leq c$, $c = 128, 192, 256$. For example, the ring $\mathbb{Z}_{2^{128}}$ accommodates parameter settings ranging from $(\ell, \sigma) = (48, 32)$ to $(\ell, \sigma) = (30, 40)$, with the soundness parameter σ goes from 32 to 40. These parameter settings have the same efficiency (Runtime, Comm. and Mem.) due to the fact that the low-level codes implementing them run in the same ring $\mathbb{Z}_{2^{128}}$. Here the higher soundness region with σ approaching 40 with bit-length ℓ around 30 renders us with choices of fixed-point number scale smaller than recommended in [22]. This is not an issue because of the floating-point number aided precision enhancing component described in 3.2.2. Switching complicated computations to floating-point number before converting back to fixed-point number can easily tolerate several bits of precision loss.

Table 1 shows the graceful degradation of performance as the low-level coding domain goes from $\mathbb{Z}_{2^{128}}$ to $\mathbb{Z}_{2^{192}}$ and then to $\mathbb{Z}_{2^{256}}$, supporting increasingly wider range of (ℓ, σ). We leave out the matrix multiplication optimization in the first part of benchmarking so that we can contrast these performance against the optimized protocols in the second part, where we conduct an apple-to-apple comparison between our framework over $\mathbb{Z}_{2^{192}}$ and Mystique over 61-bit Mersenne prime number field.

5.2 Comparison with Mystique

Base Protocols. With the parameters setting, our framework actually performs arithmetic operations over $\mathbb{Z}_{2^{128}}$, $\mathbb{Z}_{2^{192}}$, $\mathbb{Z}_{2^{256}}$ which, due to the larger size and lack of hardware-level optimizations, inherently incurs higher computational overhead compared to Mystique's atomic arithmetic operations that operate over a 61-bit Mersenne prime $2^{61}-1$. To quantify this overhead, we conducted a focused comparison of the arithmetic components of both frameworks, implemented in the same programming language, on the same hardware, and under identical network conditions. We tested the proof of 1000 multiplications and recorded the total time cost, communication, and memory usage.

Table 2. Comparison of conversions. Runtime is measured in microseconds (μs) and memory usage in gigabytes (GB).

	Runtime						Mem.	
	200 Mbps		500Mbps		1Gbps			
	Ours	[28]	Ours	[28]	Ours	[28]	Ours	[28]
A2B	45.19	46.73	41.87	44.09	26.32	36.31	6.98	5.71
B2A	49.90	50.32	41.58	41.61	30.00	37.57	7.00	5.73
Fx2Fp	143.55	159.59	136.94	155.93	136.37	148.71	2.38	1.18
Fp2Fx	133.97	129.21	130.55	126.35	119.30	118.85	2.38	1.20

The base protocol of our framework over $\mathbb{Z}_{2^{192}}$ (implementing $(\ell, \sigma) = (64, \geq 40)$) for arithmetic operations incurs approximately 4× higher runtime overhead (e.g., 5.09 s vs. 1.25 s at 200Mbps), 40% more communication (5.98MB vs. 4.32MB), and 4× higher memory usage (1.32GB vs. 0.33GB) compared to Mystique. This result is expected due to the much bigger size of the ring. Importantly, while we cannot narrow the gap at this base protocol level, we can reduce

Table 3. Comparison of building blocks. Runtime is measured in microseconds (μs) and memory usage in gigabytes (GB).

	Runtime						Mem.	
	200Mbps		500Mbps		1Gbps			
	Ours	[28]	Ours	[28]	Ours	[28]	Ours	[28]
ReLU	54.40	141.09	49.37	141.82	42.37	136.84	6.98	5.71
Truncation	55.22	351.43	51.91	393.177	51.91	389.72	6.98	5.72
MaxPooling	1448.77	1675.73	677.03	861.23	538.086	877.41	6.99	5.72
BN	391.32	4788.65	369.45	4870.47	378.06	4992.25	7.05	5.74
LN	1933	11086.90	1895.62	11349.00	1776.79	11137.00	7.05	5.73

the overall gap in total overhead through optimizations at higher-level building blocks and application layers, effectively amortizing these costs across the system.

Conversions. The performance of our framework over $\mathbb{Z}_{2^{192}}$ and Mystique in various conversion operations is summarized in Table 2. The data represents the average time cost of executing each operation 10,000 times, with time units in microseconds. In contrast to the significant overhead in pure arithmetic operations, our framework demonstrates competitive or even superior performance in conversion tasks. For arithmetic-to-Boolean and Boolean-to-arithmetic conversions, our framework achieves faster runtimes (e.g., 26.32 μs vs. 36.31 μs and 30.00μs vs. 37.57μs at 1Gbps, respectively) while maintaining comparable communication and memory costs. Similarly, for fixed-point-to-floating-point conversion, our framework outperforms Mystique in runtime (136.37μs vs. 148.71μs at 1Gbps) with only slightly higher resource usage. Even in floating-point-to-fixed-point conversion, where Mystique has a slight edge in runtime (118.85μs vs. 119.30μs at 1Gbps), the gap is minimal. This improvement is attributed to the inherent advantages of $\mathbb{Z}_{2^k}$ and the optimizations detailed earlier. While communication and memory overheads remain higher, they are approaching Mystique's levels.

Building Blocks. The performance of our framework over $\mathbb{Z}_{2^{192}}$ and Mystique in various building blocks is summarized in Table 3. Due to space constraints, only a subset of results is presented here. For ReLU, truncation, and max pooling, our framework consistently outperforms Mystique in runtime. Notably, for ReLU, our framework achieves 3.2× faster runtime (e.g., 42.37μs vs. 136.84μs at 1Gbps), and for truncation, it achieves a remarkable 7.5× improvement (51.91μs vs. 389.72μs at 1Gbps).

For batch normalization and layer normalization, our framework also shows substantial runtime improvements. For batch normalization, our framework achieves a 12.9× speedup (e.g., 369.45μs vs. 4870.47μs at 500Mbps), while for layer normalization, it achieves a 6.4× improvement (1895.62μs vs. 11349μs at 500Mbps). However, it is worth noting that for batch normalization, the runtime

Table 4. Comparison between our framework over $\mathbb{Z}_{2^{192}}$ with matrix multiplication optimization and Mystique. Runtime is measured in seconds (s), communication in megabytes (MB), and memory usage in gigabytes (GB).

Network	Runtime						Comm.		Mem.	
	200Mbps		500Mbps		1Gbps					
	Ours	[28]	Ours	[28]	Ours	[28]	Ours	[28]	Ours	[28]
LeNet-5	34.10	37.41	32.86	36.78	32.43	35.97	64.70	71.66	6.99	5.75
ResNet-50	419.33	1067.72	283.75	994.13	262.56	997.06	5861.35	8251.21	8.33	6.81
ResNet-101	566.81	1591.11	383.02	1451.49	353.47	1385.39	8199.43	12528.04	8.62	6.81

slightly increases with higher bandwidth (e.g., 369.45μs at 500Mbps vs. 378.06μs at 1Gbps). This is because the computation overhead dominates the overall cost, and the results are more sensitive to machine load than network bandwidth. Similarly, for layer normalization, the runtime decreases only marginally with higher bandwidth (e.g., 1895.62μs at 500Mbps vs. 1776.79μs at 1Gbps), as the computational complexity remains the primary bottleneck.

The distinction between batch normalization and layer normalization is rooted in their definitions. Batch normalization relies on the mean (μ) and variance (σ^2) obtained during the training phase, allowing the normalization and subsequent linear operation $\gamma \cdot (x - \mu)/\sqrt{\sigma^2} + \beta$ to be simplified to $(\gamma/\sqrt{\sigma^2}) \cdot (x - \mu) + \beta$, where $\gamma/\sqrt{\sigma^2}$ can be precomputed. This simplification reduces the computational overhead. In contrast, layer normalization must compute μ and σ for each input during inference, making it inherently more complex and computationally expensive. This explains the higher runtime and resource usage observed for layer normalization compared to batch normalization.

Proof of Inference Applications. To assess the practical performance of our framework, we evaluated it on three standard neural network architectures: LeNet-5, ResNet-50, and ResNet-101. LeNet-5 is a compact network with 5 layers and approximately 62,000 parameters, while ResNet-50 and ResNet-101 are deeper architectures with 50 and 101 layers, containing 23.5 million and 42.5 million parameters, respectively. These models were trained and tested on the CIFAR-10 dataset, which consists of 60,000 32×32 color images distributed across 10 distinct classes.

The performance of our framework and Mystique in proof of inference applications is summarized in Table 4. For LeNet-5, our framework demonstrates competitive performance, achieving faster runtimes (e.g., 32.43 s vs. 35.97 s at 1Gbps) and smaller communication (64.70 MB vs. 71.66 MB) while incurring modestly higher memory costs.

For larger networks such as ResNet-50 and ResNet-101, our framework achieves significant runtime and communication improvements. For ResNet-50, our framework is **3.8 × faster and 1.4x less communication** at 1Gbps (e.g., 262.56 s vs. 997.06 s; 5861.35 MB vs. 8251.21 MB), and for ResNet-101, it achieves a **3.9 × speedup and 1.5x less communication** (e.g., 353.47 s vs. 1385.39 s at 1Gbps; 8199.43 MB vs. 12528.04 MB). These gains are particularly notable given the computational complexity of these architectures. While our framework requires slightly higher memory (both Mystique and Ours use less than 10 GB memory for all networks), the substantial runtime improvements demonstrate the effectiveness of our optimizations in handling large-scale proof of inference tasks.

The performance gains can be attributed to the structural advantage of $\mathbb{Z}_{2^k}$ as well as the optimizations detailed earlier. These results underscore the scalability of our framework and its ability to handle increasingly complex neural network architectures while maintaining competitive performance.

Acknowledgments. The work was supported in part by the National Natural Science Foundation of China under Grants 12361141818, 12426302 and 12271084, the National Key Research and Development Program of China under Grants 2023YFE0123900 and 2022YFA1004900.

A Appendices

A.1 Functionality $\mathcal{F}_{\text{authZK}}^{\mathbb{Z}_{2^k}}$

Functionality $\mathcal{F}_{\text{authZK}}^{\mathbb{Z}_{2^k}}$

This functionality is parameterized by an integer k and a sufficiently large s for achieving ρ soundness.

Input: On receiving (Input, x) from $\mathcal{P}$, store x and send $[x]_{2^k}$ to $\mathcal{P}$ and $\mathcal{V}$.

Affine Combination: On receiving $(\text{Affine}, c_0, c_1, \ldots, c_n, [x_1]_{2^k}, \ldots, [x_n]_{2^k})$ from $\mathcal{P}$ and $\mathcal{V}$, check that $[x_1]_{2^k}, \ldots, [x_n]_{2^k}$ are valid and abort if not. Compute $y = c_0 + \sum_{i\in[1,n]} c_i \cdot x_i$ in $\mathbb{Z}_{2^k}$, store y, and send $[y]_{2^k}$ to $\mathcal{P}$ and $\mathcal{V}$.

Multiply: On receiving $(\text{Mult}, [x]_{2^k}, [y]_{2^k})$ from $\mathcal{P}$ and $\mathcal{V}$, check that $[x]_{2^k}, [y]_{2^k}$ are valid and abort if not. Compute $y = x \cdot y$ in $\mathbb{Z}_{2^k}$, store z, and send $[z]_{2^k}$ to $\mathcal{P}$ and $\mathcal{V}$.

Output: On receiving $(\text{Output}, [z]_{2^k})$ from $\mathcal{P}$ and $\mathcal{V}$, check that $[z]_{2^k}$ is valid and abort if not, otherwise send z to $\mathcal{V}$.

A.2 Modified Definition of zk-PoI

In order to be able to cater for customized application needs, we formally present a modified notion of zero-knowledge proof of inference (zk-PoI) with decoupled discretization ring and proof soundness as a cryptographic primitive. We define our modified zk-PoI using the bit-length of the fixed-point representation as one of the key parameters. The proof soundness error ε measures the probability of a wrong statement passes the verification over the randomness of the verifier challenge. We say that a zk-PoI protocol has ρ bits of security if its soundness error is upper bounded by $\varepsilon \leq 2^{-\rho}$. Finally, the zero-knowledge error is parameterized by λ.

Let $\mathcal{C}$ represent the computation of a prediction for a data sample $\mathbf{a}$ using the model weight $\mathbf{w}$. Let $[M]$ be the set of all target classifications. We treat the inference algorithm as a mapping that takes a data point $\mathbf{a}$ to $\mathcal{C}(\mathbf{a}, \mathbf{w}) \in [M]$.

A zero-knowledge proof of inference protocol with parameters (ℓ, ρ, λ) (or simply an (ℓ, ρ, λ)-zk-PoI protocol) consists of the following algorithms:

- $\mathrm{pp} \leftarrow \mathrm{zkPoI}.\mathcal{G}(1^\ell, 1^\rho, 1^\lambda)$: given the parameters, generate the public parameter pp.
- $(\mathcal{R}, \mathcal{Q}) \leftarrow \mathrm{zkPoI}.\mathcal{QS}(\mathrm{pp})$: pick a cryptography-friendly finite ring $\mathcal{R}$ and generate a quantization scheme $\mathcal{Q} : \mathit{float} \to \mathcal{R}$ that accommodates fixed-point arithmetic of bit length ℓ.
- $\mathrm{com}_\mathbf{w} \leftarrow \mathrm{zkPoI.Commit}(\mathbf{w}^\mathcal{Q}, \mathrm{pp}, r)$: commit to the quantized model weight $\mathbf{w}^\mathcal{Q}$ with a random point r generated by the prover.
- The prover and the verifier engage in generating a pair of proving key and verification key (pk, vk) (this step can be performed in an offline phase).
- $(y_\mathbf{a}, \pi) \leftarrow \mathrm{zkPoI}.\mathcal{P}(\mathbf{a}, \mathbf{w}, pk, \mathrm{pp}, r, \mathcal{Q})$: given a data sample $\mathbf{a}$, run the inference algorithm involving the quantization scheme to get $y_\mathbf{a} = \mathcal{C}^\mathcal{Q}(\mathbf{a}, \mathbf{w})$ and the corresponding proof π.
- $b \leftarrow \mathrm{zkPoI}.\mathcal{V}(\mathrm{com}_\mathbf{w}, \mathbf{a}, y_\mathbf{a}, \pi, vk, \mathrm{pp}, \mathcal{Q})$: validate the prediction of $\mathbf{a}$ given $y_\mathbf{a}$, the transcript π and a verification key vk.

Definition 1. *We say that a protocol is an (ℓ, ρ, λ)-zk-PoI for a machine learning model represented by $\mathcal{C}(\cdot,\cdot)$ if the following guarantees are satisfied.*

Completeness. *For any model weight $\mathbf{w}$ and a data point $\mathbf{a}$, an honestly computed inference and its corresponding proof should always be accepted:*

$$\Pr\left[b = 1 \;\middle|\; \begin{array}{c} \mathrm{pp} \leftarrow \mathrm{zkPoI}.\mathcal{G}(1^\ell, 1^\rho, 1^\lambda) \\ (\mathcal{R}, \mathcal{Q}) \leftarrow \mathrm{zkPoI}.\mathcal{QS}(\mathrm{pp}) \\ \mathrm{com}_\mathbf{w} \leftarrow \mathrm{zkPoI.Commit}(\mathbf{w}^\mathcal{Q}, \mathrm{pp}, r) \\ (y_\mathbf{a}, \pi) \leftarrow \mathrm{zkPoI}.\mathcal{P}(\mathbf{a}, \mathbf{w}, pk, \mathrm{pp}, r, \mathcal{Q}) \\ b \leftarrow \mathrm{zkPoI}.\mathcal{V}(\mathrm{com}_\mathbf{w}, \mathbf{a}, y_\mathbf{a}, \pi, vk, \mathrm{pp}, \mathcal{Q}) \end{array} \right] = 1.$$

ρ-Soundness. *A PPT malicious prover $\mathcal{A}$ cannot convince the verifier to accept an incorrect inference except with probability upper bounded by $2^{-\rho}$:*

$$\Pr\left[b = 1 \;\middle|\; \begin{array}{c} \mathrm{pp} \leftarrow \mathrm{zkPoI}.\mathcal{G}(1^\ell, 1^\rho, 1^\lambda) \\ (\mathcal{R}, \mathcal{Q}) \leftarrow \mathrm{zkPoI}.\mathcal{QS}(\mathrm{pp}) \\ (\mathbf{w}, \mathrm{com}_\mathbf{w}, \mathbf{a}, y_\mathbf{a}, \pi) \leftarrow \mathcal{A}(1^\ell, 1^\rho, 1^\lambda, pk, \mathrm{pp}, r, \mathcal{Q}) \\ \mathrm{com}_\mathbf{w} \leftarrow \mathrm{zkPoI.Commit}(\mathbf{w}^\mathcal{Q}, \mathrm{pp}, r) \\ b \leftarrow \mathrm{zkPoI}.\mathcal{V}(\mathrm{com}_\mathbf{w}, \mathbf{a}, y_\mathbf{a}, \pi, vk, \mathrm{pp}, \mathcal{Q}) \end{array} \right] \leq 2^{-\rho}.$$

Zero-knowledge. *The proof π should not reveal anything about the private model parameter. In particular, for security parameter λ, let* $\mathrm{pp} \leftarrow \mathrm{zkPoI}.\mathcal{G}(1^\ell, 1^\rho, 1^\lambda)$ *and* $(\mathcal{R}, \mathcal{Q}) \leftarrow \mathrm{zkPoI}.\mathcal{QS}(\mathrm{pp})$. *For a simulator $\mathcal{S} = (\mathcal{S}_1, \mathcal{S}_2)$ such that, a model weight $\mathbf{w}$ and an adversarial verifier $\mathcal{A}$, consider the following two experiments:*

$\text{Real}_{\mathcal{A},\mathbf{w}}(\text{pp}, \mathcal{Q})$:

$$\text{com}_{\mathbf{w}} \leftarrow \text{zkPoI.Commit}(\mathbf{w}^{\mathcal{Q}}, \text{pp}, r)$$
$$\mathbf{a} \leftarrow \mathcal{A}(\text{com}_{\mathbf{w}}, \text{pp}, \mathcal{Q})$$
$$(y_{\mathbf{a}}, \pi) \leftarrow \text{zkPoI.}\mathcal{P}(\mathbf{a}, \mathbf{w}, pk, \text{pp}, r, \mathcal{Q})$$
$$b \leftarrow \mathcal{A}(\text{com}_{\mathbf{w}}, \mathbf{a}, y_{\mathbf{a}}, \pi, vk, \text{pp}, \mathcal{Q})$$
$$\text{Output } b$$

$\text{Ideal}_{\mathcal{A},\mathcal{S}^{\mathcal{A}}}(\text{pp}, \mathcal{Q})$:

$$\text{com} \leftarrow \mathcal{S}_1(1^\lambda, \text{pp}, \mathcal{Q})$$
$$\mathbf{a} \leftarrow \mathcal{A}(\text{com}, \text{pp}, \mathcal{Q})$$
$$(y_{\mathbf{a}}, \pi) \leftarrow \mathcal{S}_2(\text{com}, \mathbf{a}, \text{pp}, \mathcal{Q}), \text{ given oracle access to}$$
$$y_{\mathbf{a}} = \mathcal{C}^{\mathcal{Q}}(\mathbf{a}, \mathbf{w}).$$
$$b \leftarrow \mathcal{A}(\text{com}, \mathbf{a}, y_{\mathbf{a}}, \pi, vk, \text{pp}, \mathcal{Q})$$
$$\text{Output } b$$

For any PPT algorithm $\mathcal{A}$ and any model weight $\mathbf{w}$, *there exists simulator $\mathcal{S}$ such that*

$$\left|\Pr\left[\text{Real}_{\mathcal{A},\mathbf{w}}(\text{pp}, \mathcal{Q}) = 1\right] - \Pr\left[\text{Ideal}_{\mathcal{A},\mathcal{S}^{\mathcal{A}}}(\text{pp}, \mathcal{Q}) = 1\right]\right| \leq \text{negl}(\lambda).$$

References

1. Abbaszadeh, K., Pappas, C., Katz, J., Papadopoulos, D.: Zero-knowledge proofs of training for deep neural networks. In: CCS 2024, pp. 4316–4330. ACM (2024)
2. Baum, C., Braun, L., Munch-Hansen, A., Razet, B., Scholl, P.: Appenzeller to brie: efficient zero-knowledge proofs for mixed-mode arithmetic and Z2k. In: CCS 2021, pp. 192–211. ACM (2021)
3. Baum, C., Braun, L., Munch-Hansen, A., Scholl, P.: Moz $\mathbb{Z}\_2^k$ arella: efficient vector-ole and zero-knowledge proofs over $\mathbb{Z}\_2^k$. In: CRYPTO 2022. Lecture Notes in Computer Science, vol. 13510, pp. 329–358. Springer (2022)
4. Bendlin, R., Damgård, I., Orlandi, C., Zakarias, S.: Semi-homomorphic Encryption and Multiparty Computation. In: Paterson, K.G. (ed.) EUROCRYPT 2011. LNCS, vol. 6632, pp. 169–188. Springer, Heidelberg (2011). https://doi.org/10.1007/978-3-642-20465-4_11
5. Cramer, R., Damgård, I., Escudero, D., Scholl, P., Xing, C.: SPD Z_{2^k}: efficient MPC mod 2^k for dishonest majority. In: CRYPTO 2018. Lecture Notes in Computer Science, vol. 10992, pp. 769–798. Springer (2018)
6. Dalskov, A.P.K., Escudero, D., Nof, A.: Fully secure MPC and ZK-fliop over rings: new constructions, improvements and extensions. In: CRYPTO 2024. Lecture Notes in Computer Science, vol. 14927, pp. 136–169. Springer (2024)
7. Diaa, A., et al.: Fast and private inference of deep neural networks by co-designing activation functions. In: USENIX Security 2024. USENIX Association (2024)

8. Escudero, D., Xing, C., Yuan, C.: More efficient dishonest majority secure computation over Z_{2^k} via Galois rings. In: CRYPTO 2022. Lecture Notes in Computer Science, vol. 13507, pp. 383–412. Springer (2022)
9. Feng, B., Qin, L., Zhang, Z., Ding, Y., Chu, S.: ZEN: efficient zero-knowledge proofs for neural networks. IACR Cryptol. ePrint Arch, p. 87 (2021)
10. Garg, S., et al.: Experimenting with zero-knowledge proofs of training. In: CCS 2023, pp. 1880–1894. ACM (2023)
11. Hao, M., et al.: Scalable zero-knowledge proofs for non-linear functions in machine learning. In: USENIX Security 2024. USENIX Association (2024)
12. Hussain, S.U., Javaheripi, M., Samragh, M., Koushanfar, F.: COINN: crypto/ml codesign for oblivious inference via neural networks. In: CCS 2021, pp. 3266–3281. ACM (2021)
13. Jia, Y., Li, S., Xing, C., Yao, Y., Yuan, C.: Polynomial commitments for Galois rings and applications to snarks over Z_{2^k}. In: to appear in CRYPTO 25. Springer-Verlag (2025)
14. Lee, S., Ko, H., Kim, J., Oh, H.: VCNN: verifiable convolutional neural network based on ZK-snarks. IEEE Trans. Dependable Secur. Comput. **21**(4), 4254–4270 (2024)
15. Li, Y., et al.: Sublinear distributed product checks on replicated secret-shared data over Z_{2^k} without ring extensions. In: CCS 2024, pp. 825–839. ACM (2024)
16. Lin, F., Xing, C., Yao, Y.: More efficient zero-knowledge protocols over Z_{2^k} via Galois rings. In: CRYPTO 2024. Lecture Notes in Computer Science, vol. 14928, pp. 424–457. Springer (2024)
17. Liu, T., Xie, X., Zhang, Y.: ZKCNN: zero knowledge proofs for convolutional neural network predictions and accuracy. In: CCS 2021, pp. 2968–2985. ACM (2021)
18. Lu, W., et al.: Bumblebee: secure two-party inference framework for large transformers. In: NDSS 2025. The Internet Society (2025)
19. Ng, L.K.L., Chow, S.S.M.: Gforce: GPU-friendly oblivious and rapid neural network inference. In: USENIX Security 2021, pp. 2147–2164. USENIX Association (2021)
20. Nielsen, J.B., Nordholt, P.S., Orlandi, C., Burra, S.S.: A new approach to practical active-secure two-party computation. In: Safavi-Naini, R., Canetti, R. (eds.) CRYPTO 2012. LNCS, vol. 7417, pp. 681–700. Springer, Heidelberg (2012). https://doi.org/10.1007/978-3-642-32009-5_40
21. Qu, W., et al.: ZKGPT: an efficient non-interactive zero-knowledge proof framework for LLM inference. In: To Appear in Usenix Security 2025 (2025)
22. Rathee, D., et al.: Cryptflow2: Practical 2-party secure inference. In: CCS 2020, pp. 325–342. ACM (2020)
23. Sun, H., Li, J., Zhang, H.: ZKLLM: zero knowledge proofs for large language models. In: CCS 2024, pp. 4405–4419. ACM (2024)
24. Tan, S., Knott, B., Tian, Y., Wu, D.J.: Cryptgpu: fast privacy-preserving machine learning on the GPU. In: SP 2021, pp. 1021–1038. IEEE (2021)
25. Thaler, J.: Time-optimal interactive proofs for circuit evaluation. In: Canetti, R., Garay, J.A. (eds.) CRYPTO 2013. LNCS, vol. 8043, pp. 71–89. Springer, Heidelberg (2013). https://doi.org/10.1007/978-3-642-40084-1_5
26. Wang, H., Hoang, T.: EZDPS: an efficient and zero-knowledge machine learning inference pipeline. Proc. Priv. Enhancing Technol. **2023**(2), 430–448 (2023)
27. Wang, X., Malozemoff, A.J., Katz, J.: Emp-toolkit: efficient multiparty computation toolkit (2016)

28. Weng, C., Yang, K., Xie, X., Katz, J., Wang, X.: Mystique: efficient conversions for zero-knowledge proofs with applications to machine learning. In: USENIX Security 2021, pp. 501–518. USENIX Association (2021)
29. Weng, J., Weng, J., Tang, G., Yang, A., Li, M., Liu, J.: PVCNN: privacy-preserving and verifiable convolutional neural network testing. IEEE Trans. Inf. Forensics Secur. **18**, 2218–2233 (2023)
30. Yang, K., Sarkar, P., Weng, C., Wang, X.: Quicksilver: efficient and affordable zero-knowledge proofs for circuits and polynomials over any field. In: CCS 2021, pp. 2986–3001. ACM (2021)
31. Zhang, J., Fang, Z., Zhang, Y., Song, D.: Zero knowledge proofs for decision tree predictions and accuracy. In: CCS 2020, pp. 2039–2053. ACM (2020)
32. Zhang, J., et al.: Secure transformer inference made non-interactive. In: NDSS 2025. The Internet Society (2025)

Author Index

F. -H. Liu (Ed.): CT-RSAC 2026, LNCS 16496, pp. 339–340, 2026.
https://doi.org/10.1007/978-3-032-22931-1

Zeitfracht Medien GmbH
Ferdinand-Jühlke-Straße 7
99095 Erfurt, Deutschland
produktsicherheit@kolibri360.de